The Development of Thought in Pan Africanism

Second Edition

Boatamo Mosupyoe
California State University, Sacramento

Mogobe B. Ramose
University of South Africa

Kendall Hunt
publishing company

Cover images © 2007 JupiterImages Corporation. Bottom left image courtesy of the author.

Kendall Hunt
publishing company

www.kendallhunt.com
Send all inquiries to:
4050 Westmark Drive
Dubuque, IA 52004-1840

Printed in the United States of America
10 9 8 7 6 5 4 3

 # Contents

Acknowledgments *vii*

Dedication *ix*

CHAPTER 1: Women's Multicentric Experiences *1*

Introduction to Chapter One *3*
Boatamo Mosupyoe

Intersection of Race, Class, and Gender *6*
Boatamo Mosupyoe

Mixed Messages: Gender Paradigms and Everyday Life in the Contemporary
United States *22*
Michele Renée Matisons, Ph.D.

Symbolic Gender Relations: Zion Christian Church and Traditional Bapedi Structures *33*
Boatamo Mosupyoe

Women's Perception of Patriarchy and Non-Sexism: South African Case *53*
Boatamo Mosupyoe

Is the Glass Ceiling Cracked Yet? Women in Rwanda, South Africa, and the United States
1994–2010 *72*
Boatamo Mosupyoe

Chapter One Questions *77*

CHAPTER 2: Liberated Pan-African Thought *79*

Introduction to Chapter Two *81*
Boatamo Mosupyoe

Development of Thought on Pan Africanism *83*
Boatamo Mosupyoe

The Struggle for Reason in Africa *87*
Mogobe B. Ramose

Defending Whiteness: Protecting White Privilege in Post–Civil Rights Society *94*
Rita Cameron Wedding, Ph.D.

I Doubt, Therefore African Philosophy Exists   *114*
　Mogobe B. Ramose

The Philosophy of Ubuntu and Ubuntu as a Philosophy   *126*
　Mogobe B. Ramose

Chapter Two Questions   *135*

CHAPTER 3: Reclamation and Self-Definitions   *141*

Introduction to Chapter Three   *143*
　Boatamo Mosupyoe

Toward the Black Renaissance   *147*
　Randall Robinson

'African Renaissance': A Northbound Gaze   *165*
　Mogobe B. Ramose

The Brazilian National Context: Harbingers of Change   *175*
　David Covin

Is Western Democracy the Answer to the African Problem?   *181*
　Marie Pauline Eboh

A Voyage of Discovery: Sacramento and the Politics of Ordinary Black People   *187*
　David Covin

Recent African Immigration   *194*
　Boatamo Mosupyoe

The Zion Christian Church in Post-Apartheid South Africa   *202*
　Boatamo Mosupyoe

Chapter Three Questions   *209*

CHAPTER 4: Racialized Societies, Concepts and Decisions   *215*

Introduction to Chapter Four   *217*
　Boatamo Mosupyoe

I Conquer, Therefore I Am the Sovereign: Reflections upon Sovereignty, Constitutionalism, and Democracy in Zimbabwe and South Africa   *219*
　Mogobe B. Ramose

Afrikaans Language Conflict   *253*
　Boatamo Mosupyoe

Racialized Societies   *264*
　David Covin

Brown v. Topeka Board of Education: Fifty Years Later   *271*
　Otis. L Scott

Bias Impact on Decision Makers in Child Welfare   *281*
　Rita Cameron Wedding, Ph.D.

Chapter Four Questions   *297*

CHAPTER 5: Pan-African Epistemology   *303*

Introduction to Chapter Five   *305*
   Boatamo Mosupyoe

Wisdom in War and Peace   *306*
   Magobe B. Ramose

Human Rights in Africa   *319*
   E. Oyugi

Elusive Quest? The Political Economy of Reconciliation in Post-Genocide Rwanda   *326*
   Patrick Cannon, Ph.D.

Toward a Philosophical Study of African Culture: A Critique of Traditionalism   *338*
   Oladipo Olusegun

Globalization and Economic Fundamentalism   *347*
   E.J. Kelsey

Proverbs as a Source of African Philosophy: A Methodological Consideration   *356*
   Heinz Kimmerle

Morality in Yoruba Thought: A Philosophical Analysis   *364*
   Oladipo Olusegun

The Need for Conceptual Decolonization in African Philosophy   *370*
   Kwasi Wiredu

Chapter Five Questions   *377*

Acknowledgement

My appreciation goes to all the contributors who made this second edition possible. Morakane Mosupyoe deserves special mention for her unwavering support of this project.

Dedication

In honor of the memory of Dr. Alexandre Kimenyi and his contribution to Linguistics, African Studies, Social Justice and Human Rights.

Women's Multicentric Experiences

Introduction to Chapter One

Boatamo Mosupyoe

Women and men's experiences are varied and informed by different contexts that reflect the dynamism of their environments. In the process of constructing and defining their role in society they contend with ideologies, traditions, and structures constructed on varied forms of equality and inequalities. In the process of addressing to rectify the hegemonies and solidify egalitarianism, they oscillate in fluid process marked by differing priorities. The shared space demand of them to synthesize conflicting paradigms and find ways of achieving mutual inclusivity without denying the differences and similarities.

The articles in this chapter add to that discourse of gender equality. The article, "Intersection of Race, Class, Location, and Gender" by Mosupyoe addresses the complexity of the intersectionality of race, class, location, and gender. The article elucidates on how the mutually constitutive nature of these four variables have historically operated to marginalize women and prevent them from participating in decision making. The article also sheds light on how women from different backgrounds have misunderstood each other when they fail to acknowledge the impact of race and class on their different experiences. Pertinently, the experience of Sojourner Truth and Francis Gage presents a unique illustration of a contextual experience where race and class can function as dual complimentary opposites to reaffirm racial attitudes and practices and yet transform those very attitudes to benefit gender equality. The Native American, Mexican American, and South African women's experiences also exemplify women's multicentric experiences. The struggle about knowledge construction and production becomes clear with the focus on the concept of feminism; obviously different points of view highlighted the need to contextualize experiences. Contextualizing experiences should not translate into a denial of biological sex differences, but should enhance the understanding of how concepts and paradigms are socially constructed and intersect to impact gender relations. The misunderstanding of the intersectionality is not limited to men; misunderstandings among women abound. The first women's conference best demonstrated the need for a dialogue between women of the north and women of the south to bridge the gap.

The article by Matison, "Mixed Messages: Gender Paradigms and Everyday Life," underscores the need to understand paradigms and how they work to impact gender inequality. Matison argues that in order to transcend old and ineffective frameworks of analyzing gender, mixed messages about gender require new tools that will address varied human experiences. In this article Matison employs three paradigms—genderblindness, planetary, and gender diversity paradigms—as those tools of analysis that can help in understanding gender dynamics. Matison equates genderblindness to colorblindness myth. Both approaches deny the historical impact of gender and race on institutions, policies, and practices. Genderblindness logic assumes that if we cease to see differences in our biological makeup, then the institutionalized gender inequality that has been systematically incorporated in our thinking, policies, and practices will disappear. Matison sees the denial of the existence of these biological realities as hard to ignore, if not impossible. She then continues to explore the next paradigm, the planetary paradigm.

Here Matison examines John Gray's book *Men are from Mars, Women are from Venus,* and finds a parallel between some of his arguments with the 1970s cultural feminist arguments. Both are

3

essentialist, positing the fundamental biological differences between men and women; however, they part company in their view about the capacity to transform. Gray believes change is possible and that constitutes the main focus of his book, whereas cultural feminists opt for a new institution that will reflect feminist traits of "peace, cooperation, mutual recognition, and support." Matison finds the planetary approach useful to the extent that it accentuates the difference between men and women as a way to contribute toward political awareness. She, however, laments its inadequacy inasfar as it fails to acknowledge different backgrounds, structural factors that give rise to various gender arrangements, and limited universal applicability. Matison then turns her attention to the gender diversity paradigm as an approach "that transcends the flaws" of the above-mentioned paradigm. By exploring the biological, anthropological, and political diversity arguments, she concludes that gender is not only socially constructed but it is biologically fluid. Without denying the limited merits of the genderblindness and planetary paradigms, Matison sees the gender diversity approach as encompassing and more effective in addressing persistent gender inequalities.

In the article "Women's Perception of Patriarchy and Non-Sexism," Mosupyoe continues the gender equality discourse in her exploration of how women in the Zion Christian Church of South Africa interpreted the call to non-sexism before its independence in 1994. The discussions show how these women were engaged in a contradictory process of articulation as they struggled to mediate their social, religious, and historical practices with the political call of non-sexism. Age, level of education and rural/urban dichotomy all played a part in how various women constructed their notion of non-sexism and how it should be approached and implemented. To some the concept was novel and potentially explosive; it also injected contradiction that could best be addressed by the bishop, to whom they looked for guidance. The limitation of this approach was acknowledged by women of different ages, education levels and locations. The latter notwithstanding, the symbols such as the badge (greetings of peace)

that helped shaped their worldview kept them centered and united, even though their understanding and process of articulation defy a neat unitary arrangement.

In the article "Symbolic Gender Relations in the Zion Christian Church of South Africa," Mosupyoe outlines how the confluence of the traditional Bapedi structures informed the construction of the structures of the Zion Christian Church (ZCC). This reciprocal process of construction reinforced gender hegemonies in some instances in altered forms. The efficacy of the process was enhanced by the lack of tension since the founder of the church, Engenase Lekganyane, was a Mopedi and a traditionalist. The dialectic interplay of the two entities generated reinforcement, reproduction, and change. The African cultural elements of the church attracted members, symbols of prohibitions, taboos, and polygamy and constitute examples for part of the social structure of both the Bapedi traditional structures and the ZCC. All of these contain elements that perpetuate gender inequalities. Similarly, with some variation, the leadership structures show preference to men than to women. The leaders of the ZCC follow a hereditary line of succession echoing the traditional Bapedi succession practice, for example. Linguistic phrases in the social and leadership structures of both the Bapedi and the ZCC contribute toward the persistent gender inequalities. The religious structures of both are no exceptions. In the final analysis the article shows that the ZCC and the Bapedi traditional structures informed each other and in most instances in ways that perpetuated gender inequality.

The last article, "Is the Glass Ceiling Cracked Yet?", reflects that change towards gender equality is possible but has to go through a process of mediation and tension. The article traces the challenges and achievements of Rwanda and South Africa on gender equality and compares them in some instances to the United States. In terms of representation in government, it seems that while Hilary's 18 million votes has delivered some cracks in the glass ceiling, Rwanda and South Africa have gone beyond and their reality challenges the gluey floors/glass ceiling dichotomy to include metaphors that reflect the change. Change is possible; the mere fact that cracks were made in the "highest, hardest glass ceiling" is an indication of a movement towards change. Change is achieved by acknowledgment that informs mechanisms to redress and transform. The discourse requires an understanding of paradigms and variables that function to either perpetuate or promote gender equality.

The Intersection of Race, Class and Gender

Boatamo Mosupyoe

The Purpose

The purpose of this article is to offer an introductory definition and explanation of what the intersection of race, class and gender means. The article will trace the historical development of thought on the three concepts and briefly analyze their impact on men and women relationships and status.

Much has been written about the impact of racism on people of Asian, African, Mexican, Native American descents. The debate about what is important in gender relations has spanned the discourse of ages. Views have varied from looking at race as the most salient, and class and gender as less salient. As time progresses views changed, in other words views moved from isolating the three to putting them on the same par. Progressive feminists and scholars like bell hooks, (1984) Cornell West (1993) and most recently Cole and Guy-Sheftall (2003) have stressed the importance of an analysis that focuses on the confluence of race, class, and gender in understanding the complexities of communities of color in the U.S. and the challenges that they face. In order to fully understand the impact, the three variables have to be considered. Institutionalized racism, economic injustices, and gender all play a role in the relegation of people to secondary status in societies like the United States.

Explaining the Topic

Historically race has been defined on the basis of how people look. In other words, race has been

"The Intersection of Race, Class and Gender" by B. Mosupyoe from *Introduction to Ethnic Studies*, edited by B. Baker, B. Mosupyoe, et al., 2004. Reprinted by permission of Kendall/Hunt Publishing Company.

defined around intrinsic criteria that use phenotypes attributes ascribed by birth to distinguish people from one another. The classifications went a step further to assign and associate certain behavior and skills with certain races. Some scholars of European descent argued that Euro phenotypes reflect highest forms of beauty, in other words people of Euro-descent are the most beautiful of all the people on earth. They are the standards of beauty against which everybody should be measured. Their "fine" hair, sharp noses, "pink skin" which they described and still describe as "white," represented the ultimate forms of beauty. White also came to mean "pure," "innocent," and "less likely to do evil and wrong deeds." Further, it was argued that because of the size of their skulls people of Euro-descent possess superior intellect. The logic centered around the intrinsic nature of the phenotypes, and therefore were presented and explained as biologically determined. Since they are biologically determined, they cannot be changed and have to be accepted as factual and static.

This way of thinking influenced how important political, economic, educational, social, cultural, etc. decisions were made. People of Euro descent were said to be the "norm," the "supreme," the "yard stick," and the "natural." Other people who are not of Euro-descent were not only classified but were also described in comparison with the Euro model in the most unfavorable ways. People were looked upon as inferior precisely because they were not of Euro-descent. Much has been written to dispel the myth of race as a biological construct. Race is a social construct. Although the classification uses obvious physical characteristics to group people, it is very illogical and arbitrary to conclude that the shape of somebody's nose, the color of their skin and the size of their skull give them genetic advantage in terms of intellect, beauty, and behavior over the others.

The definition of race in biological terms was clearly designed to institute and maintain a system of social inequality that ensured and still ensures the preservation of racism. It guaranteed that only people who look a certain way will have access to resources and maintain control. Moreover, this classification influences how people interact with one another. Associating physical characteristics with behavior often leads to discrimination based on race. Joy James in her article "Experience, Reflection, Judgment and Action: Teaching Theory, Talking Community," writes in part:

"I seem continuously challenged to "prove" that I am qualified. Comparing my work experiences with those of other African American Academics, I notice that in spite of being hired through a highly competitive process, we seemed to be asked more routinely, almost reflectively, if we have Ph.D. We could attribute this and have to our "diminutive" height, youngish appearances, or casual attire. Yet I notice that white women about our height, unsuited, and under sixty seem not to be interrogated as frequently about their qualifications." (D Bell and Klein Radically Speaking, 1996, p 37).

Clearly from this quote Joy James qualifications and credentials are questioned precisely because she is not of Euro descent. In simple terms, the motivation of questioning her qualifications are racist. This explains and indicates the unfair and irrational privilege the color of the skin confers on people of Euro-descent. As much as I want to write about this in the past tense, the fact of the matter is, it still happens today.

Together with race, class can function and has functioned as a form of discrimination. The tendency to socially rank people according to their relative economic system gives rise to classism. The class ranking system, unlike race, is often considered extrinsic to the individual. It is also looked upon as situational and fluid and therefore allows an individual to choose her or his position in the class hierarchy system. This is not necessarily true since class does not happen in a vacuum.

It intersects with other variables that influences the status of people in a society. More often than not, in all systems of stratification, the top ranked group controls the economic resources and also enjoys the highest prestige and privilege. Historically, in societies where race has been used to rank people, people who were favored by the race classification as superior, become the people who are also favored by the class system. In societies like the United States and South Africa male of Euro-descent have been the favored group that also defined and determined policies. Policies favored those who looked like them skin wise and gender wise. This favoritism resulted in systems of race and gender inequality that take struggles to penetrate and overcome.

Gender refers to a social construct whereby certain characteristics, behavior, and actions are assigned and associated with people based on their biological sex. "Gender also refers to the experiences of women and men, cultural definitions of womanhood and manhood and the interconnections between race, gender, sexual orientation, age, class, and other oppression." (Cole and Guy-Sheftall, 2003, p xxii). Gender constitutes one of the most salient modes of organizing inequality among the sexes. Vouching for gender as the most quintessential of the three undermines the interconnection of the three, that is, race, class and gender. The three have to be considered in an analysis of discriminatory practices. Experiences of the system and of the intersection of the different systems articulating the actual experiences of inequality, will necessarily be different from man to man, woman to woman, and man to woman. In addition, the experience will be different from one group to another, as well as from groups within a society. Women and men's experiences across class and race have both similarities and differences. It is important not to deny the differences of experiences.

Feminism as a Concept

This section examines the development of the concept of feminism and global feminism from the 1960's onwards. The examination best exemplifies the complexities of the confluence of race, class, and gender. The efforts of the United

Nations Commission on the status of women are well known. Despite sometimes fruitless attempts, the Commission was relentless in its efforts to represent women's issues to the United Nations. It's efforts were eventually successful. The advocates of women's rights eventually managed to convince the United Nations General Assembly to declare 1976–1985 the decade of women. In addition, the advocates and women were able to convince the United Nations to fund an International Women's Conference in 1975 in Mexico City. The theme of the conference was "Equality, Development, and Peace." The theme was intended to be inclusive of world's women's issues; however, what it achieved was a clear picture of dissimilarities of women's experiences world wide.[1]

The conference highlighted the differences in thought and experiences between women of Euro-descent, who I will refer to as women of the north and the others, who I will refer to as women of the south.[2] The theme Equality became the focal point of women of Euro descent. Their definition of equality in relation to men formed an important area of focus for them. Other women could not identify with the priorities and the agenda as determined by women of Euro-descent. They looked upon them as, and indeed, they were, part of the oppressive dominant structures that women of the south sought equality from. After all, most of the governing structures where the delegates came from composed of people of Euro-descent. That also meant to most if not all women at the time, women of Euro-descent represented an extension of those oppressive structures. In addition, their priorities were to be liberated from racial oppression and not gender oppression. **At that time,** race and not gender seemed to form the salient variable for women of the south. Of course, later the approach would evolve to recognizing the importance of the intersection of race, class and gender, as this discussion will later illustrate.

Conversations about feminism centered around the definition of the term. To women of the south the term would be irrelevant to their experiences if its translation meant to "be like a man and act like a man." It sounded to women of the south as if women of Euro-descent wanted to be men, in a nutshell. The women of the south did not want to be men; instead they saw an urgent need just to be treated like human beings, to have roofs over their heads, to earn wages that would enable them to feed their children, as priorities. The women of the south's arguments have been articulated outside of the conference by scholars like Lewis (1977). She describes the way in which race is more often a salient feature of oppression in African American women's lives. Lewis **then,** further argued that gender relations in communities of color cannot be interpreted in the Eurocentric terms that reflect the experiences of women of Euro-descent. Historically, African American women have tended to see racial discrimination as a more powerful cause of their subordination. In the 1980's and 1990's scholars like bell hooks also articulate experiences that are similar to those articulated by women of the south at the Mexico conference. In her book *Feminist Theory*, from margin to center (1984), bell hooks writes in part:

When I participated in feminist groups, I found that white women adopted a condescending attitude towards me and other non-white participants. The condescension they directed at black women was one of the means they employed to remind us that the women's movement was "theirs"—that we were able to participate because they allowed it, even encouraged it, we were needed to legitimate the process. They did not see us as equals. They did not treat us as equals. And though they expected us to provide first hand accounts of black experiences, they felt it was their role to decide if these experiences were authentic. Frequently, college-educated black women (even those from poor and working class backgrounds) were dismissed as mere imitators. Our presence in movement activities did not count (p 11).

Sentiments such as these articulated by hooks, were present in the Mexico conference. The agenda and the access were seen as determined by women of Euro-descent. These actions clearly indicated and proved to others that women of Euro descent were oppressive. Others in discussing Chicana women's experiences also confirmed the primacy of race in determining an individual's position in the economic order in the United States. Similar experiences by women of Asian descent and Native American women also abound.

The other two themes, Peace and Development, seemed to resonate more with women who were not of European descent. The different themes and the different experiences of women in these contexts then brought into question the universal applicability of the term feminism to women's issues. The visibility of the differences intensified during the mid-decade world conference on women held in Copenhagen in 1980. Women were determined to unite and resolve their differences. The determination, notwithstanding, the difference were present and they needed to be confronted. As part of the solution the intersection of race, gender, together with their implication on access and privilege had to be acknowledged. The discourse and the process proved difficult then as it does today in the 21st century. Cole and Guy-Sheftall (2003) notice the difficulty even today. These two remarkable women have been involved both in the civil rights and women's movements, and have been committed to the elimination of racism, sexism, classism and heterosexism in all of their professional lives. They write in part,

We have been engaged in difficult dialogues with white feminists about the importance of understanding the particular experiences of women of color, and the need to take seriously the intersection of race, class and gender in the lives of all women, not only women of color" (xxviii)

Arguably, most women of Euro-descent refuse or find it difficult to acknowledge the privilege their skin color confers to them in societies like the United States. Much has been debated about the origin or root of the denial. I will posit the views of two Euro-American women, one that I know personally and have interacted with extensively, and the other who I am acquainted with through her work. The first woman Kyzyl-Fenno-Smith is a respected librarian and scholar; she often articulates how as a woman of Euro-descent she recognizes the tremendous effort spent in maintaining the advantage accorded by the 'pink' Euro skin by Euro-American women.

From Fenno-Smith's point of view the unconscious claim reflects one symptom of the concerted effort to maintain the privilege. She succinctly points out that women we are talking about are smart and articulate in ways that demonstrate a

deeper level of understanding sexual discrimination, institutionalized and otherwise, what then blinds them to racial discrimination? Fenno-Smith argues that some women of Euro-descent become so skilled in the art of perpetuating their own privilege that they believe it is natural and self perpetuating. What complicates matters is the undeniable fact that women of Euro descent have also been discriminated against by Euro-male dominated structures. However, Fenno-Smith cautions that this should not be confused with or equated to something in the unconscious level. The often uttered phrase "I am doing the best I can," in the discussion of the intersection proves that the domain where the privilege exists is the conscious level. Fenno-Smith also says that it benefits Euro-American women to maintain the privilege, since most of the time Euro-American men, and not women, are blamed for the exclusion and discrimination. It is, she concludes, to the benefit of the women to maintain the status quo.[3]

Peggy Mackintosh in her article "White Privilege, Unpacking the Invisible Knapsack," posits a different view from Fenno-Smith's. Her divergent view is mirrored in her statement:

After I realized the extent to which men work from a basis of unacknowledged privilege, I understood that most of their oppressiveness was unconscious. Then I remembered the frequent charges from women of color that white women whom they encounter are oppressive.

Mackintosh and Fenno-Smith with their divergent views represent those women of Euro-descent who recognize the existence of racism in woman to woman relationship and therefore, offer hope for the achievement of an ideal. Problems of denial or lack of awareness or consciousness resulted in women from the south's reluctance to embrace the term feminism. The problems had linguistic, definition, and substantive implications as well. English constituted the first language of some and not all of the delegates; this impacted the efficacy of translation. The different experiences and agendas impacted the substance of the term.

The controversy surrounding the relevance of the concept feminism to "poor people" precipitated the International Women Tribune Center

(IWTC) to hold a forum made up primarily by women from North and South America on "What is Feminism?" These group of women decided that feminism should not be viewed as a list of separate issues, but as a political perspective on women's lives and the problem of domination. Focusing on the problem of domination, then women have to contend with the domination of women of Euro-descent over other women. In the United States, Australia, New Zealand, and South Africa, for example where systems still use skin color to confer privilege, women of Euro-descent had to acknowledge the privilege and its implications. When this is achieved then women can work for a definition with the contribution from everybody. This then eliminates confusion and engenders common ownership of the word.

It is worth mentioning here that it is now ten years since South Africa has been freed from a brutal blatant racist system of apartheid that classified and treated people based on the color of their skin. The progress in South Africa remarkable as it is, it takes more than ten years to transform or even eradicate a system that has been in place for 342 years. Further, Euro-Africans will be super humans to just automatically and miraculously rid themselves of the deeply socialization process that taught them that they are superior because of their race. South Africa and the United States are comparable. In spite of the civil rights movement, the U.S. is still battling different manifestations of racism, classism, and sexism.

Towards the Intersection of Race, Class and Gender

Increasingly, recent scholarship suggests a shift without denying race as one of the important variables in understanding gender and racial relationships. The scholarship has no choice but to shift, since the intersection dates from time immemorial. What has been missing is the acknowledgement of its existence. In the case of the United States like in South Africa, with racist pasts, it became difficult for women and men of color to acknowledge the intersection. Instead, what happened in such situations racial oppression seemed to take primacy over gender oppression. This is true for most communities of color in the United

States and elsewhere. Women were faced with a difficult choice, (that should not have been a choice at all), of addressing either gender oppression and risk being labeled collaborators with the Euro enemy or just sticking to addressing racial oppression in the face of patriarchy and sexism from men of color. Anyway, the intersection manifested in various forms. I will first examine the intersection as it found articulation between women and women and then between men and women.

The experiences of Sojourner Truth and Francis Gage best exemplify the intersection that was present in the long history of racial, class, and gender relationships in the United States. Their experiences also prove the complexities of the relationships and the difficulty of assigning hierarchies to oppression. However, I am very much aware that some women of color in the United States will still maintain that in a racially divided society, race and not gender becomes more prominent in creating experiences of discrimination. This paradigm becomes clear in the analysis of Sojourner Truth's experiences in Akron Ohio. At this conference that was attended mostly if not exclusively (except for Sojourner) by Euro-American women and men, men were giving reasons why Euro-American women should not be given the right to vote. One man after the other stood in the podium and justified the exclusion of women from participating in making decisions that affected their daily lives.[4]

Arguments for the exclusion of Euro-American women included the sin of the first mother, Eve was created second and sinned first, that was a powerful reason for the exclusion, one man reasoned. One man referred to the birth of Jesus Christ. Jesus Christ was not a woman; therefore, women should not be given the right to vote. Other arguments pertained to the physical weakness of Euro-American women, since men helped them over puddles of water, opened doors for them, and pulled chairs for them to sit. Arguments about women's inferior intellect were also cited as the reason. After the men made their arguments, Euro-American women were paralyzed into silence, until Sojourner Truth decided to go to the podium to respond. When she stood up, Euro-American women protested, not the men, but the women. They whispered to Francis Gage to stop Ms. Truth from going to the podium because they did not want their course to be mixed up with "the Negro's" course, they declared, very upset.

Francis Gage, an equally remarkable Euro-American woman ignored the Euro-American women's pleas and did not stop Sojourner from going to the podium. Once on the podium Sojourner addressed every argument that men cited. When she said that Jesus Christ was made by a woman and God, and man had nothing to do with it, there was a thundering applause even from those who had earlier on objected. She continued to even more applause when she addressed the sin of the first mother, by saying that, if one woman was able to turn the world upside down like that, then the women of the north and of the south will be able to turn it back right, if men would allow them.

Perhaps the most applause came when she declared that nobody helped her over puddles of water, and nobody opened doors for her; she could work from sun rise to sun set with somebody, a slave owner, beating her up on her back with a lash; not only that, she also saw most of her children sold into slavery and continued to ask, "And, Aint I a woman?" Sojourner rescued Euro-American women from the men that day in Ohio. Initially, her race as an African American woman, invoked rejection from Euro-American women. To them she was a Negro, period, her gender and her support for their course was irrelevant. Sojourner knew that she would not be part of those who would be granted the right to vote. The struggle for the right to vote at that time was for women of Euro-descent. That notwithstanding, she saw the struggle as that of all women. She and Miss Gage saw the intersection that others failed to see. In this context one would be justified to say that race seem more salient here than gender. Be that as it may, they both exist in the equation.

Rollins (1985), in her ethnographic work on black domestics in the United States, shows a different manifestation of the intersection of race, class and gender between women and women. Aspects of inequality as played out in the relationship between an African American woman employee and her Euro-American woman employer manifest in ways that blends the three variables. Phenotype distinctions, that is, race becomes an instrument that the employer uses to dehumanize her African American employee. The Euro-American employee treated the African American as invisible, as though she does not exist. The employers' skin color translated into a symbol of success, which made it easier for her to achieve with her African American employee than with other women of Euro-descent. Further, gender (female to female) blended together with class (/servant/employee to master/employer) and phenotypes (skin color, etc.) in determining the dynamics of the relationship. The African American employee would exhibit extreme forms of deference to the Euro-American employer, on one hand. On the other hand the Euro-American employer will display condescending maternalism towards her African-American employee. In addition, the employer will feel entitled to intrude into her employee's life.

The invasion served to empower the employer and reaffirmed her self worth as she continued to demean her employee who was under pressure to develop affective bonds. One other dynamic that manifested in this relationship was the need for the African American employee to perpetuate the false notion of their employer's superiority and their (African American) inferiority in their employer's mind. They would not reveal their economic successes to their Euro-American women employers, e.g., children in college, owning a car. They understood the need of their employer to feel superior in the face of the Euro-American male patriarchy and sexism. Similarly, Segura (1994) in her discussion of Chicana' women's triple oppression in the contemporary USA also sees race as playing a decisive role in the access of Chicana women to jobs. Segura sees the confluence as important and like the others she acknowledges that racial discrimination sometimes makes race more salient in determining an individual's position in the economic order in the USA.

The intersection of gender relations is very complex. The complexity increases as it relates to men and women of color relationships, especially in a racially divided society like the United States and South Africa. In their book Gender Talk, Cole and Guy-Sheftall (2003) write:

"We have also been engaged in difficult dialogues with Black men about their sexism, problematic conceptions of Black manhood, and

their own gender privilege, even within a culture
that continues to be deeply racist and demonizes
them" (xxxii).

Confronting sexism and forms of patriarchy in
communities of color has historically posed a
challenge. The saliency of race functioned to both
preclude and undermine the importance of addressing the forms of patriarchy and sexism as
practiced by men of color. Both Chicana and African American women talk about how the men in
their communities will label them traitors and
collaborators with the Euro system that brutal-
izes them on the daily basis when they attempted
to address sexism as they experienced it from the
men of color. The same dynamic also manifested
in Asian American communities. Chow in her article "The Development of Feminist Consciousness Among Asian American Women" writes:

> *As Asian women became active in their commu-*
> *nities, they encountered sexism. Even though*
> *many Asian American women realized that they*
> *usually occupied subservient positions in the*
> *male-dominated organizations within Asian com-*
> *munities, their ethnic pride and loyalty frequently*
> *kept them from public revolt. More recently*
> *some Asian American women have recognized*
> *that these organizations have not been particu-*
> *larly responsive to their needs and concerns as*
> *women. They also protested that their intense*
> *involvement did not and will not result in equal*
> *participation as long as the traditional domi-*
> *nance by men and the gendered division of labor*
> *remain (Ngang-Ling Chow, 1987, p 288).*

The arguments varied. In the video *Black is Black
Ain't*, (1995) bell hooks clearly articulates the presence of gender inequality in the African American communities and the energy that is directed
at making it a taboo subject. She recalls an incident where her father unilaterally ordered her
mother to leave the house. The incident confused
her and conflicted with her perception of marriage as a partnership. In the same video bell
hooks continues to take issue with males of color
equating the reclamation of the race to the redemption of an emasculated male identity. Ironically, when male identity is defined as such, it
encompasses forms of oppressions that marginalize women of color. In the same video Angela

Davis also talks about how women subordination
in the African American community needs to be
addressed, and how African American males
should take equal responsibility.

Often men will cite traditional values to justify
sexism, even in the U.S. Chicana women will be
told that they are betraying La Rasa. Elizabeth
Martinez (1998) notes that in situations where
Chicano and Chicana are faced with racism,
fighting for women's rights is relegated to secondary status. She states "women will feel an impulse towards unity with rather than enmity
towards their brothers" p. 183. Confronting sexism in the communities of color also translated
for men into the desire by women of color to be
like women of Euro-descent, adopting their values and ideals. This was just another way of
silencing the women from addressing the sexism
and patriarchy in their communities. Examples
of instances where women of color are silenced
when they try to address sexism within their own
communities are many. Women are often told
that they should not air dirty linen in public, because the enemy will use it against the race.
Again here this quote from Cole and Guy-Sheftall
elucidates the issue: *"whatever differences that
we have as Black brothers and sisters should and
can be worked out behind closed doors, and not
be aired in public, as if we need to be validated
by whites or the white media."* (xxxii). This was
said by an African American male journalist, re-
acting to statements made by an African American woman about O.J. Simpson and Clarence
Thomas.

In the Asian American women's protest
against sexism within the community will be criticized as *"weakening of the male ego, dilution
of efforts and resources in Asian Communities,
destruction of working relationships between
Asian men and women, setbacks for the Asian
American cause, cooptation into the larger society—in short the affiliation with the feminist
movement is perceived as a threat to solidarity
within their own community."* (Ngan-Ling
Chow, 1987, p 2).

Since there are similarities and also differences
in the experience of women of color with South
African women, I will in the next section examine the experiences of women in South Africa for
comparative purposes.

The South African Case

For a long time indigenous African women in South Africa faced the same dilemma. It became very difficult for women to address the subordination of women within the movements that were fighting against the racist policies of the South African Apartheid Government. Apartheid was the system that divided people based on the color of the skin and treated them accordingly. The indigenous Africans were placed at the bottom of the ladder in the hierarchical structure of oppression hierarchy and relegated to the margins. It was a brutal racist system that treated Africans as secondary citizens with no rights at all. The apartheid racist system was also very sexist. Women were denied many legal rights. At some point African women were legally denied the right to occupy a house if the husband died and the woman did not have a son. An African woman could not purchase anything on credit unless her husband also co-signs. Outside of the apartheid sexist and raciest laws, African women were also faced with forms of patriarchy from within their own culture. Much has been debated about the origin of the sexism and patriarchy. Granted some of it was inherited and imposed by the Euro-Africans during colonialism and apartheid era. Be that as it may, it existed and it impacted women's lives. It needed to be addressed.

The preference was to talk about the contributions of women to the liberation struggle, but not to address the gender inequality among the Africans. Often three different views prevailed. One view preferred that the close door or closet resolution of the problem. In other words, if men and women publicly confronted patriarchy and sexism, the evil apartheid agents will use it against them. The second view opted for the problem to be left to individual couples married or single to resolve. The advocates of the view opposed turning the issues into a systemic problem within the movement. The last view saw women's subordination and exclusion as an important but not as an urgent problem; or as unimportant. To them overthrowing the racist regime superceded any kind of struggle.

The then liberation movements in South Africa made efforts and strides in gender issues. Indeed, the African National Congress Women's Charter and the Women's League bear testimony to this. However, on a daily basis, women did face some of the similar difficulties that women in the United States faced. Shahrazad Ali's ideas in her book *The Black Man's Guide to Understanding Black Women* (1990), about the relationship between African American men and women, echoed what African women had to face when they dared address sexism within their own community. Ali posits that men must rule and women must submit to their natural and traditional roles, as well as to the man's will. These ideas are presented as traditional roles. Any woman who was seen to violate these roles was then described as embracing evil Western ideas. In South Africa women faced the same obstacles as well.

What should be understood is, women experience sexism and patriarchy. The experience and not the western ideas prompts their objection to the dictates that put them in the situation. It is common knowledge that I lost a husband and son on the same day, and at the time when I was expecting one of my daughters. During that period I was required to sit in a very hot room with my head bowed to show my grief. I was pained in the most terrible way; I did not need to have my head bowed all the time. I felt I needed to go outside and get some fresh air. I was pregnant and it was very hot. While my mother was very reluctant to go against the dictates of my late husband's mother, and could not bring herself to rescue me, I was fortunate that my sister was there. Mary Grace, my sister would tell everybody that I needed to take a walk and needed fresh air. That caused a lot of tension that my mother avoided, but to my sister my comfort was most important. She knew I was grieving. She could not even comprehend the extent of my grief, because she said to me after the tragedy, "Ati (my name) I am feeling so much pain, and Simmy (my late husband) and Thami (my late son) are just my brother-in-law and nephew, I cannot even imagine what pain you are feeling right now." My sister knew I was grieving whether my head was bowed 24 hours a day or not. A widow then was not allowed to go outside because that would undermine the extent of her grief, while a widower could go about and even sit under a tree, in a shade. If this was tradition, it was a tradition that was oppressing me and I needed it changed.

I was experiencing it as oppressive that is why I wanted it changed, not because some Euro-woman told me it was oppressive. I don't need a Euro-woman to tell me about my experience.

In 1996 I was invited to speak to a multiracial audience at University of Witwatersrand on my research that focused on the mediation of patriarchy and sexism by women in South Africa. During the talk I referred to the differential treatment of widows and widowers, and to this experience. While I love my culture very much, I am aware of oppressive tenants in it. At the end of my talk an African man stood up and berated me on embracing Western values and undermining the fundamentals of the African culture. He told me that he would be damned to listen to somebody who has just come from the US to lecture him on sexism. Needless to say, I did not have to respond to this man, because all the women in the audience of all descents and colors responded to him and lectured him on patriarchy and sexism. The only thing that I said at the end was to ask the women if they have been to the U.S. and the answer was no. That was an attempt to silence me. The man was obviously oblivious to the intersection of racial and sexual oppression.

Conclusion

Clearly, attempts to silence existed and still exists when the intersection of race, class, and gender are addressed. This should not be the case. Acknowledging the existence of sexism, patriarchy, and gender inequality will lead us to solutions and better relationships. The call to the recognition of the intersection does not constitute an oblivion to women of Euro-descents' subordination. However, it is important for Euro-American women to recognize the existence of privilege for a true sisterhood and brotherhood to be forged. It is in order here that I conclude by referring to MacKinnon (1996) disturbing claims that really prove her lack of awareness to the intersection of race, class and gender.

MacKinnon fails to understand or see the presence of race when she was given the statistics that African American women are raped twice as Euro-American women by Euro-American men. She asked "when African American women are

raped twice as white women are they not raped as women." Her question indicates that she marginalizes the racial component in the whole equation. Her lack of awareness becomes even more apparent when she continues to claim that she views the whole experience as a composite rather than a divided unitary whole. Her line of argument still fails to acknowledge the meaning of the intersection of race, class, and gender. To the extent that patriarchal atrocities sometimes affect other women more than the others, points to different contexts created by multiple factors. Those multiple factors, race and class being the two of them need to be addressed together with sexual inequality. The fact that the tendency is to subject women of color with PhD's to more interrogation than women of Euro-descent to proof their qualifications, the fact that Euro-American women ideas will be embraced quicker, the fact that African American or Mexican women are raped twice more than Euro-American women, demand the approach that takes race, class, and gender into account.

Men of color too should take responsibility. Addressing sexism and patriarchy does not mean women hate men. I personally love men to death, and that should not stop me from addressing sexism in as much as it should not stop me from addressing racism, classism, and heterosexism and their intersection.

Notes

1. Mosupyoe (1999).
2. The north and south characterization follows the debate at the United Nations in the 1970's. The intention was to move away from the political and economic valuation of other countries as inferior. People claimed confusion with New Zealand and Australia. They were both regarded as northern and therefore part of the west. The north in this article refers to "western-Euro" and the south to indigenous and/or different from western-Euro."
3. ibid.
4. Mosupyoe, (1999).

References

Cole, J. B. and Guy-Sheftall 2003, *Gender Talk, The Struggle for Women's Equality in African American Communities*, New York: Random House Publishing Group.

hooks, bell 1984, *Feminist Theory from margin to center*, Boston: South End Press.

Joy James 1996, "Experience, Reflection, Judgment and Action Teaching Theory, Talking Community," in D. Bell and Klein *Radically Speaking: Feminsim Reclaimed*, p 37 ed. Australia: Spinifex Press.

MacKinnon, P. 1996, "From Practice to Theory, or What is White Anyway" in Bell, D. and Klein, R. *Radically Speaking: Feminism Reclaimed*, pp 45–54 ed. Australia: Spinifex Press.

MacKintosh, P. 1990, White Privilege: Unpacking the Invisible Knapsack" an excerpt from working papers 189. *White Privilege and Male Privilege: A Personal Account of Coming to See Correspondence through Work in Women's Studies.*

Marlon Riggs et al. 1995, *Black is Back Ain't*. California: California Newsreel.

Martínez, E. De Colores Means All of Us Latina Views for a Multi-Colored Century. Cambridge: South End Press.

Mosupyoe, B. 1999, *Women's Multicentric Ways of Knowing, Being, and Thinking*, 2nd Edition. New York: McGraw-Hill Companies, Inc.

Ngan-Ling, E 1987, "The Development of Feminist Consciousness Among Asian American Women" in *Gender and Society, Vol. 1. No. 3 September 1987* 284–289, 1987 Sociology for Women Society.

Segura, D. A. 1994, Working at Motherhood: Chicana and Mexican Immigrant Mothers and Employment. London: Routledge.

Chapter 1 Bibliography

Banton, M.
     1967 *Anthropological Approaches to the Study of Religion*. London: Tavistock.
Bantu Authorities Act, no 68, 1951.
Bardhan, K.
     1986 "Stratification of Women's Work in Rural India: Determinants, Effects and Strategies." In *Social and Economic Development in India: A Reassessment*. New Delhi: Sage Publications.
Barrett, D.B.
     1968 *Schism and Renewal in Africa: An Analysis of Six Thousand Contemporary Religious Movements*. Nairobi: Oxford University Press.
     ———. 1970 AD 2000: 350 Million Christians in Africa. In *International Review of Missions*. Nairobi: Oxford University Press.
Barret, J., et al
     1985 *South African Women on the Move*. London: Zed Books Ltd.
Barth, J.A.
     1979 "Introduction." In *Ethnic Group and Boundaries*, edited by Barth, F. Bergen-Oslo: Universitetforgalet.
Bay, E.
     1982 *Women and Work in Africa*. Colo.: Westview Press.
Beattie, J.M. and Middleton, J.
     1969 *Spirit Mediums and Society in Africa*. London: Routledge and Kegan Paul.
de Beauvoir, S.
     1953 *The Second Sex*. Harmondsworth: Penguin.
Bell, D. and Klein, R.
     1996 *Radically Speaking: Feminism Reclaimed*, eds. Australia: Spinifex Press.
Bellah, R.
     1970 *Beyond Belief: Essays on Religion*. New York: Harper.
Bellman, B.L.
     1977 The Social Organization of Knowledge in the Kpelle Ritual. In *The New Religions of Africa*, edited by Jules-Rosette, B. New Jersey: Albex Publishing Corporation.
Burja, J.
     19 "Urging Women to Redouble their Efforts." In *Class, Gender and Capitalist Transformation in Africa*. London: Tavistock.
Buvinic, M., Lycette, M. & Mcgreevey, W.P.
     1983 *Women and Poverty in the Third World*. Baltimore: John's Hopkins University Press.
Breidenbach, P.S.
     1973 *Sumsum Edumwa, the Spiritual Work: Forms of Symbolic Action and Communication in Ghanian Movements*. Northwest: University Press.
Brookes, E.H.
     1956 *The History of Native Policy in South Africa*. Pretoria: Van Schaiks Limited.

     ———. 1967 *The Color Problems of South Africa*. Johannesburg: Johannesburg Publishers.
Cairnos, J.
     1974 *After Polygamy was Made a Sin*. London: Routledge and Kegan Paul.
Carr, M.
     1954 *Appropriate Technology for African Women*. Addis Ababa: Economic Commission for Africa, United Nations.
Carrillo, R.
     "Feminist Perspectives on Women in Development." In *Persistent Inequalities*, edited by Tinker, I. New York: Oxford University Press.
Caulfield, M.D.
     1974 "Imperialism, the Family and Cultures of Resistance." *Socialist Revolutions* 4 (20): 67–85.
     ———. 1983 "Equality, Sex, and Mode of Production." In *Social Inequality*, edited by Berreman, G., New York: Academic Press.
Chodorow, N.
     1978 *The Reproduction of Mothering*. Berkeley: The University of California Press.
Cohen, S.
     1955 *Folk Devils and Moral Panics*. New York: African Publishing Corporation.
Cohn, N.
     1978 *The Pursuit of Millennium*. London: Secker and Warburg.
Colson, E.
     1969 Spirits Possession Among the Tonga of Zambia. In *Mediums and Society in Africa*. Beattie, J.M. and Middleton, J. Spirit eds. London: Routledge and Kegan Paul.
Collins, P.
     1988 "The Emerging Theory and Pedagogy of Black Women's Studies." *Feminist Issues*, 6.
Comaroff, J.
     1956 *Body of Power Spirit of Resistance*. Chicago: Chicago University Press.
Comaroff, J. and J.
     1991 of *Revelation and Revolution: Christianity Colonialism and Consciousness in South Africa*, Volume One Chicago: The University of Chicago Press.
     ———. 1997 of *Revelation and Revolution: Christianity Colonialism and Consciousness in South Africa*, Volume Two. Chicago: The University of Chicago Press.
Constitution of the Republic of South Africa.
     As adopted on 8 May 1996 and amended on 11 October 1996 by the Constitutional Assembly. South Africa: ANC Government Printers.
Coser, R.
     "Authority and Structural Ambivalence in the Middle Class Family." In *The Family: Its Structures and Function*, ed. by R. Coser New York: St. Martin's Press.
CrossRoads
     1994 July/August No 43 *Building the New South Africa*.

Curtin, P.D.
1971 Jihad in West Africa: Early Phase and Interrelations in Mauritania and Senegal. *Journal of African History* 13 (4): 647–658.

Dachs, A.J.
1972 Missionary Imperialism: The Case of Bechuanaland. *Journal of African History* 12, 1, 11–24.

Daneel, M.L.
1970 (a) *Zionism and Faith Healing in Rhodesia*. The Hague: Mouton. vol 1.
———. 1970 (b) *The God of the Matopo Hills*. Leiden: Africa Study Center.

Fry, P.
1976 *Spirits of Protests: Spirits Medium and the Articulation of Consensus Among the Zezuru of Southern Rhodesia (Zimbabwe)*. London: Cambridge University Press.

Geertz, C.
1966 Religion and Cultural Systems. In *Anthropological Approaches to the Study of Religion*, edited by Banton, M. London: Tavistock.

Gerson, G.
1985 *Hard Choice*. Berkeley: University of California Press.

Gerth, H. and Mills, W.
1953 *Character and Social Structure: The Psychology of Social Institutions*. New York: Harcourt, Brace and World.

Giddens, A.
1976 *New Rules of Sociological Methods: A Positive Critique of Interpretive Sociologies*. New York: Basic Books.

Gluckman, M.
1956 *Custom and Conflict in Africa*. Oxford: Blackwell. 1972 Moral Crisis: Magical and Secular Solutions. In *The Allocation of Responsibility*, edited by Gluckman, M. Manchester: University Press.

Goody, J.
1962 *Death, Property and the Ancestors*. London: Tavistock.

Groves, C.P.
1954 The Planning of Christianity in Africa. *Africa 2*. London: Lutterworth Press.

Gusfield, J.R.
1973 *Utopian Myths and Movements in the Modern Societies*. Morritown, N.J.: General Learning Corporation.

Hackett, R.I.J.
1987 *The New Religious Movements in Nigeria*. New York: Edwin Mellen Press.

Haliburton, G.M.
1971 *The Prophet Harris*. London: Longman.

Hall, S. Jefferson, T. and Robert, B.
1976 *Resistant Through Ritual*. London: Hutchison.

Hammond-Tooke, W.D.
1953 *The Bantu Speaking People of South Africa*. London: Routledge and Kegan.

Hunt, D.R.
1931 The Development of the Bapedi. *Bantu Studies* Vol V 1931 4 276.

Huntington, S.
1975 "Issues in Women's Role in Economic Development Critique and Alternatives." *Journal of Marriage and the Family* 37 (4) 100–12. International Labor Office, 1984 *Rural Development and Women in Africa*. Geneva: International Labor Development.

Jabavu, D.D.T.
1942 *An African Independent Church*. Lovedale.

Jules-Rosette, B.
1976 (a) *African Apostles: Ritual and Conversion in the Church of John Maranke*. Ithaca: Cornell University Press.
———. 1975 (b) Marapodi: An Independent Religious Community in Transition. *African Studies Review*, 45, 2, 150–165.
———. 1975 (c) Song and Spirit: The Use of Songs in the Management of the Ritual Settings. *Africa*, 45(2), 150–165.
———. 1976 The Conversion Experience. *Journal of Religion in Africa*, 7: 132–164.
———. 1977 Grass Roots Ecumenism: Religious and Social Cooperation in Two Urban African Churches. *African Social Research*, 23: 185–216.
———. 1978 Prophecy and Leadership in an African Church: A Case Study in Continuity and Change. In *African Christianity: Patterns of Religious Change and Continuity*. Bond, G., Walker S. and Johnson W. eds. New York: Academic Press Inc.

James, J.
1996 "Experience Reflection, Judgement and Action: Teaching Theory, Talking Community" in *Radically Speaking: Feminism Reclaimed*. Bell, D. and Klein, R, 37–44 eds. Australia: Spinifex Press.

Jaquette, J.
1982 "Women and Modernization Theory." *World Politics* 34(2): 267–284.
———. 1990 "Gender and Justice in Economic Development." In *Persistent Inequalities*, edited by Tinker, I. New York: Oxford University Press.

Loutif, M.
1980 *Rural Women: Unequal Partners in Development*. Geneva: ILO.

Lukhaimane, E.
1980 *The History of the Zion Christian Church*. Unpublished Masters Thesis. Pietersburg: University of the North.

Mac Cormack, C.
1977 (a) "Biological Events and Cultural Control." In *Women's Education in the Third World: Comparative Perspectives*, Elliot, C. and Kelly, G.P. eds., 331–343 Albany: SUNNY Press.
———. 1977 (b) The Public of A Secrete Society. In *The New Religions of Africa*, edited by Julles-Rossette, B. New Jersey: Ablex Publishing Corporation.
———. 1981. "Development with Equity for Women." In *Women and World Change*. Black, N., and Cotter A.B. Albany: SUNNY Press.

————. 1982 "Control of Land, Labor and Capital in Rural Southern Sierra Leone." In *Women and Work in Africa* edited by Bay, E.G.

Mac Cormack, C. & Strathern, M.
1980 *Nature Culture and Gender.* Cambridge: Cambridge University Press.

MacKnight, J.D.
1967 Extra Descent Group Ancestor Cults in African Society. *Africa,* 37 (1):1–21.

MacKinnon, C.A.
1996 "From Practice to Theory, or What is a White Woman Anyway." In *Radically Speaking: Feminism Reclaimed* Bell, D. and Klein, R. eds, 45–55. Australia: Spinifex Press.

MacKintosh, P.
1990 White Privilege: "Unpacking the Invisible Knapsack." In *Working Papers 189 White Privilege and Male Privilege: A Personal Account of Coming to See Correspondence Through Work in Women's Studies.*

Madala, A.
1965 *Amayo Amafutshane.* Cape Town: Oxford University Press.

Magubane, B.
1965 A Critical Analysis of the Indices Used in the Study of Social Change in the Study of Colonial Africa. *Current Anthropology* 12, Introduction, 22 415–445. 1979 *African Independent Churches.* Hammanskraal: St. Peters Seminary. Mail and Guardian 1996 September Khumalo, S. "You tout Dr. Mamphela Ramphela—" Mosala, I. "Letting Down Steve Bilko" Ramphela, M. "Can Steven Biko Arbitrate From the Grave."

Makhathini, D.L.
1965 *Ancestors, Umoya, Angels in Missiology Institute: Our Approach to the Independent Church Movement in South Africa.* Mapumolo: Lutheran Theological College.

Malinowski, B.
1922 *Argonauts of Western Pacific.* London: Routledge and Kegan Paul
————. 1957 *The Sexual Life of Savages in N.W. Melanesia.* London: Routledge and Kegan Paul.
————. 1961 *Sex and Repression in Savage Society.* London: Routledge and Kegan Paul.
————. 1978 *Crime and Custom in Savage Society.* London: Routledge and Kegan Paul.

Maranke, J.
1953 *The New Witnesses of the Apostles.* Rhodesia (Zimbabwe): Bocha.

Martin, M.
1964 *The Biblical Concept of Messianism and Messianism in Southern Africa.* Pietersburg: Morija.
————. 1968 Prophetism in the Congo—Origin and Development of An African Independent Church. *Ministry: Theological Review of Africa,* 8(4).
————. 1971 The Mai Chaza Church in Rhodesia. In *African Initiatives in Religion* edited by Barret, D.B. Kenya: East African Publishing House.

————. 1975 *Kimbangu—An African Prophet and his Church.* London: Oxford Press.

Marwick, M.
1970 *Witchcraft and Sorcery: Selected Readings.* London: Penguin.

Marx, K.
1964 *The Communist Manifesto.* New York: Russel.
————. 1967 *Capital: A Critique of Political Economy,* 3 Vols. New York: International Publishers.

Massiah, J.
1958 "Defining Women's Work in the Commonwealth Caribbean." In *Persistent Inequalities,* edited by Tinker, I. New York: Oxford University Press.

Mayer, M.
1961 *Townsmen and Tribesmen.* Cape Town: Oxford University Press.

Mazumdar, V.
1985 *The Emergence of Women's Questions in India and the Role of Women in Development Countries.* New Dehli: Center for Women's Development Studies.

Mazumdar, V. & Sharma, K.
1990 "Sexual Division of Labor and the Subordination of Women: A Reappraisal from India. In *Persistent Inequalities,* edited by Tinker, I. New York: Oxford University Press.

Mbiti, J.S.
1969 *African Religions and Philosophy.* London: Heineman.

Meli, F.
1988 A History of the ANC: South Africa Belongs to us. Harare: Zimbabwe Publishing House.

Mendosa, E.
1977 Elders Office Holders and Ancestors Among the Sisala of Northern Ghana. *Africa,* 46, 57–65.

Mernissi, F.
1976 "The Moslem World, Women Excluded from Development." In *Women and World Development.* New York: Praeger Publishers.

Mies, M.
1986 *Patriarchy and Accumulation on a World Scale: Women in the International Division of Labor.* London: Zed Press.
————. 1988 "Women's Work and Capitalism." In *Women: The Last Colony.* Mies, M., Bennholdt-Thomsen, V, and von Werlhof, C. eds. London: The Zed Book Limited.
————. 1988 "Social Origins and the Sexual Division of Nature" In *Women: The Last Colony.* London: The Zed Book Limited.
————. 1988 "Class Struggle and Women's Struggle in Rural India" In *Women: The Last Colony.* London: The Zed Book Limited.
————. 1980 *Indian Women and Patriarchy.* New Delhi: Concept Publishing Company. Mies, M., Bennholdt-Thomsen, V., von Werlhof, C. 1988 *Women: The Last Colony.* London: The Zed Book Limited.

Mills, W.
1959 *The Sociological Imagination.* New York: Oxford University Press.

Mitchell, C.
The Meaning of Misfortune for Urban Africa. In *African Systems of Thought*. Fortes, M. and Dieterlin, G. eds. London: International African Institute.
———. 1969 *Social Network in Urban Situations*. England: Manchester University Press.
———. 1970 Towards a Sociology of African Independency. *Journal of Religion in Africa*, III: 99. 2–21.

Mofokeng, T.
1990 Black Theology in South Africa: Achievements Problems and Prospects. In *Christianity in South Africa*, edited by Prozenky, M. Berglei: Southern.

Mokoka, H.
1967 *Dipuku tsa Bapedi*. Pretoria: Bosele Printers.

Molland, E.
1955 *Christendom*. London: Oxford University Press.

Moller, H.J.
1992 *God en die Voorouergeeste in die Lewe van die Stedelike Bantoe*. Pretoria: Human Science Research Council.

Mönnig, H.O.
1967 *The Pedi*. Pretoria: Van Schaik Limited.

Morgan, S.
1989 *Gender and Anthropology*. Washington D.C.: AA Association.

Morris, C.
1962 *The End of the Missionary? A Short Account of the Political Consequences of Missions in Northern Rhodesia*. London: Cargate.

Muntemba, M.
1960 "Women and Agricultural Change in the Railway Region of Zambia: Dispossession and Counterstrategies, 1930–70." In *Women and Work in Africa*, edited by Bay, E. Colo.: Westview Press.

Murdock, G.P. 1949 *Social Structure*. New York: Macmillan.

Murphee, M.
1969 *Christianity and the Shona*. London: Anthlone Press.
———. 1971 Religious Independency Among the Budja Vapostori. In African Initiative in Religion, edited by Barret, D.B. Nairobi: East African Publishing House.

Mzimba, L.
1940 The African Church. In *Christianity and the Natives of South Africa*, edited by Taylor, J.D. Pretoria: Van Schaiks.

Nash, J. & Kelly, P.
1983 *Women and the International Division of Labor*. Albany: SUNNY Press.

Nash, J. & Safa, H. eds.
1985 *Woman and Change in Latin America*. Mass.: Bergin and Garvey.

Ndiokwere, N.I.
1981 *Prophecy and Revolution in the Role of Prophets in the African Independent Churches and in Biblical Tradition*. London: Oxford University Press.

Neame, L.E.
1905 Ethiopianism: *The Danger of a Black Church*. *Empire Review*, New Nation News Paper. Johannesburg 1998.

Ngubane, H.
1977 *Body and Mind in Zulu Medicine*. Cambridge: Cambridge University Press.

Nida, E.A.
1971 New Religion for Old. In *Church and Culture Change in Africa*. edited by Bosch, D.J. Pretoria: Lux Mundi.

Norbeck, E.
1961 *Religion in Primitive Society*. New York: Harper and Row.

Norton, G.R.
1940 The Emergence of New Religious Organizations in South Africa, *Journal of the Royal African Society*.

Nthabu, B.Y. (now Mosupyoe)
1989 *Meaning and Symbolism in the ZCC of South Africa*. University of California, Berkeley.

Obbo, C.
1980 *African Women*. London: Zed Press
———. 1990 "East African Women, Work, and the Articulation of Dominance." In *Persistent Inequalities*, edited by Tinker, I. New York: Oxford University Press.

O'Dean, T.F.
1966 *The Society of Religion*. Englewood Cliffs: Prentice Hall.

Ogbu, J.U.
1974 *The Next Generation: An Ethnography of Education in an Urban Neighborhood*. New York: Academic Press.

Ogbu, J.U.
1977 "African Marriage Family, Fertility and Economics" In *Current Anthropology*. 18 (2). 259–287.

Ogbu, J.U. and Simons, H.D.
1994 *Cultural Models of School Achievement: A Quantitative Test of Ogbu's Theory*. University of California at Berkeley.

Okeyo, A.P. (Formerly Pala).
1961 *Towards Strategies for Strengthening the Position of Women in Food Production*. Nairobi: Institute of Development Studies.

Ollman, B.
1971 *Allienation*. Cambridge: Cambridge University Press.

Omoyajowo, J.A.
1984 *Cheribum and Seraphim: A History of An Independent Church*. New York: Lagos.

Ramose, M.B.
1987 *Kgotso Ga e Ate*. Unpublished Manuscript: University of Zimbabwe.
———. 1988 *The Ontology of Invisible Beings*. Unpublished Pro Manuscript, Zimbabwe University.

Ranger, T.
1963 The Early History of Independency in Southern Rhodesia. In *Religion in Africa* edited by Watt, W.M. University of Edinburgh: Center of African Studies.
———. 1970 The African Voice in Southern Rhodesia. Evanston: Northwest University Press.

———. 1975 *Dance and Society in Eastern Africa 1890–1970*. London: Heineman.

Resknin, B. and Padavic,
1994 *Women and Men at Work*. Thousand Oaks: Pine Forge Press.

Rigby, P.
1968 Some Gogo Rituals of Purification. In *Dialectic in Practical Religion* edited by Leach E.R. England: Cambridge University.

Robertson, C., Berger, I.
1986 *Women and Class in Africa*. New York: Africana Publishing Company.

Rosaldo, M. & Lamphere, L.
1974 *Women, Culture and Society*. Stanford: Stanford University Press.

Rubin, G.
1975 "The Traffic in Women: Notes on the Political Economy of Sex. In *Towards an Anthropology of Women*. New York: Monthly Review Press.

Sacks, K.
1979 *Sisters and Wives*. Connecticut: Greenwood Press Inc.

Safa, H.I.
1977 "Introduction" In *Women and National Development: The Complexities of Change*. Chicago: The University of Chicago Press.
———. 1987 "Women and Change in Latin America" in Latin America: Perspectives on a Region ed. J. Hopskin. New York: Holmes and Meier.

Sahlins, M.
1976 *Culture and Practical Reason*. University of Chicago Press.
———. 1981 Historical Metaphors and Mythical Realities: *Structure in the Early History of the Sandwitch Island Kingdom*. Ann Arbor: University of Michigan Press.

Schapera, I.
1953 *The Tswana*. London: International Institute.

Schlosser, K.
1958 *Eingeborenenkirchen in Sud-und Sudwest Afrika*. Inhre Geschichte und Sozialstruktur, Kiel.

Scott, H.
1984 *Working Your Way to the Bottom: The Feminization of Poverty*. Boston: Pandora Press.

Scott, J. and Tilly, A.
1975 "Women's Work and the Family in the Nineteenth Century Europe." In *Comparative Studies in Societies and History* 17:36–64 Sechaba: *An Official Organ of the African National Congress South Africa*. United Kingdom: Sechaba Publication 1987 June Vol 22 No 6 and December Vol 22 No 12, 1989 Feb Vol 23 No 22, September Vol 23 No 9 and October Vol 23 No 10, 1990 August Vol 24 No 8.

Sibisi, H.
1977 "How African Women Cope with Migrant Labour in South Africa" In *Women and National Development: The Complexities of Change*. Chicago: The University of Chicago Press. South African *Bantu Authorities Act*, 1951 no 68.

Sundkler, B.
1948 *Bantu Prophets in South Africa*. London: Oxford University Press.
———. 1961 *Bantu Prophets in South Africa* 2nd edition. London: Oxford University Press for the International African Institute.
———. 1976 *Zulu Zion and Some Swazi Zionists*. London: Oxford University.

Star News Paper
1985 April 15 Johannesburg.

Stein, C.
1992 *Spiritual Healing: A Comparison Between New Age Grouped and African Initiated Churches in South Africa*. Pretoria: University of South Africa.

Thorbek, S.
1987 *Voices From the City* London: Zed Book Ltd.

Tinker, I. & Bramsen, B.
1976 (a) *Women and World Development*. New York: Praeger.

Tinker, I.
1976 (b) "Women in Developing Societies: Economic Independence is Not Enough." In *The Foundation For Equal Rights* edited by Chapman, R.
———. 1983 *Women in Washington: Advocates for Public Policy* Calif.: Sage Publications.
———. 1990 *Persistent Inequalities*. New York: Oxford University Press.

Urdang, S.
1989 *And Still they Dance*. New York: Monthly Review Press.

Van Warmelo, N.J.
1953 *The Bantu Speaking Peoples of South Africa*, edited by Hammond-Tooke, W.D. London: Routledge and Kegan.

Van Wyk, J.H.
1965 *Die Separatisme en Inheemse Kerklike Bewegings Onder die Bantoe van die Sothogroep*, 11: 855–856.

Wadley, S.
1980 *The Power of Tamil Women*. Syracuse: Maxwell School of Citizenship and Public Affairs.

Wallace, A.
1956 *Religion: An Anthropological View*. New York: Random House.

Warren, K.B.
1986 "Capitalist Expansion and The Moral Order: Anthropological Perspectives." In *Christianity and Capitalism: Perspectives on Religion, Liberalism and Economy*. Chicago: Center for Scientific Study of Religion.

Weber, M.
1993 *The Theory of Economic and Social Organization*, edited by Parson, T. New York: Oxford University Press.

Wellesley Editorial Committee
1977 *Women and National Development: The Complexities of Change*. Chicago: The University of Chicago Press.

West, M.
1975 *Bishops and Prophets in a Black City*. Claremont, Cape Town: David Phillip Publishers.

West, C. and Zimmerman, H.
   1979 "Doing Gender." In *Gender and Society* 1;
   125–51.
Westmore, J. and Townsed, P.
   1995 "The African Women Workers in the Textile Industry in Durban." *South African Labor Bulletin*. 2
   (4): 18–32.
Wilson, M. and Thompson, L.
   1971 *The Oxford History of South Africa*. Oxford:
   Oxford University Press.
Workers' Union 1997 and 1998 July. Cape Town:
   SAMWU.
Wright, C.
   1989 Precursors to adjustment, Revitalization, and
   Expansion: an under the carpet view of the education
   crisis in Sub-Saharan Africa. In *Zimbabwe Journal of
   Educational Research*. Volume 1, Number 1 Reconstruction and Development Programme" 1994 Johan-
   nesburg: African National Congress.
Zion Christian Church
   1985–1996 ZCC *Messenger*. ZCC Publications.

LIST OF ABBREVIATIONS

ANC	African National Congress
AIC	African Initiated Church
AICs	African Initiated Churches
AID	African Independent Churches
AZAPO	Azanian People's Organization
FEDSAW	Federation of South African Union
RDP	Restructuring and Development Program
SAMWU	South African Municipal Union Workers
ZAC	Zion Apostolic Church
S.A.Z.C.	South African Zionist Apostolic Church
ZAFM	Zion Apostolic Faith Mission ZCC
ZCC	Zion Christian Church

Some Abbreviations on Chart 1:2–1:4
I explain in the text how I use the abbreviations that refer
to the names of informants.

Prophet.	Prophetess
Adult. Liter.	Adult Literacy
Att/ville	Atteridgeville
Compl. Hs	Completed High School
DO	Drop Out
FW	Factory Worker
Hammans.	Hammanskraal
Hosp.	Hospital
Nurs.Ass.	Nursing Assistant
PR.	Place of Residence
Union Aff.	Union Affiliation

Mixed Messages: Gender Paradigms and Everyday Life in the Contemporary United States

Michelle Renée Matisons, Ph.D.

Introduction: Mixed Messages

Women who work on cars, men who cook a mean chicken dinner, girls who climb trees, boys who play with dolls. We are all familiar with idealized notions of gender associated with the categories "male" and "female"—men are strong and rational, women are weak and emotional, etc.—and we are equally familiar with the limits of these categories. No one lives up to these ideals and, on an individual level, we witness daily the transgression of strict gender categories in our own lives and the lives of people around us. It can be argued that because of varying family constellations, class privilege, religious and cultural standards, racial and ethnic identities, and sexual practices, no two people are subjected to the exact same gender expectations. For example, if your mother was a "women's libber" in the 1960s, you may have a different understanding of what it means to be a man or a woman than your best friend who was raised in a traditional midwestern Catholic family. Given the wide range of family arrangements and political ideologies within the United States, it is difficult to summarize how gender plays out on an individual basis. If gender is a complex and multilayered social phenomenon why do some people keep trying to present it as if it is so simple?

Gender, like race, has been historically presented as a fixed biological condition; you are

either a man or a woman, right? What's the big deal? There are a variety of academic fields and theories producing research on the idea that gender is not based on biological processes but on social and cultural processes instead. The fields of biology, anthropology, law, and politics provide fresh views on gender. What does it mean to say that gender is not biological but social? Aren't there a variety of physical differences between men and women? Many advocates of the view that gender is socially constructed would answer this question with a tentative "yes, but. . . ."

Like race, the solution is not to deny that physical differences exist and insist on a colorblind approach to race relations. Instead we should ask: "So what?" What does it really tell us about a person if his skin is black or she has a vagina instead of a penis? Does it mean that he cannot be trusted? Does it mean she is physically weak? Of course not! We can all think of concrete examples that contradict these pernicious stereotypes. Social policies and attitudes inspired by fixed gender ideals exist despite our everyday experiences with a diverse array of gendered behaviors. This interface between the reality of our gendered lives and the ideologies and discourses that support and reinforce the contemporary American two-gender system is explored in this chapter.

In parts one and two of this chapter we consider two contrasting gender paradigms. The "genderblindness paradigm" denies differences between men and women and the "planetary paradigm" emphasizes fundamental differences between the genders. In part three we explore an approach to gender that transcends this focus on fundamental sameness or fundamental difference— the "gender diversity paradigm." The idea of gender diversity is found in biological, anthropological, legal, and political scholarship. It is offered as the most adequate approach to studying contemporary gender arrangements in the United States, although it, too, embodies contradictions and problems that shape the parameters of current debates in the field of Women's Studies.

Because there is such a variety of approaches to analyzing gender dynamics, there is much confusion about the scope of and solutions to gender oppression. On the one hand, mixed messages about gender cause oppressive attitudes, miscommunication, anxiety, and conservative, simpleminded, and authoritarian solutions. On the other hand, these mixed messages are also celebrated in new frameworks that point us beyond an antiquated two-gender system that masks and undermines the variety of human experiences in society. Our ability to distinguish between various gender paradigms is necessary to help establish political goals in the context of these shifting and competing mixed messages about gender.

Part One: The Genderblindness Paradigm

Chapter one discusses and criticizes the colorblind approach to contemporary race relations in the United States. There are many criticisms of the colorblind approach and these criticisms were recently highlighted in the successful campaign to defeat California's Proposition 54, the Racial Privacy Initiative. Many have argued that colorblindness—the idea of "not seeing color" but the attributes of the individual instead—is actually an effort to deny contemporary racism and discredit race-based legislation such as antiracial profiling initiatives and affirmative action in education and employment. The colorblindness argument states that despite our history of slavery, colonization, and genocide we are all working on an even playing field now. One of the most misleading aspects of this argument is that on the surface it sounds quite reasonable. Who wants to be singled out for their skin color instead of their unique individual characteristics? In fact, Dr. Martin Luther King Jr.'s words about "judging a man by the content of his character and not by the color of his skin" appears to be compatible with the colorblindness approach. However, colorblindness is highly incompatible with King's own vision of racial equality since it obstructs efforts to analyze and address contemporary racism.

While colorblindness is one prevalent attempt to deny race-based discrimination, genderblindness denies gender-based discrimination in much the same way. The idealistic appeal to "not see gender" is also used to justify sexism in employment, education, and our other major social institutions. If people can claim that they hire the best person for the job regardless of gender, they can continue to favor the male gender which, as a general group, has access to higher education and better paying jobs. Genderblindness suggests that the more we talk about gender the more we contribute to women's lack of social and political progress. It is based on a set of universal criteria that can be used to determine the best person for admission, the job, etc., while denying the historical inequalities that continue to shape women's experiences in society. Criticisms of both colorblindness and genderblindness focus on the significance of historical discrimination in shaping today's "uneven playing field" for white women and men and women of color.

While the genderblindness paradigm ignores discriminatory practices occurring under the artificial rubric of an even playing field, it plays an important role in another aspect of public life: hostile work environment and sexual harassment legislation. As more U.S. women have entered the workforce, the regulation of sexual conduct has become a central and frequently contentious issue. Ideally, a harassment free environment is a gender-neutral or genderblind territory where women and men can work together without distraction and the subsequent abuses of power that result from exploiting differences.

A pure genderblind approach is difficult to achieve because gender differences are a large part of our dominant popular culture, racial and ethnically specific cultures, and languages. Even if a work environment has achieved a modicum of genderblindness it is still next to impossible to avoid subtle or even unconscious references to gender difference. An example will help illustrate this point. A male boss enters a room and greets his employees. "Hello, Frank," he says, "I see you are almost over your cold." "Bill, did you finish that report for this afternoon's meeting?" "Hi, Ann. Did you do something different to your hair?" This is just one example of how difficult it is to avoid noticing gender and communicating these differences. Regardless of these difficulties, the quest to create a genderblind environment in the context of workplace ethics is a positive one. In general, the genderblind paradigm has its pros and cons depending on how it is being applied. Ultimately it is naïve to believe that we can completely ignore gender differences, and this insight leads us to consider the strengths of the next prevalent paradigm—the planetary paradigm.

Part Two: The Planetary Paradigm

While the genderblindness paradigm tends to be used in the job sector to negatively govern employment decisions and, more positively, to shape workplace etiquette, a competing paradigm can be found in popular psychology. This paradigm has influenced popular culture—especially the talk shows—and it shapes many people's views about gender dynamics. John Gray's best-selling book, *Men Are from Mars, Women Are from Venus: A Practical Guide for Improving Communication and Getting What You Want in Your Relationships*, is the most influential of these popular psychology texts. Gray's book describes contemporary U.S. gender relations using a humorous intergalactic metaphor. He argues that the best way to understand gender dynamics is to accept that men and women are different; it is as if we are from two different planets. Gray writes:

> *Imagine that men are from Mars and women are from Venus. One day long ago the Martians, looking through their telescopes, discovered the Venusians . . . They fell in love and quickly, invented space travel, and flew to Venus . . . The love between the Venusians and the Martians was magical. They delighted in being together, doing things together, and sharing together. Though from different worlds, they reveled in their differences . . . For years they lived together in love and harmony . . . Then they*

> *decided to fly to Earth. In the beginning everything was wonderful and beautiful. But the effects of Earth's atmosphere took hold . . . Both the Martians and the Venusians forgot that they were from different planets and were supposed to be different . . . since that day men and women have been in conflict (Gray 1992, 10).*

Gray's story of an intergalactic culture clash captures the spirit of much popular discourse about U.S. gender relations (or the battle between the sexes, as it is often referred to). He does not venture into the rocky terrain of explaining why these differences exist. Instead he opts for the much safer assertion that "there are many answers, ranging from biological differences, parental influence, education, and birth order, to cultural conditioning by society, the media, and history" (Gray, 7).

While he does not take a position on the issue, his strong emphasis on difference echoes cultural feminist beliefs about gender. Cultural feminism argues that men and women are fundamentally biologically different and this results in different value systems. (Gray assumes people can change, though, and if these characteristics are completely biological, then change is unlikely.) Based on this biological analysis, cultural feminists advocate breaking away from male society as much as possible and establishing alternative institutions based on feminine characteristics of peace, cooperation, mutual recognition, and support. This type of feminism emerged in the mid 1970s and is not as popular today.

The idea that biology and society both play a role in determining why these differences exist is the extent of Gray's efforts to tackle the great question "why?" His concern is more with educating people about these differences so they can change. He includes chapter by chapter breakdowns of many themes: values, coping skills, fundamental motivating factors ("men are motivated when they feel needed while women are motivated when they feel cherished"), linguistic differences (he includes a Martian/Venusian translation dictionary), sexual intimacy, emotional variations, arguments, scoring points in the relationship, and communication skills.

Most people in intimate relationships with the opposite sex (he has very little to say about the relevance of his model for gay, lesbian, and queer relationships) can see at least a grain of truth in many of the things that Gray describes in the book. In fact, his theory is the basis of a very successful theatre performance called *Defending the Caveman*. This one-man show starring Rob Becker uses the metaphors of hunting and gathering to describe behavioral differences between men and women. The logic is probably familiar to the reader, which is what makes it such a successful show. Women like to talk a lot and men are more comfortable with silence. Men don't listen to women and women are always trying to change men. After recently attending a performance of *Defending the Caveman* in Sacramento, California, I could not help but observe that the people in attendance (mainly heterosexual white middle class young professionals and middle aged couples) were aided by this humorous, however simplistic, summary of heterosexual relationships.

The positive contribution of the planetary paradigm, as opposed to the genderblindness paradigm, is that it allows for a discussion of differences. It encourages gender awareness as opposed to denying it under the genderblindness paradigm's insistence on universal sameness. As the critics of colorblindness and genderblindness argue, different histories result in different experiences and different political needs for groups today. Simply stated, the planetary paradigm helps get the conversation started, but it only encourages the conversation to stay on a superficial level.

One major problem with this paradigm is its political limitations. It is important to keep in mind that Gray's planetary paradigm is focused on interpersonal relationships where the goal is to achieve equality and balance. However, he oversimplifies or underestimates the way that structural forms of oppression shape our personal relationships. According to *The Penguin Atlas of Women in the World*, in the U.S. there are approximately 90,000 reported rapes with the actual number of rapes estimated at 700,000 annually. In 1998 approximately 900,000 women filed assault reports against male partners. Regarding work, white women earn 73 cents to the white man's dollar, African American women earn 63 cents, and Hispanic women earn 53 cents by comparison. In 2001, women spent an average of 27 hours per week on housework while men spent 16 hours per week. These are just a few of the recent statistics that reveal structural gender inequality as a fundamental aspect of our society. Gray does not consider these facts. Instead, he faults the feminist movement for its one-sidedness when addressing these issues:

Though important advances have been made, many books are one-sided and unfortunately reinforce mistrust and resentment toward the opposite sex. One sex is generally viewed as being victimized by the other. A definitive guide was needed for understanding how healthy men and women are different (Gray, 4).

Here, it is clear that Gray's agenda is interpersonal and not necessarily political, while the feminist movement has always held that the "personal *is* political." Sure, in a relationship, resentment is not helpful and it is important to provide tools to help people work out their problems. However, is it possible to separate the conflict-ridden structural inequalities manifested in the public sphere from the domestic home front? Wouldn't a woman's anger about making less money than her male counterparts carry over into the home? Doesn't the threat of rape influence our sex lives? Gray has little to say about how "society creeps into the bedroom." New communication skills are a poor substitute for a political analysis that can push the discussion to a much deeper level. By focusing on men and women as two distinctive cultures with different languages and rituals he neutralizes the gendered power relations in society and discourages an analysis of how power is reproduced in our personal lives.

The next major problem with Gray's analysis is that his main social categories are "men" and "women." He has little to say about how the categories of race, class, nationality, religion, ability, and age intersect with these two categories to create a constellation of different types of masculinities and femininities. The fields of Women's Studies and Ethnic Studies are currently undergoing an explosion of "gender, race, class" scholarship that collectively criticizes the universal categories "men" and "women." It is especially striking that although he describes communication differences as languages, he is not sensitive to his theory's lack of applicability beyond his own white middle class experience.

Women of color have initiated the strongest arguments against the universal categories "men" and "women." For example, Angela Davis addresses the debate about how the slave system shaped contemporary gender relations among African Americans. Some scholars argue that slavery was a great neutralizer of gender differences among the enslaved because men and women worked side by side performing grueling physical labor. This argument is frequently used to criticize white feminists' own generalizing talk about men and women. Davis maintains that enslaved women had to contend with the gender specific hardships of childbirth, motherhood, and rape on the plantations, and this illustrates that there are important historical differences between black men and women that shape their relationships today.

While this debate about gender and slavery continues, it is just one reminder that race and class play important roles in the study of masculinities and femininities. Gray does admit that some couples have reported not fitting into the planetary paradigm, but he simply suggests that they have "role reversal" which allows them to still work within the planetary paradigm. He advises that they just need to reverse its terms! But this is not a good enough response to the criticism of his theory's lack of universal applicability. He never reflects on the fact that different group histories may yield different gender arrangements and communication patterns than what he describes in the book. His research is based on over 25,000 participants in his relationship seminars, but he makes no mention of the class and racial composition of these participants. While the planetary paradigm emphasizes differences between men and women, which can benefit political awareness, it does not go far enough in considering structural factors or the full spectrum of social differences that shape gender relations and complicate an analysis of contemporary masculinities and femininities.

Part Three: Gender Diversity Paradigm

A third paradigm exists that transcends the flaws of both the genderblindness and planetary paradigms. The gender diversity paradigm emphasizes that gender is a flexible, socially constructed (as opposed to biologically predetermined), and historically specific concept. Not only is this paradigm clear that the two-gender system cannot be supported using biological evidence, it also emphasizes the range of expressions that constitute culturally specific gender systems. Instead of ignoring gender (genderblindness paradigm) or viewing it in a simplified and polarized fashion (planetary paradigm), the gender diversity paradigm sees gender variety everywhere and emphasizes the real and possible forms of gender expression that transcend the U.S.'s legally enforced two-gender system.[1] This paradigm embodies several scholarly discourses that emerge from distinct fields: biology, anthropology, and law and politics. The following sections will briefly summarize how these three main discourses advance ideas about gender diversity.

The Biological Argument for Gender Diversity

In *Sexing the Body: Gender Politics and the Construction of Sexuality*, feminist biologist Anne Fausto-Sterling argues that the two-gender system cannot be supported by biological evidence. Instead she claims, ". . . labeling someone a man or a woman is a social decision" (Fausto-Sterling 2000, 3). We can use scientific knowledge to aid this decision, but she argues that, ultimately, this knowledge is grounded in social ideas about gender. The common assumption in the U.S. is that there are two forms of genitalia (penis and vagina) and thus two genders (male and female). However, the existence of "intersexed" individuals—defined by Fausto-Sterling as "bodies having mixtures of male and female parts"—reminds us that there is no simple equation between genital composition and gender.

There are fleshy and hormonal combinations that blur the simple dualistic categories of male and female, and these combinations are much more common than we might think. We are probably more familiar with the fact that there are some people who are born with mixed genitalia. People with mixed genitalia were called "hermaphrodites" but today they are more likely to be called "intersexed people" or "intersexuals."

Hormonal conditions like Androgen Insensitivity Syndrome (AIS) are less well known. Women suffering from this condition have the Y chromosome and they produce testosterone but their bodies are incapable of acknowledging this. AIS usually includes feminization or undermasculinization of the external genitalia at birth, abnormal secondary sexual development in puberty, and infertility.

It is estimated that around 1.7 percent of all births can be classified as intersexed births, although the frequency of intersexed births is not internationally uniform. According to Fausto-Sterling, "a city of 300,000 would have 5,100 people with varying degrees of intersexual development" (Fausto-Sterling, 51). Usually, people with mixed genitalia endure immediate operations or treatments to "fix" their intersexed status, which is considered the only viable medical option in a society that is so insistent that there should only be two genders based on two distinctive genital compositions. Later in life intersexed people may encounter conflicts between their own gender identity and that which was assigned to them at birth. Thus, intersexed people share common experiences with transgendered people.

Intersexed activists are at the forefront of challenging how the medical establishment treats intersexed infants, including establishing new guidelines for physicians. Using examples of biological diversity, they are calling for an abandonment of the two-gender system because it is used to justify surgical intervention of intersexed infants. They also point out that all human bodies are different and have ambivalent characteristics, including facial hair and Adam's apples in women and high-pitched voices and shortness in men. Why should intersexed infants be stigmatized for not fitting gender norms when so many of us have characteristics that do not fit specific gender ideals?

The Anthropological Argument for Gender Diversity

In addition to biological evidence, the gender diversity paradigm also includes anthropological research to argue that gender is a complex and multifaceted phenomenon. Anthropologists interested in studying how societies operate outside a two-gender system have found widespread evidence of this in places as diverse as India, Polynesia, Thailand, Philippines, Brazil, and native North America. Regarding native North America, research reveals that third and fourth genders existed and were documented by Spanish explorers who brought with them their own notion of appropriate gender roles. Berdache is a term used to describe people who were classified as third and fourth genders (Roscoe, 1998), however, today many Native Americans advocate noncolonial terms to describe third and fourth genders, such as "two-spirit."

What exactly is meant by a third or fourth gender? There are several myths about these gender variant individuals regarding their genital composition, sacred powers, and sexual practices. Since the association between genitalia and gender roles is so strong, many assume that gender variant individuals have mixed genitalia. The early European colonists assumed that they were intersexed people. Later research suggests that they did not necessarily have mixed genitalia, but instead were individuals who dressed in a unique blend of the masculine and feminine dress of their tribes. Their dress differed from tribe to tribe and individual to individual but it was common to witness more of a blending of masculine and feminine tropes among gender variant people as opposed to the quest to "pass" completely as the opposite gender. (There are exceptions here as well, including the Navajo male gender variants who sought to pass as women, down to female physiological traits.) Gender variant individuals were usually drawn to labor and activities that were associated with distinct roles. They were usually accepted in their communities so long as they contributed to the livelihood through food preparation, hunting, artistic endeavors such as rug weaving, or fighting in battle (Roscoe 1998).

In some cases they were not merely tolerated but revered by the community for having sacred healing powers. In *Gender Diversity: Crosscultural Variations*, Serena Nandy summarizes the association of a gender variance with spiritual powers. She writes:

Sometimes, by virtue of the power associated with their gender ambiguity, gender variants were ritual adepts and curers, or had special ritual functions. . . . Gender variants did not always have important sacred roles in Native North America, however. Where feminine qualities were associated with these roles, male gender variants might become spiritual leaders or healers, but where these roles were associated with male qualities, they were not entered into by male gender variants (Nandy 2000, 20).

There is diversity in the association of gender variation and sacred powers, yet it is notable that indigenous North American tribes were generally more accepting of gender variation and even conferred unique powers to gender variant individuals who were seen as leaders and visionaries for the entire group.

There was also a lack of uniformity among Native American gender variants when it came to sexual practices. European observers tended to associate gender variants with homosexuality but this was not necessarily the case. Nandy writes:

Some early reports noted specifically that male gender variants lived with and/or had sexual relations with women as well as men; in other societies they were reported as having sexual relations only with men, and still in other societies, of having no sexual relations at all" (Nandy, 17).

Despite the widespread assumption that gender variants would practice homosexuality, anthropological evidence reveals that a link between gender and sexual preference is not easily established. This is also the case today for transgendered people. A female-to-male transgendered person may prefer sex with women and therefore identify as heterosexual, for example.

In summary, if we contrast the dominant two-gender system in the contemporary United States with gender variation among Native Americans, we are reminded that our current system is not natural but instead enforced through a variety of ideological, social, cultural, legal, and economic measures. While gender variation was a complex phenomenon that differed from tribe to tribe, variation itself was generally more accepted than it is in the dominant European culture of the United States. The examples of biological and anthropological diversity briefly described in this chapter reveal that our two-gender system is culturally (European in origin) and historically specific. It takes on a universal quality as it is reinforced by a variety of social institutions and represented as natural and normal. The third major discourse that constitutes the gender diversity paradigm—the political argument—focuses on and challenges the institutional enforcement of the two-gender system in the media, economy, education, marriage and family, and religion.

The Political Argument for Gender Diversity

Drawing from the fields of biology and anthropology, and further including legal and social considerations, the political argument for gender diversity intersects in many ways with the American feminist movement's concerns. Both challenge how power is distributed through gender identity categories and both emphasize how masculinity and femininity are ideals impossible to achieve, let alone sustain. However, the feminist movement's particular focus on women's issues can conflict with the gender diversity paradigm and the U.S. transgender movement's own application of these ideas.

Informed by biological examples of intersexuality, anthropological examples of multiple gender systems, and personal experiences, the transgender movement challenges the two-gender system and highlights the wide variety of alternative gender expressions in the contemporary U.S. The term "transgender" came into circulation at the same time that scholarship and politics began emphasizing gender as a social construct, not a biological given. It includes those who identify as trangendered; they may or may not have body-modifying surgeries, take hormones, or dress or identify with the gender other than the one on their birth certificate. The transgender movement acknowledges the struggles of gender variant individuals in the areas of education, medicine, and law and politics, seeking to expand the civil rights of those who do not identify with the gender that they were assigned at birth. Because of widespread discrimination and miseducation on the issues, transgendered people are more likely to be low income, suffer from health neglect, and experience hate crimes ranging from verbal assaults to physical abuse and murder. In *Transliberation: Beyond Pink or Blue*, trans activist Leslie Feinberg summarizes the health care crisis among transgendered people due to medical discrimination and neglect:

> *Throughout the U.S. masculine females and feminine males, crossdressers, transsexuals and intersexuals are home alone dealing with pain, fevers, the trauma of gang rape and beatings, and other emergencies, hoping the symptoms will go away so they don't have to reveal themselves to a venomously hostile doctor or nurse (Feinberg 1998, 80).*

In addition to medical and employment discrimination, there are a number of legal complications faced by transgendered people. For example, legal documents that include one's "sex"—either "M" or "F"—can be contradictory. Since we use these documents regularly for identification, authorities and employers can impede travel and employment efforts when they challenge the authenticity of the documents. Since identification is increasingly important in this post 9/11 world, legal advocacy around gender identifying documents is a big focus of transgender legal activism. In New York City, activists are trying to change the requirement that one needs genital surgery in order to change their sex on their birth certificates. Other areas of legal activism focus on housing issues, the treatment of transgendered people in juvenile facilities and prisons, bathroom issues, and educational discrimination.

In addition to legal concerns, the transgender movement also has philosophical concerns about staying within or transcending the two-gender system. It is widely assumed by many transgendered and nontransgendered people that "passing" as the other gender is a major goal in many transgendered people's daily lives. If you are trying to get away from your assigned gender identity, you are trying to "be" the other gender, goes the logic. Transgendered people have a variety of responses to the issue of staying within the two-gender system or refusing its terms, for example, by refusing to identify as either male or female. The point is not to decide which position is

better, but to ensure that people can express themselves in a way that reflects their own gendered experiences.

In "2 Legit 2 Quit," Dean Spade, the director of the *Sylvia Rivera Transgender Law Project*, criticizes the transgender movement's fixation on passing and argues for more fluid gender identity boundaries in society and in our gender variant communities. He was arrested in Grand Central Station for standing in line in a male bathroom (Dean is a female-to-male transgendered person). When he reported this violation of his civil rights to the transgender community, he was shocked to discover that some people were less than sympathetic about his arrest. He writes:

> *Although I firmly believe I would have been arrested even if . . . my ID had said "M," I still must observe that the regulatory processes needed to achieve such a gender change are unfathomably [messed] up. In many states a gender change would not be possible without spending . . . hundreds of thousands of dollars . . . [what about] people like me who don't want a gender-cohesive, gender normative state-sanctioned body and mind (Spade 2004a, 2)?*

Spade not only rejects the "blame the victim mentality" of those who are unsympathetic because he was accosted in the men's bathroom, he also challenges the assumption that passing as the other gender is financially feasible or philosophically desirable. Spade reiterates this point in "More Gender More of the Time" when he challenges the desire to inhabit a singular and specific gender identity. He writes:

> *I know that for some trans people, transition is a process of moving into a new 'fully inhabited' identity category, where the goal is to be accepted and fully integrated into that category. For me, though, and a lot of other trans people I know, it's not about following a new set of rules closely, but about colliding identities, occupying multiple identities, and throwing the rules into crisis . . . I think a lot of non-trans people similarly want to (and do) shift and multiply, access varying communities, and define themselves with pleasure, intention, and no eye toward continuity (Spade, 2004b).*

Here we witness the radical and most threatening implications of the gender diversity paradigm. It is already challenging enough that many people have refused the gender identity assigned to them at birth and insisted that they be able to live as a member of the "opposite" gender. As Spade points out, many people cannot afford the costly surgeries and treatments that they need to achieve this goal. Beyond financial obstacles, many people are not interested in moving completely to the opposite gender. They instead question the values of a society that insists we must "be" a man or a woman.

In this spirit, many trans scholars have indicated that society usually holds them up to higher gender standards than non-trans people. "He's a female to male transgender? He doesn't look like one!" But, as we know, many nontransgender people do things every day that defy socially sanctioned gender ideals. Men can cook and care for children and cry. Women can fix cars, own firearms, and refuse to shave or wear make-up. If you look around you, each individual is a unique combination of characteristics associated with masculinity and femininity. Thanks to the gay, lesbian, bisexual, transgender movement and the feminist movement we have been able to broaden the range of experiences and behaviors for men and women. But it is clear that more work needs to be done around all of these issues because discriminatory attitudes still exist toward gender variant individuals and groups.

Conclusion: Gender Diversity and Feminism

On the surface it makes sense to view the feminist movement—which challenges male power and privilege interpersonally and institutionally—as compatible with the transgender movement. But it is disappointing to report that this is not necessarily the case. Since the emergence of the modern women's movement, cases for and against alliances with transgendered people have been made. What could the objections possibly be to working with and/or supporting transgender struggles? Don't those fighting against the hierarchical gender system in the name of feminisms of all stripes find affinities with those who daily (and viscerally) endure the restrictive two-gender regime? While many have observed the connections between these movements, others have strongly resisted a political alliance.

The idea that there is something "inherently male" about all men and that masculine traits are undesirable is advanced by cultural feminism. As Alice Echols describes in *Daring to Be Bad: Radical Feminism in America, 1967–1975*, cultural feminism emerged in the mid 1970s after political movements began to fade out and is not predominant today. But the idea that biology is the strongest factor in gender behavior is alive and well. Some feminists who do not support transgender issues argue that biological men are fundamentally masculine, even if they try to be feminine or a woman. Others may argue that masculine characteristics—including competition and aggression—are learned, not inborn. Either way, men and masculinity are fundamentally questioned and even rejected. There are serious political ramifications behind this hotly debated issue about gendered qualities—be they socialized or biological.

For example, in 1976 the "Michigan Womyn's Music Festival" was founded as a women-only space where women could camp out, attend cultural events and educational workshops in a safe, empowering space. In recent years this very popular event has served as ground zero in a struggle waged by the transgendered festival attendees who seek inclusion in this women-only space. The transgender community protested the festival's "womyn-born womyn only" policy by setting up "Camp Trans" outside the festival boundaries. Female-to-male and male-to-female transgendered people who have "come out" at the festival have encountered hostility and some have been asked to leave. Camp Trans activists seek a policy that allows anyone who is "woman identified" to attend the festival. Identifying with women or as a woman becomes an individual decision and it is flexible too. It can accommodate biologically born females who identify as women, biologically born males who identify as women, female-to-male transgendered people, and people who identify as male and female.

Instead of creating an environment marked by a commitment to gender diversity and gender variant lifestyles, the festival's policy tacitly endorses a view that transgendered people have something to hide—as if something sinister is afoot. While many feel that the policy of "womyn-born womyn only" is hostile to all transgendered people, others defend it because they do not want the festival overrun by men. They are concerned that if the festival doors are opened and all are welcomed then men would abuse this and exploit the all-female environment. Others suggest that a male-to-female transgendered person is a threat to the festival environment because they may still have their male genitalia (not all transgendered people have operations) and therefore can potentially be perpetrators of sexual violence or make attendees feel uncomfortable. Many attendees claim they seek a "safe space" from male dominance and the threat of sexual objectification and violence.

Regarding female-to-male transgendered people, some are worried that male-identified biological women will detract from a female-centered environment that emphasizes supposedly female traits such as cooperation, compassion, mutual recognition, and care. Yet considering the biological and anthropological evidence for gender diversity—isn't this focus on "femaleness" itself problematic? What makes a woman? Can a biological male experience girlhood instead of boyhood? Aren't some women more aggressive than some men? Where do we draw the lines? Why do we have to draw lines? What is at stake here?

Women-only space is a political phenomenon with roots in a movement that seeks to expand autonomy and self-determination for women in all aspects of our lives. If we were genderblind and thus ignored gender inequality, then the women-only space would be a moot point. If we don't see gender inequality, then we don't see the need for women to organize separately as women. Those who support the current festival policy appear to be operating from some version of the planetary paradigm, which emphasizes and simplifies the differences between the two official genders—men and women. Whether one thinks it's a biological difference, a socially constructed difference, or a combination of the two, policy supporters argue there are differences. People are weary that the festival will lose its political significance if it opens its gates to all gender variants. But what are we losing by clinging

to a two-gender system that suppresses the diverse gender identities and experiences that constitute the transgender and feminist movements? Isn't more free expression for more people without fear of ridicule, punishment and death a righteous goal for any social justice movement? These are some of the dilemmas that have yet to be settled in the transgender/feminist women-only space debate. The debate reaches past the Michigan festival—it recently emerged during San Francisco's Dyke March, for example—although Michigan's policy is emblematic of the general problem.

The mixed messages that currently circulate about gender may emerge from or be defined by the genderblind, planetary, and gender diversity paradigms. We encounter contradictory ideas about gender each day, and we can benefit individually and collectively from identifying the types of arguments we are hearing. Next time you hear someone talking about gender, ask yourself: "Do they acknowledge that society values masculine over feminine traits? That women are paid less than men (of similar racial and ethnic backgrounds) for the same work? That there is rampant sexual violence against women and gender variant individuals?" If they answer "no" to these and other gender conscious questions, then they are genderblind. They don't see how gender arrangements structure society. If they answer "yes" to the questions then they might be using a version of either the planetary or the gender diversity paradigms. The main difference between these two paradigms is the amount of complexity they allow for. The planetary paradigm emphasizes one fundamental form of difference—the differences between men and women. It overlooks how racial and ethnic, class, and sexual preferences intersect with gender to create an array of masculinities and femininities.

This is the focus of the gender diversity paradigm, which views gender as socially and biologically fluid. It considers individual and group gender variance and allows flexibility in the application of concepts. It also implies that the quest for fundamental clarity about gender dynamics is misguided. Clear politics can only emerge from admitting that gender identifications are sometimes unclear and that clarity is not everyone's experience or goal. Gender diversity facilitates an awareness of the complex relationships between the enforced two-gender system, individual and group identities, and experiences that transcend this system, and the discourses—both oppressive and liberating—that emerge politically when we try to articulate our identities and desires.

It is the contention of this chapter that the gender diversity paradigm is the most comprehensive paradigm, and thus the most useful. However, the genderblind and planetary paradigms have merit too. Genderblindness can support a sexual-harassment-free environment (although one wonders if gender diversity isn't a better paradigm for this topic), and the planetary paradigm offers some groups of people helpful ways to start discussions about gender. Gender diversity's fundamental inclusiveness and acceptance of a range of variations raises the level of debate and holds the most promise for those seeking recourse from persistent and oppressive gender norms.

Notes

1. This chapter will use the term "gender variant" to refer to individuals whose biological composition, behavior, or laboring activities cannot fit neatly into traditional dual male and female roles. The term "transgender" is

an inclusive category. A much-debated term, it refers to all forms of thinking and behavior across gender lines. It is more inclusive because it does not focus strictly on one's surgical or anatomical status but how individuals identify themselves.

References

Echols, Alice. 1990. *Daring to be bad: Radical feminism in America, 1967–1975*. Minneapolis: University of Minnesota Press.

Fausto-Sterling, Anne. 2000. *Sexing the body: Gender politics and the construction of sexuality*. New York: Basic Books.

Feinberg, Leslie. 1998. *Trans liberation: Beyond pink and blue*. Boston: Beacon Press.

Gray, John. 1992. *Men are from Mars, Women are from Venus: A practical guide for improving communication and getting what you want in your relationships*. New York: Harper Collins.

Johnson, Allan. 1987. *The Gender knot: Unraveling our patriarchal legacy*. Philadelphia: Temple University Press.

Nandy, Serena. 2000. *Gender diversity: Crosscultural variations*. Prospect Heights, Illinois: Waveland Press.

Roscoe, Will. 1998. *Changing ones: Third and fourth genders in native North America*. New York: St. Martin's Press.

Spade, Dean. 2004a. 2 legit 2 quit. http://www.makezine.org/2legit.html.

Spade, Dean, 2004b. More gender, more of the time. http://www.makezine.org/bibi.html.

Symbolic Gender Relations: Zion Christian Church and Traditional Bapedi Structures

Boatamo Mosupyoe

Introduction: Reflective

The discussion in this chapter focuses on the symbolic reproduction and contradiction of African cultural elements in the Zion Christian Church (ZCC). The reproduction reflects a continuity of patriarchy, albeit in altered forms in some instances. It can be argued that the similarities in both structures present continuity in cultural practices. Logically the Zion Christian Church members will be influenced by both since it can also be argued that most members joined the church precisely because of the retention of African traditional practices. The badge and *magadi*, two different entities, achieve the same purpose of unifying the groups within these two institutions. *Magadi* establishes in law relationships where such relatives refer to one another as *metswalle*, as does the Zion Christian Church badge. Zion Christian Church members identified by the badge refer to one another as *metswalle*. In this case symbols produce what can be perceived as equality in gender relations. However, other symbols perpetuate patriarchy.

African symbols of prohibitions and preferences, for example as they occur in both structures reflect persistent gender inequalities. While Bapedi structures involved an extensive and more complex construct that included the sororate, levirate, ghost, and preferred marriages that also transformed the fraternal relationship into filial relationships, the Zion Christian Church reflects a similar but less complex structure. Visions through dreams controlled a choice of marriage partners in the Zion Christian Church. Common to both is the valorization of the patriarchy over matriarchy. Polygamy and not polyandry constitutes the cultural norm, the birth of a son translates or translated into a completion of marriage, and patrilineality as manifest in whose surname the children assume, who inherits, and who ascends to power has primacy over matrilineality. In addition, even in the face of cultural change, authority of the family centers around the father, the continuity of the male relatives through the retention of the name remains paramount. Women always take the men's name, albeit in a hyphenated fashion; my research has never uncovered a case where a man chose to take over the woman's name.

Contradictory parallels also abound in leadership structures. Although the traditional Bapedi leadership structure proved to be more democratic and consensual than the autocratic Zion Christian Church's, males dominate in both structures. Inner councils and decision-making bodies constitute male confines. In both structures the network of kinship central to the running of both institutions also reflects patrilineal preferences over matrilineality. Both structures place or placed a high value on succession through patrilineal kinship structures, with no history of a woman ever succeeding to the highest leadership position. Correspondingly, in both structures men's prominence overshadow women's authority. Mutual sayings in both institutions, such as "*If led by a woman it falls into a pit*" and "*There are never two bulls in a kraal*," curtail and undermine women's visibility in areas where they have authority.

Moreover, the conception of God as male in both religious structures points to similar perceptions of women. Indeed, only women possess heat and are a receptacle of impurity, necessitating their isolation until purified. Men make up important diviners and prophets while women occupy peripheral positions such as *Mapale*. Perhaps the most telling sexism manifest is the Zion Christian Church requirement of women to reach menopause before they can hold pivotal positions as prophets. The logical implication then becomes, I will maintain, that the absence of menstruation in menopause equals purity. Since men can hold office at all times with proper qualifications, I can only assume that their biological constitution, obviously devoid of menstruation, translates into a symbol of purity that gives them an unfair advantage over women. Again a woman's biological makeup results in social constructs that limit her participation in structures and decision making.

The discussion contains all the reasons why patriarchy has persisted over the years. For example, the division of labor, the association of men with culture and women with nature, and modernization as in the hyphenated surname. The latter could be regarded as progress. It will be more notable if the choice extended to how the children assume their last names. Modernization still fails to resolve the actual primacy of men over women, like I have alluded before, still the continuity of the men's family becomes paramount. The importance of the influence of the two structures on women's perceptions of non-sexism cannot be relegated to the margins. The variety of their responses derives from both structural forces and socialization, or from a combination of both. Also, the influence of the development approach to non-sexism molded some answers; I am referring to conscious efforts women make to reach decisions that construct and reconstruct their perception of social educational reality. Indeed, the following discussion elucidates on the influence of the structural forces on women's lives.

Symbolic Aspects of Sex Differentiation

Membership

One of the least studied aspects of the African Initiated Churches is the question of membership, which has a bearing on the most studied leadership question. In order to analyze the symbolic aspect of women in the Zion Christian Church, looking at membership becomes an important first step. An examination of this factor offers a background that elucidates on sex differentiation in execution of women and men's roles. Barrett (1968), Lewis (1971), Brandel-Syrier (1984), Murphree (1971), Jules-Rosette (1979), and Mosupyoe (1999) noted the predominance of women in the African Initiated Churches. Their findings are either at a direct variance with or caution studies by Lagerwerf (1982)[1] and Hacket (1987a), who concur that contrary to popular academic opinion, women do not always outnumber men in the African Initiated Churches and play an important role. Kalu (1995) subscribes to the latter view, and further asserts that churches with complex bureaucratic and hierarchical structures reflect higher male attendance, at least in West Africa.

In the context of the above varying theories, the Zion Christian Church presents a unique entity. It has a complex bureaucratic and hierarchical structure partially in concert with Kalu's position. The Zion Christian Church, however, also diverges from her findings as in part it fits the other scholars' assertion, namely, women in the church do outnumber men. Membership in the Zion Christian Church is open to everybody—men, women, and children. Children, however, should be 18 years or older in order to join on their own, without their parents. Most children become members by virtue of their parents' membership.[2] From its inception women in the Zion Christian Church have outnumbered men. Comaroff (1980), in her study of the Tshidi reports that Zion Christian Church memberships in this particular congregation are composed of more men than women. However, on the whole evidence shows that in the Zion Christian Church women outnumber men.[3] In spite of the latter, the final determination of who becomes a member rests with the priests.

Both Daneel (1987) and Jules Rosette (1978) note males' pivotal role in sponsoring membership into the church of the Zionist kind. The process of becoming a member as explained to me by a number of Zion Christian Church congregants mirrors Daneel's and Jules-Rosette's accounts. To become a member both males and females have to inform the priest, who will then assign a sponsor to the prospective member. The assignment of sponsors is dichotomized along gender lines, with females sponsoring women and males sponsoring men. The sponsorship entails a period of probation and orientation about the church's teachings, rules, and regulations. In addition religious attendance to church services and meetings forms a mandatory part of this period for the prospective member.

The church expects compliance with the requirements from everybody regardless of gender. Violation of the prerequisites results in an extended period of orientation and probation. A person could be refused membership because of failure to regularly attend meetings and services. Upon completion of the orientation or probation the sponsor recommends baptism. The prospective member answers questions from elders other than the sponsor. Here two females quiz women and males quiz men to test their knowledge of the church's expectations. The high priest determines the final acceptance of members into the church by giving his approval in matters of baptism. Baptism by immersion, carried out exclusively by male priests, confers full membership. The act of baptism initiates an individual into a member of the congregation. It is also viewed as a method of cleansing of all of the pollutants that an individual has acquired from the unclean world with which he or she associated before becoming a member.

Comaroff (1980), Sundkler (1968), and all refer to the symbolic meaning of baptism in the African Initiated Churches. The most important symbolic aspect of baptism centers around the power the male priests possess. The power enables male priests to dissolve the new member of his or her former identity. Through the process the new member symbolically experiences the dual transformation of death and rebirth. This could only happen through the power endowed in the priest and transferred only to the new member. Women in the Zion Christian Church lack such symbolic abilities of transforming death to rebirth, a factor that gives an additional reason why women cannot be priests. After baptism, sponsors then give new members their uniforms. The importance of wearing uniform in the Zionist churches has been noted by Sundkler (1961: 213), Comaroff (1980: 205), West (1975: 18), and Bergelund (1967), among others. Much like in the Zionist-type churches, a uniform in the Zion Christian Church is believed to be "in-fused with power that encases the body of the wearer like a shield" (Comaroff 1985: 206). The women reiterated the sentiment and truly believe in the symbolic protective nature of the uniform.

For men the uniform comprises a khaki suit, a brown hat, and white boots. Women wear a green and yellow suit, black shoes, and a green scarf. Several women explained the symbolic meaning of the color of their uniform. West (1975 18) explained the importance of the role of color in the Zionist churches' symbolic order. Much like Comaroff (1980) and Sundkler (1968), they attribute the choices of colors to the racial conflict that existed between whites and blacks in the particular areas that they studied. For example, West (1978) asserts that black signifies churches of the spirit while white stands for churches of the law, implying that the black churches represent authentic holiness whereas white ones do not. The explanations that I received from the women in the church depart from the binary racial explanation. The color yellow these women said symbolically represents the sun and a flower like the sunflower. The sun is a sign of happiness that will always shine on the church. Green symbolizes wealth and plenty, implying that the church will continue to grow in membership and members will gain spiritual wealth. Women who sing in the choir wear blue. Blue signifies the clear sky and clarity of the mind. The symbolic meaning translates into the spiritual intelligence of Zion Christian Church members.

Although women wear black shoes, one member further claimed black represents ill luck. The women wear scarves on their heads at all times, especially when attending church services and meetings. In addition, they are required to cover the upper part of their bodies, that is, they should not expose their shoulders. The woman's body in the church symbolizes God's temple and should be treated as such; men do not have an equivalent analogy. Both men and women receive the badge after baptism and as further discussions show, they all have to wear it at all times. Men wear hats that they take off when entering a house. Women are not allowed to touch the man's hat. Such gender-based practices also find expression in other procedures of the church. Most notably, the hierarchical leadership structures show a clear demarcation of symbolic spheres of men and women, like Hacket (1987a) posited.

Priesthood, Prophets, and Prophetesses

As earlier discussions have illustrated there is a clear demarcation of the symbolic spheres of men and women's activities in the African Initiated Churches (Nthabu 1989). The evidence points to monopoly of political and administrative positions by men. Similarly, priesthood in the Zion Christian Church is a male domain. Never in the history of the church has a woman ever qualified to be a priest. Neither has the church ever had a male bishop. However, both a man and a woman qualify to be either a prophet or a prophetess, respectively. The high priest reported that any man over the age of 21 who exhibits skills and abilities can become a prophet. In addition to the skills, they further posited, the man must have "a call." The latter is a spiritual calling that causes an individual to experience change. The transformation entails a new social and spiritual identity, a symbolic rejuvenation that connects the player to the direct powers of the "living and dead,"[4] the bishop and God.

Jules-Rosette (1977) observes that in the African Initiated Churches a woman's power increases after her childbearing period has ended. Daneel (1970) concurs with Jules-Rosette. In his observation of the AIC among the Shona in Zimbabwe, he equates the phenomenon to the traditional Shona custom. He contends that Shona custom already contained precedents of an older "neuter" medium figure through whom God spoke, thereby removing all of her sexual characteristics. I found a similar paradigm in the Zion Christian Church. Only post-menopausal women can be prophetesses. Menstruation symbolically translates into placing a woman in the state of impurity and therefore disqualifies them from becoming prophetesses, and even priests. This paradigm could represent dual purposes, I will argue. It could, on one level, represent the symbolic order that seems to reform rather than reinforce the natural qualities of a woman. On another level, however, it could have the power to reverse the hegemonies by moving women from their periphery to the center. In addition, despite the fact that a woman past menopause has to go through the same spiritual experience as a man in order to be accepted as a prophetess, charismatic attributes could give her an advantage over a

prophet. Charisma has also accorded a woman to eminence, admiration, and respect in the Zion Christian Church. The charismatic promise of several prophetesses sustained their female leadership positions.

That notwithstanding, both men and women who wish to be prophets or prophetesses can report their wishes to priests. A male prophet would then be assigned to apprentice the woman in the profession, since males primarily take ritual precedence over women. Although the church has more prophetesses than prophets, only prophets serve as apprentices. The orientation involves an elaborate process of observation and practice. One could also become a prophet or prophetess through a vision seen by either the bishop or one of the priests or prophets. This ensures an accelerated way of being ordained by the church. When women appear in such visions or dreams they are immediately assigned a sponsor for apprenticeship.[5] Such orientation could take fewer than three months since the endorsement came through the power of the vision affirmed by the male. This differs from the instances where a woman proclaims herself that she has to be ordained. In such cases a number of prophets and prophetesses need to verify her claim. The process could take several months as others would sometimes say they need more time in order to see clearly whether she qualifies. A man, on the other hand, is immediately assigned the apprentice. The standards for ordination also seem to be higher for women.

I observed a process where prospective prophetesses were trained and accepted. They had to prove their visionary divining skills as well as their ability to prescribe *ditaelo*[6] in an effective way. To prove their visionary and divining power, women engaged in the process of relating to the higher priests facts about members of the congregation picked randomly. One member explained how the number of the affirmative responses the prophetesses' received for her re-counts will determine her acceptance. Their ability to prescribe *ditaelo* also had to be verified by members who will attest to having experienced healing or change after taking water or coffee that was prescribed by the prophetesses.

While people most of the time responded positively, the disparity lay in the fact that prophets are exonerated from the process. They receive ordination on the basis of what the sponsor says. Instances of prophetesses attaining prominence through a male sponsorship in the Zion Christian Church abound. Lukhaimane (1980) gives an account of the famous Maria Sefuthuma. Maria became a prophetess and was frequently sought after. She became Engenase's favorite and achieved prominence in the church. If you remember she accurately predicted the splitting of the church into two. Through Engenase's endorsement and sponsorship she achieved prominence and enjoyed a great amount of respect, one priest from Atteridgeville explained. However, after the death of Engenase her prominence diminished. She was replaced by others during Edward's tenure. The pattern continues even to the present. I also observed in various locations that those women who were favored by priests commanded a lot of respect. The privilege and power these women enjoy as mediums of revelation act as a leveling mechanism within the hierarchical framework of the church.

Some women prophetesses acquire prominence by virtue of their marriages to high priests. Here we find the familial symbolism that Jules-Rosette (1976) observes. Indeed, in the Zion Christian Church too, the familial connection legitimized authority, while at the same time it reaffirmed the division between female spiritual authority and historical male supremacy and political control. Such dual paradox of prophetesses' power and powerlessness occurs in other instances as well. For example, the prophetesses cannot administer *diatelo*. She can only do so in the absence of a minister and in cases of emergency. Yet only the prophetesses can prescribe what a "patient" should take to heal his or her ailment; the prophet cannot. In addition, the prophetesses are not allowed to hear and mediate disputes whereas prophets can. Further, while prophets can marry additional spouses after they appear to them in their dreams, the same is not expected from the prophetesses.

Despite the above limitations the prophetesses' position also commands power and respect. The prophetesses enjoy respect and deference by virtue of their age. Both men and women display obeisance to them. Priests of a younger age as well as any younger male member also defer to

their authority. In this particular case, the focal role of their divining, visionary prescriptive abilities in this symbolic process make them "mistresses" of ritual power. The latter is possible because in the Zionist symbolism such skills construct the human form into the prophetesses' image of the world according to a revealed vision of agency, power, and collective well-being. Church services can also become the domain of power for the prophetesses. During mixed-gender church services women enter through the back door, sit on the left side of the church, and are excluded from preaching. Only males can preach. However, I have observed a prophetess interrupting priests' sermons by just raising a hand to declare her intention to divine and testify about an important member of the congregation. Even the highest-ranking priest defers to this action when it happens. Such testimony, which Sundkler (1961: 192) noted a while ago and is still true today, "replaces formal preaching or clerical exegesis," to borrow from Comaroff's insights.

By this action the prophetess transfers her position from the periphery to the center. In this even her authority exceeds that of the male priest because it is believed to come from the spirits. This phenomenon departs from the above idiom of familial symbolism where the influential position of the prophetess either comes from the male sponsorship or marriage to a priest. While prominence does depend on male sponsorship in most instances, we cannot ignore their symbolic power in other spheres. Thus within the Zion Christian Church we find positions of the prophetesses assuming an ephemeral form, however, they have the ability to alter that marginal position through mediation to achieve the central focus. In the context of the theme of mediation towards non-sexism, evidence supports the claim that such negotiation cannot be divorced from the broader traditional, social, and political mix. The possibility of the role of the prophetess in the Zion Christian Church to be used as a strategic and symbolic vehicle to achieve non-sexist goals should be assessed within that background.

Theorists like Daneel (1987) insist on equating such binary positions of power in the African Initiated Churches to African traditional practices. Other scholars in much more detail than

Daneel continue the debate about the equation of the tradition and the symbolic power of women in the African Initiated Churches. Jules-Rosette (1975) argues that parallels between social change and the freedom of women in the AIC exist, but require careful approach. Fabian (1974), on the other hand, denies such correlation. My findings in the Zion Christian Church follow Jules-Rosette's contention that complexities of the complementary gender situation in the African Initiated Churches sometimes lead to traditionalistic revitalistic responses. In such cases some women tend to want to reassume the trappings of the conventional roles, as this study will later show, with more force than before. One could argue that such is a symbolic effort to hang on to the familiarity of tradition or reconstitutes a lost sense of community. However, the study will also reflect that other women opted to become prophetesses as an alternative to pursuing school education. This manifestation, in slight contrast to the above traditional revivalistic responses, implicitly reflects the women's ability to discern the potential of traditional practices to transform into the symbolic rubric through which change could occur. The women saw possibilities of advancement of their social status in becoming prophetesses.

Such a possibility in these women's minds was analogous to that achieved through formal education. It is important to note that their choice was conscious and derived from their familiarity with the traditional functions of the position. Becoming a prophetess requires skill and a "spiritual call," as we have learned in the discussion about membership. However, possessing such attributes as a prerequisite did not seem paramount to these women. Becoming a prophetess presented such a viable promising future that obstacles would be tackled as they occur. The latter suggest that these women saw the possibility of engaging in a process of simultaneous social reproduction and transformation, reaffirming Jules-Rosette (1975) and Daneel's (1987) argument of the strong links between the traditional structures and activities in the African Initiated Churches. The following discussions that juxtapose the Zion Christian Church and Bapedi structures offer further information on that correlation and the symbolic position of women.

Gender Relations in Social Structures

A comparison of both social structures reflects that while archetypes of fundamental Bapedi structures are reproduced in the Zion Christian Church, the end product differs. Sometimes the less complex and complete end product of the Zion Christian Church structure comes across as the facsimile and other times as the prototype of the traditional Bapedi social structure. This is so because of the dynamic nature of cultures, and the fact that the Zion Christian Church constitutes part of and not the entire social dimension of the lives of the Bapedi members. Systems of prohibitions and preferences, as revealed in the Zion Christian Church social systems, illustrate cultural elements that are based on the Bapedi practices; they might be similar to, but less comprehensive than, those of the Bapedi.

Like in most societies the choice of a marriage partner among the Bapedi was and still is socially organized and controlled. The system of prohibition and preferences that governed marriage depended primarily on patrilineal and secondarily matrilineal lines of descent. This did not imply that marriage requirements necessarily derived from biological and classificatory considerations, but rather from social conceptions that valorize direct lines of patrilineal descent. For example, historically, while a man used the term *kgaitsedi* to refer to his father's brother's daughter and sister, the marriage with the former was preferred and a union with his sisters was prohibited. In the common case where two brothers married sisters, a son from the union was allowed to marry a daughter from the marriage. In this case the Bapedi argued that the emphasis was on the father's brother's daughter's relation and not on the mother's sister's daughter (Mönnig 1988).

Historically, the difference between biological and social determination was reflected in the contradictory prohibitions associated with, on the one hand, marriage, and on the other, sexual intercourse. The levirate custom[7] permitted, for example, marriage, while the intercourse law prohibited sexual intimacy between a man and his late brother's widows (Mönnig 1988). Meant to perpetuate the family name, the marriage redefined biological relationships, so that what northerners would call a step or half relation translated into an original and direct relation. What was, for example, a fraternal relation became filial when a man married one of his brother's widows with a child. The new husband was considered, without semantic qualification, "father," as if he had completely replaced the true biological father. The lack of qualifiers implied a biological relation. The valorization of the patrilineal over the matrilineal in a need to maintain a protectively coherent familial structure points to the primacy of the men's line of descent over the women's. The families desired to keep the children as part of the men's family; therefore the marriage of the widow to her living brother was more important than the wishes of the woman.

An extended family benefited from maintaining its wealth through marriages between patrilineal-related family members, while avoiding matrilineal-related alliances. In addition to the primary marriage, Bapedi contracted secondary unions, which fell out of the nature of the dual function of marriage as both the establishment of alliances between two groups of relatives and enabling procreation. Consistent with these functions, the Bapedi practiced sororal and levirate customs, but without making a clear distinction between the two. Based on the evidence, it would seem that the two customs were inextricably interwoven. They translated into the right or privilege of a man to marry his wife's sister, the right or privilege of a man to claim his wife's sister as a substitute, and the right of privilege or a man to claim his deceased wife's sister as an ancillary.

Although the principle underlying the levirate marriages had what others would consider useful functions—that is, to perpetuate marriage, protect orphaned children, produce children with the objective of preserving the name that would have otherwise died in the case of barrenness or death—I argue that it had other implications. The woman or a widow did not have the same right or privilege accorded a man or a widower. To the extent that the practice is confined to men only and excludes women, it falls within the purview of the current definition of sexism within the context of South Africa. The same principle extends to "ghost marriage," in which the brother of the deceased king married, in the name of the deceased what should have been the deceased's principal wife, defined as the daughter of a neighboring nation's king.

This kind of marriage was contracted for a king who died without issue, especially one who died without having married his principal wife. Pertinent to the focus of this chapter, the custom still excluded women from receiving the same right, again rendering the custom sexist. Although the discussion thus far may have suggested monogamy as a uniform practice among Bapedi, polygamy as a form of marriage co-existed with monogamy, with a few still practicing polygamy today. Polygamy gave rise to a complex family, in which each wife from a primary marriage had her own homestead, and in which each unit functioned as a separate family with the husband as a common and uniting factor.

The polygamous marriage was disparate, since each wife had her own independent status and the wives were not equal in rank. The basis of the ranking of wives depended on the date of marriage, and the assignments of status to the individual depended on this ranking. In less comprehensive ways marriages in the Zion Christian Church are socially organized and controlled by the church to a certain extent. Polygamy is allowed; Engenase, the founder, was himself a polygamist. The genealogy of Jesus' birth vindicates polygamy as a sanction from God, the church believes. Each of the prospective wives of a male member will most likely be revealed to him in visions from, originally, Engenase or Edward, and more recently from Barnabas, Ignatius, or God. Polygamy formed an attraction to members who sought to perpetuate this valued Bapedi custom in danger of displacement by northern cultural imposition. The Zion Christian Church accommodates polygamy much more explicitly than one found in both in terms of the South African Apartheid Civil Law, and in other African Initiated Churches. I further argue that the apartheid laws rendered this African custom a necessity or at the least encouraged it to continue.

Section 10 Apartheid laws made it impossible for husbands and wives to live with each other. These laws were responsible for the division of black families; a man and a woman who could not find work in the same city or town were not allowed to live together. This culminated in men having multiple wives. Arguably it also provided the second wife as a caretaker for all the children, since the principal wife and the father worked as living employees, who on the meager salary offered could not afford to travel home and see their children, except once a week. Similarly, because of the apartheid it would be illegal for the children to visit their parents at their places of employment unless they have permission, which was rarely granted. Most ministers are polygamists; this facilitates their work. The church required ministers to abstain for three months from eating food prepared by a woman who has just given birth. She is considered impure. In addition, ministers are not allowed to come into contact with or eat food prepared by a menstruating woman. Polygamy allowed them to stay with other wives while serving the church as well. Members of the church see this as a fulfillment of God's requirement contained in the bible chapter of Leviticus 12:1–5. As one woman, a wife to one of the ministers, said:

> *"My marriage to my husband was sanctioned by God. He was not the only one who saw a vision—directing him to marry me—I did too. The same vision directed me to be a prophetess. My husband is a priest, God requires that a priest should have several wives to perform his duties efficiently—contact with "hot" women prevent such efficacy."*

While this particular woman completely accepts the practice, and the church expects chosen wives and first wives to comply with the wishes of such dreams, others defy it. I witnessed a case where a priest's wife from the Pretoria area vehemently objected to her husband taking a second wife. The woman said she's been married to the man for twenty years, in which period she bore children for the marriage. During that period the man efficiently executed his priestly duties and never did once complain about the woman obstructing his priestly duties because of the fact that she menstruates and bears children. She pointed out that they always knew how to comply with the church's requirements without violating the "ban." She viewed her husband's declaration of a vision as a fabrication prompted by his mother, who unsuccessfully tried to control their finances for the past five years. She continued to say that her mother-in-law perceived her as an obstacle that prevents her (mother-in-law)

from gaining control of their finances and now her only recourse was to push her out. When the man reiterated the sincerity of his vision a host of instruction ensued, directing the woman to obey and facilitate the legitimization of the second marriage.

She was to form part of the family that was going to complete the marriage process. Her unmistakable defiance prompted the council to allow the man to go ahead and marry without her participation. The man later revealed to me that he contracted a church exogamous marriage, a factor that he viewed as a disadvantage. Marrying endogamously, he said, secures sustainable marriages. Exposure from an early age to the church's expectations of gender roles minimizes the differences in perceptions and expectations. Consequently, such a marriage will be less controversial and troublesome. The woman's attitude, I argue, reflects the dynamic nature of the church's and traditional structures. In addition, it points to the diversely held views and paradoxes with regard to polygamy in the church and in the South African society in general. While other women and men condemned the woman's action, some agreed with her. Of those who supported her was an elderly woman from the rural area, who said:

> *"My child, things change—I personally do not wish to say anything bad about her. What she said was not even considered. It is a man's world."*

Those who disagreed with the woman from Pretoria said that her actions violate God's and the church's cultural practices. Indeed, the discussion on the Bapedi reflects that polygamy constituted a cultural practice as well as that of other indigenous South African cultures. One woman reminded me that in accordance with both the traditional Bapedi culture and the Zion Christian Church practice, women who are menstruating and who had just bore children attract polluting heat, which threatens the health of others and affects the social order. She directed me to read Leviticus in the bible and assured me that it will reaffirm the authenticity of the practice. The bishop, Barnabas, who also performs priestly duties, I was told also has to observe the ban. On that basis I logically inferred that Barn-abas too must be a polygamist. Nobody would discuss with me the marital status of the bishop. The Pretoria woman later told me that she felt a sense of loss but no regret for having to end her marriage. She did not see any way she could tol-erate her husband having a second wife. The fact that she disbelieved the authenticity of the dream made her even more determined in her actions. She alluded to the fact that on many occasions she has dreamt of being married to different men, and wondered if her wishes will be granted. She looked forward to the non-sexist South Africa, where there will be gender equality.

An examination of how marriage is contracted, how boys and girls are perceived, and how famil-ial relations function in both social structures re-veals in some instances a more fundamental reproduction than the above discussion. The dis-cussion of these issues reveals a pentimento where the lines that trace the portrait of a Christian fam-ily also mirror, even as they alter and suppress the hidden, shapes of an older, original portrait. The Bapedi traditional marriage custom emerges from and revolves around *magadi*. *Magadi* forms Ba-pedi traditional marriage custom by which a man and his family exchange with the bride's family originally cattle but recently money to legalize marriage. Misinformed and ethnocentric descrip-tions of similar customs throughout Africa viewed this practice as wife purchasing Ogbu (1977) laid that argument to rest when he urged that this practice is a way of legitimizing marriage, in the same way as northerners sign a piece of paper. Un-fortunately, most northern anthropologists and other northern scholars see the African culture through their northern eyes. Most of the concepts that deviate from what they are accustomed to is misinterpreted or interpreted using their own ex-periences as a yardstick.

The Bapedi social structure emerges from and revolves around this contract, which in addition establishes paternity, confers the husband and wife with conjugal rights, and defines powers, duties, and obligations of two groups of relatives involved. As it defines a series of relationships between individuals, and by extension, their families' *magadi* produces the framework, fi-nally, of the whole social structure. With some modifications because of changes, the family among the Bapedi, as elsewhere, remains a cohe-sive, corporate group, practicing its own subsis-tence economy and performing its internal religious and jural functions. (I should note, however, since the 1994 elections and the adop-tion of the constitution in 1997, the government of South Africa took aggressive approach to rem-edy gender inequality.) The husband remains pri-marily the member of his own group and the wife joins his group.[8]

The children, although related to the mother's relatives, become mainly members of the father's group. Lately, women take hyphenated names, but the offspring still use the father's and not the mother's name. If a case exists where the children assume a hyphenated name, my research did not uncover such an instance. Clearly this further demonstrates the ascendancy of men over women in familial relationships. The family's internal func-tions, obligations, and duties are intertwined with the communal functions, obligations, and duties that it performs within the larger social groups to which it belongs. Rather than considered or dis-cussed as primarily a separate social unit, the fam-ily formed an extension of the existing kin group, and the main vehicle for the continued existence of the group as such. Even with cultural changes, the survival of the old tradition can still be found in the current Bapedi culture as in the rest of South Africa. Similarly, the kinship system extended to all people among whom some genealogical link could be established. In practice, the whole wide network of an individual's relatives had little impact on his or her daily life. The ties of kinship, as expressed in terms of mutual interdependence, were effective mostly in the close categories of relationships asso-ciated with the family. For the Bapedi, closer rela-tives fell into three major categories: agnatic, maternal, and affinal. Within each of these cate-gories the Bapedi distinguished degrees of relation-ship (Ogbu 1977).

Within the primarily important group of ag-natic kin, in which patrilineality determined a person's relationship, a closer unity existed be-tween those descended from one mother, catego-rized as children of one breast, *bana ba letswele*. Despite the hierarchical arrangement of relation-ships, with the older brother considered superior to the younger brother, an obvious strong bond and reciprocity of service existed among them.

A strong and socially determining bond also existed between a person and his or her cognates. This group *ba ga malome*, those of my mother's brother, also included persons directly descended from the maternal grandmother, referred to as *bana bam pa e tee,* the children of one womb, and the children of co-wives who were sisters. Characterized by great mutual affection, gift exchange, and mutual sympathy, the maternal relationship took precedence over the affinal, the least significant kin group (Nthabu 1989).

Generally, the assignment of status to the individual was based on the basic kin group, the patrilineally related children of one mother from where it radiated out to the position of this group within the compound family, and the position of the compound family within the agnatic group. Among full parallel siblings, two individuals could never be of equal status, and this fact was recognized through the system of age-grading, where full parallel siblings belonged to different age-grades to underline the difference in their status. Like the traditional Bapedi structures, the Zionists require the birth of a son to carry on the father's surname and family. Succession in the church depends in practice, if not theory, to a great extent, on Bapedi succession rules. The birth of sons in the Zion Christian Church has guaranteed and continues to sustain longevity as well as continuity of the top structures of the church, since the Zion Christian Church inception women never succeeded to head the church (ibid).

On the other hand, the function of the badge, one of the primary symbols of the Zion Christian Church, symbolizes much more the same that *magadi* does. Introduced in 1928 by Engenase as a form of recognition, identification, solidarity, and unification, as well as loyalty to the church, it symbolizes the social contract among members of the religious community, like *magadi* in the Bapedi community. Coming across somebody wearing a badge immediately establishes a brother and sister relationship in Lekganyane, *metswalle,* which translates into relatives, in much the same way as *magadi* establishes a network of relations in the Bapedi social structure. The badge has multiple functions. It serves as disciplinary measure, functions as interdict of bad behavior, and shields against peril. Members wearing it will supposedly not dare to smoke or drink liquor. They also help

each other find employment. Members hold the conviction that wearing the badge all the time precludes mishaps such as being robbed. The idea follows from, I believe, the inherent unreasonableness of robbing someone in one's own family. Traveling through South Africa, in taxi ranks, train stations, and bus stations, the affinity among people wearing the badge becomes as apparent as the filial relationship established by *magadi*. The following remarks by some members affirm the extent of the badges' function:

"A fellow Zion Christian Church member is my family member."

"Seeing someone wearing a badge like me is like seeing my mother, brother, father, or sister—no mistakes there."

Throughout the years different emblems were used. The current one replicates the original that was substituted, without any given reason, by a light pink badge with a red round top. Fear of familiarity and difficulties in obtaining the material prompted the church authorities to revert to the original light green badge with a round Black top. The 1949 schism resulted in two churches using two different emblems: Edward chose the five-point star, struck from metal and superimposed on the Black and green material as an emblem, while Joseph's followers sport a metal dove on similar material (Lukhaimane 1980).

The badges, given to every member after baptism, also served to work against the preferred South African Apartheid Government policy of divide and rule, because of their panethnic nature. The badge, worn by baptized church members of any ethnic group, effectively achieves such unity, even if not so intended by the Zion Christian Church hierarchy. The uniforms associated with the Zion Christian Church, like the badges, both create and reproduce the social contract among its members. In addition, the badge constitutes one of the few symbols that attempt to bridge the gap between genders. All members use a single identical badge with no differentiation based on gender. The same cannot be said about other things, like the uniform, for example, khakhi suits distinguish male members from women who in turn wear a green and yellow uniform. Nomenclature also plays a role.

The Zion Christian Church greeting achieves the same as the badge in terms of gender relations. The greeting *khotso,* peace, followed by the response *A e ate,* "let it spread," used by every member, fosters solidarity. The significance of the greeting finds concrete testimony in the peaceful behavior of the mass gatherings at Moria, especially during Easter Weekend and September. Despite the total lack of thuggery and theft, the greeting further indicates the familial bond reflected in the Zion Christian Church's material and metaphorical expressions of solidarity. Thus the contact of the two organizations transformed the nature of the social structures through the complex process of complementary and contradictory reproduction of cultural elements.

A similar image appears in the leadership structures and functions of the traditional Bapedi and the Zion Christian Church. As the two establishments articulate their divergence and convergence with external, internal, and mutual forces, paradoxical ideological and experiential realities become revealed. An examination of the political hierarchy, the quintessential contradictory parallel, leads the discussion on the broader topic of leadership structures.

Gender Relations in Leadership Structures

The power of the Bapedi king was complex, and in his various roles he depended on the assistance of officeholders whose co-operation he needed for the effective exercise of the central power. He ruled through a severely restricted central authority by means of various institutions that included councils and the hereditary or appointed offices held by other members of the nation group. Thus the composite centralized authority became counterbalanced by the large measure of autonomy exercised by the constituent groups in the nation group. The whole network of the political structure worked not only for the operation of the nations' affairs, but also for the protection of law and the control of all abuse of power. The various councils and officeholders allowed for the representation, directly or indirectly, of both sectional and majority interests in the conduct of government. On all levels there were men who were entitled to be consulted by the king or other officeholders and without

whose active support no measures would have any force. In the execution of his central authority the king was assisted in his various roles by a number of special functionaries who were not only appointed to these offices, but who were entitled to them by virtue of their birth, rank, and status (Mönnig 1988).

The executive functions were in these offices. Foremost of these officials was *mokgomana,* literally, the highest noble male member of the group. *Mokgomana,* who by virtue of his rank and status was inferior only to exclusive class of the kingdom, led the nation in the capacity of this lifelong position. *Mokgomana* could be substituted during his absence and illness by the next man in rank, *molatedi wa mokgomana,* the follower of *mokgomana,* and often when the principal officeholder became very old such a follower frequently deputizes for him. A host of other executive positions existed. To name but a few, *morongwa,* also a male member, occupying a minor non-hereditary position assisted *mokgomana* by procuring services of the rainmaker during a period of drought. *Mofa-masemo,* the giver of land and noble male member of considerable seniority, controlled the agricultural activities of the nation (Mönnig 1988).

An assistant or follower to *mofa-masemo* called *molatedi wa mofa-masemo,* usually a younger brother or relative, substituted for him in his illness or absence. High-ranking male servants formed part of the ruling body. Some of these were *mohlanka wa lapa* (servant of the household), *moletsa phalafala* (caller or crier), and *mohlanka wa kgoro* (a man of the house). These blood relatives, usually half brothers of the king or his fathers, did not themselves do menial work but enjoyed a considerable amount of status. Their positions were hereditary through the male line of descent. The latter servant officials were respectively responsible for control of the households of the king, the entertainment of the king's guests, and blowing of the king's war horn, which assembled the men, called *lekgotla la teng la kgosi* or *kgosi le bo tatagwe,* the inner council of the king, or the king and his fathers, respectively, assisted the king. This private and secret inner council, consisting of *mokgoma,* the *kgoro* and *lapa* servants, and the *mofa-masemo,* helped the king to formulate policy and discuss beforehand any measure that was later referred to wider councils. In instances of great importance and confidential nature, the king and the inner council consulted a wider body of male councilors known as *lekgotla la thopa*, or private council.

This council confirmed policy decisions taken by the inner council, but also added its advice, and thus could accept, modify, or reject such decisions. The private council therefore sanctioned policy or laws, and could be described as the ruling nucleus of the nation. In theory the king could override the decisions of this council, but rarely attempted to do so, as such action would have led to fission in the nation group. The co-operation of this council was essential for the successful government of the nation group, and the council provided possibly the greatest check on the behavior of the king. All matters of public concern were finally dealt with before a general assembly of men. There was a slight distinction between two types of nation gatherings. The first informal gathering, called *lekgotla la banna* (council of men), constituted a court of law, it was not compulsory to attend a court of law. The men present at the king's gathering place could also discuss nation affairs in an informal manner and may thus initiate political activities (Mönnig 1988).

The second formal type of general assembly, called *pitso*, was assembled by the king and attendance was compulsory. Any man who did not attend or who had not previously arranged to be excused on sufficient grounds was liable to be fined by the court. Such formal nation gatherings met to discuss and finally accept new laws or nation policy. The king, who normally did not participate in the discussions, opened the proceedings by putting the matter that he had previously discussed with his inner council before the meeting. Any man could take part in the ensuing debate; generally the nation would find itself in agreement with the king and his councilors, and very little debate would follow after the king had outlined the matter. Where differences of opinion became apparent, the official councilors of the king attempted to bring the men around to their opinion. Often the weight added to arguments and their positions normally prevailed. Should there be great differences of opinion and very strongly expressed feelings on an issue, the king would assess the majority opinion, and allow discussions to proceed until he had a fair indication. He would then close the discussions and give his decisions accordingly. Many instances can be quoted of kings acting contrary to their own desires but in keeping with the wishes of the group of men (Mönnig 1988). The opposite was rarely the case. The above discussion demonstrates the extent to which the official running of the Bapedi nation was men's domain. Arguably the Zion Christian Church leadership structures appear to follow along similar lines of authority.

In comparison with the Bapedi king, the Zion Christian Church bishop's authority said to be derived from the inspiration of the Holy Spirit seems absolute. Although assisted in his duties by only the male prophets, ministers, and inner council (constituted mainly by members of his family), the bishop alone interprets the church's laws of procedure, proclaims and implements new rituals, and punishes violators. He does not normally adhere to the drawn constitution for a number of reasons, including the fact that until the most recent bishop none were fully schooled in the northern sense. In addition, the constitution was created primarily to comply with governmental regulations, and not to satisfy an internal need of the church. The obvious similarity of the constitution of both leadership structures by councils of male relatives with no women does not preclude the more fundamental deviation expressed through the autocracy of the bishop. The Bapedi king ruled with more consensus than the Zion Christian Church bishop.

In addition to appointing and ordaining ministers and prophets, the bishop has the power to veto the council's discussions and to suspend or expel any member who disagrees with or disobeys him. Any opposition warrants expulsion, synonymous with excommunication. The latter action impacts members so severely that one woman described it as "*comparable to expulsion from heaven.*" Thus the bishop's power reflects a significant transformation of the more consensual and democratic methods employed by Bapedi kings. Furthermore, the power of the bishop reveals the level of internalization by the Zion Christian Church leader of the authoritarian tendencies of the previous South African apartheid system of rule. It becomes very obvious that the Zion Christian Church axiologies were created through a process that oscillated between the traditional structures, the church's initiatives, as well as the apartheid regime's influence.

There are, in addition to these differences, equally and/or powerful parallels to the traditional Bapedi political structures. One of the most striking finds expression in the ties of kinship responsible for the unification of various nation units. The distinction of the political role of the division of sexes and the age differentiation system form additional similarities. The cleavage of wealth, privilege, and status synonymous with the distribution of power and authority was founded on the ties of kinship originating in the king. This network of kinship formed the basis of all power and authority throughout the nation structure categories of the church's authority. The traditional concept of king-ship among the Bapedi revolves around kinship. *Kgoro*, composed around a core of such kin, formed the most significant political unit. Political authority within *kgoro* tallied with the kinship ties within the unit. The political hierarchy in the whole nation group ascended in similar fashion towards the senior unit of the core around which the nation group was constituted, where it attained its summit in the position of the king. The proximity of each unit to the king defined the extent of its political authority. In other words, the closer the unit was to the king in hierarchy, the more power it possessed (Mönnig 1988).

The whole political structure comes from ties of kinship. The web of kinship supported the kingdom and the private advisers, who were close relatives of the king. They upheld his power if he was incompetent or a waster. They would protect him to make sure that no one supplants him. This was necessary because any change or alteration would have inevitably altered the entire structural order. Similar to the traditional Bapedi structure, the leadership structures in the Zion Christian Church are largely based on ties of kinship. The Zion Christian Church bishop rules the church with the assistance of a family council made up of brothers and uncles. Second to the family council, there is the church council, made up of local elders of the church (who are mostly blood relatives of the bishop) appointed by and responsible to the bishop. The elders, who live near the bishop's headquarters, attend to matters brought about by different congregations to the council for arbitration.

The council applies severe judgment as a repellent to disobedience, and fixes fines in the same way as nation court fines. The manner of address between the Zion Christian Church bishop and his congregation evokes that of the traditional king and his nation. He was ceremonially addressed by different honorific personification titles such as *sebatakgomo* or *tau*, which means wild beast and lion, respectively, and his deeds were exalted in special laudatory poems recited at important assemblies. The king's functions were wide and varied and united as a single whole in the kingdom. A strong fusion of his priestly, political duties, executive office, and his ritual duties existed. The fact that the king was described as the father of the nation effectively reflected the reciprocal relationship between him and the nation. He was not only the executive head of his group, but also the legislator, the supreme judge, and the religious and ceremonial leader. Like the king, who was addressed by various honorific titles in which he personified various noble animals, the Zion Christian Church bishop is often publicly addressed as, for example, *Sebatakgomo* (Wild Beast), and other emotionally emulative terms that elevate him to a respectable status befitting a king. Thus, the congregation's prayers are often characterized by *"Barnabas Morena"* (Barnabas King and *Morena* could also mean God). While this points to the Zion Christian Church philosophy of religion, I am not suggesting that the Zion Christian Church sees the bishop as God. The latter merely points to the great respect accorded the bishop.

Another area in which the Zion Christian Church follows the pre-colonial kingly authority was that of succession based on kinship rather than on charisma. With very few recent exceptions, traditionally the order of succession to all political offices among the Bapedi kingdom was hereditary in the male line of descent, in accordance with the normal principles of the kinship system. The manifestation of sex differentiation was highly visible in the Bapedi political system. The principle sanction of the king was manifest in his command of the regimental system evolving from the system of age grading. In this manner the king was in command for all organized forces in the nation group. However, this was often interpreted as beneficial to the majority of the community. To avert disputes commonly related to succession, the Bapedi distinctly prescribed succession to kingdom unilineally within a royal descent group, with membership of the dynasty transmitted only through the male line. The limitation of eligibility through the designation of one son and heir served as a buffer from confusions that might arise from the complexities evolving from polygamy, I argue. Indeed, practices like these kept dispute of succession in control and to a minimum.

The only eligible heir was the eldest son of the principle wife *mohumagadi*. *Mohumadi* is/was not necessarily the first married wife because marriage happened through accession on the advice of the king counselors. In addition, the whole nation figuratively married *mohumagadi* by virtue of their contribution towards her *magadi*. It was required that she be a daughter of a king, a factor that makes the marriage exogamous, that is, from outside the group. To emphasize her royal status that distinguished her marriage from ordinary marriages, a symbolic renewal and rebirth of the whole nation became necessary. To achieve this all the fires were extinguished and relighted during her marriage ceremony. It is easy to see the parallel to the Zion Christian Church succession. The children from Engenase's two subsequent marriages were not recognized as rightful heirs to the church leadership, although they were permitted to participate in the brass band, an important position in the church. As Comaroff (1980) rightly points out, the long line of Zion Christian Church leadership follows directly in the Lekganyane line, a fact that reaffirms Sundkler's (1968) assertion that the king-type leadership, insofar as African Initiated Churches are concerned, lasts longer than the prophet-type. Charisma was not such a determining factor; this resolves the problem of establishing the hereditary legitimacy of charisma.

By treating succession to leadership in the Zion Christian Church as hereditary, Lekganyane was extrapolating from the traditional Bapedi kinship system, primarily because he was, at the very minimum, remotely connected with the Bapedi kingdom line. However, he regards himself as the king of his church and, as a Mopedi himself, he found it relatively easy to apply the traditional Bapedi principles of succession to his church. In light of this, Bapedi tradition took precedence over the constitution as far as succession was concerned. In both leadership structures, visibility of women leaves a lot to be desired. The principal wife of the Bapedi king held political office and authority only over female activities. She arranged free labor of the women who have to weed and harvest the king's land. In performances of her tasks the *mohumagadi* was assisted by one or more women known as the helpers of the principal wife. These helpers were usually also wives of the king who come from the same nation as the principal wife and accompanied her during the time of her marriage. The youngest of the helpers attended to the homestead of the principal wife and cooked food for her and her children or arranged for the cooking and maintenance of the homestead. Similarly, it is inconceivable for women in the Zion Christian Church to be part of the inner and church councils. The post-menopausal prophetess' power is largely confined over other women. In cases where women do exercise their power over all, it is superseded by that of men. The following statements from interviews demonstrate how men justify the exclusion of women in the councils:

> "If led by a woman, it falls into a pit, there are never two bulls in the kraal."
>
> "Women have their own role to play, which in this church they know, and are satisfied about. It is not us men who wanted that way, but God—and women in this church know that. Look at it this way—women are impure—they go to the moon [meaning they menstruate]—how can they expect a person with such a handicap to perform such an important duty as to serve in the council."[9]

Gender Relations in Religious Structures

The Bapedi and Zion Christian Church gender relations in the religious structures also mirror as they conflict with one another. The conception of God as male in both structures forms an appropriate commencement point. Mönnig (1967) states that before Christianity the Bapedi accepted without a doubt the existence of a Supreme Being, a creator, *Kgobe*. After the introduction of Christianity the word *Modimo* substituted the word *kgobe*. Bapedi conceived of Modimo as male who fathered only one son, *Kgobeane*, which is diminutive of *Kgobe*. Bapedi God, in its original conception, had very little direct practical personal relationship to humanity, a perspective clearly different from Christianity's. In proximity, *Badimo*, the living dead (the departed) were nearer to God than the living, and thus acted as mediators. Even in God's capacity as creator of life and death, he is not attributed with the termination of life in its particular manifestation on Earth. This distance of Bapedi God from humanity, I argue, extended into Bapedi conceptions of death. Bapedi did not believe that God can create people only to punish them eternally after a short period on Earth. Before the Christian influence, the concept of hell was not an aspect of death to Bapedi, and indeed to the entire South African indigenous cultures. Their model of the hereafter, like the rest of the people of South Africa, reflects a comfortable place where the dead looked over the well-being of the people on Earth.

The Zion Christian Church structures reveal the impact of the previously discussed African heritage. The Zion Christian Church conception of God and Jesus Christ replay the traditional religious structures of Bapedi, as does the style of interaction between God, *Badimo*, and the living. In this case a male Jesus Christ claimant to the second personhood of a triune male God head forms the object of Christian religious faith. Jesus Christ occupies the center of this faith. In earlier times of the Zion Christian Church, Jesus Christ was conceptualized in the same way as Bapedi Supreme Being, the creator, *Kgobe* or *Modimo*, with the personal contact and relationship mediated by *Badimo*. Though the Zion Christian Church in its early constitution, acknowledged the presence of Jesus Christ and Engenase often preached about Him, few confused followers place Jesus Christ and Engenase on par. Others believed that God empowers the bishop, who mediates between Christ and the congregation like the *morongwa*, the traditional Bapedi messenger who mediated between the chief and the nation. Or like *Badimo* mediated between the living and God.

In both structures, God is remote and his impact on human life comes through mediation. The distance here does not preclude an opposite but equally important characterization of the relationship between God and people, on another level, as profoundly intimate, or even almost equivalent. I'm referring to a Zion Christian Church dynamic, which equates God and humanity in the person of the bishop and God's representative. This dynamic recalls, as it emerges from, the way in which Bapedi traditionally maintained a relatively fluid limit between the living and the dead, and I argue that most indigenous South African cultures still do. Those who used to belittle this practice are now eating a humble pie. Pope John Paul II of the Roman Catholic Church in the 1990s announced that the Church should make the religion relevant to the context of the people. Although I believe the Pope was way too late, the South African Catholic Churches in their liturgy, indeed, now also call upon *Modimo le Badimo*—God and *Badimo*. Whereas people used to belittle the Zion Christian Church for refusing to see a conflict in evoking both *Badimo* (the living dead) and *Modimo* (God) in prayer, the majority is now arguing for the same position that the Zion Christian Church has long stood for. There is a lot to learn from this church.

Bapedi held that the living and the dead reciprocally influence one another, so that souls of the dead people become living spirits, *Badimo*, which ultimately find their way to an undefined world, similar to, but superior than, the living world. The influence of the living on the dead, though limited, formed a fundamental element of all rites linked with the living dead's spirits. Good health and prosperity was often an indication of the positive influence of the living dead on the living. Respect and obedience to the living dead came with those benefits. The living dead were the guardians of the social code. To those who neglected the prevailing social code, they would be visited by sickness, economic loss, or some other misfortune. Hence, in order to retain the favor of the living dead they had to be particularly propitiated. Regarded as intermediaries of God, the powerful *Badimo* communicated with the living through dreams, by means of *moya* and *seriti*, which were two real giving attributes that each person receives from God. Detached from the body through death, *moya* could speak, while *seriti* was a configuration of the deceased manifest in the dreams of the living only. When *Badimo* repeatedly occurred in a person's dream, it was an indication of their discontent and thus they needed to be appeased. *Badimo* sometimes could also pronounce their desire through whirlwind and hail, which signified displeasure and omen, respectively. Sacrifice constituted one means of appeasing God and *Badimo* (Mönnig 1988).

Only the senior male head conducted ceremonies because he was logically "nearest" in terms of proximity to death in the world of the living *Badimo*. The head of the family, almost exclusively a male, sacrificed and called upon *Badimo* at their graves whenever they reveal themselves through dreams or calamity, or in some other form that the diviner interpreted as a signal of offense. The manner of address to *Badimo* mirrored the way peers addressed each other among the living, a familiarity that reflected the fluidity of the limits between the living and the dead. Although all other *Badimo* were called upon for help, those of the rulers related to living kings were particularly honored. To the extent that the king and his relatives guided their fortunes on earth, so spirits of the rulers from whom he descended were held by Bapedi to afford supernatural protection and assistance to the people they had once ruled (Mönnig 1988).

We find a similar fluidity in the Zion Christian Church mode of prayer, which characteristically invokes God and the bishop's name simultaneously (e.g., *"O God of Engenase, I stand here in front of you"* or *"I will end here in the name of Barnabas"*). This tendency to metaphorically aggrandize the bishop's powers derives from, I would argue, a perception among Zion Christian Church members that the bishop wields exceptional, even divine, healing powers. Accounts of his miraculous healing skills, kept reverently present in common memory, constitute the core of the Zion Christian Church philosophy of religion and, more pertinent to my theme of comparison, parallel the traditional Bapedi valorization of male divine healing and healers. That the parallel is profound and virtually complete seems to me clearly evidenced in an equality of what may be the most fundamental

characteristic of both Bapedi and the Zion Christian Church faiths. In both, the accounts of miracles performed by divinely gifted men and women healers simultaneously constitutes and "proves" (by reasserting the miracle stories as true) the presence of a higher power. We can thus begin to shape an understanding of the Zion Christian Church's deeply rooted perception of the bishop's supernatural healing capacities, enabling the same faith for which members not only visit Moria, the church's headquarters, in Polokwane (which can be compared to Muslim's Mecca), to receive all these benefits from their "Messiah's representative," but also roll down where the bishop has passed to be healed or blessed.

Even though the Zion Christian Church members also use the name of Jesus Christ as the son of God when they baptize, there is no clear distinction between Father and Son. Baptism is mainly understood, by the followers, to mean admission into the church, and not reconciliation between God and humans. However, after Engenase's death the position of Jesus Christ was slightly altered. Members try to revive the name of Jesus by constantly calling his name. In pragmatic terms, the holy spirit in the Zion Christian Church is a replication of the *Badimo* spirit or living dead. The concept of the holy spirit *moya o mokgethwa* in the Zion Christian Church translates into God's guidance, and differs in meaning from *moya*, which could mean air. Although in some instances confused with, and often subordinated to, *Badimo*, the holy spirit plays a dominant role in the development of the Zion Christian Church. The holy spirit has the power to heal, the ability to exorcise evil spirits from possessed persons, and gives people the "ability" to prophecy. Engenase and, currently, his successors are construed to have complete control over the holy spirit, which endows prophets with preaching skills. It should be noted that prophetesses are perceived to have less spiritual powers than male prophets. The bishop possesses the power to extract the spirits from prophets, thereby terminating their profession.

Further, both Bapedi and Zion Christian Church religious structures are explicitly, inextricably tied to concepts like impurity, taboo, magic, divination, and medicine, which are in other religions often implicit. I mean to explore the associative chain that links the conventional to the less conventional aspects of both religious organizations, beginning with Bapedi's. Bapedi believed in the supernatural. Their concept of the supernatural included the condition of impurity, signified by the word *ditshila*. *Ditshila*, referred to a state of impurity exclusive of moral consideration of proper or sinful conduct. This infectious condition posed a threat to the social order. Impure conditions included, for example, a woman giving birth, an unborn child, the placenta, the house where birth takes place, a woman who has had a miscarriage, a woman who intentionally had an abortion, children who were born with teeth, breech children (born with feet first), pregnancy through prostitution, sickness, and death.

According to this logic the condition of *ditshila* primarily occurred in women and children, and men could be contaminated through contact. Men would also be considered to be in the condition of *ditshila* after a loss of a spouse. To the extent that the latter logic follows the dichotomous association of women with nature and men with culture, I argue, it constitutes sexism. Death rendered both men and women *ditshila*, however, for women an additional standard different from men's functioned to isolate them. In the case of women their biological makeup and bodily functions over which they have no control operated to isolate and stigmatize them in society. Contact with a woman who was on a period, who had just given birth, etc., was said to contaminate people. They would only be allowed to be in contact with others after they have undergone purification. The condition of impurity was closely linked to the dual concepts of heat and coolness, drought and rain. The Bapedi rain symbolized goodness while drought denoted all hardships, suffering, and evil. *Ditshila* implied, then, heat and drought, and needed to be made pure by means of ritualistic application of coolness emanating from rain. Cutting across the concepts of impurity, heat, and coolness was the concept of taboo. The fact that it contains both the condition and the act of impurity made it distinct from *ditshila*. In fact, taboo, I argue, served the purpose of preventing or avoiding contact with impurity.

It was prohibited, for example, for a "pure" man to have intercourse with a menstruating woman, a woman who has had an abortion or a miscarriage, a pregnant sex worker, or a widow; all of these are considered "hot." It was also taboo for any person in a condition of impurity to enter the cattle kraal, to work on the lands, or to be present at any religious rite ceremonies. An examination of this clearly shows that the latter is taboo and not a condition. It also implies that breaking the taboo constitutes willful action. *Badimo* sanctioned actions that were willfully taken, in a way that they did not for conditions of impurity, in which the individual had no particular will. To rectify a broken taboo, therefore, included both sacrifice to *Badimo* and magical action, where purification of impurity *ditshila* depended only on magical ritual involving coolness.

Emerging from the combination of taboo and impurity was the concept of *boloi*. *Boloi*, or witchcraft, like taboo, related to both the action and condition of impurities. The witches were willful conductors of heat, an innate trait with which they were born. Similar to impurity, witchcraft derived its charge from socially threatening transitional states between, for example, walking and sleeping, or inside and outside. The two kinds associated with witches both embodied combinations of distinct categories. *Dithuru*, for example, were objects made from dead people's bodies, and had no will of their own, but depended on the will of the witches. They were, as it were, the dead brought to life. *Dithongwa* combined savagery and civilization, in that they were animals like wildcats, dogs, snakes, owls, and bats which could be made docile by the witches, and served as their sentries and steeds (Mönnig 1988).

The Bapedi distinguished between day witchcraft and night witchcraft. Day witchcraft, which was practiced mainly by men, involved the learned ability of application of magical and medicinal practices solely to the detriment of others. Night witchcraft, on the hand, practiced mainly by women, evolved from the incomprehensible or complex inborn trait of heat and a unique ability of performance; for example, a night witch's infant had the claws of cats to cling to the wall. Thus the difference between the two lay in the methods employed and not in the time of operation. Protection against witchcraft was provided by a medicine man or *ngaka*. Since most events were interpreted in terms of supernatural sources, *ngaka* had to possess a keen foresight and proper avertive methods to have genuine control over forces of witchcraft.

Ngaka, or diviner and healer, who was usually male, enjoyed a prominence given by the plurality of causes coming from various supernatural forces. His various functions included inter alia, the divination of causes of events, the recommendation of remedies or aversion/preventive measures, the naming of witches, and the prescription of protection measures against the witches, the cure of damage done by the witches, and the divination of the witches' prescription of sacrifices to *Badimo*. The diviner was the dispenser of leachcraft, and possessed the knowledge of good magic to the advantage of those who employed his services. Of the various methods of divination the most common by far was the use of bones, called *dikgara* or *ditaola*, which could be broken down into a number of groups. Pertinent to my theme of comparison and exposure of mutual reproduction of gender relations, the selection of *ditaola* reflected equality in terms of gender representation (i.e., in most cases every male part was matched by a female part). Consequently, the fundamental, indispensable group was a set of four pieces representing a man, his wife, and their son and daughter. The pieces for a man and a woman were pyramidically shaped, and were cut from the tip of a hoof of a bull and a cow, respectively (Mönnig 1988).

The two pieces for the son and daughter were flat oblong pieces, formerly made from ivory, and currently from the tibia of a bull or cow, or the fang of a pig. Less essential units of the set came from the astragali of various animals. One important pair was taken from a male and female baboon. This particular pair represented witches and provided information on witchcraft. Unfortunately, the sole male ant-bear piece presented a deviation. The piece upset the whole almost perfect gender equality in *ditaola*. This piece was referred to as *modimo*. The association of the ant-bear piece with only the male diviner perpetuated gender hegemony. In addition, the perception of and reference to this piece as *modimo*, god, and a symbolic representation of the diviner himself, further punctuated the ascendancy of men over women, I maintain.

Very few women became *dingaka*. In fact, *dingaka* normally came from a family of diviners, although anyone who wished to pay a price of a beast to a *ngaka* of his acquaintance may also learn by apprenticeship. A significant exception to the rule of apprenticeship is the king, who was automatically considered to be the principal *ngaka*, and an inheritor of a ceremonial divination set. Because he lacked the skills of interpretation, his position was also ceremonial and he relied on the expertise of his subordinates for his readings. The position of the diviners was both honored and respected in Bapedi society, and second only to the king's power and influence. In addition to the diviners, *Bapedi* had *Mapale* or *Malopo*, who divined through direct spiritual contact with Badimo. In contrast with diviners, *Mapale* were frequently women. Their task involved exorcising spirits sent by Badimo and witches, from possessed people. In the process of exorcising spirits, the possessed person was simultaneously cured and initiated to become *Mapale*, by means of intensive dancing. The dancing ended with the consultant falling into a trance and a chant; the latter two were interpreted as a communication with *Badimo*. *Mapale* did not share the special status attached to *ngaka*, maybe because her duties were more restricted than that of the diviner, or because of attitudes towards women.

The Zion Christian Church immersed in healing that assumes primarily two forms, divine and faith healing. The two, I suggest, depends upon and recreate as they emerges from Bapedi traditional concepts of the supernatural, expressed through taboo, impurity, witchcraft, magic, divination, and medicine. Divine healing, initially practiced solely by the founder of the church, who as you remember was a male, evolved into an eventually duplicated faith healing. Both methods of healing involve the use of symbols, as will become clear in the discussion that follows. Divine healing in the Zion Christian Church followed a similar pattern as in all the Zionist and Ethiopian churches, as described by Hanekom (1975) and Sundkler (1976): through laying bare hands on consultants. The basis of this practice is found in both St. Mark 16:17, 18 and St. Matthew 10:7, 8 where it is expressed that people will be cured through the laying of hands on them. In the Zion Christian Church, however, the idea pragmatically assumed a different dimension. The concept, interwoven with traditional traits, involves certain taboos that govern the laying of hands on consultants. Ministers who had attended a funeral cannot lay hands on people and have to observe a period of seven-day abstinence before they can continue with the execution of their duties. Similarly, living with and eating food prepared by a woman with less than a three-month-old baby constitutes a threat to the social order, and prohibits ministers to lay their hands on people. If you remember, the latter accounted for a large number of polygamists among ministers and prophets, since it provided for an alternative wife, and avoided forestalling duties. The ban on menstruating women, based on the book of Leviticus 12:1–5, prohibits such women to shake hands with ministers and to mix with the congregation. It also forbids ministers who have had such contact to carry on their duties. At businesses owned by the Zion Christian Church such women used to be allowed to work only after seven days.

The laying of bare hands was discontinued in 1930, because it threatened Engenase's power. Ministers, who were successful in healing consultants through laying hands, took credit for the deed. The consultants who were healed were more inclined to believe in the power of the Ministers and undermine Engenase's power. To counter this Engenase banned the use of bare hands. To ensure that all power of healing in the church will be attributed to him, he introduced pieces of khaki cloths that were blessed by him. The cloths, regarded as the only legitimate healing tools, could be confiscated by Engenase if he disqualified you as a healer. With the increase of membership, these pieces proved expensive, and were substituted by ordinary green papers or newspapers. Further, faith healing is inextricably interwoven with the use of tools believed to possess healing powers. One faith healing method involved pricking by a needle. The needle is especially designed and blessed by the bishop and is used in conjunction with a six-centimeter-long and one-and-a-half-centimeter-thick piece of wood, *kotana*. The use of the needle, also confined to male prophets, serves to extract impure blood by piercing primarily the elderly patients' legs and hands.

Kotana serves to apply healing through hitting all painful parts of the body. This method of healing is comparable to the traditional method called *lomega*. The method was used to extract blood from a person's body that was perceived as a source of general bodily pain, headache, and eye disease. This was done by sucking through a cut artery, or joint. As an alternative to pricking, coffee and tea, with or without milk, also serve as blood purifiers. The effect of water as a healing implement in the Zion Christian Church primarily depends on its source, type, and availability. Water drawn directly from distant seas and rivers is said to produce more satisfying results than water from taps, for example. Members go to great lengths to fulfill instructions of obtaining such water, not only because of their belief in its effect, but also because water from taps falls short of curing specific sicknesses. Blessed water from whatever source heals through various forms. One important form is through drinking, called *mogabalo* (Nthabu 1989).

Other methods used were blessed walking sticks and strings or strips of waist cloths. These served as a form of protection against mishaps and witchcraft, respectively. Engenase, the founder of the church, is said to have healed a cripple in Johannesburg through the powers of his walking stick and the music from his band. Members gave accounts of similar miracles performed by Barnabas, the current bishop. The strips of waist cloths, on the other hand, maintained their protective powers, as long as they were not washed with soap. In addition to this, a blue square cloth called *khouseane*, meaning "hidden," is attached in a hidden place inside the clothes served to protect individuals from assaults and lightning.

One of the high priests suggested that this is associated with Act 19:12 in the Bible, where Paul's clothes are used to cure diseases. The church members cling to the belief that power is transferred first from the objects, and then go to the person. Barrenness, which, to a certain extent, still holds a detrimental effect in terms of the perpetuation of a marriage, comprises one of the most important reasons of faith healing in the Zion Christian Church. Apart from healing this through water, bishops utilize a small blessed twig, *thupana*, which barren women look at and make a knot, representing the child, in their small blankets. Members who have been through this profess the authenticity of the whole process. Some of the Zion Christian Church bishops, especially the founder, Engenase, are said to possess the power of making rain. An example is cited where he made rain for a certain chief Matlala, who testified about this in front of the congregation. This act attracted and still attracts more members to the church. Various other methods are used: Newspapers cut into strips and blessed are burned in the faces of the consultants to purify objects, stop fights between husbands and wives, and to heal. Most houses of the church members could be identified by blessed copper wires above entrances of homes to safeguard against lightning. Sanctified papers are used to bless the food. All these methods have to be prescribed by prophets, priests, and bishops in an interaction that evokes that of traditional diviners.

Notes

1. Also see Lagerwerf (1975: 48–49).
2. Information from informants including a prophetess from Ratjiepane.
3. Information from informants including the high priest in Soshanguve. Also my field observation church events that I attended, women outnumbered men.
4. In the souls of the people who died, this illustrates the fluidity between the living and the dead.
5. Field observation.
6. *Ditaelo* refers to directives inspired and conferred by the holy spirit on male ministers to prepare and administer medicine prescribed by the prophetess to cure and rectify afflictions.
7. Levirate where a brother marries his deceased brother's wife.
8. Even in the new South Africa, patrilineality, though accepted by the larger society, translates in most part as a sign of a woman joining the men's group.
9. Information from the high priest from Soshanguve and one from Atteridgeville.

References

Barret, B. David. 1968. *Schism and Renewal in Africa: An Analysis of Six Thousand Contemporary Religious Movements.* Nairobi: Oxford University Press.

Brandel-Syrier, Mia. 1984. The Role of Women in African Independent Churches. *Missionalia* 12(1): 13–18.

Bergelund, Alex I. 1967. *Rituals of an African Zionist Church.* Johannesburg: University of the Witwatersrand, African Studies Program.

Comaroff, John, L. 1980. Bridewealth and the Control of Ambiguity Tswana Chiefdom. In John L. Comaroff (Ed.), *The Meaning of Marriage Payments.* London: Academic Press.

Comaroff, Jean. 1985. *Body of Power Spirit of Resistance.* Chicago: University of Chicago Press.

Daneel, Marthinus L. 1987. *Old and New in Southern Shona Independent Churches: Leadership and Fission Dynamics.* The Hague: Mouton.

Hacket, Rosalind. 1987a. Beyond Afternoon Tea: Images and Roles of Missionary Women in South-Eastern Nigeria. In P. Kulp (Ed.), *Women Missionaries and Cultural Change.* Williamsburg, VA: Department of Anthropology, William and Mary College.

Hacket, Rosalind. 1987b. Women and the Spiritual Churches. In *New Religious Movements in Nigeria.* New York: Edwin Mellen Press. pp.1–17.

Hanekom, C. 1975. *Krisis en Kultus: Geloofsopvattinge en seremonies binne 'n Swart Kerk.* Pretoria: Kaapstad en Pretoria.

Jules-Rosette, Bennetta. 1978. *African Apostles: Ritual and Conversion in the Church of John Maranke.* Itaca, NY: Cornell University Press.

Kalu, O. 1995. *The Dilemma of Grassroot Inculturation of the Gospel:* A Case Study of a Modern Controversy in Igboland, 1983-1988. *Journal of Religion in Africa.* 25: 48-72.

Lagerwerf, Leny. 1982. *They* Pray for You: Independent Churches and Women in Botswana. Leiden : Interuniversitair Instituut voor Missiologie en Oecumenica.

Lewis, Ioan M. 1971. *Ecstatic Religion: An Anthropological Study of Spirit Possession and Shamanism.* London: Penguin.

Lukhaimane, Khelebeni Elias. 1980. The Zion Christian Church of Ignatius (Engenase) Lekganyane, 1924 to 1948: An African Experiment with Christianity. PhD dissertation, University of the North.

Mönnig, Hermann O. 1988. *The Pedi.* Pretoria: Van Schaik.

Mosupyoe, Boatamo Y. *Mediation of Patriarchy and Sexism by Women in South Africa.* New York: McGraw-Hill.

Murphee, Marshall W. 1971. Religious Independency Among the Budja Vapostori. In David B. Barret (Ed.), *African Initiative in Religion.* Nairobi: East African Publishing House.

Nthabu, Boatamo Y. 1989. *Meaning and Symbolism in the Zion Christian Church of South Africa.* Master's thesis, University of California, Berkeley.

Ogbu, John. 1977. "*Marriage* payment: Riddle for Anthropologists. In Journal of *African* Studies, 5 (2): 151-172.

Sundkler, Bengt. 1961. *Bantu Prophets in South Africa.* London: Oxford University Press.

West, Martin. 1975. *Bishops and Prophets in a Black City.* Claremont Cape Town: David Phillip.

Women's Perception of Patriarchy and Non-Sexism: South African Case

Boatamo Mosupyoe

Introduction: Reflective

The discourse in this chapter focuses on how women in the Zion Christian Church of South Africa perceived patriarchy and non-sexist concepts before their independence in 1994. There was a discrepancy between the call for non-sexism in the current South Africa with Zion Christian Church institutional structures and social cultural practice. The call for non-sexism in essence emanates from a construct of gender relations as hegemonies. The gender relations are not only perceived as hierarchical and unequal but also as a conflict between the interests of men and women (Reskin & Padavick 1994). The diverging and converging influence of the interplay of the multiple structures of the pre-colonial South Africa, the Zion Christian Church, the colonial apartheid and the current became evident in how the women conceptualize their reality.

To this end, some women in the Zion Christian Church parted company with the construction of gender relations as symbolic polarities. Such a position proved both fallacious and divisive, in these elderly women's world. Actions like male priests opening prayer services that are meant for women not only essentialize men's superiority over women, nor do they create a hegemonious social hierarchy; on the contrary, it points to the division of labor with no reference to male power. The latter notwithstanding, ambivalence common to situations where people are faced with different forms of structural ambiguity marked these women's responses. Oakley (1974: 81), referring to this dilemma as "structural ambivalence" (Pheko 2005; Phalane

2009), notes how such inconsistencies characterize women's positions in modern societies. The mutually exclusive nature of structures from which women have to choose compound the situation since the achievement of one can mean defeat of the other (Oakley 1974). Similar ambivalence prompted these women on several occasions to concede that they will welcome change when directed by the bishop. However, on the whole they rebuked the equation of gender roles to the apartheid racial discrimination. To them gender roles and institutional practices of men and women in the church reflected a non-competitive duality and non-dichotomous hierarchies binarily ranked in opposition to each other.

The non-sexist call, on the other hand, sounded to them like a potentially explosive practice that will violate the basic *khotso* principle of the church and transform a system of peaceful co-existence into a system of rivalry. The fact that they could recall the practices from pre-colonial times and the bible served as an added reaffirmation of the authenticity of their construction of gender roles, thereby giving credence to Parson's (1954) claim, even today after so many years, of adult rigid conformity to tradition as a result of socialization. To these women the nature of their transformation to conform to the new definition of gender relations as manifest in the non-sexism concept would directly flow from the visionary guidance of their bishop. Consequently, one could conclude that they were not completely opposed to change or oblivious to some inequalities, but they exercise some extreme caution not to violate the rules of the church. For the middle-aged women as well as younger rural women, the mediation of the conflict displayed transient alliances and loyalties. Their desire for transformation was expressed in subtle ways. Maintaining the peace in the church superseded the desire for conformity with the call for non-sexism. This was done without completely obliterating the presence of the wish for transformation. These women completely align themselves with the elderly women in their loyalty to the power of the bishop's guidance. At diametric opposition with the latter are young urban women's views. They more than welcome the call for a non-sexist South Africa since their conceptualization of gender roles corresponds with that of the new government's. What they perceive as a disjuncture between the two structures could be mediated by bringing the social cultural practice of the Zion Christian Church in conformity with the non-sexist call. They see such a move creating a supportive alliance in compliance with the peace theme of the Zion Christian Church. Although they recognized and respected the bishop's influence in effecting change, they made very little if at all reference to his pivotal role.

The disjuncture in terms of perception of the division of labor among young and old, urban and rural can be traced to how the women frame the nature of men and women relationships. Urban and mostly younger women perceive income inequality between the sexes as sexist and an unfair practice that needs transformation. The man's ego becomes a non-issue, men have to adapt to women earning equal or more. These younger women give little or no consideration at all to the benefits that accrue from an educated husband or man. Their views, while acknowledging Gerson's (1985: 99) assertion to the effect that *"income inequality between the sexes reinforces a traditional sexual division of labor and supports the priority of the male career on practical grounds,"* also refuse to see this as insurmountable. Older women, on the other hand, choose to ignore the disparity in pay and concentrate on the peace that they enjoy.

The influence of the church's teachings extended to how these women perceive sexism as it plays out in the education of young men and young women. The rural older and middle-age women would still choose educating a young

man over a young girl when circumstances dictate. They would do this even in the context of a non-sexist society, reaffirming their support for the structures of female domesticity. They see rewards in being married and disadvantage at being a spinster, *lefetwa*. They therefore encourage religious endogamous marriages for their daughters. Since this carries a lot of importance, I argue that these women see marriage as an identity (Lopata 1973; Nthabu 1989) essential for their survival. Younger urban women will rather focus their attention on educating the society about the sexist nature of the nomenclature like *lefetwa* and not sacrifice their educational ambitions in favor of marriage. Spinsterhood, efficacy, and self-sufficiency seem more attractive to them than struggling to look for an educated prospective husband in the church. They advocated for choices about who should be educated in the face of hardship to be based on other factors besides the sex of an individual. Factors like who studies harder and who shows more interest in academics should play a major role.

While rural women and older urban women avoided referring to the impact of apartheid on education, urban women did not. The latter pattern reflects the degree of loyalty and adherence to Zion Christian Church values. Rural and older women displayed a certain amount of rigidity, while urban young and middle-aged women showed more flexibility. Urban women want change. The middle-aged want change but they want it to be achieved within the parameters of the khotso theme. Younger women see sexism as gross violation of the peace theme, and that peace between themselves and men will not be an authentic khotso until Zion Christian Church structures are brought into reconciliation with the dictates of non-sexism. On the other hand, women in the rural areas and older women in the urban areas will most likely wait for the bishop to direct them. What I cannot ignore, in most of these women's responses, including urban middle-aged women, but not urban younger women, is the constant reference to the bible and the old traditional culture as a factor of endorsement in their beliefs. Durkheim (1995) recognized the tremendous power invested in this, many years back. Describing the endurance and sustainability of such traditional beliefs and systems, he maintained that because of the ready-made transmission from previous generations, such beliefs receive immediate and ready acceptance and adoption. Indeed, the Zion Christian Church women's responses make this old-age insight true today as it was then.

It was obvious that their collective and ancient nature invested them with a particular authority that education teaches that they should be recognized and respected. The latter phenomenon became very conspicuous in the Zion Christian Church women's perceptions and conclusions. Practices like polygamy, deference to males and authority, which they do not oppose, mirror to varying extents the old traditional structures. Furthermore, the administrative composition and function of bodies like bursary funds, literacy centers, referred to as *lekgotla*, resemble the traditional administrative structures not only nominally but substantively. It becomes clear that traditional beliefs fashion responses of elderly and rural women, especially. In addition the general operation of the church reflects the old political structural traditions. The overall objective of the study centers on an evaluation of Zion Christian Church women's conceptualization and mediation of patriarchy and sexism with their education and social development. The abundance of literature on gender socialization and women's subordination developed through time reflects an in-depth discourse of convergent and divergent views. These ideas in turn reveal a variety of substantive paradigms that attempt to understand how men and women relate and have related throughout history. Some anthropologists, like Chodorow (1978), stress the psychodynamic process of development of the unconscious as a determinant in how different genders arrive at a decision. Mead (1949), on the other hand, refers to the importance of the psychological conditioning, with little emphasis on the unconscious. Other anthropologists like Ortner (1974) and a long time ago de Beauvoir (1953) subscribe to the universal association of men with culture and women with nature as the influential force that drives men and women to the kind of decisions they make.

There are many instances that can be quoted to illustrate the validity of the claim of the exclusion and negative portrayal of women based on the association of women with nature and men with culture. For example, Smith and Padula (1996) relate how menstruation and women's reproductive powers were perceived by some Cubans to drive men to madness and how menopause ironically saved women from such acts. These cultural biases have in many instances developed into social values that guided decision making. Some employers adopted informal segregation codes that kept women from supervising men. Despite these instances, we must also acknowledge individual life histories, cultural specificity, and contexts as additional tools of analysis in understanding gender relations. This theory that was also articulated by Wright Mills (1959: 143) examines how biographies and histories intersect with social structures to persuade decisions among genders.

My analyses of the women's varied responses defy and de-naturalize any one theory as sufficient in the comprehension of how Zion Christian Church women construct and mediate factors that make up their world. Their conception and process of articulation of the concepts cannot be represented as a neat unitary formation (Foaster-Carter 1978), but rather it is a set of complex conceptual order motivated by a variety of factors. The women's responses reflect the validity of McCormarck's (1977) claim of the need for cultural specificity, I will also add of individual particularity as well.

Foundations That Shape Women's Perceptions

Religious Instruction

The construct and conceptualization of the concept of non-sexism by women in the Zion Christian Church produced answers that varied according to age, level of education, degree of exposure, and commitment to the Zion Christian Church religious instruction, as well as rural/urban dichotomy. Women provided varied and diverse responses that displayed an evident epistemological foundation that was heavily influenced by the interpretation of religious instruction and the theme of peace *khotso*. Both served as the sources of knowledge production and the construct of cultural logic. In addition, both played a pivotal role as mechanisms of socialization that shaped how members construct the concept of non-sexism. On frequent occasions women will refer me to the bible and biblical teachings as expressed in the church to affirm their answers. In addition to the bible, most women from Polokwane will also refer to the traditional practices of the Bapedi as to further authenticate their beliefs and practices. The common response from elderly and middle-aged women would be:

> "The Bible is my guide, and what I do not understand the bishop and ministers will clarify."

These women believed that the ministers, when involved with the word of God, cannot go wrong, since they are inspired by the Holy Spirit. When I asked about the elements that might negatively affect them as a result of the religious practices of the church, they ascribed the differences to the division of labor, saying:

> "It is just like in the workplace. You have a manager, a supervisor, and a subordinate. This does not translate into oppression, but a natural division of labor."

In attending church services, it became apparent that though seniority defined by relative age assumes primacy with regard to the role that church members play, the role of gender as an organizing principle still manifests. For example, while there are male ministers across the age range who show deference to and respect to the elderly ministers, there are no women ministers. Priesthood in the Zion Christian Church is a male preserve, as we have learned. Consequently, only males can preach during church services, women cannot even by virtue of their age preach to a mixed audience that included males. Responses like the following were commonplace among both the middle age and older women:

> "We do not envisage a stage where a woman will be a priest or a bishop in the church" and "It really does not matter whether a woman becomes a priest or a bishop."

When I inquired as to whether the call of non-sexism by the government will at some stage compel the church to change its position and ordain women as priests, a lot of skepticism punctuated the varied answers. Thus a general passive resignation among some women to the monopoly of priesthood by men priests was obvious. Women seem to have internalized their role as distinctly different from men, with total disregard to their differential treatment. The prospect of a non-sexist society loudly and clearly also advocates priesthood for women. To a few women in the church the possibility exists; to others, especially the elderly, it is an impossibility that will only attract God's wrath and poverty for women.

The latter follows the social value that finds expression in the New Testament and reads:

> "Let a woman learn in silence with all subjection. But I suffer a woman not to teach, nor to usurp the authority over the men, but to be in silence."[1]

Violating such a command to some Zion Christian Church women will invite poverty. Those who held this view believed that the call to non-sexism will alienate men and therefore cause the loss of their financial support for families. Yet to most, the actualization of non-sexism will depend on the directive from the bishop, who will have a vision that will define the context within which the transformation to a non-sexist society should be addressed. If the bishop sees a holy vision that would be a sanction that a woman can be a priest that will be accepted without question. These women hoped that the bishop will act accordingly to the demand of the moments' requirement and by doing so the bishop will ensure their stability. During a period of accelerated social change, people do not usually draw from childhood experiences of socialization, but act to fit their present circumstances. Gerth and Mills (1953) found this to be true in their study of socialization.

Conditions in the church also sometimes dictate responses that breach church practice and induce behavior and responses appropriate to the demands of immediate needs. Functions of male and female elders demonstrate this. Zion Christian Church women elders, regardless of their status, still relationally enjoy respect and deference from younger males, including young ministers. The deference, however, does not extend to the realm of responsibilities like *ditaelo*. *Ditaelo* refer to directives inspired and conferred by the holyspirit on male ministers to prepare and administer medicine prescribed by the prophetesses to cure and rectify afflictions. However, in case of emergencies, like in a life-threatening situation, where a member needs urgent medical attention and a male minister cannot be found, a woman elder can administer *"ditaelo."* As a 62-year-old woman elder, who has been in the church for 34 years and supports herself and her family by selling food to schoolchildren, asserted:

> *"I have personally witnessed older women handling coffee, tea, and other healing devices where a male priest could not be found. The women have to be past menopause."*

Women prophetesses and elders can only prophesy and preach at women-only services that are held on Wednesdays. Even then, these meetings are opened by a male elder priest, who regardless of his relative age to the woman elder, possess the privilege of opening the women's meeting. Women elders assume that role only in the absence of a male. Furthermore, I have alluded to the practice where on Sundays and Wednesdays women are not allowed to use the front door to enter the church, and only male ministers, male church elders, and dignitaries can use the door. All the other ordinary male members have to observe the same practice as women, meaning, they do not use the front door to enter the church. Older and middle-age rural women members gave no credence to this practice. They perceive it as a commonplace practice where dignitaries everywhere enjoy special privileges like walking on the red carpet. The absence of women in the midst of those dignitaries constitutes no offense; neither does it in their eyes diminish their status as women. Some women contended:

> *"When you travel with the president, you do not expect to get the same treatment. He is the president you are a common person. It is done everywhere. It is not unique to the Zion Christian Church."*

These women members perceive this interplay of gender and seniority as relational and not necessarily hierarchical. At variance with Chodorow's (1978) theory of the unconscious as determining choices, these women see their perception as deriving from the level of consciousness. One woman elder, a 54-year-old rural woman who married into the church and has been a member for more than 15 years, remarked that what other people perceive as male privilege, like male ministers opening services points to the division of labor with no reference to male power. That God's reception of and answer to prayers is nondiscriminatory since it gives equal hearing to prayers of anybody who prays to him, legitimizes her claim, she posited. Another much older rural woman, gave a more specific response that may suggest men's superiority to women:

> *"Men are the head of the household. It is not only cultural but the Bible also states so. It has been like that all my life. There are things that I do that men cannot do. And things that I can do that they cannot."*

A general agreement with the above view prevailed, while views diverged as to whether a transformation should be effected to conform to the concept of a non-sexist South Africa. This woman and most women in her age group do not feel the need to oppose the practice. Opposing the practice violates the basic principle of peace that constitutes the fabric of the Zion Christian Church structure. She conceived the move toward non-sexism as a danger to peace or *khotso* and as a potential precipitator of fights that are not tolerated in the church. The majority of middle-aged women, on the other hand, would welcome change achieved within the parameters of the church's dictate and/or through a vision seen by the bishop from God. All males can potentially become prophets; only women past menopause, as indicated previously, qualify as prophetesses. In this case power as conferred by women's seniority manifest in a situational and relational fashion. As the discussion has demonstrated, the prophetess enjoys enormous authority and respect from any younger members and congregants, regardless of gender. In addition to civility, seniority gives women prophetesses a measure of control that guarantees them obedience from all subordinates and reinforces their position and leadership.

Here again the Zion Christian Church religious organizational structure reflects both seniority and gender as organizing principles that determine power in situations and relationships. For males both seniority and gender make up the criteria that confer leadership status, while for women only seniority plays a pivotal role in determining their leadership. Charisma works for men in obtaining leadership status and also to a lesser extent it can play a pivotal role in enhancing a woman's status as a leader. Like in other African Initiated Churches in West and East Africa, for example, the Harrists' movement, and Legio Maria, respectively, the Zion Christian Church shows occasions of the ephemeral rise of women to leadership with the support of a male kin. In the Weberian (1947) sense the charismatic potential for women is routinized in the group as a whole, but not with respect to their specific positions or cultural contributions. Usually charismatic promise sustains the female leadership positions.

At the time of my research, for most men and women the amount of years of school education was minimal. Most of the male ministers had less than four years of school. Ngubane (1977) argued that the Zion Christian Church, like many other AICs, vindicated the superiority of their religious and cultural value by referring to practices and symbols in the bible. The initial lack of interest in school can be traced from such roots. Mr. A.M. Kgathi, a staunch member of the Zion Christian Church who not only holds two university degrees but is also an advocate for providing school education to church members writes:

"The Bible is central to all teachings of the Zion Christian Church . Unfortunately not all members of the clergy have been trained in the ministerial work. In fact the majority of the priests are not literate." (Zion Christian Church Messenger, September 1985)

In concert with the above assertion traditionally in the Zion Christian Church the acquisition of education was not considered a prerequisite for ministry. As one member of the congregation from Garankuwa put it:

"Jesus never attended school, preaching comes through the inspiration of the holy spirit—you do not need school for that."

This pervasive conceptualization of knowledge production resonates with the traditional cultural logic that rationalized that the production of knowledge, wisdom, and efficacy derives primarily from seniority and life experience. In addition, it affirms that both gender and seniority function together in determining positions of authority, albeit differentially. Obeisance to superiors is highly visible and seems to facilitate acquiescence with the church's religious prescriptions. Similarly, peace as a preeminent religious mandate and the foundation of the cultural logic in the Zion Christian Church social, political, and religious intercourse facilitates conformity with the teachings of the church and this becomes clear in the next discussion.

Peace-Khotso

That the base of the Zion Christian Church's axiological logic on all levels derives from the peace or *khotso* theme becomes evident in the writings, among others, of one of the staunch members of the Zion Christian Church, Jan Mukhondo, who asserts:

"Some joined us and boarded the Zion Christian Church peace train whereas others did not because they despised our Church. Some went amok thinking that they had better mechanisms for bringing peace in their territory, homes and at their work, but up to now they have not yet brought peace in their environments. Why? Because they are not turning their hearts and souls to Jesus who is the only Prince of Peace." (II Thessalonians 2:14–17; Zion Christian Church Messenger, 1992, Issue No. 22: 8)

Mukhondo goes on to posit in the same issue that the church believes in Jesus Christ as the only prince of peace and it invites anybody who seeks peace to join them and they will achieve everlasting peace. All teachings, in church, schools, and meetings, are preceded by the greetings of peace. Consequently peace as the fundamental epistemological basis for the Zion Christian Church sociocultural logic necessarily has varied construction of meaning by the members. By some members, mostly older members, the thematic translation includes acceptance of the church's teachings without any opposition, while others, like younger members, contrary to the latter, apply its usage to advocate transformation. The latter factor became very clear when I asked members if they agreed or disagreed with any teachings of the church. The most common response emphasized the centrality of the bishop, thus if the church mandates an order through the holy guidance of the bishop, nobody has any business to even suggest an opposing stance. At one instance a younger male university student, as the discussion later reflects, questioned the management of the bursary fund by the committee members appointed by the bishop. The response from one of the male elders of the church echoed the notion that what has been mandated by the bishop equals infallibility and should not be questioned.

Such manner of settling thorny and controversial issues, that is depending on and not daring to question the bishop's views and directives, frequently manifested in most elderly women's responses on how they perceived the fate of non-sexist South Africa. These women in their late 50s and 60s cannot bring themselves to accept the call. Their acceptance and non-acceptance will be mandated by the bishop. In this way uniformity that will guarantee peaceful interaction will be maintained, they argued. One woman went to great lengths to explain to me the advantages bestowed by the consistent observance of a peace theme, as well as its relevant application to men and women relationships within the church. Congruent with the notion of *khotso*, she asserted, the bishop and the church highly condemn physical abuse of women and children by men. She reminded me of the many times I have been to church services with her and heard ministers preaching about the fact that a man who engages in physical abuse of his family loses the power of peace and will never be eligible to be a priest. She further remarked that the new South Africa is aspiring for an element of gender equality, which the church has long achieved, because of peace. Women are also encouraged to resolve problems with their children through communication, and to resort to spanking only in extreme cases. Spanking does not comprise abuse but depicts a form of acceptable discipline.

Women with regard to this practice referred me to traditional practice where they *bata* disobedient children. Indeed, the word does not connote cruelty but it is a method of calling a child to order with very mild spanking. Again, they drew my attention to the age-old tradition, which could not mean they were wrong. It was at this stage that one of these women drew my attention to the fact that the whole country debates the issue of polygamy, an element of the Zion Christian Church cultural practice sanctioned by the bishop and God, according to these women. Bishop Tutu, Nobel Laureate and Archbishop of the Anglican Church, then argued for the practice to be accepted by the World Council of Churches as an authentic African cultural practice, one woman reminded me.[2] I then solicited their response to the practice within the church. A 62-year-old rural woman who also supports herself and her family by selling food to schoolchildren offered her response:

"I know of men who practice polygamy in the church for a reason. The reasons could be a barren wife or a lazy one."

Others agreed with her. They saw polygamy as an authentic African cultural practice that agrees with the teachings of the Zion Christian Church. Polygamy in AIC is a form of an expression of spiritual independence; an assertion of freedom of African traditional practices as against monogamy has been noted by many scholars (Barret 1968; Mosupyoe 1999; Isichei 1995; Ndou 2000). Indeed, to these elderly women in the Zion Christian Church, monogamy posits a lot of disadvantages that engender conflict in marriages. To them monogamy as the only marriage option of cultural practice translates into an imposition from the north. Even then northerners themselves cannot practice what they preach. They practice polygamy in a form of "cheagmy" (i.e., having extramarital affairs). Come to think of it, northerners redefined polygamy into bigamy, thereby transforming an agreeable cultural practice into a criminal act. Even they themselves cheated on their wives and continue to do so, yet they claim monogamy. The women continued to direct my attention to the prevalent infidelity in monogamous relationships. In addition, they related at great lengths the stress that accompanies confronting a cheating spouse. In such situations they all agreed, women have to fight to preserve the resources, like when a cheating spouse spends money on a mistress. Furthermore, they contend, the injured woman has to go for therapy. Whereas in polygamous marriages the first wife will be informed of the husband's intention and where she gives her consent she plays a pivotal role in the process of legitimizing the marriage. As one of the two co-wives of one minister succinctly put it:

> *"We do not have to worry about a husband who sneaks out and wastes money on entertaining another woman. We have each other for support. We do not need to pay money to speak to psychologists or psychiatrists. The support we need is right here. I would not sit here and listen to people putting down our culture."*

These women's responses partially typify some of the responses stated previously. As these more mature and mostly rural women, some in monogamous and others in polygamous marriages, accept the practice, younger women opposed it with the same amount of vigor. They discern the custom as not only insensitive to women, but also as according men even more undeserved privileges. These young women referred me to the healing practice in the Zion Christian Church that uses water as a healing device. One reminded me that one of the reasons for a man to take a second wife has to do with the claim of a woman's incapability to conceive, in other words her barrenness. In cases where a couple cannot conceive the woman bares the blame. Men's sterility, on the other hand, never comes up as a factor to be acknowledged and addressed. Motivated by the above information, I engaged in participant observation where healing was conducted. I observed several ministers about this issue. Among those I observed were two high priests. They attended to many patients, some of whom had problems with conception. Indeed, in concert with what the younger women had said, women and not men were said to have the problem of conceiving, in cases where couples did not have children. In all these cases water was prescribed as a form of cure. The water had to be taken through a drinking

process called *mogabalo*. The drinking of such water every morning and evening is supposed to avert misfortunes and diseases, and help barren women to become pregnant. I was curious to know if the water ever helped sterile men. To this effect I asked one of the ministers. His answer was preceded by a detailed account of his involvement with the church.

He told me he is not an actively practicing economist even though he is an economist by profession. Instead, he currently operates as one of the highly educated priests of the Zion Christian Church. He was born in the church, which he abandoned in his youth. Later because of the constant misfortunes that he encountered and the vision through a dream of his deceased parents, he decided to go back to be an active member of the church of his "father and mother." Then he finally gave an answer that deserves to be reported in its entirety. He responded as follows to my question as to whether men can be sterile:

> *"God intended everybody to have children— there is technically no sterile man as much as there is no barren woman—something happens that blocks a woman's tubes and prevents her from getting pregnant—our water serves the purpose of unblocking the dirt that blocks the woman's tube and enables her to have children."*

I then asked if a man can be blocked, and consequently require the blessed water to unblock him. He then impatiently answered in the negative and emphasized the efficacy of the Zion Christian Church water in this regard; the efficiency that even, as far as he is concerned, supersedes Professor Mokgokong's abilities. Professor Mokgokong is a celebrated South African gynecologist who was based at Medical University of South Africa and has helped women with the problems that prevented them from conceiving.

The other minister's answer, though slightly different, also implied the same sentiments. He emphasized that the church never had a case where it was a man's fault. If such a case should come to their attention, he assured me the Zion Christian Church will do for the man what it does for the women. In addition, the church has never failed to help women to conceive. He told me that the blessed water in the Zion Christian Church does something that the hospital can never do for anyone. The water works in conjunction with belief and the friendly attention of the priests who attend to these women consultants. They relax and they also believe that they are going to be helped by God of Engenase, Edward, and Barnabase, and that produces results.

It is to such interpretation that the younger women object and also view as differential to women. They contend men can be sterile like women can be barren. In their opinion, such views violate peaceful gender existence and interaction, and the basic principle of peace as espoused by the church. To the contention that a man can take a second wife if the first one exhibits laziness, these young urban school-educated members of the Zion Christian Church unanimously agreed that they would like to be accorded the same privilege. After all, one maintained, Queen Modjaji of the Lobedu nation, in one of the South African provinces has had several husbands. She practices polyandry. Therefore, they concluded, polyandry forms an authentic African cultural practice that should not be viewed as foreign and should also be applied to women. These women perceived monogamy, polygamy, and polyandry as legitimate African practices. Practicing both forms of marriage in the South African culture would engender equality for both men and women. The differential right of men to have more than one wife as happens in polygamy will be balanced by the right of women to have more than one husband as manifest in polyandry, at least the choice should be evident and real. This will be in line with the concept of non-sexism that the government advocates, as well as the peace principle of the Zion Christian Church.

Body as God's Temple

The discourse on the dress code expectations followed the same pattern of response that I received in relation to the peace theme. Responses on the expectations by the church of dress codes continued to vary according to age. The girls and women are taught to respect their bodies by wearing long skirts and dresses, covering their heads with scarves especially during church services, and avoiding wearing pants since they expose part of their bodies. Treating their own bodies as a temple is emphasized. One elderly woman in her late 50s explained that a woman's body symbolizes God's temple. Therefore the onus falls on a woman to respect herself so as to be respected by men and the public. The conduct and practice will also ensure that women present less temptation to men. When I asked about the responsibility of men in terms of controlling their own temptation, several women between the ages of 54 and 60 responded that women should not expose themselves to danger, banking on the fact that men will control themselves. While men are indeed expected to take that responsibility, women should also do their part. The fact that women respect their bodies and guarantee their own safety does not for these women translate into putting an extra burden of expectation on women to the advantage of men. To them the practice amounts to taking care of oneself and should not be genderized. They compare this to protecting one's house against thieves by locking your doors. The following remark represents the sentiments of both elderly and middle-aged women from both the urban and rural areas:

"You do not depend on the good will of the thieves to take moral responsibility not to steal your belongings."

On the other hand, younger urban Zion Christian Church members' views diverge from the above view. They strongly feel that they will wear whatever they want, and their choices of attire should not be sanctioned by fear of being attacked by men. These young urban women perceived this cultural axiology as constructed on social relational hierarchy that endows men with unfair privilege. The absence of an equal expectation from men seems to be a point of reaffirmation for these young urban women's views. One even maintains: "Clearly younger women like to see an equivalent expectation of dress code for men, while older women see a relational and not a differential practice of dress code."

Education

Women's General Views on Education

Some priests had preached that a woman should not be more educated than a prospective husband or a husband. Quotes from the bible predominated to reaffirm the assertion that God intended a woman to be subordinate to a man. The saliency for the message from 1 Timothy 2:11–1-2 that directs a woman to be subservient to the man also found articulation through quotations from John Knox's expression. Thus expressions such as *"The same God that denied power to the hand to speak, to the belly to hear, and feet to see, had denied to woman power to command a man"* (Starr 1991) were invoked. Not surprisingly, some women from age 50 both urban and rural with little school education agreed with the idea. Inasfar as they were concerned; sometimes being more educated than a man precipitates insecurities in a man that results in constant arguments in the household.

This particular view by women supports recent studies done by Knox and Schacht (2009), Blumstein and Schwartz (1983), and Huber and Spitze (1983), focusing on northern societies, all demonstrate that on average women will enjoy an amount of support for their success from their husbands. However, husbands tend to experience discomfort when wives' income equals or exceeds theirs. Important to note, men alone cannot be held responsible for the persistence of these patriarchal tendencies, since some women uphold the marriages to protect and accrue their own interest. The above pattern became apparent in the Zion Christian Church women's answers. They considered an environment where a man feels he is the main provider as more conducive to a peaceful and economically prosperous existence than if the opposite holds true. Elevated to an imaginary higher position a man tends to be agreeable and very generous, to a woman's advantage, some women posited. However, this study will later reflect a shift from this way of thinking in women in younger generations and women who have spent more years in school. The teachings at that time encouraged women from competing with men, both domestically and in the workplace. Any woman who strives to be more educated than her husband and possesses over ambitiousness runs a risk of being called competitive. Such a competition, they contended, brings tensions in and instability to marriages because they argued a more educated wife tends to undermine her husband. Women should acquire just enough education to

complement and not compete with men and current husbands.[3] Recently, however, the Zion Christian Church stresses the importance of education; the stress, however, at the time proved disparate in favor of men/boys. Boys are told to work hard and get the education that will enable them to provide for their families.

Commonly in the rural areas I encountered women of varied ages who had to leave school after third or fourth grade because of lack of sufficient funds in the family. Their families considered it prudent to continue financing the education of their brothers rather than theirs. The assumption is that church endogamous marriages will guarantee them educated husbands who will care for them. Most of the young women in the rural areas who were in the ninth and twelve grades considered this a good idea. They said getting married forms an essential inevitable step that every respectable young woman should aspire to. This view was shared by some middle-age women with fewer than four years of school. High education in a woman tends to repel and intimidate prospective husbands, they maintained. Furthermore, spinsterhood carries a stigma that engenders isolation and contempt, a risk too high to take. Most of the women feared to be referred to as *lefetwa*, a term that literally translated means "an individual who has been passed for marriage." *Lefetwa* is a non-gendered or gender-neutral nomenclature that nevertheless exclusively in usage refers to women who have never been married. On the other hand, men who have never been married are just single, as indicated by the word *lekgwathla*. When subjected to a thorough analysis, the word *lefetwa* is a socially constructed word that evaluatively demeans a woman's status. It carries the implication "she has been passed by men for marriage." Culturally that state of having been passed is looked down upon. Therefore, the word reaffirms the status. Conversely, the word *lekgwathla* is devoid of such implications.

Most of the young women in the rural areas generally agree with older women. They displayed loyalty to the church's values with which they completely aligned themselves. When asked how they will reconcile the contradictions in the church with a vision of a non-sexist South Africa, which advocates equal amount of education for all, they gave some of the following responses:

"The ministers will tell us if that is okay" (10 yr. old) *"That is not right, because a man is a man and a woman is a woman—she is made out of a man and she must obey him"* (11 yr. old) *"Even if a woman is clever than a man, but she is not allowed to rule him—the church and God say so—you can be clever, but a man has to rule you—I don't know it's the law"* (12 yr. old).

On the other hand, the responses of young women of school age in areas around Garankuwa, Atteridgeville, and Mamelodi were very different. Some responded:

"The church has an obligation to teach what it has to. I do not have to agree with everything. I am to get as educated as I want. A husband is not going to limit my educational ambition" (17 yr. old woman) *"Some of the teachings of the church are old fashioned. I love my church and I am going to marry within the church and be more educated than the men"* (15 year. old girl).

These young women were less concerned with being spinsters, but more troubled by the terminology employed to refer to women who have never married or those who are at an age considered inappropriate to be single. Inter alia the names include *lefetwa, letekatse,* and *sefebe.*[4] They assert that they could be single, educated, and very respectable women. The latter view obviously deviates from those of young women in rural areas of the same educational standard. In addition to these general perceptions informed by the church's teachings, the Zion Christian Church had to, like other institutions, contend with the apartheid laws. The trichotomous confluence of the indigenous, colonial, and apartheid historical periods precipitated a dynamic within the Zion Christian Church, with its own unique epistemological milieu. The Influx Control Laws as well as the Migratory Labor System affected the Zion Christian Church schools like all the others (Unterhalter 1989). To contextualize the women's responses to these laws, an overview of the composition of the Zion Christian Church schools is in order. All the Zion Christian Church schools

are in Polokwane, within the area of the headquarters of the church. The first school started its first operation in 1964. These schools are mostly served and are staffed by church members. At one time the schools were staffed and served exclusively Zion Christian Church members. Other members reported that they joined the church because they wanted their children to have access to the schools. These members highly praised the church and made it a point to let me know that they have not regretted their decisions since.

The Zion Christian Church schools were mostly staffed by male teachers at higher levels. Some of the teachers, mostly males, were well qualified for their positions. However, others were not well qualified; they just had a junior high school education. The female teachers were mostly confined to primary schools. Male teachers tended to outnumber females in high schools. This is not unusual and it is not only confined to the Zion Christian Church. Cligent and de Miranda (1977) conclude that the degree and form of labor and education for women stems from social, cultural, and historical factors. They employ structural and Marxist analysis to examine women's educational status in the Cameroon, the Ivory Coast, and Brazil, respectively. They observe that more often economic development or development in general fails to accord women participation at the same level of equality with men in education and in the labor force. Akin to their analysis, the Zion Christian Church at that time made efforts to "develop" its members in a way that still reinforced patterns of sexual differentiation. When I specifically pointed out the above disparity in terms of teachers along gender lines to the Zion Christian Church women, the responses implicitly showed the impact of the apartheid migratory labor and influx control laws. Women gave their answers with much care not to indict the apartheid system. They avoided acknowledging the fact that the church cooperated with the apartheid regime, and forbade its members to fight against apartheid. They, however, admitted that men have no option but to move away from home to go to the workplace. They also alluded to the low salaries earned by men, which (a far cry from their white co-workers) made frequent visits home impossible for the migrant laborers.

It was clear in their carefully worded answers that the influx control system, which made it illegal for a husband's family to move in with or even visit him at his place of employment, ensured both the destruction and separation of families. More often men ended up creating new families near places of employment. The responsibility to manage households and send children to schools with meager salaries fell on the women. Encouraging women to marry early as a strategy to lessen the financial burden developed into a cultural pattern, while young men viewed it as a source of security and were encouraged to continue with their education. The latter factor played a part in the disproportionate representation of genders with both the teachers and students. Furthermore, women alluded to the fact that young women and girls are sufficiently qualified after they have acquired skills in sewing and cooking. The fact that these composed an important part of the school preliminary curriculum to them justified their actions of withdrawing girls from school earlier than boys. Analyzed within the context of apartheid laws and the Bantu education system, this attitude was also formed and shaped by apartheid laws. With the exception of religious instruction, the school curriculum in the Zion Christian Church schools followed the South African Bantu education syllabus. The Bantu education system, specifically designed for South African blacks, prepared the latter not to compete with but to be servants to their white counterparts. From this system of education the former apartheid regime gained both a huge pool of unskilled and semi-skilled African labor, as well as a small African professional and managerial class.

Unterhalter (1989) describes Bantu education as gutter tutelage to the masses specifically produced and fashioned to make it extremely difficult or impossible for blacks to get out of the gutter because of illiteracy and low paid employment. The range of subjects offered clearly reflects Bantu education's ultimate goal. The subjects offered illustrate the intent of the education very clearly. Lower primary schools (i.e., first grade to fourth), for example, offered algebra, needlework, mothercraft, domestic science, Afrikaans, English, Vernacular, and religious instruction, designed to generate competent

current maids for the white population. I will also argue that the system also produced competent "housewives." Unfortunately, such a background provides these women with a frame of reference that advances their justification to perpetuate discontinuance of women's education. The framework not only justified their actions but they also felt compelled to make decisions that accounted for their gender incongruity. In addition, the women cited the high cost of education, again with great caution not to assign blame to the apartheid laws, however applicable. When I suggested that a great disparity existed in government funding among different racial groups, none of them was prepared to engage me on that level, except to say that that may be, but in their main point focuses on the expensive education, and not causal matters.

The fact of the matter is the apartheid government spent approximately $1,000 annually for every white child's education as opposed to approximately $50 for every black child.[5] Furthermore, Blacks, unlike whites, had to pay for their education from elementary up to university, while whites had free elementary and high school education. Textbooks were free for whites and not for the Africans. In addition, Africans had to travel for very long distances to reach their schools while whites did not have to.[6] The gender–wage differential that paid men more than women in all labor occupations, in professional and non-professional fields, functioned as an additional reason why the education of boys was encouraged more than that of girls. An inquiry into how women perceive these differences in the context of the education for women in current non-sexist South Africa again prompted varied answers, divided along age, and rural/urban dichotomous variables. Rural older women's answers proved to be in concert with their urban counterparts as they revealed loyalty and trust in the bishop's ability to guide and lead in matters of policy. These women believed that a vision will be disclosed to the bishop. The answer from one urban middle-aged woman reads as follows:

"Like with everything else the bishop will see the light will give us guidance. As of now things are working just fine. Educating boys more and

not girls is not such a great loss since both will work together to take care of each other. In fact it is not a loss at all if you look at it as a matter of peaceful cooperation and not conflict. What we have to do is wait, like I said the bishop will tell us what is right."

The others nodded in agreement and one further maintained:

"Even in your new non-sexist South Africa we still have Mandela at the top. We have to make decisions in life that involve choosing one over the other for the benefit of all. Can you tell me of an instant in life where people are completely the same?"

The women further said that they regard the education of women as important as that of men, and that will be of great pleasure to them if both can be equally educated. However, with the problems that they have presented to me above, like expensive education, they will still make the same decisions, meaning they will continue to privilege the education of boys instead of girls even in the context of a non-sexist South Africa. They further revealed their confusion and skepticism about the concept of non-sexism. One remarked that what we are espousing as non-sexism conflicts with the notion of peace *khotso*. At this stage, as I prompted them further by referring to the comparison with the non-racial concept, their dispositions displayed passive resignation as they echoed their faith in the bishops' guidance. To these women the two calls of non-racialism and non-sexism depict distinct concepts that should not be confused. They conceptualize gender harmony and equality as dependent upon division of labor, which by and large also dictates decisions about the education of boys and girls. Inherent in the sentiment is the belief that in case of marriage the couple will use their different skills as acquired through education to complement and not compete with each other. Conversely inasfar as racialism goes the whites from the beginning had no intention at all to either share or complement Africans in any way. Their plan centered on subjugation. Some of them continued to explain that when they met their husbands the intention of staying and working together to raise children

was clearly stated. One middle-aged urban woman remarked:

"My husband did not say to me: 'I want to marry you to subjugate you.' He said I love you and want to marry you, live with you, have children with you that we could raise together, and take care of each other."

Thus the decision to educate boys over girls, they maintained, in that context does not translate into sexism. I also posed the question about equal remuneration, or differential remuneration based on skills, merit, and experience, which could in some cases, mean that women earn more than men. Either way for these women is fine as long as one does not humiliate the other. However, they all agreed that if a woman earns more the potential for conflict could increase more than if the opposite is true. Culturally and religiously a man should be the main provider. Again to them the inability of some men to accept the woman as the main provider does not prove gender inequality, or lack of reason on the part of the man. He would merely be aspiring to fulfill his natural duties as a man that is the main provider. Middle-aged women express a strong desire for change of attitude and practice. However, their caution and cognizance of such a transformation to be carried out within the parameters of the church's law and the bishop's vision from God could not be ignored.

Similarly, younger rural women favor change that will be within the dictates of the church's theme of peace. In addition, they displayed the same amount of faith and trust in the guidance of the bishop, in the same way as the elderly women. Although they very much would like to earn according to their skills, merit, and experience, albeit earning more than men or husbands, these young women place a higher amount of responsibility on themselves to maintain the balance and peace in the household more than on men. As one of them put it:

"If I earn more education and more money than my husband, I will be very careful that I do not use that to humiliate him. I will also not abrogate the responsibility as a woman, like doing dishes, lest he should think that earning more money gives me airs."

On whether in the current non-sexist South Africa boys should be preferred over girls when decisions are made as to who should continue with schooling, their answers largely echoed the above. They still maintained that they will get married endogamously to educated men who will look after them. They further remarked that this was in concert with the teachings of the church and God. Unlike the older women, these young rural women understand the concept of non-sexism as something that people outside of the church define as unequal relationship between men and women. While they acknowledged that might be so, because they are informed by their church's teachings they have to view it as relational division of labor, and not as a divisive culture practice, even though they would welcome the change. Younger women from urban areas, on the other hand, see the current state of affairs as a vehicle to transform these differences in practice. Being afforded the same educational opportunities as young men will benefit the country as well as the church. Earning an equivalent or more money than the man where they are more skilled would serve as an incentive for them to excel at work and in their education. The majority of these young women feel very strongly that men should not be bothered or be overly concerned when a woman earns more than they do. They understand the concept of non-sexism as a vehicle that will create equality and rectify imbalances in the schools as well as in the home and work place.

The above view defies Durkheim's (1995) old explanation of socialization and social facts, respectively. He argued that education that socializes comes from without the individual and exists outside the individual consciousness. In addition, Durkheim contends the education gives the historical fashion in which a social being is constituted. These women's responses, by their very contradiction of the socialization norms of the Zion Christian Church, demonstrated that resisting and contradicting the norm can also serve as a powerful form of socialization that comes consciously from within. Their responses and approach rather match Farzaneth's (2008) view that recognizes the three stages of socialization that includes individuals as active players.[7] They therefore conceive of the concept of non-sexism as something that will change perceptions

and attitudes, to the extent that it will not matter whether the man or the woman earns more. In addition, family decisions about who should continue with schooling in cases where a shortage of resources exists should depend on other factors, other than whether somebody is a girl or a boy. The views of these young women concurred with those of Zion Christian Church members who had education beyond 12th grade, and are mostly employed as teachers and nursing assistants. The Zion Christian Church authorities seem to agree with the position that education forms an essential part of life, since they took upon themselves to establish means that will enhance their members' education. How that manifests along gender lines is examined in the next topic of discussion.

Women and the Zion Christian Church Literacy Campaign

Despite the fact that the Zion Christian Church schools have been in existence now for more than four decades, a substantial number of members at the time of my research still did not have "school education." I am employing the usage "school education" to deconstruct reference to people as "illiterate."[8] In 1980 Lukhaimane described the Zion Christian Church followers as "underprivileged, rural and illiterate." Numerous newspapers and even Zion Christian Church members themselves echo the reference to members as both "illiterate," "rural," and "underprivileged." The high priest from Soshanguve maintains that "the majority of members in the Zion Christian Church have an average of six school years, with a high percentage of women with very little school education. One very well-educated member who told me he is a medical doctor[9] admits to the fact that most members have very little school education. The Zion Christian Church members themselves as well as the bishops have had concerns about the amount of school education its members possess. The 1988 September issue of their magazine, *Messenger*, remarking on the campaign for literacy, states in part:

> *"This campaign will fight adult illiteracy within the church and raise the level of education*

within the Zion Christian Church, thereby meeting the challenge that the Zion Christian Church has more than its fair share of people who cannot read or write." (11: 13)

Thus, responding to such criticism of its members bursary funds, administrative staff management training and adult education centers were established. The next discussion focuses on how women feature into these literacy efforts by the Zion Christian Church.

Women and the Zion Christian Church Bursary Funds and Merit Awards

The name of the fund, called Bishop Edward Lekganyane Bursary Fund, honors bishop Edward Lekganyane, the deceased father of the current bishop of the church. His courage of attending school at a very late stage to satisfy the apartheid regime requirement of ministers to at least have two years of schooling before the church can be a registered and recognized functioning body played a determining role in the choice of the name. The bishop appointed the committee of the fund that is composed of six men. Any attempt to question the functioning and structure of the committee evokes rebuke. This became very evident when a final-year law student and a member of the church at one university questioned among others the qualifications as well as the allocation of money. According to the student's estimation, the current allocation would culminate in the exhaustion of funds after the first year of its life. Consistent with the perception of the bishop's infallibility, the student was thus in part told:

"I still cannot believe that a long standing and allegedly dedicated member of the church can dare challenge a project which has been initiated and blessed by His Grace The Bishop." (The Zion Christian Church Messenger 1991)

Even though the bishop chose the name (Lukhaimane 1980) it was insisted that:

"the concept was born, nurtured and made into reality by men and women of foresight and love for their fellow human beings." (The Zion Christian Church Messenger, November 2, 1992)

Notwithstanding, I proceeded to ask how women felt about the fact that only men make up the deciding body of who should be awarded the bursary. The responses to this question suggest that older women in the rural areas do not feel qualified to even dare to voice objection to something that has been dictated by the bishop. They had faith that the holy spirit will guide the members of the committee to do the right thing. If women were needed as members, they maintained the bishop would have seen that before the committee was constituted. The fact that the bishop did not see the need reflected how unnecessary women's inclusion is. Older women in the urban areas views slightly diverge from their rural counterparts. Although completely in agreement with the bishop's decision, they believed that women's presence in the committee would make a difference in the decision making. For instance, one offered, if more boys are given scholarships than girls, a woman would be more sensitive to that than a man, in her estimation. They echoed the rural women's belief that the need for women's presence would if necessary have been made clear to the bishop.

For the first time the younger women from both the urban and rural areas agreed. They considered the inclusion of some women in the bursary committee as needed. However, the reasons given for the inclusion differed. Most young women from the urban areas perceived such incorporation as a fair non-sexist practice well overdue. On the other hand, ambivalence on the part of the young rural women thrived. Some were of the view that the inclusion of women would facilitate the men's responsibilities because they believe that women make excellent secretaries. Other young rural women displayed discomfort and great ambivalence. They asserted that the composition of such a secular committee should not necessarily be bound by religious dictates. This, of course, implicitly challenges the bishop's authority. An interesting observation is in sharp contrast with views expressed by some of their counterparts with exposure to similar socialization processes. Such diversity of views demonstrates the fluidity, conflict, and ambivalent nature of human personalities belonging to the same organization. A factor that should caution social scientists against oversimplifying the psychoanalytical postulations of conditioning that comes out of socialization. While internalization, a psychological aspect of socialization, may instill feelings that correspond to feminine psychic structure, it does not guarantee that the behavior will match the feelings. Individuals are not robots in the process of socialization (Andersen & Taylor 2007), and these women displayed that. In line with this claim, these young rural women, well vested with the supremacy of the bishop's directive within the church more so than their urban counterparts, in a very rare move gave responses that do not conform to the expectations of the female Zion Christian Church.

The bursary fund has two sections. The first section, called the merit award, a grant given to the three best 12th grade or matric students, best translates into obtaining a minimum of four distinctions in the final examinations. The loan grant is partially a loan and partially a grant. Fifty percent of the grant will be payable when the bursar completes the education program for which the money was granted. The conditions of receiving any of the grants include being a practicing member of the Zion Christian Church and continuing to be so while still in receipt of the bursary. The bursary board requires that merit and need constitute the criteria used to distribute the money. In their words:

> "Students who show academic merit but are disadvantaged by financial circumstances are the target group of the bursary fund, whereas sex, age, and choice of academic stream are not considered."

An examination of who has benefited from the fund most clearly shows that more young men than women benefit from the fund. In the 1988 distribution only four young women out of thirty recipients obtained the loan award. The trend still continued at the time of my research. Although I could not obtain the latest official statistics, during field research I hardly found any young women who were recent recipients. Or did I not try hard enough? The merit award since its inception has been awarded to young male students only. The trend through the years has mirrored the 1980s. Since merit determines the selection of those awarded the merit grant,

young women from the urban areas point to the attitudes and cultural practices as partially responsible for the pattern.

The culture expects girls to do more chores than boys. For instance, girls had to clean the house every day, cook, and wash the dishes. In addition, they had to do laundry, including the boys' laundry. Consequently, young women had less time to study because of cultural attitudes and expectations. Men and young women who engaged in so-called "women house chores" were still stigmatized; worse still adults in most households still held similar views. These attitudes and perceptions partially accounted for young men doing much better than young women in school. Young women from the rural areas were divided in their views on the reasons that account for the gender disparity in the distribution of funds. Some agreed with the young urban women, while a few thought that boys naturally are more intelligent than girls. The latter thinking that clearly emanated from the teachings of the church seemed to influence the responses of rural older women. While they concurred that cultural attitudes and expectations might be attributable to the persistent unequal distribution of funds, they nevertheless also alluded to the fact that men possessed more intelligence than women. Older urban women regard cultural attitudes as well as the possibility that girls did not apply for the bursary as much as boys did as the causes of gender disparity in the distribution of bursary awards.

The bursary committee made up one of the church councils *lekgotla la kereke*. This body, like all the other bodies, had absolute respect and showed complete deference to the person and office of the bishop. The impact of such respect and deference, referred to as "non-negotiable first essential" (Morongwa 1985), become apparent in the answers of both rural and urban older women. All their answers were preceded by reference to the holy guidance of the bishop and his wisdom. The wisdom and the guidance would then automatically transfer on the decision-making body, that is, the bursary committee. In sum, transformation of any practice or law has to be mediated with the bishop's directive. The degree to which compliance with the bishop's instructions are carried out cannot be underestimated. Indeed, the Zion Christian Church Adult Education Literacy Centers, the establishment of which was mandated by the bishop, bears testimony of his influence.

Women and the Adult Education Literacy Centers

The bishop initially appointed inspectors J.M. Mamabolo and I. Kutoane to serve as heads of the adult literacy campaign within the Zion Christian Church.[10] They served as chairman and secretary, respectively. The bishop ordered that every branch of the church should establish an adult literacy center. As expected the branches heeded the call and centers were established, as illustrated in the tables at the end of the book. Men made up the governing structures as well as the functionary staff of all these centers, with the exception of just very few women, who taught sewing or needlework. However, women of varying ages from age 21 and up almost exclusively made up the student body. The curriculum still reflected the Bantu education structure with few additions. The additions included extra classes that train male ministers to conduct funerals and marriages in a uniform way.

Classes for women revolved around learning how to master basic writing and reading skills, as well as sewing, mothercraft, and home economics. That the above subjects promote servitude is efficiently articulated by C. Wright (1989). In his article "An Under the Carpet View of the Education Crisis in Sub-Saharan Africa," he writes about how education in many countries in African promotes the virtues of services to others than self and orients learners toward seeking employment rather than creating it. Wright further argues that the latter paradigm entails values of selfless sacrifice, conformity, and dependency. I assert that helping each other is a virtue to be admired and encouraged, however, if the purpose leans toward precluding people to participate in other structures that could develop more of their potential beyond domestically oriented duties, then I will part company with such a view. The school curriculum in Zion Christian Church schools, a mirror of Bantu education, did just that, fitting into Wright's criticism about education in Sub-Saharan Africa.

As indicated above most of the students are women. Some centers show poor retention of students. The most notable exception to this pattern was the Rakopi Adult Education Center at Thabamoopo, a district of Polokwane. As the tables show, the retention in this center for 1990 and 1991 is above 55%. The center in 1999 continued to have an even higher rate of retention. In most centers the pattern had been men dropping out, leaving the classes without male students at the end of the sessions. Given such a situation, I then posit that the trend indicated that given the opportunity, access, and conducive cultural practices to education and social development, women will seize the opportunity. As far as I am concerned that demonstrates the desire for women in the Zion Christian Church to advance, educationally and socially. It shows they value education. Since also the adult literacy centers came into being through the order of the bishop, it proves how influential he can be in encouraging the move toward non-sexism. The attitude of women to the fact that males constituted their administrators and trainers remained that of passive resignation. They feel that the appointed men have the qualifications to teach. In addition, since married men conducted the night classes it made perfect sense that the wives look after the home and children. Again, the practice translated to them into a clear division of labor and not an objectification of discordant representation of gender. The latter notwithstanding, they also submitted that when women have acquired the skills to train, they will welcome them as trainers and managers, if the bishop and the church endorsed such a practice.

The Administrative Staff Management Training

The administrative staff composition reflected a reproduction of the Bapedi leadership structures both nominally and substantively. *Kgoro*, made up of an inner council of related male kin, like I mentioned earlier, also benefited from the education campaign of the Zion Christian Church. To keep in touch with the larger world and to expose the council to the technological era, the bishop invited Damelin College to the headquarters in Moria for the purpose of enhancing their skills.[11] The initial invitation entailed an analysis study conducted by the Damelin staff to assess the efficiency of the systems that the Zion Christian Church had. In addition, they had to recommend ways in which improvement can be achieved as well as to update ways that will be in line with the larger technological world. To this end the Damelin personnel interviewed the staff of *kgoro* as well as the bishop about their record-keeping, banking, and cash-flow practices. After the appraisal Damelin presented their report and the proposal for training and meeting educational needs of the Zion Christian Church *kgoro* staff. They proposed an in-service training program that would take place within a period of seven months. Personnel management, bookkeeping, accounting, finance, principles of management, business English, and law composed the entire curriculum. The training occurred two months after the proposal was presented to the bishop.[12]

Members attested to the training visible benefits. Since *kgoro* is at the headquarters mostly people in the rural areas have exposure to its staff. Urban members come into contact with the staff on special occasions, like Easter. Even then it is extremely rare since on those instances millions visit the place. Women who come into contact with this male staff emphasized the bishop's efforts to improve the church. When I mentioned that Damelin trained men and not women, the general response was that you have to start somewhere. None of the women would be critical or question neither the constitution of the *kgoro* nor the decision of the bishop.

The following chapter on how Zion Christian Church women as minorities in the educational institutions that do not belong to the church demonstrates how the traditional practices of the Zion Christian Church impact strategies that young women adopt to deal with the conflict that affects their educational aspirations. The discourse will also show that the very historical practices influence how the community at large perceived the Zion Christian Church members. The discussion proves Kanter's (1977) argument. He argues that the dominant groups or groups in the majority often exaggerate the differences when the minority comes into what they (majority) perceive as their space. He calls it boundary heightening.

Notes

1. New Testament (1 Timothy 2:11).
2. Bishop Tutu's attendance at the church was reported on the Internet and in the *South Africa Star*, July 19, 1998.
3. Information obtained from participant information in church meetings at Atteridgeville and Soshanguve.
4. I hesitate to give an English translation because it can incorrectly convey the meaning of the words. The words are derogatory, suffice it to say.
5. For more information, see Price and Rosenberg (1980).
6. Things have changed and continue to change but the legacy of apartheid is still felt and unfortunately denied by people like Helen Zille.
7. Also see http://www.suite101.com/content/the-influence-of-society-on-the-individual-a70121.
8. I was motivated to change the usage because of how members gave me a look of displeasure at the characterization of members as illiterate.
9. The member is from Garankuwa.
10. Also see *The Zion Christian Church Messenger*, 1992.
11. Damelin is one of the reputable adult training colleges in South Africa.
12. Also see Zion Christian Church *Morongwa*, 1991, 13.

References

Barret, B. David. 1968. *Schism and Renewal in Africa: An Analysis of Six Thousand Contemporary Religious Movements*. Nairobi: Oxford University Press.

Andersen, Margaret L. and Taylor Howard F. 2007. *Sociology: the essentials*. Belmont: Thomson Wadsworth.

Blumstein, Phillip, and Schwartz, Pepper. 1983. *American Couples: Money, Work, Sex*. New York: William Morrow.

de Beauvoir, S. 1953. *The Second Sex*. Harmondsworth, UK: Penguin.

Chodorow, Nancy. 1978. *The Reproduction of Mothering*. Berkeley: The University of California Press.

Durkheim, Emile. 1985. *Rules of the Sociological Method*. New York: Free Press.

Durkheim, Emile. 1995. *The Elementary Forms of Religious Life*. New York: Free Press.

Arash, Farzaneth. 2008. The Influence of Society on the Individual: The Processes of Socialization of Max Weber and Emile Durkheim. September 2008, http://www.suite101.com/content/the-influence-of-society-on-the-individual-a70121, accessed April 2010.

Gerson, Kathleen. 1985. *Hard Choices: How Women Decide About Work, Career, and Motherhood*. Berkeley: University of California Press.

Huber, Joan, and Spitze, Glenna. 1983. *Sex Stratification: Children, Housework, and Jobs*. New York: Academic Press.

Kanter, Rosabeth, M. 1977. *Men and Women of the Corporation*. New York: Basic Books.

Isichei, Elizabeth. 1995. *A History of Christianity in Africa from Antiquity to the Present*. London: SPCK.

Knox, David, and Schacht Caroline. 2009. *Choices in Relationships: Introduction to Relationships and the Family.* Belmont, CA: Wadsworth.

Lopata, Helena Z. 1973. Self Identity in Marriage and Widowhood. *Sociological Quarterly 14* (Summer): 407–418.

Mead, Margaret. 1949. Character formation and diachronic theory. In: *Social Structure: Studies Presented to A. R. Radcliffe-Brown,* ed. Meyer Fortes, 18-34. Oxford: Clarendon Press.

———————————*Male and Female: A Study of the Sexes in a Changing World.* New York: Morrow.

Mukhondo, Jan. 1992. *Zion Christian Church Messenger.* Polokwane: Moria.

Ndou, Mothupei R. 2000. *The Gospel and Venda Culture: An Analysis of Factors Which Hindered or Facilitated the Acceptance of Christianity by the Vhavenda.* PhD dissertation, University of Pretoria.

Ngubane, Harriet. 1977. *Body and Mind in Zulu Medicine.* Cambridge, UK: Cambridge University Press.

Nthabu, Boatamo Y. 1989. *Meaning and Symbolism in the Zion Christian Church of South Africa,* Master's thesis, University of California, Berkeley.

Oakley, Ann. 1974. *The Sociology of House Work.* London: Martin Robertson.

Ortner, S. 1974. Is Female to Nature as Nature Is to Culture? In M. Zimbalist Rosaldo and Louise Lamphere (Eds.), *Woman, Culture, and Society.* Stanford, CA: Stanford University Press.

Phalane, Manthiba. 2009. *Gender Structural Adjustment and Informal Economy Sector Trade in Africa: A Case Study of Women Workers in the Informal Sector of North West Province of South Africa.* PhDdissertation, University of Limpopo.

Pheko, M. 2005, September 18. Another Year of More Talk, Less Implementation. *City Press.*

Price, Robert M., and Rosenberg, Carl G. (Eds.), 1980, *The Apartheid Regime: Political Power and Racial Domination.* Berkeley: Institute of International Studies, University of California.

Reskin, Barbara, and Padavick Irene. 1994. *Women and Men at Work.* Thousand Oaks, CA: Pine Forge Press.

Smith, Lois, M., and Padula, Alfred. 1996. *Sex and Revolution: Women in Socialist Cuba.* New York: Oxford University Press.

Starr, Tama. 1991. *The Natural Inferiority of Women: Outrageous Pronouncements by Misguided Males.* Poseidon: Pr.

Unterhalter, Elaine. 1989. Contradictions in Bantu Education. *Sechaba Official Organ of the African National Congress* 23(2).

Weber, Max. 1947. *The Theory of Social and Economic Organization.* Translated by A. M. Henderson and Talcott Parsons. New York: Free Press.

Wright Mills, C. 1989. Precursors to adjustment, Revitalization, and Expansion: an under the carpet view of the education crisis in Sub-Saharan Africa. *Zimbabwe Journal of Educational Research* 1(1).

———————1959. *The Sociological Imagination.* Oxford, UK: Oxford University Press.

Is the Glass Ceiling Cracked Yet? Women in Rwanda, South Africa and the United States, 1994–2010

Boatamo Mosupyoe

"Making gender equality a reality is a core commitment of UNDP. As a crosscutting issue, gender must be addressed in everything the organisation does. Why? Because equality between women and men is just, fair and right—it is a worthy goal in and of itself, one that lies at the heart of human development and human rights; and because gender inequality is an obstacle to progress, a roadblock on the path of human development. When development is not 'en-gendered' it is 'endangered'.... There are two complementary approaches to achieving gender equality: mainstreaming gender and promoting women's empowerment. Both are critical."
(United Nations Development Programme, 2002)

We are in the 21st century and the issue of gender equality remains salient in global education, economic, political, scientific, cultural, academic, and other discourses and agendas. As recent as in 2008 when Hillary Clinton lost to Barack Obama she remarked that although the effort to shatter the glass ceiling failed, it, however, culminated with 18 million cracks (Milbank 2008). Her failure to reach the highest office in the United States of America indicates the strength and formidability of the glass ceiling, even in a country that perceives itself as the leader of the world. Hillary's 18 million votes failed to break the glass ceiling, prompting Mosupyoe to assert "one area in which the USA has failed to lead is in having a person other than a male of European descent to its highest office. It

is also worth mentioning that the second office, that of the Vice President has suffered the same fate" (2008: v). The glass ceiling refers to the challenge women face to achieve equal and fair representation with men in senior executive positions in the workplace. Berry and Frank (2010) define the glass ceiling as an invisible obstruction that stands in the way of women's ability to occupy the highest executive jobs.

This invisible obstruction mutually operates with the problematic sticky floors that locate women at the bottom of the economic pyramid. In variable forms the obscured glass ceiling is discernable in different parts of the world, manifesting in and informed by different contexts. Equally true, cracks have been made to the ceiling, to borrow Hillary Clinton's words, in different ways. Turning to Africa, this paper examines how two African countries, Rwanda and South Africa, have negotiated and attempt to synthesize the tripartite and mutually constitutive paradigms: glass ceilings, sticky floors, and cracks. The analysis also makes few comparisons with the United States. The question remains, have Rwanda and South Africa delivered a crack or completely crumbled the imperceptible stubborn configurations of women's inequality? Have the two countries advanced beyond the metaphorical glass ceiling, cracks, and sticky floor variables to new realities and emblematic formations that will offer novel descriptions?

An analysis of the following can help us formulate our understanding: (1) a brief historical background of the events of 1994 that led to self-determination in both countries; (2) post-conflict approaches to gender equality and men's and women's participation in the reconstruction; (3) the pronouncement of the constitutions of both countries on the status of women, (4) the function of the dual legislative/electoral voluntary/involuntary allocation of percentages to gender shared governance, and (5) the representation of women in government, informal, and private sector. Both countries have made a concerted effort to address gender equality. Akin to the UNDP statement on gender, in principle both countries seem to understand that "when development is not `en-gendered' it is `endangered.'" In development transformation is achieved by an acknowledgment that informs mechanisms to redress inequalities. The discourse requires an understanding of paradigms and variables that function to either perpetuate gender inequality or promote gender equality. To give context to Rwanda and South Africa's achievements and challenges on gender equality, a brief history is in order.

A juxtaposition of the 1990 events of the two countries reveals that at the end of April while South Africa celebrated its independence from centuries of discrimination of indigenous people by a white minority, Rwanda experienced genocide that culminated in the death of almost a million Tutsis. It could even be argued that the attention of the world on the "miraculous" transformation in South Africa contributed toward the diverted focus from the inhumane genocide in Rwanda. Nevertheless, the Rwandan Patriotic Front (RPF) managed to gain military victory in July 1994. The post-conflict reconstruction in both countries assumed forms and approaches that included security, justice and reconciliation, individual healing, governance, etc. In an effort to bridge the divide engendered by race, class, ethnicity, gender, etc., the two countries established somewhat similar administrative processes. The processes' main intent was to build consensus and avoid further division among the citizens of the respective countries.

The 1994–2003 Rwandese Broad Based Government of National Unity mirrors in principle and intent the 1994–1997 South African provision for a Government of National Unity. In the South African election of April 27, 1994, the African National Congress obtained the majority of seats in the National Assembly, and together with the other parties, including those that supported and perpetuated the racist apartheid system, formed a Government of National Unity. Clause 88 of the interim Constitution of South Africa made a provision for broad participation of political parties. Any party with 20 or more seats in the National Assembly was entitled to one or more cabinet portfolios as membership in the government. More pertinent to the theme of my analysis, both the interim and final constitution states in part that "The Republic of South Africa is one sovereign democratic state founded on the value of Non-Racialism and non-sexism" (Mosupyoe 1999: 53). Furthermore, the part of the Constitution on Commission on Gender Equality states:

(1) There shall be a Commission on Gender Equality, which shall consist of a chairperson and such number of members as may be determined by an Act of Parliament. (2) The Commission shall consist of persons who are fit and proper for appointment, South African citizens and broadly representative of the South African community. (3) The object of the Commission shall be to promote gender equality and to advise and to make recommendations to Parliament or any other legislature with regard to any laws or proposed legislation which affects gender equality and the status of women. (Constitution of the Republic of South Africa Act 200 of 1993, repealed by Constitution of the Republic of South Africa, [No. 108 of 1996], G 17678, December 18, 1996)

An examination of the processes of Rwanda reveals the same spirit of commitment to gender equality. According to http://www.gov.rw/page.php, the official website of the government of Rwanda, on July, 19, 1994, the RPF established the Government of National Unity with four political parties: the Liberal Party (PL), the Social Democratic Party (PSD), the Christian Democratic Party (PDC), and the Republican Democratic Movement (MDR). Subsequently a 70-member Transitional National Assembly consisting of representatives of the RPF, the four other original parties plus three other smaller parties—namely, the Islamic Party (PDI), the

Socialist Party (PSR), and the Democratic Union for Rwandese People (UDPR)—as well as six representatives of the Rwandese Patriotic Army (RPA) came into being. Here again relevant to the thesis of my investigation, the 2003 Rwandan Constitution adopted on May 2003 clearly and unequivocally pronounces gender equality as follows:

"Reaffirming our adherence to the principles of human rights enshrined in the United Nations Charter of 26 June 1945, the Convention on the Prevention and Punishment of the crime of Genocide of 9 December 1948, the Universal Declaration of Human Rights of 10 December 1948, the International Convention on the Elimination of All Forms of Racial Discrimination of 21 December 1965, the International Convention on Civil and Political Rights of 19 December 1966, the International Covenant on Economic, Social and Cultural Rights of 19 December 1966, the Convention on the Elimination of all Forms of Discrimination against Women of 1 May 1980, the African Charter of Human and Peoples' Committed to ensuring equal rights between Rwandans and between women and men without prejudice to the principles of gender equality and complementarity in national development." (http://www.rwanda-hope.com/constitution.pdf)

In addition, Article 9 of the Rwanda Constitution obligates 30% of posts for women in decision-making bodies and Article 82 reserves 30% of seats in the Senate for women. Rwanda's legislative milestone also reflects in the bills aimed at ending domestic violence and child abuse. Thus, while Rwanda's constitution has a constitutional involuntary gender-shared governance allocation, South Africa does not. However, both countries have clear and precise constitutional pronouncements on gender equality and the status of women, but approach shared governance allocation differently.

The notion of gender-based shared governance percentage allocation in Africa has been common since the 1990s. Kandawasvika-Nhundu (2009) notes that the desire for visible impact of women's contribution necessitates the practice. The efficacy of the constitutional mandate becomes evident with an analysis of Rwanda's achievements. Rwanda occupies the highest position in the world, with its highest number of women parliamentarians, also leading Europe, North America, and Asia. Women constitute 56.3% of parliamentarians in the Lower House and 34.6% in the Senate. The latter is an improvement from 48.8% and 30%, respectively, before the 2008 elections. The South African constitution, unlike the Rwandese constitution, does not mandate a percentage of gender-shared representation for elected public officials. Even in the absence of such a provision South Africa in terms of numbers has made strides. The representation of women in the local government has improved from 19% after 1995 to 40% after the 2007 elections (Letsholo & Nkwinika 2006: 21; Chikulo & Mbao 2006: 54); and from 27.5% in 1994 to 43% in the National Assembly in 2009. Compared to the United States, both countries, with Rwanda leading, possess a decisive numerical strength of women representation in parliament. As of October 2010, of the 100 members of the U.S. Senate only 17 are women, while the 111th United States Congress consists of 541 elected officials, only 75 are women. Furthermore, in the U.S. federal government, women occupy 44.1% of available positions but only hold a mere 13% of Senior Executive Service (SES) positions (Annual Report on the Federal Workforce, 2009). In this area it is safe to say that Rwanda and South Africa have delivered a much more powerful blow to the ceiling than the United States, with Rwanda's glass ceiling at a more advanced stage of destruction. The glass might be cracked, but sticky floors remain, as persistent gender inequalities can still be traced to other areas in government. Both Rwanda and South Africa have not had a woman occupying the highest office of the presidency. However, South Africa has had two women Vice Presidents, and three women Speakers of the House. Rwanda has a woman as the Speaker of the House, and of course the United States also has a woman as a speaker of the house. While change is evident, it would be premature to declare a total destruction of the glass ceiling with its complimentary opposite sticky floors.

The South Africa ruling party, the African National Congress (ANC), has adopted a voluntary gendered shared governance to negotiate the sticky floors. This is done on the party and not the government level. The results of the 2008 census underscored the need. The 2008 census reveals that while women outnumber men across all salary levels in government at 54.76%, men still hold 67.8% of senior management positions. The census also shows that in the private sector the employment of women in executive positions has slightly improved but leaves a lot to be desired. The other area to measure achievements and challenges is the informal economy sector. The informal economy sector is "the part of economic activity that is neither taxed nor monitored by government, and it is not included in government's Gross National Product (GNP); as opposed to a formal economy" (Phalane 2009: 2). South African women make up 40.4% of the street traders according to the 2007 national estimates (Phalane 2009: 43; Braude 2004: 7; StatsSA 2007: 33).

The informal economy sector also offers a clear indication of persistent inequalities that still demand a consideration of the intersectionality of race and class 16 years after South African indigenous people freed themselves from white oppression. In this sector low wages and lack of benefits locate women at the bottom of the economic ladder. African (black) women make up 50% of people employed in the informal economy sector, domestic sector, and subsistence agriculture. These statistics—11.4% of African women work as domestic workers as compared to 7.7% of Colourdes, .03% of Indians, and 0.2% of white women (Phalane 2009: 45)—remind us that aftermaths of white privilege accorded to white women during apartheid remain part of the discourse and tension to be negotiated. The ANC purposeful 50/50 2005 Get the Balance Right campaign produces visible impact on government gender equity; the informal economic sector and the private sector need more attention, perhaps a gendered campaign that also takes the intersectionality into consideration.

As in South Africa, in Rwanda women also constitute the majority in the informal sector. Inter Press Service News Agency (2010) reports that the Rwandan government aims to register 900,000 informal businesses to increase tax revenue. To that effect they have embarked on registering the informal sector businesses through an agency called Rwanda Development Board. One of its tasks is "the sensitisation and mobilisation of women to invest in doing business" (http://ipsnews.net/africa/nota.asp?id-news=51756).

Rwandese women also form cooperatives that allow them to sell their goods to stores like Macy's in the United States. The famous peace basket has improved how women conduct business and has allowed them to get loans through the Women's Guarantee Fund. Some rural women have complained about the efficacy of the program but that notwithstanding Rwanda has made progress in the informal sector and through legislation it has repealed laws that prevented women from inheriting land, and thus improving economic growth and freedom for Rwanda's women. The new laws also allow them to sign for bank loans.

The discussions show that although gender inequalities persist, the gluey floors/ glass ceiling dichotomy experienced a shift that calls for new definitions of the degree and intensity of formidability. The transformation in Rwandan and South African governments defy the crack allegory because of the visible gaping holes in some places. The application of the metaphor should not obscure areas where gender parity exists as a result of transformation. In countries where women's involvement with knowledge production and construction transcends party affiliation and engagement with the media intensified to provide a gender sensitivity lens, the glass ceiling metaphor demands a definition that highlights the achievements of gender parity in areas where it has occurred. In conclusion, one must acknowledge that the glass ceiling/gluey floor dichotomy works with patriarchal traditions that also need mediation as they contribute to the slow progression of women into senior-level positions. The latter include society's social expectations of women entering traditionally male-dominated positions (Gherardi & Poggio 2001) and internalized sexism where women locate themselves at the bottom of the hierarchy (Conrad et al. 2010). This personal orientation regarding the hierarchical structure may affect the chances of women advancing more so than the glass ceiling. Conrad et al. (2010) state that anything that is perceived as real is real in all of its consequences.

References

Aimable Twahirwa and Kudzai Makombe 2010 *Inter Press Service News Agency*, "Women Win by Formalising Businesses.

Annual Report on the Federal Workforce. 2009. http://www1.eeoc.gov//federal/reports/fsp2009/index.cfm?renderforprint=1, accessed October 2010.

Berry, P. & Franks, T. 2010. Women in the world of corporate business: Looking at the glass ceiling. *Contemporary Issues in Education Research*, 3(2), 1-9. Retrieved May 19, 2010 from EBSCOhost database.

Braude, W. 2004. *South African Country Analysis, A Naledi Global Poverty Network Workforce Development Study.* South Africa: Naledi.

Chikulo, B., and Mbao, M. 2006. North West: Gender. In *EISA Election Update: South Africa.*

Conrad, P., Carr, P., Knight, S., Renfrew, M. R., Dunn, M. B., and Pololi, L. 2010.

Hierarchy as a Barrier to Advancement for Women in Academic Medicine. *Journal of Women's Health* 19(4): 799–805.

Constitution of the Republic of Rwanda, http://www.rwandahope.com/constitution.pdf, accessed July 2010.

Constitution of the Republic of South Africa Act 200 of 1993, repealed by Constitution of the Republic of South Africa, [No. 108 of 1996], G 17678, 18 December 1996, http://www.info.gov.za/documents/constitution/index.htm, accessed July 2010.

Gherardi, S., and Poggio, B. 2001. Creating and recreating gender order in organizations. *Journal of World Business 36*: 245–259.

Kandawasvika, Nhundu, R. 2010. Expert Opinion: Strategies and Legislation Adopted in Africa that Call for the 30% Quota, http://www.iknowpolitics.org/en/node/9289.

Letsholo, S., and Nkwinika, T. 2006. Gauteng Gender Issues. In *EISA Election Update: South Africa.*

Milbank, D. 2008, June 8. A Thank-You for 18 million cracks in the glass ceiling. *Washington Post*, p. 1.

Mosupyoe, Boatamo. 1999. *Women's Multicentric Way of Knowing, Being, and Thinking.* New York: McGraw-Hill.

Mosupyoe, Boatamo. 2008. Introduction. In Rita Cameron-Wedding and Y. Boatamo (Eds.), *Institutions, Ideologies, and Individuals*, eds. Dubuque, IA: Kendall/Hunt.

Phalane, Manthiba, M. 2009. *Gender, Structural Adjustment and Informal Economic Sector Trade in Africa: A Case Study of Women Workers in the Informal Sector of North West Province, South Africa.* PhD dissertation, University of the North.

Statistics South Africa (Stats SA) 2007: 33

The UN Development Programme (UNDP). 2002. Gender Equality Practice Note. New York: United Nations Development Programme.

Chapter One Questions

1. What does the genderblindness paradigm mean?

2. What does gender diversity mean?

3. Identify where from the readings this quote comes from: "The trichotomous confluence of the indigenous, colonial and apartheid historical periods precipitated a dynamic within the Zion Christian Church with its own unique epistemological milieu." Explain how the three systems affected women in the Zion Christian Church.

4. What is your understanding of the glass ceiling/sticky floor dichotomy?

5. Briefly discuss how the concept applies to Rwanda, South Africa, and the United States.

6. What is your understanding of the intersectionality of race, class, and gender?

7. Choose one concept from the traditional Bapedi structure and explain how it parallels a similar symbol in the Zion Christian Church to perpetuate gender inequality.

CHAPTER 2

Liberated Pan-African Thought

Introduction to Chapter Two

Boatamo Mosupyoe

The articles in this chapter contextualize the legacy of Euro-centric tradition of defining and constructing knowledge of and about people of African descent. The marginalization of African knowledge, existence, and thought that coalesced through European domination, colonialization, and scholarship faces challenges as people of African descent increasingly engage in knowledge production and distribution.

The chapter starts with the "Development of Thought in Pan Africanism," by Mosupyoe. She starts by tracing the spirit and ideology of the term Pan Africanism and its historical emergence. Although the term came into being as a reaction by people of African descent to their domination and subjugation by people of European descent, it evolved and adapted. As it did so, distinguishable paradigms from people like Dubois, Padmore, Appiah, Nkrumah, Kenyatta, and Lumumba became evident. Mosupyoe briefly analyzes the various conferences since 1900 that shaped the ideology of Pan Africanism and examines what Pan Africanism means in the 21st century. Akin to the new vibrant African scholarship, the article discerns new concepts and forms that still seek to peripherize voices of Africans but also concedes change and remarkable achievements of people of African descent.

Ramose recognizes the latter in his interrogation of European standards of knowledge production in relation to Africa. In my observation, Ramose goes beyond just the interrogation and situates his scholarly views and findings in this discourse as appropriate, authentic, and long overdue. In his article "The Struggle for Reason in Africa," Ramose traces the struggle to the time when Aristotle declared that "man is a rational animal." He notes that Aristotle's definition of man excluded African, Amerindians, Australians, and women. Taking the opportunity as an African to speak for and about Africans, Ramose challenges the notion that African philosophy does not exist. The explicit and implicit racist connotation undermines the humanity and intellect of Africans. The persistent debate of the question by Africans and non-Africans raises concerns about the intent of both. Supporting his argument with strong evidence of annotations from Aristotle, Pope John Paul II as recently as 1998 Ramose concludes that non-Africans continue to deliberate the question to perpetuate the false perception of non-reasoning, non-human, and therefore non-philosophical Africans. Some Africans, on the other hand, persistently pursue the inquiry for empirical reasons. Ramose contends that African philosophy exists independent of Western philosophy and "to deny the existence of African philosophy is to reject the very idea of philosophy." He is, however, not oblivious to the tenacity of those who seek to perpetuate the myth of African inferiority and assign exclusive right to reason to people of European descent.

Cameron-Wedding's observations in her article "Defending Whiteness: Protecting White Privilege in Post–Civil Rights Society" reaffirms Ramose's assertions, albeit in a different context. She posits that under the guise of colorblindness, the United States engenders old racism in new forms. These forms find expressions in themes of patriotism and insidious covert institutionalized arrangements that undermine the impact on the justice system, and processes the results in pay disparity, education, social welfare, and government agencies. The United States Cameron-Wedding accurately notes, owes its foundation to racial/racist ideologies that shaped and continue to mold the laws and the social fabric that associates black with criminality, questions in much more the same way that Ramose does the efficacy of people of African descent to produce reasoned knowledge, and even more disturbing their ability to authentically articulate their experience of racism even in the 21st century. The association of Tom Brokaw, a white male with objectivity, neutrality, and implied superior intellect, as compared to the correlation of Jessie Jackson, a black man with polar opposite attributes of "troublemaker, biased, and race baiter," eloquently illustrate this artificial and yet real hierarchical hegemonic order. The dismissal of the voices amounts to the persistent deliberate effort to protect white privilege as much as it is designed to silence and rename those who experience racism and fight for social justice. Equating colorblindness to pro-American patriotic sentiments effectively serves the agenda of suppression of the impact of new forms of racism clearly discernable in ideologies, practices, policies, and laws pertaining to anti-affirmative action, anti-immigration, English-only, and race privacy initiatives. The preservation of white privilege shapes and informs the thread of the discourse, for example, the colorblindness paradigm essentially denies the racial history of the United States and its impact and repudiates the experience of discrimination by people of color, Cameron-Wedding concludes.

In the article, "I Doubt, Therefore African Philosophy Exists," Ramose continues the discourse. By refocusing the dialogue on African philosophy on the Africa/African duality Ramose offers insights of why the term "Africa," though widely used and considered "settled," is problematic and expresses the experience of Europeans about Africa and fails to articulate the experience and self-definition of, by, and about Africans themselves. The latter gave rise to ideologies that grossly constituted Africans with false distorted identities informed by Western hegemonic premises. Ramose elects to retain the term "Africa" while asserting African self-definition, self-articulation, and representation, as echoed in the eloquent call to reconstruction edifice "I Doubt, Therefore African Philosophy Exists." In impressive details Ramose questions Shutte's dichotomous logic that distinguishes between "African wisdom" and "Western philosophy" in the book *Philosophy for Africa* (1993) and his conception of *Ubuntu* in a different publication titled *Ubuntu: An Ethic for a New South Africa* (2003). In part Ramose sees Shutte's reasoning as scientifically flawed, methodologically problematic, and imbued with contradictions. These contradictions manifest in Shutte's struggle for identity. While he was born and raised in South Africa, his European descent and education orientation explains the lack of harmony in his thoughts and view of African philosophy. His views reflect a paradoxical dual proximity to and distance from African ideological/cognitive processes that offer insights. Despite the latter,

Ramose notes that Shutte's inquiry into "the question of justice" for indigenous people of South Africa or "people of without cold continent" qualifies him to be part of the methodic doubt construction "I Doubt, Therefore African Philosophy Exists." In this way he can give content and meaning hopefully without denying the existence of African philosophy.

The chapter concludes with Ramose's examination "The Philosophy of Ubuntu and Ubuntu as a Philosophy." Ramose starts with an investigation of the linguistic structure of the word. In essence the seemingly morphologically disparateness of the prefix -*ubu* and stem -*ntu* in the word *Ubuntu* belies their profound mutual inclusivity. Ramose argues that the structural logic of the word as -*ness* and not -*ism* and as simultaneously gerund and gerundive reflects reconciled and not fragmented entities of being human and becoming a human being. The premise provides the basis to judge human worth and constitutes the foundation of African philosophy. While he concedes to the binary interpretation of musical rhythm as rational and emotional, Ramose not only rejects the attribution of the emotional as a defining attribute of African philosophy but he also sees that as unrelenting racism rooted in Western philosophy. Ramose further argues that the response to music and rhythm by Africans indicates reasoned aesthetic judgment and the quest for harmony. Seen through the Western lens, unfortunately the "ontological–epistemological difference" of passive Western reaction to music as opposed to African active reaction through dance assumed racist tones. The definition of African intellect as emotional and therefore irrational became the false canon.

At best the articles in this chapter reflect the engagement of people of African descent with their self-determination and self-definitions. The stubborn ideologies that still seek to define Africans as inferior in the 21st century are unfortunate. One wonders why the Euro-centric approach persists in this endeavor. Cameron-Wedding perhaps has the answer; the profoundness of the need to preserve white privilege should not be underestimated. Her discussion of U.S. society indeed reflects the various sophisticated ways in which this is done, and equally informative are Ramose's articles.

Development of Thought on Pan Africanism

Boatamo Mosupyoe

This article intends to give a brief historical development of the concept of Pan Africanism. The concept of Pan Africanism endured the ages, displaying a range of conflicting ideologies that sometimes cohere. The dialectic convergence and divergence of what constitutes Pan Africanism is evident in the selected descriptions or definitions by three prominent scholars:

> *"Pan-Africanism is a political and cultural phenomenon that regards Africa, Africans and African descendants abroad as a unit. It seeks to regenerate and unify Africa and promotes feeling of oneness among the people of the African world. It glorifies the African past and inculcates pride in African values."* (Esedebe 1982: 5)

> *"The national, unified struggle and resistance of African peoples against all forms of foreign aggression and invasion. The primary goal of Pan-African Nationalism is the total liberation and unification of all Africans and people of African descent under African communalism."* (Nantambu 1998: 569)

> *"The idea that people of African descent the world over shared a common destiny; that our forced dispersal through the transatlantic slave trade, our common oppression under colonialism in Africa and the Caribbean, and under Jim Crow segregation in the United States, through the exploitation of our labor power under capitalism, and the denial of political rights, had created parallel contours for struggle. Our kinship was also cultural, social and historical, and we found within ourselves the genius and grace of being which was denied us by the racist standards of the white world. By renewing our connections, we forged a consciousness of resistance which could be felt across the globe."* (Marable 1995)

Earlier definitions or descriptions also include phrases like "industrial and spiritual emancipation of the Negro" (*Crisis*, November 1933: 247), "rehabilitation of African Past," "solidarity among men of African descent" (Esedebe 1982: 5); and, most recently, definitions that give primacy to the 21st century trends and consider the dynamic role of Africa in the changing world predominate. Thus we see the nomenclature emphasizing the contributions of Africans and those in the diaspora to the modern world; transformation in post-African conflicts; intersection of race, class, and gender; African scholarship; etc. The theme of unity occupies the center of this array of views on Pan Africanism. The ideology embedded in the spirit of the concept predates the articulation of the concept. I marvel at how scholars assume the originator of the concept as a man, Esedebe (1982: 5), for example, asserts, "The man who first expressed pan-African sentiments will never be known." As much as I would like to think that here "the man" represents "humans," I doubt the saliency of "the woman" as in female manifested anywhere in the fore front of Esedebe's mind.

Redeemably, in 2003 the African Union concomitantly adopted the Protocol on the Rights of Women with the role of the African Diaspora in the future of continental Africa (Reddock 2007). While the originator of the concept is hard to identify, the conferences that followed to maintain the movement and ideology are not. Although most literature regard the 1900 London conference as the first conference on Pan Africanism, Esedebe (1982) reminds us of the week-long Chicago Congress on Africa in 1893 as the pioneer of the convention on Pan African-ism. Esedebe's claim finds validation in the wording by Frederick P. Noble in the *Advance*, a Chicago newspaper, which applied the term *pan-* as a prefix to all diverse denominations that were present and to also indicate participation of wide-ranging people of African descent.

With some disagreement, largely the convening of the 1900 London conference is credited to Sylvester Williams. Williams was a Trinidadian Pan-Africanist, a lawyer who ironically married an Englishwoman, Agnes Powell, and lived in many countries including South Africa, promoted the ideals of Pan Africanism until his death on March, 26, 1911 (http://www.itzcaribbean.com/history_hs_williams.php). Conference topics identified the following, among others, as problems: discrimination on the basis of color, equal opportunity in education, self-government for Africans and African countries, greed for gold that caused subjugation and enslavement of Africans, to the use of religion as a tool to subjugate and obscure the ruthless exploitation of people of African descent (Esedebe 1982; Legum 1963). Thirty-two delegates constituted attendees at the conference from the United States, Haiti, Trinidad, St. Lucia, Dominican Republic, Nigeria, African exiles from England, South Africa, Sierra Leone, former Gold Coast, Liberia, etc. Important historical figures participated in the conference, we normally hear of names like W. B. Du Bois and Marcus Garvey. Women also attended, among them Annie J. Cooper from Washington, D.C., and Anna J. Jones from Missouri. Nevertheless, W. B. Du Bois's prediction of the color line as one of the primary problems of the 20th century accentuated the thematic focus of the conference (Esedebe 1982).

The second conference convened by W. B. Du Bois in Paris February 19–21, 1919, had a toned-down approach that annunciated controversial stands by the Senegalese delegate Blaise Diagne who advocated an embrace of the colonial systems. His acceptance of the French cultural and political hegemonic system received explicit and implicit derision from the approach, scholarship, and paradigms of many people including Léopold Senghor in years to follow.[1] The latter notwithstanding, the 57 delegates demanded reforms and committed to convening the next conference. Unlike the 1919 conference the third Pan African

conferences, held in Paris in February 1921, and in Brussels from August 31 to September 2, 1921, mirrored the post-war sentiments for freedom. Interesting was the reaction to the following resolution by delegates from both conferences:

> Either the complete assimilation of Africa with two or three of the great world states, with political, civil and social power and privileges absolutely equal for its black and white citizens, or the rise of a great black Africa State founded in Peace and Goodwill, based on popular education, natural art and industry and freedom of trade; autonomous and sovereign in its internal policy, but from its beginning a part of a great society of peoples in which it takes its place with others as co-rulers of the world. (*The Crisis*, November 1921: 8–9)

Controversial and colonial accommodationist Blaise Diagne lacked complete support in his rejection of any wording of what he perceived to be revolutionary, while the more restrained Du Bois enjoyed support for his motion and through his deference saved the conference from dismay. From this conference Du Bois won the support and praise of the European media. If I am to identify one of the concrete outcomes of the conference, a committee that included Du Bois and presented a petition to the League of Nations in Geneva deserves a mention. Also worth noting is the threat experienced by the European powers and the United States government who sent spies to survey the participants and the contents of discussions (Esedebe 1982).

The 1923 fourth Pan African conferences in London and Lisbon called, among other things, for treatment of black folk as men. Most noticeable is the shift from "assimilation" to independence as expressed in eight general and irreducible needs articulated as: "own government, land, equality before the law, free elementary education, training in technology, higher training in select talent," development of Africa for Africans and not for the benefit of Europeans, eradication of enslavement and traffic in liquor, world disarmament, the organization of commerce and industry to benefit the many and not enrich the few (West Africa, November 1923: 1377; Esedebe 1982: 93).

By the time the fifth Pan African Congress took place in 1927 in New York, a growing criticism of the main players developed with venom. These attacks by both capitalists and communists of the players who they sought to control but failed to could not dampen the thematic resolution of the fifth conference that paralleled the one from the previous conference. With the aging of people like W. B. Du Bois, the influence of Africans from the continent like Kwame Nkurumah could not be ignored at the Manchester Congress of October 15, 1945. At this conference the numerical representation of delegates counted more than at previous conferences, with continental Africa outnumbering all delegates and participating organizations. The transformation also found expression in the old militancy revealed in a new strategy that engaged (1) the nationalist organizations in the continent and the Caribbean, (2) advocated for the struggle to be fought in Africa and not in the Western countries, (3) called for unity between the intellectuals and the masses, and (4) embraced trade unions as an essential component of the resistance to imperialism.

The specificity of the regional thematic focus and its inclusivity also differentiates the Manchester conference from the previous ones. Deliberations focused on "the color problem in Britain," "imperialism in North and West Africa," "oppression in South Africa," "the East African picture," "Ethiopia and the black republics," and "the problem in the Caribbean." The loud, clear, and uncompromised demand for equal rights, universal franchise, autonomy, and condemnation of colonialism also characterized the framework of the congress; in stark contrast to the colonial accommodationist approach of Blaise Diagne's during the 1921 Brussels conference. The fact that Britain and the United States had just produced a blueprint postwar statement through the Atlantic Charter affirmed the hopeful spirit and moral stance of the participants (Esedebe 1982; Legum 1963).

After all, the eight points of the Charter that included the right to self-determination by all people, and refrain from territorial gain, global economic cooperation and promotion of social welfare, and freedom from want and fear (Morton 1945) also paralleled the demands of oppressed and marginalized people of African descent. After the Congress African leaders began to meet on a regular basis and the formation of the Organization of African Unity (OAU) on May 25, 1963, in Addis Ababa institutionalized the Pan African ideology. The organization called for unity among Africans and people of African descent as they continued to fight for self-determination and human dignity (King 1973).

The 1950s and 1960s experienced the rise of the Black Power Movement, most notably in South Africa and the United States. In South Africa Robert Sobukwe formed the Pan African Congress, a liberation movement that encouraged Africans to refrain from dependence on non-Africans in their quest to liberate themselves. His ideology influenced the Black Consciousness movement that was led by many, including Steven Biko. Steven Biko, like Kwame Ture (Stokley Carmichael) of the United States, repudiated the persistent European ideals that continued to marginalize everything African. During this period old forms of racism reared their heads in transformed sophisticated appearances that still peripherized. Most of Africa also gained its independence and began to struggle with adaptation to environments that contained remnants of colonial influence. Africa and people of African descents continued to redefine and reconstruct their identity, economy, political system, etc., and faced problems of corruption and ethnic divisions.

New nomenclature to define new paradigms fashioned the framework that negotiated problems engendered by post-colonial dynamics. To mention but a few, neocolonialism critiques the arrangements through World Bank and International Monetary Fund by former colonial power to maintain their control on former colonies; paternalistic neocolonialism, a critique of the continued political and economic hegemonic control of former colonies by former colonial power on the pretext that the former colonies derive benefit from the occupation; dependency theory perceives the center as composed of wealthy states that continuously exploit resources of the poor states who occupy the periphery; and cultural colonialism refers to the tendency of northern nations to manipulate and control the axiology of poor nations through media, language, education, and religion. Africa had to still deal with corrupt leaders.

South Africa in the meantime was still fighting blatant legal racism against a white minority apartheid government and had liberation movements outside the country in exile. The struggle against apartheid in South Africa intensified in the 1980s. Two significant historical events happened in the 1990s. In 1994, while South Africa gained its freedom and independence and Mandela was inaugurated as the first African president, Rwanda experienced genocide.

With such developments, leading towards the 21st century the Pan African philosophy had to saliently include in its agenda issues of gender equality, conflict resolution, transitional justice, poverty, HIV/AIDS, environmental issues, etc. Africa continues to confront the challenges through many avenues, including the African Union. In 2002 the Organization of African Union was disbanded by its then president Thabo Mbeki who is also a former president of South Africa and was replaced by the African Union (AU). The AU is an intergovernmental organization comprised of 53 African countries. Some of the objectives of the AU are "to accelerate the political and socio-economic integration of the continent; to promote and defend African common positions on issues of interest to the continent and its peoples; to achieve peace and security in Africa; and to promote democratic institutions, good governance and human rights" (http://www.africa-union.org/root/au/index/index.htm). The Pan African Parliament forms one of the decision-making bodies of the AU.

In conclusion, the articles in this edition of the *Development of Thought in Pan Africanism* continue the dialogue on the ideology as they also offer suggestions of how to mediate the tension created by the conjuncture of old and new structures. Hopefully the days of Africa pessimism are gradually moving behind us.

Note

1. Certainly the writings of people like Steven Biko, Mogobe's "Philosophy of Ubuntu and Ubuntu as Philosophy," Randal Robinson's article "Towards Black Renaissance," Ramose's article "African Renaissance: A Northbound Gaze," Marie Pauline Eboh's article "Is Western Democracy the Answer to the African Problem?: The Need for Conceptual Decolonization in African Society," reflect the rejection of that approach.

References

Esedebe, P. Olisanwuche. 1982. *The Idea and Movement 1776–1963.* Washington, D.C.: Howard University Press.

King, Kenneth. 1973. *Pan-Africanism from Within.* London: Oxford University Press.

Legum, Collin. 1963. *Pan Africanism: A Short Political Guide.* Washington, D.C.: Frederick A. Praeger.

Morton, H.V. 1945. *Atlantic Meeting.* Methuen & Co.

Reddock, Rhonda. 2007. Gender Equality, Pan-Africanism and the Diaspora. *International Journal of African Renaissance Studies: Multi-, Inter-, and Transdisciplinarity* 2(2): 255–267.

The Struggle for Reason in Africa

Mogobe B. Ramose

For centuries discourses on Africa have been dominated by nonAfricans. Many reasons account for this state of affairs and, not least, the unjustified violence of colonization. Since colonization Africans have had almost an infinity of spokespersons. These claimed unilaterally the right to speak on behalf of the Africans and to define the meaning of experience and truth for them. Thus Africans were reduced to silence even about themselves. On the face of it, decolonization removed this problem. However, on closer analysis it is clear that decolonization was an important catalyst in the breaking of the silence about the Africans. It is still necessary to assert and uphold the Africans' right to define the meaning of experience and truth in their own right. In order to achieve this one of the requirements is that Africans should take the opportunity to speak for and about themselves and in that way construct an authentic and truly African discourse about Africa. In this introduction focus is placed first upon some of the main reasons why Africa was reduced to silence. This is followed by the speech, the discourse, of Africans about the meaning of experience and truth for them. The essays contained in this section constitute this discourse. We now turn to consider some of the principal reasons why colonization considered itself justified in silencing and enslaving Africa.

"Man Is a Rational Animal"

One of the bases of colonisation was the belief that "man is a rational animal" was not spoken of the African, the Amerindian and the Australasians: all the indigenous peoples of their respective countries

from time immemorial. Aristotle, the father of this definition of "man" did not incur the wrath of women then as they probably were astounded by the fact that for him the existence of his mother appeared to be insignificant. It was only much later in history, namely, at the rise of feminist thought and action that the benign forgiveness of Aristotle by the women of his time came to be called into question.[1] Little did Aristotle realsie that his definition of "man" laid down the foundation for the struggle for reason not only between men and women but between the colonialists and the Africans,[2] the Amerindians,[3] and the Australasians.

Aristotle's definition of man was deeply inscribed in the social ethos of those communities and societies which undertook the so called voyages of discovery apparently driven by innocent curiosity. But it is well-known that these voyages changed into violent colonial incursions. These incursions, unjustifiable under all the principles of the theory of the just war, have had consequences which are still with us today. It seems then that the entire process of decolonisation has, among others, upheld and not jettisoned the questionable belief that "man is a rational animal" was not spoken of the African, the Amerindian and the Australasian. In our time the struggle for reason is rearing its head again around the globe especially in the West under the familiar face of resilient racism.

For example, the term African philosophy renders the idea that history repeats itself easy to believe. More often than not the term tends to revive innate skepticism on the one hand and to stimulate ingrained condescension on the other. The skeptic, unswervingly committed to the will to remain ignorant, is simply dismissive of any possibility let alone the probability of African philosophy. Impelled by the will to dominate the condescendor—who is invariably the posterity of the colonizer—is often ready to entertain the probability of African philosophy provided the judgement pertaining to the experience, knowledge and truth about African philosophy is recognised as the sole and exclusive right of the condescendor. Of course, this imaginary right, supported by material power designed to defend and sustain the superstition that Africa is incapable of producing knowledge, has got far-reaching practical consequences for the construction of knowledge in Africa. The self-appointed heirs to the right to reason have thus established themselves as the producers of all knowledge and the only holders of the truth. In these circumstances, the right to knowledge in relation to the African is measured and determined by passive as well as uncritical assimilation[4] coupled with faithful implementation of knowledge defined and produced from outside Africa. The condescendor currently manifests the will to dominate through the imposition of "democratisation," "globalisation" and "human rights." Such imposition is far from credible if one considers, for example, the fact that democracy became inadvertently the route towards the inhumanity as well as the irrationality of the holocaust.

Historically, the unjust wars of colonisation resulted in the forcible expropriation of land from its rightful owners: the Africans. At the same time the land expropriation meant loss of sovereignty by the Africans.[5] The close connection between land and life[6] meant also that by losing land to the conqueror the African thereby lost a vital resource to life. This loss was aggravated by the fact that by virtue of the so called right of conquest the African was compelled to enter into the money economy. Thus the so called right of conquest introduced an abrupt and radical change in the life of the African. From the condition of relative peace and reasonable certainty to satisfy the basic necessities of life, the African was suddenly plunged into poverty. There was no longer the reasonable certainty to meet the basic necessities of life unless money was available. Having been thus rendered poor by the stroke of the pen backed by the use of armed force, the African was compelled to find money to assure not only individual survival but also to pay tax for owning a hut, for example. In this way, the African's right to life— the inalienable right to subsistence—was violated. Since all other rights revolve around the recognition, protection and respect of the right to life, talk about human rights based upon the continual violation of this right can hardly be meaningful to the African. To be meaningful, human rights discourse must restore material and practical recognition, protection and respect for the African's inalienable right to subsistence. The 1994 Kampala conference on reparations to Africa is a pertinent example of Africa's demand for the material and practical restoration of her inalienable right to subsistence. Reparations, though not technically due to the conquered, is in this case morally and legally appropriate. It proceeds from the premise that there is a historical and conceptual link between colonization, racism and slavery. It was therefore demanded that these items be included in the agenda of the United Nations conference on racism to be held in the city of Durban, South Africa in August 2001. The necessity to include this demand prompted the United States of America to threaten to boycott the conference. It must be emphasized in favour of the United States and, with particular reference to hostile sentiment towards Israel or the world Jewry, that it is ethically imperative to oppose vigorously anyone who contemplates a repeat of the irrationality and the inhumanity of Hitler's holocaust. However, it is the United States which undermined her own ethically laudable position by insisting on the exclusion from the United Nations agenda deliberations on restitution arising from the injustice of colonization and slavery. Surely, these experiences of humanity were also by every test both irrational and inhuman? There is no hierarchy in measuring the value of one human life over another. Thus the question persists: why is it that the African's right to life continues to be denied, derecognised and remains practically unprotected by the beneficiaries of the violence, irrationality and the inhumanity of colonisation? In the end the United States sent an official delegation to the Durban conference. Israel and the United States withdrew their delegations from the conference. The majority of the Western countries present at the conference insisted that the prevailing inhumanity of the global structural violence and poverty should be maintained. This they did by ensuring that conference would adopt resolutions that would absolve them from both the moral and the legal guilt of the violence of colonization and the inhumanity of racism. That Africa relented in the name of compromise clearly underlines the urgent need for authentic African philosophy aimed towards the liberation of Africa. Thus the struggle for reason is not only from outside but also from within Africa.

"All Men Are Rational Animals"

The struggle for reason—who is and who is not a rational animal—is the foundation of racism. Despite democracy and the culture of human rights in our time, the foundation of the struggle for reason remains unshaken. Biological accidents like blue eyes, skin colour, short hair or an oval cranium are all little pieces of poor evidence to prove the untenable claim that only a particular segment of humanity is rational. This conventionally valid but no less scientifically untenable proof was used to justify both colonisation and the christianisation of the colonised. This imaginary justification proved unsustainable because of a basic contradiction in the internal logic as well as the intent of both colonisation and christianisation. If the colonised are by definition without reason then it may be justified to turn them into slaves. But they must be seen as slaves of a particular kind, namely, sub-human beings who because of lack of reason can have no will of their own and therefore no freedom either. To teach them anything that human beings can understand and do by virtue of their rationality would be a contradiction in terms. It would be tantamount to redeeming them from the status of sub-human beings and to elevate them to parity with human beings. This is precisely why the ensuing stalemate in the christianisation of the colonised was overcome when the Papal bull, Sublimis Deus gave in to the law of logic and removed the contradiction by unreservedly declaring that "all men are rational animals."[7] The Papal declaration together with the defeat of scientific racism do, however, have great and fundamental significance. Both may be seen as the triumph of reason in the affirmation that all human beings are rational animals. On this basis, it is clear that there is indeed only one race, the human race.

The Papal declaration, just like the defeat of scientific racism by science itself, failed to eradicate and erase the struggle for reason from the social consciousness of successive generations of the former colonisers: be they in the colonizing mother countries or in the former colonies. The will and determination to wish away Sublimis Deus and the victory over scientific racism is no more than a sustained endeavour to enliven and sustain the myth that only a particular segment of humanity has a prior, exclusive and superior right to rationality. According to this reasoning, the myth that within the species homo sapiens there are humans proper and sub-humans means that there cannot be one human race. In our complex global village of today, biology through the reproductive route shall eventually vindicate the reality that the human race is one. Children shall continue to be born from mothers and fathers with accidental biological differences and different cultural backgrounds. Provided humanity does not sink into the ultimate irrationality of self-annihilation through an unwinnable nuclear war, human reproductive power shall in the distant future of evolution march inexorably towards the defeat of the myth that the human race is not and cannot be one.

Why did the teaching of Western philosophy in African universities fail for so long to address the concrete experience of racism in the continent in the light of philosophical racism? For too long the teaching of Western philosophy in Africa was decontextualised precisely because both its inspiration and the questions it attempted to answer were not necessarily based upon the living experience of being-an-African in Africa. Yet, the Western philosophers that the teaching of philosophy in Africa emulated always drew their questions from the lived experience of their time and place. Such questioning included the upkeep and refinement of an established philosophical tradition. In this sense, Western philosophy has always been contextual. But this cannot be said without reservation about the teaching of Western philosophy in Africa since it was—and still is—decontextualised to the extent that it systematically and persistently ignored and excluded the experience of being-an-African in Africa. The mimetic and the decontextualised character of the teaching of

Western philosophy in Africa calls for a radical overhaul of the whole epistemological paradigm underlying the current educational system. To evade this duty is to condone racism which is a form of injustice. The injustice is apparent in the recognition that there is neither a moral basis nor pedagogical justification for the Western epistemological paradigm to retain primacy and dominance in decolonised Africa. The independent review and construction of knowledge in the light of the unfolding African experience is not only a vital goal but it is also an act of liberation.[8]

Is There an African Philosophy?

The question whether or not African philosophy is possible or exists continues to be debated. It is curious that the debate seems endless even though strong arguments have been advanced to demonstrate the actual existence of African philosophy. Non-Africans are the principal initiators of this question. They remain the ones who continue to keep the question alive. Thus it is pertinent to ask, (i) why they persist in raising this question and, (ii) what is the meaning of this question. In answer to the second question we reply that it is evident that there are many African philosophers around if by that we mean people schooled in the discipline of philosophy. For this reason it is unlikely that the non-Africans are posing this as an empirical question. The question pertains more to the capability of the African to philosophise. In other words, it is doubtful that Africans can philosophise. If Africans were exposed to philosophy they could not cope with its requirements. This is because by their nature, their very being what they are, it is impossible for Africans to do philosophy. In this way the question assumes an ontological character: it calls into question the humanity of the African. The question is thus another way of saying that it is doubtful if Africans are wholly and truly human beings. The majority of the non-Africans continue to choose the answer that Africans are not wholly and truly human beings. Proceeding from this premise it was a matter of course for them to write the history of Western philosophy without due consideration for the African component in it. For example, Pope John Paul II in his Fides et Ratio, Vatican 1998 implies that

Africa provides nothing remarkable or worth recalling in the history of philosophy since antiquity to the contemporary period. The Italian D. Composta and Copleston also give neither credit nor scientific status to African philosophy in antiquity. Copleston "totally rejects a historical and scientific African philosophy of ancient Black Egypt and its subsequent influence on and relation with early Greek philosophy. . . . F.C. Copleston (1907–1985), an American Catholic clergyman, is a typical 20th-century European representative of the view which denies and severs all historical philosophical links of ancient Egypt with Greece and Rome. . . . Furthermore, Copleston would not accept even the personally documented testimonies of the ancient Greek philosophers. In his Metaphysics (1.1,981b 14–24), Aristotle clearly recognizes the Egyptian origin of the philosophical sciences of mathematics and astronomy. . . . If Copleston ignores the personal and firsthand literary testimonies of ancient Greek philosophers, he would certainly be less ready to accept the secondary reports of later past authors like Herodotus . . ."[9] Thus in the name of science many spurious excuses were found as to why there could not be and never was an African philosophy. The history of Western philosophy was seen from this perspective and continues to be done within the framework determined by the premise that Africans are not wholly and truly human. African historical reconstruction is a response and a challenge to this tradition. It is a questioning of the standards used in the reconstruction of the history of Western philosophy. It is an interrogation of the manner and extent to which the standards have been used to produce a less than truthful picture of the history of Western philosophy especially the Ancient and Medieval periods.

The African Historical Reconstruction

Like the defenders of Black philosophy in the United States of America, the proponents of African historical reconstruction were asked to justify their claim that there is an African philosophy. This demand for justification clearly presupposed "a specific understanding of the nature of the philosophical enterprise and the appropriate standards and methods for philosophizing."[10] There was thus an implicit distinction between Philosophy and philosophy the latter being the suitable label for the African's claim. But is there any scientific ground for this kind of distinction? Who determines the "scientificity" of the distinction? The demand for the protection of standards arising from this situation is weakened by its very lack of objectivity. It is also devoid of legitimacy since it arises from the questionable premise that Africans are not wholly and truly human. Arguing for the legitimacy of the African historical reconstruction Osuagwu posits that "African history of philosophy is an existential, call it an ontological, memorial of the ways our scholarly ancestors thought and lived life through, the way they attempted to understand and master themselves and their world."[11] The deeper meaning of the word "memorial" in this context is that there is an inextricable connection between memory and the construction of individual or collective identity. Thus self-knowledge can never be complete without reference to one's roots, to the past which is one's history. It is because of their adherence to the image of their identity that human beings sometimes prefer to lose their lives rather than suffer the loss of their identity. For this reason the study of one's history is necessary. On this reasoning, the blurred and dotted picture of the history of Western philosophy is a deformation of the African identity. African historical reconstruction is a corrective to this. It is intended to present the true picture of the African identity. "In conducting their historical essay, African philosophers want to rectify the historical prejudices of negation, indifference, severance and oblivion that have plagued African philosophy in the hands of European devil's advocates and their African accomplices. African historical investigations in philosophy go beyond defense, confrontations and corrections. They are also authentic projects and exercises in genuine scientific construction of African philosophy concerning diverse matters of its identity and difference, problem and project, its objectives, discoveries, development, achievements and defects or failures."[12] Historical investigations such as Cheik Anta Diop's The African Origin of Civilization, M. Bernal's Black Athena,

T. Obenga's Philosophie Africaine de la Periode Pharaonique 2780–330 avant notre ere, and, I.C. Onyewuenyi's The African Origin of Greek Philosophy, must be studied in this light.

Towards the Liberation of Philosophy

To deny the existence of African philosophy for the sake of maintaining the existing standards in education is to undermine the very nature of education and science. It is at the same time to make the questionable claim that the curriculum is free from ideological tension. The opponents of the protection of the existing standards of education recognise that the educational curriculum is by definition the terrain of ideological struggle. For the sake of the liberation of those who bore the burden of learning under the imposed Western epistemological paradigm, they urge for the transformation of the curriculum. Resistance to this is tantamount to the rejection of liberation. It is precisely standing firm in the position of the de-liberation of philosophy. But the de-liberation of philosophy must be challenged through transformation. Parallel with the Black experience in the United States of America, "a philosophy that reflects and/or endorses the white experience dominates the discipline. Accordingly, to call for a black philosophy, . . . is to launch an implicit attack on racism in philosophy, especially in its conceptual, research, curricular, and institutional expressions. . . . to advance a black philosophy is to affirm that the black perspective has been devalued and omitted from the recipe of Western philosophy and that that which has been ignored is a necessary ingredient for authentic philosophizing."[13] Authentic philosophizing is possible only through the inclusion of that which was deliberately ignored and omitted and, in our example, this is African philosophy. The inclusion is necessary for the liberation of philosophy from the overwhelming one-sidedness of the history of Western philosophy.

To deny the existence of African philosophy is also to reject the very idea of philosophy. It is to foreclose in advance the doors of communication with what we do not know. Yet, if the philosopher is the lover of wisdom surely it is common sense that one cannot acquire wisdom by improving one's skills to avoid listening to others. Hearing others is one thing but listening to them is quite another matter. The latter involves the possibility for communication. Accordingly, to deny oneself the opportunity for dialogue is to reject the possibility condition of becoming a philosopher. Dialogue being the basis of deliberation, it is clear that the liberation of philosophy is possible only through dialogue. For this reason it is imperative to take seriously Gracia's warning to Continental and Anglo-Saxon philosophers, namely, that ". . . the sorts of questions raised by Continental philosophers are frequently dismissed by analysts as illegitimate, and the questions they regard as legitimate are dismissed by Continental philosophers as trivial, . . . This technique of dismissal is a serious matter, for it clearly points to a kind of antiphilosophical dogmatic attitude that runs contrary to the very nature of the discipline as traditionally conceived. . . . To reject at the outset any attempt and possibility of communication with those who oppose us is something that always has been criticized by philosophers and that, nonetheless, is generally accepted in the profession today. The curiosity to understand those who don't think as we do is gone from philosophical circles to the detriment of the discipline. The situation, therefore, is intolerable not only from a practical standpoint but more important, because it threatens to transform the discipline into one more of the many ideologies that permeate our times, where differences of opinion are settled not through argument but through political action or force."[14]

Conclusion

In reading what follows both the curious and the adherents to the view that only one segment of humanity has a prior and exclusive claim to reason might feel urged to raise a number of questions and even objections. One of the questions might be that what is presented as African philosophy is so familiar to Western thought that one still wonders what exactly is African afterall. First of all, this question is a strange way of preferring to ignore the fact that African philosophy is by any stretch of the imagination linguistically and philosophically distinct from whatever

might be termed Western philosophy. Second, one of the unstated presuppositions of this question is that African philosophy is not only an expression of the already familiar in Western philosophy but that it also relies upon it for its existence. To discover familiarity between Western and African philosophies is not the same thing as to affirm identity between them. The two philosophies are not and cannot be identical since to be identical they must dissolve into one philosophy only. Such dissolution might be possible only if (a) two separate conditions may be found to be exactly the same in all respects at one and the same time; (b) if human freedom and, therefore the inherent unpredictability of human action, were to be completely removed from the human experience. For as long as requirements (a) and (b) cannot be fulfilled at the same time in specific circumstances relating to a particular human experience, the point that familiarity is not identity remains intact. Furthermore, the fact that human experience is time and space bound allows for the possibility of similar insights arising out of dissimilar experiences. This means that although insights might be similar, they are always ineluctably clothed and coloured by different experiences. Tinctured insights are the possibility condition for dialogue and communication. But they are not the reason for the assimilation, integration or even dissolution of one experience into another. Yet, over the centuries since conquest in the unjust wars of colonisation this has been the course preferred by the non-Africans in their relations with the Africans. The former, ignoring the tinctured character of insights and refusing to recognise the basic distinction between insight and argument, persistently argue that since the insights are the same, the African must in the name of "development," "democracy" and "human rights," for example, simply dissolve and become Western. This kind of demand sometimes under the guise of "methodological" objections is based on the fallacy that one experience is both prior to in terms of temporal or historical sequence and superior to the other in terms of an artificial hierarchical order. This kind of demand is morally questionable. That it is an objection epistemologically untenable requires no special pleading. However, it is understandable that it should come from a people who in the name of science have not only confused but insist on the identification of reason with absolute obedience to the convention to rely on the authority of references. The insistence is implausible because reason manifests itself first through the spoken language. Writing is an invention which depends on the prior existence of the spoken language. Accordingly, the speaking human being (homo loquens) precedes the writing human being (homo scriptans). Therefore, where there are no footnotes there is no reason is the fallacy underlying the demand of the non-Africans to assimilate and integrate the African into the West. At bottom this fallacy is expressive of the wish to appropriate experience and history for the sake of sustaining the undying myth that only one segment of humanity has a prior, superior and exclusive right to reason. Without this wish there is no need to posit the question whether or not there can be an African philosophy.

Notes

1. McMillan, Carol, *Women, Reason and nature*, Basil Blackwell Publisher Limited: Oxford 1982. P. 1–15 and 80–151

2. Hume, D., "Of national characters," in Norton F.N. and Popkin, R.H., (ed.) *David Hume: Philosophical Historian*, The Bobbs-Merrill Company, Inc.: New York 1965. p. 47

3. Williams, R.A., *The American Indian in Western legal thought*, Oxford University Press: Oxford 1990.

4. This is precisely the same structural circumstance in which the Amerindian and the Australasians find themselves. By claiming the sole and exclusive right to reason the erstwhile conqueror continues to hold epistemological primacy and dominance. In this way holding the key to knowledge practically means holding the key to power. See, Bondy, A.S., "The meaning and problem of Hispanic thought (Can there be a Latin American philosophy?)" in Gracia, J.J.E. (ed.) *Latin American philosophy in the twentieth century*, Prometheus Books: New York 1986. p. 243

5. In his discussion of "the evolution of the international personality of the new African states," in the precolonial period, Okoye argues against the denial of "any status in classical international law" to the ancient and medieval states outside "Europe." He notes pertinently that, "Again European powers concerned in the acquisition of African territories in the nineteenth century took the opinion that native populations had rights of sovereignty over the territory." Okoye, F.C., *International law and the new African states*, Sweet and Maxwell: London 1972. p. 5

6. Brueggemann, W., *The land*, Fortress Press: Philadelphia 1977. p. 48. Fanon, F., *The wretched of the earth*, (trans.) Farrington, C., Penguin Books Ltd.: Harmondsworth, Middlesex 1961. p. 34

7. Hanke, L., *Pope Paul III and the American Indians*, Harvard Theological Review, Volume XXX 1937. p. 71–72.

8. Altbach, P.G., "The distribution of knowledge in the third world: a case study in neocolonialism," in Altbach, P.G. and Kelly, Gail, P., (ed.) *Education and the colonial experience*, Transaction Books: New Brunswick (U.S.A.) and London 1984. p. 230–231

9. Osuagwu, I.M., *African historical reconstruction*, Amamihe Publications, Imo State, Nigeria: 1999. p. 87, 94, 95, 96

10. Jones, W.R., *The legitimacy and necessity of Black Philosophy: some preliminary considerations*, The Philosophical Forum, Volume IX, Nos. 2–3 1977–78. p. 151

11. Osuagwu, I. M., *African historical reconstruction*, Amamihe Publications: Imo State, Nigeria 1999. p. 22

12. Osuagwu, I.M., *African historical reconsctruction*, Amamihe Publications: Imo State, Nigeria 1999. p. 25

13. Jones, W.R., *The legitimacy and necessity of Black Philosophy: some preliminary considerations*, The Philosophical Forum, Volume IX, Nos. 2–3 1977–78. p. 153

14. Gracia, J.J.E., *Philosophy and its history*, State University of New York Press: New York 1992. p. 25

Defending Whiteness: Protecting White Privilege in Post–Civil Rights Society

Rita Cameron Wedding, Ph.D.

For most of its existence, both as European colony and as an independent nation, the U.S. was a racial dictatorship. From 1607 to 1865—258 years—most nonwhites were firmly eliminated from the sphere of politics. After the Civil War there was the brief egalitarian experiment of Reconstruction which terminated ignominiously in 1877. In its wake followed almost a century of legally sanctioned segregation and denial of the vote, nearly absolute in the South and much of the Southwest, less effective in the North and far West, but formidable in any case. These barriers fell only in the mid-1960s, a mere quarter of a century ago (Omi and Winant 1994, 66).

Race is the basis upon which U.S. society was organized, and it remains central to the stratification of society even today. Racial stratification was achieved through the establishment of racially based laws, social institutions, and ideologies which rationalized and justified a racial hierarchy and the inequitable distribution of societal resources. *"The legal affirmation of whiteness and white privilege allowed expectations that originated in injustice to be naturalized and legitimated. The relative economic, political, and social advantages dispensed to whites under systematic white supremacy in the United States were reinforced through patterns of oppression of blacks and Native Americans. Materially, these advantages became institutionalized privileges; ideologically, they [remain] . . . part of the settled expectations of whites—a product of the unalterable original bargain* (Harris 1995, 287).

"Defending Whiteness: Protecting White Privilege in Post–Civil Rights Society" from *Institutions, Ideologies, and Individuals: Feminist Perspectives on Gender, Race, and Class* by Rita Cameron Wedding and M.R. Matisons, 2004, Reprinted by permission of Kendall/Hunt Publishing Company.

The link between white privilege and racism is inextricable. In contemporary society, the relative absence of the more blatant acts of discrimination such as lynching and cross-burning (though they still occur) is evidence to some that racism no longer exits. But racism in contemporary society must be understood according to much different terms. Racism should not be thought of in terms of a single act but, instead, a system of elaborate intersections in private and public spheres. Racism should not be thought of as merely the acts of a few misguided individuals, such as skinheads or white supremacists, nor should it be defined only as those acts deemed as official hate crimes. It is neither random nor coincidental. Modern day racism operates like a wolf in sheep's clothing: it looks innocent but it is not. *In the post–civil rights movement era racial discrimination in employment and housing, racially segregated schools, racism in the health care and criminal justice systems, environmental racism, transportation racism, racial discrimination in voting procedures, racial bias in the mass media, race-based hate crimes, and plain old "everyday racism" in daily social interactions remain ubiquitous features of U.S. society* (Neubeck 2002; Bonilla-Silva 2001; Fegin and Vera 1995).

Despite the insidious and ever present nature of racism, conservatives argue that we are living in a colorblind society. Common to all modern race projects or efforts of conservatives to stymie the civil rights movement is the claim of colorblindness and the covert manipulation of racial fears in order to achieve political gains (Omi and Winant 1994, 58). Colorblindness is probably the most efficient race project of contemporary society. Colorblindness has not only suppressed the public discourse on race but by reframing the historic applications of race and racism it also sets the parameters around which race can be understood

Civil Rights: equal opportunity to all.

and articulated. Therefore political campaigns presented as pro-American and colorblind, such as anti-affirmative action, anti-immigration, English-only and race privacy initiatives, have as their primary objective the protection and preservation of white privilege. They garner support by inducing the fear within whites that their rights and privileges are threatened and need to be protected. Modern race projects position whites as the new victims of racism. Minorities and civil rights projects such as affirmative action are often blamed for a shrinking job market and the loss of professional, technological, and industrial jobs. But these jobs have not been taken over by minorities but by corporations who have exported these jobs to cheaper labor markets.

Thus modern race projects designed as a defense of whiteness are not race neutral. Initiatives such as "The Civil Rights Initiative" (the anti-affirmative action initiative) and "The Racial Privacy Initiative" (the initiative designed to eliminate racial classifications) have names that deliberately mask the intentions of these propositions. Where overt expressions of white racial privilege were once commonplace, debates favoring "new racism" argue that race should not be taken into account. Yet nowhere in these debates have any social reparations been proposed to realign historic racial inequality. Obviously, without such considerations colorblind projects work to keep existing inequitable social arrangements intact.

Modern race projects allow conservatives to position themselves as the real defenders of justice and civil rights. Their belief systems are hegemonic and reflect the prevailing social, political and even religious viewpoints of society at large. As their beliefs are reiterated by the public discourses in academia, government bureaucracies, the press, the courts, and popular culture they are accepted as normal and common sense. Controlled by elite groups, these public discourses typically count as legitimated knowledge (Collins 1998, 49). On the other hand, those who reject the ideologies of colorblindness and interrogate their inherent contradictions do so with virtually no social and moral authority. Their challenges, always impeachable, are subverted by ideological depictions of themselves as race baiters and as the new racists. The purpose of this chapter is to examine the methodologies of new racism and to

explore the modern struggle to preserve and to fight America's greatest social problem—racism.

This chapter focuses on race even though in reality race overlaps and intersects with other systems of oppression such as gender and social class in ways that cannot be isolated. All systems of oppression produce inequitable outcomes. Understanding the complexities of race and racism in contemporary society enables us to better recognize the confluent effects of gender and social class in creating and reproducing inequality.

The focus on blacks should in no way suggest that race can be understood only in terms of "black" and "white." All racial and ethnic groups, including white ethnic groups, have experienced various forms of discrimination. Although this chapter discusses the racialization process as it was and is still applied to African Americans, many of the insights apply to other historically racialized groups as well.

- *The new racism*

  Racial meanings which reiterate the inherent value of whiteness and simultaneously devalue blackness have resulted in racial inequalities that can be correlated to poverty, wealth, etc. Such differences are the outcome of social structure, not biology. There is no such thing as race from a biological standpoint. Race is a social, not a biological construct that was developed to produce and rationalize the inequitable distribution of societal resources according to phenotypes such as skin color. Race holds immense social significance imbued with meanings and connotations that inform our common sense. Even though race is constructed through historic meanings and social interactions it is as much a part of our national character as themes of patriotism.

- *In contemporary society, racism has been transformed but not eliminated.*

  In order to fulfill the ideals of a racial democracy, the transition from a system which utilized direct forms of violence and coercion to one which relies more (but not exclusively) on abstract forms of racism was essential. Racism as it was initially understood (as actions and attitudes which were irrefutably racist) still exists but such actions are often overshadowed by modern or institutionalized forms of racism which are insidious and very hard to detect. Institutional racism *"consists of established laws, customs, and practices which systematically reflect and produce intentionally and unintentionally racial inequalities in American society"* (Carter 1997, 200). Institutional racism is hard to detect because it utilizes policies and practices which on the surface appear neutral but can nonetheless result in racial disparities. *"The structural form of racism is difficult to perceive easily, because it does not use race as the subordinating mechanism, but uses other devices only indirectly related to race"* (Carter 1997, 200).

- *Identifying racism in contemporary society is tricky.*

Racism is typically defined by a direct link between discrimination and domination. Shifting from definitions based on a direct cause and effect relationship (or actions directly resulting in discrimination or subordination) to one where the action can't show an immediate subordinating outcome is the crux of modern day racism. "But as long as actions can be understood in a racial context, they offer the possibility that racism can be promoted even though the intention or action can be argued as not being at all linked to race" (Carter 1997, 200). Therefore, if racism is defined only by a direct link between race and vilification (e.g., racial epithet), or race and discrimination (e.g., denial of a job), few acts even though they produce racist outcomes would fit the criteria. Unlike the blatant discrimination of the past such as lynching, cross-burning, and signs that read "blacks need not apply" (acts which are incontrovertibly racist), contemporary racism is subtle and often indetectable. In contemporary society, while the old definitions of racism still apply, new racism must be critiqued and understood in ways that reveal the systematic, often indirect and oblique, relationship between race and discrimination. Old definitions of

racism allow new racism to go undetected because it doesn't leave much evidence. Even lawyers argue that if you can't show a direct link between race and discrimination it can't be racism.

- *Proof of racism found in patterns of disproportionality.*

Despite the fact that most of the overt systems of discrimination have been dismantled, racism is reflected in all of our major social institutions such as education, criminal justice, housing, healthcare, economics, and labor force participation. Even though it may be hard for some to connect the dots between race and oppression, the persistence of racism is irrefutably evident in patterns of racial disproportionality. *"If it can be shown that distinct racial differences exist, then what is observed is institutional racism"* (Carter 1997, 200). If we fail to recognize that institutional racism produces racial disparities we are left to conclude that patterns of disproportionality can be explained through superiority–inferiority paradigms. Such ideologies rationalize inequality according to inherent deficits of blacks and the implied superiority of whites, or meritocracy theory which argues that whites fare better as a group because they work harder and are therefore more deserving. Both of these theories ignore the structural nature of racism. Without structural analyses to examine forces such as racism and capitalism, gross racial disparities appear random and coincidental.

How Racism Persists Virtually Undetected

Perhaps the most important quality of modern day discrimination is its ability to persist virtually undetected. This chapter identifies four interacting factors that are essential to the maintenance of racial arrangements under new racism: 1) rearticulating a new racial politic by distorting meanings of race, racism, and civil rights; 2) constructing and deploying colorblind ideologies; 3) the colorblind/color conscious paradox; 4) how racism is operationalized within institutions.

1. *Constructing a New Racial Politic*

Rearticulating the Terms and Conditions of Civil Rights

The civil rights movement symbolized an end to a racial dictatorship. Incontrovertible forms of discrimination were no longer an acceptable means for achieving the desired social order. According to Omi and Winant's *Racial Formation in the United States*, in an attempt to eliminate racial discrimination the government legitimated group rights, established affirmative action mandates, and spent money on a range of social programs that supposedly debilitated rather than uplifted its target populations. In this scenario, the victims of racial discrimination had dramatically shifted from racial minorities to whites, particularly white males. Such actions, clearly a threat to the "original bargain," were met with a racial reaction that coopted civil rights language. Opponents of civil rights infused civil rights themes with new political meaning linked to other key elements of conservative ideology (Omi and Winant 1994, 117).

Reframing civil rights language allowed conservatives to strategically undermine the civil rights movement. They had the ability to rationalize any distortions in social relations by passing and reinterpreting laws, social policy, and even the constitution. They control the media, appoint Supreme Court Justices, and garner the consent of everyday people to act as agents of the new racism through the use of cleverly articulated racial projects. Their positions were reconstituted by law which held to the basic premise that those in positions of power, beneficiaries of racially conferred privilege, have the right to establish norms for those who have historically been oppressed pursuant to those norms (Harris 1995, 287). Their authority to rearticulate the debate according to long-standing hegemonic terms represented a comfortable compromise particularly for the many whites who perceived themselves as egalitarian and fair but who at the same time worried about the diminution of white privilege. These whitewashed versions of civil rights allowed them to reconcile any conflict they may have had while leaving their liberal identities in tact.

Affirmative action was designed to offset the consequences of historic white racial preferences that resulted in race-based arrangements in which whites disproportionately occupied the most favorable positions. But affirmative action was not able to redistribute the benefits which accrued to whites under institutionalized privileged systems to other groups. When blacks assert their rights to equality such assertions are used against them. Ideologies which represent whites as meritorious are juxtaposed to ideologies of lazy blacks "who wanted something for nothing," "who had an entitlement mentality" and "thought the world owed them something." These ideologies maligned both black people and any program designed to promote equality.

Clearly conservatives fought fire with fire. By redefining the terms and conditions of equality, opponents of civil rights effectively colonized the civil rights movement. They linked themselves symbolically to Dr. Martin Luther King by evoking his famous *I Have a Dream* speech. But instead of a society that had truly transcended the boundaries of race they applied their definition of colorblindness to practices that surreptitiously preserved a racial hierarchy. Colorblindness in contemporary society means that we will pretend not to notice race even while the racialization processes continue. The conservatives' brand of colorblindness was used to denounce any recognition of race that could be used to redistribute racial values. Now that blacks are being positioned to demand group rights the law says that "nobody's race should matter" (Harris 1995, 287).

Of course this was simply a ruse because the value of whiteness had already been purchased and guaranteed through the erection of racial hierarchies which were firmly in place. Historic preferences for whites were entrenched in the social structure and a hegemonic order was firmly intact. Without the interference of civil rights projects like affirmative action programs, the new racism would be as effective and efficient in preserving the racial order as were conditions of the past.

Affirmative Action

The Civil Rights Act of 1964 was the first nationwide attempt to provide equal opportunity to all Americans. Title VII of the Civil Rights Act, which prohibits discrimination by any employer or labor union on the basis of race, color, religion, sex, or national origin, provided the initial foundation for affirmative action programs. This law stimulated affirmative action programs in the public and private sector. Affirmative action encompasses any measure, beyond simply ending a discriminatory practice, that establishes programs to identify qualified individuals who have either historically or actually been denied those opportunities and/or to prevent the recurrence of discrimination in the future. The goal of affirmative action is to prevent discrimination before it happens. Opponents of affirmative action argued for its elimination on the basis that discrimination statutes already outlaw discrimination. But such laws offer a remedy only after the discrimination occurs. Moreover, these statutes provide no proactive mechanism to redistribute racial value (Proposition 209 Manual).

Affirmative action was designed to correct historic racial inequality by giving people of color and white women the same access to opportunities as white men. As Cheryl Harris puts it, affirmative action was designed to delegitimate the inherent property interest in whiteness (Harris 1995, 288).

Affirmative action affirmed and legitimated the rights of historically disenfranchised groups and by doing so offered the possibility of destabilizing the status quo. But affirmative action, as it was superimposed upon existing systems of inequality, was never itself institutionalized. Its effectiveness was weakened by an onslaught of court cases that contested it ostensibly on the basis that the law should be colorblind. But, in reality, it was contested on the basis that racial entitlements to whites would be compromised. Although affirmative action programs played a major role in providing access to members of previously disenfranchised groups, once the programs were dismantled it appeared that the systems they sought to change remained virtually undisturbed.

In Supreme Court decisions on affirmative action we again see how rearticulated meanings of colorblindness were used to weaken, and in some states dismantle, affirmative action. In the context of new racism it was important to reinterpret the meaning of race. After nearly four centuries of

racial constructions, race had come to embody connotations, codes, and cues so powerful that the words white or black symbolized a host of ideological messages that were commonly understood by most members of society. But despite this the Court, on the basis of newly articulated definitions of colorblindness, legitimated race to be narrowly construed to mean skin color devoid of any historical, political, or economic value or determination of history (Crenshaw 1998, 284). Therefore any historical or structural conditions that institutionalize injustice, such as inadequate education or poverty, are considered irrelevant, asserting instead that we are now all on a level playing field—and we need to be blind to color (Cameron Wedding 2003, 58). This is the final blow in the depolitization of race. By positioning race as skin color outside the context of historical precedents and connotations, government can (and has) relinquished its responsibility for insuring equality. But racism must be understood from a political context because state actions have treated people in very different ways according to their race, and therefore the government cannot retreat from its policy responsibilities in this area. It cannot suddenly declare itself "colorblind" without in fact perpetuating the same type of differential, racist treatment (Omi and Winant 1994, 57). Racism de-linked from the social structure requires that each case be interpreted as individual or coincidental.

Redefining race as neutral allowed for the emergence of "reverse discrimination" discourse which is arguably the most effective defense against civil rights. Charges of reverse discrimination was the call that mobilized a defense of white privilege. Reverse discrimination is based on the presupposition of white entitlement. Charges of reverse discrimination attempt to negate discrimination claims made by people of color by asserting that white people are the new victims of racism. In the Allan Bakke case (one of the first cases based on reverse discrimination), the defendant claimed discrimination on one basis—whiteness (Hurtado and Stewart 1997, 304). Other selection criteria, like applicants being the offspring of wealthy donors, went unchallenged, largely because these hierarchies are perceived as legitimate. In Professor Harris's words, *"Bakke expected that he would never be disfavored when competing with minority candidates although he might be disfavored with respect to more economically privileged whites . . . that is, competition among whites is fair because they are his equals"* (Hurtado and Steward 1997, 304).

Many whites believe that they have been victims of reverse discrimination. The term "reverse discrimination" implies that it is the mirror opposite of "discrimination," the only difference being that the victims are white. It is not uncommon for students to say "it's not only minorities who experience discrimination, everyone has experienced some kind of discrimination." This is true, but not all discrimination is equal. Racial discrimination is not random, it is institutionalized, historically sanctioned by law or social practice, and supported by ongoing race projects which target members of particular groups for differential treatment. While it is true that everyone experiences discrimination, whites as a group are not targets of systemic discrimination that will result in a loss of economic or social power. Many whites who have made charges of reverse discrimination assume that any time they are passed over in favor of a minority that it is reverse discrimination. This is due to the fact that some whites feel that blacks are inherently inferior to them and therefore no fair decision could allow them to be deselected in favor of a less deserving "minority." Moreover, charges of reverse discrimination often occur in the absence of any objective criteria that could prove that they were in fact the most qualified; their possession of whiteness seems to be the basis of their defense.

Reverse discrimination fuels new racism because it pits whites against nonwhites. The threat of a loss of race privilege insures that all whites are recruited in the fight against programs construed to grant preferential treatment to nonwhites. Stories of reverse discrimination (which are included in every white person's "invisible knapsack of privilege") serve as reminders to all white people that they are at risk. Frequently, people tell stories about how they or someone they know didn't get a job because the company hired a "minority." The use of the word minority in this case almost always implies "less qualified." Recently after assisting a white student with a law school application, the student expressed concern about getting admitted. She cited numerous examples of friends telling her that she would not get into law school because she is not a minority. We suggested that she call some law schools to get their racial profile. Until the racial demographics shift from being disproportionately white, as they are currently at nearly every law school in the country, to disproportionately "minority," which has never been the case, being white should not be seen as a disadvantage to law school admission but rather a prerequisite. Such stories are common to colorblind parlance. Even though there is no evidence to support the reverse discrimination theory as it applies to law school admissions it can be argued that even one "minority" (constructed as less qualified) is one too many.

Whites can experience racism on the basis of race but such actions are individualized and not backed by the force of law or social custom in ways which can produce systemic inequalities. Reverse discrimination theories contradict all socioeconomic indices which document that whites fare consistently better on most quality of life measures—including wealth, education, health—than any other group.

California's Proposition 54— The Race Privacy Initiative

California's Proposition 54, also known as the Race Privacy Initiative, was on California's notorious ballot that recalled Governor Gray Davis in 2003. This proposition was possibly more controversial than the recall of the governor. Had it passed, it would have banned the state from classifying any individual by race, ethnicity, color, or national origin except under specified circumstances. This proposition was based on the argument, as are all modern race projects, that we are living in a colorblind society so race doesn't matter. It reaffirms the legal mandate that rights are given to individuals and not groups. People of color had historically been denied rights on the basis of group membership. Redefining the meaning of group rights would allow the state to continue to deny blacks access to group rights that had historically privileged whites. Even though the rights of whites as a group have been codified and protected by law, the recognition of group rights is disallowed when asserted by racially oppressed groups. The law is then interpreted to mean that "equality mandates only the equal treatment of individuals under the law" and the idea of rights of social groups has no place (Harris 1995, 287). This obviously denies the role of government in affirming and privileging whites and promotes the myth that the position whites occupy in society is derived solely from individual merit. Attempts to invalidate group membership would become a key issue in later colorblind debates.

Diminishing group identity makes it harder for groups to mobilize around common themes of oppression. Historically, social policies regulating racial identities such as "drop of blood" doctrine, rule of hypodescent, and state enforced matriarchy (a practice during slavery which required that children born to a slave inherit the status of the mother), left no doubt about racial identity. However, in contemporary society racial identity is intentionally ambiguous. The new flexibility around racial identification allows blacks and mixed race people to self-identify, which on a personal level is a good thing, but politically can mask the perpetuation of discrimination. The ambiguity of these more flexible racial classifications allows people to symbolically situate themselves outside rigid race constructs while ignoring the ways in which they are simultaneously being reconstructed solely in racialized terms. On a political level the point is not whether they are "mixed race" or bi-racial, or even Mexican or Asian, the point is that they are not white. Conservatives are not concerned about cultural identity but rather their ability to preserve the privileges which accrue to whiteness.

But the real problem is not the racial categories per se but rather in historic racial constructions which would have persisted even if Proposition 54 had passed. In other words, eliminating racial classifications without deconstructing racial hierarchies will only exacerbate the problem because the systems which preserve racism will remain intact. What we will lose is the only systematic way to measure the impact. Without racial classifications we can claim that we are a racial democracy because the data on patterns of racial disproportionality, and even data documenting racial progress, would be lost.

Even though Proposition 54, The Race Privacy Initiative, failed this year we should keep in mind that at least in California one such initiative appears on every ballot each election. Whether these ongoing race projects succeed or fail at the polls they are still effective. They rearticulate notions of colorblindness and offer new themes, defenses and clichés for defending the status quo. These themes resemble themes of civil rights, resonate principles of social justice and equality, and are easy to sell in a colorblind society.

Because modern race projects mask their anti–civil rights objectives they often receive broad support even from liberals who otherwise support genuine social justice reforms. What resistance there is to modern race projects like anti-affirmative action initiatives, anti-immigration policies, and English-only initiatives, typically comes from people who have considerably less power and credibility to assert and argue their position. Negative images of angry, loud people of color in protest marches denouncing the government is to some further proof that these people are the problem, not racism.

As we can see from this discussion, because of the rearticulation of racial politics, race and racism are not as they appear. Those fighting for the real civil rights agenda appear to be the obstacle to racial harmony. Conservatives point the finger at civil rights activists for protesting against so-called colorblind legislation and construe them as race baiters and people who just want to sow the seeds of unrest. Conservatives want people to believe that racial classifications represents the last vestige of racism. But, in fact, the elimination of racial classifications themselves will do little to disrupt inequality. Civil rights activists understand that eliminating racial categories does not signal that we are living in a racial democracy. To the contrary, they know that the informal elements of white supremacy have been much more difficult to intervene against than the formal, legally sanctioned racial system. If people can be persuaded by colorblind ideology that racism no longer exists even when they are surrounded by hard evidence of racial disproportionality in every sphere of social life, there is no question that the fight for civil rights would be lost with the passing of laws which outlawed the collection of racial data.

A comparison between Brazil, which had a more informal system of racism, and the U.S., where race was a matter of state policy, offers important insights into how racism can persist even when it appears that the state has no investment in preserving racial arrangements.

The U.S. transitioned from a system which established and policed the color line through slave codes and slave patrols under slavery, segregation in the pre–civil rights period, and equal opportunity and affirmative action policies in the post–civil rights era (Winant 1999, 98). "In Brazil by contrast the state and the political system have been extremely reluctant at least since abolition either to enforce or suppress racial boundaries; far more prevalent has been the blanket denial that racism exists there" (Winant 1999, 99). The informality of the Brazilian system went a long way to mask a system that suppressed (or even entirely averted) any demand for the extension of full rights to blacks (Winant 1999, 102–103). According to Winant the Brazilian myth of racial democracy retained a greater grip on its black subjects than white supremacist ideology did on U.S. blacks (Winant 1999, 102). It was precisely the formality of the U.S. racial order, its politicization and enforcement by the state, that provided the black movement with a suitable target for mobilization. Thus, when the link between state enforcement and race is blurred, and principles of colorblindness take center stage, the fight for civil rights can be totally subverted.

2. Colorblind Ideologies Create the Social Conditions for New Racism

Colorblindness emerged as the so-called solution to ending race-based politics, but instead it should be understood as a system of strategies developed to preserve and protect racial hierarchies in the post–civil rights era. Ideologies of colorblindness control and regulate the public and private discourses on race and set the necessary conditions for colorblind laws and social policies that enforce patterns of inequality.

The following list of strategies is common to colorblind society. How many do you recognize?

Colorblind Strategies Used to Control Race Discourse

1. *Silencing those who fight for social justice.*

Individuals who speak out against racism are often seen as a problem greater than racism itself. "Playing the race card" is an accusation used to attack, discredit, and silence anyone who raises the specter of race discrimination. Terms like *militant* and *femi-nazi* are also used to label people involved in social justice movements. While the word *militant* targets black men, the word *femi-nazi,* made popular by conservative Rush Limbaugh, specifically targeted white women. Feminist and social justice movements have formed racially diverse coalitions to fight racism and sexism. But any demonstration of activism by women puts them in violation of gender role prescriptions. Strong women and feminists are often vilified as men haters and lesbians. A favorite way to discredit feminists is to associate them with lesbianism. "*. . . [W]hen the label 'lesbian' is used to smear and dismiss feminists and feminism, it silences women who fear being labeled if they identify themselves as feminists or even talk openly about patriarchy*" (Johnson 1997, 108). Perhaps it is no surprise that so many women say, "I believe in equality but I'm not a feminist." In this way we see how hegemony can mobilize to weaken any individual or movement that threatens the status quo.

2. *Slandering affirmative action and shaming those who benefited.*

Affirmative action gave millions of people of color and white women access to the playing field for the first time in history. Some whites have intrinsic notions of superiority and feel that minorities who "made it" did so at their expense because affirmative action allowed them to jump to the head of the line. As a consequence, the legitimacy of these programs was always highly contested. But also under attack were those who were considered beneficiaries. Ironically, very little attention has been paid to the fact that white women largely benefited from affirmative action programs which were designed to protect against both race and gender discrimination. Because white women typically marry white men, white families benefited greatly from a program associated mostly with blacks. Drawing from the body of ideological constructions which depict minorities as being inferior to whites, it was then relatively easy to enforce the notion that affirmative action candidates are minorities and therefore inherently undeserving and unqualified. Thus affirmative action programs and minorities were yoked and as a result both were tarnished reputationally. This strategy supported the anti-affirmative action movement by shaming minorities and stigmatizing them as "recipients" who were inherently unqualified. Consequently many people who should have benefited from these programs instead (at least in theory) rejected them because they did not want to be stigmatized.

3. *Attacking "political correctness."*

Political correctness was an ideological framework based on tolerance, inclusivity, and cultural sensitivity. It is amazing how the political right could destroy the one ideological approach to building sensitivity and make it the butt of jokes and fodder for late night TV. Being "politically correct" became a laughing matter.

4. *Renaming the racist.*

Social justice vernacular which utilizes terms such as racism, or racists, is restricted under colorblind culture. Naming someone or something racist is seen as a seditious act. Who is the racist? Because talk about racism is censored under colorblind ideology, the person who utters race first is the racist in the room. Conservatives associate racism with the actions of skinheads, white supremacist hate groups, and the KKK while making off limits the use of the terms racism and racist as they might apply to the actions of everyday people, which makes modern oppression possible. Aversive racism is a form of modern prejudice that explains how many whites who regard themselves as nonprejudiced and liberal minded can nevertheless discriminate in subtle rationalizable ways. While many people would not discriminate in ways that are overtly racist, most people do discriminate in ways that require implicit agreements that can be achieved from little acts of discrimination not directly linked to oppression (Gaertner 1997, 168). Modern day acts of racism are often small incremental actions which alone would hardly appear racist but accumulatively can produce pervasive racial disparities. New racism involves the participation and complicity of all members of society to some extent or another—including those who are hurt by it. Modern day racism remains efficient because it involves little personal culpability; aversive actions are a normal and routine aspect of interpersonal interactions.

5. *Litmus test for racism: the question of intentionality.*

Consider this statement made by Rush Limbaugh: *"I don't think he's been that good from the get-go"* (referring to Donovan McNabb the black quarterback for the Philadelphia Eagles). *"I think what we've had here is a little social concern in the NFL. The media has been overly desirous that a black quarterback do well. There is little hope invested in McNabb, and he got a lot of credit for the performance of his team that he didn't deserve. The defense carried his team"* (http://www .Sportsline.com/nfl/story/7000602.html). This comment was considered by some to be racist. What many conservative pundits argued is that no one knows if Rush's statement was racist because to know this we would have to know "what's in his heart." In other words the new litmus test for racism is that of intentionality. Was the statement intended to be racist? Asserting that statements or actions can't be racist unless they were "intended" as such will protect even the most racist actions because no one can ever really know what's in anyone's "heart."

6. *Who is the minority?*

In a society in which the majority of the population is represented by people of color, the term *minority* which refers to nonwhite populations, has truly outlived its usefulness. Historically the term may have referred to a statistical minority or a nonwhite group or groups smaller in number than whites. But the term has also been used to refer to power differentials denoting that whites as the "majority" group were more powerful and dominant compared to the nonwhite "minority" or "subordinate" group. Despite the fact that immigration policies have historically favored European immigration in ways that allow whites to stay in the "majority" the majority of people in the U.S. are nonwhite. Not only is the term *minority* statistically obsolete, but it's problematic in the way that it reinforces the inherent nature of superiority for whites and inferiority for so-called minorities.

7. *Regulating public discourse that names whiteness.*

While it is routine to discuss minorities, the disadvantaged, single parents, and welfare mothers, exposing whiteness and white privilege is protected under the "white male bashing act" of colorblindness. Thus any academic discussions which critique this most privileged group are often seen as white male bashing.

8. Why can't we all just get along?

Many people think that the problem of racism is an individual problem and that if we as individuals would just be nicer to one another the problem would be resolved. But racism is more than an individual problem, it is structural. Racism does rely on individuals to transmit racial values and give their consent to practices and laws which legitimate racial hierarchies, but where does the incentive for individuals to do so come from, and what is the collective stimulus for a society to act in such a uniform fashion? Clearly the core of such actions can be found in the hegemony, a social structure; laws, policies, and practices that normalize race hierarchies and allow them to be seen as common sense and just, despite the fact that such systems reproduce racial inequalities. Individuals are then taught to see these inconsistencies as the outcome of failings of individuals who as members of certain groups just can't seem to get it right. In the video *Color of Fear*, David the white former vineyard owner described his perception of how people of color cling to their ethnic identities instead of just being Americans. *"How can I be an American I can't so I won't, is this clinging to the problem? Why can't they [people of color] just be individuals and go out and make a place for themselves?"*

While individuals could become more aware of how they are complicit in racism on a day-to-day basis, their ability to identify and perceive racism is determined by which side of the color line they are on. If individuals could understand the historical and structural constructions of race they could then "just say no" to laws, public policies, and institutionalized racism and sexism as it occurs. Most scholars will argue that this is unlikely because the inequitable distributions which oppress some operate to privilege others. We all have a personal stake in racism.

9. Denying racism and blaming the victim.

There is a tendency for whites to think that the solution to ending racism lies in the attitudes of blacks. We are once again reminded by David from *The Color of Fear*, *"the world is open to you but you think the white man is a dam and a block to your progress. He is not. I think you put a block and dam your progress in regards to the white man."*

10. Ahhhhhh.

This sound is caused by a release of air from the mouth of a person who has just heard something that violates colorblind protocol such as naming racism or sexism, or calling an individual or an institution racist. This sound, which is typically accompanied by a look of incredulity or a scowl, symbolizes that what they have just heard is out of bounds and that this discussion has summarily ended. This response is an extremely common and effective means of controlling interpersonal discourse because of its ability to regulate speech or shut it down admonishes the violator. The "ahhhhhh" effect can be achieved by any verbal or nonverbal action that brings a halt to conversations that are perceived to violate the rules of colorblindness.

Controlling the race discourse through colorblind principles insures their standardization. As these ideals are normalized and reiterated by "culture makers" and policymakers or "the white men in positions of influence and power; political leaders, editors, novelists, educators, ministers, military leaders, doctors, and business men" (Takaki 1990, vii), and even Dr. Phil, colorblindness provides the context through which new racism is understood and articulated.

The broad acceptance of colorblind beliefs and assumptions as the way things are and the way things are supposed to be is assured by the endorsement of people in positions of power and authority who not only control the means of production but also the production of ideas (Jewell 1993, 18). According to Patricia Hill Collins (Hill Collins 1993, xi), within hierarchical power relations, the ideas produced [and reported] by elite groups about community, difference in voice, justice and many other topics matter (Hill Collins 1993, xi).

Take, for example, the difference between the voice of Tom Brokaw and that of Jessie Jackson. Mr. Brokaw as a member of the social elite is considered a legitimate leader who is objective, neutral, and well-informed. Mr. Jackson on the other hand is called a race baiter, a troublemaker, and biased. The assumed neutrality and honesty of Mr. Brokaw is implied not only because his viewpoints are situated within the context of hegemony (and therefore validated) but also because he, by virtue of his occupational status, race, gender, and social class, is constructed through ideological hegemony as legitimate and inherently trustworthy. Thus to the extent that he reiterates (or at least works within the confines of) established hegemonic order he and other social intelligentsia are in the best position to situate colorblindness within broader values of capitalism and patriotism. Moreover, because his beliefs are well-represented and reiterated by the hegemony, he rarely has to speak out against or challenge hegemonic discourse. Once again this allows him to appear to always have a calm and balanced demeanor. On the contrary, Mr. Jackson works to correct social injustice so he is typically fighting against the status quo. It's likely that you will only see him when he is involved in controversy, thus his rabble-rousing image is well-earned. Finally, while it's easy to assume that people like Mr. Jackson can only speak to one issue, it's important to realize that he and others like him don't control airtime. These decisions are controlled by the media so that about the only time you really see blacks giving their opinions is when it relates to minorities and civil rights (Parenti 1993, 11).

3. Colorblindness/Color-Conscious Paradox

New racism requires the redefinition of colorblind ideologies and the promotion of color-consciousness through racial ideologies that denigrate blacks and normalize and valorize whites. Racial hypersensitivity and colorblindness certainly on the surface appear mutually exclusive. Despite the fact that colorblindness is based on the premise that race doesn't matter and we shouldn't notice race, color-consciousness reinforced by racial ideologies or stereotypes is a central feature in all private and public interactions. Day-to-day practices of color-conscious behavior inform our decisions about who to date, who to marry, where to live, who to trust, standards of beauty, assumptions of competency, and the type of TV shows we watch—all while we are supposedly blind to color.

Though they may appear to be contradictory in nature, colorblindness and color-consciousness are in fact interconnected and interdependent systems. Colorblindness is the process which sets the tone and methodology and prescribes the conduct for a colorblind culture, and racial coding or color-consciousness tells us what can be expected of groups on the basis of race. These systems operate simultaneously. Although they appear contradictory they are in fact complementary. Race and corresponding gender and social class constructions depend upon the rationalizations provided by ideologies. What appear to be antithetical and oppositional principles are in fact mutually beneficial. Colorblindness does not "blind" us to race but instead suppresses the public and private discourse and allows the functions of ideological racial constructions to operate undisturbed.

Ideological Constructions of Blackness

The new hegemony has become a part of the established and accepted patterns of social life, and an aspect of the socialization of every member of society. *"Few can escape the cultural and cognitive forces that promote racial bias"* (Gaertner 1997, 168). It seems that most people in society are influenced by the ideological connections between black men and criminal behavior. Last semester in my Ethnic Studies course I had a student who always appeared nervous and uncomfortable. Whenever I would look her in the eye, she would divert her eyes away from mine. While lecturing on certain topics, particularly those which dealt directly with racism, she would often cross her arms over her chest assuming a posture that could best be described as defiant. One day while lecturing on discrimination I posed a particular question and asked her for a response. She told me that she had nothing to say. I asked her if it was more the case that she didn't want to share her thoughts. Clearly I struck a nerve. Eventually she blurted out that she believed that blacks committed more crimes. She then went on to recount a recent incident. Leaving a sports arena one night, she noticed that there were two black men walking behind her (probably along with a number of people filing out of a sports arena) and she was afraid that they were going to rape her. I asked her if there had been any provocation which produced this fear or if she had ever been hurt by a black man and she said no and that she otherwise had no exposure to black people ("except you," she quipped). Despite the fact that more crimes are committed by whites, white men are not pathologized as a threat to society but black men have historically been attached to what we think of as a crime.

The ideological connections between black men and criminal behavior are a part of our collective awareness. My student is not alone. In Michael Moore's *Stupid White Men* he states ". . . when I turn on the news each night what do I see again and again? Black men alleged to be killing, raping, mugging, stabbing, gangbanging, looting, rioting, selling drugs, pimping, hoing, having too many babies, dropping babies from tenement windows, fatherless, motherless, godless, penniless. I believe we've become so used to this image of the black male predator that we are forever ruined by this brainwashing" (Moore 2003, 29). Ideologies make it easy to dismiss or ignore mistreatment or violence directed at blacks, resulting in presumption of their guilt as plausible and their mistreatment rational.

The most compelling aspect of such ideologies is how they normalize bias. In Michael Moore's *Stupid White Men* he describes the powerful effect of racial ideologies as revealed in his first film, *Roger & Me*. In this film there is a scene in which a white woman on social security clubs a bunny rabbit to death so that she can sell him as "meat" instead of as a pet. Moore says that he was deluged with calls expressing outrage for the violence displayed in the scene. But less than two minutes after the bunny lady "does her deed" there is footage of a scene in which the police in Flint (Michigan) open fire and shoot a black man wearing a Superman cape and holding a plastic toy gun (Moore 2003, 29).

The complete pervasive, commonsense acceptance of black men as deviant rationalizes racial disproportionality in our nation's prisons and it also makes them seem deserving of the mistreatment they receive in the hands of law enforcement. Incidents of police brutality are sadly an all too common event in America. According to Moore, not once did anyone say to him, "I can't believe you showed a black man being shot in your movie! How horrible! How disgusting! I couldn't sleep for weeks!"

The conditioning that allows us to connect blacks to violence requires that we normalize ideologies of black criminality so that they don't conflict with our values of justice and fairness. This allows the outcomes, including death, to appear rational. Even while the U.S. positions itself as the model for social justice to the world, liberty and justice are not distributed equally to all Americans. For example, the U.S. incarcerates a higher percentage of black men, by a factor of six, than did South Africa's Botha government during apartheid (Guinier 2002, 263). This glaring example of racism is morally reprehensible and yet through the insidious mix of ideologies of colorblindness and color-consciousness these inconsistencies can be justified within principles of "liberty and justice for all."

Social theories portraying black people as intellectually inferior, criminally inclined, and sexually deviant have informed ideological constructions in ways that set up conditions for their mistreatment in all spheres of social life, e.g., education, child welfare, political life, and legal system. Ideologies inform even the most discreet and seemingly inconsequential social interactions. Take for example the following story. In class a student stated that she had just attended the worst job interview of her life. She described the interviewer as rude, disorganized, and sloppy. She told the exact same story to her roommate. The next day the roommate called to tell the student that the "black lady" called about the job; my student asked, "what black lady?" My student said she never told the roommate the interviewer was black, because she was in fact white. Why did the roommate assume the interviewer was black? What descriptors provided symbolic cues for blackness? Even when race is not mentioned the ideological processes continue.

Ideological Constructions of Whiteness

In this quote from David in *The Color of Fear* he tries to neutralize the meaning of whiteness by suggesting that a color is a color when it comes to race. *"What is the big deal about color? I'm a color, I'm white. That's a color."* Colorblind ideology prohibits any frank discussions that expose the true meaning of whiteness; such talk is counter-hegemonic. It is, however, acceptable to criticize minorities, the underprivileged, at-risk populations, the disadvantaged, and even the poor. But talking about those who are "overprivileged" is taboo. Although there is a gag order on discussions which expose white privilege as unnatural rather than natural, not to discuss it leaves no room to question and critique the role, function, and form of white privilege which is at the heart of all racial projects.

Though David from *The Color of Fear* thinks that race is simply about phenotypes or skin color and that all races are equal, "I'm a color, you're a color," we are reminded by critical race theorist Cheryl Harris that the essential meaning of whiteness is its ability to subordinate. Inherent in the concept of being white was the right to own or hold whiteness to the exclusion and subordination of blacks. Because identity is continuously being constituted through social interactions, the assigned political, economic, and social inferiority of blacks necessarily shaped white identity (Harris 1995, 283).

- *Pro-whiteness as a racial ideology*

  Thus hegemony and all of its manifestations are designed to protect and preserve the privileges accorded to whiteness, and to continually reproduce racial group identity as an instrument of exclusion and exploitation (Carter 1997, 200). Ideologies frame racial discourse and rationalize the racial order; whether groups are ranked as good, bad, right or wrong, trustworthy, or simply unworthy is determined by ideology. Pro-white ideology is *"the conscious and unconscious conviction that white Euro-American cultural patterns and practices, as reflected in values language, belief systems, interpersonal styles, behavior patterns, political, social roles, economic, music, art, religious tenets, and so forth, are superior to those of other visible racial/ethnic groups"* (Carter 1997, 200). Because these assumptions are not associated with anti-group sentiments they can easily conceal racial biases which promote white privilege. Such attitudes cannot be seen as neutral because they rank cultural patterns, practices, and values of other groups based on how closely the approximate those of the privileged class (Jewell 1993, 6).

- *Ideological hegemony positions whites as "just people" while reinforcing nonwhites as the "racialized other."*

A significant point about pro-white ideologies is how they construct whites as normal and neutral, and position whites and their interests as superior to all others. As whites control the production of ideas they have the ability to rank their projects above all others using criteria seemingly unrelated to their race. They control the dissemination and ranking of knowledge. For example the "great works" in literature, philosophy, and the arts are by and large the work of white men. Though these works are not specified according to race and gender or referred to as "white literature," for example, they have the ability to reiterate the history of whites in manners which appear to be racially neutral. Thus whiteness is often interchangeable with values of Americaness. Through this process the works of whites are represented as those most worthy of adopting and studying and are considered essential knowledge for anyone considered an educated person.

Pro-white ideologies elevate the status of whites and their projects, practices, and patterns as superior to others. Ideologies of whiteness mask the racialization of whites and position them instead as just people. This allows benefits that accrue to them as a result of race to be seen instead as the consequences of individual merit, circumstance or even coincidence. Take, for example, the recent court case of former CEO executive Andrew Fastow. Mr. Fastow and his wife have been sentenced to serve time in prison. But the courts are currently negotiating an arrangement whereby the Fastows will not have to be incarcerated at the same time in order that their children will not be displaced from both parents. This is certainly an example of how race intersects with class to produce outcomes consistent with values associated with whiteness. In this case the obvious conclusion is the concern the courts have for the well-being of the children of convicted felons—as long as they are white and wealthy.

• *Many whites claim that "whiteness" does not bring unearned privileges.*
Peggy McIntosh in her article *White Privilege Male Privilege* describes the privileges that accrue to whiteness as an invisible knapsack of unearned privilege (Hurtado and Stewart 1997, 305). Most whites deny that privileges accrue to them because they are white and argue instead *that whatever privileges are accorded to whiteness are earned through merit because whites, as a group, perform better than people of color in all kinds of arenas* (Hurtado and Stewart 1997, 301). As whites often see their success in the context of "merit" they have a tendency to assume that when blacks do well that it is because of some type of preferential treatment.

The ability of ideological constructions to de-link whites from race ideologies allows whites to not see themselves as a group in general but rather as individuals. This individual versus group identity contributes to their tendency to deny that they benefit from any group privilege. Acknowledgement of the privileges that accrue to whiteness is more evident when there is a threat that these privileges will be lost. It is when group privileges are threatened that whites are more likely to mobilize to protect their group status, as in the peculiar construction of "reverse discrimination strategies." "It is in the process of being dislocated and making sense of that dislocation that whites [respondents] begin to fully acknowledge the privileges they previously denied whiteness brought them" (Hurtado and Stewart 1997, 301).

Since whites benefit from ideological representations of merit and neutrality, even the most deviant whites, benefit from the positive ideological constructions of their group. Group membership has a much different consequence for blacks. Blacks as a group and as individuals are "foreshadowed by omnipresent racial signs and symbols that have no meaning other than pressing them to the lowest level of the racial hierarchy" (T. Morrison, as cited in hooks 1995, 3).

A few years back *Sixty Minutes* did a piece on Ruth Simmons who had just been appointed as the first African American president of Brown University, one of our nation's premier institutions of higher education. During the interview Dr. Simmons described an incident in which she was racially profiled in a department store for shoplifting. Such stories recounted by the most renowned African Americans are a reminder that ideological constructions problematize all individuals within the racialized group. Therefore all blacks must negotiate negative racial constructions. Even the most accomplished blacks are judged first by ideological assumptions and must prove that they are an exception to the rule.

Racial ideologies that explain juxtaposing definitions of whiteness and blackness promote a hyper-consciousness of race which has existed since slavery. Colorblind framework requires that whiteness be positively representative of the human race. In this way whites are neutralized and their privileges are seen to accrue to them as individuals not as a racial group, while simultaneous depictions of blacks draw direct and negative connotations of race. But ideologies of race, no matter how they are constructed, are essential to the survival of all modern race projects.

4. How Racism Is Operationalized within Institutions

The consequences of colorblindness and color-conscious ideologies are reflected in the policies and practices of all social institutions and organizations because individuals create and apply standards and procedures within institutions that reproduce racist outcomes (Carter 1997, 200). This means that all individuals have been socialized to interpret, understand, and react to race in ways which are insidious and operate to keep the color line intact. To the extent that institutional practices emulate those of broader society, individuals can reenact them with little or no awareness. Such transactions become an integral part of institutional culture, especially when compliance is enforced from the top. For example, most school cultures reflect social and academic arrangements based on race (as well as gender and social class). What would happen in a school in which the majority of the students who are in detention, expelled or labeled with emotional disorders were disproportionately white instead of black and if statuses typically reserved for white students such as "outstanding student of the month" were awarded as frequently to black students? Let's assume that this shift not arbitrarily, but accurately, reflects student behavior and performance. The extent to which these changes violate school culture is likely to ruffle feathers even though the changes are fair and just. Thus any teacher or school administrator trying to institute social justice reforms will be scrutinized and reminded often indirectly of the racial practices which need to be adhered to. Policies and practices which seem neutral to race, such as school disciplinary policies and procedures, can be applied and interpreted in ways which appear rational but reproduce racialized outcomes. Individuals who breach these implicit agreements may themselves be seen as the problem.

Institutional Racism Absolves Individuals of Personal Accountability

A teacher involved in a scenario similar to the one described above may need to learn to practice aversive racism so she can abide by prescribed and accepted school culture. By learning how to "not notice race," individuals can participate in routine race practices under the guise of "just following the rules" and feel no personal culpability for decisions which may in fact be based on race. Because racism is de-linked from government mandates, individuals and society in general can appear to be neutral to race while operationalizing racism as part of everyday social and public life.

Colorblind culture requires more or less the cooperation of every individual. Even those disadvantaged by such systems are pressed into service unwittingly to protect the very system that results in disadvantages to them. Individuals ratify and replicate social arrangements of race in every major social institution. Whether the individuals in these institutions are members of the dominant group is irrelevant to the fact that their ability to do their jobs as teachers, counselors, social workers, politicians, or correctional officers are linked to their ability to uphold the wishes of the dominant group; thus many assimilate, acculturate, and embrace the dominant values upon which criteria for good employees is based. In this way we all become agents of a raced, gendered, and classed system that we are taught to view as neutral or "professional" and void of power relations.

The practices by which individuals operate must comply with value systems which emerge from the cultures of those in charge. The individual-institutional relationship results in the reproduction of social arrangements in the broader society. The attitudes which reproduce these arrangements in all institutions reflect the tension between values of equality and allegiance to a racial order within which noncompliance will be punished. Individuals will apply their interpretation of race and gender in every private and public interaction unless they consciously and intentionally work against it. Ideological belief systems infused into laws, customs, and social practices produce intentional and unintentional race and gender inequalities (Cameron Wedding 2003, 63).

This final section examines the role of institutions as an important element in the formulation of new racism. The relationship of institutions to racism can be inadvertent and unwitting, as described above, or it can reflect the utilization of race as a tool or conduit to manipulate social, political, and economic objectives. The first example describes the "aversive" form of institutional racism or the tendency for institutions like government and education or business which, though they have strong opposition to racism (at least in theory), can still practice racism in subtle and indiscriminate ways.

Practices of Aversive Racism within Institutions

This is clearly demonstrated in the selective application of institutional policies in ways that produce differential outcomes. All organizations, businesses, and social institutions have rules which can be applied or implemented arbitrarily. When rules designed to control and regulate are disproportionately enforced for members of certain groups, such actions can easily be defended as "simply following policy." A good example of this is consumer racism. Most stores have policies that require sales clerks to check identification prior to completing a credit card or check transaction. This policy is obviously intended to protect against fraud. In recent years the concern about identity theft has resulted in salesclerks having less discretion in whether or for whom they will check identification, but prior to this, it was commonplace for identification to only be checked for people whose race (people of color) or demeanor (whites differentiated by class or behavior) would remind the salesclerks of the reason for which such policies were in place. The occasional but not systematic surveillance of whites allows for the possibility that such practices can be defended against charges of racism.

- *Subtle and selective applications of institutional policies and procedures exact an emotional cost for racism and a financial cost as well.*

  In October 2003 an article in the Sacramento Bee reported that African Americans paid on average more than 2.5 times the amount in "subjective markup" compared with white buyers—$656 versus $244. The report cited one case in which a black consumer paid an actual $12,425 markup on a 60-month loan with $23,530 financed, or an overall markup of 17.46%.

- *Aversive racism is essential to the enforcement of state laws which mandate colorblindness.*

  Can the state deliver on its promise not to discriminate on the basis of race or gender? In 1996, Proposition 209, also known as The California Civil Rights Initiative, eliminated affirmative action in California. The law reads that *"The state shall not discriminate against, or grant preferential treatment to any individual or group on the basis of race, sex, color, ethnicity, or national origin in the operation of public employment, public education or public contracting."* If more positive or neutral assumptions accrue to whites, is it possible for race not to be a consideration in hiring and employment? Even though the state has outlawed discrimination on the basis of race and gender, can such a law really be enforced? Who is the State? The individuals who are "agents" of the State bring with them their own brand of racial constructions. They engage in racial politics on a daily basis. How do we shift from utilizing race to inform our daily decision making, both ordinary and significant, to colorblindness? How can we avoid being influenced by hegemony that positively positions whites as superior and allows their whiteness to be encoded as "just people"? In a job interview if the word race is never uttered, is it possible that people don't notice race? Moreover, is it possible that positive racial constructions of whites or negative racial constructions of blacks that everyone in society is predisposed to will not play a role in the way the candidate is perceived by the "State"? Is it possible to see skin color detached from any connotative meaning?

Can any one of us really not notice race or do we just pretend? Can we leave our racial biases at the door or do they influence our perceptions about who we are the most comfortable with, who we feel we have the most in common with, who we feel the most familiar to, and ultimately who we perceive as the "most qualified person"? Is the determination of the "most qualified" a purely objective decision or do these subjective considerations consciously or unconsciously come into play? Even though it is against the law our interpretations and internalization of racial constructions can influence our overall decision making. In this hegemonic culture there is no such thing as racial neutrality or colorblindness. Purely objective perceptions about the most qualified person for the job cannot occur unless we dismantle the ideological constructions which correlate superiority and inferiority paradigms to race.

Institutional racism occurs as a result of law, practices, or "policies" which can be applied arbitrarily. But even when they are applied evenly the consequences, negative or positive, can have a differential effect according to where people are positioned economically. Because people of color are disproportionately poor, social polices can have a disparate (though sometimes indirect) impact on them because they do not have the personal means to fill in the economic gap between public and private resources.

Most public policy decisions, particularly those which lead to budgetary shortfalls in school funding, such as preschool education or other social services programs that are known to impact educational achievement, will result in negative social and economic consequences for these groups.

Other groups may not be disadvantaged by the exact same policy because they can resort to other economic options. When kids lag behind academically and ultimately drop out and are ill-prepared to go on to college we often see it as a failing of the race rather than a failure of social policy.

Secondly, because public policies may have a neutral effect on some groups but not others, these policies can be argued as being neutral to race. Arguments pointing at long-term consequences are often ignored until the damage has already been done. Such policies like Proposition 209 that make it illegal to consider race in hiring and education make it permissible for people to ignore racial outcomes and attribute them to other factors even when the policies are obviously flawed. Initiatives such as Proposition 54 which would outlaw data collection on race would make the documentation of such disparities impossible. Bias masked by institutional policies protects against personal culpability—as even the most racist individuals can argue—"that's not racism, we're just following the rules."

A simple analysis of California's unprecedented budget cuts in education reveals how such cuts may systematically produce unintended (and possibly intended) racial consequences. Linking the consequences of these cuts to institutional racism is problematic because the effects will occur over time and may be difficult to verify. But as discussed earlier, if these budget cuts "produce gross and identifiable disparities [in areas such as drop-out rates, academic achievement, and college-going rates] on the basis of racial group membership then what is observed is institutional racism" (Carter 1997, 200).

First to Worst (2004), a documentary on California's public school system, presented a very bleak picture of a school system beset with problems. Once the nation's premier educational system, California now hovers at the bottom. Despite the centralized school funding system, dramatic inconsistencies in the quality of schools with stark racial disparities are unmistakable. Structural barriers such as spending caps imposed by Proposition 13 have created conditions (like those found in third world countries) such as overcrowding, leaking roofs, malfunctioning plumbing, dirty bathrooms, and dirty floors, in addition to having

no counselors, nurses or librarians, credentialed teachers or textbooks. It is important to point out that even the wealthiest schools face obstacles. However, individual wealth and access, family contributions, extensive fundraising, and the ability to get the bond measures needed to increase tax revenues have resulted in striking dissimilarities between the wealthier districts which are mostly white and poorer districts which are disproportionately people of color. The wealthier schools are representative of what California's schools should look like. They have adequate levels of staffing including qualified and credentialed teachers, nurses, librarians, resources such as computer labs, music and art programs, textbooks, and clean bathrooms with functioning plumbing.

It is highly predictable that the poorer schools with grossly inadequate resources are more likely to be low-performing schools and as a result will represent a smaller proportion of the college bound students compared to schools augmented with private financing. Students from low-performing schools will face a series of institutional barriers that will directly impact their adult occupational options. With lower test scores coming out of the sixth grade, they will be ineligible (in most cases) for college prep courses in high school. Consequently, the chances of them getting admitted to a four-year college or even attending a community college directly out of high school, or graduating from college even later in life will be greatly diminished. While the causal relationship between public school funding and institutional racism may be difficult to measure, it is a safe bet that it will add to the burgeoning level of racial disproportionality in every aspect of social life.

Intentional Use of Racism as a Tool to Effect Institutional/Government Objectives

The second goal of this section is to look at institutional racism, not according to how race is obscured by institutional policies and practices in ways that might be considered inadvertent or unintentional, but rather the intentional use of race as a tool to rationalize and manipulate social outcomes. Ideologies of race inscribe and encode whole systems of meanings and assumptions.

Ideologies which define race symbolize meanings which even if unstated are connoted in the words black, white, Mexican, Asian, etc. These words provide a context for understanding individuals according to their group membership in ways which are implicitly understood.

This chapter has mentioned several times the commonsense perception of blacks as criminals and drug addicts. The media's reinforcements of these connections allow them to become so ingrained that the link between blacks and drugs, either directly or by insinuation, is just a given. Blacks represent approximately 15% of drug users but 50% of network news stories on drugs focus on African Americans (Parenti 1993, 11). Perhaps this can explain how in Tulia, Texas, 13% of the adult African American community was arrested for drug sales in a town of 5,000 people, without a single shred of evidence. In this example we can see how ideologies as information systems can be useful to organizations and government in assisting them in meeting their economic and political agenda.

In 1999 an undercover officer named Thomas Coleman identified mothers, fathers, and grandparents—all from the same neighborhood, all black, and all of whom, according to Coleman, sold him drugs. These people, rounded up in the middle of the night, were taken into custody in front of the media who had been alerted that the bust would be taking place. Many were hardly dressed, many were in their pajamas. "So what's the big deal?" you might ask, "These people must have done something wrong." There was no proof or a shred of material evidence corroborating the allegations made by Coleman; no drug paraphernalia, no money (in fact one defendant at the time of her alleged drug sale was in a neighboring town withdrawing $8.00 from a bank), no weapons, or any evidence of drug dealing. Thomas Coleman, who himself was in trouble with the law, offered no video, eye witness testimonies, or fingerprint evidence. He named people who at the time of the alleged drug transaction were later proven to have been 50 miles away, or whose physical descriptions did not match those in his report. In one case he described one defendant as a tall black man with bushy hair. This man, in fact, was 5'7" and bald.

A total of 46 residents were convicted by all-white juries of drug sales and given from 20 to 341 year sentences. The first trial resulted in the conviction of 60-year-old Joe Welton Moore who was sentenced to 90 years in prison. Mr. Moore, labeled a "drug king pin," had lived in a one room shack all of his life.

To say that this was a miscarriage of justice is an understatement. Eventually, every single one of these convictions was thrown out, but only after some of the defendants had served more than three years of what would have been life sentences for crimes they did not commit. The obvious question is how Mr. Coleman was able to pass off such an unbelievable travesty of justice to the police, the judge, the jury, and the community without someone asking, "What the heck is going on?"

The Panhandle Regional Narcotics Trafficking Task Force that was handing out money to fight drugs in rural communities, and the town, stood to gain a lot of money from these convictions. The more arrests and convictions, the more money the town would get the following year to be used in any way it saw fit. Blacks were an easy target. Forty-six black people being arrested and convicted for sale of drugs in one small town with absolutely no corroborating evidence is mind-boggling unless you understand the function of ideologies in constructing guilt. This does not mean that everyone in the town was on the take. It just means that ideologies can make even the most implausible circumstances plausible, especially when people are not required to be intentional and thoughtful about race and racism (*Sixty Minutes*, Tulia Texas, 2004).

The misapplication of laws in ways that distort legal outcomes can only be construed as racist. Take, for example, the case of Marcus Dixon who was convicted of aggravated child molestation for having consensual sex with a minor, his high school classmate (act4justice.com). Marcus, who is black, was eighteen and his then girlfriend, who is white, was three months away from her sixteenth birthday at the time they had sex. Of course, laws regulating sexual relationships between an "adult" and a "minor" are on the books for some very good reasons but the statute used to convict Marcus had never been applied to consensual sex between two teenagers with less than three years age difference until this case. Marcus, who had never been in trouble with the law, had been offered a scholarship to Vanderbilt University but instead faces ten years behind bars. Did race play a role in his conviction? Even if it was decided that "the law is the law" and the law is colorblind, are there other ways to punish this offense? Was justice really served?

Social institutions, such as education, social welfare, the criminal justice system, and even government agencies reproduce social arrangements based on race and gender because the individuals who staff and run these institutions bring to them a consciousness informed by ideological belief systems that rationalize racial disparities. Pervasive ideological constructions of race create preconditions for how individuals are perceived and treated. When institutional arrangements mirror those of broader society they can be seen as normal and inevitable outcomes (Cameron Wedding 2003, 66). Whether racism is aversive or intentional individuals can participate in policy decisions under the cover of "just following the rules." Strict application of the law for some and not for others allows racist practices to go unnoticed.

In contemporary society we have rendered invisible the ideological and structural dynamics that determine racial outcomes. The relative absence of old forms of discrimination such as racial epithets, segregated housing, cross burnings, etc., is proof enough for some that racism no longer exists. This allows us to continue to debate the legitimacy of racism even though its persistence is irrefutably evident in patterns of racial disproportionality found in every aspect of social life. The way new racism is structured makes it easy for some people to ignore. This is precisely why modern race projects are so successful. Our society is very sophisticated in how it constructs, defines, and practices racism, making new racism and its oblique and disguised set of values, practices, policies, and laws as effective in regulating the color line as were race regimes of the past.

References

Cameron Wedding, R. 2003. Colorblindness: Challenging the discourse of contemporary U.S. racism. In *Readings in race, class, and gender,* edited by R. Cameron Wedding, E. Vega, and G. Mark. Iowa: Kendall/Hunt Publishing.

Carter, R. T. 1997. Expressions of racial identity. In *Off white: Readings on race, power and society,* edited by M. Fine, L. Weis, L. Powell, and L. Mun Wong. Great Britain: Routledge Press.

Civil Rights Coalition and "No on 209 Campaign." N.d. *Training manual: No on 209.* Los Angeles, CA: Author.

Collins, P. H. 1998. *Fighting words: Black women and the search for justice.* New York: The News Press.

Color of Fear. 1994. Video, directed by Lee Wah, produced by Lee Wah and Monty Hunter. Berkeley, CA: Stir-Fry Productions.

Crenshaw, K. W. 1998. Color Blindness, history, and the law. In *The house that race built,* edited by W. Lubiano. New York: Vintage Books.

Edmon, L. 1999. Providing access to success. *Los Angeles County Bar Association: President's Page.* Retrieved March 4, 2004, from http:www.lacba.org/lalawyer/apr99/president/ html.

Fight injustice: Save Marcus Dixon. 2004. *http://www.act4justice.com.*

Gaertner, S. L. 1997. Does white racism necessarily mean anti-blackness: Aversive racism and pro-whiteness. In *Off white: Readings on race, power and society,* edited by M. Fine, L. Weis, L. Powell, and L. Mun Wong. Great Britain: Routledge Press.

Guinier, L. 2002. *The miner's canary: Enlisting race, resisting power, transforming democracy.* Cambridge: Harvard University Press.

Harris, C. 1995. Whiteness as property. In *Critical race theory,* edited by K. Crenshaw, N. Gotanda, G. Peller, and K. Thomas. New York: New York Press.

hooks, b. 1994. *Teaching to transgress.* New York: Routledge Press.

Hurtado, A., and Stewart, A. 1997. Through the looking glass: Implications of studying whiteness for feminist methods. In *Off white: Readings on race, power and society,* edited by M. Fine, L. Weis, L. Powell, and L. Mun Wong. Great Britain: Routledge Press.

Jewell, K. S. 1993. *From mammy to Miss America and beyond.* New York: Routledge Press.

Johnson, A. 1997. *The gender knot: Unraveling our patriarchal legacy.* Philadelphia: Temple University Press.

Moore, M. 2003. Kill whitey. In *Readings in race, class, and gender,* edited by R. Cameron Wedding, E. Vega, and G. Mark. Iowa: Kendall/Hunt Publishing.

Neubeck, K. 2002. Attacking welfare racism/honoring poor people's human rights. In *Lost ground*, edited by R. Albelda and A. Withorn. Cambridge Mass: South End Press.

Omi, Michael and Howard Winant, ed. *Racial formations in the United States from the 1960s to the 1990s*, 2nd ed. New York: Routledge Press, 1994.

Parenti, Michael. 1993. *Inventing reality: The politics of news media*. 2nd ed. New York: St. Martins Press.

Takaki, Ronald. 1990. *Iron cages: Race and culture in 19th century America*. New York: Oxford University Press.

Winant, Howard. 1999. *Racial democracy and racial identity: Comparing the United States and Brazil*, ed. Michael Hanchard. Durham, NC: Duke University Press.

I Doubt, Therefore African Philosophy Exists

Mogobe B. Ramose

ABSTRACT

In this essay the question whether or not African philosophy exists is considered through an examination of the meaning of doubt. In St. Augustine and Descartes the basic presupposition with regard to doubt is the indubitable certainty that the doubting subject must exist before there can be any doubt at all. By parity of reasoning, African philosophy must first exist before it can doubt its own existence or be doubted by another. The origin and meaning of the term "Africa" is then examined. This culminates in the thesis that, once the indigenous conquered peoples of the continent choose to retain the term "Africa," then they are entitled to give content and meaning to it.

Introduction

In the search for knowledge and its justification Augustine, "the great African Doctor" (Copleston, 1962:55) is said to have argued that one cannot doubt if one does not accept that one exists in the first place. Doubting then is impossible without at the same time acknowledging that the one who doubts, recognizes himself or herself as existing. "In this way St. Augustine anticipates Descartes: *Si fallor, sum*" (Gilson, 1955:75). Augustine here is recognized as "the great African Doctor" that is, an African by origin even though his philosophy is presented mainly as an integral part of Western philosophy. In this sense Augustine is an African but does not, as presented, espouse African philosophy. Instead, he anticipates the methodic doubt of Descartes, yet another figure in Western philosophy. Descartes's *si fallor, sum* (if I doubt, then I am or exist) echoes not only Augustine as a figure in Western philosophy but it also evokes, albeit dimly, the memory of Augustine as an African. Indeed when later on the question of African philosophy arose, that is, can there or is there an African philosophy, Augustine

"I Doubt, Therefore African Philosophy Exists" by M.B. Ramose in *South African Journal of Philosophy*, Vol. 22, No. 2, pp. 113–127(2003). Reprinted by permission.

was named, among others, to prove the existence of African philosophy (Osuagwu, 2001:83–85). This may be construed as the use of Augustine's methodic doubt to prove both the existence and the philosophy of Africans. This then is the meaning of "I doubt, therefore Africa exists."

For a very long time the question of African philosophy focused more on "philosophy" and much less, to put it mildly, on "African." The meaning of African was taken for granted. It is the purpose of this essay to focus more on the meaning of "Africa/African" with particular reference to the expression. "African philosophy." Our argument in this connection is that the appellation "African" is by no means an innocent geographical designation. There is an historical meaning of the term "African." This suppressed or ignored meaning is still at the core of the question of "African philosophy." In support of this argument we will focus on specific texts from South Africa that belong to "African philosophy."

The Meaning of the Term "Africa"

The geographic meaning of Africa is widely accepted as settled. However, questions and problems arise as soon as expressions such as "Arab

Africa," "Mahgreb Africa" or "sub-Saharan Africa" are used. These expressions are the manifestations of the historical meaning of Africa. For example, one may ask: does "Arab Africa" mean that the Arabs have an unquestionable title to a specific portion of the territory of Africa? When and how did they acquire such a title? If we assume that the Sahara desert is not the natural birthmark of Africa as a territory, is there some justification in the conjecture that Arabs and sub-Saharan African peoples lived close to one another in the distant past? Do existing studies in natural history, linguistics, archeology and philosophy—to name but a few—lend some credence to this assumption? The intention here is not to even attempt to answer these questions. Rather it is to suggest that the meaning of the term Africa may not be taken for granted. Our problem though is precisely that the geographic meaning is generally taken so much for granted that it seems idle and futile to problematise the term "Africa." Our contention is that it is scientifically legitimate to problematise the term. Surely, the name "Africa" is much more than a matter of etymological inquiry. It is also a question of history, of interaction among human beings, that is, why, how and when did the continent receive the name "Africa?"

With regard to the historical meaning we read that: "In antiquity, the Greeks are said to have called the continent Libya and the Romans Africa, perhaps from the Latin *aprica* (sunny), or the Greek *aphrike* (without cold). The name Africa, however, was chiefly applied to the northern coast of the continent, which was in effect regarded as a southern extension of Europe. The Romans, who for a time ruled the North African coast, are also said to have called the area south of their settlements, Afriga, or the Land of the Afrigs—the name of a Berber community south of Carthage. Another explanation occasionally offered is that the name applied to a productive region of what is now Tunisia and meant Ears of Corn. The work Ifriqiyah is apparently the Arabic transliteration of Africa" (Encyclopaedia Britannica, 1974:117).

From the above citation we note that: the Mediterranean sea provided a platform for cultural interaction between and among the Romans and the Greeks and, the peoples of what was later to be called north Africa. It was also the platform for cultural interaction between and among the Romans and the Greeks, the peoples of "north Africa" and the Arabs. It is in the course of this cultural interaction in the Mediterranean cultural space that the name "Africa" emerged. It referred to the north coast of the continent only and thus not to the whole continent. In terms of the interaction and relations between the Greeks and the Romans on the one hand and the peoples of "north Africa" on the other it is clear that the name "Africa" is a description of the Greek and Roman experience, respectively, of the climate of the particular region. It does not directly and immediately refer to the inhabitants of this region and their philosophy. It is a description based upon the Roman conquest of "north Africa." It is therefore reasonable to infer that the name Africa does not arise from the indigenous conquered inhabitants of the region, let alone the whole continent.

In the course of time this description became part of the everyday vocabulary of the peoples of southern Europe. As the Roman Empire expanded so was the description spread to other parts of Western Europe including the United Kingdom. Talk of "Africa" also extended from the "north coast" to the entire continent. The unjust wars of colonization were thus focused on "Africa" the "sunny," "without cold" continent. Like the Roman conquest of "north Africa," the colonial conquest of other parts of "Africa" also followed the logic of ignoring the culture and philosophies of the conquered. The will to ignore the philosophies of the various inhabitants located in different parts of the continent was strengthened by adherence to the description of the climate of the continent. This made it possible to speak of Africa as if it comprised of only one ethnic group of people having a single common culture. That this is one of the continuing problems concerning the identity of "Africa" is exemplified by the fact that in most cases, at independence African countries change their names, for example, into Namibia, Tanzania or Zimbabwe. The change of name is significant in that it may be compared to a child who has lived for a long time with foster parents who deliberately and systematically concealed the fact that they were not the biological parents of the child. Surely, when the child ultimately discovers its biological parents its relationship with the foster parents will change for better or worse. The same is true with regard to its relationship with its newly discovered biological parents.

Furthermore, the term "Africa," applied to the entire continent, could have had a different significance if the "Arigs" were to be held responsible for its reference to the entire continent. Against this background the discovery that "Africa" is not only a description by an outsider but also an imposition by the same outsider will generate many reactions. One of the reactions is that it is rather funny that the study of "African" philosophy simply means the study of "sunny" or solar philosophy! No doubt anyone interested in the impact of a climate "without cold" upon the philosophy of a people living under such a climate may propound a theory about that. But this is not the same thing as the philosophy expressed by the peoples of such a climate in their own right. In other words, it is one thing to talk about the philosophy of the Bantu, the San or the Akan peoples and quite another to theorize on solar philosophy. This point is not idle since some of the critics of "African" philosophy aver that it is impossible to speak of such a philosophy precisely because Africa comprises of multiple and diverse ethnic groups. Of course, the critics take the meaning of the term "Africa" for granted whereas we in this instance do not.

The term "Africa" speaks more to the West European historical experience with the peoples of the continent and much less to the experience of the peoples of the continent with regard to their own self-understanding. In other words, the history of "Africa" is mainly the history of West European experience of "Africa" and only incidentally is it the story of the peoples of the continent about themselves. No wonder then that the resurgence of "African philosophy" occurs only after the attainment of independence by various countries in the continent. While some scholars regard the era of decolonisation as the opportunity to reassert continuity between the past and the present philosophies of the various peoples of the continent others consider decolonisation as the landmark underlining the beginning of "African philosophy": meaning that the various peoples of the continent may now give expression to their own philosophies. From this point of view it makes even better sense to speak of certain aspects of Bantu philosophy in Rwanda, (Kagame, 1955) Zimbabwe (Samkange, 1980) or South Africa. In

short, particularity must be accorded precedence over universality with regard to talk about "African philosophy." This is necessitated by the fact that experience is the basis for philosophy. But experience is always bound to time and space in the first place (Jimoh, 1999, 31–37). This is the particularist dimension from which philosophy starts. However, the particularity of experience does not preclude the possibility that a similar, as opposed to identical, experience may occur elsewhere. Questions pertaining to such experiences, the answers to such questions as well as the insights gained illustrate that particularity does not by definition or necessity exclude the possibility for universality. Osuagwu underlines this reasoning through his definition of African philosophy

> as scientific philosophy scientifically done the African way, by African authors in Africa on African issues within the African context of time and space to generate African doctrines. . . . In and by these formal scientific factors, we seek, on the one hand, for the genuine philosophicality of African philosophy, and on the other hand, for its authentic scientific Africanity. These scientific criteria make African philosophy to bear the dual essential characters of universality and particularity. By its philosophicality, African philosophy is a universal expression, determination, order, mission, vocation and destination. By its Africanity, it is a particular, that is to say, a particular reflection, concentration, concretization, contextualization, experience, identification and differentiation of the philosophic, scientific universal. . . . In being African, philosophy does not search for meaning or truth which is exclusively African, which belongs to or is valid for Africans only. Because African philosophy is an objective science, it cannot but seek for the scientific universal in the particular African natural/cultural issues (Osuagwu, 2001:26–29).

Yet another scholar argues the same point thus:

> An emerging African philosophical tradition needs to be rooted in, and also to be nourished within, the context of the African culture, history and the experience of the people. In fact, the raw materials of any tradition of philosophy are to be found in the totality of the

practitioners' own culture and life experience. For this reason, the search for an African philosophy has to be home-based and conducted from within the African experience. . . . However, despite these cultural specifics, it seems obvious, on grounds that blend the a priori with the empirical, that there are certain universals which cut across all human cultures. Indeed, to say that a human is a rational being is to imply that humankind as a whole shares in common certain features whose absence in a given group raises the question as to whether such a group is human by definition (Sogolo, 1993:xiv–xv).

Yet, it is precisely reason that has been denied and continues to be denied the "African" thereby putting into question the humanity of the "African" (Ramose, 2002:1–32). The thesis underlying this denial is that because the "African" is defective in its ontology, that is, a being without reason, it cannot qualify as a human being. Following upon this is the conclusion that the "African" cannot therefore have a philosophy. (Masolo, 1994:1) This is the meaning of the question posed by those coming from outside the continent and continue to experience it as "without cold" or "sunny." Their perennial question, posed with regard to Latin America as well, (Bondy, 1986: 240–243) is: "can there be or, is there an African philosophy?" Let us take one example to illustrate this denial of "reason" to the inhabitants of the continent.

From volume six of the Encyclopaedia Britannica under the rubric 'history of Egypt' we read: "The Egyptians were a practical people, and they reveal through the products of their arts and crafts their particular genius. In classical times these early Egyptians were also credited by the Greeks with great knowledge and wisdom; but the evidence provided by Egyptian writings does not support this Greek opinion. It is probable that Greek travellers in Egypt, impressed by the grandeur and antiquity of the monuments of the land and misled by the accounts of past ages given to them by their priestly guides, grossly misinterpreted the evidence and jumped to unwarranted conclusions. Unlike the Greeks, the Egyptians were not philosophically inclined, intellectually inquisitive, or prone to theorizing . . ." (Encyclopaedia Britannica, 1974:461). First, the author

here contradicts "Greek opinion" on the facts which s/he does not care to bring to light except to refer to them vaguely as "Egyptian writings." Second, it was not only "Greek travellers" who visited and sojourned in Egypt. Aristotle, by his own admission, (Metaphysics, 1.1, 981 b 14–24) acknowledged the Egyptian origin of the philosophical sciences of mathematics and astronomy. Apparently, it is testimony like this which the author of the entry cited either ignores deliberately or denies. S/he is by no means alone in this. Even Copleston, a towering figure in the history of Western philosophy, has shown similar disregard and implicit denial of first-hand testimony from the ancient Greeks. Commenting on this, Osuagwu argues thus: "Copleston totally rejects a historical and scientific African philosophy of ancient Black Egypt and its subsequent influence on and relation with early Greek philosophy. F.C. Copleston (1907–1985), an American Catholic clergyman, is a typical 20th century European representative of the view which denies and severs all historical philosophical links of ancient Egypt with Greece and Rome. Furthermore, Copleston would not accept even the personally documented testimonies of the ancient Greek philosophers. . . . If Copleston ignores the personal and firsthand literary testimonies of ancient Greek philosophers, he would certainly be less ready to accept the secondary reports of later past authors like Herodotus . . ." (Osuagwu, 1999:87, 94–96) It goes without saying that the author of the entry just cited falls within the same category as Copleston. The point about both the entry in the Encyclopaedia Britannica and Copleston's rejection, denial, disregard or even misinterpretation of ancient Black Egypt is to arrogate philosophy and reason exclusively to the West. It is precisely this will to appropriation which impels the author of the entry into the Encyclopaedia Britannica to assign "wisdom" but not thought or reason to ancient Black Egypt. It is the same will to the appropriation of reason which permits the author to give himself/herself the licence to ascribe, later in the same paragraph of the above citation, "magic" to the body of knowledge of ancient Black Egypt. This will to appropriate reason as the exclusive quality and right of the West European is one of the robust pillars of Western philosophy. Taking the cue from Aristotle's definition of the human being as "a rational animal," it inspired the philosophy of colonization and has survived decolonisation. In effect, it is alive in our time although in somewhat more subtle manifestations.

Two crucial points may be extracted from the arguments of Osuagwu and Sodipo cited above. For these two and very many "African" philosophers, the critical question in "African philosophy" pertains to the meaning of "philosophy." The meaning of the term African is at best neglected though in fact it is not considered at all. Yet, a consideration of this term, as we have done above, shows that it too requires the close attention and scrutiny of the indigenous conquered inhabitants of the continent. It has emerged in the course of our considerations above that the term "African" is of Greek and Roman origin. It does not arise from the indigenous conquered inhabitants of the continent. The term does not describe or define the identity of the "African" as this is ignored by the unswerving focus upon the climate rather than the peoples living under it. The question then is this: since the term "African" is silent on the identity of the indigenous conquered peoples of the continent, why does it seem to be accepted as if it is an adequate or reasonable description of their identity? Our answer to this question is that the term "African" has been foisted onto the indigenous conquered peoples of the continent. Instead of being a reasonable, fair and adequate description of the conquered peoples it became the bearer of misrepresentation, disfiguration and distortion of the identities of the conquered peoples. In accepting this term the latter at the same time recognize the ethical-political duty to put the record straight by assuring that they will speak for themselves in their own right. They will give a description of themselves and provide their own definition of themselves even if they might need the conqueror or the other as their mirror. The post-colonial condition throughout the continent provides the opportunity for this. On this basis it may not be necessary to abolish the term Africa. Instead, we may declare confidently that "I doubt, therefore African philosophy exists." This methodic doubt thesis on African philosophy is the call for the reconstruction of the history of Africa in general, and the history of African philosophy in particular (Diop, 1974). It is the ethical-political imperative to reaffirm and

assert the humanity and the dignity of the African peoples, that is, the indigenous peoples conquered in the unjust wars of colonization. It is the inauguration of a specific period in the history and politics of Africa. It is not the period of the "African Renaissance" (Oladipo, 1999:11–13), because this is clothing African philosophy in Western robes (Ramose, 2000:47–63). Furthermore, it is an implicit refusal to be free from Western tutelage. As such the "African Renaissance" is contrary to one of the basic tenets of "I doubt, therefore African philosophy exists" namely, the liberation (Ramose, 2002:33–39) of philosophy, and indeed the entire African epistemology from the centuries-old epistemicide (Ntsoane, 2002: 22–24) committed in the name of the colonial conqueror's questionable "right of conquest." African philosophy today is situated in the historical moment known as the period of the birds: the *Mokoko-Hungwe* period. It is the hour to reaffirm the humanity and the dignity of the African without any obsequious defense of being an African. It is the moment to seize the initiative and remedy historical injustice with justice. Against this background we now turn to consider specific South African texts on African philosophy.

Voices from South Africa

The book, *Philosophy for Africa* appeared in 1993 under the authorship of Augustine Shutte. We intend focusing on the methodology and the express intent of the author. In stating that we shall focus on methodology, we mean that we shall investigate the methods, procedures, concepts, aims and the principles of reasoning that Shutte uses in his book. We mean, therefore, to examine, for example, the title of the book itself and try to discover if there is a relationship between the title and the contents of the book: what is the stated aim of Shutte in writing the book and, what does it mean to posit the particular aim?

Shutte states that he "was born and brought up in Africa," and presumably in South Africa (Shutte, 1993:8). So we may state that Shutte being born and brought up in South Africa is a South African. We shall take the liberty to state that Shutte speaks English even though Afrikaans might very well be his mother tongue.

Furthermore, we shall also take the liberty to state that having been "born and brought up in Africa," Shutte is an African. Shutte is a philosopher. By this route we have established that Shutte is a South African and a philosopher. In view of the title and contents of the book, could we justifiably state, by combining the two identities of Shutte, that Shutte is an African philosopher?

Just like the writer of the Foreword to his book, Hurley, Shutte also upholds both a distinction and a division between "African wisdom" and "Western philosophy" and, with particular reference to the latter, they uphold a distinction and separation between "African wisdom" and "modern Thomism." One might say, therefore, that for both Hurley and Shutte Africa has got "wisdom" and the Western world possesses "philosophy." Accordingly, "philosophy" cannot be ascribed to Africa since Africa is—for those who share Hurley's and Shutte's view—known never to have had its own "philosophy." This view inspires and underlies Shutte's aim which is to provide African thinkers with an "appropriate philosophical setting for the analysis in depth of traditional African values" (Shutte, 1993:2). How is the appropriateness of the envisaged "philosophical setting" to be determined? By whom shall such a determination be made? There is a link between these questions and the title of the book, *Philosophy for Africa*. We have the picture of someone having "philosophy" to offer to Africa. The question is whether or not the offer is an unsolicited donation or a prescription from someone possessing either superior power or superior knowledge. By what right or title has the superiority of either power or knowledge been established?

It is the aim of Shutte "to outline a philosophical conception of humanity that incorporates and systematises the African insights I think so important" (Shutte, 1993:9). It is, therefore, apparent that Shutte can set out "to outline a philosophical conception of humanity" only if he proceeds from the assumption that there is no "philosophy" in "traditional African values." If the "traditional African values" have in the past resulted in an African philosophy then Shutte's outline of a "philosophical conception of humanity" must either be an extension of African philosophy or an alternative African philosophical conception of humanity. But Shutte does not make an explicit

and sustained claim to any one of these two alternatives. Instead, he prefers to stick to the "European" philosophical tradition in which he was "trained." Only by doing so can he be quite explicit on the point that his aim is to provide an "appropriate philosophical setting" for the African "insights" and "traditional values." For the achievement of this aim Shutte will proceed to "incorporate" and "systematise" some "African insights" which he considers to be "important." Does Shutte perhaps imagine that "African insights" must be "incorporated" into something like *Thomism* because they cannot stand on their own? Are we justified in defining Shutte's incorporation and systematisation procedure as scientific or as philosophical colonisation? The Angelic Doctor, Saint Thomas Aquinas himself "metamorphosed," in our context *colonised*, the philosophy of Aristotle before its widespread transmission into the Christian West. Aristotle, "the pagan" was, as it were, christianised by Aquinas before he was proclaimed as a great philosopher of the West. There is a striking parallel between this and Shutte's procedure. Leopold Senghor will be elevated to "philosophy" and even be christianised via Teilhard de Chardin, before he may be proclaimed a "philosopher."

Our definition of his procedure as philosophical colonisation appears to be much more than appropriate. Shutte, it seems, simply sticks to the long established Thomist tradition. However, the appeal to tradition can hardly serve as a defence since Shutte surely must justify his procedure if he wishes to acquit himself of the charge of philosophical colonisation. In other words, Shutte must remove all reasonable doubt with regard to his claim that:

> Of course, such traditional conceptions have not, by and large, undergone rigorous philosophical scrutiny and assessment. Traditional thought simply assumed their coherence and truth and did not seek to systematise or prove them.

Surely, an argument must be made to make good the claim that the coherence and truth of unspecified traditional conceptions were taken for granted. The plain meaning of this unsubstantiated claim is that "traditional conceptions" do not qualify as philosophy. Thus talk of African philosophy is either misguided or unjustified. This is so because "Philosophy as a rigorous, self-critical intellectual discipline is a comparative newcomer to modern Africa. But in the last thirty or forty years significant attempts have been made by African philosophers to subject such traditional conceptions to philosophical analysis and systematisation" (Shutte, 1993:8). We find similar affirmations in the following citations: "On the other hand the attempt to use European philosophical tools and techniques on traditional African conceptual systems might—in addition to producing an African philosopher—result in a philosophical 'discovery' or creation that would otherwise have never happened" (Shutte, 1993:20). Also, "It is not difficult to see the way in which Teilhard's theory of all energy being in the last resort 'psychic' could be used to articulate the traditional African idea of force. Senghor uses it precisely for this purpose, delighted to find a scientific and philosophical vindication of his anti-materialist position" (Shutte, 1993:31). Shutte underlines his philosophical colonisation thus: "The kernel of this book, then, is my attempt to outline a philosophical conception of humanity that incorporates and systematises the African insights I think important. I use the particular European philosophical tradition in which I have been trained for this purpose. It is the tradition in which Aristotle and Aquinas are the classical figures . . ." (Shutte, 1993:9).

Shutte's aim to "systematise" some "African insights" could gain both credibility and plausibility if he were to demonstrate that "African insights" were never "systematised." But as he freely admits, in one of the above citations, that attempts at systematisation have already been made in the past, it is difficult to understand why *Thomism* should be superimposed upon the already existing edifice of systematisation without at the same time acknowledging that such superimposition is an extension of African philosophy. This difficulty is compounded by the fact that many African philosophers such as Abanda Ndengue, Abiola Irele, Alexis Kagame, Mulago gwa Cikala Musharhamina, Lufuluabo, Chiri, Ntumba, Towet, Mongameli Mabona, N'daw, Nkrumah, Nyerere and many others have contributed to the already existing edifice of African philosophy. It would seem though that these

latter have, nevertheless, not yet attained the status of "philosophy."

In addition Shutte aims to help the Anglo-American philosophical tradition "to overcome its inability and unwillingness to engage with the human issues that arise in our present context in South Africa" (Shutte, 1993:7). In the light of these aims, Shutte takes the position that "The main practical task of the book is to show that philosophy can provide insight and guidance in the present predicament in which we find ourselves in South Africa. The first half of the book is taken up with constructing the philosophy, the second with applying it" (Shutte, 1993:10).

The division between "African wisdom" and "philosophy," in this case, Western philosophy, is to be maintained in order to find "fields of contact between African wisdom and modern Thomism in two profound all-pervading African values: that of the life force that permeates the universe, manifesting itself especially in human persons, and the importance of community (Shutte, 1993: 1–2). Nowhere in the book do we find an argument addressed specifically to the belief that the division between "African wisdom" and "Western philosophy" is philosophically and scientifically sound. Instead, it is simply assumed that Africa does not have "philosophy." But if philosophy means, at least, etymologically, love of wisdom then it is difficult to understand the basis for the assumption that Africa does not have philosophy. In other words, to ascribe "wisdom" to Africa is at the same time to concede that Africa does have a philosophy. One could maintain otherwise only at the risk of upholding the self-contradiction that although philosophy means love of wisdom, and wisdom is the quintessence of Africa, it is nevertheless true to say that Africa does not have a philosophy. Paradoxically, this is precisely what Shutte upholds implicitly. We therefore must look elsewhere in order to resolve the self-contradiction and to remove the paradox.

In upholding the division between "African wisdom" and "Western philosophy," Shutte evidently bases this division upon his concept of philosophy. According to Shutte, philosophy is "a rigorous, self-critical intellectual discipline . . ." (Shutte, 1993:8). It is—he continues—a description of interpersonal transactions that form the necessary conditions for personal life and growth.

These descriptions are philosophical in the sense that: "they are derived from reflection on and analysis of our own fundamental and unavoidable experience of being a person, namely of self-realisation. They are thus ideal and abstract rather than realistic and concrete . . ." (Shutte, 1993:75). On this definition of philosophy it is clear that human experience is the inescapable source of all philosophy and science. It is thus remarkable that Shutte's concept of philosophy excludes the African through the subtle suggestion that although Africans had experience of being a person, this was never constructed into descriptions showing that the African did reflect upon and analyse the experience. This suggestion is untenable because contemporary studies on the history of Africa in general and the history of African philosophy in particular show that there was "scientific" philosophy long before the Roman conquest of "North Africa" or the incursions of colonization. Yet, Africa is not just simply excluded from "philosophy" but it ought to be excluded. This prescriptive exclusion may be interpreted from at least two perspectives. First, it is unnecessary, arbitrary and self-contradictory. As Gyekye put it: "To deny African peoples philosophical thought is to imply that they are unable to reflect on or conceptualize their experience, whereas the proverbs that, as I shall argue below, can be used with other materials as a source of African philosophical ideas are the undeniable results of reflection on their experience in the world. Philosophy proceeds from the facts of experience . . . African thought, if it is thought at all, must encompass philosophy . . ." (Gyekye, 1987:8).

Second, as a faithful disciple of "the particular European philosophical tradition in which I have been trained . . . ," (Shutte, 1993:9) Shutte appears to feel comfortable with the distinction and division between "philosophy" and "traditional African values" or "insights." It is submitted, in agreement with Outlaw, (Outlaw, 1987:34–35) that such comfort and complacency is unwarranted and philosophically unjustified.

There is a methodological necessity compelling Shutte to exclude Africa from "philosophy." The title of the book may help to illuminate this point. The title may best be explained in terms of the doctor-patient relationship in Western medicine. In this kind of relationship the doctor is regarded to be qualified and competent to prescribe specific medicines for the cure of the patient. It is simply inordinate, irregular and even unthinkable that the patient would suddenly decide to prescribe specific medicines for the doctor whose health condition the patient could hardly have examined competently before taking the bold step of prescribing medicine. So this kind of relationship is like a one-way road. It is only the doctor who prescribes. Shutte stands in a similar relationship to what he variously terms "African insights" or "traditional African values." He has placed himself in the position of the doctor so that he can prescribe a philosophical remedy to the supposedly un-philosophical African "insights" and "traditional values." In order to be a credible prescriber, the helplessness as well as the incompetence of the patient—in this case African "insights" and "traditional values"—must be exposed and then be shown to be in need of a cure; a philosophical cure. In these circumstances, the knowledge, ability and competence of the doctor must be placed beyond reasonable doubt and, should be supported by the claim that they can be applied for the good of the patient. On this basis, we may understand why, (a) Shutte upholds the division between "African wisdom" and "Western philosophy"; (b) this division is particularly relevant to the title of the book; (c) the title of the book would, especially in the light of its content, otherwise be empty, meaningless and inept; (d) Shutte himself would rather be "helped to be African," and not claim to be an African (see *dedication*). If he were to claim unreservedly to be an African then he would immediately become a philosophical patient. As a result, he would also lose his position as the doctor, the prescriber of the philosophical cure. His careful denial of his African credentials is a methodological necessity as well. "What has brought me to this view has been my own recent experience of Africa, or, if that sounds odd coming from one who was born and brought up in Africa, it has been my own recent awakening to African thought, African values and African culture through my encounters with black colleagues and students, black fellow-parishioners of a township church, and philosophy written by black authors in Africa . . ." (Shutte, 1993:8).

We can also discern a hierarchy here. By refraining from the explicit claim that he is an African,

Shutte thereby secures for himself a position outside, beyond and higher than the African. If he were to assume either an equal or lower position to the African then he would lose his assumed title to prescribe "Philosophy for Africa." Thus the hierarchy of superior/inferior is also a methodological necessity for Shutte. In the light of the foregoing, the answer to our question: is Shutte an African philosopher, must be in the negative. It remains to show, albeit briefly, the relationship between the argument from methodology and the structure and content of the book.

Shutte's book consists of thirteen chapters. Chapters one until six are mainly concerned with "philosophy" in Africa. Chapter seven, the number seven being reminiscent of the end of the Christian God's act of creation, is the highpoint of Shutte's philosophical investigation of philosophy in Africa. The very title of this crucial chapter, namely, "A philosophy for Africa" has more than a semblance of prescription. This is hardly surprising since it has been shown in chapter one that there is a difference between "philosophy" and Africa. This is the significance of the title of chapter one, namely, "Philosophy and Africa." Shutte appears not to think about philosophy *in* Africa. When he does in fact deal with "Philosophy in Africa" in chapter two, the dichotomy between "philosophy" and Africa is preserved in two ways. First the nature of philosophy must be determined and only after such determination can the "position and importance" of philosophy in Africa be defined. What is clear here is that Shutte has in mind the "import" to Africa called philosophy. In the light of this it is understandable, though not necessarily acceptable, that Shutte should state the following: "I think philosophy needs to be defined both by its method and by its content. I will presently explain why. It is because of this that my interest in philosophy in Africa can be expressed by two distinct questions. Can traditional African thought be of help to contemporary philosophy? I think it can. And can contemporary philosophy be of help to Africa? I think it can. I also think the two questions are connected. It is only when it allows itself to learn from traditional African thought that contemporary philosophy will be able to give Africa the help she really needs and which is its proper task to give" (Shutte, 1993:20). It is difficult to avoid the inference that

there is in this citation a dichotomy, a difference between "traditional African thought" and "contemporary philosophy" even though Shutte at times uses the term "philosopher" with regard to an African, "the Senegalese philosopher . . . Leopold Senghor" (Shutte, 1993:20). In this way the idea of the "import" called philosophy is retained. Second, the citation serves to identify the patient with reference to our doctor-patient analogy. "Traditional African thought" is the patient. "She really needs" the cure, the "import" called philosophy. It is the inviolable sacred task, yes, the exclusive and superior prerogative of "contemporary philosophy" to provide and administer this cure. No wonder then that the philosophy of Senghor is portrayed in chapter three to be in dire need of a philosophical cure which it finally receives in the philosophy of Teilhard de Chardin. Through Teilhard de Chardin, Shutte realises his "incorporation" and "systematisation" procedure.

In chapter four Shutte examines "contemporary European" philosophy with a view to identifying "a critical inadequacy" with regard to its conception of human nature. Beyond this point, Shutte would give "an alternative" couched in "a recent development of the Thomist tradition" (Shutte, 1993:34). Having achieved his aim in chapter four, Shutte proceeds in chapter five to "offer a corrective to the dominant views in contemporary European philosophy" (Shutte, 1993:46). This corrective is found in two aspects of traditional African thought. The first is the African proverb, *umuntu ngumuntu ngabantu* and the concept of *seriti*. This latter Shutte claims, "is the Xhosa term . . ." (Shutte, 1993:46). Here we beg to differ and suggest that the word *seriti* cannot be described as a "Xhosa term." On the contrary, it is a term in the *Sotho* language group. In the *Nguni* language group one could refer to *isithunzi (Zulu)* and *[i]sidima* (Xhosa) as acceptable synonyms of *seriti*. Of course, this raises important questions concerning the reliability of Shutte's research not only in terms of linguistic competence but also in terms of his portrayal, especially of African philosophers, including Setiloane the theologian, who must needs be patients in order to make his "incorporation" and "systematisation" procedure credible. No wonder then that Setiloane, A Tswana (Sotho) speaking theologian is presented as "struggling to express this conception of a person . . ."

(Shutte, 1993:55), in his competent discussion of the Tswana term *seriti*. All the African "strugglers" we have had discussed thus far can no longer hide their ailment. They are all in need of a philosophical cure and this is administered in chapter six with their baptism in Thomism. From this point onward the way is clear for Shutte to offer his "alternative" to pronounce his prescription in chapter seven, namely, "A philosophy for Africa."

In the light of the foregoing, we suggest that Shutte's enterprise, "Philosophy for Africa" is methodologically problematical. Its substance is contentious with regard to many fundamental points, in particular, his concept of philosophy and his apparent willingness to take the meaning of "Africa/African" for granted. In spite of this Shutte nevertheless finds it "odd" that he does not regard himself as "African" even if he is "born and bred" in South Africa. Here it is not specifically the term "Africa/African" which receives his primary attention. Rather it is the character of his relationship with Africa which is at issue. It is also problematical that the prescriptive "for" in Shutte's title does not augur well for a genuine dialogue between and among different philosophies, in this case the Western and the African. In what manner and to what extent does Shutte meet this criticism? To answer this question we now turn to his recent publication, *Ubuntu an Ethic for a New South Africa* (Shutte, 2001). I have already done an in-depth analysis of this work elsewhere (Coetzee and Roux, 2002:326–329). The reader is therefore advised to regard the following as an adumbration of the analysis provided elsewhere.

As in *Philosophy for Africa,* Shutte is still in search of a philosophy that will guide contemporary South Africa out of her "present predicament." This time he has found *ubuntu,* supported by the "European" understanding of freedom, as that particular guide. It is specifically an ethical guide. One of the core theses of Shutte is that the combination of *ubuntu* and the "European" understanding of freedom is an ethical guide not only to the "new" South Africa but to the whole of humanity on the planet Earth. (Shutte, 2001: 2) "Ubuntu is an African conception, but it embodies an insight that is universal. And I believe that it provides us with the key to overcoming the great division in the world of today, as well as undoing the divisions in South Africa created by

apartheid." (Shutte, 2001:9) No doubt "apartheid" in South Africa is historically much younger than the structural divisions created by colonization in its various manifestations in South Africa. Indeed some scholars have even described "apartheid" as a form of "internal colonization" thereby preserving the historical link between colonization and "apartheid." It follows then that "our present predicament" and the prevailing "divisions" in the "new" South Africa may not justifiably be placed at the doorstep of "apartheid."

From *ubuntu* Shutte wants specifically to extract "the idea of community, that persons depend on other persons to be persons" whereas from Western Europe he will take "the idea of freedom, that individuals have a power of free choice." No doubt both cultures—or, "traditions" as the preferred term of Shutte—do have the idea of "community" as well as the idea of "freedom." It would seem therefore that the borrowing that Augustine proposes to do relates more to what is emphasized in one culture than the claim that one culture is particularly deficient either of the idea of "community" or "freedom." Shutte himself does not make this particular observation. The reader is thus left to guess. Does the proposed borrowing arise from the deficiency of one culture in contrast to the other or, does it stem from the fact that both "ideas" are found in the two cultures but each one places special emphasis on the one rather than the other? Perhaps this might not be important for Shutte since his primary aim is not to be "critical" of any of the two cultures as far as the ideas of "community" and "freedom" are concerned. No doubt, "Ethics, as a branch of philosophy, is always critical. So what I am presenting is a critical interpretation of both traditions, the African and the European. But my ultimate aim is creative rather than critical. I want to create and apply an ethic of *ubuntu* that is based on the genuinely universal insights of European and African thought, which, because the insights themselves can be reconciled, will be able to reconcile the different elements of a new South African culture." (Shutte, 2001:10)

Having thus stated his aim, Shutte then proceeds to achieve it. However, with particular reference to *ubuntu,* he once again adopts the position of a stranger, an outsider as he did in his *Philosophy for Africa.* "Because I myself have been brought up and educated in the European tradition, I have been especially careful to test what I have written on African colleagues and friends" (Shutte, 2001:10). Despite his position as a stranger, Shutte does eventually achieve his "creative" aim. He reaches this point by constituting "community" and "freedom" as equal partners in a "creative" dialogue. This is a significant departure from the prescriptive standpoint of *Philosophy for Africa*. Through this "creative" dialogue on the basis of equality Shutte has in effect done the following. First, he has endorsed dialogue, that is, the willingness to be honest and truthful about oneself and the readiness to listen to rather than just hear the other, as the principle of philosophy (Gracia, 1992:25). Second, he has acknowledged the independent existence of African philosophy. This acknowledgement is consistent with Shutte's consistent search for an ethical guide that may lead to the resolution of the problems facing the "new" South Africa and the world at large. This aspect of Shutte's philosophical temperament is already more than apparent in his *Philosophy for Africa*. Its significance lies in the fact that without degrading the importance of abstract speculation in philosophy, Shutte nevertheless underlines the crucial importance of philosophy also as a means to clarify and contribute towards the resolution of the problems of everyday life. No wonder then that he is especially focused on ethical questions. This is precisely what places Shutte at the center of one of the major concerns of contemporary African philosophy. Beginning with *Philosophy for Africa*, Shutte has demonstrated that he takes the African experience seriously. His philosophical concerns revolve around this experience and he understands clearly the universalist implications of taking the African experience seriously. He writes: "No matter how universal an ethic may be, it still has to be applied in a particular time and place." And, he continues,

> The gap in wealth, health, education, security, is enormous and growing all the time. In previous ages such things as poverty, disease, ignorance, danger, were inevitable, part of the order of nature. Now however, they are not. Science and technology have given humanity the power to provide a simple but satisfying life for everyone on the globe. That is not in doubt. The problems

of production and distribution are technical problems well within our power to overcome. . . . But it does not happen. Why?" (Shutte, 2001: 6–7).

In this way Shutte poses the question of justice. From the point of view of colonial history in Africa this is the question of both restorative and distributive justice. It is an African philosophical question *par excellence*. It is therefore understandable modesty that Shutte should appear so sensitive about not being an African. However, this modesty must give way to the recognition that his willingness and ability to raise fundamental and critical questions that people with a sense of justice and history continue to raise in this "without cold" continent undoubtedly make him an African philosopher. He has every reason to be part of the declaration, "I doubt, therefore, African philosophy exists."

Conclusion: *Ex Africa semper aliquid novum*

The above sub-heading is susceptible to at least two interpretations. One is that it is simply a statement asserting that there is always something new from Africa. Another is that if it is couched in the form of a question then it is not only asking if there is always something new from Africa but that it is also suggesting that nothing new will ever come from Africa. Well, *Philosophy from Africa*, now in its second edition has come out of Africa. It is edited by Coetzee and Roux. The present writer freely admits active participation in the editorial work pertaining to the second edition. It is precisely because of the "from" in the title that the present writer requested that his name should not appear as one of the editors. His argument was that the "from" in the title is not only reminiscent of the "for" in Shutte's title but that it is also a subtle expression of doubt that philosophy "proper" can ever come from Africa. In other words, it is an expression of doubt about the meaning of "African philosophy." Yet, the essays contained in this volume more than testify to the existence of African philosophy. They also establish the point that historically, the term African must include peoples of African origin in the diaspora. This inclusion is significant because it is, among others, the recognition that the Harlem Renaissance (Masolo, 1994:10) remains one of the important antecedents to the resurgence of African philosophy in the continent "without cold." In view of the fact that Philosophy from Africa contains the voices of many Africans philosophizing over a wide spectrum of philosophical questions, one wonders why it should hang onto the "from" thereby doubting the existence of African philosophy. Yet, by its intent and content the book is yet another loud declaration that "I doubt, therefore African philosophy exists."

References

Bodny, A.S., 1986. The meaning and problem of Hispanic American Thought, Can there be a Latin American philosophy? in, Gracia, J.J.E., (ed.) *Latin American Philosophy in the Twentieth Century*, New York: Prometheus Books.

Cheikh Anta Diop, 1974. *The African Origin of Civilization*, (trans.) M. Cook, Westport: Lawrence Hill & Company.

Cheikh Anta Diop, 1987. *Precolonial Black Africa*, (trans.) H.J. Salemson, Trenton, New Jersey: Africa World Press.

Encyclopaedia Britannica, 1974. Volume 1, Macropaedia, Chicago: William Benton Publisher.

Encyclopaedia Britannica, Volume 6, Macropaedia, 1974. Chicago: William Benton Publisher.

Coetzee, P.H. and Roux, A.P.J. (ed.), 2002. *Philosophy from Africa*, Oxford: Oxford University Press.

Copleston, F., 1962. *A History of Philosophy*, Volume 2, New York: Image Books, A Division of Doubleday & Company, Inc.

Fuze, M.M., *The Black People*, 1979. (trans.) Lugg, H.C., (ed.) Cope, T.A., Pietermaritzburg: University of Natal Press.

Gilson, E., 1955. *History of Christian Philosophy in the Middle Ages*, London: Sheed and Ward.

Gracia, J.J.E., 1992. *Philosophy and its History*, New York: State University of New York Press.

Gyekye, K., 1987. *An Essay on African Philosophical Thought: The Akan Conceptual Scheme*, Cambridge: Cambridge University Press.

Jimoh, A., 1999. *Context-dependency of Human Knowledge: Justification of an African Epistemology*, WAJOPS, West African Journal of Philosophical Studies, Volume 2.

Kagame, A., 1955. *La philosophie bantu-rwandaise de l'Être, Memoire présenté à la séance du 20 juin.*

Masolo, A.D., 1994. *African Philosophy in Search of Identity*, Bloomington, Indianapolis: Indiana University Press.

Ntsoane, O., 2002. *Colonial education and the production of rural misfits, in Teaching Endogenous Knowledge*, (ed.) Crossman, P., Pretoria: Africa Research Centre, KULeuven, Belgium, University of the North and Centre for Indigineous Knowledge, University of Pretoria.

Obenga, T., 1990. *La philosophie Africaine de la periode pharaonique*, 2780–330 avant notre ere, Paris: Editions L'Harmattan.

Oguejiofor, J.O., *Fundamental considerations for a history of African philosophy*, WAJOPS, West African Journal of Philosophical Studies, Volume 3, December 2000. p. 5–26.

Ogunmodede, F.I., 2000. *Philosophy re-examines its ancient origins*, WAJOPS, West African Journal of Philosophical Studies, Volume 3.

Onyewuenyi, I.C., 1993. *The African Origin of Greek Philosophy*, Nsukka, Nigeria: University of Nigeria Press.

Oladipo, O., 1999. *Knowledge and the African Renaissance*, WAJOPS, West African Journal of Philosophical Studies, Volume 2.

Osuagwu, I.M., 1999. *African Historical Reconstruction*, Amamihe Lectures, Volume I, Owerri, Nigeria: Amamihe Publications.

Osuagwu, I.M., 2001. *Early Medieval History of African Philosophy*, Amamihe Lectures Volume II, Owerri, Nigeria: Amamihe Publications.

Outlaw, L., 1987. African "Philosophy" Deconstructive and reconstructive challenges, in Floistad, G. (ed.) *Contemporary Philosophy*, Volume 5, African Philosophy, Dordrecht: Martinus Nijhoff Publishers.

Ramose, M.B., 2000. *'African Renaissance': a northbound gaze*, Politeia 19(3), 47–63.

Ramose, M.B., 2002. *African Philosophy through Ubuntu*, Harare, Zimbabwe: Mond Books Publishers.

Samkange, S. and Samkange, T.M., 1980. *Hunhuism or Ubuntuism: A Zimbabwe Indigenous Political Philosophy*, Salisbury: Graham Publishing.

Shutte, A., 1993. *Philosophy for Africa*, Cape Town: UCT Press (Pty) Ltd.

Shutte, A., 2001. *Ubuntu, An Ethic for a New South Africa*, Pietermaritzburg: Cluster Publications.

Sogolo, G., 1993. *Foundations of African Philosophy*, Ibadan, Nigeria: Ibadan University Press.

Van Sertima, I., (ed.) 1988. *Black Women in Antiquity*, USA Journal of African Civilizations Ltd., Inc.

Williams, C., 1976. *The Destruction of Black Civilization*, Chicago: Third World Press.

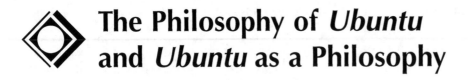

The Philosophy of *Ubuntu* and *Ubuntu* as a Philosophy

Mogobe B. Ramose

Ubuntu is the root of African philosophy. The be-ing of an African in the universe is inseparably anchored upon ubuntu. Similarly, the African tree of knowledge stems from ubuntu with which it is connected indivisibly. Ubuntu then is the wellspring flowing with African ontology and epistemology. If these latter are the bases of philosophy then African philosophy has long been established in and through ubuntu. Our point of departure is that ubuntu may be seen as the basis of African philosophy. Apart from a linguistic analysis of ubuntu, a persuasive philosophical argument can be made that there is a "family atmosphere," that is, a kind of philosophical affinity and kinship among and between the indigenous people of Africa. No doubt there will be variations within this broad philosophical "family atmosphere." But the blood circulating through the "family" members is the same in its basics.[1] In this sense ubuntu is the basis of African philosophy.

In this chapter we shall focus upon the elucidation of the view that ubuntu is simultaneously the foundation and the edifice of African philosophy. Just as the environing soil, the root, stem, branches and leaves together as a one-ness give meaning to our understanding of a tree, so is it with ubuntu. The foundation, the soil within which it is anchored, as well as the building must be seen as one continuous whole-ness rather than independent fragments of reality. Accordingly, African ontology and epistemology must be understood as two aspects of one and the same reality. We shall adopt a philosophical approach in our clarification of ubuntu philosophy.

In terms of geographic demarcation we agree partially with the delimitation of De Tejada. Thus the ubuntu philosophy we are about to discuss "goes from the Nubian desert to the Cape of Good Hope and from Senegal to Zanzibar."[2] However, this delimitation is questionable since the Sahara desert is not the indelible birthmark of Africa. For this reason the meaning and import of human interaction before the birth of the Sahara desert must be taken into account. We shall not, however, pursue this line of inquiry in the present essay.

Philosophy in Ubuntu

It is best, philosophically, to approach this term as an hyphenated word, namely, ubu-ntu. Ubuntu is actually two words in one. It consists of the prefix ubu- and the stem ntu-. Ubu- evokes the idea of be-ing in general. It is enfolded be-ing before it manifests itself in the concrete form or mode of ex-istence of a particular entity. Ubu- as enfolded be-ing is always oriented towards unfoldment, that is, incessant continual concrete manifestation through particular forms and modes of be-ing. In this sense ubu- is always oriented towards -ntu. At the ontological level, there is no strict and literal separation and division between ubu- and -ntu. Ubu- and -ntu are not two radically separate and irreconcilably opposed realities. On the contrary, they are mutually founding in the sense that they are two aspects of be-ing as a one-ness and an indivisible whole-ness. Accordingly, ubu-ntu is the fundamental ontological and epistemological category in the African thought of the Bantu-speaking people. It is the indivisible oneness and whole-ness of ontology and epistemology. Ubu- as the generalized understanding of be-ing may be said to be distinctly ontological. Whereas

126

-ntu as the nodal point at which be-ing assumes concrete form or a mode of being in the process of continual unfoldment may be said to be the distinctly epistemological.

The word umu- shares an identical ontological feature with the word ubu-. Whereas the range of ubu- is the widest generality umu- tends towards the more specific. Joined together with -ntu then umu- becomes umuntu. Umuntu means the emergence of homo-loquens who is simultaneously a homo sapiens. In common parlance it means the human be-ing: the maker of politics, religion and law. Umuntu then is the specific concrete manifestation of umu-: it is a movement away from the generalized to the concrete specific. Umuntu is the specific entity which continues to conduct an inquiry into be-ing, experience, knowledge and truth. This is an activity rather than an act. It is an ongoing process impossible to stop unless motion itself is stopped. On this reasoning, ubu- may be regarded as be-ing becoming and this evidently implies the idea of motion. We propose to regard such incessant motion as verbal rather than the verb. -ntu may be construed as the temporarily having become. In this sense -ntu is a noun. The indivisible one-ness and whole-ness of ubu-ntu means, therefore, that ubuntu is a verbal noun.

Because motion is the principle of be-ing for ubuntu do-ing takes precedence over the do-er without at the same time imputing either radical separation or irreconcilable opposition between the two. "Two" here speaks only to two aspects of one and the same reality. Ubuntu then is a gerund. But it is also a gerundive at the same time since at the epistemological level it may crystallize into a particular form of social organisation, religion or law. Ubuntu is always a -ness and not an -ism. We submit that this logic of ub-ntu also applies to hu- and -nhu in the Shona language of Zimbabwe. Therefore it may not be rendered as hunhuism[3] as Samkange has done. The -ism suffix gives the erroneous impression that we are dealing with verbs and nouns as fixed and separate entities existing independently. They thus function as fixations to ideas and practices which are somewhat dogmatic and hence unchangeable. Such dogmatism and immutability constitute the false necessity based upon fragmentative thinking. This latter is the thinking—based on the subject-verb-object understanding of the structure of language—which posits a fundamental irreconcilable opposition in be-ing becoming. On the basis of this imputed opposition be-ing becoming is fragmented into pieces of reality with an independent existence of their own.

Without the speech of umuntu, Ubu- is condemned to unbroken silence. The speech of umuntu is thus anchored in, revolves around and is ineluctably oriented towards ubu-. The language of umuntu 'relevates,' that is, it directs and focuses the entire epistemological domain towards the ontology of ubu-. This it does by the contemporaneous and indissoluble coupling of ubu- and umuntu through the maxim *umuntu ngumuntu nga bantu (motho ke motho ka batho)*. Although the English language does not exhaust the meaning of this maxim or aphorism, it may nonetheless be construed to mean that to be a human be-ing is to affirm one's humanity by recognising the humanity of others and, on that basis, establish humane relations with them. Ubuntu understood as be-ing human (human-ness); a humane, respectful and polite attitude towards others constitutes the core meaning of this aphorism. Ubuntu then not only describes a condition of be-ing, insofar as it is indissolubly linked to umuntu but it is also the recognition of be-ing becoming and not, we wish to emphasise, be-ing and becoming.

In this sense it is simultaneously a gerund and a gerundive since the latter is implied in the imperative, *nga bantu*. In other words, be-ing human is not enough. One is enjoined, yes, commanded as it were, to actually become a human being. What is decisive then is to prove oneself to be the embodiment of *ubu-ntu (botho)* because the fundamental ethical, social and legal judgement of human worth and human conduct is based upon ubu-ntu. The judgement, pronounced with approval or disapproval respectively, is invariably expressed in these terms: *ke motho or gase motho*. In the original language, in this case the Sotho cluster in the Bantu-speaking grouping, these expressions may not be interpreted literally since in literal terms they mean he/she is a human be-ing or she/he is not a human be-ing. A literal interpretation boils down to an affirmation or negation of the obvious if we restrict ourselves to the biological definition of a human being. Even worse, the negation would ultimately be meaningless since its assertion neither abolishes nor alters the biological definition of nature of a human being. Thus the affirmation or negation of *ubu-ntu (bo-tho)* is a metaphor for ethical, social and legal judgement of human worth and human conduct. In the sphere of politics, the veritable arena for the making of law, ubu-ntu is reaffirmed as the basis of judgement in the three mentioned domains of human life by the maxim: *kgosi ke kgosi ka batho,* meaning, the source and justification of royal power is the people.[4] Even here ubu-ntu recurs with stubborn consistency because *ba-tho (ba-ntu)* is simply the plural form of *mo-tho (umu-ntu).* Accordingly, the sphere of politics and law is not only suffused with ubu-ntu but it is also based upon it. Cumulatively, these considerations together constitute the basis for our submission that ubuntu is the philosophical foundation of African philosophy among the Bantu-speaking peoples.

Against the Fragmentation of Be-ing

One of the primary functions of language is to break the silence of be-ing. Only if and after language had broken the silence of being is it possible to commence conversation with or about be-ing. The following emerges in the execution of this function. We have the structure of the doer engaged in the activity of doing and, frequently the doing is directed towards the object. Thus we have the noun[5] (subject)—the verb[6]—the object as the apparent structure of language. This structure is supposed to be inherent to language. Furthermore, the general view appears to be that this apparent structure of language determines the sequence of thought. Thought is supposed not only to follow this pattern but also to reveal the separate and independent existence of the noun on the one hand and the object on the other. So the idea arises that the subject—object distinction is a fundamental and ineradicable ontological datum. According to this reasoning, the verb then functions as the vehicle of mediation between the subject and the object. On this reasoning, the logic of separate, distinct and independent existence is already ontologically established. What is required, therefore, is only an elucidation of this logic.

Feeding upon this putative ontological verity, the elucidation unfolds in the positing of the noun as the source of all activity in relation to be-ing.

This places the doer, the noun or subject, in the position of moulding and ordering be-ing. Be-ing as a wholeness is thus the object of the subject. Moulded being becomes then the reality. It becomes the representation and the order of be-ing because the represented shifts originally be-ing systematically to the remotest background. The do-ing, just like be-ing as the possibility condition for moulding and ordering, recedes progressively and almost imperceptibly to the background. This obliviousness of do-ing and the imperceptible derecognition of be-ing as the possibility condition for moulding and ordering is what we mean by the fragmentation of being as a wholeness.

Positing the noun as the source of all activity in relation to be-ing also involves the idea that the noun (subject)—in this case the human being—is the center of the universe. This idea is, however, questionable because in all probability the universe has got no center at all.[7] Therefore, neither as the noun nor the gerund may the doer be construed as the center of the universe. The stubborn persistence and tenacity of this idea means that the human being, as the noun, is the causative factor in the establishment and preservation of political and social organisation.

Seen from an ontological and epistemological point of view, the in-istence[8] of the subject through language, as the cause of political and social organisation, is based upon a false opposition between be-ing and becoming. Instead of recognising only be-ing becoming, that is, infrangible incessant motion, language insists upon the fragmentation of be-ing becoming into be! and becoming. The critical point to note here—and this is our view as well—is that: 'Being and Becoming are not to be opposed one to the other; they express two related aspects of reality.'[9] According to the imposed separation and opposition between be-ing and becoming, be! is order and becoming is chaos. The divide between the two is not only complete but it is perceived as a fundamental and irreconcilable opposition between them. This kind of opposition precludes the possibility of the birth of order out of apparent chaos. Order can therefore not come out of nonequilibrium perceived as chaos.

Be-ing becoming, the incessant flow of motion is perceived as chaos since it is considered to provide neither certainty nor equilibrium. The experience of nonequilibrium is thus the basic problem of human existence. To solve this problem language invokes the concept of order as the means to establish and maintain equilibrium in human relations. But since the projected order is based upon an unbridgeable opposition between be-ing and becoming, how then can "order" come out of chaos? The question cannot be answered unless we ground "order" in the very experience of fundamental disequilibrium in be-ing. By so doing we may well hold that order not only can but does indeed come out of apparent chaos.[10]

Language crystallizes into the imperative that be-ing becoming must be!' that is, it must cease becoming and remain only be!: it is. This be! it is; is a veritable caricature of be-ing becoming. It is the linguistic order which is no more than the fragmentation and thus a distortion of originary be-ing. The separation of be-ing becoming and the invention of the opposition, be-ing and becoming, through the insertion of be! is ontologically and epistemologically questionable. Pursuant to this line of questioning we propose to attempt an answer to the following question. What would reality look like if be-ing becoming were not at all fragmented? For a tentative but no less plausible answer we now turn to consider the rheomode language.

The Rheomode: The Philosophical Language of Ubuntu

The rheomode is derived from the Greek verb 'rheo' meaning to flow. It is a 'new mode' of language . . . trying to find out whether it is possible to create a new structure that is not so prone toward fragmentation as is the present one.'[11] It is a critique of a thought and language structure which assumes and imposes a strict divide and a necessary sequence in terms of subject-verb-object. It is an appeal for the understanding of entities as the dimensions, forms and modes of the incessant flow of simultaneously multi-directional motion. This understanding speaks to be-ing rather than be! It sustains and at the same time preserves the whole-ness and not the whole of be-ing. Whole cannot appropriately describe be-ing since it already implies the fixation of be-ing and its replacement by being. Precisely because motion cannot be stooped since in the very act of stopping motion is already present we cannot talk about the whole

of be-ing as though be-ing had attained to the state of complete stagnation: absolute rest. The suffix -ness is indispensable since it underlines the importance of this logical impossibility and puts into sharp relief the ancient opposition between motion and rest as principles of being.[12]

In contrast to the subject-verb-object linguistic structure that we have discussed already the rheomode language takes the verb as its point of departure. In this way the incessant flow of motion as be-ing is preserved because the verb pertains to do-ing rather than do! Together the suffixes -ing and -ness preserve the idea of be-ing as a whole-ness.[13] Since there is always the doer in the doing the rheomode language understands the verb as the verbal noun, that is to say, the gerund.

In our view the verb not only presupposes but it is also the embodiment of the doer. The activity or action of the verb is, minus the effect of certain illnesses, inseparable from the doer. The doer do-ing; present continuous tense is in itself at any given moment the embodiment of the potentiality for an infinite variety of an unceasing activity of merging and converging. The present tense be-ing itself only a specific mode of incessant motion is always continuous. To use a biological metaphor, we may say that the present continuous tense is like an infinite chain of dangling babies, youth and adults all perpetually connected to their mothers through unseverable umbilical cords. Accordingly, we hold that the gerund rather than the verb is the ontological basis of the rheomode language.

The logic of ubu-ntu is distinctly rheomodic in character. It is the logic of and for the preservation of be-ing as a whole-ness. Accordingly, it is against the fragmentation of be-ing through language. The rheomodic character of ubu-ntu underlies the widely recognised view that the African philosophic view of the universe is holistic. Here it must be emphasised that the correctness of this view would be enhanced by discarding hol-ism as either the definition or description of the African philosophic view of the universe. Instead, the term holon-ness should be used. It is appropriate as it speaks directly against the fragmentation of be-ing, especially through language, and defines the African philosophic understanding of be-ing as a whole-ness. Epistemologically, be-ing is conceived as a perpetual and universal movement of sharing and exchange of the forces of life. The African philosophic conception of the universe is, to borrow from the Greek, pantareic. On this view, "order" cannot be once established and fixed for all time.[14]

The African philosophic conception of the universe is not only pantareic but it is musical as well. It is thus rooted in "its musical conception of the universe."[15] This makes it dynamic. We certainly agree with De Tejada's suggestion that the musical conception of the universe can result in two interpretations of the musical rhythm, namely, the rational and the emotional. However, we definitely disagree with his ascription of the "emotional" as a distinctive feature of Bantu law and, by extension African philosophy. First, the ascription is an uncritical repetition of the tradition of philosophic racism in Western philosophy. The basic thesis of this tradition is that Aristotle's "man is a rational animal" was not spoken of the African, the Amerindian and the Australasians: all the indigenous people of their countries from time immemorial. His not infrequent use and appropriation of "unserer Logik," "unserer rationalen Logik"[16] coupled with his express ascription of Bantu thought to the "magical" and the emotional speak to an exclusivism[17] which is psychologically more revealing. Historically, it is an inadvertent transmission of a fundamentally questionable tradition. Second, the ascription does to a large extent undermine his own powerful criticism of researchers and scholars of Bantu philosophy who were bent to find European thought patterns and institutions in Africa rather than recognise what Bantu philosophy was in its own right.[18]

Third, De Tejada's ascription is inconsistent with our understanding of be-ing as a whole-ness. It undermines its own foundation because the African worldview upon which ubuntu philosophy is based is fundamentally holonistic. As such it is a criticism of fragmentary thinking; precisely what De Tejada has fallen prey to by maintaining a radical opposition between the "rational" and the "emotional." African philosophy would not subscribe to the radical opposition between reason and emotion. Discourse on the psychosomatic is meaningful even to the Western mind. Understanding thought as a system means recognising it as a whole-ness which includes not only the indivisibility but also the mutual dependence of the "rational" and the "emotional."[19]

Music: The Conception and Harmony of Be-ing in African Philosophy

The dance of be-ing is an invitation to participate actively in and through the music of be-ing rather than being a passive spectator thereof. This explains the difference of both attitude and reaction towards music (the dance of be-ing) between the African and the non-Africans. For the Africans the invitation of the dance of be-ing is undeclinable since it is understood as an ontological and epistemological imperative. Indeed in Northern Sotho, for example, one of the Bantu-speaking languages, there is a saying that *Kosa ga e theeletswe o e duletse* (you don't listen to music seated). This underlines the African attitude and reaction towards the dance of be-ing as an ontological and epistemological imperative to be in tune. To dance along with be-ing is to be attuned to be-ing.

Instead of understanding and underlining this African attitude towards music the prevailing explanation holds tenaciously to the naive view that Africans are by nature a people governed by emotion. Hence, so the naive view continues, Africans spontaneously dance to music and the rhythm of their dance consistently rhymes with the music. Accordingly, so the naive view continues, Africans are persistently in search of harmony in all spheres of life. The conclusion that Africans are persistently in search of harmony in all spheres of life is pertinently true of African thought. The concrete expression of African thought is the continual quest for consensus aimed to establish harmony. Harmony gives excellence and beauty to music. To posit excellence as an aim and to actually achieve it is by every test a rational act. So it is also with the creation of beauty. Although aesthetic judgement might be spontaneous, it is by no means necessarily devoid of reason. The drum as a basic instrument in African music is a pertinent example here. The premises upon which De Tejada discusses Bantu thought are questionable in so far as they amount to the restriction of reason to the West. Our criticism in the context of this questioning applies to De Tejada's otherwise adequate description of the drum as the basic instrument in the Bantu understanding of be-ing as musical harmony.[20] Reasoned spontaneity is a familiar theme in poetics. Accordingly, the African philosophic conception of the universe as a musical harmony cannot but be the expression of reason through emotion.

It is therefore understandable why many Africans not only display lack of interest in but also remain expressly surprised by the habit of non-Africans to be glued for hours as passive spectators to the musical rendition of Bach, Mozart, Händel or Beethoven. The African surprise then speaks not only to attitudinal difference but more importantly, it reveals the underlying ontologico-epistemological difference. We are fully aware that the inherent limitations of our musical metaphor—after all non-Africans dance to pop and even Reggae music—might be somewhat exaggerated. However, we hold that passive spectatorship on hearing the music of be-ing is understandable only as a necessary posture for the fragmentation of be-ing. It is a prior and necessary condition for the fragmentation of be-ing. Despite its imagined necessity, this condition is by no means sufficient because the unlimitable elasticity as well as the infinite resilience of be-ing guarantee the failure of every effort to fragment it.

The Rheomode and Its Implications for Our Overall Worldview[21]

One of the implications of the rheomode language for the dominant worldview based upon fragmentative thinking is that our idea of fact and truth must change. It is no longer unproblematical to hold that a 'fact' is an objective state of affairs susceptible to verification and, by implication falsification. To make such an assertion without reference to the relationship—and a complex one at that—between the supposedly ob-jective state of affairs and the declarant is to ignore unduly a crucial dimension in the construction of 'facts.'[22]

Our idea of truth must be reviewed from the standpoint of rheomodic thought. According to rheomodic thought, truth may be defined as the contemporaneous convergence of perception and action.[23] Human beings are not made by the truth. They are the makers of the truth.

Even perception is not wholly neutral. In this sense it is more appropriate for humans to live the truth rather than living in and by the truth. The former captures the basic tenet of African philosophy whereas the latter speaks to the prevailing

feature of Western philosophy. To put it in another way; the expression "African time" it its negative connotation, for example, misses the basic point pertaining to the philosophic difference between African and Western philosophy. For African philosophy human beings make time and they are not made by time. Therefore, it is both natural and logical to live time. But for Western philosophy primacy is accorded to living in time. Quite often time is already there as an empty space to be filled. Hence the proliferation of diaries to note appointments and all that needs to be done to fill up the space of time until death. (It is salutary to note that consonant with contemporary scientific research into time-space Western philosophy may in the long run persuade the Westerner to live time rather than live in it.)[24] Seen from this perspective, truth is simultaneously participatory and interactive. It is active, continual and discerning perception leading to action.[25] As such it is distinctly relative rather than absolute.

The Metaphysics of Ubuntu Philosophy

Umuntu is the embodiment of the ontology and epistemology of ubu-. Ubu- as the generalized and widest be-ing is marked by uncertainty. This is because it is by definition motion involving the possibility of infinite unfoldment and concrete manifestation into a multiplicity of forms and organisms. Umuntu is one such organism in the whole-ness of be-ing as fundamental uncertainty.

A specific element of the experience and concept of whole-ness in ubuntu philosophy is the understanding of be-ing in terms of three interrelated dimensions. We find the dimension of the living—umuntu—which makes the speech and knowledge of be-ing possible. The second dimension is that of those beings who have passed away from the world of the living. These beings departed from the world of the living through death. It is thus understood that death has discontinued their existence only with regard to the concrete, bodily and everyday life as we know it. But it is believed that death does not totally discontinue the life of these departed beings. Instead, they are believed to enter into and continue living in a world unknown to those left behind. On the ground of this belief the departed are called the living-dead *(abaphansi)*. A rather contested term, "ancestors" continues to be used as a synonym of the living-dead. The living-dead continue to live despite their departure from the world of the living. In this sense they are immortal. The third dimension is that of the yet-to-be-born. These are beings of the future. It is the task of the living to see to it that the yet-to-be-born are in fact born.

Because the ubuntu understanding of be-ing involves three levels of human existence, we call it the onto-triadic structure of be-ing. Since two of these levels pertain to beings which are either unknown or unseen, we may refer to it as the ontology of invisible beings. The ontology of invisible beings is the discourse about the unknown from the standpoint of the living. The unknown remains unknowable on the side of the living. Yet, it is believable and because of this belief it has a direct influence on the life of the living. In this sense, the belief in the unknown unknowable is metaphysics. It is a claim, based upon belief, to knowledge about beings outside the domain of the world of the living. The ontology of invisible beings is thus the basis of ubuntu metaphysics.

According to the ubuntu understanding of be-ing, the world of metaphysics is the world of *u-nkulu-nkulu:* the greatest of the great; the ineffable. The ineffable is neither male nor female. But if it must be genderised at all it is female-male (hermaphroditic) according to the logic of u- (Nguni languages) or mo- (Sotho languages). The main point though is that *u-nkulu-nkulu* is neither definable nor describable. This preserves the essence of *u-nkulu-nkulu* as unknowable. Therefore, it is best to remain quiet about the unknowable and simply recognise the ineffability of *mo-dimo (unkulunkulu)*. This, it is submitted, is a basic starting-point to explain why ubuntu philosophy and religion have got no theology.

The Implications of the Ubuntu Onto-triadic Conception of Be-ing

The nature of human relations in the world of the living is based upon and influenced by the onto-triadic understanding of be-ing. Uncertainty, fear, joy and sorrow, solitude and companionship, ill and good health, are some of the phenomena which define the fundamental instability

of the world of the living. The question is: how does one respond to the fundamental instability of be-ing?

In ubuntu philosophy a human being in the world of the living must be umuntu in order to give a response to the challenge of the fundamental instability of be-ing. Umuntu cannot attain ubuntu without the intervention of the living-dead. The living-dead are important to the upkeep and protection of the family of the living. This is also true with regard to the community at large. For this reason, it is imperative that the leader of the community together with the elders of the community must have good relations with their living-dead. This speaks to the ubuntu understanding of cosmic harmony. It must be preserved and maintained by translating it into harmony in all spheres of life. Thus African religion, politics and law is based on and suffused with the experience and concept of cosmic harmony. Religion, politics and law must be anchored upon the understanding of the cosmos as the continual strife for harmony. It is such anchorage which gives them authenticity and legitimacy. And this is the basis for consensus as the distinctive feature of ubuntu philopraxis. Peace through the concrete realisation of justice is the fundamental law of ubuntu philosophy. Justice without peace is the negation of the strife towards cosmic harmony. But peace without justice is the dislocation of umuntu from the cosmic order.

We now turn to consider the presence and role of ubuntu philosophy in the spheres of religion, medicine, law, politics and ecology.

Notes

1. Ki-Zerbo, J., quoted by De Tejada, F.E., in "The future of Bantu law," in ARSP, Beiheft Neue Folge, Nr. 11 1979. p. 304.
2. De Tejada, F.E., ARSP, 1979. op. cit., p. 304.
3. Samkange, S. and Samkange, T.M., Hunhuism or Ubuntuism: A Zimbabwe indigenous political philosophy, Graham Publishing: Salisbury 1980.
4. For an extended discussion of this topic see, Ramose, M.B., "African democratic tradition: oneness, consensus and openness: a reply to Wamba-dia-Wamba," in Quest, Volume VI Number 2 December 1992. p. 62–83.
5. We adopt the meaning of the term "noun" as explained in the Shorter Oxford English Dictionary, Third Edition, Volume II, Oxford University Press: Oxford 1973.
6. We adopt the meaning of the term "verb" as explained in the dictionary referred to in note 5 above as well as

that contained in The Oxford Dictionary of English, Second Edition, Volume X 1989.

7. Cantore, E., Scientific man, ISH Publications: New York 1977. p. 403.

8. I am indebted to Verhack for the hyphenated use of the term. It is clearly a departure from the ordinary usage in terms of spelling and meaning. However, as is evident in the present essay, Verhack and I do not necessarily attach the same meaning to the term. See, Verhack, I., "Freiheit und Ek-in-sistenz," in Schadel, E. and Voigt, U. (ed.) Sein-Erkennen-Handeln, Band 7, Peter Lang: Franfurt am Main 1994. p. 649–657.

9. Prigogine, I., Stengers, I., Toffler, A., (et al.), Order out of chaos, man's dialogue with nature, Fontana: London 1985. p. 310.

10. Prigogine, I., et al., op. cit., p. 287.

11. Bohm, D., Wholeness and the implicate order, Routledge and Kegan Paul: London 1980. p. 30–31.

12. Charles-Saunders Peirce states: "I start from and in and with and as Motion. For me, in the 'spiritual' as well as the physical world, there is of course no Rest as the ultimate goal or as the antithesis of Motion. The changeless is less than the dead, it is the non-existent. . . . I often say that I am determined to be free and free to be determined. Why? Because of the unnamed Third yet lying in the womb of Motion, to which both the determinate and the indeterminate have reference. . . . To me the idea of the new, the young, the fresh, the possible, are deeper than any time-import, and are indeterminate only in a special sense. . . . The best I can do is say, 'I wish of the Future, we could begin to talk of the Unreached as the Yet distant.'" in Kevelson, R., Law as a system of signs, Plenum Press: New York 1988. p. v.

13. Bohm, D., wholeness and the implicate order, op. cit., p. 30.

14. Griaule, M., Conversations with Ogotemmeli, Oxford University Press: Oxford 1965. p. 137.

15. De Tejada, F.E., ARSP 1979, op. cit., p. 306–307.

16. De Tejada, F.E., "Bemerkungen uber der Grundlagen des Banturechts," in ARSP Volume 46 1960. p. 522–523.

17. Adam, L., "Modern ethnological jurisprudence in theory and practice," in Journal of Comparative Legislation and International Law, Third Series, Volume XVI 1934. p. 221.

18. De Tejada, F.E., "Bemerkungen uber die Grundlagen des Banturechts," in ARSP Volume 46 1960. p. 510–514.

19. Bohm, D., Thought as a system, Routledge and Kegan Paul: London 1994. p. 18.

20. De Tejada, F.E., ARSP, op cit., 1960. p. 522–527.

21. This subtitle is borrowed verbatim from Bohm's chapter 2 on the rheomode.

22. We have already stated our intention not to discuss the correspondence theory. However, we believe that Bohm's critique of this theory, evidently from the perspective of rheomodic thought, is worth noting. See, Bohm, D., The undivided universe, Routledge and Kegan Paul: London 1993. p. 16–17.

23. Bohm, D., Thought as a system, op. cit., p. 181.

24. Kimmerle, H., "The concept of time as a key-notion for new ideas about development," in Diange, S.B. and Kimmerle, H. (ed.) Time and development in the thought of Sub-Saharan Africa, Studies in Intercultural Philosophy, Volume 8 1997. p. 21.

25. Bohm, D., Thought as a system, op. cit., p. 183.

Chapter Two Questions

Choose one answer.

1. Ramose posits that the term "Africa" speaks more to
   a. the Romans who for a time ruled the North African Coast the North Coast of the continent
   b. the western European historical experience with the people of the continent
   c. the Mediterranean Sea
   d. scientific etymological inquiry

2. Ramose posits that the term "Africa" speaks much less to
   a. the experience of African self-understanding
   b. the western European historical experience with the people of the continent
   c. African philosophy
   d. ears of corn
   e. land of the Afrigs

3. By the concept of "I Doubt and Therefore African Philosophy Exists," Ramose essentially
   a. abolishes the term Africa
   b. acknowledges that the term Africa will never be abolished
   c. reconstructs African history in general and the history of African philosophy in particular
   d. reaffirms African Renaissance
   e. clothes African philosophy in Western clothes

4. Ramose posits that the Harlem Renaissance is
   a. one of the forerunners of African philosophy
   b. the voices of Africans in the Diaspora
   c. philosophy
   d. the struggle for reason
   e. the rebirth of Africa

5. The unjust war of colonialization resulted with
   a. the loss of sovereignty and land for the Africans
   b. the imaginary rights of Africans
   c. Aristotle's definition of man
   d. African philosophy
   e. Western philosophy

6. One of the most important catalysts in breaking silence of and about Africans was
   a. Aristotle
   b. decolonialization
   c. "man is a rational being"
   d. the unjust war of colonialization
   e. Hitler's Holocaust

7. Which of these best describes what Ramose sees as the basis for racism?
   a. Colonialization
   b. The law of logic
   c. Western philosophy
   d. The struggle for reason—who is and who is not a rational animal
   e. Africans

8. The following factor(s) will result in the dissolution of both African and Western philosophies.
   a. Familiarity between the two
   b. Indistinguishable characteristic
   c. Tinctured insights
   d. Assimilation
   e. Integration

9. What does Ramose consider as the deeper meaning of "memorial" in the African historical reconstruction context?
   a. Collective identity and memory
   b. Individual identity and memory
   c. The past
   d. Ontology
   e. Indivisible link between memory and individual or collective memory

10. What does Cameron-Wedding see as the crux of modern racism?
    a. Racial profiling
    b. The Civil Rights Initiatives
    c. Shifting and denying the link between discrimination and domination
    d. The Racial Privacy Initiative
    e. Old definitions of racism

11. The intent of Race Privacy Initiative was actually to
    a. Make it harder for marginalized people to mobilize against racism
    b. To protect the privacy of whites
    c. To protect the safety of the minority group
    d. To celebrate diversity
    e. To stop the use of the word *minority*

12. Affirmative Action's objective was to
    a. Punish whites for the sins of their fathers
    b. Discriminate against whites
    c. Encourage minorities and women to achieve
    d. Counterbalance the impact of historic white racial preferences
    e. Perpetuate discrimination

13. Cameron-Wedding asserts that in the modern-day United States it is easy to perpetuate racism by
    a. Supporting Affirmative Action
    b. Supporting colorblindness
    c. Equating colorblindness to patriotism
    d. Playing basketball
    e. Supporting Tom Brokaw and not Jessie Jackson

14. Cameron-Wedding posits that the modern-day United States conservative effectively undermines the civil rights movement by
    a. Supporting Affirmative Action
    b. Compromising hegemonic terminology
    c. Reframing civil rights language
    d. Fighting fire with fire
    e. By linking themselves to Dr. Martin Luther King

15. The Pan-African concept came into being because
    a. Africans were troublemakers
    b. Reaction to Euro-Domination
    c. Europeans needed Africans to self define
    d. Reaction to Euro domination that undermined everything African
    e. None of the above

16. The First Pan African Congress was held in
    a. 1919
    b. 1963
    c. 1994
    d. 1997
    e. None of the above

17. The theme of all Pan African Conferences has been
    a. Unity
    b. European domination
    c. Corrupt African leaders
    d. Racism
    e. African independence

18. The Fifth Pan-African Congress was held in
    a. Manchester in 1945
    b. Ghana in 1998
    c. South Africa in 1999
    d. New York in 1927
    e. Lisbon in 1923

19. The conclusion by Ramose that Africans are consistently in search of harmony is
    a. pertinently true of African thought
    b. false
    c. questionable
    d. an indication of confusion
    e. an indication of excellence

20. Ramose sees Western philosophy and African philosophy as
    a. identical
    b. similar but not identical
    c. fragmented
    d. reconciled
    e. None of the above

21. The first person to win the Noble Peace Prize was
    a.   former President Nelson Mandela of South Africa
    b.   President Barack Obama of the United States
    c.   former Secretary-General of the United Nations Kofi Annan of Ghana
    d.   Ralph Bunche of the United States
    e.   Wangari Mathai of Kenya

In 100 words, describe the link between white privilege and colorblindness.

In 100 words, describe institutionalized racism and give examples.

Describe the contribution of Pan Africanism against Eurodomination.

What are the basic tenets of the methodic doubt construction "I Doubt, Therefore African Philosophy Exists"?

What is your understanding of "Philosophy of Ubuntu and Ubuntu as a Philosophy"?

What difference and similarities do you see between the African struggle against racism and the United States?

Name at least 10 achievements of people of African descent.

CHAPTER 3

Reclamation
and Self-Definitions

Introduction to Chapter Three

Boatamo Mosupyoe

A quest by Africans and people of African descent to reconstruct, redefine, and reclaim their rightful place in the universe marks the development of thought in Pan Africanism. No doubt the colonialization of Africa by Europeans as well as the European enslavement of African people adversely impacted on African ideologies, institutions, individuals, and communities. Failed post-colonial policies reveal human flaws as manifest in corruption but also display the strength of the aftermath of colonialism and gave rise to constructs like neo-colonialism, cultural theory, the dual conservation and neo-colonialism theory, and critical theory to capture the ongoing dialogue. As Africans struggled with developing national identities, ideologies, and edifices that would rid them of images as inferior people who deserved to be subjugated, new tensions emerged. The mediation of that tension happened in different areas, including discourse in academia. The articles in this chapter represent the continuing pursuit.

Randal Robinson's article "Toward Black Renaissance" notes the aftermath of both the colonialization and enslavement of African people. His article elucidates on the horror of enslavement and how that legacy continues today. He argues that African Americans use the right to vote to support the Democratic Party that rarely if ever advances the African American agenda. Randall uses federal housing statistics to illustrate the continuing disparity in wealth between the European Americans and African Americans. This disproportionality, also evident in white-collar salaries, etc., renders the argument that "it is too late" to demand reparations for African Americans irrelevant and ill placed. The saliency of the issue of reparation can be seen through the efforts of Congressman John Conyers, an African

American Democrat from Detroit. He introduced a bill that never made its way out of the Subcommittee on Civil and Constitutional Rights. The bill called for the acknowledgment of the "injustice, cruelty, brutality, and the inhumanity of slavery" and also to admit the impact of the racial and economic discrimination against African Americans. Preceding the Congressman's efforts was a book by Yale professor Boris Bittker, *The Case for Black Reparations*. Robinson observes that the book received little attention and even more notable silence from white liberal professors. Also worth noting are the efforts of James Foreman to bring light to the issue when he interrupted a predominantly European American church in New York to read a *Black Manifesto* demanding churches and synagogues to recompense African Americans for the injustices perpetrated on them. Realizing the degree of resistance to even the mention of reparations, Robinson suggests that fighting for reparation might not equal winning reparations even though a strong case can be made and he knows "no statute of limitation either legally or morally that would extinguish" the obligation to recompense African Americans, Africans, and Africans in the Diaspora.

A brief juxtaposition of Robinson's "Toward Black Renaissance" and Ramose's article "African Renaissance: A Northbound Gaze" reveals convergent and divergent views as the dialogue on black and/or African Renaissance continues. Both articles give primacy to the experience of people of African descent; Robinson focuses on reparations while Ramose questions the linguistic appropriateness of the word *renaissance* as it applies to Africa. Ramose outlines the historical usage of the word and its fist application in the African context. Ramose annotates the absence of the term "African Renaissance" in different types of literature, including eight volumes of UNESCO's *General History of Africa*. He attributes the absence of the term in these bodies of literature to lack of conceptualization of the concept. Abdel-Malek used the term "the renaissance of Egypt." Ramose notes that the "r" is in lowercase. The significance of this observation develops in the context of his argument. Ramose argues that if Africa has to give meaning and content to its experiences, including the reclamation, then Africa has to self-redefine, self-reconstruct, and self-name. The linguistic, experiential, historical, philosophical, and cultural richness of Africa obviously make this possible. The tendency to turn to the West or North to supplant concepts to the African experience proves problematic and results in a construct indicative of internalized racism and confusion, like Seme's dual "backward with the advanced" analogy of Africa and Europe, with Africa as backward and Europe as advanced; and Abdel-Malek's binary "R" and "r" application. Ramose emphasizes that African linguistics terminology *Mokoko-Hungwe* aptly (a) captures the "period of restitution and reparation to Africa," (b) rejects northern prominences and leadership, (c) preserves Africa's right to choose from her experience, (d) accepts multicentric interpretation of history, (e) affirms the dignity of African humanity as second to none, and (f) more importantly offers an indigenous concept of understanding "contemporary African history and politics."

Covin's article "The Brazilian National Context: Harbingers of Change," articulates how the Afro-Brazilian were excluded from meaningful participation in leadership positions even though they are in the majority. The Afro-Brazilians, in their struggle to find a place for themselves in their society, had to negotiate the "contradictory dominant myth" of a society that claims racial democracy and yet implicitly and explicitly demands "whitening" as a prerequisite to improving one's position in society. Despite claims of a non-racialized society, Brazil is racialized. The latter was evident by the absence of Blacks in leadership positions. Those African Brazilians who whitened themselves through association with white friends, obtaining higher education or success in the arts, were accepted into organizations but not as decision makers. Consequently in the words of

Abdias do Nascimento, "for black people to begin to play an active role in organizations or movements which were dedicated to their deepest concerns, they were going to have to either join the nascent black organizations, or they were going to have to build entirely new ones."

Marie Pauline Eboh's article "Is Western Democracy the Answer to the African Problem?" continues the theme of the need to accord primacy to African experience and contribution in resolving Africa and people of African descent's problems. Eboh basically argues for the efficacy of all society to contribute to human development, institutions, and ideologies. She observes that the Western or northern tendency to impose "democracies" on African nations belies the notion of democracy if indeed it means a government of the people, by the people, and for the people. She highlights the fact that U.S. democracy also manifests problems. She traces the historical manifestation inherent in U.S. democracy to Mary E. Lease's observation that Wall Street and not the people of the United States owns the country. In 1990 Porter McKeever underscores Lease's observation decades later, his comparison of the 1988 U.S. presidential election with Eastern Europe and Tiananmen Square led him to conclude that the vibrancy of democratic ideals in the United States pale. Dr. Kissinger's statement to the effect that the United States as a unilaterally and dictated world order is unsustainable further affirms Eboh's argument that Western democracy is not the answer to the African problem; instead, she reasons, "Thus far, there seems to be a sort of mutual agreement that Western democracy is not the answer to the African question. The answer lies in taking the bull by the horn—tackling the African socio-economic and political reality and giving democracy an African flair."

David Covin's: "A Voyage of Discovery: Sacramento and the Politics of Ordinary Black People" mirrors inasmuch as it affirms the reclamation and self-definition of people of African descent. In his speech given at the 40th anniversary of Ethnic Studies at California State University, Sacramento, in part Covin says, "This afternoon I'm going to talk about a Voyage of Discovery that has taken place over the past 40 years. It is the voyage of my discipline, Pan African Studies." He then proceeds to analyze findings of his research on the Sacramento area and how the historical social narratives and memories empowered by the historical Civil Rights and Black Power Movements were not grounded into mere ephemera. The empowerment translated into a visible and undeniable reclamation of social spaces and programs as their own to advance their own and others' agendas even where they were not in the majority. The first part of Covin's speech draws our attention to the road to the establishment of the Pan African Studies Program at California State University, Sacramento. Pertinent to the development of thought in Pan Africanism, this statement by the faculty then offers parallels and invaluable insights: "On this campus, the faculty said, let's make it clear, explicit, that Black Studies means the study of African people\s-*wherever they are.* Let's call ourselves Pan African Studies. They changed the program's name from Black Studies to Pan African Studies." The process leading to the establishment of Black Studies, Africana Studies, Africology, Afro-American Studies also indicate the varied multicentric ways of black people's or people of African descent's pathways of self-definition and reclamation.

The thematic self-definition and reconstruction focus persists in Mosupyoe's article "Recent African Immigration in the United States of America." Mosupyoe examines the immigration trends of Africans and the reasons behind the resettlement. The voluntary migration cultivated new environments, spaces, and relationships whose dynamics require new tools of analysis. The new immigrants' interaction with descendents of Africans who were brought to the Americas against their will produce tensions that require mediation. Reproductions of colonial paradigms such as concepts of divide and conquer appear in new forms simultaneously with cognitive distances engendered by varied views; these differing views are a product of convergent and divergent socialization processes that transcend common phenotypes. Despite the obvious challenges that have to be negotiated, the two groups share a space and resources that also spells out the desire to connect with people from "the mother land." This allure is undeniable. At best its articulation of the link and interaction between African Americans and recent African immigrants from 1950 to the present depicts in some parts of the United States and the Diaspora in Covin's axiom, the irrational dynamic of "persistent, perpetual, and relentless appeal for Black Unity that emerges from African peoples." Indeed, the divergent African country origin and city origin, linguistic diversity, variant thoughts accent the absurdity.

The chapter ends with the article "The Zion Christian Church in Post-Apartheid South Africa." In this article Mosupyoe examines how a church that previously identified with a regime that was oppressive to the African majority by a few European Africans, successfully reconstructed, reidentified, and redefined its self and its position to align with a new government in South Africa. The church's reconstructive success indicates its malleability and the government's determination to create new identities that promotes a peaceful transition to a new society.

Toward the Black Renaissance

Randall Robinson

Looking over the courses of study of the public schools, one finds little to show that the Negro figures in these curricula. . . . Several miseducated Negroes themselves contend that the study of the Negro by children would bring before them the race problem prematurely. . . . These misguided teachers ignore the fact that the race question is being brought before black and white children daily in their homes, in the streets, throughout the press and on the rostrum. How then, can the school ignore the duty of teaching the truth while these other agencies are playing up falsehood?

— Carter G. Woodson, *The Mis-Education of the Negro* (1933)

The little black girl who was Khalea's friend was told at age nine that she had failed to measure up, that she had not "cut" it. She was indisputably bright, disarmingly personable, and sun-clean of spirit, but she could not read well enough to get into the school she'd been led to believe she would one day attend. Rejected at nine.

Not knowing how to do otherwise, she no doubt blamed herself, further eroding a fragile self-esteem that had been under assault for the long heavy ages she could not know she already had borne. For in the person of a single half-soft-half-resilient child could be discerned the cumulative experience of a whole race of long-abused people.

These thoughts are about her and Sarah and Robert and Billy and the millions of children like them. They, before whom has been strung seriatim for centuries every conceivable hardship, are the future of the black race. Take no comfort from what you may see as examples of conspicuous black success. It has closed no economic gap and is statistically insignificant. It is the children of the black poor, the bulk legatees of American slavery, that we must salvage—or, in our time, we will have marked time but accomplished nothing.

It is not enough to say what needs to be done. That has been done before, brilliantly even, and gotten us little. Nonetheless, in a moment I will burden you with some of my thoughts on program recommendations. But such is not my strength. Nor is it the central point here. After all, we all pretty much know what needs to be done. Blacks know this and whites know this.

Trouble is, those who exercise control over our national public policy see no reason why they should care very much about taking steps to fix what America has done to blacks. The problem is not in preparing a black policy agenda for those who receive our votes. The Joint Center for Political Studies has done this. National black leadership summits have done this. More black groups than I can name have done this, along with gifted political thinkers like Ron Walters.

The politics of black people are controlled by the Democratic party and organized labor because these entities foot the bill. In fact, there is a formula: blacks supply the votes as a reliable part of the Democratic party coalition, fueled by the funding by Democrats and labor, often determining victory for Democratic candidates. Then, when blacks demand that their agenda be fulfilled, there is an impasse because they do not own their political resources and as such cannot really "demand." The end result amounts to a sophisticated form of begging.

— Ronald Walters, University of Maryland

We give our votes. We give our recommendations. We get little in return from those whom our votes help elect. The reason is the *politics* that connect votes to policy outcomes. In other words, we blacks don't *own* our politics, and thus have little leverage at the end of the day to enforce our policy recommendations. As long as our community must depend on the Democratic Party and other entities outside the black community to pay for voter mobilization within the black community, we will have little to no leverage to influence what gets placed on the legislative table and comes out as public policy.

In off-year national elections, it costs as little as five million dollars to run national voter education and voter mobilization efforts in the black community. Such efforts are carried out by black church, civic, and social organizations. Little of the money to fund the political work of these organizations comes from the black community, although it would seem that there is ample wherewithal to do so. Thus, we don't *own* the politics between *our* votes and *their* policy, and have, alas, little leverage over the latter. The reason? Our heads. The heads of those who could easily fund and own, in our name, our own community's politics. The heads of our children and all the rest of us. It is another price of slavery and its aftermath. We have no connecting mantra, no secular religion, no common tenets. No complete and satisfying knowledge of ourselves. With exceptions, most of us who have a little money to give have done better renovation work to our outsides than to our insides, or to our heads. As the colloquial expression goes: "it's a head thing."

I've talked enough about why this is the case. The profound consequences constitute still another particular in a long bill of them against the government of the United States and others who benefited from slavery. But this is why I have expended so much time here on the issue of reparations, for the very discussion engendered will help an embattled nine-year-old to know finally what happened to her, that she is blameless, that she has had something taken from her that has a far more than material value.

Perhaps it would help her place herself in context if she could read a letter I came upon in the wonderful book *Strong Men Keep Coming* by Tonya Bolden. The letter is dated August 7,

1865, and was written by Jourdon Anderson, once a slave in Big Spring, Tennessee, to his former owner, Colonel P. H. Anderson, who had written to the ex-slave in Dayton, Ohio, where he had resettled with his wife and children. The colonel had written to persuade Anderson to return to Big Spring and work for him as a free man:

Sir: I got your letter, and was glad to find that you had not forgotten Jourdon, and that you wanted me to come back and live with you again, promising to do better for me than anybody else can. . . .

I want to know particularly what the good chance is you propose to give me. I am doing tolerably well here. I get twenty-five dollars a month, with victuals and clothing; have a comfortable home for Mandy,—the folks call her Mrs. Anderson,—and the children—Milly Jane, and Grundy—go to school and are learning well. . . . Now if you will write and say what wages you will give me, I will be better able to decide whether it would be to my advantage to move back again.

As to my freedom, which you say I can have, there is nothing to be gained on that score, as I got my freedom papers in 1864 from the Provost-Marshall-General of the Department of Nashville. Mandy says she would be afraid to go back without some proof that you were disposed to treat us justly and kindly; and we have concluded to test your sincerity by asking you to send us our wages for the time we served you.

I served you faithfully for thirty-two years, and Mandy twenty years. At twenty-five dollars a month for me, and two dollars a week for Mandy, our earnings would amount to eleven thousand six hundred and eighty dollars. Add to this the interest for the time our wages have been kept back, and deduct what you paid for our clothing, and three doctor's visits to me, and pulling a tooth for Mandy, and the balance will show what we are in justice entitled to. . . .

Please send the money by Adam's Express, in care of V. Winters, Esq., Dayton, Ohio. If you fail to pay us for our faithful labors in the past, we can have little faith in your promises in the future. We trust the good Maker has opened your eyes to the wrongs which you and your fathers have done to me and my fathers, in making us toil for you for generations without recompense. . . . Surely there will be a day of reckoning for those who defraud the laborer of his hire. . . .

Say howdy to George Carter, and thank him for taking the pistol from you when you were shooting at me.

Colonel Anderson never paid Jourdon Anderson what he owed him for his labor, nor had any of the other slaveholders (including George Washington and Thomas Jefferson) who had stolen the labor of tens of millions of blacks and, by so doing, robbed the futures of all who would descend from them. The United States government was complicit in this massive injustice of defrauding "the laborer of his hire." Of course, the injustice would not end with the lives of the colonel and Jourdon Anderson, for the colonel's heirs did not pay the debt to the heirs of Jourdon Anderson either. Thus the value of Jourdon Anderson's stolen labor was to compound itself toward the future of today through the blood lines of the white man who had owned him against all immutable notions of natural justice.

If the nine-year-old girl or Sarah or Robert or Billy is not the great-great-great-grandchild of Jourdon Anderson, she or he is the descendant of somebody like him. They are owed, not just for the value of their forebears' labor, or for the humiliation of performing it, but for every devastating failure since, engendered by their government on the basis of race.

As the psychoanalyst would exhort the patient troubled in adulthood by some unspeakable, but repressed, violation in early life—

If you're ever to get past this, it must be gotten out and dealt with. Whatever awful thing was done to you must be drawn out and exorcized.

The chant becomes a mantra.

You are owed. You were caused to endure terrible things. The fault is not yours. There is nothing wrong with you. They did this to you.

Such is the emotional value to blacks of the call for reparations, a call now expanding to a chorus that includes, among others, the National Association for the Advancement of Colored People and the National Bar Association. Imagine all the liberating insights rising to the surface in the tear-washed foam of this long-suppressed national discussion on slavery, its unjust economic penalty, and its searing social price. Billy could learn now why there is no slavery museum on the Mall, no monument to Harriet Tubman, no memorial for Nat Turner—indeed, why he and everyone he knows are poor. Sarah could dream of herself as descended, just maybe, from the Queen of Sheba, of whom, before the discussion, Sarah had heard, but without knowing she was black and from Ethiopia.

The scale of the truth-tale balancing now, if only a little, in a cleansing new wind, Robert could glimpse the unproud side of European history, washing him deep, persuading him, where no one could have witnessed his previous shame, that, when averaged, no racial group is, or ever has been, superior or inferior to another.

Among the instances of [cannibalism] reported with some authority: in 1476, in Milan, the unpopular tyrant Galeazzo Maria Sforza was dismembered and eaten by a crowd; in 1572, after the St. Bartholomew's Day Massacre, Huguenot body parts were sold at auction and reportedly eaten in Paris and Lyon; in 1617 the body of Marshal d'Ancre was eaten in France. . . . Montaigne asserts in "On Cannibalism" that both Catholics and Protestants ate each other during the sixteenth-century Wars of Religion, but he does not pretend to offer proof of it, perhaps because it seemed so believable.

—Kirkpatrick Sale, *The Conquest of Paradise*

I, like the *"if I were French"* student at Howard, had never read Carter G. Woodson's *The Mis-Education of the Negro* in college. No professor I'd had at the black schools I'd attended (Norfolk State College and Virginia Union University) had put it on a syllabus. I had read the book on my own. I was stirred by Woodson's thinking but depressed as well by the still-apt fit of his views, sixty-seven years after he had written them. Progress of the "head," slavery's first casualty, seemed small. How long must a few lonely blacks whistle wisdom through the lightless centuries?

The catharsis occasioned by a full-scale reparations debate could change all that, could launch us with critical mass numbers into a surge of black self-discovery. We could wear the call as a breastplate, a coat of arms. We could disinter a buried history, connect it to another, more recent and mistold, and give it as a healing to the whole of our people, to the whole of America.

> *Upon examining the recent catalogues of the leading Negro colleges, one finds that invariably they give courses in ancient, medieval, and modern Europe, but they do not give such courses in ancient, medieval, and modern Africa. Yet Africa, according to recent discoveries, has contributed about as much to the progress of mankind as Europe has, and the early civilization of the Mediterranean world was decidedly influenced by Africa.*
> —Carter G. Woodson, *The Mis-Education of the Negro* (1933)

And then, of course, there are the billions of dollars owed to Africa and the descendants of slaves for pain and suffering, for the value of slaves' work, and for wealth lost in a postslavery environment of government-approved racial discrimination.

With respect to the question of compensation to African Americans, it has been proposed by Robert Westley, in "Many Billions Gone," that a private trust be established for the benefit of all African Americans. The trust would be funded out of the general revenues of the United States to support programs designed to accomplish "the educational and economic empowerment of the trust beneficiaries (African Americas) to be determined on the basis of need."

Professor Westley further suggests that the trust be funded for a period of no more than ten years. He does not name amounts. He is right not to do so. That should come later after an assessment can be made of what it will cost to repair the long-term social damage. By the same token, I believe that such a trust would have to be funded for at least two successive K-through-college educational generations, perhaps longer. Among other programs funded from the trust would be special K–12 schools throughout the United States with residential facilities for those black children who are found to be at risk in unhealthy family and neighborhood environments. The curricula for these schools would be rigorous, with course requirements for English, advanced mathematics, the sciences, and foreign languages. Additionally, the schools would emphasize the diverse histories and cultures of the black world. For blacks who remained in the public schools, much the same would be provided by special-purpose schools funded to supplement public-school offerings in a fashion not dissimilar to the role performed by weekend Hebrew schools for the Jewish community. All fees for these schools would be fully funded from the trust. Further, all blacks who qualified academically and were found to be in financial need would be entitled to attend college free of charge.

On the private side, a study funded by the trust would be undertaken to determine the extent to which American and foreign companies, or the existing successors to such companies, or individuals, families, and public institutions, were unjustly enriched by the uncompensated labor of slaves or by the *de jure* racial discrimination that succeeded slavery. Compensation would then be sought from those companies, institutions, and individuals—and sought with the same vigor that Undersecretary of State Stuart Eizenstat demonstrated on behalf of Jewish survivors of the Nazi holocaust, inducing sixteen German companies under pressure from the U.S. to establish a fund a 1.7 billion dollars to compensate mainly Jews used as slave laborers during the Nazi era.

Proceeds of a recovery from private interests on behalf of the descendants of black American slaves would go into the trust fund.

Now a final thought about additional programs that would be funded from the trust. The broad civil rights advocacy necessitated by a persistent climate of American racism would be generously funded, as well as the political work of black organizations seeking, as Ron Walters has suggested, to "own" the *politics* of the black community.

Lastly, I would urge the United States government to begin making amends to Africa and the Caribbean by initiating discussions that might constructively start with an American commitment toward full debt relief, fair trade terms, and significant monetary compensation.

The ideas I have broached here do not comprise anything near a comprehensive package. Nor was such my intention. What I have proposed does constitute a new starting point for a discussion with and among those who should feel some moral obligation to atone for slavery and what followed it, along with a commitment to close the social and economic gap between the races, opened and maintained by some 350 years of American racialist policies. One might reasonably ask how anyone could realistically expect the United States to take such a course when, at home, it is rolling back affirmative action programs and, abroad, providing in development assistance to poor countries but fifty cents per capita compared to the Nordic countries' sixteen dollars?

Blacks should come broadly to know that we do not approach this looming national debate as supplicants. The appeal here is not for affirmative action but, rather, for just compensation as an entitlement for the many years of heinous U.S. government-embraced wrongs and the stolen labor of our forebears. We make only the claims that other successful group complainants have made in the world. Put simply, we too are *owed*. Let us as a national society have the courage to approach the future by facing up at long last to the past.

If blacks are to have any chance for success here, we must make it clear to America that we will not allow ourselves to be ignored. I would offer in this connection a tactical suggestion: In addition to building our case on factual evidence, precedents, and serious scholarship, we would more effectively project our demands upon Washington policy makers were we to launch what I will call, a Year of Black Presence. Every black church, organization, and institution would commit to choose one day of the 130-odd days that the Congress is in session and bring on that day one thousand African Americans to walk the halls of Congress in support of compensation measures designed to close the economic and psychic gap between blacks and whites in America. The Congress, for one year, would never stop seeing our faces, never stop hearing our demands, never be relieved of our presence.

Unlike those who came to America of their own volition, African Americans are underrepresented in the councils of political power and finance. If we are to win our battles, we must fight them with the one asset that we have in abundance: our bodies.

We must do this in memory of the dark souls whose weary, broken bodies endured the unimaginable.

We must do this on behalf of our children whose thirsty spirits clutch for the keys to a future.

This is a struggle that we cannot lose, for in the very making of it we will discover, if nothing else, ourselves.

◇ ◇ ◇

On January 5, 1993, Congressman John Conyers, a black Democrat from Detroit, introduced in Congress a bill to "acknowledge the fundamental injustice, cruelty, brutality, and inhumanity of slavery in the United States and the 13 American colonies between 1619 and 1865 and to establish a commission to examine the institution of slavery, subsequent *de jure* and *de facto* racial and economic discrimination against African Americans, and the impact of these forces on living African Americans, to make recommendations to the Congress on appropriate remedies, and for other purposes."

The bill, which did not ask for reparations for the descendants of slaves but merely a commission to study the effects of slavery, won from the 435-member U.S. House of Representatives only 28 cosponsors, 18 of whom were black.

The measure was referred to the House Committee on the Judiciary and from there to the House Subcommittee on Civil and Constitutional Rights. The bill has never made it out of committee.

More than twenty years ago, black activist James Foreman interrupted the Sunday morning worship service of the largely white Riverside Church in New York City and read a *Black Manifesto* which called upon American churches and synagogues to pay $500 million as "a beginning of the reparations due us as people who have been exploited and degraded, brutalized, killed and persecuted." Foreman followed by promising to penalize poor response with disruptions of the churches' program agency operations. Though Foreman's tactics were broadly criticized in the mainstream press, the issue of reparations itself elicited almost no thoughtful response. This had been the case by then for nearly a century, during which divergent strains of black thought had offered a variety of reparations proposals. The American white community had turned a deaf ear almost uniformly.

Gunnar Myrdal, a widely respected thinker, wrote of dividing up plantations into small parcels for sale to ex-slaves on long-term installment plans. He theorized that American society's failure to secure ex-slaves with an agrarian economic base had led ultimately to an entrenched segregated society, a racial cast system But while Myrdal had seen white landowners being compensating for their land, he never once proposed recompense of any kind for the ex-slave he saw as in need of an economic base. In fact, in his book on the subject, *An American Dilemma,* Myrdal never once uses the words: reparation, restitution, indemnity, or compensation.

In the early 1970s Boris Bittker, a Yale Law School professor, wrote a book, *The Case for Black Reparations,* which made the argument that slavery, Jim Crow, and a general climate of race-based discrimination in America had combined to do grievous social and economic injury to African Americans. He further argued that sustained government-sponsored violations had rendered distinctions between *de jure* and *de facto* segregation meaningless for all practical purposes. Damages, in his view, were indicated in the form of an allocation of resources to some program that could be crafted for black reparations. The book evoked little in the way of scholarly response or follow-up.

The slim volume was sent to me by an old friend who once worked for me at TransAfrica, Ibrahim Gassama, now a law professor at the University of Oregon. I had called Ibrahim in Eugene to talk over the legal landscape for crafting arguments for a claim upon the federal and state governments for restitution or reparations to the derivative victims of slavery and the racial abuse that followed in its wake.

"It's the strangest thing," Ibrahim had said to me. "We law professors talk about every imaginable subject, but when the issue of reparations is raised among white professors, many of whom are otherwise liberal, it is met with silence. Clearly, there is a case to be made for this as an unpaid debt. Our claim may not be enforceable in the courts because the federal government has to agree to allow itself to be sued. In fact, this will probably have to have come out of the Congress as other American reparations have. Nonetheless, there is clearly a strong case to be made. But, I tell you, the mere raising of the subject produces a deathly silence, not unlike the silence that greeted the book I'm sending you."

Derrick Bell, who was teaching at Harvard Law School while I was a student there in the late 1960s, concluded his review of Bittker's book in a way that may explain the reaction Ibrahim got from his colleagues:

Short of a revolution, the likelihood that blacks today will obtain direct payments in compensation for their subjugation as slaves before the Emancipation Proclamation, and their exploitation as quasi-citizens since, is no better than it was in 1866, when Thaddeus Stevens recognized that his bright hope of "forty acres and a mule" for every freedman had vanished "like the baseless fabric of a vision."

If Bell is right that African Americans will not be compensated for the massive wrongs and social injuries inflicted upon them by their government, during and after slavery, then there is *no* chance that America can solve its racial problems—if solving these problems means, as I believe it must, closing the yawning economic gap between blacks and whites in this country. The gap was opened by the 246-year practice of slavery. It has been resolutely nurtured since in law and public behavior. It has now ossified. It is structural. Its framing beams are disguised only by the counterfeit manners of a hypocritical governing class.

For twelve years Nazi Germany inflicted horrors upon European Jews. And Germany paid. It paid Jews individually. It paid the state of Israel. For two and a half centuries, Europe and America inflicted unimaginable horrors upon Africa and its people. Europe not only paid nothing to Africa in compensation, but followed the slave trade with the remapping of Africa for further European economic exploitation. (European governments have yet even to accede to Africa's request for the return of Africa's art treasures looted along with its natural resources during the century-long colonial era.)

While President Lincoln supported a plan during the Civil War to compensate slave owners for their loss of "property," his successor, Andrew Johnson, vetoed legislation that would have provided compensation to ex-slaves.

Under the Southern Homestead Act, ex-slaves were given six months to purchase land at reasonably low rates without competition from white southerners and northern investors. But, owing to their destitution, few ex-slaves were able to take advantage of the homesteading program. The largest number that did were concentrated in Florida, numbering little more than three thousand. The soil was generally poor and unsuitable for farming purposes. In any case, the ex-slaves had no money on which to subsist for months while waiting for crops, or the scantest wherewithal to purchase the most elementary farming implements. The program failed. In sum, the United States government provided no compensation to the victims of slavery.

———

Perhaps I should say a bit here about why the question of reparations is critical to finding a solution to our race problems.

This question—and how blacks gather to pose it—is a good measure of our psychological readiness as a community to pull ourselves abreast here at home and around the world. I say this because no outside community can be more interested in solving our problems that we. Derrick Bell suggested in his review of Bittker's book that the white power structure would never support reparations because to do so would operate against its interests. I believe Bell is right in that view. The initiative must come from blacks, broadly, widely, implacably.

But what exactly will black enthusiasm, or lack thereof, measure? There is no linear solution to any of our problems, for our problems are not merely technical in nature. By now, after 380 years of unrelenting psychological abuse, the biggest part of our problem is inside us: in how we have come to see ourselves, in our damaged capacity to validate a course for ourselves without outside approval.

Meanwhile, the cotton the slaves produced had become not only the United States' leading export but exceeded in value all other exports combined. After the slave trade was outlawed in 1807 approximately one million slaves were moved from the states that produced less cotton (Maryland, Virginia, the Carolinas) to those that produced more (Georgia, Alabama, Mississippi, Louisiana, Texas)—a migration almost *twice as large as that from Africa to the British colonies and the United States. With the increase in cotton production, the price of slaves went up, to such an extent that by 1860 capital investment in slaves in the south—who now numbered close to four million, or one third of the population—exceeded the value of all other capital worth, including land.*
—Yuval Taylor, *I Was Born a Slave*

The issue here is not whether or not we can, or will, win reparations. The issue rather is whether we will fight for reparations, because we have decided for ourselves that they are our due. In 1915, into the sharp teeth of southern Jim Crow hostility, Cornelius J. Jones filed a lawsuit against the United States Department of the Treasury in an attempt to recover sixty-eight million dollars for former slaves. He argued that, through a federal tax placed on raw cotton, the federal government had benefited financially from the sale of cotton that slave labor had produced, and for which the black men, women, and children who had produced the cotton had not been paid. Jones's was a straightforward proposition. The monetary value of slaves' labor, which he estimated to be sixty-eight million dollars, had been appropriated by the United States government. A debt existed. It had to be paid to the, by then, ex-slaves or their heirs.

Where was the money?

A federal appeals court held that the United States could not be sued without its consent and dismissed the so-called Cotton Tax case. But the court never addressed Cornelius J. Jones's question about the federal government's appropriation of property—the labor of blacks who had worked the cotton fields—that had never been compensated.

Let me try to drive the point home here: through keloids of suffering, through coarse veils of damaged self-belief, lost direction, misplaced compass, shit-faced resignation, racial transmutation, black people worked long, hard, killing days, years, centuries—and they were never *paid*. The value of their labor went into others' pockets—plantation owners, northern entrepreneurs, state treasuries, the United States government.

Where was the money?

Where *is* the money?

There is a debt here.

I know of no statute of limitations either legally or morally that would extinguish it. Financial quantities are nearly as indestructible as matter. Take away here, add there, interest compounding annually, over the years, over the whole of the twentieth century.

Where is the money?

Jews have asked this question of countries and banks and corporations and collectors and any who had been discovered at the end of the slimy line holding in secret places the gold, the art, the money that was the rightful property of European Jews before the Nazi terror. Jews have demanded what was their due and received a fair measure of it.

Clearly, how blacks respond to the challenge surrounding the simple demand for restitution will say a lot more about us *and do a lot more for us* than the demand itself would suggest. We would show ourselves to be responding as any normal people would to victimization were we to assert collectively in our demands for restitution that, for 246 years and with the complicity of the United States government, hundreds of millions of black people endured unimaginable cruelties—kidnapping, sale as livestock, deaths in the millions during terror-filled sea voyages, backbreaking toil, beatings, rapes, castrations, maimings, murders. We would begin a healing of our psyches were the most public case made that whole peoples lost religions, languages, customs, histories, cultures, children, mothers, fathers. It would make us more forgiving of ourselves, more self-approving, more self-understanding to see, *really see,* that on three continents and a string of islands, survivors had little choice but to piece together whole new cultures from the rubble shards of what theirs had once been. And they were never made whole. And never compensated. Not one red cent.

Left behind to gasp for self-regard in the vicious psychological wake of slavery are history's orphans played by the brave black shells of their ancient forebears, people so badly damaged that they cannot *see* the damage, or how their government may have been partly, if not largely, responsible for the disabling injury that by now has come to seem normal and unattributable.

Until America's white ruling class accepts the fact that the book never closes on massive unre-

dressed social wrongs, America can have no future as one people. Questions must be raised, to American private, as well as, public institutions. Which American families and institutions, for instance, were endowed in perpetuity by the commerce of slavery? And how do we square things with slavery's modern victims from whom all natural endowments were stolen? What is a fair measure of restitution for this, the most important of all American human rights abuses?

> *The founders of Brown University, Nicholas and Joseph Brown, got their wealth by manufacturing and selling slave ships and investing in the slave trade.*
> —*The Black Holocaust for Beginners,* S. E. Anderson

If one leaves aside the question of punitive damages to do a rough reckoning of what might be fair in basic compensation, we might look first at the status of today's black male.

For purposes of illustration, let us picture one representative individual whose dead-end crisis in contemporary America symbolizes the plight of millions. At various times in his life he will likely be in jail or unemployed or badly educated or sick from a curable ailment or dead from violence.

What happened to him? From what did he emerge?

His great-great-grandfather was born a slave and died a slave. Great-great-grandfather's labors enriched not only his white southern owner but also shipbuilders, sailors, ropemakers, caulkers, and countless other northern businesses that serviced and benefited from the cotton trade built upon slavery. Great-great-grandfather had only briefly known his mother and father before being sold off from them to a plantation miles away. He had no idea where in Africa his people had originally come from what language they had spoken or customs they had practiced. Although certain Africanisms—falsetto singing, the ring shout, and words like *yam*—had survived, he did not know that their origins were African.

He was of course compulsorily illiterate. His days were trials of backbreaking work and physical abuse with no promise of relief. He had no past and no future. He scratched along only because some biological instinct impelled him to survive.

His son, today's black male's great-grandfather, was also born into slavery and, like his father, wrenched so early from his parents that he could scarcely remember them. At the end of the Civil War, he was nineteen years old. While he was pleased to no longer be a slave, he was uncertain that the new status would yield anything in real terms that was very much different from the life (if you could call it that) that he had been living. He too was illiterate and completely without skills.

He was one of four million former slaves wandering rootlessly around in the defeated South. He trusted no whites, whether from the North or South. He had heard during the war that even President Lincoln had been urging blacks upon emancipation to leave the United States en masse for colonies that would be set up in Haiti and Liberia. In fact, Lincoln had invited a group of free blacks to the White House in August 1862 and told them: "Your race suffers greatly, many of them, by living among us, while ours suffer from your presence. In a word we suffer on each side. If this is admitted, it affords a reason why we should be separated."

Today's black male's great-grandfather knew nothing of Haiti or Liberia, although he had a good idea why Lincoln wanted to ship blacks to such places. By 1866 his life had remained a trial of instability and rootlessness. He had no money and little more than pickup work. He and other blacks in the South were faced as well with new laws that were not unlike the antebellum Slave Codes. The new measures were called Black Codes and, as John Hope Franklin noted in *From Slavery to Freedom,* they all but guaranteed that

the control of blacks by white employers was about as great as that which slaveholders had exercised. Blacks who quit their job could be arrested and imprisoned for breach of contract. They were not allowed to testify in court except in cases involving members of their own race. Numerous fines were imposed for seditious speeches, insulting gestures or acts, absence from work, violating curfew, and the possession of firearms. There was, of course, no enfranchisement of blacks, and no indication that in the future they could look forward to full citizenship and participation in a democracy.

Although some blacks received land in the South under the Southern Homestead Act of 1866, the impression that every exslave would receive "forty acres and a mule" as a gift of the government never became a reality. Great-grandfather, like the vast majority of the four million former slaves, received nothing and died penniless in 1902—but not before producing a son who was born in 1890 and later became the first of his line to learn to read.

Two decades into the new century, having inherited nothing in the way of bootstraps with which to hoist himself, and faced with unremitting racial discrimination, Grandfather became a sharecropper on land leased from whites whose grandparents had owned at least one of his forebears. The year was 1925 and neither Grandfather nor his wife was allowed to vote. His son would join him in the cotton fields under the broiling sun of the early 1930s. They worked twelve hours or more a day and barely eked out a living. Grandfather had managed to finish the fifth grade before leaving school to work full time. Inasmuch as he talked like the people he knew, and like his parents and their parents before them, his syntax and pronunciation bore the mark of the unlettered. Grandfather wanted badly that his son's life not mirror his, but was failing depressingly in producing for the boy any better opportunity than that with which he himself had been presented. Not only had he no money, but he survived against the punishing strictures of southern segregation that allowed for blacks the barest leavings in education, wages, and political freedom. He was trapped and afraid to raise his voice against a system that in many respects resembled slavery, now a mere seventy years gone.

Grandfather drank and expressed his rage in beatings administered to his wife and his son. In the early 1940s Grandfather disappeared into a deep depression and never seemed the same again.

Grandfather's son, the father of today's black male, periodically attended segregated schools, first in a rural area near the family's leased cotton patch and later in a medium-sized segregated southern city. He learned to read passably but never finished high school. He was not stigmatized for this particular failure because the failure was not exceptional in the only world that he had ever known.

Ingrained low expectation, when consciously faced, invites impenetrable gloom. Thus, Father did not dwell on the meagerness of his life chances. Any penchant he may have had for introspection, like his father before him, he drowned in corn spirits on Friday nights. He was a middle-aged laborer and had never been on first-name terms with anyone who was not a laborer like himself. He worked for whites and, as far as he could tell, everyone in his family before him had. Whites had, to him, the best of everything—houses, cars, schools, movie theaters, neighborhoods. Black neighborhoods he could tell from simply looking at them, even before he saw the people. And it was not just that the neighborhoods were poor. No, he had subconsciously likened something inside himself, a jagged rent in his ageless black soul, to the sagging wooden tenement porches laden with old household objects—ladders, empty flowerpots, wagons—that rested on them, often wrong side up, for months at a time. The neighborhoods, lacking sidewalks, streetlights, and sewage systems, had, like Father and other blacks, preserved themselves by not caring. Hunkered down. Gone inside themselves, turning blank, sullen faces to the outside world.

The world hadn't bothered to notice.

Father died of heart disease at the age of forty-five just before the Voting Rights Act was passed in 1965. Like his ancestors who had lived and died in slavery in centuries before, he was never allowed to cast a vote in his life. Little else distinguished his life from theirs, save a subsistence wage, the freedom to walk around in certain public areas, and the ability to read a newspaper, albeit slowly.

Parallel lines never touch, no mater how far in time and space they extend.

They had been declared free—four million of them. Some had simply walked off plantations during the war in search of Union forces. Others had become brazenly outspoken to their white masters toward the war's conclusion. Some had remained loyal to their masters to the end. Abandoned, penniless and unskilled, to the mercies of a humiliated and hostile South, millions of men, women, and children trudged into the false freedom of the Jim Crow South with virtually nothing in the way of recompense, preparation, or even national apology.

It is from this condition that today's black male emerged.

His social crisis is so alarming that the United States Commission on Civil Rights by the spring of 1999 had made it the subject of an unusual two-day conference. "This is a very real and serious and difficult issue," said Mary Frances Berry, chair of the commission. "This crisis has broad implications for the future of the race."

The black male is far more likely than his white counterpart to be in prison, to be murdered, to have no job, to fail in school, to become seriously ill. His life will be shorter by seven years, his chances of finishing high school smaller—74 percent as opposed to 86 percent for his white counterpart. Exacerbating an already crushing legacy of slavery-based social disabilities, he faces fresh discrimination daily in modern America. In the courts of ten states and the District of Columbia, he is ten times more likely to be imprisoned than his white male counterpart for the same offense. If convicted on a drug charge, he will likely serve a year more in prison than his white male counterpart will for the same charge. While he and his fellow black males constitute 15 percent of the nation's drag users, they make up 33 percent of those arrested for drug use and 57 percent of those convicted. And then they die sooner, and at higher rates of chronic illnesses like AIDS, hypertension, diabetes, cancer, stroke, and Father's killer, heart disease.

Saddest of all, they have no clear understanding of why such debilitating fates have befallen them. There were no clues in their public school education. No guideposts in the popular culture. Theirs was the "now" culture. They felt no impulse to look behind for causes.

———————

Q: What were the five greatest human rights tragedies that occurred in the world over the last five hundred years?

Pose this question to Europeans, Africans, and Americans, and I would guess that you would get dramatically divergent answers.

My guess is that both the Americans and the Europeans would place the Jewish holocaust and Pol Pot's extermination of better than a million Cambodians at the top of their list. Perhaps the Europeans would add the Turkish genocide against Armenians. Europe and America would then agree that Stalin's massive purges would qualify him for third, fourth, or fifth place on the list. The Europeans would omit the destruction of Native Americans, in an oversight. The Americans would omit the Native Americans as well, but more for reasons of out-of-sight than oversight. Perhaps one or both would assign fifth place to the 1994 Hutu massacre of Tutsis in Rwanda. No one outside of Africa would remember that from 1890 to 1910 the Belgian King Leopold II (who was viewed at the time in Europe and America as a "philanthropic" monarch) genocidally plundered the Congo, killing as many as ten million people.

All of these were unspeakably brutal human rights crimes that occurred over periods ranging from a few weeks to the span of an average lifetime. But in each of these cases, the cultures of those who were killed and persecuted survived the killing spasms. Inasmuch as large numbers, or even remnants of these groups, weathered the savageries with their cultural memories intact, they were able to regenerate themselves and their societies. They rebuilt their places of worship and performed again their traditional religious rituals. They rebuilt their schools and read stories and poems from books written in their traditional languages. They rebuilt stadia, theaters, and amphitheaters in which survivors raised to the heavens in ringing voices songs so old that no one knew when they had been written or who had written them. They remembered their holidays and began to observe them again. They had been trapped on an island in a burning river and many had perished. But the fire had eventually gone out and they could see again their past and future on the river's opposite banks.

The enslavement of black people was practiced in America for 246 years. In spite of and because of its longevity, it would not be placed on the list by either the Americans or the Europeans who had played a central role in slavery's business operations. Yet the black holocaust is far and away the most heinous human rights crime visited upon any group of people in the world over the last five hundred years.

There is oddly no inconsistency here.

Like slavery, other human rights crimes have resulted in the loss of millions of lives. But only slavery, with its sadistic patience, asphyxiated memory, and smothered cultures, has hulled empty a whole race of people with inter-generational efficiency. Every artifact of the victims' past cultures, every custom, every ritual, every god, every language, every trace element of a people's whole hereditary identity, wrenched from them and ground into a sharp choking dust. It is a human rights crime without parallel in the modern world. For it produces its victims *ad infinitum*, long after the active stage of the crime has ended.

Our children have no idea who they are. How can we tell them? How can we make them understand who they were before the ocean became a furnace incinerating every pedestal from which the ancient black muses had offered inspiration? What can we say to the black man on death row? The black mother alone, bitter, overburdened, and spent? Who tells them that their fate washed ashore at Jamestown with twenty slaves in 1619?

But Old Massa now, he knows what to say. Like a sexually abusing father with darting snake eyes and liquid lips he whispers—

I know this has hurt and I won't do it again, but don't you tell anybody.

Then on the eve of emancipation, in a wet wheedling voice, Old Massa tells the fucked-up 246-year-old spirit-dead victims with posthypnotic hopefulness—

Now y'all just forget about everything. Gwan now. Gwan.

Go where? Do what? With what? Where is my mother? My father? And theirs? And theirs? I can hear my own voice now loud in my ears.

America has covered itself with a heavy wet material that soaks up annoying complaints like mine. It listens to nothing it does not want to hear and wraps its unread citizens, white and black, in the airless garment of circumambient denial, swathing it all in a lace of fine, sweet lies that further blur everyone's understanding of "why black people are like they are."

America's is a mentality of pictorial information and physical description placed within comprehensible frames of time. We understand tragedy when buildings fall and masses of people die in cataclysmic events. We don't understand tragedy that cannot be quantified arithmetically, requiring more than a gnat's attention span.

The Negro is an American. We know nothing of Africa.
    —Martin Luther King Jr.

Culture is the matrix on which the fragile human animal draws to remain socially healthy. As fish need the sea, culture, with its timeless reassurance and its seeming immortality, offsets for the frail human spirit the brevity, the careless accidentalness of life. An individual human life is easy to extinguish. Culture is leaned upon as eternal. It flows large and old around its children. And it is very hard to kill. Its murder must be undertaken over hundreds of years and countless generations. Pains must be taken to snuff out every traditional practice, every alien word, every heaven-sent ritual, every pride, every connection of the soul, gone behind and reaching ahead. The carriers of the doomed culture must be ridiculed and debased and humiliated. This must be done to their mothers and their fathers, their children, their children's children and their children after them. And there will come a time of mortal injury to all of their souls, and their culture will breathe no more. But they will not mourn its passing, for they will by then have forgotten that which they might have mourned.

————

On April 27, 1993, under the auspices of the Organization of African Unity (a body comprised of African governments), the first pan-African conference on the subject of reparations was convened in Abuja, Nigeria. Among the hundreds who attended from thirty countries and four continents were Abdou Diouf, chairman of the OAU and president of Senegal, and Salim Salim, OAU's secretary general. My friend Dudley Thompson, the Jamaican human rights lawyer, served as rapporteur for the three-day conference. The delegation at the end of their deliberations drafted a declaration that was later unanimously adopted by Africa's heads of state at a summit meeting.

I should like to quote for you parts of that declaration, for it accomplishes at least two important purposes. First, it makes known the victim's (in other words, Africa's) very public witness, which has been long suppressed. Second, it introduces what I believe to be a just and legitimate claim against the United States and the countries of western Europe for restitution:

Recalling the establishment by the Organization of African Unity of a machinery for appraising the issue of reparations in relation to the damage done to Africa and to the Diaspora by enslavement, colonialism and neo-colonialism; convinced that the issue of reparations is an important question requiring the united action of Africa and its Diaspora and worthy of the active support of the rest of the international community;

Fully persuaded that the damage sustained by the African peoples is not a theory of the past but is painfully manifested from Harare to Harlem and in the damaged economics of Africa and the black world from Guinea to Guyana, from Somalia to Surinam;

Aware of historic precedents in reparations varying from German payments of restitution to the Jews, to the question of compensating Japanese-Americans for the injustice of internment by the Roosevelt Administration in the United States during World War II;

Cognizant of the fact that compensation for injustice need not necessarily be paid entirely in capital transfer but could include service to the victims or other forms of restitution and readjustment of the relationship agreeable to both parties;

Emphasizing that an admission of guilt is a necessary step to reverse this situation;

Emphatically convinced that what matters is not the guilt but the responsibility of those states whose economic evolution once depended on slave labour and colonialism and whose forebears participated either in selling and buying Africans, or in owning them, or in colonizing them;

Convinced that the pursuit of reparations by the African peoples on the continent and in the Diaspora will be a learning experience in self-discovery and in uniting political and psychological experiences;

Calls upon the international community to recognize that there is a unique and unprecedented moral debt owed to the African peoples which has yet to be paid—the debt of compensation to the Africans as the most humiliated and exploited people of the last four centuries of modern history.

The declaration was ignored by American media, and I confess that I knew nothing about it until Dudley Thompson brought it to my attention after my speech in March 1999 at the University of Technology in Kingston. I cannot say that I was surprised that American media had not covered the conference. News decision-makers no doubt decided that such deliberations were unimportant, even though they had for years heaped attention upon the appeals of other groups in the world for compensation as wronged parties. As you can see, such claims were hardly unique in the world and many had been pursued successfully, resulting in billions of dollars in compensation.

After World War I the allies made successful claims against Germany, as would Jews after World War II. The Poles also laid claims against the Germans after being used by the Nazis during the Second World War as slave labor. Japanese-Americans recovered from the United States government. The Inuit recovered from the Canadian government. Aborigines recovered money and large areas of land from the Australian government. Korean women, forced into prostitution by Japan during World War II, were compensated as well.

According to Dudley Thompson, international law in this area is replete with precedents.

Not only is there a moral debt but there is clearly established precedence in law based on the principle of unjust enrichment. In law if a party unlawfully enriches himself by wrongful acts against another, then the party so wronged is entitled to recompense. There have been some 15 cases in which the highest tribunals including the International Court at the Hague have awarded large sums as reparations based on this law.

Only in the case of black people have the claims, the claimants, the crime, the law, the precedents, the awful contemporary social consequences all been roundly ignored. The thinking must be that the case that cannot be substantively answered is best not acknowledged at all. Hence, the United States government and white society generally have opted to deal with this *debt* by forgetting that it is owned. The crime—246 years of an enterprise murderous both of a people and their culture—is so unprecedentedly massive that it would require some form of collective insanity not to see it and its living victims.

But still many, if not most, whites cannot or will not see it (a behavior that is accommodated by all too many uncomplaining blacks). This studied white blindness may be a modern variant of a sight condition that afflicted their slaveholding forebears who concocted something called *drapetomania,* the so-called mental disorder that slaveholders seriously believed caused blacks to run away to freedom. America accepts responsibility for little that goes wrong in the world, least of all the contemporary plight of black Americans. And until America can be made to do so, it is hard to see how we can progress significantly in our race relations.

On my behalf, my old friend Ibrahim called Robert Westley, a black law professor at Tulane Law School in New Orleans. Westley had been on the verge of publishing in the *Boston College Law Review* a detailed legal analysis of the case for reparations he believes the United States government owes African Americans as a group. Within a week of Ibrahim's call to Westley, I received from Westley a one-hundred-page draft of his article, "Many Billions Gone," which measured, with quantitative data compiled by respected academic social researchers, the cumulative economic consequences to African Americans of three and a half centuries of U.S. government–backed slavery, segregation, and *de jure* racial discrimination. The moral and legal merits of Westley's arguments were compelling, particularly when measured against those of claims for reparations that have been successful. One such ground-breaking claim, which had been formulated by Jewish organizations and leaders before the end of World War II, resulted in September 1952 in the Luxemburg Agreement. The claimants were two entities: the state of Israel, on behalf of the five hundred thousand Nazi war victims who had resettled in Israel, and the Conference on Jewish Material Claims Against Germany (the Claims Conference), on behalf of victims who had settled in countries other than Israel. The Claims Conference also represented the interests of the Jewish people as a whole who were entitled to indemnification for property that had been left by those who had died without known heirs.

Westley wrote of the treaty:

Wiedergutmachung [literally, "making good again"] was unprecedented in several respects. . . . The treaty obligation by which Israel was to receive the equivalent of one billion dollars in reparations from West Germany for crimes committed by the Third Reich against the Jewish people reflected Chancellor Konrad Adenauer's view that the German people had a moral duty to compensate the Jewish people for their material losses and suffering. Secondly, the sums paid not only to Israel but also to the Claims Conference showed a genuine desire on the part of the Germans to make Jewish victims of Nazi persecution whole. Under Protocol No. 1 of the Luxemburg Agreement, national legislation was passed in Germany that sought to compensate Jews individually for deprivation of liberty, compulsory labor and involuntary abandonment of their homes, loss of income and professional or educational opportunities, loss of [World War I] pensions, damage to health, loss of property through discriminatory levies such as the Flight Tax, damage to economic prospects, and loss of citizenship.

Israel's prime minister, David Ben-Gurion, was to say of the agreement:

For the first time in the history of relations between people, a precedent has been created by which a great State, as a result of moral pressure alone, takes it upon itself to pay compensation to the victims of the government that preceded it. For the first time in the history of a people that has been persecuted, oppressed, plundered and despoiled for hundreds of years in the countries of Europe, a persecutor and despoiler has been obliged to return part of his spoils and has even undertaken to make collective reparation as partial compensation for material losses.

The principle, set forward in the agreement and amplified by Ben-Gurion for other reparation claims that would follow, was simple. When a government kills its own people or facilitates their involuntary servitude and generalized victimization based on group membership, then that government or its successor has a moral obligation to materially compensate that group in a way that would make it whole, while recognizing that material compensation alone can never adequately compensate the victims of great human rights crimes.

Some would argue that such an obligation does not obtain in the case of the black holocaust because the wrongful action took place so long ago. Such arguments are specious at best. They can be answered in at least two ways, the second more compelling than the first.

Beginning with the question of late amends-making, in 1998 President Clinton signed into law the Sand Creek Massacre National Historic Study Site Act, which officially acknowledges an 1864 attack by seven hundred U.S. soldiers on a peaceful Cheyenne village located in the territory of Colorado. Hundreds, largely women and children, were killed. The act calls for the establishment of a federally funded Historic Site at Sand Creek. While not providing for payment to the victims' heirs, the apology/restitution measure, coming 134 years after the event, does counter the "it's too late" objection.

In the early years of the twentieth century, it was becoming clear that the Negro would be effectively disfranchised throughout the South, that he would be firmly relegated to the lower rungs of the economic ladder, and that neither equality nor aspirations for equality in any department of life were for him.

The public symbols and constant reminders of his inferior position were the segregation statutes, or "Jim Crow" laws. They constituted the most elaborate and formal expression of sovereign white opinion upon the subject. In bulk and detail as well as in effectiveness of enforcement the segregation codes were comparable with the black codes of the old regime, though the laxity that mitigated the harshness of the black codes was replaced by a rigidity that was more typical of the segregation code. That code lent the sanction of law to a racial ostracism that extended to churches and schools, to housing and jobs, to eating and drinking. Whether by law or by custom, that ostracism extended to virtually all forms of public transportation, to sports and recreations, to hospitals, orphanages, prisons, and asylums, and ultimately to funeral homes, morgues, and cemeteries.

—C. Vann Woodward, *The Strange Career of Jim Crow*

In 1994, seventy-one years after the Rosewood massacre in which white lynch mobs during a weeklong orgy of hate, killed six blacks and drove survivors into the swamps near a prosperous black community in Florida, Governor Lawton Chiles signed into law a bill (House Bill 591) that provided for the payment of $2.1 million in reparations to the descendants of the black victims at Rosewood.

Indeed, slavery itself did not end in 1865, as is commonly believed, but rather extended into the twentieth century to within a few years of the Rosewood massacre for which reparations were paid. As Yuval Taylor has pointed out in *I Was Born a Slave:*

Although they were not called *slavery,* the post-Reconstruction Southern practices of peonage, forced convict labor, and to a lesser degree sharecropping essentially continued the institution of slavery well into the twentieth century, and were in some ways even worse. (Peonage, for example, was a complex system in which a black man would be arrested for "vagrancy," another word for unemployment, ordered to pay a fine he could not afford, and incarcerated. A plantation owner would pay his fine and "hire" him until he could afford to pay off the fine himself: The peon was then forced to work, locked up at night, and, if he ran away, chased by bloodhounds until recaptured. One important difference between peonage and slavery was that while slaves had considerable monetary value for the plantation owner, peons had almost none, and could therefore be mistreated—and even murdered—without monetary loss.)

The foregoing precedents for reparations would be less sustaining, however, had the enormous human rights crime of slavery (later practiced as peonage) not been overlapped and extended by a century of government-sponsored segregation and general racial discrimination.

What slavery had firmly established in the way of debilitating psychic pain and a lopsidedly unequal economic relationship of blacks to whites, formal organs of state and federal government would cement in law for the century that followed. Thus it should surprise no one that the wealth gap (wealth defined as the net value of assets) separating blacks from whites over the twentieth century has mushroomed beyond any ability of black earned income ever to close it. This too is the fruit of long-term structural racial discrimination, government-sponsored in many cases, acquiesced to in others.

The evidence of this discrimination is so overwhelming that one hardly knows which examples to select to illustrate the point. Westley writes in "Many Billions Gone":

Based on discrimination in home mortgage approval rates, the projected number of credit-worthy home buyers and the median white housing appreciation rate, it is estimated that the current generation of blacks will lose about $82 billion in equity due to institutional discrimination. All things being equal, the next generation of black home owners will lose $93 billion.

As the cardinal means of middle class wealth accumulation, this missed opportunity for home equity due to private and governmental racial discrimination is devastating to the black community.

Of course, benefiting intergenerationally from this weather of racism were white Americans whose assets piled up like fattening snowballs over three and a half centuries' terrain of slavery and the mean racial climate that followed it.

Indeed, until 1950 the Federal Housing Authority provided subsidies to white mortgage holders who were bound by restrictive covenants to exclude blacks from any future ownership of their real property. This device alone caused blacks to miss out on billions, in home equity wealth accumulation. Since 1950 American residential apartheid and middle-class wealth-building discrimination have been maintained through, among other means, the practice of redlining.

It follows unavoidably from this that the black middle class would be almost wholly dependent upon the gossamer filaments of salary to suspend it over rank poverty's chasm below. Consider. College-educated whites enjoy an average income of $38,700, a net worth of $74,922, and net financial assets of $19,823. College-educated blacks, however, earn only $29,440 annually with a new worth of $17,437 and $175 in net financial assets.

Attributing the black middle class's sickly economic condition to mortgage and other past and existing forms of racial discrimination, Westley reports:

Blacks who hold white collar jobs have $0 net financial assets compared to their white counterparts who on average hold $11,952 in net financial assets. Black middle class status, as such figures indicate, is based almost entirely on income, not assets or wealth. Thus, the black middle class can best be described as fragile. Even blacks earning as much as $50,000 per year have on average net financial assets of only $290 compared to $6,988 for whites. Moreover black families need more wage earners per household to attain the living standards of white households of similar income. Thus whether poor or "middle class," black families live without assets, and compared to white families, black families are disproportionately dependent on the labor market to maintain status. In real life terms, this means that blacks could survive an economic crisis, such as loss of a job, for a relatively short time.

So you can see that an unbroken story line of evidence and logic drawn across time from Jamestown to Appomattox to contemporary America renders the "it's too late" response to reparations for African Americans inadequate. For blacks, the destructive moral crime that began in Jamestown in 1619 has yet to end.

Let's not mince words here. The racial economic gaps in this country have been locked open at constant intervals since the days of slavery. The gaps will not close themselves. To close them will require, as Norman Francis, president of Xavier University of Louisiana, has said, a counterforce "as strong as the force that put us in chains."

During the centuries of the Atlantic slave trade, Africa was denuded of tens of millions of its ablest people, a massive pillage from which Africa has

yet to recover. During the century-long period of colonial exploitation that followed on the heels of slavery, Africa saw its theretofore viable social, political, economic, and agricultural systems destroyed by the colonizing powers of Western Europe. The magnitude of this long-running multi-dimensional human rights crime continues to define not only the crushing dilemmas of contemporary Africa but the here-and-now burdens borne by the scattered descendants of her sold-off issue as well. For black people, no human rights wrongdoing stands before slavery and what followed it.

———————

Our lives—all of our lives, all races, all classes—have a regular course to them. They are habit-shaped. There is habit in the way we see ourselves, the way we see and relate to each other, as genders, as classes, as races. Habit has to it a silence, a soothing transparency. In our cluttered modern lives, charged with the burdens of the clock and the cool embrace of electronic socialization, habit relieves us of the myriad social decisions we've neither the time nor the energy to make or remake. Why throw the rice at the bridal couple? Who knows anymore? But everyone throws it. Harmless, eh? Most customs are, and habits as well. Habit does not alleviate pain. It does, however, cause us often to forget its source.

———————

Well before the birth of our country, Europe and the eventual United States perpetrated a heinous wrong against the peoples of Africa—and sustained and benefited from the wrong for centuries. Europe followed the grab of Africa's people with the rape, through colonial occupation, of Africa's material resources. America followed slavery with more than a hundred combined years of legal racial segregation and legal racial discrimination of one variety or another. In 1965, after nearly 350 years of legal racial suppression, the United States enacted the *Voting Rights Act* and, virtually simultaneously, began to walk away from the social wreckage that centuries of white hegemony had wrought. The country then began to rub itself with the memory-emptying salve of contemporaneousness. (If the wrong did not *just* occur, it did not occur at all in a way that would render the living responsible.)

But when the black living suffer real and current consequences as a result of wrongs committed by a younger America, then contemporary America must be caused to shoulder responsibility for those wrongs until such wrongs have been adequately compensated and righted. The life and responsibilities of a society or nation are not circumscribed by the life spans of its mortal constituents. Social rights, wrongs, obligations, and responsibilities flow eternal.

There are many ways to begin righting America's massive wrong, some of which you must already have inferred. But let there be not doubt, it will require great resources and decades of national fortitude to resolve economic and social disparities so long in the making.

Habit is the enemy. For whites and blacks have made a habit now, beyond the long era of legal discrimination, of seeing each other (the only way they can remember seeing each other) in a certain relation of economic and social inequality.

American capitalism, which starts each child where its parents left off is not a fair system. This is particularly the case for African Americans, whose general economic starting points have been rearmost in our society because of slavery and its long racialist aftermath. American slaves for two and a half centuries saw taken from them not just their freedom but the inestimable economic value of their labor as well, which, were it a line item in today's gross national product report, would undoubtedly run into the billions of dollars. Whether the monetary obligation is legally enforceable or not, a large debt is owed by America to the descendants of America's slaves.

Here too, habit has become our enemy, for America has made an art form by now of grinding its past deeds, no matter how despicable, into mere ephemera. African Americans, unfortunately, have accommodated this habit of American amnesia all too well. It would behoove African Americans to remember that history forgets, first, those who forget themselves. To do what is necessary to accomplish anything approaching psychic and economic parity in the next half century will not only require a fundamental attitude shift in American thinking but massive amounts of

money as well. Before the country in general can be made to understand, African Americans themselves must come to understand that this demand is not for charity. It is simply for what they are *owed* on a debt that is old but compellingly obvious and valid still.

Even the *making* of a well-reasoned case for restitution will do wonders for the spirit of African Americans. It will cause them at long last to understand the genesis of their dilemma by gathering, as have all other groups, all of their history—before, during and after slavery—into one story of themselves. To hold the story fast to their breast. To make of it, over time, a sacred text. And from it, to explain themselves to themselves and to their heirs. Tall again, as they had been long, long ago.

Hazel and I went to the third-grade commencement of one of Khalea's friends last night. Imagine that. These prestigious private schools start building a child's portfolio early. We sat in folding chairs under a merciful May sun in the school's manicured courtyard. Some eighty gaily dressed nine-year-olds sat on the brick steps of a broad terrace and listened brightly to the headmistress tell them how promising their futures would likely be. At least ten of the boys and girls were black. When the students' names were called, they strode across the terrace toward the headmistress to receive their first diploma amidst flashing bulbs and whirring camcorders. A few aging alumni had grumbled privately that the school was no longer the old place they had cherished so dearly. A tad too dark it had gotten. But the headmistress, to her credit, had stood her ground, and the grumbles died before finding anything near to a broader audience. All but one of the black children came from families not unlike in their socioeconomic circumstance the other families seated there on the courtyard lawn. Theses black children had done uniformly well, and most had been admitted to the fourth grade in schools of their choice. The black parents were doubtless proud of their children, and proud as a group as well, even while not losing sight of their economic lack of representation of the black community as a whole. The program culminated with a formal group photograph of the class of 1999, following which the children retrieved from their various classrooms the paper products of a year's work in art, science, computer studies, and other subjects. A climate of bonhomie held parents and children together for a time on the lawn before they began to slowly make their way toward expensive cars that had been parked along the school's long, sloping driveway. As we turned finally onto the street, I saw in the distance two figures standing at a bus stop. It was a black mother and the daughter on scholarship she had just seen receive her diploma waiting to catch one of two buses they would have to ride that night before reaching home in a poor section of the city. The daughter, Khalea's friend, was bright and personable, and gave every appearance of being blessed with rich potential. But she had not done well at the school and had fallen below grade level in reading and math for many of the reasons that had explained the failure of Sarah, the twelve-year-girl I had known in Boston many years before.

What harm was done to Khalea's nine-year-old friend, and millions like her, was done long ago for profit, and with her country's complicity. Now it must properly be the country's responsibility to undo the damage and make victims like Khalea's friend whole.

But first the victims must be noticed. They must be *seen*. Early in the fall of the first grade, the mother of the little girl in this story came to the school and told her daughter's teacher that her child was having reading problems. The teacher assured the mother that the child was doing fine in reading. Unconvinced, the mother returned to the school twice in the following week to voice the same concern. She was assured on both occasions that her daughter was doing adequately well in mastering the basic reading skills. Early in the third grade, the child's final year at the school, the mother was informed that her daughter was not "cutting it" in reading and therefore would not be recommended for acceptance into the fourth grade of the school the child would normally have attended next.

The child, clutching her diploma at the bus stop beside her disappointed mother, had been cast into limbo at age nine. Of course, what happened to her happened to more than a few students at the school, white and black. In those cases, however, the parents ignored the school's assurances, sought and paid for outside help. Such options are not available to the poor, whether in public schools or private schools with vouchers or scholarship assistance. And a disproportionate segment of these child victims are black, struck down tender in a hail of figurative bullets with little idea of the direction from which the gunfire had come or why they had been selected out for special treatment.

'African Renaissance': A Northbound Gaze

Mogobe B. Ramose

ABSTRACT

The mid-nineties have seen the revival of the 'African Renaissance' by Thabo Mbeki, President of South Africa. The multiple resurrection of the 'renaissance' gives rise to the question if this is the appropriate key concept for understanding and interpreting the evolution of history and politics in Africa. The present article is an attempt to answer this question. It argues that at best the 'renaissance' has dubious linguistic roots in the soil of Africa. Thus, focusing upon the 'renaissance' is the appropriation of an historical concept which does not in the first place belong to the history of Africa. Such appropriation is made possible by fixing the gaze to the North, meaning the West, where this concept has its proper place in the history of ideas. The sequence, 'African Renaissance' gives first place to Africa. But Africa is denied the right to choose from its own experience a key concept for understanding and interpreting its history and politics. Thus the sequence does not remove the methodological and historical obstacles that need to be overcome before we can be comfortable about the use of the term 'African Renaissance.' *Mokoko-Hungwe* is an indigenous African concept capable of aiding our understanding and interpretation of contemporary African history and politics.

1 The African Roots of the 'Renaissance'

Biological anthropologists, linguists and historians might find difficulty in supporting a research proposal seeking to establish that *ubuntu* is deeply rooted in the Indo-European languages. The same kind of caution and reserve might be expressed with regard to the claim that the deepest roots of the term 'renaissance' are to be found in the soil of the ancient languages of Africa or the *Ur-Bantu*. What would justify this initial reaction of scepticism? The research proposal first. There are two basic reasons for this scepticism. One is that *ubuntu* does not appear at all either as a group or a branch of the Indo-European languages. It does not appear, for example under the Anatolian, Italic or

Germanic groups. It is thus not even remotely connected to the Latin and its modern representatives: the Romance languages consisting of French, Italian, Spanish and Portuguese. So the search for the roots of *ubuntu* in this direction is problematic since there is no apparent basis for the assumption that its ancestry lies in these languages. Another reason is that the single language from which the Indo-European languages evolved is unrecorded and split into a number of dialects by about the 3rd millennium BC.[1] Thus the two basic reasons together mean that the principal problem is both methodological and historical. By what method could we piece together the constituent parts of an ancient unrecorded language? Since the languages that evolved from the original do not themselves suggest any historical connection with *ubuntu*, what is the point of establishing a connection from the position of a historical void? What is the reason for uprooting *ubuntu* and trying to implant

"African Renaissance: A Northbound Gaze" by M.B. Ramose as appeared in *Politeia*, Vol. 19, No. 3, 2000, pp. 47–61. Reprinted by permission of Unisa Press.

it within a historical soil unsuitable for its growth and development? Is there anything unnatural about the environment from which it continues to grow and develop from the beginning of time? Second, exactly the same questions apply, in reverse order, to the claim that the deepest roots of the term 'renaissance' are to be found in the soil of the ancient languages of Africa or the *Ur-Bantu*. Our first basic point, then, is that there are methodological and historical obstacles that need to be overcome before we can be comfortable about the use of the term, 'African Renaissance.' The discomfort stems from the fact that using this term before the obstacles are overcome, is at the same time denying that the African experience is the appropriate source from which we can choose a key concept to understand and interpret African politics. Does Africa not have the right to choose such a key concept from its own historical experience? Why the persistence of this Northbound gaze? The philosophical and political implications of this denial are what we wish to explore in some detail.

2 Renaissance or Renascence?

Most dictionaries and other standard reference works distinguish between the Renaissance and renascence. The first remarkable point is that most of them concur that the distinction lies in the first place in the appearance of the two words. The first appears with the capital letter 'R' and the second with the small letter 'r.' However, most dictionaries concur that at one level, the two words share a common meaning, namely, rebirth, renewal or revival. Even at this level, none appears willing to deprive the first of the capital letter 'R.' This means that there is another level of meaning at which renascence cannot have the same meaning as the Renaissance. It is the level at which the Renaissance is an historical concept signifying a specific period[2] in the history of Europe. It is specifically a European historical movement that originated in Italy and spread through other parts of Europe. It is noteworthy that even Italian standard reference works reserve the capital letter 'R' to this phenomenon, namely, the *Rinascimento*.[3] In using the capital 'R' for Renascence, Matthew Arnold acknowl-

edged that 'I have ventured to give to the foreign word *Renaissance* an English form.'[4] Arnold's venture does not neglect to grant the capital letter 'R' to his Renascence. As an historical concept the Renaissance is deeply rooted 'in Europe'[5] and has Europe as its primary reference point. Other parts of the world are its secondary reference point in so far as it had ramifications for them and had an impact on them.[6] It follows then that as a historical concept, the Renaissance must retain the capital letter 'R.' Specific philosophic currents were special features of this history. In this sense the Renaissance was also a philosophical movement. Conceptual clarity can be preserved and a great deal of confusion avoided if any other period of revival anywhere in the world could be given another name than the Renaissance. But this is not the virtue of the 'African Renaissance.'

The term 'African Renaissance' does not appear as a specific entry under this title in the eight volume *Cambridge History of Africa*. Nor does it appear anywhere in the four volume *Encyclopedia of Africa South of the Sahara*. It also does not appear in Jean Jolly's three volume *Histoire du Continent Africain*. It is more than curious to note that the 'African Renaissance' does not feature specifically under this title as a topic in anyone of the eight volumes of the UNESCO *General History of Africa*.[7] Could it be that the galaxy of experts responsible for this undoubtedly erudite work on the history of Africa had all forgotten that Africa also had a Renaissance? Perhaps it was not a question of collective amnesia. The experts simply did not predict that the 'African Renaissance' was yet to come. What appears in this eight volume series is Abdel-Malek's 'The renaissance of Egypt.'[8] This is clearly specific and limited in scope than the general and all-embracing 'African.' Furthermore, the author of this entry does not give reasons for his adoption of the term 'renaissance.' However, he is careful not to use the capital letter 'R.' Why this borrowing which creates a lack of conceptual clarity and sows confusion? Matthew Arnold did not venture into wholesale borrowing but adapted the Renaissance to his native language. Even this option appears to have been foreclosed to the 'African Renaissance.' The question is: is there something unnatural about the natural environment of Africa such that the history of Africa cannot be described and defined by concepts originating from Africa?

3 The Regeneration of Africa

In this section we propose to place in historical perspective the current and problematical 'African Renaissance.' The point is also to establish a context within which the two questions contained in the two paragraphs of the preceding section could be answered. Africa continues to have periods of rebirth, of revival. Africa has its own renascence. Among the earliest traces of this is the thesis of 'African regeneration.' This was posited by the South African, Pixley ka Isaka Seme in an article in *The African Aboard*, April 5, 1906.[9] According to Seme, Africa should not be compared to Europe. The reason is that comparison assumes that there is a 'common standard' and this exists, if at all, only in an imperfect way. Since Africa cannot be and is not identical to Europe, so Seme continued, it is best to judge Africa in its own right than by reference to Europe as the standard for Africa. He then enumerates some of the historical and cultural monuments of Africa which 'are the indestructible memorials of their [her] great and original genius.' Already in 1906 Seme wrote that the African 'giant is awakening! . . . A great century has come upon us. No race possessing the inherent capacity to survive can resist and remain unaffected by this influence of contact and intercourse, the backward with the advanced.' In declaring the dawn of this century Seme had at the same time fallen victim of his own caution and warning. By reference to 'the backward with the advanced,' he had compared Africa to Europe. Yet, he decried comparison between the two. What 'common standard' did he use for the comparison? Clearly, the attraction to the North, the Northbound gaze, was already very much alive in Seme and many others then, as the whole tenor of his article shows. Despite ignoring his own caveat, Seme's warning deserves serious consideration. The twentieth century regeneration of Africa is for Seme a period of optimism reflecting the glory of the rising sun of Africa from all the corners of the African experience. For Seme, the regeneration of Africa means 'the entrance into a new life, embracing the diverse phases of a higher, complex existence. The basic factor which assures their regeneration resides in the awakened race-consciousness. This gives them a clear perception of their elemental needs and of their undeveloped powers. . . . The African people, although not a strictly homogeneous race, possess a common fundamental sentiment which is everywhere manifest, crystallizing itself into one common controlling idea.' Here we find a great omission which is at the same time a loss. This is that Seme did not identify and specify the 'common fundamental sentiment' which the African people are said to possess. Is this loss irretrievable? Seme emphasised that the African regeneration means that 'a new and unique civilization is soon to be added to the world. . . . The most essential departure of this new civilization is that it shall be thoroughly spiritual and humanistic—indeed a regeneration moral and eternal!' From Seme's thesis we can extract the following as the features of the twentieth century African renascence: Africa has the right to establish its own credentials and must be judged in its own right; there is tension between Africa asserting the right to be herself from the standpoint of the African experience and the temptation to abandon this in favour of understanding Africa according to the standard imposed by Europe; there is a common fundamental sentiment that all Africans possess (apparently this is the humanism that will be the hallmark of the 'new civilisation'); the 'rising sun' evokes the imagery of light penetrating and replacing darkness, the regeneration of Africa is the age of light overcoming darkness. It is crucial to understand that for Seme the term African excludes the non-African, that is, the European.

Almost thirty years after Seme launched the theme of the African regeneration, the same thread was picked up by Gilbert Coka. This appeared in the form of an article under the title, 'The African Liberator, Our Message,' published in *The African Liberator*, October 1935.[10] Coka noted in his article that the imminent outbreak of the Second World War contained the possibility to liberate the African. 'The hour of African freedom has struck. . . . But this good time coming, will not come of its own volition. It will be brought by Africans themselves.' In order to translate this hope into reality, Coka urged the Africans to free themselves of pettiness and inferiority complex. This is necessary for African unity and solidarity. These will encourage and strengthen self-reliance among Africans. Because of the very high premium he placed upon the achievement of these aims, Coka criticised uncritical Africans who imitate the non-Africans. 'We take the monkey apings of our so-called distinguished men for progress. There is no progress in Africans aping Europeans and telling us that they represent the best in the race, for any ordinarily well trained monkey would do the same.' He urged Africans to realise that the philosophy of imitation and obsequious behaviour is in reality a sign of lack of confidence in oneself; it is the supreme expression of an inferiority complex. Self-confidence and self-reliance are the cure for both the African and the non-African because the latter 'respect Africans who work out their salvation.' In pursuing their quest for liberation Africans are urged by Coka to always take into account the fact that 'Money at present is the ruling power of the world.' Therefore, the just wage and the just price are two of the indispensable items in the struggle for liberation. Coka's vision of liberation included 'equal democratic rights for all South Africans irrespective of colour, creed, or race.' As Seme before him, Coka declares the African renascence: 'Africa is opening another era in human history.' The following are the features of the twentieth century African renascence as perceived by Coka: Liberation is a necessity and Africans must be the authors of their own liberation—an essential corollary to this is that Africans must have confidence in themselves, be self-reliant and act in unity and solidarity; the abandonment of imitative or mimetic[11] philosophy and its corresponding action; recognition of the status and influence of money in the conduct of domestic and international politics; and the establishment of a colour blind, rights-based democracy regardless of creed. It is significant that Coka does not include gender equality in his vision of liberation. Seme and Coka concur on the dawn of a new Africa. They also agree on the point that the African experience is the fertile ground from which the new Africa can and must draw inspiration, in the first place. Coka expressly called this the liberation of Africa. Thus liberation stands out as one of the specific features of the African renascence. Despite the apparent contra-

diction in Seme, he is, as Coka, against mimetic philosophy and its corresponding action. They thus share the implication of this position, namely, that as a human being the African is second to none and must therefore assert this right to equality with the utmost self-confidence. Africa has the prior and exclusive right to determine its own destiny even in the sphere of international relations.

Outside of South Africa and even earlier than Seme and Coka, Edward Wilmont Blyden stood out as an exponent of the 'regeneration of Africa.' Having established his sojourn in Liberia in 1850, Blyden argued that the former slaves returning to Africa from the United States of America would, together with the indigenous West African peoples, set the regeneration of Africa in motion. Blyden posited the thesis that the regeneration of Africa should acknowledge cultural differences among the races. Upon these differences Africa should assert its dignity and build its personality. He was thus a 'Pan-Negroist.'[12] He argued that Africa should draw from the African experience to build the image of an African church, to construct African history and culture, and to draw up an African educational curriculum. When colonialism became firmly established in the West Africa region around 1900 there was a shift of emphasis from the cultural to political aspects. This meant that strategies of resistance to colonial rule became the primary issue. In this sense the theme of the liberation of Africa became one of the specific features of the regeneration of Africa even before it was espoused by Coka. The period of the regeneration of Africa, represented by Blyden, Seme and Coka may thus be said to come to a close after the end of the Second World War. Decolonisation was the next period.

4 The 'New African Renaissance'

With the advent of Nkrumah we come to the express use of the term the 'new African renaissance' by an African head of state. In his celebrated *Consciencism*[13] Nkrumah writes, 'In the new African renaissance, we place great emphasis on the presentation of history. Our history needs to be written as the history of our society, not as the story of European adventure. African society must be treated as enjoying its own integrity; its history must be a mirror of that society, and the European contact history must find its place in this history only as an African experience, even if as a crucial one. That is to say, the European contact needs to be assessed and judged from the point of view of the principles animating African society, and from the point of view of the harmony and progress of this society.' It is significant that Nkrumah refers to the 'new African renaissance' as if there were an 'old' one in the past. But the idea that there was an 'old' African renaissance is not supported, for example, by the UNESCO *General History of Africa*. So why the use of the word 'new'? The answer is to be found in the fact that the text used by the present writer has the term 'renaissance' with the small letter 'r.' Two inferences can be made from this. One is that the use of the word 'new' is intended to distinguish the African renaissance from the European Renaissance. The latter is the old Renaissance and the former the new. Another is that the term 'renaissance' is spelt with small letter 'r' precisely to underline the distinction between the African renaissance and the European Renaissance. In this way Nkrumah has shown awareness of the historical and philosophical problems pertaining to the use of the capital letter 'R' with reference to the history of Africa. By so doing, he had at the same time avoided the philosophical problems connected to such usage. We therefore submit that the 'new African renaissance' of Nkrumah refers to the rebirth and renewal of Africa. It is thus analogous to the 'regeneration of Africa' espoused by Blyden, Seme and Coka. What then are the main features of Nkrumah's new African renaissance?

It is the period which accords primacy to the African experience. It is thus the reaffirmation of the thesis that the African experience can be and should be the primary source from which to draw concepts to understand and interpret its politics, history and philosophy, to name but a few. The principles animating African society should be used as the basis for rebuilding Africa and also for judging it. The point that there are principles animating African society is the reaffirmation of the insight expressed earlier by Seme, namely, that there is a common fundamental sentiment which Africans possess. We have noted

already that Seme appears to have African humanism in mind. On the basis of a philosophical analysis of *ubuntu*, the present writer has reservations about the suffix '-ism' attached to human-ism, *hunhuism* or *ubuntuism*.[14] Having noted this reservation, the present writer submits that Nkrumah's 'principles animating African society' refer to African 'humanism.' In answering the question whether or not these principles should be preserved, Kwasi Wiredu, replied: 'It would profit us little to gain all the technology in the world and lose the humanist essence of our culture.'[15] Nkrumah recognised Africa's encounter with Europe, Christianity and Islam. He maintained however that this encounter should be seen as part of the African experience. It should not be allowed to assume primacy over the African experience. Nor should it serve as the superior standard by which to understand and interpret the African experience. In this way Nkrumah rejected mimetic philosophy and its corresponding action. This is underlined by his thoroughgoing reaffirmation of the dignity of the African person in his celebrated, 'The African Personality' appearing in his *I Speak of Freedom*. Here Nkrumah leaves no doubt of his conviction that as a human being, the African is second to none. Similar to his predecessors in the period of the regeneration of Africa, he emphasised the necessity for unity and solidarity among Africans. It is to Nkrumah's credit that this culminated in the establishment of the Organisation of African Unity.

Nkrumah's new African renaissance is the period of the phased achievement of freedom. The first phase is the achievement of political freedom to be followed by the economic. 'Seek ye first the political kingdom and all things shall be added unto you' is the well-known prescription of Nkrumah's philosophy for decolonisation. It is curious that Nkrumah adopted this separation and timing in spite of his acute awareness that the political kingdom without the economic is empty.[16] The unfolding experience of Africa proved Nkrumah's prescription to be 'partially right.'[17] The lesson from this experience is that that attainment of political independence is inseparable from economic independence. Laying down the foundation of economic independence must thus be part and parcel of the moment of political independence. It may not be postponed. The curious point is that many other African states, including South Africa, which attained independence afterwards, ignored this lesson. They preferred Nkrumah's prescription and this is called appositely by Mazrui, 'Kwame Nkrumah's immortal imperative.' In theory and practice this prescription meant condoning the injustice of conquest based on lawlessness, inhumanity and lack of morality. This is the conquest of the meridian line drawn arbitrarily by the European conqueror to demarcate the define the sphere of truth and justice. Beyond that line these were inoperative. As Carl Schmitt put it: 'the only matter (the parties) could actually agree on was the *freedom* of the open spaces that began beyond the line. This freedom consisted in that the line set aside an area where force could be used freely and ruthlessly. . . . The general concept was then necessarily that everything which occurred 'beyond the line' remained outside the legal, moral and political values recognized on this side of the line.'[18] Lawlessness, inhumanity and lack of morality were allowed beyond the meridian line, the line that experienced the voyages of discovery and colonisation. The basic flaw of this condonation is that the attainment of political independence was nowhere in formerly colonised Africa the reversion to unencumbered and unmodified sovereignty to the same quantum and degree as at conquest.[19] Thus Africa acquired limping[20] sovereignty burdened in particular by the inheritance of an unpayable foreign debt owed to its former conqueror. Makonnen makes a relevant point with regard to Kenya. 'Kenya paid compensation for land reacquired from the 'alien' land holders . . . the British Government provided Kenya with loans from its own sources and also from the World Bank, in order to finance the compensation for the transferred alien property, which amounted in fact to outright repurchasing of Kenya by the Kenyans.'[21] This point, however, applies to the whole of decolonised Africa precisely because state succession was not the basis for granting independence to African states. This is not only incomprehensible but also basically unfair because, 'the question whether a state gaining territorial sovereignty (the successor state) inherits, together with the territory concerned, the rights and obligations of another state (the

predecessor state) arises if this latter is actually considered to be extinct. This question leads to the problems of state succession. . . . The states emerging from colonial status to independence are new subjects of international law; the problems to be solved in connection with them are those of state succession.'[22] Why was the state of the conqueror not considered extinct at independence? The attainment of political independence in formerly colonised Africa was thus a transition from slavery by coercion to slavery by consent. Nkrumah's prescription also meant the loss of an opportunity to demand restitution and restoration. These are the plain demands of natural justice arising from unjustified conquest based on lawlessness, inhumanity and lack of morality. The question is: can the new African renaissance provide a remedy for these mistakes?

Three clerics, Smangaliso Mkhatshwa, Maurice Ngakane and Allan Boesak, also used the term 'Renaissance.' They were the motor and organisers of a conference, the 'Black Renaissance Convention.' This was held in Hammanskraal, South Africa, in 1974. It is significant that these clerics chose 'Black' instead of African. However, the pre- and postconference documentation does not offer an argument devoted specifically to this choice. The Reverend Allan Boesak's predilection for 'Black' crystallised in the publication of his doctoral dissertation whose subtitle contained the significant words, 'black theology and black power.'[23] In time he and Mkhatshwa abandoned 'Black' and chose 'African' through their membership of the African National Congress. The present author is unaware of a written argument by either justifying the choice of 'African.' Since the focus of their 'Renaissance' was rather diffuse and blurred, there is no point in bringing it under the prism of critical analysis. Suffice it to say that their use of the term leads directly to the historical and philosophical problems we have dealt with above. Their importance lies then in helping us determine the frequency of the term 'African Renaissance.'

President Thabo Mbeki can be said to be the second African head of state to use the term the 'African Renaissance.' It is thus the third time, counting from Nkrumah, that this term is used. Is it the multiple resurrection of the renaissance: a Northbound gaze which is impossible to discard? Or, is it an indication that some of the problems that have been noted already in the period of the regeneration of Africa remain unsolved? The ideas of President Mbeki about the 'African Renaissance' can be gathered partly from his own writings and partly from his foreword, singular and plural, to other works by Africans. For example, his foreword to *Mokoko*[24] contains some of his ideas on the 'African Renaissance.' They may also be culled from the book, *African Renaissance,* edited by Makgoba. The book is the result of a conference held recently under the same title.[25] One of the key ideas of President Mbeki's 'African Renaissance' is Africa first. We see this translated into practice in the South Africa that he is leading. For example, a study of the composition of key functionaries in his office and his advisers shows that primacy is accorded the African. Similarly, the enactment of the Equity Act is not only a question of according primacy to the African but also of rectifying plain and manifest injustice. The President is yet to address the *matyotyombe* phenomenon; the so-called squatters problem.[26] It is curious that the Africans refuse to be called squatters. They prefer to call themselves *baipei*.[27]

The Africa of which South Africa forms part also deserves primacy. It is the Africa of the Southern African Development Community, the Africa of War in the Congo, Ethiopia versus Eritrea, the troubles in the Sudan, deepening poverty and increase in preventable deaths, the Africa plagued with AIDS, it is the Africa of disjointed reconciliation, it is the Africa of racial strife and tension, the Africa which has caused 'donor fatigue' and has thus been renamed the forgotten continent. It is the Africa that is stampeded by globalisation. It is the nuclear weapons free Africa. Yet, the inescapable victim of an irrational nuclear war to be waged exclusively by non-Africans. It is the Africa still licking the wounds of Nkrumah's deadly prescription. Perhaps the time has come to move beyond the new African renaissance because it is no longer the correct instrument to deal with all these problems. Even if we may retain the small letter 'r' in our use of the renaissance the closeness with the capital letter is a source of discomfort. It is the temptation to fix our gaze to the North. Continuing in this way is problematical because even the European Renaissance did come to an end. It was followed by the Enlightenment,[28] the Age of Reason.[29] It was the age when authority was challenged and superstition was reportedly eliminated from European culture. It was the time when human beings dared to reason. And this was always reasoning from their own experience first of all. If we retain the 'renaissance' and thus preserve our Northbound gaze it should come as no surprise that the North should insist on continuing to be in the leadership. The justification, though questionable, is on hand: 'You are still in the renaissance. We have long made the transition to man as a rational animal. We have established ourselves in the Age of Reason. We are entitled to universal leadership.' Since reason is not an exclusive European or Northern quality, the time has come for Africa to move beyond the renaissance. It is time to enter the period of the birds.

5 Mokoko

Mokoko is the Sotho language term for a cock. It is also the title of the book by Makgoba, to which we have already referred. The title is apposite because in many cultures the cock-crow carries the significance of a warning or the fulfillment of a prophecy. For example, we read in the Bible that by the time the cock crows Peter will have betrayed Jesus. Indeed when the cock crowed Peter remembered with regret that the words of Jesus had come true. In African culture the early morning cock-crow proclaims the passage from darkness to light. It is the message of the beginning of a new day, a new life. And everyone is invited to rise up the occasion and be an active part of the new life. Indeed, the 'Makgoba affair' at the University of the Witwatersrand spread throughout South Africa like a conflagration. It was the real crow of *Mokoko*. It raised many issues concerning the nature and function of a university. Issues under debate ranged from an honest presentation of a curriculum vitae, transformation, affirmative action, the maintenance of educational standards to the preservation of social and political values. It raised basic questions about the meaning and function of South African society. The land question, though raised expressly in the book, received the least attention. Another issue which received little attention was the question of whether the African is also a rational animal.

Before the start of the voyages of discovery, Aristotle's definition of man as a rational animal was deeply rooted in the European culture.[30] When the voyagers met other human-like animals, they refused to attribute rationality to them. Aristotle's definition was given a restrictive interpretation. Only the European was held to be the rational animal. Combined with the ideology that law, morality and humanity did not apply beyond the meridian line, this restrictive interpretation of Aristotle justified conquest and slavery the other side of it. The universalist impulse to turn everyone in the world into a Christian brought about an unintended challenge to the restrictive interpretation. It was this. If only some men are rational animals then it is irrational to Christianise human-like animals. The best course is to leave the human-like animals to their own devices and desist from Christianising them. The debate in 1550 at Valladolid, Spain, between Sepulveda and Las Casas, was the highpoint of this dilemma. In the result Pope Paul III issued the bull, Sublimis Deus.[31] This declared expressly that 'all men are rational animals.' It thus justified Christianisation. Yet, its necessary implication, namely, that law, morality and humanity also apply to the African, was not recognised. The conviction that man is a rational animal was not spoken of. The African had acquired the status of an ineradicable superstition. It is precisely this superstition that lay at the heart of the Makgoba affair. We are not concerned here with the pros and cons of the individual struggle. The Makgoba affair was not just the simple struggle of an individual against a big institution. It was the struggle for the assertion of the right of the African as a human being second to none. It was the struggle for the right of the African to be African in Africa. It was the struggle for the reaffirmation of the dignity of the African; of the African's right to give primacy to the African experience in Africa. By this struggle Makgoba ushered in the *Mokoko* period, the period beyond the 'African Renaissance.'

6 Hungwe—The Zimbabwe Bird

Hungwe is the Shona name for the bird regarded as sacred among the Shona. It is to the indigenous Zimbabwean what the cross is to a Christian.

The *hungwe* is an indispensable point of contact with the ancestral gods: the gods who gave the land to the indigenous Zimbabweans from time immemorial. The land and sovereignty over it were lost at conquest based on lawlessness, inhumanity and lack of morality. In time the conqueror returned—under the Lancaster Agreement—the land half-heartedly to its original rightful owners. This did not please the ancestral gods. They instructed the *hungwe* to sing from the national flag of Zimbabwe. It sang from all other places and sites where it was perched. The song was, 'the gods shall never sleep until the return of the land to original and rightful owners.' Neither the government nor the indigenous Zimbabweans could ignore this song. They could not erase from memory the injustice of unjustified conquest based upon lawlessness, inhumanity and lack of morality. When the people took action to remedy this historical injustice they unintentionally assisted the United Kingdom to remember the conquest of Rhodesia. In memory of this conquest, the United Kingdom declared herself ready to receive back to their ancestral home, Great Britain, at least twenty thousand Rhodesians. The present writer does not accept that the approach of the Zimbabwean government on the return of the land is the correct one. It contains basic flaws which call for urgent remedies. The first is that by going along with the situation initiated by the people the government has reduced the matter of the collective right of the indigenous Zimbabweans to a simple question of private law. It has become the question of the right to private property with particular reference to the land. Second, the violence that accompanies land occupation is unjustified. It should be clear then that the song of the *hungwe* shall survive President Mugabe. It is indifferent to the outcome of the forthcoming elections. It is a demand from all the ancestral gods of Africa that a remedy to Nkrumah's prescription is long overdue. This is the significance of the Mokoko-Hungwe period of African history and politics. It is the period of the birds. It is the hour to assert and reaffirm the dignity of the African precisely by seizing the initiative to remedy historical injustice with historical justice. It is the season of the return of the land to its original rightful owners; the period of reversion to unmodified and unencumbered sovereignty. It is the age of restitution and reparation to Africa. It is the age of African memory functioning as the critique of history. Thus 'reparations,' as a structure of memory and critique, may be regarded as a necessity for the credibility of Eurocentric historicism, and a corrective for its exclusionist worldview. What really would be preposterous or ethically inadmissible in imposing a general levy on South Africa's white population?[32] Sure the question applies to all decolonised Africa.

Conclusion

We have argued that the marriage between African and 'renaissance' is an uneasy one. It is a marriage that is full of historical and philosophical problems. The attempt to implant the 'renaissance' into Africa is an implicit denial of Africa's right to choose from her experience terms and concepts that can be used to understand and interpret African history and politics. At the same time this denial is a covert adherence to the linear interpretation of history. Thus one of the results of the fixation of the African gaze to the North is that Africa thereby concedes prominence and leadership to the North. This marriage must be dissolved because there is no philosophical and historical justification for it. The humanity and dignity of the African is second to none. African history has yielded and continues to yield fertile experience from which to extract key analytical concepts. Even if we were to concede the period of the African 'renaissance' this has passed. It is now superseded by the *Mokoko-Hungwe* period. The period in which the question of historical justice has emerged in very sharp relief. It is the period for Africa's reversion to unmodified and unencumbered sovereignty. It is the period of restitution and reparation to Africa.

Notes

1. 1987, The *New Encyclopaedia Britannica*, Volume 6, 15th Edition, pp. 295–296.
2. 1902, The *Cambridge modern history*, Volume 1, The Renaissance, Cambridge University Press, Cambridge, p. 532.
3. MCMXXXVI *Enciclopedia Italiana di Scienze*, Lettre ed Arti, XIV, p. 346.

4. 1989, *The Oxford English dictionary*, Volume XIII, Clarendon Press, Oxford, (see, Renaissance).
5. 1966, *Standard dictionary of the English language*, International Edition, Volume 2, Funk & Wagnalls Company, New York, (see, Renaissance).
6. 1902, *The Cambridge modern history*, Cambridge University Press, Cambridge, pp. 7–66.
7. Here the present writer refers to both the UNESCO/ Heinemann and the Curry editions of this series.
8. Abdel-Malek, A. 1989, 'The renaissance of Egypt, 1805–81,' in: Ade Ajayi, J. F. (ed) *General history of Africa*, Volume VI, Heinemann, California, UNESCO, p. 325–355.
9. Pixley ka Isaka Seme. 1972, The regeneration of Africa, in: Karis, T. and Carterm G. M. (eds), *From protest to challenge*, Volume 1, Hoover Institution Press, Stanford University, California, pp. 69–71.
10. Coka, G. 1973, 'The African Liberator, Our Message,' in: Karis, T. and Carter, G. M. (eds), *From protest to challenge*, Volume 2, Hoover Institution Press, Stanford University, California, pp. 16–18.
11. Ramose, M. B. 1999a, *African philosophy through ubuntu*, Mond Books Publishers, Harare, pp. 128–135.
12. van Hensbroek, P. B. 1998, African Political Philosophy, 1860–1995, dissertation presented to the University of Groningen for the attainment of the degree of Doctor of Philosophy, p. 52.
13. Nkrumah, K. 1979, *Consciencism*, Panaf Books Ltd, London, p. 63.
14. Ramose, M. B. 1999a, *African philosophy through ubuntu*, Mond Books Publishers, Harare, pp. 49–66.
15. Wiredu, K. 1980, *Philosophy and an African culture*, Cambridge University Press, Cambridge, p. 21.
16. In his foreword to Oginga Odinga's *Not yet uhuru*, Nkrumah writes, 'A turning point has now been reached in Africa's history. After years of patient effort to achieve the total political and economic emancipation of the continent by peaceful means, only limited results have been achieved, and it has become essential to adopt a more militant and positive strategy. 'A Union Government of Africa backed by organised military power with sound continental economic planning is bound to compel nations outside Africa to respect our collective interests.' Although political independence is a noble achievement in the struggle against colonialism, neocolonialism, and imperialism, its effectiveness is superficial unless economic and cultural independence is also achieved.'
17. Mazrui, A. A. 1993, 'Seek ye first the political kingdom,' in: Mazrui, A. A. and Wondji, C. (eds) *General history of Africa*, Volume VIII, Heinemann, California, UNESCO, pp. 105–126.
18. Schmitt, C. 1996, 'The Land Appropriation of a New World,' *Telos*, number 109, pp. 36–37. The following, from the already cited The Cambridge Modern History, portrays and underlines the meaning of the meridian line during the so called voyages of discovery. 'The tidings of his voyage were joyfully received both in Spain and at Rome; and a petition was preferred to Pope

Alexander VI for a confirmation to the Spanish Crown of the district comprising the newly-found islands, *subject only to the rights of any Christian communities* which might happen to be included in it. In answer to this two separate bulls were issued. One simply contained the confirmation desired; the other was framed in similar terms, but limited the area of Spanish enterprise to *a meridian line* to be drawn one hundred leagues west of the Azores and the Cape Verde Islands (emphasis added, p. 23).

19. We hold, contrary to Alexandrowicz, that a proper understanding of conquest beyond the meridian line cannot but construe such reversion as an exigency of natural and fundamental justice. See Alexandrowicz, C. H. 1969, 'New and original states, the issue of reversion to sovereignty,' *International Affairs,* vol. 45, no. 3, pp. 471–473.

20. Ramose, M. B. 1999b, 'Sovereignty and constitutional democracy: South Africa and Zimbabwe,' *Thamyris,* vol. 6, no. 2, pp. 168–175.

21. Makonnen, Y. 1983, *International Law and the new states of Africa,* UNESCO, pp. 363–364.

22. Bokor-Szegš, Hanna 1986, 'identity and succession of states in modern International Law,' *Questions of International Law,* vol. 3, p. 18 and 40.

23. Boesak, A. A. 1984, *Farewell to Innocence, a socio-ethical study of Black Theology and Black Power,* Orbis Books, Maryknoll, New York. Boesak, A. A. 1977, *Afscheid van de onschuld, een sociaal-ethische studie over zwarte theologie en zwarte macht,* (vert/trans) Frese, Like, Kok, Kampen 1977.

24. Makgoba, M. W. 1997, *Mokoko: The Makgoba affair,* Vivlia Publishers, Johannesburg.

25. There are various possibilities for dialogue with most of the essays contained in the book mentioned. However, a dialogical encounter has been avoided deliberately in order to (i) make as complete a statement as possible on the perspective adopted here; (ii) to question at least the implicit assumption, apparent in almost all the essays, that the usage 'African Renaissance' is historically and philosophically unproblematical. See Makgoba, M. W. 1999, *African Renaissance: the new struggle,* Mafube & Tafelberg, Cape Town.

26. Gutto, S. and Roux, T. 2000, 'Our northern neighbour offers key lessons for SA, write Shadrack Gutto and Theunis Roux,' *Business Day,* 18 April.

27. Ramose, M. B. 1999b. 'Sovereignty and constitutional democracy: South Africa and Zimbabwe, *Thamyris,* vol. 6, no. 2, pp. 179–180.

28. Copleston, F. 1964, *A history of philosophy,* Volume 6, Part II, Image Books, New York, pp. 207–209.

29. Kant, I. 1959, *Foundations of the metaphysics of morals and what is Enlightenment?,* (trans.) Beck, L. W., Bobbs-Merrill Company, Indianapolis, p. 85.

30. Hanke, L. 1959a. *Aristotle and the American Indians.* Henry Regnery Co., Chicago, p. ix.

31. Hanke, L. 1937b, 'Pope Paul III and the American Indians,' *The Harvard Theological Review,* volume XXX, pp. 71–72.

32. Soyinka, W. 1999, *The burden of memory: the muse of forgiveness,* Oxford University Press, New York, p. 39 and 25.

The Brazilian National Context: Harbingers of Change

David Covin

The Setting

The seeds that sprouted into the MNU were planted in a society operating under a contradictory dominant myth that it was a racial democracy within which one could improve one's position by *whitening*. A prominent belief was that the society was *not* racialized. The racialized character of the society can nevertheless be understood by looking at the politics of the republic during the last years before the military coup that resulted in 20 years of military dictatorship.

Brazilian politics were turbulent during the years 1961–1964. They coincided with the Goulart administration, an administration which entertained an increasingly populist agenda. It was a populist agenda which favored the unorganized rural poor, the organizing rural poor, the organized urban workers, and the semiorganized urban populations. What that means *in Brazil* is that it was an agenda which favored black and brown people, African-descended people. They constituted the overwhelming majority of the rural poor— organized, organizing, and unorganized. This is particularly true in one of the areas of their greatest political influence at the time, Pernambuco, a northeastern state which is overwhelmingly black. There, peasant leagues threatened significant change to the prevailing social order. While most *organized* urban laborers in the southeast were not black, a significant percentage of them were, and the predominant semiorganized and unorganized people in the southeast were African descended. The Goulart agenda was increasingly a *black* agenda, one which would give greater influence to black populations and which would place significant numbers of black people in positions of political leadership.

Those most fiercely opposed to the Goulart reforms were the giant landowners of the northeast, the military officer corps, and the governmental technocrats. These were all categories which were largely white— and whose leading and upper echelons were entirely white. The struggle from 1961–1964 was a struggle over incorporating the black population into the political equation. But, as in the case of the U.S. Constitution, it was never couched in those terms.

One only has to *look* at the populations involved in the two sides of the struggle *to see* what was going on. The actual character of the fight was cloaked by the leadership on both sides— all of whom were white. This was not a deliberate masking. They did not *see* the racial character of the contestation.

Black people, a majority of the population, had no role in political leadership. They were excluded from substantive participation. This exclusion operated under the guise of the disenfranchisement of the rural poor, the illiterates, the urban slum dwellers. But who were these people? They were not just anyone— they were black. Even those who were not physically black were black in the minds of the social elites because they lived like black people among black people.

Such political exclusion represents the place and role of black people during the most liberal and liberalizing years of the republic— absolutely omitted from the national political leadership and, indeed, from the substantive political process. The political was a world which belonged to white people, "white folks' business."

That recognition speaks to the character of black life. That it was marginalized there can be no doubt. Indeed, the word, "marginal," had come to be (and still is) synonymous with black. It was a code word without the need for a code. Everyone understood what it meant. Everyone also understood what "good appearance" meant. It was not a code. It was an established value. This is racialization so entirely incorporated into the normal operations of society that its racial quality is not perceived.

In 1961 the Afro-Brazilian population was still mostly a rural population. It consisted primarily of agricultural laborers. They worked land owned by others. Whole families worked. Their work on one landholding was often not sufficient to support themselves, so many family members often had to find other work as well, particularly seasonally. It was largely an illiterate population, suffering from many diseases and physical injuries, short life spans, and high infant mortality rates. It was absolutely impoverished.

While this rural, poor, black population was found all over the country, it was concentrated in the northeast, particularly in the states of Maranhão, Ceará, Rio Grande do Norte, Paralba, Pernambuco, Alagoas, Sergipe, and Bahia. The northeast was the poorest part of the country. When the pressures on the land became too great, or when a particular area was beset by drought or flood, northeasterners moved in droves to the metropolitan areas of their states, and to the southeast, particularly the great cities of Rio de Janciro and São Paulo.

In 1961 there was also a substantial urban black population. This population too was impoverished, though a bit more likely to be literate. They performed the most arduous and least compensated labor. Many of the women were domestic workers. Both men and women sought heavy labor and street work of various kinds. They lived, for the most part, on the peripheries of the cities where they built their own settlements without public services of any kind. They had no water, sewage, electricity, sidewalks, streets, garbage service, police, firefighters, or health services. They were *favaledos*, slum

dwellers. Large numbers of the children were street children, children without permanent homes. They lived where and as they might, with no official records of their existence. Street children in urban Brazil were a long-standing phenomenon, a continuation of a pattern arising during slavery.

There was a relatively small group of skilled black, urban laborers, many unskilled laborers, many unemployed, and a tiny collection of professionals and solvent entrepreneurs. But the people in the latter two categories were so few as to be statistically invisible.

In the political world, local, state, and national, those who decided the fates of these black people were white. One feature of the racialized character of the society was that this white monopoly of political power was seen as perfectly normal.

In the national government the PSD, PTB, and UDN political parties contended for influence and dominance. Minor parties such as the PSB, PST, PTN, and the PCB, strove to have some impact on national policy. These groups haggled and wrestled over policies which would have critical implications for the black population, while the black population itself was entirely a witness to the process, denied a presence in public life.

One feature of the personal, clientelist, patrimonial, influence-centered characteristics of Brazilian politics and political parties of the era is that none of them sought to build a mass base for anything other than voting. Since illiterates were denied the franchise, they could be ignored altogether. But even for eligible voters, the objective of the political parties was merely to secure their votes through established leadership patterns rather than to mobilize, to engage the population itself in politics. To do that would have meant incorporating the black population into politics— a prospect which was inconceivable.

In many senses, the struggles of 1961–1964— particularly with the increasingly leftward lean of the PTB under Goulart, a lean driven by Leonard Brizola, and the struggles against that lean by the PSD, the UDN, the major rural landholders, and the military leaders— were struggles over race. Was the black population to be admitted to citizenship? Was the black population to be entitled to full participation in political activity and leadership? Were the material circumstances of the black population going to be addressed? Aside from personalities and rivalries between cliques, these were the deeper and nationally more germane questions of the Goulart presidency. But they were never the questions which were articulated or examined. In fact, they were never even perceived as salient questions. The particular manifestation of racialization in Brazil prevented anyone from recognizing what underlay the rhetoric about the working class, the rural peasantry, the dispossessed. This was the state of affairs during the republic *before the military dictatorship.*

What, then, transpired with the military's assumption of power?

First of all, the ousting of the civilian regime and the military takeover answered the racial questions. The black population was not to be admitted to citizenship. Indeed, citizenship in general was to be much more greatly circumscribed. The black population was to be excluded from full participation in political activity and leadership. The material conditions of the black population were not going to be addressed. Additionally, the further step was taken of assuring that no one was going to be allowed to take positions which would raise such questions— not even in the traditional form— which was to call for improving the material conditions of the poor and increasing their political participation while avoiding the issue of race altogether.

One can see the racial nature of these contestations inside the military. One of the major factors which influenced some of the military leaders who had been opposed to the military's removing the elected head of state was a revolt of navy and air force noncoms who seized control of Brazilia. Their principal demand was to be eligible to run for elective office. They were eventually arrested. They appeared, however, to have the support of the Goulart government. Even junior officers were opposed to the noncoms. When officeholders in the sailors and marines association were arrested for attending a meeting at a Communist Party Union headquarters, subsequently released without penalty, and paraded through the streets of Rio; and when Goulart spoke to a meeting of military police subofficials

and sergeants, the die were cast. The military stepped in. Officers of all ranks, all white, united against the "mutiny" of noncoms, sailors, marines, subofficials and sergeants of the military police. The latter groups were all composed of marginals. In this decisive alignment, race was never publicly mentioned.

Port workers, rural workers, largely black, as well as organized labor, military noncoms, private sailors and marines, were all being increasingly organized, increasingly mobilized, increasingly involved in entering the political process. The rising black tide had to be stemmed. The whites who ruled Brazil would be in no position to prevail in a genuinely popular politics. Yet *no one* in these struggles, either elite or downtrodden saw the struggles as racial. *Racial ideology* in Brazil obscured *racial practice* in Brazil, rendering it invisible to every element of the Brazilian population.

For Afro-Brazilians one aspect of life did not change drastically once the military was installed. In Brazil, whether under colonialism, monarchy, civilian, or military regime, the forces of order: the police, the militia, the military police, and the military when necessary, have always been ruthless to the dangerous classes. The dangerous classes are very visible. They have always been at the absolute mercy of the forces of order. That did not change under the military presidency initiated in 1964.

The military regime, however, meant that black *leaders* were specifically targeted for serious sanctions. As a member of the dangerous classes, it was safer to be part of the herd than to be set apart as a bellcow, an agitator, a communist sympathizer.

But for most Afro-Brazilians their lives were no more perilous than ever. Because what was always dangerous about the dangerous classes were their daily lives. This continued to be every bit the case under the military regime.

The Lives of Black Folk

None of this looks like ferrile soil for the emergence of a black consciousness movement. It wasn't. It was very poor soil indeed. But wherever there is free space, there is room for visions of alternative possibilities. There are places for those visions to be shared. That's what made Palmares possible, and other *quilombos*, *mocambos*, and *palengues* that peppered the Brazilian landscape. That's what enabled the 1835 Male Rebellion in Salvador and the literally hundreds of other African tebellions throughout the duration of slavery in Brazil, and in every area of the country. It's what led to *Candomble terreiros*, *capocira* schools, and samba schools. It made possible the FNB, and for the period at hand, the TEN.

The TEN, *Teatro Experimental do Negro*, the Black Experimental Theater, was the creation of Abdias do Nascimento, perhaps the most significant and influential Brazilian black consciousness propagator in the 20th century. Nascimento was a member and participant in a wide range and number of political and cultural organizations, events, and campaigns. He joined the FNB in its waning days; hence, he was present in the hallmark black political organization of the first half of the century.

Throughout the 1930s, '40s, '50s, and '60s, until his self-exile in 1968, Nascimento was a gadfly picking at the consciousness of the white elites and the white left. He was an instigator in the African Brazilian population trying to stimulate and originate black political and cultural organizations and activities.

In 1944 he created the Black Experimental Theater (TEN). The organization's name is decidedly misleading. The TEN, developed in Rio de Janciro, was a theatrical group, but it was also a literary group, an organizing entity, a newspaper publisher, a beauty contest organizer, a propaganda machine, the sponsor of the Black Christ Art Contest, the host of the National Black Convention, the organizer of the First National Congress of Blacks, the originator of the Afro-Brazilian Democratic Committee, and a training school for black cultural workers and organizers.

The TEN flourished until 1968, four years after the start of the military government— up to the point when the most serious repression began. At that time Nascimento took the occasion of an invitation to travel to the United States as an opportunity to stay abroad. He was not to return, permanently, until 1978, appearing at the launching of the MNU.

The TEN is instructive because it is representative of the kinds of activities a minuscule stratum of the Afro-Brazilian population was engaged in from the 1930s through the 1960s. So few in number they barely made a ripple on the Brazilian political and cultural scene, they were nevertheless hard at work in the country's urban centers: Rio de Janeiro, São Paulo, Pôrto Alegre, Recife, and Salvador. Usually not as comprehensive as the TEN, separate organizations in other locations did the same kinds of things the TEN did in Rio. A tiny cadre of Afro-Brazilians, present in every major metropolitan area of the country, began focusing on concerns which were racially oriented. They began connecting with each other, particularly at the local levels, and to a lesser degree, regionally and nationally.

Black Folk in Academia

Simultaneously with the development of the TEN and its smaller and more obscure counterparts around the country, another space opened up to small numbers of African Brazilians, the academy— the world of the university and white intellectuals. Nascimento knew that world. He earned a degree in economics, a rarity for a black person at that time. He knew its rarity, but there were other black people who knew it as well.

As indicated in the last chapter, some white intellectuals had begun to develop an interest in Afro-Brazilian culture. They began to go into the *favelas*, into rural black communities, to study the inhabitants. They visited *Candomblé terreiros*. They began talking with black people, scouring archives, digging up old public records. UNESCO commissioned some to do a study on race relations in Brazil with a hope that through uncovering the secrets of the racial democracy, they could find ways to reduce racial problems elsewhere in the world. Once the Braziliah sociologists had conducted their studies, their findings, simply put, were that if a racial paradise existed, it wasn't in Brazil. The myth of racial paradise camouflaged a pit of racial hell. Some black intellectuals and black students participated in this work. They came to see their country with new eyes.

They began to participate in black organizations such as those, like the TEN, which had begun developing all over the country. They started participating in *Candomblé* and *umbanda* themselves. Some started forming new organizations in the settings they were most familiar with— in universities and among the intellectuals with whom they worked. Not a great deal is known about what many of the people and organizations involved in these developments did during the '60s. The little that is currently known suggests startling possibilities for significant discoveries.

Some of these organizational efforts are identifiable, and there are people who cite names of figures involved. Nascimento alone identifies over a score of people.

During the dictatorship, Afro-Brazilians, in addition to developing new organizational forms and spaces, continued to work with their white counterparts, primarily leftists of every stripe, including socialists and communists, many of whom were active in the formally approved political parties.

Regime Change

For this study, the main point about the military regime is that the incipient popular activities which appeared threatening to the elites in 1964, and which resulted in a military coup, were largely dormant between 1964 and 1974. They were gradually reawakened from 1974–1984. In January, 1985, an electoral college selected the first nonmilitary president in 20 years. By then, popular forces had become fully unleashed in the country, despite the continuation of military rule.

This awakening included black people. Not all of their activities ceased under the dictatorship. Many were disguised. Some went underground. Indeed, the dictatorship seemed to serve as a pressure cooker which compressed activists together and made them ready to explode into activity when the pressure was released. Among the organizations that served as the vehicles for that explosion was the MNU.

The military government had begun, from 1964 to 1967, by silencing the opposition. By 1968 it moved into a repressive phase. Under increasing economic difficulties and associated social pressures, the repression was lifted slightly beginning in 1974. The process of cutting back on repressive measures was expanded from 1979 to 1985. It was in the first month of 1985 that the regime change formally took place.

The process of change had begun with the selection of Geisel as the leader of the military government in 1974. The most repressive phase of the dictatorship began to come to an end. Geisel sought a decompression, *distenção*. One of the major obstacles to the decompression was the question of how to begin to rein in the mechanisms and people responsible for internal security. Accomplishing this objective would reduce the hostility directed toward the government as well as the military and enable the loyal opposition to function in good conscience, to really contribute to the government rather than plotting against it and engaging in foot-dragging.

Over time— and with the presidency of Figueiredo in 1979, the regime moved from a policy of *dissenção* to one of *abertura*, opening. The policy of opening was intended to encourage increased political participation, to indicate that broader freedoms would be permitted. For example, censorship of the press was curtailed. The long-suppressed leftists rushed into this window of opportunity. They avoided directing most of their efforts to political parties, which were still limited to the two officially approved and sanctioned by the state (ARENA and MDB); instead, they involved themselves in a popular politics, identified as social movements. Some of these activities were explicitly identified as urban social movements. Among the activists in the social movements was an almost invisible scattering of black people.

The Imprint of Racialization

Racialization did not legally bar Afro-Brazilians from any public spaces. At the same time, it did not give them legitimacy in many public spaces. Those public spaces in which they had most legitimacy were entertainment and sports. The public news media also featured their presence in criminal activity. Popularly, they were assigned roles as members of the dangerous classes. When they were present in explicitly political public spaces, they were not legitimate participants unless they met criteria which established them as having been whitened to a particular degree.

Most Afro-Brazilians who were active in the left during the *abertura* had achieved some degree of whitening. They had assumed leadership roles in some kinds of activities. Or they had a lot of white friends and associates. They had higher educations. Or they had experienced some degree of success in the arts or political writing. Some combined all of these attributes. They had whitened themselves enough to be accepted— not just tolerated, but accepted— into the leftist organizations and sometimes into the higher circles of those organizations. They were not, however, accepted as decision makers in those organizations. The mantle of leadership was not bestowed upon them. They were legitimate participants as long as they accepted their role— which was to do as they were told. Every single recorded Afro-Brazilian militant who cut eye teeth in the leftist movements made the same recognition.

Benedita da Silva said, "The left has not paid attention to the racial question in its organizational structure. In Brazil, none of the parties.... Right ... center, or ... Left— makes race their referent point."

Thereza Santos wrote,

I realized that these people had a very condescending relationship with me, as well as with the other blacks who were on the Left. It was a kind of paternalism, as if we were ... stupid, and they were in charge of protecting us, guiding us ... Many times when I expressed an opinion, somebody would interrupt and ... translate what I was thinking.

Ivanir dos Santos says. "I learned that a black man with a conscience within a political party dominated by a white intellectual middle class of students is never accepted....

Arani Santana was a member of a group of African Brazilians who were more or less privileged for the time. They had jobs, professions.

She said, What the group had in common was that inside our heads we all had this preoccupation with racism. We'd experienced discrimination in the university, at work, and even in the theater. We felt this type of discrimination very thoroughly because we were in Bahia, a state that is overwhelmingly Black, and still in the theater there were few colored people.

Abdias do Nascimento's statement is,

African Brazilians were always treated as outsiders. At best we were the left's "folklore." At worst we were "divisionists" potentially responsible for the pulverization of working class unity.

When political and social movements began to develop during the *abertura*, because the country was racialized, they could not be genuinely inclusive movements. White people were privileged in them. Black people in those movements were what they were in the society at large— marginalized. For that reason, for black people to begin to play an active role in organizations or movements which were dedicated to their deepest concerns, they were going to have to either join the nascent black organizations, or they were going to have to build entirely new ones.

Their breaks with their white mentors were often not clean. Influences lingered, especially for those whose mentors had been their professors. As students they had idolized their teachers. The white academics in the social movements were not only intellectually brilliant, they were also activists. They had committed their lives to social struggle. Many of them had been arrested, jailed, tortured, exiled. These were not tawdry characters. They were inspirational. Severing those bonds was extraordinarily difficult, and often never fully achieved. Like Adam and Eve, black people were driven from racial paradise because they were not deemed worthy. Reluctant refugees from a paradise which had denied them both justice and peace, their creation of explicitly black organizations, rooted in racial identity, was the last resort of a desperate people, grasping for hope.

Is Western Democracy the Answer to the African Problem?

Marie Pauline Eboh

Introduction

Just as one hears of Greek philosophy, Western philosophy, African philosophy, one also hears of Greek democracy, Western democracy, African consensus democracy etc. This tends to suggest that like philosophy, democracy is culture relative. Yet there is something in both philosophy and democracy which transcends the various cultures within which they are practised. In the case of democracy that "something" is freedom. Freedom is a cultural universal. Democracy without a reasonable amount of freedom is unthinkable. That is why some people argue that such an independent and autonomous development as democracy cannot be achieved in the IMF-dominated continent of Africa. Paradoxical enough, it is only in terms of constraints or inhibitions emanating from other human beings or institutions that freedom can be meaningfully defined. For instance, a person who is marooned in an island cannot talk of his/her freedom of speech as no one is there with him/her to encroach on his/her liberty. Nor does he/she have to exercise appropriate restraint and show respect for the opinions of other people. Such a person will be self-governed, but cannot be said to practise democracy. It takes more than freedom to effect democracy. The bottom line is people. As peoples of the earth differ in their frames of reference so also do their cultural practice of democracy vary. "If the relevant claim to freedom is properly limited to a subset

of human beings, its ultimate validation must rest on their peculiar needs presented by their institutional setting in order for them and their institution to function effectively to achieve their own purposes or mission."[1] Missions are not always the same; that is why lectures, for instance, hammer away academic freedom while journalists emphasise freedom of the press, and developing nations stress economic freedom.

America is known as the land of freedom, and there is a tendency to think that US is the home of true democracy. In addition, US has made it her business to champion the cause of democracy all over the world, and has thereby earned the title: "The Policeman of Democracy." When President Babangida, who had instituted a transition programme from Military to democratic rule, faltered by annulling the June 12th presidential election which was meant to usher in democratic rule in Nigeria [an election supervised by the outside world and seen to be free and fair], America and Britain were very quick to impose sanctions on Nigeria. What Babangida was doing, they said, was not in keeping with the democracy they know of. What they did, of course, pleased many Nigerians who are pro-democracy. And these Nigerians called for more sanctions to complement the efforts of Nigerian political activists who were hellbent on terminating Babangida's dictatorship. On the other hand, other well-meaning Nigerians saw the foreign intervention as a new way to reimpose colonial hegemony and to have a naval base in Port Harcourt and they asked our trading partners to keep off Nigeria's internal affairs. This incident aroused sober reflections: Is there only one route to democracy? Should democracy be imposed from outside? Does true democracy obtain in the US? Is Western capitalist democracy the Answer to the political instability of African nations? etc.

Is There Only One Route to Democracy?

As counter-reaction to US' and Britain's universalizing move and their use of overweening socio-economic pressure to enforce compliance, President Babangida was quick to say that there is no single route to Democracy. Hence in his message to the O.A.U. [Organization of African Unity] summit held in Cairo, he warned against a wholesale importation of Western democracy because it ignores cultural values and differences. A uniform set of democratic rules will lead to the dissolution of global differences in economic and axiological sense.

As to whether democracy should be imposed from outside, if by common definition, democracy is "government of the people, by the people, for the people," how authentic is it when dictated from outside? A democracy which is practised under the huge legs of a colossus cannot but be preposterous. It is a sham. Little wonder why Wamba-dia-Wamba deftly proposes the displacement of the "social epistemology of domination"[2] by a new philosophical paradigm as the condition of possibility of an emancipative politics in Africa. For a democracy to be authentic, the political process must be free and fair; freedom must not be shackled either overtly or covertly. Democracy, Nyerere says, "is a declaration of faith in human nature." Western style democracy is not an authentic expression of contemporary African political culture, which must address so many peculiar issues. For instance, the politics of emancipation of Africa cannot afford to ignore the human dignity of the whole people of Africa, both male and female, and it has to be characterised by the humanistic *cum* latitudinarian value-system of the traditional African polity. It must redress the socio-economic and political malaise which plagues contemporary Africa. Any thing to the contrary would not be liberating but rather shortsighted. At any rate, there cannot be political stability without economic stability. And so long as instability prevails, military dictators can always find excuses to seize power.

Does True Democracy Exist in the US?

As far back as 1890, Mrs. Mary E. Lease, the Leader of the Farmers (People's) Party of the United States of America observed that "Wall Street owns the country. It is no longer a government of the people, by the people, and for the people, but a government of Wall Street, by Wall Street, and for the Wall Street."[3] As regards improving democratic elections in the United States, Porter Mckeever, former aide to Adlai Stevenson and Washington Observer, said while addressing the City Club, Cleveland, Ohio, on June 15, 1990:

In 1988 Presidential elections . . . voter turnout was the lowest in 64 years. Barely half of those eligible to vote bothered to register a choice as to who should be President of the United States. . . . According to a recent poll 70 percent of adult Americans believe that Congress is devoid of integrity. Worse, one in every four believe at least half of all Senators and Congressmen are financially corrupt. . . . Nor does one need polls to be aware of the cynicism that has seeped into and corrodes our entire political process. And this is happening at a time when democratic ideals and institutions have before them the most far-flung opportunity since humanity began its struggle towards freedom. It is a supreme irony that the fervor for democratic ideals and processes seems to be far more vibrant and alive in Eastern Europe, and far more dramatically affirmed in Tiananmen Square, than here in democracy's homeland (America). . . . More important than on personal longings, however, is the fact that the quality of our leadership has fateful consequences for the entire planet.[4]

With regard to America's performance in the Gulf War, Dr. Henry Kissinger commenting on George Bush's idea of NWO said that he admired Bush's skill and fortitude in building (Gulf War) coalition, but doubted whether "the idealistic expectations accurately described what happened in the Gulf crisis." Kissinger further observed: "US Policy makers must recognise that the New World Order cannot be built to US specifications. America cannot forcefeed a global sense of community where none exists. American preponderance cannot last. Nor can the American economy indefinitely sustain a policy of essentially unilateral interventionism.[5]

If nothing else, the reaction of the erstwhile US secretary of state, Henry Kissinger, tends to suggest that the American populace must have been propagandized while their leader went ahead to do his own thing in the Gulf. US unilateral bombing of Iraq in Bush's last days in office ignoring the consensus reached by the coalition is also indicative that even in the US true democracy is a thing of the future. Questions are even raised as to whether the **New World Order** is not a synonym for **The American Empire,** especially in the light of the erstwhile US Senator, Beveridge's declaration:

> Have we (Americans) no mission to perform, no duty to discharge to our fellowman? Hawaii is ours; Porto Rico is to be ours; at the prayer of her people Cuba finally will be ours; in the islands of the East, even the gates of Asia . . . the flag of a liberal government (of the United States) is to float over the Philippines. . . . The commercial supremacy of the (American) Republic means that this nation is to be the sovereign factor in the peace of the world. For the conflicts of the future are to be conflicts of trade-struggles for markets—commercial wars for existence. So Hawaii furnishes us a naval base in the heart of the Pacific, Manila another at the gates of Asia—Asia, to the trade of whose hundreds of millions American merchants, manufacturers, farmers have as good right as those of Germany or France or Russia or England; Asia whose commerce with the United Kingdom alone amounts to hundreds of millions of dollars every year. . . . We cannot retreat from any soil where providence has unfurled our banner, it is ours to save that soil for liberty and civilization.[6]

Could this be the philosophy behind the democracy whose cause US is championing all the world over? Are human right activists of any rich "soil" being covertly gingered up to pray US "to save that soil for liberty and civilization?" Is "this nation" [US] not presently proving "to be the sovereign factor in the peace of the world" by intervening in the internal affairs of fellow sovereign nations like Nigeria?

Is Western Democracy the Answer to the African Problem?

In view of all the foregoing, there is little wisdom in expecting too much from Western capitalist democracy. For as our people put it, he who went to the house of a toad and requested for a seat, did he find the toad sitting on any chair?

The importation of ideologies and foreign systems has not helped, and will not help Africa establish good governments. At best, what we can do, is to adopt a symbiosis of the best values, drawn from Europe and other civilizations, which harmonize with our own cherishable African systems or cultural institutions.[7]

The traditional consensus democracy is generally affirmed, not only as being a form of consultative debate which enabled the equal participation of all adult males in the decision making of the tribe, but also as a system full of checks and balances which ensured that nobody could abuse power or grab it for his own benefit.[8]

Ruch has it that our democracy is neither to be a mere return to traditional Africa, nor exactly that of the Western countries. It cannot be purely traditional because both the size of our modern countries and their type of unity is different from the traditional one. It cannot be Western model because we have to fight an especially bitter battle against the divisive forces of traditional tribalism and we must create a unity where there is no natural foundation for it. Moreover, our traditional values demand that we aim at consensus decisions.[9] Ruch is fundamentally correct. However, the reasons he gave to back up his position are hardly sustainable. Because if tribe is rightly understood as a "social division of a people defined in terms of common descent, territory, culture etc.," and tribalism is taken to mean "loyalty to a tribe or tribal values," then, tribalism is not an African preserve. It is even more pronounced in the US where colour bar mars the political career of some talented persons of African descent. Perhaps someone may say that we are mixing up tribe and race, tribalism and racism. The divide between the two is very marginal. For race simply means "a group of people with common ancestry distinguished from others by physical characteristics," while racism is "abusive or aggressive behaviour towards members of another race" on the basis of superiority complex. The very "divisive forces of traditional tribalism" form part and parcel of racism and US *modus operandi* exhibits a fair share of it—Whites versus Blacks and other non-Whites. US community is not homogeneous. True to its name, "God's own country," all God's children are there—the Indians, the Anglo-saxons, the Africans, the Polish, the Irish, the Spaniards, the Dutch, the Italians, the Jews, the Arabs, name it. If all these races, which congregated in this "Galilee of the nations," could patch it up, then, *a fortiori,* Africans can. So, there must be other reasons why "our democracy" will neither be the pristine African traditional type nor Western style. However, the important thing is that Ruch recognized that it cannot be "exactly" Western model.

Western democracy e.g., the US model is a two party system, with the second party acting as opposition. "Opposition" does indeed often mean systematic rejection of whatever the government does because the governing party is "the enemy," rather than participation in the construction of the nation for the common good of all. Politics is a notoriously fickle game.[10]

What is necessary for democracy is not an organized opposition, which, in order to offer itself an alternative government, adopts every obstructive and even at times destructive measures and maneuvers to overthrow a government that . . . is unprepared to make mistakes to encourage the growth of a strong opposition. What is necessary for democracy to be maintained is the opportunity to criticize or speak one's mind without fear or favor, the opportunity to share in the government by exercise of your franchise without fear or favor, the opportunity to change those who govern by the use of your vote.[11]

"The test of a democratic regime in Africa might not necessarily be the actual presence of a second party or several parties, so much as whether or not the regime tolerated individualists. This is the crucial point, for societies are not built or improved by conformists."[12] "The basis of human progress throughout history has been the existence of people, who regardless of the consequences to themselves, stood up when they believed it necessary, and said 'that was wrong; this is what we

should do . . .'"[13] A one party system democracy could still be censured through a free press and not necessarily through an opposition party. At any rate, institutionalizing opposition as checks and balances is not a bad idea in view of the one party totalitarian government of the then Eastern bloc. However, it could also be counter productive. For, when one is over supervised, the one tends to make unnecessary mistakes. Besides, there is no reason to presuppose that the members of the opposition party will always be above board and so can never be swayed by any incumbent government if it means to.

"Africa cannot move from one extreme to the other extreme without mapping out its own original path while taking due cognizance of developments in other social formations."[14] The economic problems of contemporary Africa constitute a serious cog in the wheel of genuine democracy. They are *inter alia* servitude to foreign financial clubs and institutions, unmanageable debt servicing on account of high interest rates resulting in penury, political instability, military dictatorship, disaffection between the government and the governed etc. These are intertwined. As those who have the guns call the shots, vassalage to foreign nations explains Africa's political instability and the constant military interventions in most African states. Immanuel Kant foresaw this long ago.

In his treatise *Perpetual Peace*, Kant advocated the abolition of standing armies, and the prohibition of foreign debts, warning that otherwise bankruptcy would be inevitable in the long run: since the rich state would take the advantage to grow in strength against its debtors; and that would pose a big threat. Foreign debts destabilize debtor governments. He who pays the piper determines the tune: hence creditors, such as the International Monetary Fund (IMF), always give conditionalities, which, most of the time, impose stringent measures, that make the citizens of the borrowing nations disillusioned, to the point of losing confidence in the good intentions of their rulers. A case in point is the . . . anti-SAP (Structural Adjustment Programme) crisis, which led frustrated Nigerian masses to burn down and to loot many government establishments.[15]

Of course, disaffection is not only the result of loss of faith in the ability of the African governments to alleviate the plight of the common man, but also a natural outcome of the imposition of military dictatorship on a people, who are customarily democratic from time immemorial. Dictatorship rends not only the solidarity or unanimity which is the linchpin of African traditional politics, but also erodes the people's equality and freedom of expression. Democracy cannot thrive under economic and political instability because democracy connotes emancipation which purports autonomy or the freedom to be oneself.

Wamba emphasizes a redefinition of democracy and politics in general in a non-state-centered way. The state is to be held accountable to the people. As he rightly said, unless society has some autonomy from the state, it cannot control and limit the state powers.

My proposal is to focus on political processes (of the people) rather than on the political system (of the state); on democratization, that is, on the people's treatment of differences among themselves in society, rather than on democracy as a form of state. It is an attempt to define the main lines of a possible emancipative/progressive mode of politics through which democratization can be given a new meaning. The dominant modes of politics, which are now in crisis, have been centered around the seizure of state power and distribution of state positions and have not been about the transformation of the state in favour of the people's social and political emancipation.[16]

We cannot agree more. However, we do not fully approve of some of Wamba's non-statist or anti-statist development strategies. For instance this one: In Africa, we must move away from the unpatriotic territorial nationalism [Wamba-dia-Wamba (1991)] of comprador modernizers. This is a process of 'nation-building-from-above,' which is rooted in colonial legacy and insists on political unanimity seen as a basis for national unity. This process has blocked people's creativity and mass enthusiasm and has made the treatment of differences among the people by the people themselves complicated. For example, citizens of one state may be required to treat their relatives of a neighbouring country as refugees or enemies.[17]

We do not appreciate the fact that colonial masters amalgamated tribes that had nothing in common and we therefore endorse the right to self-determination of any tribe that is being treated as better-gone-away in the country in which it finds itself by mere accident of history. But the rest, who are okay in the new dispensation should remain. Boundaries *per se* do not bring about enmity. Even in the pre-colonial African society, there were boundaries separating village from village, town from town, tribe from tribe etc.

Persons from Town-X were visitors in Town-Y and if they sought sanctuary, they were accorded the status of refugees. For although they mix up freely and share everything in common with the host community, they would not **inherit** land in Town-Y even if the persons involved were to be relatives. If we try to revoke every "unpatriotic territorial nationalism" we may have many wars in our hands and also have as many countries as the number of tribes in Africa, some of which might not be viable. We should rather emphasize the opening up of the minds and hearts of Africans to justice[18] [equitable distribution of goods and services] which bears a human face.

Thus far, there seems to be a sort of mutual agreement that Western democracy is not the answer to the African question. The answer lies in taking the bull by the horn—tackling the African socio-economic and political reality, and giving democracy an African flair.[19]

It may be pertinent to mention that on the Nigerian scene, even while democratic elections seemed to be a their peak in the country, many political activists were busy propagating the idea of splitting Nigeria into many federations. They do not even see the present democratic process as an answer to the Nigerian problem.

Conclusion

The global community has come to regard democracy as not only a civilised value to be fostered, but also as a principle upon which to build the new World Order. The difficulty is not in the new idea of a just World Order, but that the political leaders of powerful countries are finding it difficult to escape from the old ones. [They] have been politically committed to conservative ideology and it would, therefore, be naive to believe that they can usher the dawn of a new World Order without dismantling their conservative political structures. What is therefore urgently required of the

US Western powers is that they correct their policy to suit the demands of new world realities, instead of forcing the world to suit their outdated ideological perspectives.[20]

If there must be democracy worldwide, the global community has to address the issue of the uneven development of the nations of the earth, and material inequality. If we must universalize democracy, it is necessary to universalize also the good things of the temporal order which make life liveable. It is only when this is done that individual persons/international communities can meet as equals and engage in meaningful and horizontal dialogue to their mutual edification.

The fact that no country has yet acquired true democracy, argues in favour of intercultural fecundation of democracy. Maybe by integrating the good aspects of the democratic processes of every society, the world may yet evolve a better brand of democracy. For instance, Africans could contribute their idea of true consensus while Americans contribute their ideal practice of freedom of the press, etc. Noam Chomsky would disagree with this. For, in his book: *Necessary Illusions* "Chomsky rips away the mask of propaganda that portrays the media as advocates of free speech and democracy."[21] Nevertheless, the point we are making is that every culture has something to offer.

Notes

1. W.B. Harvey: *Freedom, University and The Law. The legal Status of Academic Freedom in the University of Black Africa.* Lagos 1978, p. 1.

2. E. Wamba dia Wama: *Philosophy and African Intellectuals. Mimesis of Western Classicism, Ethnophilosophical Romanticism or African Self-Mastery?* In: Quest Philosophical Discussions 5, 1 (1991), p. 9.

3. In: Philosophy and Social Action 17 (1991), p. 74.

4. Op. cit., p. 98.

5. D. Sharma: *America's New World Order.* In Philosophy and Social Action 17 (1991), p. 8.

6. Op. cit., back cover.

7. M.P. Eboh: *A Philosophy and Political Stability Are Needed for Holistic Development. A Reflection with Reference to Nigeria.* In: AFER [African Ecclesiastical Review] 31 (1989), p. 351.

8. E.A. Ruch/K.C. Anyanwu: *African Philosophy. An Introduction to the Main Philosophical Trends in Contemporary Africa.* Rome 1981, p. 305.

9. Op. cit., p. 304.

10. Op. cit., p. 320.

11. K. Baako: *The Party.* In: CPP Journal 4–7 (1961).

12. President Olympio in *Africa Speaks.* Princeton 1961, p. 76–77.

13. Cowan/O'Connell/Scanlon (eds): *Education and Nationbuilding in Africa.* New York 1965, p. 312–313; quoted in Harvey, op. cit. (in note 1), p. 15.

14. J.O. Ihonvbere: *Is Democracy Possible in Africa? The Elites, the People and Civil Society.* In: Quest. Philosophical Discussions 6,2 (1992), p. 106.

15. Eboh, op. cit. (in note 7), p. 345–346.

16. E. Wamaba dia Wamba: *Beyond Elite Politics of Democracy in Africa.* In: Quest. Philosophical Discussions 6,2 (1992), p. 30.

17. Op. cit., p. 32.

18. Eboh, op. cit., p. 351.

19. M.P. Eboh: *Democracy with an African Flair.* In: Quest. Philosophical Discussions 7,1 (1993), p. 98.

20. Sharma, op. cit., p. 8.

21. In: Philosophy and Social Action 17 (1991), p. 79.

A Voyage of Discovery: Sacramento and the Politics of Ordinary Black People

David Covin

Good Afternoon,

Thank you for the introduction.

I am honored and humbled to be invited to speak at the 40th Anniversary of Ethnic Studies at Sacramento State University. It is a singular honor to be invited to speak at the university where I taught for 35 years, to be invited by my home department, and my home program of Pan African Studies within that department, to be invited by my colleagues. This honor is enhanced by the distinction of the department. This Ethnic Studies department is one of the most outstanding in the country. An indicator of that reality is that one of its past chairs, Dr. Otis Scott, is the only person ever elected to two consecutive terms as President of the National Association of Ethnic Studies. Another indicator is the distinction of each of the separate programs which constitute it: Asian-American Studies, Latino/Chicano Studies, Native American Studies, and Pan African Studies. My program, Pan African Studies, as currently constituted, is one of the strongest in the country. It has a sterling legacy of teachers, scholars, activists, and mentors. As a continuation of that legacy, its current composition, consisting of nationally and internationally renowned faculty members, places it in the first rank in the United States, and in the world.

Sac State's Ethnic Studies Department has a quadruple legacy of scholarship, teaching, activism, and mentoring. It is built—and operates—to serve students and to serve the community. There is no *link* between the department and the community. There is a *commonality*. That is

represented, for example, by Cooper-Woodson College—which unites students, faculty, and community residents in a mentoring and support system. In the whole country there is no counterpart.

To be chosen to speak by such an illustrious group of colleagues is, indeed, a humbling honor.

This afternoon I'm going to talk about a Voyage of Discovery that has taken place over the past 40 years. It is the voyage of my discipline, Pan African Studies. By extension, it represents the voyage made by every aspect of the Ethnic Studies department. My focus is specifically on Pan African Studies. In the course of the discussion I will use one of my books as an illustration of how a particular work contributes to the voyage.

Pan African Studies, as the field is named on this campus California State University, Sacramento, and Black Studies, as it is more widely known, elsewhere is also designated as Africana Studies, Africology, Afro-American Studies, and various and sundry other appellations. By whatever name, 40 years ago, it was virtually non-existent as an academic discipline. Beginning at San Francisco State, in 1966, the first Black Studies departments and programs were established. In 1968 and 1969 there was an explosion in their number following the assassination of Dr. Martin Luther King, Jr. The program here began as part of the broader program of Ethnic Studies, in the academic year, 1969-70. The Black Studies programs and departments established in those early years were not academic disciplines. They were part of a social movement—the Black Movement, more popularly known as the Black Power Movement.

They were not academic disciplines because there were no academic Black Studies departments or programs to produce the scholars who would populate them. If we look at the early incumbents of Black Studies positions on this campus, for example, we find Dr. William Gibson, who was a historian; Dr. Maxwell Owusu, who was an anthropologist; Dr. Addison Somerville, who was a Psychologist; Jesse McClure, who had an MSW; Dr. Fannie Canson, who was an Educational administrator; Mugo-Mugo Gatheru, who was an author and a historian; Gabriel Bannerman-Richter, who was an English teacher and writer; Dr. Allan Gordon, who was an Art Historian. Not one of them was the product of a Black Studies Department. In the cohort I came in with in 1970, there were two of us who were political scientists, an artist, a dramatist, a fine arts graduate who was a poet, and a social worker. No graduates of Black Studies departments. There weren't any.

Black Studies, as an academic discipline, had to be created. The job of early Black Studies departments was to do precisely that: *Create* Black Studies. It did not have to be done out of wholecloth because there was a rich tradition of Black scholarship which could be drawn on. But that tradition was academically diffuse. There was the incomparable and path-breaking work of Dr. W.E.B. DuBois, the historical work of Dr. Carter G. Woodson, and Dr. John Hope Franklin. There were the pioneering studies of John Henrick Clark, C.L.R. James. There was Dr. Anna Julia Cooper, the Harlem Renaissance writers, scholars, artists, musicians. There was the Negritude movement. The work of sociologists like Dr. C. Eric Lincoln and anthropologists like Dr. Sinclair Drake. The political scientist, Dr. Ralph Bunche. Dancer/scholars like Katherine Dunham. There was a rich history of scholarly investigation and artistic creativity. But there was no academic discipline devoted, particularly, to mining and developing that treasure trove.

The people I've mentioned were stars—luminaries—but there were very few foot-soldiers dedicated to this work. Most Black people who had come to maturity before the 1950s, were not high-school graduates. Those who were hired to teach Black Studies in the 1960s and 70s had to figure out the parameters, the dimensions, of this new field. That work was both driven and complicated by the reality that the field had emerged out of a social movement.

One of the constants of the human condition is that if you get two people together, they will disagree with each other—on just about anything. Add to that people who are fired up about a social movement—extremely opinionated— and others steeped in the tradition of objective academic rigor, and you have a very explosive mix indeed. Figuring out what this new discipline was going to be—the very first step in creating Black Studies—was no walk down a garden path.

Combined with this was the condition that a lot of these new faculty members were practicing "learning as you go." They hadn't read Ida B. Wells, Mary McCleod Bethune, David Diop, Paul Lawrence Dunbar, Phyllis Wheatley, Marcus Garvey. These people weren't covered in any classes taught in the colleges and universities they'd attended. The new teachers had to learn them on their own. And for several years that's what most Black Studies consisted of—drawing on the rich seed-bed of scholarship and artistic accomplishment that earlier generations of Black people had produced—but which had enjoyed a very narrow audience, accomplishment that was almost entirely excluded from traditional academia.

How do all these disparate people, doing their own basic learning, in the throes of a social movement, figure out what their discipline is going to be? They were learning almost everything as they went along. I'll use what happened here to illustrate some of what that means.

Does Black Studies (Afro-American Studies)— as many people thought, believed, and argued— mean the study of Black people in the United States? Here—on this campus—almost half the people teaching Black Studies were from Africa: Maxwell Owusu, Mugo-Mugo Gatheru, Gabriel Bannerman-Richter, John Shoka. It didn't make sense for Black Studies to be restricted to the United States. As people educated themselves they increasingly became exposed to the African *diaspora*—a term many had never even heard before they began their careers as Black Studies professors. The African *diaspora*—Black people in the United States, but also in the Caribbean,

Central America, South America, even Canada for heaven's sake—for starters. How does one convey that the field encompasses all these African peoples? On this campus, the faculty said, Let's make it clear, explicit, that Black Studies means the study of African people—*wherever they are*. Let's call ourselves Pan African Studies. They changed the program's name from Black Studies to Pan African Studies. Its mission—was to join with others—across the world—to create an academic discipline of a new type.

Let me lay out what that means. Despite the remarkable work done by pioneering Black scholars and artists, by comparison with other works produced, those by or about people of African descent were negligible. In the discipline I was trained in, political science, for example, in the two major journals of the discipline, from 1886—1990, a period of 104 years, a total of 6,157 articles were published. Fifty-four of those were focused on Black politics. 6,103 were not. Of the 54 articles on Black politics—17 were really not on Black politics at all, but were about slavery, the politics of slavery. In reality, then, only 37 articles focused on Black politics after the Civil War. Approximately ½ of 1% of all the articles. That's what I mean by negligible. 99.5% of the articles were not about Black politics. Plainly and simply, that means for most people who wanted to study Black politics, there was nothing to study.

The task that fell to these new scholars was—creating a literature, a subject matter, a body of knowledge for their discipline—even as they were trying to figure out its parameters.

How did they do?

We'll use Pan African Studies at Sac State as an indicator. CSU Sacramento is not a Research I institution. That means its primary mission, the mission of its faculty, is not research, but teaching. Community service is also a major responsibility of this university—a responsibility greatly heightened for Pan African Studies. In California, research is primarily the mission of the U.C. system. It is funded to support research. The work load of its faculty is based around research. That is not true here. Research in the CSU system, has to be torn out of faculty members' hides.

Given all that, how did the Pan African Studies faculty—who were not paid to do original research, to produce subject matter—but to disseminate it—how did they do?

Faculty members associated with Pan African Studies at Sac State since its inception have written 64 books, almost 700 articles, book chapters, book reviews, and short stories. They have produced major works of art—which have been hung, played, and performed in galleries, theaters, and concert halls all over the world. They have been consultants on projects of every kind all over the planet. They have produced films, CDs, radio and television programs. They have produced web-sites and blogs. They have created and edited journals. They have appeared in radio, television, newspaper, journal, and magazine interviews. They have had articles, even books, written about *them*.

Now, let us compare their production of Black articles over 40 years, to that of another academic discipline, political science, for the whole country—over 104 years. All of Political Science over 104 years—37 articles. Pan African Studies at Sac State over 40 years—700.

This is one program, in a non-Research I institution. Can you imagine the total amount of work produced by Black Studies scholars in colleges and universities of every description, including Research I institutions, throughout this region, throughout this state, throughout this country, and throughout the world over these 40 years? It is ... staggering. It is an academic achievement of colossal magnitude. And it is recognized ... by almost no one. That is why this anniversary needs to be celebrated and broadcast—to every village and hamlet.

This discipline has been sailing on an unprecedented—Voyage of Discovery.

I'm going to use my book, *Black Politics After the Civil Rights Movement: Sacramento, 1970–2000*, as an illustration of the kinds of places this voyage has taken us, the kind of discovery such research produces. By the way, that title is the publisher's title. I call the book, *The Politics of Ordinary Black People*. It took me 40 years to write it. So you can see I was not working on a publish or perish schedule. I would have perished. The objective of academic research is to produce new knowledge, at the very least, to produce promising and likely speculations. Most of us produce the latter: promising and likely speculations. I liken the conduct of original research to taking voyages of discovery. Their objectives are the same. What is "original" research but going somewhere no one's ever been? If somebody's already been there, it's not original.

Christopher Columbus undertook voyages of discovery. But he wasn't looking for someplace new. He was looking for some place old—the Indies, the Orient, the East. He was looking for a new "passage" to the Indies. That's what he was trying to discover. He didn't "discover" the new passage. He didn't know there was a whole hemisphere between Europe and the East. Going for the East—he ended up in the West. That's what doing original research is like. You don't know where you're going. You often end up at a different place than you thought you would. You are often surprised, and often don't know where you are once you've arrived. You may even think you're some place you're not. Columbus thought he was in the Indies. He ended up somewhere he didn't even know existed.

That's original research. Every time you begin it, you are entering the unknown. In the 40 years since the advent of Black Studies, Black Political scientists have produced a tremendous amount of research. Bearing witness to their productivity is that unlike the U.S.A., the American Political Science Association, the APSA, has had three Black presidents during that period, one of them a woman (the three followed by some forty-five years the Presidency of Ralph Bunche in 1954). Presidents of the APSA are elected on the basis of their leading role in the discipline. So the three Black presidents speak to the quality of Black scholarship over the past 4 decades. Political Science, nevertheless, remains a backwards discipline on questions of race, despite the prodigious output of Black scholars, because white scholars and *all* non-Black scholars produce articles on Black politics at about the same rate they always have. Despite the many discoveries of my colleagues in the field of Black politics, there were a number of unanswered or even unaddressed questions I wanted to explore. That's why I did the research that produced this book. Most political studies deal

with officeholders, appointed officials, bureaucracies, organizations, social movements, individual actors—variations across class, gender, age, race, public opinion, as well as connections among these variables—at the local, state, national, and international levels. I wanted to understand how ordinary Black people—who held no political office—fit into that complex aggregation of structures, activities, and orientations.

One of the salient findings of most of the major studies was that the Black politics of the 30 years between 1970 and 2000, usually referred to in the literature as the Post-Civil Rights Era, had not been worthy successors of the Civil Rights and Black Power epoch. Black politics had become increasingly dysfunctional. Some scholars also identified a declining significance of race, identified in politics, as deracialization. Some preliminary studies I had done raised questions about these findings. While it was incontestable—as other studies showed that after the late 1970s the Civil Rights and Black Power Movements had ended, it was equally incontestable that ferocious opposition to those gains persisted. Yet my work showed, and no serious work really contradicted it, that the gains of the Civil Rights and Black Power movements continued, and in most instances had been enhanced. How could that be, I wondered, if Black politics had become increasingly dysfunctional. I used Sacramento as a universe to explore these questions. A 2002 edition of *Time* magazine unintentionally validated the academic viability of the project by identifying Sacramento as the city most representative of the diversity of the national population.

Focusing on Sacramento I was able to look in much more detail at Black organizations, residential patterns, social networking, social movements, officeholders, political campaigns, and three critical elements derived from social movement research: social spaces, social narrative, and social memory, than I would have been able to do looking at the country at large, or even at a very big city. I was also able to identify national Black political efforts which were present in Sacramento, such as the War on Poverty, the Harold Washington Mayoral campaign, the Jesse Jackson Presidential campaigns, and the Million Man March. In them I could examine the relationships between national and even international political efforts and local ones. I divided the analysis by decades, in order both to make it manageable and to enable the identification of changes, trends, and continuities over time.

Let me highlight some of my principal findings:

1. The emergence of a significant Black middle class in Sacramento, beginning in the mid 1960's, and increasing rapidly in each subsequent decade.
2. A fluid Black population, with births, deaths, and people moving in and out of the area.
3. A tendency of Black people to identify certain governmental programs, governmental offices, and geographical areas as "theirs" regardless of demographic characteristics.
4. A tendency of other population groups to acquiesce to such Black claims.
5. Affronts to Black people served as powerful incentives for mobilizing Black people, with the police department most frequently the source of the affronts.
6. A high level of organization among the Black population, characterized over time by a significant decrease in the number of working class organizations and an almost geometric expansion in the number of mixed and middle-class organizations.
7. An almost total absence of organization of the Black underclass, except the Nation of Islam, and a very small number of secular organizations during the 90s.
8. A consistent increase in the total number of Black organizations and in the number of organizations intentionally founded to be specifically Black, despite widely disseminated notions of a declining significance of race.
9. No support for the proposition that for Black people, between 1970 and 2000, there was a decline in the significance of race. If anything, the data showed an *increase* in the significance of race.
10. A general and consistent lack of political involvement by Black churches throughout the whole period.
11. The Nation of Islam bucked the trend of Black religious detachment from politics from 1984 on.
12. The cathartic and empowering effect of the appeal for Black Unity.

I'll talk about a few of these findings to illustrate their explanatory power.

The tendency of Black people to identify certain social spaces as their own, and to take them over, is related to Black use of social narratives and social memory. Black people, more than any other similarly oppressed or exploited group, were empowered and mobilized by the Civil Rights and Black Power Movements. As a result, the War on Poverty, closely connected to those movements, was claimed by Black people when it came to Sacramento. For the most part, they captured it, though most poor people in Sacramento were not Black, they were white. Yet in every target area where there was a significant Black population, Black people ended up running the poverty organization whether the majority or plurality was white or Latino, because in no case was the majority or plurality Black. This is one instance of the tendency of Black people to identify certain social spaces as their own and take them over.

Another avenue that opened up such possibilities for Black people arose when the Sacramento City Council went to a district system of election, Black activists worked hard to develop two Black-influence districts. Each of those 2 districts, council district 2 and council district 5, had white super majorities. Yet Black people, using Black narrative to dominate political spaces, claimed those districts as their own and twice elected Black people in district 2, and once got a Black person appointed. In district 5 they elected 1 Black person, got another appointed, and later elected a Black person to consecutive terms. Still later, in District 8, where the plurality population was white, but in which Black people had mobilized to have boundaries drawn to make it a Black influence district, Black people elected a councilman to two consecutive terms, and when he died, elected his wife to the seat. In every single one of these electoral instances, white, Latino, and Asian populations deferred to Black assertions.

The significance of the cathartic and empowering impact of the appeal to Black Unity was revealed in the distinction between organizing and mobilizing.

There is a persistent, perpetual, and relentless appeal for Black Unity that emerges from African peoples. It is an appeal which makes no rational sense. Within the United States the Black population is too large, too dispersed, too varied, too complex, and too conflicted for Black Unity to have any possibility of being realized organizationally. Yet the appeal to Black Unity has a powerful effect as a mobilizing tool.

Black people in the aggregate crave racial unity. That's why metaphors such as house slaves, field slaves, uncle Toms, Aunt Gemimas, oreos, and handkerchief heads are so effective. That's why Clarence Thomas, Wardell Connerly, and Condoleeza Rice are such anathemas. They accent disunity, the fractured condition of the Black population.

The irony is that contested figures such as Shelby Steele and Alan Keyes accurately reflect the reality that the Black population is not monolithic. Most Black people wish it were, because they believe—if it were, they would be much more effective in achieving their collective aspirations. This is all wishful thinking, but it is powerful wishful thinking with profound implications for Black political life. It "keeps hope alive"—and raises the prospect of realizing *"The Impossible Dream."* The appeal to Black Unity can *mobilize* the Black underclass without the need to *organize* it. Whereas only the underclass has shown the ability *to organize* itself, it rarely does, and then—except for religious purposes and gangs—only for short periods of time. Appeals to Black unity, however, issued by the Black working class and the Black middle class can and do effectively *mobilize* the Black underclass.

Which brings me to ... Barak Hussein Obama. He is ... the manifestation ... of the impossible dream. How did he occur? To answer that question, one must first understand the role of the Black electorate in the Presidential election—particularly in the Democratic primaries. That means not concentrating on polling numbers, the party platform, who Ted and Caroline Kennedy endorsed, what Pfloufe's and Axelrod's strategies were. It doesn't even mean examining the effects

of the Congressional Black Caucus. It means scrutinizing the deep work of ordinary Black people. The census is misleading. In the election of Harold Washington in Chicago, the Jesse Jackson Presidential campaigns, Obama's primary victories on Super Tuesday—deep Black organizational work and appeals to Black unity resulted in Black mobilizations which by all conventional measures, were impossible, because they actually seemed—to increase the size of the Black population.

How did the realization of *the impossible dream*, the election of Barak Hussein Obama to the presidency of the United States of America, occur?

A rigorous analysis of the political work of ordinary Black people in Sacramento over a thirty year period provides critical clues for us. How did Robbie Robertson, elected in a Sacramento City Council district with an overwhelming white majority, occur? How did Dan Thompson, elected in a Sacramento City Council district with an overwhelming white majority, occur? How did Grantland Johnson, a product of this program at Sac State, elected in a Sacramento City Council district with an overwhelming white majority, occur? How did Lauren Hammond, also a product of this program, elected in a Sacramento City Council district with an overwhelming white majority—for 4 consecutive terms, occur? How did Sam Pannell, elected to the Sacramento City Council from a white plurality district for 2 consecutive terms, occur? How did Bonnie Pannell, elected in the same City Council district for three consecutive terms, occur? How did Grantland Johnson, elected to the County Board of Supervisors in a district with not only a white super majority, but with a Black population as a negligible minority, occur?

What this study shows is an extraordinary, day-to-day organizational life of ordinary Black people—organizing and mobilizing at a far greater intensity than any other population group, and across a broader spectrum of political issues, creating a dense and networked organizational infrastructure, which is effective at seizing and dominating public spaces and selected social narratives. It shows a driven, emergent Black middle class; cross-class, cross-gender, cross-sectional, cross-national mobilizations in an effort to achieve the chimera of Black Unity. All this comes from a demeaned part of the population, woefully bereft of material resources, and tremendously outnumbered—who, against all odds, assert claims to office, create a narrative to give their claims authenticity, and hyper-mobilize in a transcendent search for unity.

This study shows us that ordinary Black people do what other ordinary people do: They participate in their children's school and after school activities. They are in the PTO, or PTA, as the case might be. They coach little league, are soccer moms, referee Pop Warner football leagues. They join professional associations, hold offices in labor unions, join environmental organizations, women's organizations, and volunteer in raising funds for cancer survivors. They populate recreational leagues for softball, basketball, bowling and golf. They join the VFW and the American Legion. They are active participants in the Democratic and Republican parties. They do what everybody else does. And then—they create—in addition, a wholly alternative world. Of women's and men's organizations, health organizations, educational organizations, professional organizations, civil rights organizations, PACs, voter registration efforts, health advocacies, legal ventures, political education webs, blogs, newsletters, magazines, whole cultural venues—all of which are Black. They invest themselves—fully—in two entirely different worlds.

I mentioned the APSA. There is also the National Conference of Black Political Scientists. Black political scientists belong to, and are active in both. There is the American Sociological Association. There is also the Association of Black Sociologists. There is the American Medical Association. There is also the National Medical Association (which is Black). There is the American Bar Association. There is also the National Bar Association (which is Black). In every arena of life in this country—black people are engaged in the dominant organizations and in counterpart organizations which are Black. They also engage in Black organizations for which there are no dominant counterparts. This research shows that these tendencies have not stopped. They have not diminished. On the contrary, they increased—dramatically—between 1970 and 2000. This is an extraordinary expenditure of effort—of resources, both human and material—that goes far beyond the norm. It speaks to a felt need, because if people didn't feel an urgency for such exertions—a need for them—they certainly wouldn't engage in them.

Sometimes ... it works. Not only in this city, and this county. But in the person of the President of the United States of America—becoming the living embodiment of *the impossible dream.*

This is where we need the microscope—a kind of biological chemistry, if you will. We can't get at the root of the mysteries abiding in the continual realization of *impossible dreams* by looking only at the big people. We have to look at the little people. And to do that we have to approach research questions from outside the dominant paradigm. We must rely less, as it were, on our understandings of musculature, and develop our understandings of chemical interactions. We must have a reliable vision of the micro as well as the macro. That's how we can produce—in this arena—new knowledge, or at the very least, promising and likely speculations.

We cannot begin to understand these phenomena without the very specific scholarship Pan African Studies brings to the table.

These—are the Voyages of Discovery—on which our scholars and our students—set sail.

Recent African Immigration

Boatamo Mosupyoe

ALL MINORITIES HAVE BENEFITED FROM THE
1965 CIVIL RIGHTS ACT.

BRITTON WOOD INST.
-IMF
-WB
HAITI IS THE POOREST NATION IN THE WESTERN HEMISPHERE.

Introduction

Current immigration policy in the United States have created more opportunities for citizens of other nations to immigrate into the country (Nag 2005). This trend has increasing number of immigrants since the 1970s as natives from other countries continue to migrate to the United States. The immigrants often arrive in search of opportunities to improve their standard of living (Lee, Myers, Ha, & Shin 2005; Nag 2005). Many of these immigrants are well educated, holding managerial and professional positions in their native country prior to immigrating (Buzdugan & Halli 2009; Nag 2005). On their arrival in the United States, some of these professionals are forced to take "low skill" jobs in spite of their educational background (Adamuti-Trache & Sweet 2005).

This article draws from my unpublished research of recent African immigrants in the Bay Area, Sacramento, California, and Washington State, as well as from other sources. The article should not be seen as a report on my research, since it just borrows and does not even begin to give an exhaustive account of the research.

Areas of focus are the lives and experiences of recent African immigrants into the United States of America relative to the following issues:

- The immigration pattern of Africans in the United States.
- The motivations for immigrating to the United States.
- Collective and multiple identities (e.g., how and to what extent ties to the African continent affect the group's identity; the extent to which their views converge and diverge with their children's; their respective achievements and failures and the extent to which these are ideological or structural; issues like school performance are considered as well as the relevance of Ogbu's theory of voluntary and involuntary minority).
- The assertion that recent African immigrants are favored by institutions and are benefiting from Affirmative Action more than African American descendants of former enslaved people.
- The relationship of African Americans with their recent African counterparts.
- The challenges that recent African immigrants face, including domestic violence.
- An overview of their contribution to the U.S. economy.

Immigration Patterns

The United States is always defined as a country of immigrants. Native Americans have been very generous in accommodating people from different countries, a point never acknowledged. The United States immigration pattern reveals a historical preference towards European immigration into the United States and varied degrees of less preference towards immigrants from other parts of the world, including Africa. Salih Omar Eissa (2005) accurately observes that 19th- and 20th-century immigration policy was discriminatory and heavily Eurocentric, despite the migration of

Black Cape Verdean mariners to Massachusetts during this period.

Even when the McCarran-Walter Act of 1952 eliminated all racially specific language from the Immigration and Nationality Act (INA), and the Hart-Cellar Act of 1965 passed, national quotas remained and migration from the African continent was set at the lowest quota of 1,400 annually. Eissa (2005) further argues that of all people admitted to the United States between 1990 and 2000, only 10 percent were Africans. This notwithstanding, the number of Africans in the United States has been increasing. An examination of immigration figures shows that 30,000 Africans came legally into the United States in the 1960s, 80,000 in the 1970s, and 176,000 in the 1980s (Khalid El-Hassan 2005. Since the 1980s the number has more than quadrupled. The figures from the Immigration and Naturalization Services (INS) reveal that between 1981 and 2000 the number stood at 531,832. It is important to note that some scholars, including myself, believe the 2000 U.S. Census Bureau report fails to capture the actual number of recent African immigrants. The possibility exists that the report underreported the number of Africans by hundreds of thousands. Africans who are in the country illegally exhibit the same behavioral pattern as other immigrants. They would not participate in the census exercise or even seek government help in other matters. At all costs they avoid authorities since they seek to hide their statuses.

Motivations for Immigrating to the United States

The 2000 U.S. Census shows that most recent African immigrants come from West Africa, at 35% a year, 26% from East Africa, 20 percent from North Africa, 7% from South Africa, and less than 2% from Central Africa. They are found in major metropolitan cities as well as in small towns and are not necessarily clustered in one part. The reasons for their immigration to the United States are varied and are discussed. However, to give a context to the many issues that the recent Africans face, a very brief overview of the first African immigrants and their contribution is in order. We all know that the majority of first people of African descent to come into the United States came as people who were later enslaved. Any account about African immigrants that fails to acknowledge the foundation laid by these first Africans would be disingenuous (Mosupyoe 2005).

Europeans traded with Africans as early as 1450. In the 17th century the British started transporting Africans to North America. They were also captured from different parts of Africa, including Bight of Benin, Senegambia, and the Gold Coast in West Africa, Angola, etc. Their labor and presence transformed the sociocultural and economic patterns of the United States. By the mid-1800s the positions they occupied and the kind of work they performed varied to include teamsters, porters, domestics, and plantation workers. At this time European immigration was encouraged and favored. European immigrants were also granted citizenship, a right that was denied to Africans, through the 1857 *Dred Scott* decision (Mosupyoe 2005).

The decision declared Africans as "beings of an inferior order," and therefore deserving to be denied rights by the Constitution, including the right of citizenship. In addition, many other laws denied Africans their basic human rights. Although January 1, 1808, became the date designated for the prohibition of trade with African people, the capture and enslavement of African people continued well into the mid-19th century. The Emancipation Proclamation of 1863 permanently ended enslavement of African people. Thereafter, in 1868, the 14th Amendment to the U.S. Constitution guaranteed citizenship, due process, and equal protection under the law for people of African descent, thereby overturning the *Dred Scott* decision (Mosupyoe 2005).

In spite of all these gains, discrimination against African Americans continued in various ways, Jim Crow laws in the South being one of those. Through different organizations, such as the National Association for the Advancement of Colored People (1909), National Urban League (1911), and United Negro Improvement Association (1916), and institutions, such as Howard University, Morehouse College, and Spelman University, African Americans were able to secure for themselves their rightful place in the U.S. landscape.

These remarkable people and their descendants, who have endured tremendous adversity and displayed admirable temerity, unquestionably laid the foundations of opportunity for a new wave of immigration after slavery and desegregation. Their struggles against and triumphs over slavery, Jim Crow, and segregation, through the civil rights movement and other means, have been instrumental in transforming the sociopolitical climate in the United States. Pertinent to this discussion is the 1965 Hart-Cellar Immigration Act. The act advocates admission of immigrants based on their skills, professions, and familial relations.

The ideology of the act, in origin, substance, and final passage as law, mirrors the spirit of the civil rights movement as well as the thoughts of other Pan African activists who preceded the movement. Moreover, the African American involvement could be attributed to the direct success of a series of post-1965 immigration policy shifts that opened the doors to a steady increase in African immigration in the latter part of the 20th century. African Americans, descendants of enslaved Africans, created benefits through their struggle, which recent African immigrants like me enjoy. They produced an environment far more accepting of new immigrants. Today, approximately 50,000 Africans arrive annually from different parts of Africa for different reasons (Mosupyoe 2005).

The post-enslavement period migration of Africans falls within the purview of Ogbu's voluntary immigrants' classification (Ogbu 1993). The voluntary African immigrants came to the United States for many different reasons. In the 1950s and 1960s many Africans migrated to Europe; however, during the 1970s and 1980s most European countries experienced recessions that went along with aversion to immigration and culminated in the tightening of immigration laws. Meanwhile, with the passage of the 1965 Hart-Cellar Immigration Act, U.S. immigration policies became somewhat liberalized. The United States then became the country of choice for Africans to immigrate to.

The push to immigrate stems from various factors. In the 1970s high unemployment and devalued currencies in most African countries resulted from failed economic policies engendered by poor management and "structural adjustment" programs demanded by the World Bank and International Monetary Fund. These conditions caused disappointment in the wake of newly acquired freedoms from European domination. Some parts of Africa, like South Africa, had racist governments that blatantly and legally discriminated against blacks. Opposing the racist policies led to detention and even death. In addition, civil wars in some parts of Africa precipitated immigration into the United States. In view of this and also taking into consideration civil wars in other parts of the world, such as Bosnia, the U.S. Congress reformed its policy toward refugees.

African immigrants benefited from the Refuge Act of 1980 and the immigration Reform and Control Act of 1986. One offered new refugees permanent resident status after one year while the other legalized the status of 31,000 Africans living in the United States since 1982. It could be argued that such a step encouraged African immigrants to stay in the United States. The Temporary Protected Status (TPS) that is part of the Diversity Visa Lottery Act of 1990 also acted as an impetus for African immigration from African countries such as Sudan, Sierra Leone, Liberia, Somalia, and Burundi. The act has a provision that gives temporary refugee status to foreign nationals present in the United States who would be subject to either violence due to armed conflict or environmental disaster if repatriated.

This Diversity Visa Lottery Act of 1990, further, offers immigrant visas to high school graduates in an attempt to increase the low rates of underrepresented nations in the United States. The visa lottery thus became another vehicle through which Africans primarily immigrated to the United States. Some Africans come to the United States to study or on exchange programs and then decide to stay because they have developed love relationships that culminate in marriages. Others come with babies who grow into children and teenagers while parents are attending school. Having raised their children here, they then decide to stay. Their decision is mainly based on their conclusion that their children will find it hard to adapt to their countries of origin. Yet others come to the United States through family reunification programs.

In the 1960s and 1970s most Africans who came to the United States had strong desires to go back and contribute towards their respective countries' nation building. The trend has changed in the last two decades. Recent African voluntary immigrants chose to stay, build a life for their families, and find ways of integrating into U.S. society—the focus of the next section.

Challenges and Collective and Multiple Identities

The recent African immigrants are not a monolithic group; they come from various countries in Africa and the Caribbean. Although they speak English, they also speak different languages that are not mutually intelligible. African cultures have as many similarities as they have differences. Ideological diversity also abounds. A case in point is the view of how South Africans should deal with the post-apartheid society, how Nigeria should mediate the corruption in that country, how to raise children in the U.S. culture, and how to best integrate into U.S. society.

In most part Africans will associate and form strong alliances with those who come from the same African countries. You will also find organizations formed along those lines (e.g., you will find an Igbo organization, a Somali organization, South African in the Bay Area, etc.). Organizations formed along African country of origin lines are mostly support system groups designed to strengthen relationships and help one another in times of need. In addition, such communal organizations offer ties with people from respective homes who share a common language. It also important to note that some alliances are formed based on the different regions from the same country (e.g., in the case of South Africans, people from the eastern Cape will feel closer to one another than they would with people from Gauteng), although survival, the need for community, and fear of isolation often force collective identity based on the country of origin to be stronger and more enduring.

In addition to this collective identity defined by specific countries of origin, Africans from different parts of Africa do share a collective identity based on a continent of origin, the differences notwithstanding. Africans tend to come together to an "African party" to share their respective vibrant cultures and also to discuss difficult issues that they face as immigrants. Some of the challenges that recent African immigrants face are the same as those faced by African Americans. To start with they share some phenotypes, and in the United States discrimination on the basis of how you look persists.

Police brutality (as in the case of the death of Amadou Diallo, an African immigrant who was killed by police) and racial profiling affect them, as does the subtle perception as being inferior. Additionally, African accents are described as heavy (although as an African immigrant myself, I never understood that); this tends to invite both intrigue and repulsion from others. I personally have had students' evaluation where one student asked that the school should make me change my accent. I have also had people admire "my heavy accent."

Discussions with some of the immigrants have revealed that they are often told that "you have an accent." To some, to the extent that having an accent suggests ignorance and stupidity, this observation becomes troubling—particularly since we all have accents, a point that most U.S. people miss, in my experience. One immigrant related how a taxi driver attempted to take advantage of her in terms of pricing because he thought that since she "had an accent" her knowledge of the place and the pricing was minimal and therefore she was a prime target for exploitation.

Other problems are presented by men and women's relationships as they try to adapt to the new culture. Domestic violence is a reality in the communities of recent African immigrants. Some men come with their cultural beliefs about women as inferior and subservient. In 2005 professor Uwazie of the Criminal Justice Department at California State University, Sacramento, called a meeting that was triggered by a series of domestic violence acts committed by men on women in the Sacramento area and other parts of the United States. I was asked to be the co-moderator of the discussions.

In one of the Sacramento incidents a Ghanaian man reportedly stabbed his wife to death 22 times, after an argument. In another case, a Nigerian man drove all the way from Atlanta, Georgia, to stalk his Ondo-born wife living separately in Dallas, Texas. He eventually shot her to death in her car. Also, in August 2005 a Nigerian man used a hammer to murder his Sierra Leonean–born wife at their home in a Dallas suburb. The murder reportedly occurred in front of the couples' seven-year-old daughter. Ben Edokpayi reported on the meeting in the newspaper *Times of Nigeria* in an article entitled "An Elephant in the House." I am going to briefly summarize his report to give you insights into the thinking of recent African immigrants from different countries, both men and women, on this issue.

Edokpayi acknowledges the existence of patriarchy and male chauvinism as an epidemic in Africa. He reports that while incidents of domestic violence in African communities in the diaspora are only now coming into the limelight, the problem has long been an entrenched epidemic in African countries where male chauvinism rules. He writes that "the dominant thread that ran through many of the evening's contributions on the subject was the juxtaposition of the African and American cultures and how the two can be effectively combined by recent transplants from across the Atlantic." He goes on to give a sampling of the discussions that reflected the variety of opinions:

"The support system you have back home doesn't exist here. In order to feel comfortable here we need to know our limitations. The rules of the game are not the same as you might have say in Ghana," said Ngissah.

A Nigerian auditor who's been married to his wife for 30 years had a different perspective: *"We already know the problem. First of all you can't put old wine into new wine. You can think you can bring your Igbo culture and enforce it here? It just won't work," he said, adding rather humorously, "You go to our African parties and take a look at the face of our women. They look worn out and don't want to dance. Why? Because they spend most of their time cooking, cleaning, and taking care of the home all by themselves. That's abuse!"*

Another Nigerian, Sylvester Okonkwo, presented an interesting angle to the clash of cultures and how it frames the issue. *"Let's not make this sound as if it's an African problem,"* he said. *"The African culture has its own pluses and minuses. Most of us studied here and gained employment here. We have a proverb that says when you are in a foreign land, `learn all the good things there and leave the bad ones alone,'"* said Okonkwo.

I agree with Edokpayi's observation that "most participants agreed that it was tough to balance the two cultures, all were in agreement that the African culture was intrinsically sound and could be a good insulation against the pressures of today's microwave world where materialistic pursuits and the hurry for results tend to obfuscate everything else." The discussions offer hope to the extent that the domestic violence is acknowledged, discussed, and the determination to come with solutions salient. In her article "What it means to be an Asian Indian Woman," Y. Lakshmi Malroutu posits that among the recent Asian Indian immigrants, domestic violence is hidden and denied. This should speak well of the recent African immigrants.

Mediating the tension brought by raising children who grow up in the United States also presents paradoxes. An experience of children who grow up in the United States and have minimal to zero experience of Africa is often the discussion of common experiences. Children assume a different identity from their parents and most likely identify as African Americans, proclaiming more of an affinity in cultural experiences to African American children who are descendants of former enslaved Africans than to their parents. Often parents have to decide which behavior should be accepted and which not. In the research that I am currently conducting on this topic, a student from Ethiopia relates how her mother preferred that she and her siblings associate with other recent immigrant children who have better manners than the rest of U.S. kids. It is only recently, she says, that her mother has accepted that they are culturally U.S. and have chosen their identity accordingly.

I have two daughters, too, who grew up here. When I first came one was two weeks old and the other just a year-and-a-half old. They identify with no hesitation as African Americans. We also have different views and perspectives on things in addition to those engendered by generational differences. I would like them to offer people food when they come to visit without asking if they want food or not. People will then reject the food politely afterwards if they choose to, but they constantly remind me that they have to ask since this is "America." Most parents have a variation of these cognitive dissonances to deal with. For the most part parents identify with Africa more than their children do. In my research I found that African adults will identify as "Africans in America" and children will identify as African Americans.

Relationships with African Americans

It has also been argued that recent African immigrants perform well in school, have better study habits, and have excellent job performance rates. This behavior pattern parallels that of other immigrants of different continental origin. An assessment of the applicability of Ogbu's theory on voluntary and involuntary minority then becomes relevant here. This assessment should also take into consideration that the late Ogbu was also a recent African immigrant who came to the United States in the 1960s from Nigeria. Ogbu (1993) asserts that in understanding the performance of minorities in the United States a distinction between the types of minority status and the different types of cultural differences should be taken into account.

Voluntary minority refers to immigrants like the recent African immigrants who came to the United States through other reasons than U.S. enslavement. Involuntary minority refers to the status of African Americans who are descendants of enslaved people. Ogbu argues that there is an absence of persistent basic academic difficulties among the voluntary minorities despite the primary cultural differences with the European American culture. Involuntary minorities, on the other hand, Ogbu further posits, have difficulties because of the nature of their responses to their

forced incorporation and subsequent persistent mistreatment by the Euro-American power structures. Despite the phenomenal strides that have been made, a legacy of sanitized unequal treatment still endures. Ogbu argues that African Americans have thus formed oppositional identity and cultural frame of references that tend to impact performance.

If we are to follow Ogbu's argument, if indeed recent African immigrants are performing better, then their success could be attributed to the fact that they have a better response to the structural discrimination and unwelcoming school environments. What Ogbu's theory fails to take into consideration is the fact that some Euro-Americans feel more comfortable with recent African immigrants than they do with African Americans. When I first came to the United States as a student, an African American professor at Denison University in Ohio, at an orientation into the U.S. society, explained that in his experience there is less guilt, whether subconscious or salient, for Euro-Americans towards recent African immigrants. As a result they tend to be more receptive and friendlier to recent African immigrants. Obviously this friendly attitude has its unfair benefits. The friendly atmosphere contributes towards a learning environment conducive to producing good results, or conversely a friendly working environment. This then becomes a structural and institutional hurdle for others who are not afforded the same courtesy to overcome. I have personally experienced this, as this discussion later shows. The fact that African immigrants enter the country mostly with more than a high school diploma should also explain their relatively high level of educational attainment.

African immigrants are not immune to the adverse impact of competition for resources that often manifest in xenophobia. They have been looked at as taking away jobs from those already here and have also been victims of hate crimes. The other challenge that they have to face pertains to their relationship with African Americans who are descendants of former enslaved people. Professors Lani Guinier and Henry Louis Gates, Jr., a Harvard law professor and the chairman of Harvard's African and African-American Department, respectively, spoke at the third Black Alumni Weekend of Harvard University, which took place October 3–5, 2003, and drew more than 600 former students. Their comments illustrate the tension and challenge.

According to the Harvard University news of January–February 2004, Harvard was pleased about the 8 percent increase in black students (530 students) at the university over 2003 enrollment. However, the celebratory mood of the evening was broken by Professor Guinier, whose mother is white and whose father immigrated from Jamaica, when she advised that Harvard should reconsider its celebration since the majority of the black students were not true African Americans, but West Indian and African immigrants or their children, or to a lesser extent, children of biracial couples. Professor Gates, Jr., supported her assertions and charges (Onyeanyi, 2006).

Such comments by highly visible African Americans continued when Alan Keyes, a former right-wing Republican presidential candidate, accused Barack Obama, a senator from Illinois, of not being a true African American since his father was from Kenya. Alan Keyes is quoted in a *New York Times* article of August 27, 2004, titled "'African-American' Becomes a Term for Debate," as saying, "Barack Obama claims an African-American heritage." Mr. Keyes said on the ABC program *This Week* with George Stephanopoulos, "Barack Obama and I have the same race—that is, physical characteristics. We are not from the same heritage."

Yet another prominent African American, an administrator at the University of Columbia, Bobby Austin, was quoted in the same *New York Times* article of August 27, 2004, saying, "Some people feared that black immigrants and their children would snatch up the hard-won opportunities made possible by the civil rights movement." Dr. Austin further said, "We've suffered so much that we're a bit weary and immigration seems like one more hurdle we will have to climb. People are asking: 'Will I have to climb over these immigrants to get to my dream? Will my children have to climb?'" Perceptions and thoughts like this permeate to the other parts of the community. Oftentimes in my classes I will have African American students asking me why

do Africans hate them and vice versa. I often tell them that I do not wish to participate in this divide-and-conquer mentality that does not benefit us.

The workplace also fails to help bridge the gap between the two. I am a recent African immigrant, as I have mentioned before. Prior to coming to California State University, Sacramento, I was employed in Washington, in an institution that was predominantly Euro-American. For years I was the only faculty of African descent. Efforts to encourage a hire of African Americans were often met with, "but we have you." For years the institution and some of its people felt comfortable with me and did not find it necessary to hire an African American who was born and raised in the United States.

When I discussed my concerns about this with some of my former colleagues and expressed that I felt like a token because of their attitude and refusal to hire African Americans, they would tell me how they did not see me as a token but as a strong, highly opinionated woman. As can be expected, they missed the point. Their behavior made me fully understand what the professor in Denison meant, that hiring an African American evokes feelings that they would rather not deal with. When they did subsequently hire an African American, they displayed such racist behavior towards her that, among other issues, she was forced out.

Recently, I spoke with one of my former colleagues, Vicki Scannell, who is also from the same institution. She told me that the problem still persists and the excuse that is now being made is that the institution does not pay enough to attract African Americans. The impression created then remains that African Americans will not work for less pay while hardworking Euro-Americans would. Of course, my friend, who is also Euro-American, made a point to remind them that institutional racism, and not pay, accounts for the absence of African American professors.

African Americans, as I mentioned earlier, paved the way for contemporary African immigrants—it would benefit both groups to unite and work together. Where I am teaching students seem to do a better job of bridging the gap. Two years ago they invited me to speak at an event they organized and the thesis was "bridging the gap between people of African descent from the continent and the Diaspora. "

Despite all the challenges that I have mentioned, African immigrants do share a life with their native-born counterparts. There are many intermarriages between them. Their offspring and their unions provide an element of diversity in the United States that should not be ignored since it bridges the gap between the native born and foreign born. Second-generation Africans are commanding leadership roles in arenas large and small throughout the country. Whether members of Congress such as Barack Obama, leaders of black community and student organizations, or even up-and-coming hip-hop artists such as Akon, African second-generation immigrants are wholehearted participants in and even creators of today's African American culture.

Continuously infused with new influences from their own diaspora, [Africans are contributing to the fluid adaptability of U.S. dynamic urban culture.] In the process of redefining their race and culture in a social order far different from that of their parents, African immigrants are both giving to and taking from African American tradition in a reciprocal and mutually advantageous relationship (Eissa 2005).

They have embraced the economic opportunities offered by the United States. According to the Schomburg Center for Research in Black Culture, "Some highly educated [African] immigrants, realizing that their limited proficiency in English and their foreign degrees would make it difficult to get the American jobs they coveted, have instead opened their own businesses. This entrepreneurial spirit is deeply ingrained in Africa, where the informal economic sector is particularly dynamic." The Bay Area and Sacramento, like many other U.S. cities, have African restaurants, African hair braiding salons, nightclubs, music stores, and many other entrepreneurial ventures that provide economic stability.

Although there were about 100,000 highly educated African professionals throughout the United States in 1999, many more are also involved in jobs where less education and often less skill may be required. They work as cab drivers, parking lot attendants, airport workers or waiters, waitresses, and cooks in restaurants. Even African women who have traditionally been in the background of most traditional African family structures now find themselves at the forefront of economic opportunities in the United States and thus are playing important economic roles in maintaining the family structure both for the family members who are still in Africa and those in the United States.

Bibliography

Adamuti-Trache, M., & Sweet, R. 2005. Exploring the relationship between educational credentials and the earnings of immigrants. *Canadian Studies in Population*, 32 2, 177-201.

Buzdugan, R., & Halli, S. 2009. Labor market experiences of Canadian immigrants with focus on foreign education and experience. *International Migration Review*, 43 2, 366-386.

Edokpayi, Ben. 2006. *The Times of Nigeria*.

Eissa, Salih Omar. 2005. *Diversity and transformation: African Americans and African immigration to the United States*. Immigration Policy Brief.

Lee, S. S., Myers, D., Ha, S., & Shin, H. R. (2005). What if immigrants had not migrated? *American Journal of Economics & Sociology*, 64(2), 609-637. Retrieved October 20 2010, from EBSCOhost database.

Mosupyoe, Boatamo. 2005. *Recent African immigrants in the U.S.* Unpublished manuscript.

Nag, B. 2005. A journey across the black waters: Female migration from India to the United States. *Dissertation Abstracts International*. (UMI No. 3176796). Retrieved October 20 2010 from the University of Phoenix ProQuest Dissertations.

Ogbu, John. 1993. Difference in cultural frame of references. *International Journal of Behavioral Development* 16(3): 483–506.

Onyeanyi, Chika A. (2006, February 6). *The African Sun Times*.

The Zion Christian Church in Post-Apartheid South Africa

Boatamo Mosupyoe

During the apartheid years, that is, the years of oppression of the South African indigenous people by the minority white government, the Zion Christian Church (ZCC) enjoyed favoritism from the apartheid government. Ambivalence marked the favoritism. As an African Initiated Church, the ZCC was subjected to the restrictive policies of the apartheid regime embodied in the Native Churches Commission of 1924 (Lukhaimane 1980). To acquire permission, certain requirements had to be met. The Zion Christian Church had to go through the services of at least two lawyers before overcoming the obstacles and obtaining such permission to register the church. The malevolence of the process, manifested in the intent of the apartheid regime to curb the mushrooming of the African Initiated Churches, at the time referred to by the government as Native Separatist Churches (Nthabu 1989). The ZCC constituted one of such churches. The malevolence of the process, however, fails to supersede the more powerful benevolence that characterized the relationship of the Zion Christian Church and the apartheid government. Whereas during the apartheid era, the boundaries between the opposition and the apartheid regime were clearly defined and marked by rigid suspicion and brutality, the opposite was true for the Zion Christian Church. The favorable disposition of the apartheid regime to the Zion Christian Church was evident.

Disguising the obedience and lack of opposition to apartheid laws with elaborate explanations of liturgy, biblical injunctions of obedience of those in power, separation of the sacred and

the profane, peace/*khotso* theme, and declarations of a disciplined nonpolitical stance, the Zion Christian Church advanced the apartheid regime agenda. More explicit was the various visits by the different prime ministers of the regime to the church's headquarters in Moria during the Easter pilgrimage attended by millions of Zion Christian Church members. In different ways reaffirmation of the support of the regime enjoyed center stage. This obvious acceptance of the regime served as a retrogressive force to the struggle against apartheid. These visits by design on the part of the regime enjoyed enormous international exposure. The spectacle of millions of blacks to the international world welcoming the perpetrators of apartheid instilled doubts to others about the inhumanity of apartheid. Even more damaging was reference to these meetings by some international entities as justification of their continued support for the system. Additional overt symbioses of the regime and the Zion Christian Church manifested in its support of the Homeland leaders[1] and its condemnation of anti-apartheid activists like Allen Boesak, Nelson Mandela, and the liberation movement the African National Congress.

This stance of condemning the freedom fighters was as ambiguous as it negated the Zion Christian Church proclamation of the separation of the sacred and the profane. Its inconsistency spelled a political stance in support of the apartheid government. A bus accident in which a number of EuroAfrican kids died further proved that the Zion Christian Church at the time presented a complex confusing entity with regard to its stand towards apartheid and the white power structure. The bishop, who has never given monetary support to the efforts to free blacks from the oppression of whites, gave money to a white school after this bus accident. This particular incident increased the resentment towards the church and members of the Zion Christian Church. In the townships especially, the suspicion towards the members intensified and the label of the church as supporters of the apartheid regime was reaffirmed and comfortably justified. During my research some Zion Christian Church women referred to this label as a stigma. In any case, while the stigma resulted in an exacerbated tension between the black population and the Zion Christian Church on one hand, it increased trust toward the Zion Christian Church by the whites and their apartheid government, on the other. White employers preferred to hire the Zion Christian Church members and complaints to the police against the Zion Christian Church fell on deaf ears.

In the late 1980s and 1990s the movement against the destruction of apartheid gained momentum and with that the Zion Christian Church rhetoric transformed enormously. One of the leaders pronounced in ways that mirrored the words of South African liberation theologists. His articulation of justice and equal representation in government was as surprising as it was marking the change of times. Akin to the rhetoric, the church extended an invitation to Mandela, De Klerk, and Buthelezi to their Easter meetings.[2] The warm welcome of Mandela and the ovations that he received as compared to the somewhat cold reception of the two perpetrators of apartheid clearly indicated a pragmatic and ideological shift in the Zion Christian Church. The Zion Christian Church, accurately reading the signs of the time, initiated a process of articulation that would mediate previous tension and ensure its position in a newly constructed dialectic setting. The ANC embraced the ideation and consciously managed the discourse (Marx 1967: 71; Giddens 1979: 183) in manner that would translate into a lived symbiotic experience that sharply contrasted with their relationship during the apartheid era. This shift defines the new relationship between the ANC government and the Zion Christian Church.

What Changed?

As a conclusion to my assessment of what role could the Zion Christian Church play in the transformation toward a non-sexist society, I posited in parts:

"The women's reality and not the ANC's ideology will determine whether change within the church happens or not. A durable change that will be hard to reverse will be a change that occurs with the contribution of all in the Zion Christian Church. Most importantly the Zion Christian Church themselves must see the need to move towards a non-sexist society. If the Zion Christian Church is committed to the course of non-sexism, which will include the educational and social development of Zion Christian Church women, will asking the bishop to give such a directive be a bad idea?" (Mosupyoe 1999: 153)

The Zion Christian Church has proclaimed a clear line of demarcation between the spiritual and the worldly. The members understood the directive, were so ritualized, and lived by the creed. The same cannot be said for the leadership. The invitation of apartheid political leaders, and recently of post-apartheid politicians to their meetings in Easter, indeed brings into question the validity of the claim. More importantly, it speaks to the need to further examine the social theory of the fluid boundaries of the spiritual and the temporal world hierarchy. The Zion Christian Church struggled in maintaining that separation despite its ideological stance. The conflict between the Zion Christian Church ideology and the practice has been established (Mosupyoe 1999). Consonance on a number of issues between the Zion Christian Church and the larger black majority rarely existed. The persistent cognitive dissonance between the Zion Christian Church and the larger South African black majority in terms of the involvement of the church in the struggle against apartheid became clear at the presentation of the Zion Christian Church at the Truth and Reconciliation Commission after apartheid.[3] The presentation was made by the Reverend Emmanuel Motolla, a member of Bishop Lekganyane's council. The presentation revealed a number of issues which also inform social theories debated throughout the years. First, the presentation affirms that the Zion Christian Church forms one of the Christian movements that originated as a reaction to the Mission churches.[4] Much has been debated about the validity of the syncretic nature of the church (Anderson 1992; Mofokeng 1990; Mosupyoe 1999). Motolla underscores the assertion that syncretism exists. He stated:

> "The founder of the church, Bishop Agnus Barnarbas Lekganyane, had by then become acutely aware of the attempt by missionaries to erode African value systems and cultural beliefs. He realised that unless Christianity was interpreted in a context suitable to the African lifestyle, cultural and political development, Africans would, in due course, find themselves as a nation alienated from its roots, rich history and religious foundation." (ZCC Testimony before the Truth and Reconciliation Commission, East London, November 19, 1999)

Motolla essentially affirmed the church as a custodian of African tradition and culture. The position of course is not at variance with nor does it contradict the church's authenticity as Christian.

Second, Motolla's presentation either redefines what constituted opposition to apartheid or adds more ambiguity into the "resistance to apartheid" logic. In the post-apartheid era the church asserts that it fought against apartheid, a views that stands in stark variance with the common view of this church as a staunch supporter of apartheid. Indeed, Motolla tried to refute this view as he refers to the church's "suffering during the dark years of apartheid." He blames propaganda for the misperception of the church's lack of involvement in the anti-apartheid struggle. The claim of the church's involvement in the struggle against apartheid was undermined by the absence in his speech of the specific names of Zion Christian Church members who were in the struggle. Also the reverend could not provide the names of the programs that he claimed were in place to fight against apartheid. Troubled by this unsubstantiated claim, Reverend K. Mgojo, one of the official members of the Truth and Reconciliation Commission asked this of Motolla: "I would

have liked to have heard about what programmes were those that your church was involved in, in fighting against apartheid."

Reverend Motolla's response was imprecise. He referred to the bishop's sermons that taught the members to reject evil and injustice. Implicitly the latter saw apartheid as an evil that needed to be confronted and according to Motolla the Zion Christian Church members engaged in that struggle. At the same time contradicting his previous statement, he explicitly said:

> "Chairperson, as a church, the ZCC did not lead people into a mode of resistance against apartheid. We have not, as a church, stood up and said let's go and fight the white government, and for that omission, if it was an omission, because we thought genuinely we needed to teach our people to be able to stand upright, not to hurt others, but to refuse to be hurt by others. Bishop Lekganyane did not go and stand up in the street and say, let us fight, let us go to way, then as far as that is concerned, if that is the omission you are referring to, we plead guilty, Chairperson." (ZCC Testimony before the Truth and Reconciliation Commission, East London, November 19, 1999)

It is difficult to say what would mediate and resolve this cognitive dissonance. The Zion Christian Church sees itself as having fought against apartheid. The notion is comparable to the claim by the majority of white South Africans who allege they did not support apartheid. Given the now known inhumanity of the system, very few white South Africans want to admit that they were active players and beneficiaries, in the same way as their former allied partner the Zion Christian Church. We now have a transformed relationship of the Zion Christian Church with the white population because the white government does not exist anymore; the post-apartheid ideology denies alliance. What changed after apartheid is the fact that the Zion Christian Church perceives itself as an entity that fought against apartheid. Other things also changed.

While in the past the Zion Christian Church found it necessary to continuously affirm the separation of church and state (*Pretoria News*,

April 12, 1985), we rarely hear that today. The once more ideologically prominent separation of the spiritual and the profane is replaced by actions of fluid limits displaying mutual embrace by both the ANC government and the Zion Christian Church. The victory for freedom mediated the tension and distanced the bitter memories of acquiescence with the apartheid regime. Perhaps the desire for reconciliation explains the mutual aggrandizement of efficacy and powers by the bishop and the ANC leaders. For example, in September 2007 the bishop praised President Mbeki for his achievements in ruling the nation and in turn, the former president Mbeki urged the nation to heed the bishop's prophetic message.[5] Similarly, the mutual reciprocal newfound admiration was expressed by Premier Edna Molewa (2005a) who stated at a prayer meeting in honor of the disappearance of Zion Christian Church constable Francis Rasuge that *"The Zion Christian Church understands intimately the travails, trials, tribulations and challenges of the majority of South Africans."*[6] In turn, the bishop attends the many prayer meetings of the ruling party and gives his blessings. These meetings are also attended by huge numbers of the Zion Christian Church.[7] On April 11, 2004, the South African Broadcasting Corporation reported that President Mbeki signed a "peace pledge" with the Zion Christian Church bishop and others committing to free, fair, and peaceful election. The president's praise for the Zion Christian Church bishop was abundant.

Individual Zion Christian Church members feature prominently at various ANC celebrations. Worth mentioning here is Solly Moholo, a Zion Christian Church musician whose songs are full of praise for the ANC government. They display constant transient support of the seating ANC president; the support transfers to his dancing partners. In 2006 during the Freedom Day celebrations, Solly Moholo danced with President Mbeki, to the enjoyment of the crowd.[8] In 2007 at the celebration victory of the ANC election, he was seen dancing with president-elect Zuma[9] (*Independent*, April 24, 2009). The Zion Christian Church works openly with the ANC to promote development programs. My study was not focused on the political affiliation of the church members, nor would the church

encourage the dissemination of such data. Some members say the church sees the political affiliation as a private matter. Motolla's statement also suggests that Zion Christian Church members' political affiliation is not limited to one party. Monare (2004) reports Motolla as saying the bishop would call for Zion Christian Church members, "irrespective of their political persuasions," to strive for a peaceful South Africa. However, Democratic Party (DA) member Gibson claims that many members of his party are members of the Zion Christian Church (IoL News.co.zaApril 11, 2004).[10] The DA is mainly white and led by the controversial Helen Zille.

The Church collaborates with the government and many other agencies on development programs. In his many appearances with ANC government officials, the collaboration is acknowledged and echoed. At a prayer rally in the Northwest Province, where Bishop Lekganyane was present,[11] Premier Maureen Modiselle not only referred to the importance of the numerical strength of the Zion Christian Church but also conceded its pivotal role in modernization programs of the government (South African Government Information, May 2010). As far back as 2005 Premier Edna Molewa's collaboration with the Zion Christian Church punctuated it as a partner in reconstruction and development of South Africa. Both the government and the church committed to reviving the cultural concept of Ubuntu to boost the moral fiber of the society and encourage moral regeneration. They also agreed to promote self-reliance through integrated food security programs that will empower communities to start food gardens. An additional area of agreement revolved around the improvement of transportation (Molewa 2005b).[12] The Zion Christian Church schools and adult literacy centers continue to operate. The bishop's rhetoric also confirms the church's commitment to education and development. In one of her statements Molewa seemed to implicitly decry the need to "modernize" the members when she stated that "she wished to see ZCC accelerate its modernisation of its members" (Molewa 2005b). The bishop seemed to have heeded the call for development. His speeches in various church gatherings reflect that and an appropriate example is his speech in September

2007 addressing the more than two million congregants in Moria:

> *"To all our youth, be seen to be taking advantage of the opportunities available to make your future a success. The private sector, government and other organisations as well as ZCC, the Bishop Edward Lekganyane bursary fund, provide you with bursaries, internships as well as vacation work to engage the skills development to greater heights."*

Former president Mbeki also based one of his weekly letters on the substance of the speech.

The church's partnership with the government in fighting poverty and the scourge of HIV/AIDS found expression at yet another jointly hosted prayer meeting. Premier of the Eastern Cape Province, Nosimo Balindlela, stated:

> *"The church is a major player in these socio-political issues. I have been very impressed with the role that the church is playing in our province to work with government to fight poverty and the scourge of HIV and AIDS. The Multisectoral HIV and AIDS Partnership that we established in this province at the beginning of January is actually winning the war against AIDS. What the church is publicly saying is that AIDS is not only for those who decide not to go to church. Linked to that is the acts of the clergy to take the AIDS tests publicly. It is an indication to ordinary people that no one is safe from the disease." (Balindlela 2007)*

The above discussion proves that the government acknowledges the church's influence and role. When I published the first edition of *Mediation of Patriarchy and Sexism by Women in South Africa* in 1999, I emphasized the influence of the church and its potential in transforming the society and helping in the achievement of a non-sexist South Africa. I referred to the power and authority of the bishop and how the elders and important officials proclaim that implementing and obeying what the bishop demands constitutes *"an absolute essential."*[13] In various explicit ways the ANC government is realizing

that and is engaging in active campaign to partner with the Zion Christian Church to realize their various objectives, including addressing violence against women and poverty that affects mostly women and children. The mode of thought and practice that seems to productively inform the process of transformation mediates the contradiction that existed before. The constitution demands a non-sexist society. Since 1994 the government's commitment to transformative agenda on gender relations and non-sexist South Africa found articulation through legislation, awareness campaigns, and establishment of various institutions, etc. In this post-apartheid era the Zion Christian Church continues to be a partner. The Zion Christian Church joined a campaign of "awareness and action for the betterment of life for the women of South Africa" (Molewa 2005). The Zion Christian Church bishop also made assurances that the plight of women across South Africa and the world is also his plight.

Finally, Premier Marshoff's (2006) statement at the Zion Christian center mass prayer meeting affirmed the needed pivotal role of the church when he said:

> *"One of the most important challenges that remain for our country is the scourge of violence against women and children. The harsh reality is that the most vulnerable members of our communities and families are being targeted by the worst kinds of criminals. The key to turning the tide against these crimes is to expose the criminals so that they can be punished, and to prevent them from ever being in a position to repeat their crimes. The church can play a critical role in creating awareness on women and child abuse; it can also assist in helping victims of abuse. (1)*

No doubt this productive process of articulation possesses greater potential of defining an enduring sociocultural order that mediates the tension and produces social arrangements that would impact the non-sexist agenda; an agenda that still has a long way to go despite the visible achievements.

Notes

1. Under the homeland system, the South African govern-ment attempted to divide South Africa into a number of separate states, each of which was supposed to develop into a separate nation-state for a different ethnic group. (Leach 1986: 15).
2. Buthelezi: A former homeland leader and supporter of apartheid regime in very controversial ways. De Klerk: The last president of the apartheid regime. Mandela called him an illegitimate leader.
3. The Truth and Reconciliation Commission was estab-lished to deal with the atrocities committed during the apartheid era.
4. See Zion Christian Church Testimony before the Truth and Reconciliation Commission, East London, Novem-ber, 19, 1999. http://web.uct.ac.za/depts/ricsa/com-miss/trc/Zion Christian Chrurchtest.htm
5. Volume 7, 35: 7–13, September 2007, ANC Today On-line Voice of the African National Congress.
6. http://www.nwpg.gov.za/nwpg/premiers/media%20re-leases/Zion Christian Church PrayerService31JUL05 .pdf, accessed February 2010.
7. One such example is the approximately 1.2 million members of the Zion Christian Church have prayed for the forthcoming ANC Conference in Limpopo and im-proved service delivery in the Eastern Cape during a special mass prayer meeting at the Bisho Stadium in 2007 before the December 2007 ANC Conference in Polokwane.
8. *Mail and Guardian*, "**Freedom Day: Mbeki calls for better service delivery.**" April 27 2006, front page, 12: 27, Kimberly, South Africa.
9. *Independent*, April 24, 2009, 6: 49, Presidential candi-date Jacob Zuma dances up a storm with Solly Moholo at bash outside the party's headquarters in Johannes-burg.
10. See IoLNews.co.za, April 11, 2004, "No touting for votes in Moria" by Moshoeshoe Monare.
11. Premier Modiselle thanks Zion Christian Church for choosing North West for prayer, May 11, 2010.
12. Molewa, "Zion Christian Church a partner in recon-struction and development," *South African Govern-ment Information*, February 9, 2005.
13. I noted that a young church member in the 1990s ques-tioned the bishop's authority. Recently, *Sowetan* (Sep-tember 17, 2010) reported that Advocate Mphafolane Koma exposed brutality and human rights violations in the church and was expelled. He is taking the church to court to challenge his dismissal. This has never hap-pened before.

Bibliography

Anderson, A.H. 1992. *African Pentecostalism in a South African Urban Environment. A Missiological Evalua-tion*. Pretoria: University of South Africa.

Balindlela, Nosimo. 2007, December. Speech presented by the Premier of the Eastern Cape Province at the Zion Christian Church prayer meeting. South African Gov-ernment Information.

Giddens, Anthony. 1979. Central problems in social theory: Action, structure, and contradiction in social analysis

Marshoff, Beatrice. 2006. *Zion Christian Church mass prayer meeting*. South African Government Informa-tion.

Marx, Karl, 1967, *On the Jewish Question*, in Loyd David Easton and Kurt Guddat (eds), *Writings of the Young Marx on Philosophy and Society* (Anchor).

Mofokeng, Takatso. 1990. Black theology in South Africa: Achievements, problems and prospects. In Martin Prozesky (Ed.), *Christianity in South Africa*. Bergvlei: Southern.

Molewa, Edna. 2005a, July. Address by North West Pre-mier, EDNA MOLEWA at the Zion Christian Church prayer service for missing Constable Francis Rasuge, Odi Stadium, Mabopane. http://www.nwpg.gov.za /nwpg/premiers/media%20releases/Zion   Christian Church PrayerService31JUL05.pdf, accessed May 1, 2010.

Molewa, Edna. 2005b. *Zion Christian Church a Partner in Reconstruction and Development*. South African Gov-ernment Information.

Monare, Moshoeshoe. 2004. No Touting for Votes at Mo-ria, Zion Christian Church Rules. IoL News.co.za., April 11, 2004. http://www.iol.co.za/news/politics/no-touting-for-votes-at-moria-Zion Christian Chrurch-rules-1.210361, accessed April 15, 2010.

Mönnig, Hermann O. 1988. *The Pedi*. Pretoria: Van Schaik.

Mosupyoe, Boatamo Y. 1999. *Mediation of Patriarchy and Sexism by Women in South Africa*. New York: McGraw-Hill.

Nthabu, Boatamo Y. 1989. *Meaning and Symbolism in the Zion Christian Church of South Africa*. Master's thesis, University of California, Berkeley.

Chapter Three Questions

Choose one answer.

1. The Voting Right Act was passed in
   a. 1976
   b. 1987
   c. 1965
   d. 1960
   e. 1954

2. OAU stands for
   a. Organization of Africans United
   b. Organization of African Unity
   c. Organized African Unity
   d. Opulent American Union
   e. Organized African Union

3. Who wrote of dividing plantations into small parcels for enslaved people?
   a. Nelson Mandela
   b. Abraham Lincoln
   c. George W. Bush
   d. Gunnar Myradal
   e. Jessie Jackson

4. Who wrote the book *The Mis-education of the Negro*?
   a. Mogobe Ramose
   b. Otis Scott
   c. David Covin
   d. Alexandre Kimenyi
   e. Carter G. Woodon

5. The thesis of African regeneration was first posited by
   a. Boatamo Mosupyoe
   b. Jessie Jackson
   c. Barrack Obama
   d. Prixleey ka Isaka Seme******
   e. None of the above

6. The first man of African descent to win the Nobel Peace Prize was
   a. Nelson Mandela
   b. Barack Obama
   c. Ralph Bunche
   d. Desmond Tutu
   e. Martin Luther King

7. What best reflects Eboh's thinking about democracy?
   a. It must come from the West
   b. Is best exemplified by the United States of America
   c. It must be eradicated

    d. It must involve the global community and address uneven development and material inequality

    e. It must involve the global community and address uneven development

8. Ibrahim Babadinga is the former president of
    a. South Africa
    b. Liberia
    c. Nigeria
    d. Angola
    e. Namibia

9. Who was the only person ever elected to two consecutive terms as president of the National Association of Ethnic Studies?
    a. Boatamo Mosupyoe
    b. Annette Reed
    c. Otis Scott
    d. Patrice Lumumba
    e. Steven Biko

10. Who wrote *Black Politics After the Civil Rights Movement: Sacramento, 1970–2000*?
    a. David Covin
    b. Otis Scott
    c. Boatamo Mosupyoe
    d. Mogobe Ramose
    e. None of the above

11. What term in this form appears in the eighth edition of UNESCO's *The General History of Africa*?
    a. The African Renaissance
    b. African Renaissance: A Northward Bound
    c. The African renaissance
    d. The African Liberator
    e. Rinasscimento

12. Mokoko is a language term in
    a. Sesotho/Sotho
    b. Afrikaans
    c. English
    d. Spanish
    e. Italian

13. Hungwe is a language term in
    a. Shona
    b. English
    c. Afrikaans
    d. Italian
    e. Spanish

14. How many African immigrants came to the United States in 1960?
    a. 20,000
    b. 50,000
    c. 5,000
    d. 30,000
    e. None

15. Which act offered refugees permanent resident status?
    a. Refugee Act of 1980
    b. Refugee Relief Act of 1953
    c. Refugee Act of 1980***
    d. Immigration Reform Act of 1986
    e. Hart-Cellar Immigration Act of 1965

16. Which Act legalized the status of 31,000 Africans living in the United States since 1982?
    a. Refugee Act of 1980
    b. Refugee Relief Act of 1953
    c. Refugee Act of 1980
    d. Immigration Reform Act of 1986
    e. Hart-Cellar Immigration Act of 1965

17. Thabo Mbeki is the former president of
    a. Liberia
    b. South Africa
    c. Nigeria
    d. Angola
    e. Zimbabwe

18. Who was the first and only African woman to win the Nobel Peace Prize?
    a. Wangari Mathai of Nigeria
    b. Wangari Mathai of Liberia
    c. Wangari Mathai of South Africa
    d. Wangari Mathai of Kenya
    e. Wangari Mathai of Angola

19. Which country in Africa has the first woman president?
    a. Liberia
    b. Nigeria
    c. Benin
    d. Niger
    e. Ghana

20. Ellen Johnson Sirleaf is the president of what African country?
    a. Ghana
    b. Nigeria
    c. Botswana
    d. Liberia
    e. Morocco

Answer the following questions in about 100–150 words.

What was the main aim of the Diversity Visa Lottery Act of 1990?

What are Robinson's views on the economic gap in the United States between African Americans and European Americans?

Briefly discuss Robinson's views on reparations and how the issue should be approached.

What does Ramose mean by northbound gaze and what does he propose as a better solution?

What does Eboh see as an answer to Democracy in Africa and why does she reject Western democracy as an answer?

In post-apartheid South Africa, what changes between the Zion Christian Church and the New Government?

From Covin's speech, identify five organizational strengths of the African American Sacramento community.

Racialized Societies,
Concepts and Decisions

Introduction to Chapter Four

Racialized societies have histories that construct their axiologies based on the color of the skin. These constructs then shape the ideologies, institutions, and social practices of that society; after all, they are the value system. An examination of their historical documents also produce evidence of racialized Constitutions passed as authentic voices of the people, by the people, and for the people, despite the obvious hierarchical hegemonic order. Racialized societies for the most part also draw parallels from their histories of protesting unjust laws fashioned on the basis of race. Amendments of racism and racist language to the constitutions, abolition of racialized laws, challenges of such laws in courts, the aftermaths of such construct on post-colonial, post-apartheid, post–civil rights societies, and the emergence of sophisticated forms of biases also form part of the commonalities and the differences in transformed societies.

The theme of racialized society runs through the articles in this chapter. Ramose's interrogation of the question of sovereignty in the article "I Conquer and Therefore I am the Sovereign: Reflections upon the Sovereignty, Constitutionalism, and Democracy in Zimbabwe and South Africa" implicitly demonstrates that by racializing societies of South Africa and Zimbabwe the Europeans' claim to the indigenous people's land was justified on the contrasting dual concepts of reason/unreason, civilization/barbarism, fidels/infidels, and anomalous rationalization of "Papal mandate, discovery, or the mission to civilize." This Eurocentric construct places the indigenous people in the unreasoned, barbarism, infidels' milieu. Thus constructed and differentiated, their right of sovereignty to their own territory was thus nullified. Mosupyoe's examination of the Afrikaans language conflict accents the impact of racialized legislations on educational institutions in apartheid South Africa. Focusing on the conflict engendered by the apartheid regime's imposition of the oppressor's language, Afrikaans as a medium of instruction, she shows the impact of this decision in students, parents, school officials, the community, and the apartheid regime. A country exploded through a protest wedged by young kids who understood that quintessentially the imposition of the oppressor's language marked a design to punctuate their standard as inferior. Parallels between the South African experience and the African Americans in the United States abound, as reflected in the articles by Covin, Scott, and Cameron-Wedding.

Covin's article "Racialized Societies" through articulation of the United States as a racialized society elucidates how the racial history of the United States provides an appropriate template. From the time of the enslavement of Africans to the time of Jim Crow, racism shaped ideologies, directed the script of the Constitution, informed policies, and formed foundations of racist legislations. The article not only enhances but gives context to the understanding of both Scott's "*Brown v. Topeka Board of Education*: Fifty Years Later" and Cameron-Wedding's "Bias Impact on Decision Makers in Child Welfare." Like South Africa and Zimbabwe the Unites States' history of racism resulted in (1) the famous *Brown v. Board of Education* and its victory in 1954 as well as its shortcomings in fully realizing the benefits of the 14th Amendment and (2) the bias against African Americans in the welfare system as it adversely impacts African Americans. The United States claimed separate but equal in the education system while the South African apartheid education presented a blatant separate and unequal maxim. Scott's "*Brown v. Topeka*

Board of Education: Fifty Years Later" shows the strategy of Charles Huston to defeat Jim Crow. While their victory impacted the education system, Scott feels that more still has to be done to enhance the benefits of the May 17, 1954, decision and the 14th Amendment.

That much still has to be done and vigilance exercised to preserve the gains is illustrated well in Cameron-Wedding's "Bias Impact on Decision Makers in Child Welfare." African Americans constitute the majority in the child welfare system. Cameron-Wedding demonstrates that bias, racism, attitudes, concepts of colorblindness, and denials perpetuated institutionalized practices that negate the achievements of the civil rights movement. Brazil is no exception. Covin shows that the Brazilian society is equally racialized but the racism is manifested in different forms that still leaves blacks at the bottom of the ladder.

I Conquer, Therefore I Am the Sovereign:
Reflections upon Sovereignty, Constitutionalism, and Democracy in Zimbabwe and South Africa

Does Conquest and disregard for Morality.

Mogobe B. Ramose

Natural or fundamental justice

Compares Law to natural Law
Law ≠ Morality

The present essay is about sovereign title to territory and its constitutional implications for contemporary Zimbabwe and South Africa. It is a philosophical analysis of the history, politics, and the constitutionality of the law underlying the democratic dispensation in the two countries. It does not purport to be a juridical analysis in the first place. Instead, it will focus upon the area of tension resulting from the inclusion of some 'natural facts' and the exclusion of others from the universe of juristic facts. The purpose of this focus is to show that what people hold to be natural or fundamental justice does not always coincide with justice according to law. Legal justice will remain a contested area for as long as it does not coincide with the ordinary perceptions of natural or fundamental justice. We shall focus specifically upon historic titles in law and state recognition in the context of international law. In this context we shall consider if and to what extent the fact of conquest, in the history of the voyages of 'discovery' and colonization, has been included or excluded from the universe of juristic facts. To answer the question what are the implications of either inclusion or exclusion we shall analyse the political significance of sovereignty in relation to both the conquered indigenous peoples and their conquerors. The thesis we wish to defend is this: under whatever conception of law, the claim that the conquerors of the indigenous peoples of South Africa and Zimbabwe are the legal successors in title to wholesome and absolute sovereignty over these peoples is unsustainable either on the plea of Papal mandate,

'discovery' or the 'right of conquest.' Therefore, justice demands the restoration of title to territory to the indigenous conquered peoples as well as restitution to them.

Jurists invariably argue that moral considerations fall outside the scope of law. Law is one thing and morality another, so the argument goes. If this is a plea for the independence of the juridical method then it is understandable. However, the plea for methodological purity is not tantamount to a denial that the order that law seeks to establish and maintain is ultimately the moral commonwealth. Accordingly, law cannot totally avoid being the expression of the moral convictions of a given society. Law therefore has a necessary minimum content of morality. For this reason both the necessity and the desirability of certain laws are not in the first place the exclusive initiatives of the legal order. On the contrary, the moral commonwealth is the inescapable source of the necessity or desirability of specific laws. Accordingly, the efficacy of these latter is judged not only according to juridical criteria but also on the basis of morality. This judgement from outside the legal framework speaks precisely to the exclusion of certain 'natural facts' from the universe of 'juristic facts' and the tension that results from such exclusion. We now turn to identify the conqueror and consider the context within which the urge to conquer was nurtured.

The Cultural Context of Colonization

Reason and Unreason

One of the lines that the conqueror drew is that between reason and unreason. Aristotle, one of the major figures in ancient Western philosophy, reaffirmed this line through his definition of

Man has the ability to reason

you cannot prove or disprove "natural law"

'man.' According to him, man is a rational animal. Those animals whose being or nature includes reason as their distinctive characteristic fall within his definition. They are therefore human beings, or 'man.' Any other animal which might look like a human being but be without reason does not qualify as a human being. It is properly an animal with unreason. So the line between reason and unreason was drawn. This line indicated not only the boundary between reason and unreason but it also assigned[1] competences, rights, and obligations in agreement with reason and unreason respectively.[2] In this way it established the nature of the relationship between those inside and those outside the line of reason. The right to freedom and the competence to exercise one's will were assigned only to rational animals. In their relationship with one another rational animals had the obligation to recognize, respect, and protect the right to freedom and freedom of the will. But animals with unreason could neither claim the competences nor the rights that did not belong to them by nature. Therefore, in their relationship with rational[3] animals, the animals with unreason were disallowed in advance to demand obligations that befit only rational animals. This heritage[4] from Aristotle is the philosophy that was deeply rooted in the mind of the conqueror. In essence this philosophy denied humanity to all animals with unreason. By definition such animals could not and did not qualify to be human. This philosophy was actually applied when the conqueror came into contact with the African,[5] the Amerindian,[6] and the Australasian. According to the conqueror, Aristotle's definition that man is a rational animal excluded the African, among others. The exclusion meant the African was to be treated only as an animal because by nature the African was an animal with unreason. Accordingly, it was necessary and proper to conquer and enslave the African. I think, therefore, I conquer and enslave is the practical application by the conqueror of Descartes,' 'I think, therefore, I exist.'[7] No wonder then that conquest and the slave trade have been the main features of the relationship between the conqueror from the West and the African, especially the sub-Saharan African.

They came to stay

Unconquered = Don't Reason   Conquerors = have Reason

colonizer: Negating Humanity of the conquered people, saying that they could not reason. They then conquered the peoples.

Civilization and Barbarism

Having thus made the exclusive claim to reason, the conqueror argued that one of the competences of reason is to conquer nature. Nature was to be investigated in order to use it to improve the quality of human life. There could be no other option since the conquest of nature was a necessary response to the urge to survive individually and collectively. Any advancement designed to improve the chances of survival came to be called progress. Sustained progress growing in depth and complexity came to be known as civilization. This was possible on condition that the agent was a rational animal.[8] Animals with unreason could not make progress. They could therefore not attain any civilization.[9] This line between civilization and barbarism was an extension of the boundary between reason and unreason. The conqueror claimed the status of being the possession of a superior civilization. Accordingly, when the conqueror encountered the African their respective competences, rights, and obligations were already predetermined. The conqueror was civilized and the African was the barbarian. So in the view of the former possession of a superior civilization imposed the duty to civilize the barbarian.[10] The line between civilization and barbarism thus established the relationship of superior and inferior. Accordingly, the conqueror had competences and rights against the African but without any obligations to the African. This was a one-way relationship which precluded the possibility of reciprocity. The African had only obligations towards the conqueror but no rights.

Fidels and Infidels

Another line which the conqueror drew was that between the fidels and the infidels. This line is the special area of religion. God, however understood, is at the same time the subject and the object of any religion. The main point to grasp here is that from the beginning of time all human beings around the world tried to make sense of the experience of death. Does death mean a total, complete, and irreversible end of individual life? Does it mean the return to the purposeless darkness of the nowhere from which we come?

Might Was Right.
Courts determine Natural Law. It's Instinctual. *1066 British Rose To Power*

The experience of death brings humanity face to face with uncertainty. Can we be sure of why we were born and what is our destiny when we die? God is an invention of the human mind to answer these questions. An invention because the existence of god cannot be proved or disproved. It is something that rests on faith. Because of this, god belongs to the sphere in which the idea of proof does not make sense. God belongs to the sphere of metaphysics.[11] Since the experience of death cuts across geographical, cultural, and gender boundaries, it is clear that in the beginning there were gods. This is true of the conqueror as well. The conqueror's long tradition of the mythic gods of the pagan world was interrupted and discarded to a large extent when christianity replaced it.

Christianity justified its abandonment of paganism by appeal to reason and revelation. The former was used to show that irrationality was the basis for belief in the mythic gods. These gods were at best the highest form of aesthetic expression and, at worst mere objects of superstition. Reason therefore justified distraction from them. They had to be abandoned. This was strengthened by the claim that god had now revealed himself through Jesus. Since this provided certainty about the being and the destiny of humanity, it was no longer necessary to have faith in the mythic gods. The conviction here was that the god of Jesus was the one and only true god and this justified the burial of all other gods and their replacement by the god of Jesus.

It is remarkable that the justification of christianity side-stepped commonsense questions by demanding first faith in Christ before attempting to answer the questions. In this way theology clothed religion with the dignity of science. Rationality and, not irrationality as in the past, thus became the complement of religion. Yet, a commonsense look at some of the miracles of the christian religion shows that there is no difference in insight with regard to all the religions christianity was determined to bury. For example, the story of the virgin birth (immaculate conception) is quite problematical from a commonsense point of view. First of all, it is hardly convincing to argue that Mary got married to Joseph in order to prove to him every day the

virtue of virginity. In their time marriage was recognized as the key to sexual intercourse. It is still recognized as such in other parts of the world. Even in the so-called permissive societies the debate about pre-marital sex is still alive. It speaks to the recognition that marriage is the key to sexual intercourse. In addition, Joseph was expected to accept without objection that Mary had a secret meeting with the invisible angel Gabriel who told her that she would be pregnant and the child would be the son of god. If Mary knew beforehand that she would have such a secret meeting, did she disclose this to Joseph before they got married? If she did not have such foreknowledge why did she reportedly preserve her virginity? The Bible refers to the brothers of Jesus.[12] Whose sons were they?[13] Second is the miracle of the resurrection. All that lives must die. Jesus lived and died. But we are informed he rose from the dead and thus was Christ.[14] The Bible speaks of the empty tomb in which Jesus was buried. But what about the emptying of the tomb? How and when did Jesus leave the tomb? Instead of providing an answer to these questions, we are referred to the story of the unbelieving Thomas. This underlines the priority of faith[15] over reason. Accordingly, the line of demarcation here is not rationality and irrationality but faith and reason. And faith requires reason in order to understand the object of its belief. But reason does not require faith in order to understand the object of its knowledge. It is precisely in the domain of religion that the conqueror's exclusive claim to reason becomes clearly doubtful. The universality of death as we explained above must mean also the universality of reason wherever there are human beings. The possibility to invent one's own god is an expression of reason and freedom of the will. Thus even the conqueror's exclusive claim to freedom rests on a very weak foundation. The god of Christ is first and foremost based on faith. This is true of all other gods whoever they may be. And so the conclusion that the god of Christ is the only true god cannot hold even if it rests on revelation because the miracles connected to this cannot withstand the test of commonsense. This remains valid even if theology calls the failure to withstand the test of commonsense mystery or miracles. All it means is that a mystery is a dogmatic statement intended, either by design or default, to block further inquiry. Whereas a miracle is another name for theologized superstition. There is therefore no justification for drawing the line between fidels and infidels meaning christians and peoples of other religions. In effect the determination of christianity to bury all the other gods is misplaced arrogance, irresistible absolutism and, intolerance nurtured by dogmatism.

* No Morality *

Just and Unjust War

What is just and what is justice

War was known in the broad geographic expanse inhabited by the conqueror. Its causes and objectives differed according to time and place. And so was its devastation too. In time principles governing the humanization of war were established. These drew the line between just and unjust wars. The latter expression refers in the first place to the permissibility of war *(ius ad bellum)*. It lays down the conditions to be fulfilled before resort to war may be justified. In the second place it refers to principles regulating the conduct of war *(ius in bello)*. We shall give a brief outline of this according to Thomas Aquinas. His exposition of the doctrine of the just war is the continuation of a long established tradition. This tradition existed before the onset of the voyages of discovery. It's his opinion

According to Aquinas, war may be said to be just when (1) it is waged at the command of the sovereign; (2) there is a just cause *(iusta causa)*; (3) there is the right intention *(intentia recta)*.[16] These principles are predicated on the premise that all other means of peaceful resolution of the conflict have been exhausted. The principles must be simultaneously present and verifiable in any single act of war for it to qualify as just. The following are some of the problems associated with these principles. The principle that only the sovereign may declare war lends credence to the suggestion that war is exclusively a matter between sovereign powers. But the right to self-determination and humanitarian intervention call this exclusivity into question.[17] The principle of the just cause means that war may be initiated in order to: (1) repel an injury *(ad repellendas*

injurias); (2) gain vindication against an offence such as national honour *(ad vindicundas offensiones)*; redress an injury or regain the thing lost *(ad repetendas res)*. Any one of these may constitute sufficient cause on the basis of which war may be declared. We shall argue that vindication against an offence and recoverability *(ad repetendas res)* together underlie the ongoing struggle over land in Zimbabwe. The principle of the right intention speaks to the motivation to do good and avoid evil. Accordingly, if war is waged in order to do evil it is immediately impermissible. Impermissibility for Aquinas had theological[18] connotations as well.[19] This underlines one of the major difficulties concerning the right intention. The reason for war is to be determined exclusively by those who decide to wage it. Invariably, they would argue that the other side is in the wrong. Yet, the other side can make exactly the same claim because it is also entitled to an exclusive determination of the reason for war. Self-defence which is almost spontaneous and natural may be invoked by either side. In view of the nature and quality of nuclear weapons the invocation of self-defence[20] as the reason for resort to nuclear war is academic and thoroughly problematical.[21]

Once real war breaks out moral laws continue to speak. This is the sphere of humane conduct during war *(ius in bello)*. One of the moral laws in this context is that war should stop as soon as the aim for which it was waged is achieved. Another is that only those human beings—mainly soldiers—and other objects necessarily connected to the waging of war may be attacked. This is the principle of non-combatant immunity which does not allow attacking old people, children and women, for example. Similarly, bestiality and cruelty such as torturing the defenceless, raping and injury to human dignity are also prohibited. The principle of proportionality is particularly pertinent here as it prescribes only the use of necessary force to achieve the legitimate aims of war. It implies the principle of the double effect which stipulates that in pursuing a good aim which at the same time includes unavoidable evil then the lesser of the two evils must be chosen.[22] Thus both the *ius ad bellum* and the *ius in bello* are together an attempt to make unavoidable war as human as possible.

Pope gives permission for people to convert the world.

A Meridian Line Decides the Truth and Defines Justice

The conqueror also drew lines such as the rayas and amity lines. Geographically, these amity lines ran along the equator or the Tropic of Cancer in the south, along a degree of longitude drawn in the Atlantic Ocean through the Canary Islands or the Azores in the west, or a combination of both. It was forbidden, under any pretext, to shift the western meridian beyond the Azores. At this "line" Europe ended and the "New World" began. . . . Beyond the line was an "overseas" zone in which, for want of any legal limits to war, only the law of the stronger applied. The characteristic feature of amity lines consisted in that, different from the rayas, they defined a sphere of conflict between two contractual parties seeking to appropriate land precisely because they lacked any common presuppositions and authority. . . . the only matter (the parties) could actually agree on was the freedom of the open spaces that began beyond the line. This freedom consisted in that the line set aside an area where force could be used freely and ruthlessly. . . . The general concept was then necessarily that everything which occurred "beyond the line" remained outside the legal, moral, and political values recognized on this side of the line.[23] Thus reason, morality, civilization, law, and justice was the identity of those this side of the amity line, that is, the conqueror. Lawlessness, ruthlessness, and injustice was the identity of the conqueror beyond the amity line since, in the view of the conqueror, that zone was characterized by unreason and barbarism. Thus the meridian line decided the truth and defined justice about those this side and those beyond it. It reaffirmed the conventional truth that the conqueror had sole and exclusive power. It arbitrarily defined justice as that which was due only to the conqueror and thus imposed no obligation on the part of the conqueror to reciprocate. It follows that fraud, forgery, and the use of brute force as a means of conquest were the recognized method of acquisition of title to the territory of the indigenous conquered peoples. By virtue of this conquest the sovereignty of the indigenous conquered peoples was supplanted and their title to territory extinguished. Historically, this happened to both South Africa[24] and Zimbabwe.[25]

The question then is: may lawlessness, utter disregard for morality, manifest injustice, and the unprovoked use of armed force vest perpetually and irreversibly in the conqueror title to the territory of the conquered as well as absolute sovereignty over them? This is clearly a normative question, which may be considered either from a moral or a juridical perspective. We will pursue the latter perspective though not exclusively. According to the law of the time the answer could be only in the affirmative. It was this: a meridian line decides the truth and defines justice. At bottom this answer means that an injury inflicted malevolently may change into a right and transform the original injustice into justice *(ex injuria ius oritur)*. Thus legality was conferred upon conquest. The meridian line drawn by the conqueror established and upheld the maxim that the threat or the actual use of physical force is the true foundation of law—*auctoritas non veritas facit legem*.

Summary

The above is a brief statement on the intellectual heritage of the conqueror prior to the onset of the voyages of discovery. The drawing of lines defined identities and determined the power relations between them. The question of power is therefore part and parcel of the drawing of lines. The crucial line is that between reason and unreason. It denied the humanity of all other human beings in other parts of the earth. This justified West European conquest ungoverned by law, morality, and humanity. This was so because the just war doctrine did not apply to human-like animals endowed with unreason. The laws of natural or fundamental justice could not and would not be applied to such human-like animals.

Sovereignty since the Beginning of Time

It may well be worth our while to recognize as van Kleffens reminds us, that: 'The word "sovereign" for the highest, supreme power in a given legal order may have been a product of the feudal age, but the notion it represents had forced itself upon the human mind ever since men began to establish independent political groups, and that goes back to the dawn of time. It cannot be emphasized enough that there was sovereignty and there were sovereigns long before these terms were coined, . . . '[26] The point of van Kleffens' reminder is that we take note of both the notional status of sovereignty as a philosophical concept and its historical evolution. Philosophically, there was sovereignty before the term was coined. The coinage was an affirmation of the historical reality of sovereigns. These terms are interwoven with the construction of both individual and collective identity. To tell someone, 'Ngoni is my son' is to describe the relationship between Ngoni and myself. But this descriptive statement is at the same time normative insofar as it identifies Ngoni as son and me as the father. The normative significance of this identity is that is establishes a boundary, a line of demarcation between all other boys who are not my sons and all other senior males who are not Ngoni's father. In this way the norm draws the line. By so doing, it includes and excludes at the same time. Such inclusion also defines the rights and obligations that attach to the relationship of father and son. At the same time it excludes everyone outside this relationship from claiming similar obligations and rights from the same father and son. The crucial point to grasp about this exclusion is that it is not by necessity equal to the denial of similar rights and obligations in a parallel relationship. But it has the potential to actively deny similar rights to those outside the line. However, all it states is that within this particular boundary there are rights and obligations open only to those inside. Indeed even god draws lines.[27] The creation story in Genesis portrays god drawing lines in the construction of the identity of the various species. To each species she assigned characteristics, competencies, rights, and obligations exclusively their own. These remain in agreement with the identity of each species. One of the crucial lines that god drew is that between heaven and hell. Sure this is the ultimate line, the line between life and death; the line of divine justice. The point of this illustration is to show that human beings organize life by drawing lines all the time in everyday life. So did the conqueror. For the conqueror the logic of drawing lines served as the basis of the ideology which maintained that those on the other side of the line could not and did not have similar rights to those this side of the

line. The main question then is not about the drawing of lines but whether or not doing so results in justice to others. Justice because injustice can lead to a life and death struggle. The construction of identity and the drawing of boundaries coincide in the single, contemporaneous, and simultaneous act of inclusion and exclusion. This is what we call bounded reasoning. Independent political groups could hardly claim their independence if they lacked substantive identity found within specific boundaries. Thus the notion of sovereignty predates the coinage of this term at a particular point of history. There was sovereignty and there were sovereigns since the beginning of time. Regardless of the historical coinage of the word 'state' sovereignty is held by a people in perpetuity.[28] For us then there is a philosophical grounding for the quest for historical justice.

Universal Sovereignty without Territory

The 'Donation of Constantine' is the highpoint of the struggle for power between Constantinople and Rome.[29] Having emerged the victor of his struggle Rome invoked the Petrine Commission[30] and on this basis asserted its sole and exclusive right to universal spiritual sovereignty. The universalist thrust of this spiritual sovereignty covered all the inhabitants of the earth. Since the sovereignty here is by definition spiritual—and, the spirit if any exists at all is by definition metaphysical—it was unnecessary for Rome, the universal spiritual power (*potestas spiritualis*) to make any territorial claims. The inhabitants of the earth could, theoretically, retain sovereignty over their territory provided they submitted unconditionally their spirits to the extraterritorial metaphysical sovereignty of the Pope. One basic problem with all the successors of Peter was that even they were unable to submit their spirits unconditionally to the metaphysical sovereignty of the Pope. The reason was that their spirits could be found nowhere. Thus the only way to imagine this metaphysical sovereignty was to recognize that to be human is to be an embodied being. This meant that the spiritual sovereign had to deal with bodies located in space and time. Being fixed or located in a territory (territoriality) thus became a factor which the spiritual sovereign had to

Popes looked at Pagans as animals that needed to be converted.

contend with in order to realize the mandate from Christ. This ultimately led to clashes between the papacy and earthly princes and kings. It is clear then that the idea of universal sovereignty without territory is imaginary and metaphysical. Its impact can still be felt from the manner and extent to which the voyages of discovery and colonization affect, in the present case, Zimbabwe and South Africa.

The Papal Mandates: Discovery and Colonization

For as long as the authority of the papacy was recognized by the earthly rulers, it was the former who played an important role in legitimizing the voyages of discovery. Intent upon honouring the mandate of Christ to go and teach all the world, the papacy authorized the voyages of discovery. The yet to be discovered had only one right, namely, to submit to christianity or die.[31] Thus the bulls of Pope Nicholas V—*Dum Diversas* (1452) and *Romanus Pontifex* (1455) gave the kings of Portugal the right to dispossess and enslave Mahometans and pagans. *Dum Diversas* clearly specifies the right to invade, conquer, expel, and fight *(invadendi, conquirendi, expugnandi, debellandi)* Muslims, pagans, and other enemies of Christ *(saracenos ac paganos, aliosque Christi inimicas)* wherever they may be. Christian kings could thus occupy pagan kingdoms, principalities, lordships, possessions *(regna, principatus, Dominia, possessiones)* and dispossess them of their personal property, land, and whatever they might have *(et mobilia et immobilia bona quaecumque per cos detenta ac possessa).* They also were given the right to put these peoples into perpetual slavery *(subjugandi illorumque personas in perpetuam servitutem).*[32] Following upon the footsteps of his predecessor, Pope Alexander VI issued the bull *Inter caetera divinae* (May, 4 1494) authorizing the overthrow of paganism and the establishment of the christian faith in all pagan nations.[33] All these bulls sanctioned disseizin and killing, among others, if the prospective converts refused to become christians.[34] The voyagers modified the papal mandate by claiming title to the territory of the conquered as well as sovereignty over it even if the conquered accepted christianity.

Christopher Columbus, Vasco de Gama, and Batholomew Diaz all derived indirectly from the papal bulls their permission for the voyages of discovery. They were the bearers as well as the disseminators of the tradition of conquest, inhumanity, and disregard for justice. Following upon a heated debate between Sepulveda and Las Casas in Valladolid, Spain in 1550, Pope Paul III issued the bull, *Sublimis Deus.* It declared expressly that 'all men are rational animls.'[35] Accordingly, it erased the dividing line between reason and unreason among human beings. But the deletion of this line did not eradicate the conqueror's conviction that only some men are rational animals. This conviction survived the conquest of South Africa and Zimbabwe by the Dutch and the British. We still live with it today. It is expressed by dividing lines such as the First and the Third World,[36] the North and South countries, rich and poor countries, as well as white and black people. In this way the power relations of superior and inferior persist. Thus conquest by the Dutch and the British did not depart from this tradition. Instead it refined and solidified it. It confirmed and established the doctrine that the 'right of conquest' meant that loss of title to territory and sovereignty over it were irreversible and permanent. This doctrine acquired the status of a juristic fact. The law recognized it. This recognition thus entailed the dissolution of the sovereignty of the indigenous people over their territory. It also entailed, at independence, granting formal equal constitutional status to both the successors in title to the 'right of conquest' and the conquered indigenous people. In this way injustice came to be constitutionalized. The conquered people continue to remember this original injustice. They are like christians who continue to remember the original sin committed by Eve and Adam millions of years ago. The sin of these supposed original parents does stick even to their unborn innocent children. The beneficiaries of the 'right of conquest' are visible, active in their enjoyment of the benefits and, objectively identifiable. On what ground can they plead innocence and declare that their present privileged position has nothing to do with their historical ancestry? Instead of seeking baptism to restore friendship with god, the indigenous conquered people of Zimbabwe demand justice: the return of their land

and full sovereignty over it. It is precisely this memory of the original injustice which prompts them to seek justice beyond the Lancaster Agreement.

Historic Titles in Law

Among the modes of acquisition of territory possession since time immemorial, conquest and effective occupation are recognized by international law. Conquest may be legal if it satisfies the requirements prescribed. We shall consider the legality of conquest in the light of a radical questioning of the legal maxim that *ex injuria ius oritur*. The questioning is in fact its opposite, namely, that malevolent injury may not change into a right nor may it transform an injustice into justice *(ex injuria ius non oritur)*. The first maxim is a plea to deal with a factual situation as we find it without questioning its historical, political, and moral foundations. With particular reference to conquest this legalistic view holds that 'if conquests by their nature form a legitimate right of possession to the conqueror, it is indifferent whether the war be undertaken on just or unjust grounds.'[37] This concession of law to conquest regardless of the morality or justice thereof is challenged and opposed by the second maxim.[38]

Hall, quoted in McMahon, defines conquest as the taking of property of one state by the conquering state. The same conquering state then proceeds to claim sovereignty over the property (territory) thus taken away and to impose its will upon the conquered inhabitants. Once this claim to newly acquired sovereignty is acknowledged and established without further challenge or opposition then title to territory as well as sovereign rights come to be vested in the conquering state.[39] McMahon is critical of this definition of conquest. He argues that its particular weakness lies in the fact that it omits to mention that usually appropriation with regard to conquest is either an act of the actual use of armed force or the threat to use such force. Consequently, he continues, violent seizure is an indispensable element in any definition of conquest. Even if the condition arising from conquest may be sustained for a long time, it does not necessarily follow that conquest then is perfected into a legal right. This latter is specifically an argument against

acquiescence[40] prescribed by international law as one of the necessary elements to change conquest initially ungoverned by law into a right transforming an original injustice into justice. Accordingly, injustice may not supersede justice only because the injustice has prevailed for a long time.[41] Hall's argument here can therefore not hold because 'the general principle of law is that a right cannot arise from a wrong. Hence all the cases of revival or survival of State sovereignty despite conquest and annexation can also be explained by the maxim *ex injuria ius non oritur*. A claim to territorial title which originates in an illegal act is invalid.'[42] If one were to argue that at that time there was no law[43] and therefore no justice[44] beyond the meridian line then the conclusion is not that territory acquired then may be retained by the conqueror. Why should the reverse, namely, the return of territory to its original owners thereby restoring their sovereignty be necessarily precluded?

New Lines and Old Truths beyond the Meridian Line

The conquerors resolved their conflicts arising from appetite for more land[45] beyond the meridian by arbitrarily[46] drawing more lines dividing up the disputed[47] territories between themselves. This criss-cross of arbitrary lines was done without consultation[48] and with no regard for the sovereignty[49] of the indigenous conquered people. It was simply assumed that the original lawlessness was changed into lawfulness conferring the so-called right of conquest upon the conqueror. Similarly, it was taken for granted that the lapse of time had transformed the original injustice into justice. It was equally forgotten that international law this side of the meridian line recognized possession from time immemorial as legitimate ground for title to territory. But the memory of the indigenous conquered peoples was neither dimmed nor obliterated by decades and centuries of subjugation. They remembered that their title to territory—in this case South Africa and Zimbabwe—is deeply rooted in the unfathomable past in which their forebears occupied the territory and exercised absolute sovereignty over it. Accordingly, they were and remain by right of ancestry the rightful heirs to territory and they are the absolute sovereign over it. Therefore, under whatever conception of law, the claim that the conquerors of the indigenous peoples of South Africa and Zimbabwe are the legal successors in title to wholesome and absolute sovereignty over these peoples is unsustainable either on the plea of Papal mandate, 'discovery' or the 'right of conquest.' Memory evoked the old truth that the land and sovereignty over it belong to the indigenous conquered peoples.[50] On the basis of this truth these peoples recognized the injury and the injustice done to them through conquest: the use of armed force ungoverned by law, morality or humanity. Awareness of this truth impelled them to seek justice in the form of the reversion of title to territory to its rightful holders—the indigenous conquered peoples—the restoration of absolute sovereignty over the same territory and restitution. Implicit in this quest for justice is the assertion of the right to self-determination. 'It need scarcely be added that the transition from colonial status to independence is not regarded as secession, whether or not it is achieved by force of arms, but rather as the "restoration" of a rightful sovereignty of which the people have been illegitimately deprived by the colonial Power concerned.'[51] On this basis effective occupation and the lapse of time would not necessarily eliminate permanently this original right to territory and absolute sovereignty over it. 'The use of the right of self-determination can be important as regards title. As a manifestation through international recognition of a legal rule it is important as a constituent of statehood. As such it may deny title in situations of effective control and it imposes a duty in particular circumstances to transfer territorial sovereignty.[52] It is therefore submitted that despite the irrelevance[53] of population in the legal determination of statehood, the demand for title to territory and sovereignty over it by the indigenous conquered peoples of South Africa and Zimbabwe is vital and pertinent to the legal determination of statehood. It is an exigency of natural or fundamental justice. It is the foundation upon which the use of armed force against colonization in its various formations and manifestations is built. Since this is a statement of principle, it remains to show how in practice the transition from Rhodesia to Zimbabwe and in South Africa to a 'multiracial democracy' answered to these exigencies.

From Rhodesia to Zimbabwe

Mason identified conquest as the basic problem in what is now known as Zimbabwe.[54] The conqueror in this case was the same as in South Africa. Thus the philosophical and ideological underpinnings of conquest remain the same. When the conquest was changed into a right and the injustice transformed into justice, the conqueror in Rhodesia was—prior to 11 November 1965—recognized as an international personality[55] albeit in a limited way. However, the recognition became rather strained when Rhodesia unilaterally declared independence from the United Kingdom on 11 November 1965. The referendum of June 20, 1969 to turn Rhodesia into a republic thereby dissolving every connection with the British monarchy was supported only by the Rhodesian conqueror. In effect, the referendum result forced the British Government and others to concede that they held responsibility without power. . . . Responsibility without power had been an apt description of the relationship with Rhodesia of successive British Governments since 1923.[56] The strain pertaining to the continued recognition of the conqueror's Rhodesia was more respect for the sovereignty of the United Kingdom[57] than for the fact that extinctive prescription meant injury and injustice to the indigenous conquered people of Zimbabwe.[58] The latter drew the conclusion to assert their right to historic title through both peaceful means and the use of armed force. This led to internal unsuccessful constitutional[59] engineering and ultimately to a series of peace negotiations culminating in the Lancaster House Agreement.

The Lancaster Agreement paved the way for the transition from Zimbabwe-Rhodesia to Zimbabwe. The Agreement was made possible when the major parties to the conflict accepted, with qualification, the reversion of sovereignty to the United Kingdom. There was thus a return to legality in the sense that the United Kingdom was recognized[60] by the international community as the sovereign of Rhodesia. Zimbabwe-Rhodesia being the result of the illegal unilateral declaration of independence by the government of Ian Smith on 11 November 1965 did not acquire international personality and was therefore not recognized as the legal sovereign of Rhodesia. This remained the position despite the co-option of Bishop Muzorewa's party and his ascent to the premiership. The price that the Smith government was prepared to pay for this co-option was, among others, the renaming of the country to Zimbabwe-Rhodesia. Perhaps inadvertently for both sides this name is particularly significant in that it described the major parties to the conflict in the country. The name also identifies the basic meaning that each party ascribes to the country. For the indigenous conquered people the proper name of the country is Zimbabwe, the country that belongs to them and over which they hold title to sovereignty by virtue of ancestry from time immemorial. For the conqueror the name of the country is Rhodesia in memory of Cecil John Rhodes. Through the actions of this latter the indigenous conquered people of Zimbabwe lost their title to territory and sovereignty over it. The successors in title to Rhodes, including the government of Ian Smith, were determined to preserve and maintain their inherited title to Rhodesia and their sovereignty over it. From this point of view, it is clear that the basic problem in the country was right from the first contact with Rhodes the question of title to territory and sovereignty over it. Did the Lancaster Agreement provide a solution to this problem?

At Lancaster House the British government prescribed a settlement.[61] This consisted of (1) an entrenched 'Declaration of Rights,' and (2) loans to the new government of Zimbabwe. The 'willing seller,' 'willing buyer' principle was established to defend the 'property' rights of the conqueror in Rhodesia. Under pressure, not least from the Heads of state of the Front Line States, the Patriotic Front reluctantly accepted this particular agreement. It was not the first time that the British government imposed this kind of agreement on African states.[62] In this way the latter was forced to accept extinctive prescription as an irreversible and immutable fact. Yet, the sense of an injured consciousness and the injustice of extinctive prescription did not become completely and permanently erased from the memory of the indigenous conquered people of Zimbabwe.[63]

Did the government of Zimbabwe provide a solution to the question of title to territory and sovereignty over it after the expiry of the Lancaster Agreement? Our argument with regard to both questions is that the Lancaster Agreement did not provide a solution to the question of title to territory precisely because the British government neither raised nor entertained the question. At the expiry of the Lancaster Agreement the government of Zimbabwe did not provide a solution to the problem first by omitting to raise the question afresh and, second by addressing it as a matter of private law with particular reference to the right to property, especially the ownership of land. By so doing the government of Zimbabwe reduced the question of collective right to a matter of individual right. The problem with this reduction is that it implicitly condones the principal myth of the Lancaster Agreement, namely, that sovereignty can be conferred without the simultaneous recognition that the sovereign holds, either potentially or actually, title to a specific territory.[64] This myth and the inherent injustice that attaches to it is the legacy of the Lancaster Agreement. It is the ghost that continues to haunt decolonization in Africa and many other formerly colonized countries. The United States of America, Australia, Canada, and New Zealand are notable exceptions. The government of Zimbabwe still has the task to replace this myth with reality, namely, the restoration of title to territory to the indigenous conquered people and the necessity for the reversion to unencumbered and unmodified sovereignty to the same quantum and degree as at conquest.[65] Only in this way can restitution and reparation as exigencies of historical justice be realized in Zimbabwe. The implications of this resolution for the rest of Africa speak for themselves.

Sovereignty over Natural Resources

Article one of the Universal Declaration on the Eradication of Hunger and Malnutrition states that 'every man, woman and child has the inalienable right to be free from hunger and malnutrition in order to develop fully and maintain their physical and mental faculties.'[66] The declaration is specific on the point that this right is 'inalienable.' It is a right which even the holder may not transfer to another. Any transfer of this right would mean that the holder places themselves in a position in which it is impossible for them to fend for themselves. Yet, no one needs the prior permission of another to make sure that they continue to live.[67] Seeking permission from another to continue to live is to treat that other as the source of our life having sole authority to decide if we may continue to live. But such treatment cannot be conferred on another human being—even our parents—because we all did not choose to be born. We did not choose the necessary connection between life and death. Life for all of us is gratuitous. It is something we have without having done anything special to deserve it. It is by chance that it is ourselves in this world and not someone else instead of us. We therefore have an equal right to life. It is a right to conferred not by any individual or the state. Other individuals and the state have only the duty to recognize, respect, and protect this right. For this reason 'If the citizens of a State—that is to say, families—on entering into association and fellowship, experienced at the hands of the State hindrance instead of help, and found their rights attacked instead of being protected, such associations were rather to be repudiated than sought after.'[68] Food is produced on and from the land. No land, no food. Thus there is an indivisible connection between land and life in the organic biological sense. Life without food is not possible biologically. Land, food, and life are thus connected inseparably. In this sense the right to land means at the same time the right to food and life. Accordingly, the primary and fundamental egoistic proclamation that each individual can make against the community without moral embarrassment is the assertion of the right to food.[69] It is this indivisible interconnection between land and life which makes the right to food inalienable.[70] To take away the land of another is to deprive them of an indispensable resource of life. Also to deny someone access to land is to exclude them from the means necessary to sustain life.[71] Through conquest the conqueror in Zimbabwe violated this inalienable right of the indigenous conquered people of Zimbabwe. This violation brought about conflict between the conqueror and the conquered. The former transformed this violation into justice and thus resolved to make it irreversible and permanent.

The latter continue to regard the original violation as injustice and maintain that it is reversible and temporary.

The Principle of Recoverability

He who denies another by force access to land that originally and rightfully belonged to them provokes the necessity for self-defence on the part of those so deprived. According to the theory of the just war, the forcibly deprived may invoke the principle of recoverability (*ad repetendas res*) if every other peaceful means to resolve the conflict fails. The principle of recoverability holds that access to or ownership of land is such that there is a direct and immediate link between land and the preservation of life. For this reason the use of force, including the possibility of killing, is justified in order to recover lost land.[72] Of course, all the other principles of the theory, namely, the right intention, proportionality, and non-combatant immunity apply. The conquered people of Zimbabwe either expressly or by implication invoked this principle at the start of the first chimurenga[73] war. The war did not achieve this particular aim. The second chimurenga war did not achieve this particular aim either. It enabled political independence but denied economic independence as well. It also facilitated the renaming of the country to Zimbabwe. The transition from Rhodesia to Zimbabwe was thus another new stage in the struggle to recover land lost by conquest ungoverned by law, morality, and humanity.

The Chimurenga War

A lot of effort was made to resolve the conflict over land recovery by peaceful means. When this path failed to yield the desired results it was decided to turn to war. The primary aim of the second chimurenga or liberation war was to recover the land lost at conquest and to regain sovereignty over it. Without this the goal of economic independence would remain a permanent mirage. Other aims of the war were the elimination of racial discrimination. The aims of the war were many and concurrent. The war continued until the conqueror recognized the need for a negotiated resolution of the conflict. The first crucial step in this was the Rhodesian conqueror's admission that sovereignty vested in the United Kingdom. Strictly, this recognition was equal to the admission that the United Kingdom was the ancestral conqueror.[74] It was from this ancestral conqueror that the Rhodesian government usurped sovereignty and title to territory. Thus the Rhodesian government claimed, illegally, to be the successor in title to the United Kingdom's sovereignty. The claim was contested by the United Kingdom and the international community. Accordingly, the Rhodesian state was denied international personality. The legal point here is that although 'an entity may have all the objective characteristics which international law prescribes for statehood. This does not make it an international person. It merely has the capacity to be recognized as an international person. It is only when it is accorded recognition that it will have international personality, i.e., be the bearer of rights and duties in international law.'[75] Because Rhodesia did not have international personality, it was not recognized by the United Kingdom and the international community. Thus the insistence on the return to legality actually meant the recognition of the United Kingdom's 'right of conquest' with regard to Rhodesia.[76] This could not have been the meaning that the indigenous Zimbabweans attached to 'the return to legality.' The chimurenga war was in the first place a challenge to the 'right of conquest' whether it vested in the United Kingdom or its successor in title, Rhodesia. However, under pressure from the Front Line States the continuation of this challenge had to be through negotiations. Thus the Patriotic Front reluctantly[77] participated in the negotiations which culminated in the Lancaster Agreement. It is to be noted specially that at the time of the negotiations the United Kingdom exercised sovereignty based upon the original conquest ungoverned by law, morality, and humanity. The United Kingdom's 'right of conquest' was a juristic fact. The Lancaster Agreement did not question it. Instead, it was used as the foundation for the constitution of Zimbabwe. Through the constitutionalization of the 'right of conquest' the United Kingdom conferred equal formal status to the conqueror and the conquered. In this way it ignored the question of

historic justice and dissolved it into the precarious legal equality between the conqueror and the conquered in Zimbabwe. By this mechanism the sovereignty of the United Kingdom over Rhodesia was extinguished. It was transferred fully to the Rhodesians and partially to the indigenous Zimbabweans. For the latter, the sovereignty conferred was limping in the sense that it was not the express reversion to unencumbered and unmodified sovereignty to them over their territory. This was so because the transfer of political power did not mean the extinction of British sovereignty based on the 'right of conquest.' At independence sovereignty was transferred only to its successors in title, namely, the Rhodesians. Thus only the Rhodesians, having a claim to the nationality of the United Kingdom by virtue of ancestry, acquired full sovereignty over Zimbabwe. Yet, reversion to unmodified and unencumbered sovereignty to the same quantum and degree as at conquest was the basic demand of natural justice due to the indigenous Zimbabweans. This they did not achieve at independence. The only way to realize this was to make the transition from Rhodesia to Zimbabwe a matter of state succession.

The transition from Rhodesia to Zimbabwe was a movement away from the status of a colony to sovereign independence. Because of the so-called right of conquest the conquered people did not form part of the sovereign character of Rhodesia. The rise of Zimbabwe brought with it a new constitutional quality to the older character of Rhodesian sovereignty. By so doing, it inscribed a new identity to the new state, Zimbabwe. Thereby it abolished the old state of Rhodesia. It is submitted therefore that the transition from Rhodesia to Zimbabwe was a matter of state succession and not government succession as the Lancaster Agreement prescribed. It is worth noting the following reflections in connection with our submission. 'The question whether a state gaining territorial sovereignty (the successor state) inherits, together with the territory concerned, the rights and obligations of another state (the predecessor state) arises if this latter is actually to be considered extinct. This question leads to the problems of state succession. The significance of the question is not only theoretical but practical. The fact is that international law does not provide that territorial changes shall have an effect implying the automatic and unconditional devolution, in all cases, of rights and obligations together with the territory concerned. The establishment of the identity of a state is therefore important because in this case the continuance of rights and obligations does not become questionable. . . . As regards the particular types of territorial changes the answer is unambiguous: the states emerging from colonial status to independence are new subjects of international law; the problems to be solved in connection with them are those of state succession.'[78] Treating the transition from Rhodesia to Zimbabwe as a question of government succession conferred only formal legal equality between the Rhodesians and the Zimbabweans. This legal equality meant that the conquered would accede, on an equal plane, together with the conqueror to the rights and obligations of Rhodesia.[79] Yet, the former had not enjoyed the full benefits of either in the time of Rhodesia. This basic injustice was built into the constitutional structure provided by the Lancaster Agreement. Zimbabwe was thus necessarily destined to seek a remedy to this injustice.

Territorial Sovereignty or Land Reform?

In this section we wish to show that focus upon 'land reform,' 'land resettlement' was the primary preoccupation of the government of Zimbabwe since 1980. It could not be otherwise because this was part of its obligations under the Lancaster Agreement. Three years into independent Zimbabwe, the British government threatened to withdraw a part of its aid on land resettlement. In response the incumbent President, then Prime Minister Mugabe, left no doubt about who are the rightful owners of Zimbabwe. He vowed, 'swearing by the name of the legendary anti-British spirit medium Ambuya Nehanda, . . . that his government would confiscate white-owned land for peasant resettlement if Mrs Thatcher suspends promised British compensation . . . If they do that we will say 'Well and good, you British gave us back the land because you never paid for it in the first place. The land belongs to us. It is ours in inheritance from our forefathers.''[80] Seventeen years on the same President

upholds the same position. The deed is now being suited to the word and so the position is implemented practically. This is consistency and not opportunism. Only unhistorical imagination can regard this as part of the election manifesto to improve the chances of the ruling party to win the elections scheduled for June 2000.

'Since the mid-1980s the Government has danced defensively around the question of land reform until Independence Day in April 1993 when President Mugabe forcefully argued that land redistribution was fundamental and had to be implemented speedily. His speeches emphasized the important role that land plays in reconciling blacks and whites, in resolving the National Question by providing land rights for the majority and in guaranteeing the rural poor the basic means of their survival. Given the potentially explosive consequences of not addressing these issues in a controlled and fair manner, the President affirmed the central role that the state, as a sovereign entity, needed to play in land reform.'[81] Indeed beginning from 1980, there are four five-year phases of the land reform and resettlement programme mapped out by the government of Zimbabwe. But October 1998–September 2000 are earmarked specifically as 'two-year phasing.'[82] This focus intensified over the years and has now reached its highpoint since about February 2000. Yet, this means a shift of focus from the primary issue, namely, the return of the land to its original rightful owners—the indigenous Zimbabweans—and the restoration of their full sovereignty over it. This is the basic right of title to territory by virtue of ancestry. It imposes the imperative for the reversion to unencumbered and unmodified sovereignty to the same quantum and degree as at conquest. It is crucial to rectify the scale of priorities by according primacy to this basic right. Once the land has been returned to its original rightful owners and sovereignty over it has been restored to them, it follows that in their capacity as the sovereign the people of Zimbabwe may take appropriate legal measures to have 'land reform' and 'land resettlement.' Thus the one does not exclude the other. It is therefore not a question of either the one or the other. It is a question of both together but according to their order of priority. For this order to be logically valid and historically true, the return of the land and the restoration of sovereignty must be first. But mixing up the priorities actually blurs the issues and blunts the edge of the sovereign to cut and slice the necessary legislation.

Forget about the Past

Forget about the past is the main message of acquisitive or extinctive prescription. The problem with this message is that it makes an unequal and unjust demand. The conqueror is asked to forget about the past on the understanding that the benefits of conquest in an unjust war shall accrue exclusively to him. On the other hand, the conquered is asked to forget about the past on condition that they renounce their right to seek a remedy to the injustice of conquest in an unjust war. According to this message, justice is due only to those who acquire their rights through the use of physical military force. Thus the holder of military superiority may impose his will on the conquered and call this will law. Yet, there is no in-built guarantee that anyone will forever remain the military superior. Therefore, if time and circumstances permit, the conquered may reaffirm their right to seek a remedy to the injustice of conquest in an unjust war. This means replacing coerced renunciation with determined reaffirmation of their right to restore justice. Memory is the key to this. It serves to remind the conquered about the original injustice. The reminder preserves the determination to restore justice. The reminder is a message about a vital part of their identity, namely, a people conquered in an unjust war.[83] From this point of view, 'forget about the past' is also a demand to erase specific traits from one's identity. Some identity traits may be dispensed with and others are regarded as indispensable. Instead of giving up the latter, people would rather sacrifice their own lives. The right to seek a remedy to the injustice of conquest in an unjust war is an indispensable identity trait of the conquered people. The underlying reason for this is that to renounce this right is to deny that all human beings are equal in their humanity. This denial does not mean that some human beings are more equal than others. Even more, it means that a line is drawn between humans and non-humans. All humans are equal

but non-humans cannot by their very nature claim equality with humans. By preserving the memory of the injustice of conquest in an unjust war, the indigenous conquered people of Zimbabwe—and, indeed the indigenous conquered people anywhere in the world—actually uphold their right to equality. They reaffirm their humanity by refusing to be placed in the category of non-humans. We submit therefore that the message of 'forget about the past' is an unjustified attempt to wipe out history. It is also philosophically unsustainable because (1) it is a one-sided drawing of lines giving privileges the status of a right; (2) it is a unilateral construction of the identity of 'the other'; (3) it is the forced transmutation of an injustice into justice. It must be replaced by, 'thou shalt not kill memory.' The indigenous conquered people of Zimbabwe have decided to abide by this latter precept.[84] Accordingly, they are pursuing justice beyond the Lancaster Agreement.

Religion and Politics

African traditional religion[85] continues to play a vital role in the private and public lives of many an African. Those Africans converted to other non-African religions such as christianity are not necessarily free of at least the impact of African traditional religion on their lives.[86] In their observance of their new-found religion they cannot but take African traditional religion into account. Among others, this means considering it negatively as 'superstition' and thus constantly rejecting it. By so doing, they recognize its presence and influence on their lives. The religious culture of spirit mediums[87] is very deeply-rooted in the life of the indigenous Zimbabweans. The spirit mediums continue to be regarded as indispensable links with the living-dead (ancestors). These mediums even have names. However, as a rule they are not addressed directly by their names. Rather, their actual name is often preceded by a title of respect. This is the case, for example, with the spirit medium, Nehanda. Her title of reverence is Ambuya, meaning, grandmother. 'Nehanda has always been a woman, and affectionately called, ambuya, grandmother, by all her Zezuru adherents in Central Mashonaland among whom this particular one operated during the rebellion.'[88] Thus the spirit-mediums like Nehanda were present to the Zimbabweans in times of drought, famine or other natural disasters. They were also present to the people in matters of war and peace; in politics. That is why they feature in the 'rebellion' of 1896. They are thus present in all the spheres of the people's life. For this reason, 'Nehanda was of the same mould as the famous holy men and women about whom we read in Christian literature. She was reportedly simple, ascetic, and averse to public acclaim. And yet she had an influence over her followers that, in its own Shona way, would have been comparable to that of Mahatma Gandhi. Before her Shona men and women of every rank humbled themselves as if they were of no consequence whatever because in their eyes she was god's lieutenant and the intermediary between god and his people and also the intermediary between them and their ancestors. Indeed, they felt that she was above everyone throughout the country, black and white, above the Church as well as the Government. Little wonder that she was so exalted and her person was shrouded in such deep mysteries and secrets, open only to the very few Shona men representing the tribes whose allegiance she enjoyed.[89] Accordingly, only those with blind bravery and asinine courage would dare to disobey the guidance from Ambuya Nehanda. Obedience to her guidance came before everything else because, 'The word of the mediums was as good as law, . . . speaking with the authority of the spirits of the dead on matters of freedom, life and death.'[90] No wonder then Ambuya Nehanda played such a crucial role in the second chimurenga war.[91] This, as we have already suggested, was in the first place the war for the return of the land to its original rightful owners and the restoration of sovereignty to them. The religious basis of the war becomes apparent in the words of Jakobo. He was speaking at a family occasion having an unmistakable national significance. Jakobo addressed the gods thus: 'For reasons we have never been able to understand, you permitted this ngozi to fall upon us. . . . You allowed victory to go to them rather than to us. . . . You must know better than we do that we shall always need care, succour and safeguards against the machinations and knavishness of the white men who say they are our masters and

come into our homes as it pleases them to make criminals of us. . . .'[92] Resentment of 'the white men' and the will to defy them are unmistakable in Jakobo's address to the gods. Thus conquest in an unjust war has remained the basic theme of the politics of Zimbabwe.

The role of African traditional religion did not end at independence in 1980. One of the living reminders of this is the inscription of the Hungwe, called the Zimbabwe bird by non-Africans, in the national flag of Zimbabwe. The Hungwe also appears on many other sites of national importance. This is no accident. For the indigenous Zimbabweans, the Hungwe is a sacred bird. 'Chaminuka's medium, . . . interpreted the squawkings of Hungwe, Shirichena, ShiriyaMwari—the Celestial fish eagle, the Bird of Bright Plumage, the Bird of Mwari—on its annual visit to the shrine, as pronouncements of the deity. . . . It is also possible that these birds, some of which have a crocodile carved onto the base of their supporting columns, were the symbolic representations of the godhead himself.'[93] There is little doubt then that there is profound religious symbolism surrounding the Hungwe. It is regarded as the vital messenger from the living to the-living-dead[94] (the spirits, the gods or ancestors) and from the latter to the living. A message from the Hungwe may be disregarded only at the risk of provoking the wrath of the gods. The Hungwe is a vivid reminder of the role and influence of religion in the national politics of Zimbabwe. To all governments of Zimbabwe since 1980 the Hungwe carries the message from the gods that there is still unfinished business with regard to the Lancaster Agreement. The gods had willed a partial victory by conceding the Lancaster Agreement. But they shall be appeased and remove the ngozi (bad luck, curse, catastrophe) they have cast upon the indigenous Zimbabweans only if the latter remedy the original injustice of conquest by recovering their ancestral land and regaining sovereignty over it. And so they have sent the Hungwe to sing this song to every indigenous conquered Zimbabwean: 'the gods shall never sleep until the land is returned to its original rightful owners and full sovereignty over it is restored to them.' Thus the government of Zimbabwe, irrespective of the Mugabe Presidency, has the religious duty to engage in the politics that will put the gods to sleep.

In the light of the above, the government of Zimbabwe has got two tasks. The first is the return of the land to its original rightful owners and the restoration of their sovereignty over it. The second is the land reform and resettlement programme. This programme must be understood as a compelling state interest. That is to say, the state of Zimbabwe must launch and realize the objectives of this programme if it wants to preserve internal security, social stability and the promotion of sustainable economic well-being for all its citizens.

The Experience of the Land Reform and Resettlement Programme

The Lancaster Agreement did not address the question of title to Zimbabwean territory and sovereignty over it. Instead of dealing with this as the yet to be achieved primary aim of the chimurenga war, both the government of Zimbabwe and the people approached it as a question of private law with special reference to ownership of land. Thus the focus was on land reform and resettlement. It was therefore easy to identify farms on which the landless could be resettled and engage in agricultural activity. The following are the objectives of the land reform and resettlement programme. 'To acquire 5 million hectares from the Large Scale Commercial Farming sector for redistribution. To resettle 91 000 families and youths graduating from agricultural colleges and others with demonstrable experience in agriculture in a gender-sensitive manner. To reduce the extent and intensity of poverty among rural families and farm workers by providing them adequate land for agricultural use. To increase the contribution of agriculture to GDP by increasing the number of commercialized small scale farmers using formerly under-utilized land. To promote the environmentally sustainable utilization of land. To increase conditions for sustainable peace and social stability by removing imbalances in land ownership.'[95]

The land reform and resettlement programme was not without problems. The first challenge through the courts occurred when the Constitution of Zimbabwe Amendment Act No. 11, 1990 was contested. Section 6 of this Amendment con-

tained an ouster of the jurisdiction of the courts in these terms: 'and no such law shall be called into question by any court on the ground that the compensation provided by that law is not fair.' The challenge to this focused on the right to property and protection against compulsory acquisition of property. Further, it questioned whether designation of land without compensation amounts to acquisition of interest in property without payment of compensation. It also questioned the constitutionality of Part IV of the Land Acquisition Act 3 of 1992 of the 1980 Constitution of Zimbabwe.[96] The court was not called upon to decide the issue of historic titles in law. Rather it was called upon to determine the legality of the government action basing itself on a constitution which was founded on the dubious assumption that the 'right of conquest' was legally and equally valid for all parties to the conflict. It was held on the basis of the doctrine of eminent domain that the state was entitled to acquire land in terms of the disputed provisions. In this particular case the judge answered the question: who is the rightful owner of Zimbabwe? As noted, the court was not called upon to adjudicate the dispute as a species of historic titles in law. But the full answer of the judge deserves verbatim quotation. 'But the fact of the matter is that the facts that make land acquisition for resettlement a matter of public interest in Zimbabwe are obvious that even the blind can see them. These facts make the resettlement of the people a legitimate public interest. In my view, anybody who has lived in Zimbabwe long enough needs no affidavit to know the following facts, which are common knowledge, which make acquisition of land for resettlement imperative in public interest. These are: once upon a time all the land in Zimbabwe belonged to the African people of this country. By some means foul or fair, depending on who you are in Zimbabwe, about half that land ended in the hands of a very small minority of Zimbabweans of European descent. The other half remained in the hands of the large majority, who were Africans. The perception of the majority of Africans was that the one-half in the hands of the minority was by far the better and more fertile land, while the other half, which they occupied, was poor and semi-arable. It is also common knowledge that, when the Africans lost half their land to the Europeans, they were paid nothing by way of compensation. . . . Attempts to redress the land issue by peaceful means were not successful. The Africans took up arms and armed struggle ensued. The Lancaster House agreement marked the end of the armed struggle and the transfer of political power to the Africans. The Constitution that came out of the Lancaster House agreement imposed certain restrictions regarding the redistributions of land. As of now, the perception still exists that still large portions of the land remains in the hands of a small minority of European descent while the majority of the Africans are still crowded in semi-arable communal land. The majority of the Europeans who own land are able and willing to release some of the land to resettle Africans. They are willing to sell it to a cash-strapped Government at a premium. On the other hand, the majority Africans who are still crowded in the communal areas are more than anxious to be resettled on land they see as their own taken from them wrongly in the first place. They see no merit in having to pay for land that was taken from them without compensation in the first place.'[97] The judge makes the following crucial observations. (1) That all the land of Zimbabwe belonged to the Africans since time immemorial. Ancestry since time immemorial is thus the legal basis of their title to Zimbabwe territory and their sovereignty over it. But the Africans lost their title and sovereignty 'by means foul or fair,' meaning by conquest in an unjust war ungoverned by law, humanity, and morality. As a result title and sovereignty vested in the Rhodesians. (2) The Lancaster Agreement marks the end of a protracted armed struggle aimed specifically to regain title to territory and recover sovereignty over it. The Agreement did not meet these specific aims. Instead, it imposed the duty upon the people and government of Zimbabwe to purchase back their own land. The inherent injustice of this duty to purchase back is that 'when the Africans lost their land to the Europeans, they were paid nothing by way of compensation.' But the government of Zimbabwe did, in the name of the 'Africans,' condone this injustice as part of the Lancaster constitution. (3) The 'Africans,' evidently in possession of insufficient information about the Agreement and, hardly in a position to understand all its implications, gave

the government the benefit of the doubt. But in doing so, they were, right from the beginning 'more than anxious' to be resettled on land they regarded as their own. As they were 'more than anxious,' their patience ran out as the government delayed to deliver on its promise. (4) They therefore resolved to pursue, within the framework of land resettlement and reform, the aim of acquiring land for themselves. This obviously shifted focus away from the question of land as a matter of collective sovereign right to the issue of the individual right to private property. This shift of focus was based on the conviction of the 'Africans' that the land on which they wished to be resettled was 'their own taken from them wrongly in the first place. They see no merit in having to pay for land that was taken from them without compensation in the first place.' Thus from the point of view of the 'Africans' the government was wrong in principle and in fact to condone the injustice of 'purchasing back'—the 'willing seller, willing buyer' clause—enshrined in the Lancaster constitution. Clearly, the constitution and the law based upon it did not shake their conviction that the land belongs to them. The constitution and the law were simply a mystery[98] that often obscured the truth of their conviction. No doubt none of the 'Africans' needed the label 'war veteran' in order to understand this plain and manifest injustice. (5) The land reform and resettlement programme is a compelling state interest, that is, an 'imperative in public interest.' In these circumstances, the government was now placed in the position to catch up with the ways and means of 'Africans' to acquire their land without the obligation to pay anyone for such acquisition. (6) One of the necessary implications of this reasoning is that if there should be any talk of compensation at all then such compensation is owed, in the first place, to the 'Africans.' This already lays the basis for restitution and reparation as exigencies of historical justice.

The government of Zimbabwe took stock of this experience. This is apparent in President Mugabe's foreword to the launch of phase II of the Land Reform and Resettlement Programme. 'Zimbabwe's independence negotiations in 1979 nearly floundered because of differences on how to redress the land problem. The justiceability of land acquisition and compensation on a willing-seller–winning-buyer basis remains a problem. The Lancaster House Constitution provided for market-based and negotiated land sales. The key nations which brokered Zimbabwe's independence negotiations promised to provide the finance needed for land acquisition and redistribution on the basis of this approach. The Government of Zimbabwe transferred over three million hectares of land to over 71000 families on this basis since 1980. However, inadequate international support and limited national resources for land purchases, and a number of legal, administrative, and logistical constraints limited the pace and quality of land redistribution. As a result, racial imbalances in land ownership and use, and associated poverty remain entrenched in the country. The continuation of this state of affairs poses a threat to social stability.' The President thus made the following points. (1) There were differences on how to resolve the problem of redress with regard to the land. The compromise solution to this problem did not meet the demands of fundamental justice as seen by the conquered. This is borne out by the fact that the Lancaster constitution consists of an inherent injustice. Since he described this as a 'problem,' it clearly means that a remedy must be found for the injustice. (2) Funding received from various sources enabled the government to acquire some land and resettle some families. Problems surrounding acquisition on the basis of the Lancaster constitution resulted in the government not meeting the desired objectives. It is significant that the President does not mention corruption as one of the problems. Yet, it is common cause that some government Ministers would not come out with clean hands if investigated. The arrest of Minister Kumbirai Kangai in this connection attests to this observation. Moreover, both the draft Bill and the corresponding new law on the question of land acquisition provide for the establishment of 'an Anti-Corruption Commission.' This clearly means that the government is determined to put its own house in order for the sake of making the programme a success. In the past the government of Zimbabwe under President Mugabe established the Sandura Commission to investigate corruption. As a result some government Ministers lost their posts. Therefore, the intention to set up yet another 'Anti-Corruption

Commission' is a normal part of the political life of Zimbabwe. It hardly qualifies as opportunism. (3) The problem is cast in terms of race categories rather than the conquered and the conqueror. Our problem with the former is that it fails to capture the historical moment and nature of the conflict, namely, conquest in an unjust war. Furthermore, it can be used to promote racism and encourage racial disharmony. (4) The land reform and resettlement programme is a compelling state interest. Against this background, the government of Zimbabwe prepared a referendum seeking the opinion of the population with regard to—among others—compulsory acquisition of land.

The referendum returned a negative result. A referendum does not have the force of law in Zimbabwe. It therefore is not binding on the government. In view of the fact that the majority of the population in Zimbabwe is illiterate, using the referendum technique is rather questionable. Since the conviction of the 'Africans' that Zimbabwe is their land remains strong and undiminished, it is doubtful that they preferred to abandon this conviction simply because it was presented to them in the form of a referendum. It is clear then that the referendum was a tactical error. First, it was presented to a populace the majority of whom simply did not understand and appreciate its significance. Second, it was a mistake to ask for a yes or no vote on the referendum as a whole. If each item were to be voted for separately and counting were also done on the basis of each item it is more than likely that the result on the land question would have been positive. As a follow up to this the legislature in Zimbabwe proposed a Bill subsequently enacted into law, the Constitution of Zimbabwe Amendment (No. 16) Act, 2000. Section 16A deals with 'Agricultural land acquired for resettlement' and, subsection 1 hereof provides as follows:

In regard to the compulsory acquisition of agricultural land for the resettlement of people in accordance with a programme of land reform, the following factors shall be regarded as of ultimate and overriding importance:
(a) under colonial domination the people of Zimbabwe were unjustifiably dispossessed of their land and other resources without compensation;

(b) the people consequently took up arms in order to regain their land and political sovereignty, and this ultimately resulted in the Independence of Zimbabwe in 1980;

(c) the people of Zimbabwe must be enabled to reassert their rights and regain ownership of their land;

and accordingly:

(i) the former colonial power has an obligation to pay compensation for agricultural land compulsorily acquired for resettlement, through a fund established for the purpose; and

(ii) if the former colonial power fails to pay compensation through such a fund, the Government of Zimbabwe has no obligation to pay compensation for agricultural land compulsorily acquired for resettlement.

According to the title of this section the main topic is the acquisition of 'agricultural land for resettlement.' Yet, the first factor, refers to the dispossession of land in the sense of the entire territory. This includes 'agricultural land.' This latter is therefore part of the whole. The reference means then that unjustified land dispossession is one of the 'ultimate and overriding' factors to be taken into account with regard to the acquisition of 'agricultural land.' The question is this: since unjustified land dispossession covered the whole land why restrict land acquisition to 'agricultural land' only? This question is reinforced by factor (b) which states expressly that according to the people, the 'ultimate and overriding' aim of the armed struggle was 'to regain their land and political sovereignty.' Thus the restoration of title to territory and the recovery of sovereignty over it were the heart and soul of the struggle for Zimbabwe. Accordingly, 'the people of Zimbabwe must be enabled to reassert their rights and regain ownership of their land.' But the Lancaster constitution did not make the realization of the basic aim of the armed struggle possible. In recognition of this the legislature in Zimbabwe has placed the onus for compensation of 'agricultural land' compulsorily acquired on 'the former colonial power,' that is, the United Kingdom. If the latter fails to pay compensation then 'the Government of Zimbabwe has no obligation to pay compensation.' By this the legislature

recognized the mistake of the Lancaster compromise Agreement. It accordingly determined to rectify this mistake by holding the former colonial power responsible for compensation. Even this is still a far cry from the exigencies of restitution and reparation being the necessary demands of historic justice. This can neither be new nor surprising. After the end of the second world war, the Adenauer government in Germany agreed to pay reparation to the Jews. The state of Israel benefitted from this agreement. The agreement bound unborn Germans. The basis for this agreement having the power to impose an obligation upon the unborn was moral and not legal. Accordingly, the Zimbabweans may assert their right to restitution and reparation.

Subsection (2) weakens and blurs the above reasoning. It reads as follows:

'In view of the overriding considerations set out in subsection (1), where agricultural land is acquired compulsorily for the resettlement of people in accordance with a programme of land reform, the following factors shall be taken into account in the assessment of any compensation that may be payable—

(a) the history of the ownership, use and occupation of the land;

(b) the price paid for the land when it was acquired;

(c) the cost or value of improvements on the land;

(d) the current use to which the land and any improvements on it are being put;

(e) any investment which the State or the acquiring authority may have made which improved or enhanced the value of the land and any improvements on it;

(f) the resources available to the acquiring authority in implementing the programme of land reform;

(g) any financial constraints that necessitate the payment of compensation in instalments over a period of time; and

(h) any other relevant factor that may be specified in an Act of Parliament.'

The basic problem with this subsection is that it concedes payment of compensation. Clearly, the legislature may not repudiate the 'obligation' to pay compensation and at the same time with regard to the same subject uphold and accept the duty to pay compensation. It is true that land dispossession was in the first place unjustified. It is also true that the loss of land and other resources by the people was not met with compensation by the former colonial power. Now what is the justification for the legislature's preparedness to consider 'the assessment of any compensation that may be payable?' This question falls off and the paradox disappears only if the legislature proceeds from the assumption that the former colonial power is willing to honour the obligation to pay compensation. In that case, the assessment of any compensation payable is legitimate since the compensation will be coming from the former colonial power and not from the people of Zimbabwe.

As the legislature was busy making laws, the people were continuing to occupy farms owned by Zimbabweans of European descent. The occupations were not without violence. In view of this unfolding situation the British government disclosed that it had a contingency plan to receive at least twenty thousand Rhodesians into the United Kingdom. Instead of helping the situation this announcement exacerbated it. First, it was ill-timed as it came at a time when Britain was tightening all screws to make asylum into the country least attractive. Second, if it is true that freedom conferred can never be revoked[99] then it is difficult to understand why Britain is concerned primarily and exclusively about the well-being of Rhodesians in Zimbabwe. What about the indigenous Zimbabweans whose farms have also been occupied? Third, Britain used ancestry as the foundation of its readiness to receive the Rhodesians back home. The Rhodesians thus hold an historic title to British nationality. In this way the United Kingdom confirmed, perhaps inadvertently, that historically the conqueror does not belong to Zimbabwe. Rhodesia was the home the conqueror established in Africa through conquest ungoverned by law, morality, and humanity.[100] This memory of the past is the underlying meaning of the readiness of the United Kingdom to receive at least twenty thousand Rhodesians. Other European Union countries, as well as Australia and New Zealand, have since declared themselves ready to receive some Rhodesians as well. But the United Kingdom is not the only country with a good memory of its history. The indigenous conquered people of Zimbabwe have an equally good memory. They also remember that Zimbabwe belongs to them from time immemorial. Ancestry is the anchor of history from which they claim title to Zimbabwe and sovereignty over it. Britain did not deal with this at Lancaster. But this did not erase it from the memory of the indigenous people of Zimbabwe.

Reparations

Conquest in an unjust war remains the basis for the argument for reparations to the indigenous Zimbabweans. According to the technical understanding of reparations, the latter would still be bound to pay reparations to the conqueror regardless of the fact that the war was unjust in the first place.[101] The argument that reparations are due only to the conqueror is no longer sustainable. Why should the conqueror receive reparations for waging an unjust war in the first place? In the case of Zimbabwe and the rest of formerly colonized Africa there is simply no basis for the argument that these peoples provided the conqueror with just cause to wage war on them. When the conqueror invaded them they acted in self-defence but were defeated. They may not therefore—in the name of reparations—be held responsible for the loss of life and material suffered by the conqueror. They owe the conqueror no reparations. In order to strengthen this argument it is important to consider the question of responsibility for reparations with regard to the bombings of Hiroshima and Nagasaki. There is something to be said for the argument that Japan was the author of its own destruction during the Second World War. Equally true is the fact that the adverse effects of the bombing of the two cities are still felt more than fifty years after the war. Who now is responsible for the betterment of the lives of the non-combatants not yet born but are currently affected by the previous bombings? Our point here is to show that the logic of reparations cuts across in two ways. Depending on the circumstances, reparations may be due to the conquered. It is not only the conqueror who is invariably entitled to reparations.

The above reasoning applies to the struggle in Zimbabwe for the reversion to unmodified and unencumbered sovereignty to the same quantum and degree as at conquest. By necessity it includes reparations to the indigenous Zimbabweans. Yet, as we have already shown, the Lancaster Agreement provided for the exact opposite. This is unsustainable because of its inherent injustice. It is precisely the perception by indigenous Africans of this kind of injustice that gradually led to the Kampala conference in April 1994 on reparations to Africa. Both conquest in an unjust war and the African slave trade formed the bases for the necessity to demand reparations. 'The consequences of both enslavement and colonization are not merely themes for plenary lectures at African Studies conventions, but also the malfunctioning colonial economies in Africa and the distorted socioeconomic relations in the African diaspora. Hence the malevolent continuities of both colonialism and racism. . . . The inspiration behind the reparations movement was not change but continuity. It was the persistence of deprivation and anguish in the black world arising directly out of the legacies of slavery and colonialism.'[102] Reparations are due to Africa as a matter of fundamental justice. The former colonial conqueror has the duty to do justice to the conquered by paying reparations. The conquered have a right to justice and the conqueror has the duty to perform. For this reason it is not up to the conqueror to change this question of right to one of privilege. If this happens then the conqueror would have been granted a blank cheque to make concessions to justice in a unilateral way. Thus doing justice to the conquered would be a matter of convenience and not compliance with duty.

Reparations are also due to Africa in order to provide 'a symbol of international and racial reconciliation for future amicable interaction.'[103] The unfolding struggle for land in Zimbabwe fits perfectly into this demand. In this sense Zimbabwe is the African pioneer engaged in the endeavour to make the demand for reparations a living reality. 'Reparations . . . serve as a cogent critique of history and thus a potent restraint on its repetition. It is not possible to ignore the example of the Jews and the obsessed commitment of survivors of the Holocaust, and their descendants, to recover both their material patrimony and the humanity of which they were brutally deprived. . . . The closeness to, or distance from, a crime whose effects are still recognizable in the

present is no argument for or against the justice of reparations . . . Justice must be made manifest either for all, or not at all.'[104]

The Search for Peace in South Africa

In the beginning the indigenous conquered people of South Africa pursued the path of peace[105] in their quest for historical justice. After an assessment of the efficacy of this path it was decided to reinforce it by resort to the use of armed force.[106] In the face of this the conqueror persisted in perfecting the means of oppression and suppression. In this regard the conqueror's South Africa received extraordinary assistance from her Western allies.[107] The declaration policy of the latter censured oppression and suppression. This did not deter these allies from according the conqueror's South Africa full and complete status of international personality. On this basis South Africa enjoyed membership of international organizations such as the United Nations including a special relationship with NATO under the auspices of SACLANT (the Supreme Allied Command in the Atlantic).[108] The declaration policy of South Africa's Western allies was on the whole far from consistent with its action policy. Juridically, the conqueror's South Africa was considered in no way defective with particular reference to title to territory and sovereignty. Precisely because of this the Act of Union in 1910, the Republican status acquired in 1961 after the dismemberment of South Africa from the Commonwealth, Bantustanization, and the 1983 constitution were all regarded as evolutionary phases of South African constitutionalism. Criticism of any of these developments was more political than juridical. The reasoning underlying the juridical view appears to be this. Conquest does not necessarily and immediately vest title to territory in the conqueror. The latter may, however, exercise immediately absolute sovereignty over the territory. Either through acquiescence[109] or lapse of time title to territory may eventually vest in the conqueror. From this moment the superior claim to their territory by the indigenous conquered peoples becomes extinguished.[110] Thus extinctive prescription eliminates the superior claim of the conquered and renders it obsolete. Accordingly, a legal prohibition is imposed upon the conquered never ever to revive their claim to territorial title and sovereignty over it.[111] At the same time this prohibition perfects the conqueror's acquisition of territory by conquest. In this way the universe of juristic facts excludes, discards and ignores a matter of natural and fundamental justice. Extinctive prescription or the statute of limitation created a specific and definite area of tension precisely by the exclusion of a matter which for the indigenous conquered peoples is a question of natural and fundamental justice. This tension is sharpened particularly by the fact that the conception of law of the indigenous conquered peoples does not recognize the statute of limitation. 'Prescription is unknown in African law. The African believes that time cannot change the truth. Just as the truth must be taken into consideration each time it becomes known, so must no obstacle be placed in the way of the search for it and its discovery. It is for this reason that judicial decisions are not authoritative. They must be able to be called into question.'[112] So it is that even at the juridical level there is a conceptual clash. This would certainly exacerbate the tension created by the exclusion of a matter of fundamental justice.

The exclusion made it relatively easy to urge, on political grounds, for the extension of democracy to the indigenous conquered people. This, so the argument continued, would be achieved through the abolition of the 1983[113] constitution and its replacement by a new constitution. It was thus predetermined in advance that the new constitution would exclude and ignore the question of the reversion of title to territory as well as the restoration of sovereignty over it. Thus the basis and parameters of transition to democracy in South Africa were laid down.[114] This was the case also with regard to the negotiations leading to the transition from Rhodesia to Zimbabwe.

The Transition to Democracy in South Africa

There were only two major parties to the negotiations leading to a new South Africa. These were the conquered people on the one side and the conqueror on the other. The former term is preferred because it is historically appropriate and at the same time avoids an ethnic perspective to the problem. It includes expressly the indigenous peoples, the Coloured people, the Indian people, and all other peoples who though not vanquished at the onset of 'discovery' and colonization, were nevertheless subjugated by the conqueror. Accordingly, the characterization of the parties as it is done here is deliberately neutral as to race; a term which continues to be almost at the centre of contemporary South African and Zimbabwean politics. Another observation we wish to make is that the claim to title to territory and sovereignty over it is far from a demand to restore honour to an attenuated prestige. It may, however, not be denied that this is a secondary. The quest for justice in the form of restoration of title to territory and sovereignty over it is primarily predicated on the premise that land is the indispensable resource[115] for the sustenance of human life.[116] The right to life[117] is inseparable from the right to land. It is the most fundamental in the sense that it is the basis for and precedes all other human rights.[118] Therefore, talk about human rights must recognize that there were human beings and human rights long, long ago before the term 'human rights' was coined.

In the 'negotiations' leading to the new South Africa there were two contending paradigms, namely, the decolonization and democratization paradigms.[119] The former speaks to the restoration of title to territory and sovereignty over it. It includes the exigency of restitution. It would bring the conqueror to renounce in principle and expressly title to South African territory and sovereignty over it. In this way sovereignty would revert to its rightful heirs. The conqueror's South Africa would be dissolved. This would then lay the basis for state succession.[120] The legal consequences flowing from total state succession[121] or the Nyerere doctrine[122] (the clean slate doctrine) would then follow. By its nature then the decolonization paradigm is contrary to and inconsistent with the conqueror's claims pertaining to extinctive prescription. By contrast, the democratization paradigm conforms to and is consistent with the conqueror's claims concerning extinctive prescription. It proceeds from the premise that given the evolutionary character of constitutionalism in South Africa, the major weakness of the 1983 constitution consists in the exclusion of the indigenous conquered peoples. Therefore, democracy will be achieved through the inclusion of the latter in the new constitution. In this way non-racialism would be one of the hallmarks of the new constitutional dispensation. In its determination to achieve victory over apartheid, the democratization paradigm lost sight of the fact that the land question was a basic issue[123] long, long before apartheid was born. Despite this oversight, democratization won the day and so the question of title to territory and sovereignty over it did not become an integral part of the 'negotiations' agenda.

In these circumstances it was relatively easy for the conqueror to realize the resolve to defend and consolidate all the benefits resulting from extinctive prescription. To this end the conqueror argued for the abolition of the principle of the sovereignty of parliament. This was rather odd since the sovereignty of parliament was a basic constitutional principle[124] in South Africa for as long as the conqueror held sole and exclusive political power. This principle did not become suddenly inadequate. Instead, the conqueror feared that the indisputable numerical majority of the conquered people would probably abuse the principle. To avert this abuse abolition was considered the best solution. The conqueror's fear was based on the experience of its own abuse of this principle. It was pertinently observed in this connection that: 'Several modern critics of the South African constitution have argued cogently that the foundation fathers of the Union created the wrong sort of constitution for this sort of country, urging that greater decentralization (. . .) plus the incorporation in the written constitution of a bill of rights enforceable by a more independent judiciary endowed with testing power, all established on a much broader basis of popular consent, would have made it a more acceptable and enduring document. With these opinions we need not quarrel. The absence of safeguards of this sort resulted in the attribution of supremacy to a legislature which is not and never has been thoroughly representative, and which has since shown a disposition to use that supremacy with singular lack of restraint.'[125]

In an effort to win the support of the numerical majority population in the country, the conqueror appealed to *ubuntu*[126] and used it tactfully to remove the causes of its own fear. Here it is important to understand that the majority of the South African population continues to be nurtured and educated according to the basic tenets of *ubuntu*, notwithstanding the selective amnesia of a small segment of the indigenous elite. For example, *ubuntu* was included in the interim constitution to justify the necessity for the Truth and Reconciliation Commission.[127] Yet, the necessity for the Truth and Reconciliation Commission cannot be said to be the expression of the will of the conquered people of South Africa. This is because the necessity was a unilateral decision by the political leadership of the conquered people. The people themselves were not consulted, by way of a referendum, for example. From this point of view the decision was democratic and, therefore, it was not the execution of the will of the conquered. This is in sharp contrast to the leadership of former President De Klerk who in the heat of the 'negotiations' leading to the 'new' South Africa fielded a referendum exclusively to the conqueror in order to obtain a fresh mandate for specific items to be negotiated. So the appeal to *ubuntu* is hardly convincing especially because the term was excluded from the final constitution. Why? *Ubuntu* was again invoked by the Constitutional Court delivering the judgment that capital punishment is unconstitutional.[128] With respect, the invocation of *ubuntu* in this case was *obiter dictum* as the same conclusion could have been reached without recourse to *ubuntu*. Knowing why and how the death sentence affected mainly the conquered people in the past, the conqueror once again was driven by fear in opting for the abolition of the death sentence. These transparent tactics apart, it is curious that the final Constitution should remain completely silent about *ubuntu*. If a constitution is at bottom the casting into legal language of the moral and political convictions of a people then the mere translation of Westminster and Roman Law legal paradigms into the vernacular languages of the indigenous conquered people is not equal to the constitutional embodiment of their moral and political convictions. There is no a priori reason why *ubuntu* should not be the basic philosophy for constitutional democracy in South Africa.

Contrary to its rejection of this in the past, the conqueror now urged for the Constitution as the basic law of the country. The essence of the argument here is that the Constitution as the basic and supreme law of the country shall be above the law-making power vested in parliament. The laws enacted by parliament shall, in principle, always be subject to their conformity and consistency with the Constitution. Parliament would therefore be the prisoner of the Constitution whose principles[129] possessed the character of essentiality[130] and immutability. What then is the meaning of popular sovereignty in the form of representative parliamentary democracy? Without attempting to answer this question it is clear that the option for Constitutional supremacy by the conqueror was not simply a matter of juridical considerations. The cumulative result of the conqueror's arguments and tactics is that the democratization paradigm carried the day. Its success was in fact the victory of extinctive prescription. Thus the injustice of conquest ungoverned by law, morality, and humanity was constitutionalized. This constitutionalization of injustice places the final Constitution on a precarious footing because of its failure to respond to the exigencies of natural and fundamental justice due to the indigenous conquered people. But the constitutionalization of an injustice carries within itself the demand for justice. Accordingly, the reversion of title to territory and the restoration of sovereignty over it did not die at the birth of the new Constitution for South Africa.

Molato Ga O Bole: Challenging Extinctive Prescription

The paradox of democratization and independence in both South Africa and Zimbabwe is that the compromises that the political representatives of the conquered peoples made are philosophically and materially inconsistent with their people's understanding of historical justice. Philosophically, the peoples hold that *molato ga o bole*, that is, extinctive prescription, is untenable in the African understanding of law. Until and unless equilibrium is restored through the restoration of title to territory and the reversion of sovereignty over it even the best constitution would be fragile for lack of homegrown credentials.[131] Landlessness resulting from the arbitrary definition of truth

and justice according to the meridien line is the immediate material effect of this clash at the philosophical level. In terms of immediacy therefore it is understandable to urge for the redefinition of property and land reform.[132] But these are manifestations of the fundamental problem of the restoration of title to territory and the reversion of absolute sovereignty over it.[133] That 'in general the doctrine of reversion to sovereignty does not apply to sub-Saharan Africa' is an untenable thesis. The authority upon which the learned author relies for this thesis is burdened with an unmistakably cursory and superficial knowledge of African history. Nonetheless, he proceeds from such knowledge to draw sweeping conclusions about unspecified 'African Rulers' and 'African Chieftains.' It is also crystal clear that the authority is committed to the untenable view that because Western Europe had a supposedly superior civilization it therefore had the right to colonize.[134] The thesis that the reversion to sovereignty is neither relevant nor applicable to sub-Saharan Africa is philosophically untenable and historically empty. It is therefore submitted that the restoration of title to territory and the reversion of sovereignty over it is the basic problem.

It is still problematical that even in this second phase the government of Zimbabwe continues to deal with this problem as a matter of conflict of rights in the sphere of private property rights. This has led the government to enact a new law permitting land acquisition without compensation. Critics of this law argue that the legislature decided on this enactment contrary to the result of the referendum. What the critics omit to mention is that according to the law of the land, a referendum has got no legal force. Whatever the result it is not legally binding on the government. And the government is not necessarily the legislature. In addition, the critics fail to appreciate the fact that the majority of the indigenous conquered people in Zimbabwe are illiterate especially with their lack of understanding of the dominant epistemological paradigm of the conqueror. Against this background, it is not difficult to see that the very idea of a referendum was essentially a tactical blunder since its import could not be properly appreciated. Another blunder was at the scientific level. It was inappropriate to seek a vote on the referendum as a whole without at the same time determining that the counting will be on each issue separately. Alternatively, the people should have been asked to cast multiple votes by way of giving an answer to each item on the referendum. Since neither of these was pursued, it is fair to conclude that scientifically the referendum contained fatal flaws. No wonder then that the people went ahead and occupied land as though there never was a referendum. The critics of the government argue that such occupation is in violation of the human rights of the land 'owners.' It is important to determine if the critics belong historically to the category of the conquered or the conqueror. On the basis of such a determination it is worth reminding the critics that long before the coinage of the term 'human rights' there were human beings and these were surely not without rights. Did the conqueror show respect for any of these rights when lawlessness, lack of morality, and inhumanity were the main features of the original conquest leading to the acquisition of territory beyond the meridian line? The British government has not made matters easy by announcing the existence of an emergency plan to receive about 20 000 Rhodesians back into the United Kingdom. No doubt this announcement is tantamount to the British government's admission that there are Rhodesians in Zimbabwe who have a claim to British nationality by right of ancestry. Ironically, it is precisely the right of ancestry upon which the indigenous conquered peoples of Zimbabwe rely to urge for the exigencies of historical justice. Both the Zimbabwean government's approach and the British government's reaction to it exacerbate the conflict. But even without this it is clear, at least for those like the present writer who took time to be in the midst of the so-called ordinary people in both Zimbabwe and South Africa, that people have finally decided to go their own way to solve the problem. Following their conversations in public transport, under the tree talk, in amusement centres and private homes, there is no doubt that people argue for title to territory and sovereignty over it. This boils down to nothing less than reversion to unencumbered and unmodified sovereignty to the same quantum and degree lost at conquest ungoverned by law, morality, and humanity. It must be stated in fairness to the Patriotic Front that on this point it was long, long ago at one with the peoples. 'The Patriotic Front

relinquished under pressure many of its fundamental tenets during the conference. . . . As the government of Zimbabwe, it must operate under a constitution not entirely of its own choosing.'[135] There is evidence that both the Pan Africanist Congress and the Azanian People's Organization of South Africa concur with the peoples on this point. Unlike, the Patriotic Front, the Pan Africanist Congress did not pursue this point at the 'negotiations.' Despite its non-participation in the 'negotiations,' the Azanian People's Organization did not—even in its campaign at the last general elections—present title to territory in its election manifesto. As the political leadership in both countries continues to pursue the resolution of this conflict within the narrow and untenable epistemological paradigm of the conqueror, their peoples chartered their own route through the *matyotyombe* phenomenon which is common to both South Africa and Zimbabwe. (*Matyotyombe* is a Xhosa term that refers to a complex combination of dirt, despondency, miserability, poverty as well as unacceptable exposure to very serious health risks. In short, it refers to a condition unfit for human habitation but human beings nonetheless find themselves in that condition.) The option for *matyotyombe* is a radical questioning of the juridical epistemology of the conqueror. It is a rejection of a situation of basic injustice protected by a constitution without homegrown credentials. It is the refusal to grant such a constitution the power to preempt, proscribe, and nullify the exigencies of justice due to the conquered people.

The Reversion to Unencumbered and Unmodified Sovereignty

For the conquered people 'democratization' or independence would be incomplete and meaningless if it excluded the reversion to unencumbered and unmodified sovereignty to the same quantum and degree as was lost at conquest ungoverned by law, morality, and humanity. *Matyotyombe* is the people's expression of this: a guide to the political leadership. It is a Xhosa word designating conditions of squalor. It is descriptive of a situation of extreme poverty, dirt, and moral degradation. It signifies conditions unbefitting to human habitation and derogatory of human dignity. Concretely, this refers to houses, shacks built of ordinary plastic wood, corrugated iron, mud or even bricks. The size and structure of these edifices reflect anything but a home. Safety for the dwellers is, to say the least, lowest.

The problem with *matyotyombe* is that they proliferate relentlessly in all directions. These penetrate any area and freely fix themselves. They even fix themselves on no man's land which subsequently turns out to be another's 'private property.' The latter then defines *matyotyombe* dwellers as squatters. Both the legality and the justice of the claimant's right to 'private property' are assumed to be valid even for the so-called squatters. The injured party then seeks a remedy through the courts. The latter invariably hand down eviction orders. These evoke defiance instead of obedience from the dwellers. The reason for this may be found in the Sotho term for the same *matyotyombe*, namely, *baipei*. The latter is descriptive of people who have fixed and settled themselves into a particular place. The idea of being fixed to a place in the sense of belonging to it as of right underlies the meaning of *moipei* being the singular of *baipei*. *Baipei* does not fix themselves at any place as though they are in search of any space: a void without any history. *Baipei* assert their right to a place and not a space and the whole of South Africa is this place because it is 'space which has historical meaning, where some things have happened which are now remembered and which provide continuity and identity across generations. Place is space in which important words have been spoken and which have established identity, defined vocation and envisioned destiny . . . a yearning for a place is a decision to enter history with an identifiable people in an identifiable pilgrimage.'[136] The pilgrimage for the restoration of title to territory and the reversion of unencumbered and unmodified sovereignty over it is spearheaded by the *baipei*. Slowly the government of Zimbabwe has joined this pilgrimage of the people. It needs, however, to rid itself of the burden of dominance by the juridical paradigm of the conqueror especially with regard to the putative eternity and immutability of 'property rights.' With particular reference to both rural and urban land both the governments and the courts

of Zimbabwe and South Africa must, at the very minimum, recognize and accept together with the Catholic Bishops' Conference of Brazil that: 'The right to make use of urban land to guarantee adequate housing is one of the primary conditions for creating a life that is authentically human. Therefore when land occupations—or even land invasions—occur, legal judgments on property titles must begin with the right of all to adequate housing. All claims to private ownership must take second place to this basic need. . . . We conclude that the natural right to housing has priority over the law that governs land appropriation. A legal title to property can hardly be an absolute in the face of the human need of people who have nowhere to make their home.'[137]

Conclusion: Towards a Post-Conquest South Africa and Zimbabwe

We have shown that conquest ungoverned by law, morality, or humanity is the original basis for the conqueror's claim to title to territory by appeal to extinctive prescription. Such a claim is, from the point of view of the conquered, untenable even if one were to appeal to Papal mandate, discovery or the mission to civilize. The posterity of the original conqueror is therefore not the legal successor in title to absolute sovereignty. Extinctive prescription is inconsistent with the legal philosophy of the indigenous conquered people. It is also contrary to natural and fundamental justice. Accordingly, the restoration of title to territory and the reversion of unencumbered and unmodified sovereignty to the same quantum and degree as at conquest remains the basic demand of justice due to the indigenous conquered people. This includes the exigencies of restitution and reparations. The restoration of title to territory and the reversion of sovereignty as already indicated constitute the inescapable basis for a post-conquest South Africa and Zimbabwe.

Primarily for the convenience of the conqueror, apartheid was presented as the main problem in South Africa. By the time apartheid appeared in 1948, title to territory and sovereignty over it had established itself as the main problem in the country at least two and a half centuries back.

The elimination of apartheid solved the problem only by conferring limping sovereignty over the indigenous conquered peoples. The elimination of apartheid is not an answer to the question of the reversion of unencumbered and unmodified sovereignty to the same quantum and degree of sovereignty as was lost at conquest ungoverned by law, morality, or humanity. The transition to Zimbabwe also conferred limping sovereignty to the indigenous conquered people of the country in the same was as in South Africa. Thus a post-conquest South Africa and Zimbabwe is yet to be born in the form of a veritable state succession rather than government succession as it is at present the case in both countries. To argue otherwise is to condone the questionable maxim that *ex injuria ius oritur*. State succession must ensue with the express and unequivocal declaration by the conqueror renouncing sovereignty over territory. This is inescapably necessary in order to dissolve the categories of conquered and conqueror. But the dissolution does not create automatically equality of condition in material terms. For this reason restitution and reparation arise as distinct necessities of historical justice. If this is a novelty in international law, there surely is nothing to suggest that the corpus of this law is comprehensive, exhaustive, and definitive. The ordinary consequences of state succession must follow thereby delivering the conquered of the burdens which they neither created nor benefited from. This would create space to work out a homegrown post-conquest constitution. Restitution and reparation must be counted among the basic pillars of the post-conquest constitution. Instead of taking up the offer to return to Britain or other ancestral homelands, the former conqueror under the guise of a citizen second to none could be part of this constitution-making. A post-conquest constitution for South Africa and Zimbabwe—indeed for the rest of formerly colonized and enslaved Africa—would be predicated on the necessity to rectify the injustice of the past. Justice as equilibrium would, on this basis, appear to be an acceptable premise of constitution-making. Remove the element of responsibility then justice as experience and concept becomes totally devoid of meaning. Therefore, 'reparations . . . as a structure of memory and critique, may be regarded as a necessity for the credibility of Eurocentric historicism, and a corrective for its exclusionist world-view . . . what really would be preposterous or ethically inadmissible in imposing a general levy on South Africa's white population?'[138] This measure of restitution surely applies to Zimbabwe and seems a better option to the current land acquisition process. It is salutary to note that many academics from within the ranks of the conqueror have already raised the possibility of wealth tax. Prominent among them is the Stellenbosch University academic Professor Sampie Terblanche whose testimony to the Truth and Reconciliation Commission on the question of wealth tax deserves much more than a cursory study.

Notes

1. Hume, D., 'Of national characters,' in F. N. Norton and R. H. Popkin, eds., *David Hume, philosophical historian*, New York. The Bobbs-Merrill Company, 1965.
2. McMillan, Carol, *Women, reason and nature*, Oxford: Basil Blackwell Publisher, 1982.
3. Lange, Lynda, 'Woman is not a rational animal,' in Sandra Harding and M. B. Hintikka, eds., *Discovering reality*, Dordrecht: Reidel Publishers, 1983:1–15.
4. Hanke, L., *Aristotle and the American Indians*, Chicago: Henry Rugnery Co., 1959:ix.
5. Mudimbe, V. I., *The invention of Africa*, Indiana University Press: Bloomington, 1988.
6. Williams, R. A., *The American Indian in Western legal thought: The discourses of conquest*, Oxford: Oxford University Press, 1990.
7. Dussel, E., *Philosophy of liberation*, Tr. Aquilina and Christine Morkovsky, New York: Orbis Books, Maryknoll, 1985:3.
8. Popkin, R. H., 'The philosophical bases of modern racism,' in C. Walton and J. P. Anton, eds., *Philosophy and the civilizing arts*, Athens: Ohio University Press, 1974:128–129.
9. Hegel, G. W. F., *Lectures on the philosophy of world history*, Tr. H. B. Nisbert, Cambridge: Cambridge University Press, 1975:190.
10. Schmitt, C., 'The land appropriation of a new world,' *Telos*, 109, Fall 1996:30.
11. Gilson, E., *God and philosophy*, New Haven: Yale University Press, 1941:141.
12. Ruether, Rosemary, 'The collision of history and doctrine: The brothers of Jesus and the virginity of Mary,' *Continuum*, 7(1) 1969:94–96.
13. Novak, A. J., 'The virgin birth: ad Ruether,' *Continuum*, 7(3) 1969:443–452.
14. Ware, R. C., 'The resurrection of Jesus, II: Historical-critical studies,' *The Heythrop Journal*, xvi(2) April 1975:177.

15. Ware, R. C., 'The resurrection of Jesus, I: Theological orientations,' *The Heythrop Journal,* xvi(1) January 1975:26–27.

16. Thomas Aquinas, *Summa Theologiae,* 2a2ae, 40, 1.

17. Ramose, M. B., 'Only the sovereign may declare war and NATO too,' *Studia Moralia,* 38, 2000.

18. Russell, F. H., *The just war in the Middle Ages,* Cambridge: Cambridge University Press, 1975:258–291.

19. Steenbergen Van, F., 'The reading and study of St Thomas,' *Theology Digest,* iv(3), 1956:166–169.

20. That 'limited nuclear war' is a military illusion is a point that requires no special pleading. It is copiously documented. Again, the rationality of nuclear weapons lies precisely and only in their non-use. Accordingly, any use of these weapons will overstep the bounds of rationality. This is the essence of the well-documented rationality of the irrationality argument. Nuclear war would be irrational because it would defeat all the aims pursued by such warfare. A war that guarantees that there will be no survivers can hardly claim to be a defensive war. Yet, in answer to the following question: is the threat or use of nuclear weapons in any circumstances permitted under international law?, the International Court of Justice held as follows. 'There is in neither customary nor conventional international law any specific authorization of the threat or use of nuclear weapons; There is in neither customary nor conventional international law any comprehensive and universal prohibition of the threat or use of nuclear weapons as such; A threat or use of force by means of nuclear weapons that is contrary to Article 2, paragraph 4, of the United Nations Charter and that fails to meet all the requirements of Article 51, is unlawful; A threat or use of nuclear weapons would be compatible with the requirements of the international law applicable in armed conflict, particularly those of the principles and rules of international humanitarian law, as well as with specific obligations under treaties and other undertakings which expressly deal with nuclear weapons; It follows from the above-mentioned requirements that the threat or use of nuclear weapons would generally be contrary to the rules of international law applicable in armed conflict, and in particular the principles and rules of humanitarian law; However, in view of the current state of international law, and of the elements of fact at its disposal, the Court cannot conclude definitively whether the threat or use of nuclear weapons would be lawful or unlawful in an extreme circumstance of self-defence, in which the very survival of a State would be at stake; There exists an obligation to pursue in good faith and bring to a conclusion negotiations leading to nuclear disarmament in all its aspects under strict and effective international control.' Quoted from Burroughs, J., *The legality of threat or use of nuclear weapons,* Munster: LIT, 1997:21–22.

21. For an extended discussion of this topic see, Ramose, M. B., *The legalistic character of power in international relations: A philosophical essay on the ethics of defence in the nuclear age,* unpublished Doctoral dissertation presented to the Catholic University of Leuven (KUL), Leuven, Belgium, 1983.

22. Mangan, J. T., 'An historical analysis of the principle of the double effect,' *Theological Studies,* x(1) 1949:42.

23. Schmitt, C., 'The land appropriation of a new world,' *Telos* 109, Fall 1996:36–37.

24. Troup, F., *South Africa,* Harmondsworth, Middlesex, England: Penguin Books Ltd., 1975:33 and 53.

25. Mason, P., *The birth of a dilemma: The conquest and settlement of Rhodesia.* Oxford: Oxford University Press, 1958.

    Palley, Claire, *The constitutional history and law of Southern Rhodesia 1888–1965,* Oxford: Clarendon Press, 1966. It is significant that the first chapter of this book deals primarily with the drawing of lines by and among the European powers with regard to the demarcation of their respective 'spheres of influence.' The latter was the exclusive zone of the particular European claimant. In the second place we read about 'land purchase arrangements with local chiefs' as though the chiefs had put their land to sale out of goodwill. Almost nothing is said about why and how the conqueror finally had access to the chief. It is instructive though to compare the so-called land purchase arrangements with local chiefs with what transpired in the acquisition from the indigenous Indians of United States and Canadian territory by the conqueror from Europe. See in this connection:

    Lysyk, K., 'The Indian title question in Canada: An appraisal in the light of Calder,' *La Revue du Bureau Canadien,* LI, 1973:450–480.

    Calder, V. et al. 'Attorney-General of British Columbia 34 D.L.R. (3rd) 1973.

    Uzoigwe, G. N., *Britain and the conquest of Africa: The age of Salisbury,* Ann Arbor: University of Michigan Press, 1974.

    Quinn, D. B., *England and the discovery of America 1481–1620,* New York: Alfred A. Knopf, 1974.

26. Van Kleffens, E. N., 'Sovereignty and international law,' *Recueil de Cours,* 82, 1953:11–12.

27. This is intended solely as an example. It is not an argument from authority. As such it is not intended to suggest that since god does draw lines the creatures of this god have no other choice but to do the same.

28. Thompson, Janna, 'Land rights and Aboriginal sovereignty,' *Australian Journal of Philosophy,* 68(3) 1990:316.

29. The 'Donation of Constantine' is a vital ingredient in the papal struggle to extricate itself from the respublica Romana. Although the document is widely regarded as a forgery and a fraud, it played a significant role and perhaps even a decisive one in emancipating the papacy from the respublica Romana. It also assisted the papacy to lay claim to supreme authority in Latin Christendom. Since the detailed history relating to these questions is outside the scope of the present essay, we direct the interested reader to the following:

    Ullman, W., *The growth of papal government in the Middle Ages,* London: Methuen, 1955:75–83.

McIlwain, C. H., *The growth of political thought in the West*, New York: Macmillan, 1932:270–271.

Carlyle, R. E. and Carlyle, A. J., 'A history of medieval political theory in the West,' vol. 1, Edinburg & London: William Blackwood and Sons Ltd, mcmlxii, 158.

Spenyt, H., *The sovereign and its competitors*, Princeton, New Jersey: Princeton University Press, 1994:45.

30. Here we refer specifically to Matthew xvi, 18–19. Without any attempt at an exegetical exposition of this verse, we suggest that these words mean that Peter's authority to rule the Christian commonwealth is derived directly and immediately from Christ who is god. Therefore, Peter-pope may not be judged by anyone on earth *(papa a nemine judicetur)*. This claim notwithstanding, the problem of succession to Peter arose. The core of the problem was the argument that since the very words of Christ were addressed directly and specifically to Peter, the Petrine Commission ceased with the death of Peter. Consequently, the successors of Peter were not entitled to the authority contained in the commission. Moreover, Peter himself had not provided for the transfer of his authority. The document known as the 'Epistola Clementis' purports to answer this argument. For a detailed treatment of this see:

Ullman, W., *The church and the law in the Middle Ages*, London: Variorum Reprints, 1975:295–317.

31. Williams, R. A., *The American Indian in Western legal thought: The discourses of conquest*. Oxford University Press, 1990:67.

32. Mudimbe, V. I., 'African gnosis, philosophy and the order of knowledge: An introduction,' *African Studies Review*, 28(2/3) 1985:151–153.

33. Mudimbe, V. I., *The invention of Africa*, Bloomington and Indianapolis: Indiana University Press, 1988:45.

34. It is important to note that in March 2000 Pope John-Paul II openly and publicly asked for forgiveness for such abuses by the Roman Catholic Church. The apology could certainly have been more specific. At the same time it is curious that in asking for forgiveness the Pope mentioned nothing about the Church's readiness to consider restitution and reparation. Yet, it is customary in the Catholic Church that at confession absolution is accompanied by some burden in the form of three Hail Marys, for example, or Our Father once. Surely, redemption by Christ does not mean reconciliation and forgiveness eliminating freedom and, therefore, absolving all human of the responsibility to choose either eternal bliss or condemnation.

35. Hanke, L., 'Pope Paul III and the American Indians,' *Harvard Theological Review*, xxx 1937:71–72.

36. The designation, 'first/third world' clearly preserves the hierarchy of superior and inferior. At the same time it is not necessarily free of racism. A pertinent agreement in this connection reads as follows: 'by 1648 there was ample evidence that civilization was rapidly supplanting Christianity as standard of moral assessment of non-Christian states. This continued to be the case long after Christianity had ceased to be a relevant factor in international relations, with a hard residue of Augustinian exclusiveness and Aristotelean superiority surviving in the attitudes of European powers towards political communities encountered in their expansion overseas. This was partly reflected in the terms contained in so-called capitulation treaties. The same mentality was epitomised in the treaty relationship between European colonial powers and African tribal chiefs, who were refused recognition as subjects of international law. It survived the termination of the colonial, mandate and trusteeship systems in the second half of the twentieth century to resurface in the form of growing racial prejudice against those originating in the former 'uncivilised' fringe. In our days, lurking behind an outward benevolence, it is manifested in a generally condescending attitude towards what we are now pleased to call the "underdeveloped countries" or, relegating it instinctively to the bottom of the scale, the "third world."'

Parkinson, F., *The philosophy of international relations*, Beverly Hills, London: Sage Publications, 1977: 24–25.

37. McMahon, M. M., *Conquest and modern international law: The legal limitations on the acquisition of territory by conquest*, Washington: The Catholic University of America Press, 1940:44.

38. Blum, Y. Z., *Historic titles in international law*, The Hague: Martinus Nijhoff, 1965:4.

39. McMahon, M. M., *Conquest and modern international law*, 1940:8.

40. MacGibbon, I. C., 'The scope of acquiescence in international law,' *The British Year Book of International Law*, 1954:143.

41. Waldron, J., 'Superseding historic injustice,' *Ethics*, 103 October 1992:15.

42. Cattan, H., *Palestine and international law: The legal aspects of the Arab-Israeli conflict*, London: Longman Group Ltd., 1976:110.

43. Hyde, C. C., 'Conquest today,' *American Journal of International Law*, 30 1936:471.

44. Schwarzenberger, G., 'Title to territory: Response to a challenge,' *American Journal of International Law*, 51 1957:314.

45. Fisch, J., 'Africa as terra nullias: The Berlin Conference and international law,' in S. Forster, W. J. Mommsen, and R. Robinson, eds., *Bismarck, Europe and Africa: The German Historical Institute* London: Oxford University Press, 1988:347–375.

Wesseling, H. L., 'The Berlin Conference and the expansion of Europe: A conclusion, S. Forster et al., op cit. 1988:528–540.

46. Robinson, R., 'The Conference in Berlin and the future in Africa, 1884–1885,' S. Forster et al., op. cit. 1988: 1–32.

47. De Courcel, G., 'The Berlin Act of 26 February 1885,' S. Forster et al., op. cit. 1988:247–261.

48. Gann, L. H., 'The Berlin Conference and the humanitarian conscience,' S. Forster, et al., op cit. 1988:321–331.

49. Uzoigwe, G. N., 'The results of the Berlin West Africa Conference: An assessment,' S. Forster et al., 1988:542.

50. Memory is what urged the Jewish people to insist that historical justice demands that the state of Israel be established. This happened finally in May 1948. Similarly, after more than six hundred years the memory of the two main ethnic groups in Kosovo impels each group to claim sovereignty and title to Kosovar territory. This has led to several bloody struggles. One of them led to the bombardment of Belgrade by NATO. Despite the heavy heat and suffocating smoke of the bombs, the struggle for title to Kosovar territory continues as though NATO never dropped a single bomb. Memory also led to the war for the Falkland Islands (Malvinas) between Argentina and the United Kingdom. The latter conceding China's memory and claim to historical justice eventually recognized Chinese title and sovereignty over Hong Kong. On the basis of these few examples, it surely cannot be seriously argued that the indigenous conquered peoples of South Africa and Zimbabwe are incapable of remembering their history. Accordingly, their memory urging them to insist that historical justice demands the return of the land to its rightful owners and the restoration of their sovereignty over it may not be regarded as either irrational or exceptional. Yet, sustained efforts continue to be made to ensure that these demands of historical justice are eternally erased from the memory of the indigenous conquered peoples of Zimbabwe and South Africa. For this reason academic and by no means disinterested South African historiography remains committed to challenging the validity of the more than obvious veracity of the proposition that there are to this day identifiable original and, therefore, rightful owners of the territory on the one hand and those who are the beneficiaries of conquest on the other. This debate apart, conquest in the colonization of South Africa finds memorable expression in the following. 'The Khoikhoi sued for peace, and tried to regain rights to their pastures, "standing upon it that we (the Dutch) had gradually been taking more and more of their land, which had been theirs since the beginning of time . . . Asking also, whether if they came to Holland, they would be permitted to do the like." The Commander argued that if their land were restored there would not be enough grazing for both nations. The Khoikhoi replied "Have we then no cause to prevent you from getting more cattle? The more you have the more lands you will occupy. And to say the land is not big enough for both, who should give way, the rightful owner or the foreign invader?" Van Riebeeck made it clear "that they had now lost the land in war and therefore could only expect to be henceforth deprived of it. . . . The country had thus fallen to our lot, being justly won in defensive warfare and . . . it was our intention to retain it.' Quoted from Troup, Freda, *South Africa*, Harmondsworth, Middlesex, England: Penguin Books Ltd., 1975:33 and 53. To date the beneficiaries of this conquest have reaffirmed the intention to retain the land and never return it to its rightful owners. The same beneficiaries persist in the argument that the Bantu-speaking peoples have no just title to the territory since they have taken it away from the Khoisan. This argument is based on a mistaken understanding of the meaning of 'indigenous conquered peoples of South Africa.' It is clearly the conqueror's one-sided and self-interested misrepresentation of the history of South Africa. Even if the Bantu-speaking peoples of South Africa might have taken the land from the Khoisan it does not follow that two wrongs make a right. If the Khoisan have been conquered in an unjust war, it is essential that they themselves should say so and declare their solution. Any other interest party purporting to act in their name must show why and what interest they have in the matter. They must also prove that they act on the express request of the Khoisan.

51. Emerson, R., 'Self-determination,' *American Journal of International Law*, 65(3) July 1971:465.

52. Shaw, M., *Title to territory in Africa*. Oxford: Clarendon Press, 1986:23.

53. Marek, Krystyna, *Identity and continuity of states in public international law*, Geneve: Librairie Droz, 1968:127–128.

54. Mason, P., *The birth of a dilemma: The conquest and settlement of Rhodesia*, Oxford: Oxford University Press, 1958:209–210.

55. Devine, D. J., 'The status of Rhodesia in international law,' *Acta Juridica*, 1974:111.

56. Kirkman, W. P., 'The Rhodesian referendum: The significance of 20 June 1969,' *International Affairs*, 45(4) October 1969:648.

57. McDougal, M. S. and Reisman, W. M., 'Rhodesia and the United Nations: The lawfulness of international concern,' *The American Journal of International Law*, 62, 1968:10–11.

58. It is significant that the Zimbabwean novelist, Vambe, in his novel, *An ill-fated people*, uses the expression, 'the conquered people' with reference to the indigenous Zimbabweans at least more than twenty times.

59. Harris, P. B., 'The failure of a "Constitution": The Whaley Report, Rhodesia 1968,' *International Affairs*, 45(2) April 1969:235.

60. Devine, D. J., 'The status of Rhodesia in international law,' *Acta Juridica* 1974:111.

61. Davidow, J. A., *Peace in Southern Africa: The Lancaster House conference on Rhodesia*, Cambridge, Massachusetts: Harvard Law School, 1990:56.

62. Commenting on the imposition of a similar solution by the British government on Kenya, Makonnen argued appositely that: 'Kenya paid compensation for land reacquired from the "alien" land holders . . . the British Government provided Kenya with loans from its own sources and also from the World bank, in order to finance the compensation for the transferred alien property, which amounted in fact to outright repurchasing of Kenya by the Kenyans.' Makonnen, Y., *International law and the New States of Africa*, 1983:363–364.

63. Mandaza, I., 'Reconciliation and social justice in Southern Africa: The Zimbabwe experience,' in M. W. Makgoba, ed., *African Renaissance*, Mafube: Tafelberg, 1999:90.

64. Our understanding of title to territory is that the concept is much more than a reference to a geographically identifiable entity. It includes the people who may be defined as the sovereign. Such a definition must take into account, especially, the historical basis of the right to sovereignty. 'Territory is, of course, itself a geographical conception relating to physical areas of the globe, but its centrality in law derives from the fact that it constitutes the tangible framework for the manifestation of power by the accepted authorities of the State in question. The principle whereby such a State is deemed to exercise exclusive power over its territory can be seen as a fundamental axiom of classical international law. Territory therefore plays not only a definitional role, but a constitutive one historically as well. It is the link between a people, its identity as a State, and its international role.'
Shaw, M., *Title to territory in Africa*, London: Clarendon Press, 1986:1–3.

65. Consonant with the ideology that the meridian line decides the truth and defines justice it was claimed that the West had the sole and exclusive right to colonize. The basis for this claim was that only the West had a superior civilization. The supposed exclusive right of the West to colonize denied in advance that the peoples of Africa could have sovereignty over territory to which they held title. Accordingly, the question of the reversion of unencumbered and unmodified sovereignty to Africa as at precolonization was held not to arise. It is unnecessary to argue the ignorance about African history on the part of the proponents of this thesis. Suffice it to state that the thesis is philosophically untenable and historically empty. Among the proponents of this thesis are:
Alexandrowicz, C. H., 'New and original states: The issue of reversion to sovereignty,' *International Affairs*, 45(3) July 1969:471–473.
Devine, D. J., 'The status of Rhodesia in international law,' *Acta Juridica* 1979:403.

66. UNGAR 3348 (xxix) 1974.

67. Donnelly, J., *The concept of human rights*, London/Sydney: Croom Helm, 1985:3.

68. *Rerum Novarum*, pars. 10 and 35. To be read in conjunction with par. 43 of *Mater et Magistra* and pars. 9 and 11 of *Pacem in Terris* in D. J. O'Brien and T. A. Shannon, eds. *Catholic Social Thought*, New York: Orbis Books, Maryknoll, 1995.

69. Donnelly, J., *The concept of human rights*, 1985:13.

70. Waldron, J., *The right to private property*, Oxford: Clarendon Press, 1983:103.

71. Fanon, F., *The wretched of the earth*, Tr. C. Farrington, Harmondsworth, Middlsex, England: Penguin Books Ltd., 1965:34.

72. Sullivan, S. J., *Killing in defense of private property*, Montana: Scholars Press, 1976.

73. Beach, D. N., '"Chimurenga": The Shona rising of 1896–97,' in G. Maddox, and T. K. Welliver, eds. *Colonialism and nationalism in Africa*, New York & London: Garland Publishing, Inc., 1993:395–420.

74. This point is expressed in the following legal language. 'As far as international law is concerned, there can be no doubt that a mother state is competent to grant independence to a colony or other dependency or to a part of the territory. There can be no doubt that the United Kingdom claims to be such a mother state exercising sovereignty over Rhodesia. This claim to sovereignty over Rhodesia is recognized by practically all other states. It cannot, therefore, be doubted that the United Kingdom has the competence to grant independence to Rhodesia. Were such a grant to be made, other states need not necessarily recognize Rhodesian independence.'
Devine, D. J., 'The status of Rhodesia in international law,' *Acta Juridica*, 1979:352.

75. Devine, D. J., 'The status of Rhodesia in international law,' *Acta Juridica*, 1973:144.

76. The author cited here does not problematize the 'right of conquest.' Instead it is relegated to the sphere of 'moral considerations.' These are supposed to be irrelevant to law because they do not have the status of juristic facts. The 'right of conquest,' on the other hand, is a juristic fact cognizable by law regardless of its moral propriety. Here we part ways with the law. Our point is that all juristic facts have a minimum content of morality even if this might be ignored by the law. The criteria, if any, by which the law elevates 'natural facts' to the status of juristic facts are, at the very minimum, characteristically without a common standard. Accordingly, juristic facts are not necessarily the best measure of justice in a given situation. The 'right of conquest' is one such juristic fact. The citation that follows implies that the law takes cognizance of the 'right of conquest.' 'As far as international customary law is concerned, there is no restriction on the power to grant independence, and it is possible for a mother state to establish a newly independent state in which a minority government prevails. In customary law, the United Kingdom could therefore grant independence to Rhodesia on any terms it wished without infringing any international obligations. The competence to grand independence has however been modified by conventional obligations binding the United Kingdom by virtue of the Charter of the United Nations.'
Devine, D. J., 'The status of Rhodesia in international law,' *Acta Juridica*, 1979:359.

77. Jaster, R. S., 'A regional security role for Africa's front line states: Experience and prospects,' Adelphi Papers, Number One Hundred and Eighty, London: The International Institute for Strategic Studies, 1983:15.

78. Bokor-Szego, Hanna, 'Identity and succession of states in modern international law,' *Questions of International Law*, 3, 1986:18 and 40.

79. The transition from Rhodesia to Zimbabwe was a movement away from the status of a colony to sovereign independence. Because of the so-called right of conquest based on the ideology of the meridian line, the conquered people did not form part of the sovereign character of Rhodesia. The rise of Zimbabwe brought

with it a new quality to the older character of Rhodesian sovereignty. By so doing, it inscribed a new identity to the new state, Zimbabwe. Thereby it abolished the old state of Rhodesia. It is submitted therefore that the transition from Rhodesia to Zimbabwe was a matter of state succession and not government succession as the Lancaster Agreement prescribed. It is worth noting the following reflections in connection with our submission. 'The question whether a state gaining territorial sovereignty (the successor state) inherits, together with the territory concerned, the rights and obligations of another state (the predecessor state) arises if this latter is actually to be considered extinct. This question leads to the problems of state succession. The significance of the question is not only theoretical but practical. The fact is that international law does not provide that territorial changes shall have an effect implying the automatic and unconditional devolution, in all cases, of rights and obligations together with the territory concerned. The establishment of the identity of a state is therefore important because in this case the continuance of rights and obligations does not become questionable . . . As regards the particular types of territorial changes the answer is unambiguous; the states emerging from colonial status to independence are new subjects of international law; the problems to be solved in connection with them are those of state succession.' Bokor-Szego, Hanna, 'Identity and succession of states in modern international law,' *Questions of International Law,* 3, 1986:18 and 40.

80. *The Guardian,* 10 October 1983.
81. Moyo, S., *The land question in Zimbabwe,* Harare: SAPES Books, 1995:2.
82. Zimbabwe Land Reform and Resettlement Programme, (LRRP Phase II), Land Task Force Report, 8 October 1998.
83. The Zimbabwean historian-novelist, Lawrence Vambe, writes the following about the memory the indigenous Zimbabweans have with regard to their status as a conquered people. 'Madzidza had very little to say, except from time to time to remind anyone willing to listen that these were rotten times, unlike the good old days when there were no policemen, no money-hungry governments and therefore no taxes to pay to anyone. It was a fair point, but hardly one to give comfort to anybody. Nor did it alter anything, save only to increase the sense of bewilderment and defeatism which overlook every member of the family circle as well as most of the adult population in Mashonganyika village, who took Mizha's peremptory arrest as a gruesome reminder of our conquered status . . . Understandably, the conversation concentrated on a broad recapitulation of some of the highlights of the 1896 rebellion, its causes, effects and aftermath. . . . Listening to these reminiscences, as I did on numerous occasions, I formed the clear impression that the VaShawasha looked at white people and their ways as a perpetual pestilence. . . . As most people of Mizha's and Jakobo's generations claimed to have had personal experience of this bloody

confrontation between black power and whiter power which so decisively changed the fortunes of the Shona and the Ndebele people in my country, the amount of firsthand information available on the subject in the village was immense and colourful. Each man claimed to be a war veteran, . . . Each time I listened to this account, a whole world of human savagery, misery, injustice, blood and death was revealed to my mind.' Vambe, L., *An ill-fated people,* London: Heinemann Educational Books, 1972:19–20, 22–23.

84. No doubt it is not only the indigenous conquered people of Zimbabwe who understand the deeper meaning of this precept and live by it. The Maoris in New Zealand, the Indians in Canada and the United States, and the Aborigines in Australia also act according to this precept. Similarly, memory is what urged the Jewish people to insist that historical justice demands that the state of Israel be established. This happened after many centuries of struggle. The preservation of the state of Israel remains a vital interest of the Jewish people. Significantly, one interesting documentary film in this regard is entitled, 'IZKOR,' meaning, remember. During the first half of the year 2000 an international conference was held in Stockholm, Sweden, aimed at finding means to assist future generations to remember the holocaust. The point about this was that by remembering, the future generations would be placed in a position to avoid repeating the same. Thus memory may serve as a means to uphold the claims of justice and to absolve the guilty by making them meet the demands of justice. The same logic underlies the struggle for Kosovo. After more than six hundred years the memory of the ethnic Albanians and that of the Serbs impels each group to claim title and sovereignty over Kosovar territory. This has led to several bloody struggles. One of them led to the bombardment of Belgrade by NATO a year ago. Despite the heavy heat and suffocating smoke of the bombs, the struggle for title to Kosovar territory continues as though NATO never dropped a single bomb. Memory also led to the war for the Falkland Islands (Malvinas) between Argentina and the United Kingdom. China's memory led finally to the recognition by the United Kingdom that sovereignty over Hong Kong must revert to China. Some of these memories span over centuries. The memory of the life of Jesus is two thousand years old. Yet it dominates the global calendar. Just think of the Christmas and Easter holidays, for example. Moreover, we are told that the high point of the Catholic church service is the moment of the consecration; the change of ordinary bread and wine to the body and blood of Christ. It is more than significant that at this moment the last words in the consecration of each species are: 'whenever you do thus, do it in memory of me. . . . *in me memoriam facieties.*' Finally, what would the West lose if Socrates, Plato, and Aristotle were to be completely excluded from any and all teaching of philosophy? In view of these considerations, 'forget about the past' is an unsound devaluation of history, it rests on a dubious

pedagogical claim and, is philosophically unsustainable. There is thus no reason why the indigenous conquered people of Zimbabwe should simply 'forget about the past.'

85. Bolaji Idowu, E., *African traditional religion*, London: SCM Press Ltd., 1973.

86. Gehman, R. J., *African traditional religion in biblical perspective*, Kijabe, Kenya: Kesho Publications, 1989: 15–22.

87. The meaning and place of spirit mediums in African traditional religion is, as Vambe as well as other scholars on this subject note, a 'complex matter. Chaminuka and Nehanda are not the only known spirit mediums in the traditional religion of Zimbabwe. However, they are said to have distinguished themselves from amongst other spirit mediums and, in consequence, have become prominent. Similarly, Hungwe, the Zimbabwe bird, is not the only known bird regarded as sacred in the traditional religion of Zimbabwe. But it seems to have assumed the position of prominence as well. Like Nehanda, it is regarded as a special messenger in the two-way traffic between the living-dead and the living. In naming the birds that are thought to have this role, Dancel—to whom we shall refer specifically below, places the Hungwe first. It is uncertain if Dancel's naming follows a deliberate order of priority. This notwithstanding, it is significant that the Hungwe is named first. This is underlined by the fact that the rear outside cover of Dancel's book carries the images of the Hungwe and the crocodile beneath carved in one and the same stone. It is far from our intention to delve into any depth with regard to the traditional religion of Zimbabwe. Our intention is limited to extracting insights and beliefs from this domain and showing their relevance as well as significance to the theory and practice of politics in Zimbabwe. It stands to reason that this kind of extrapolation can hardly be limited to Zimbabwe. It applies to the whole of Africa.

88. Vambe, L., *An ill-fated people*, London: Heinemann Educational Books, 1972:118.

89. Vambe, L., *An ill-fated people*, London: Heinemann Educational Books, 1972:179.

90. Vambe, L., *An ill-fated people*, London: Heinemann Educational Books, 1972:54.

91. Lan, D., *Guns and rain, guerrillas and spirit mediums in Zimbabwe*, Harare: Zimbabwe Publishing House, 1985:4–5.

92. Vambe, L., *An ill-fated people*, London: Heinemann Educational Books, 1972:20–21.

93. Daneel, M. L., *The god of the Matopo Hills*, The Hague: Mouton, 1970:24.

94. Ramose, M. B., *African philosophy through ubuntu*, Harare: Mond Books, 1999:88–92.

95. Government of Zimbabwe, Land Reform and Resettlement Programme, Phase II, A Policy Framework, June 1998:3.

96. 1994 (2) ZLR 294 (H).

97. 1994 (2) ZLR 307–308 (H).

98. Van Horn, Alison, 'Redefining property: The constitutional battle over land redistribution in Zimbabwe,' *Journal of African Law*, 38(2) 1994:159.

99. Ndlwana v Hofmeyr, *NO and others* 1937 229 (AD) 237.

100. Mason, P., *The birth of a dilemma: The conquest and settlement of Rhodesia*, Oxford: Oxford University Press, 1958:209–210.

101. Honig, F., 'The reparations agreement between Israel and the Federal Republic of Germany,' *American Journal of International Law*, 48 1954:567.

102. Mazrui, A. A., *Global Africa: From abolitionists to reparationists*, Paper presented at the Seventh Pan African Congress, Kampala, Uganda April 3–8, 1994.

103. Tibamanya Mwene Mushanga, *Africa should demand reparation for slavery and colonial exploitation*, Paper presented to the Seventh Pan African Congress, Kampala, Uganda April 3–8 1994:17.

104. Soyinka, W., *The burden of memory, the muse of forgiveness*. Oxford: Oxford University Press, 1999: 83–84 and 91.

105. Karis, T. and Carter, G. M., *From protest to challenge*, vol. 2, Stanford, California: Hoover Institution Press, Stanford University, 1973.

106. Benson, M., *The struggle for a birthright*, Harmondsworth, Middlesex, England: Penguin Books Limited, 1963.

107. Cervenka, Z., and Robers, B., *The nuclear axis*, London: Julian Friedman, 1978:57–310.
The Star, February 20, 1980:21.
Barnaby, F., *Nuclear proliferation and the South African threat*, Geneva: World Council of Churches, 1977:19.

108. Wall, P., ed. *The Indian Ocean and the threat to the West*, London: Stacey Interntional, 1975:39–66.
El-Khawas, M. A. and Cohen, B., ed. *The Kissinger study of Southern Africa*, Westcort, Connecticut: Lawrence Hill & Co., 1976:39–40.
Crocker, C., 'Western interests in Southern Africa,' *Survival* xxiii(6), London: International Institute for Strategic Studies, 1981:279.

109. MacGibbon, 'The scope of acquiescence in international law,' *The British Year Book of International Law*, 1954:143.

110. Blum, Y. Z., *Historic titles in international law*, 1965:6.

111. Johnson, D. H. N., 'Acquisitive prescription in international law,' *The British Year Book of International Laws*, 1951:337.

112. M'Baye, 'The African conception of law,' *International Encyclopedia of Comparative Law*, vol. II, 1974:147.
M'Baye's understanding of African law with regard to prescription is confirmation of a similar understanding forty years earlier. It was expressed in these terms, 'A debt or a feud is never extinguished till the equilibrium has been restored, even if several generations elapse . . . to the African there is nothing so incomprehensible or unjust in our system of law as the Statute of Limitations, and they always resent a refusal on

our part to arbitrate in a suit on the grounds that it is too old.' Driberg, J. H., 'The African conception of law,' *Journal of Comparative Legislation and International Law,* vol. xvi, 1934:238.

113. Booysen, H. and Van Wyk, D., *Die '83 grondwet,* Johannesburg: Juta, 1984.

114. The ANC seems to have accepted these premises without question. See, 'African National Congress Draft Proposals for the Transition to Democracy, Transition to Democracy Act, 5 RADIC' 1993:208–224.
For an earlier discussion of the ANC constitutional proposals, see, for example:
Corder, H. and Davis, D., 'The constitutional guidelines of the African National Congress: A preliminary assessment,' *The South African Law Journal,* 106, 1989:633–647.

115. Jonsson, U., 'The socio-economic causes of hunger,' in A. Eide, W. B. Eide, S. Goonatilake, J. Gussow, and O. Omawale, eds., *Food as a human right,* Tokyo: The United Nationals University, 1984:24.

116. Fanon, F., *The wretched of the earth,* Tr. C. Farrington, Harmondsworth, Middlesex, England: Penguin Books, 1965:34.

117. Ramcharan, B. G., 'The right to life,' *Netherlands International Law Review,* vol. xxx 1983:297–329.

118. 'Rerum Novarum' par. 10, in D. J. O'Brien and T. A. Shannon, eds., *Catholic social thought,* New York: Orbis Books, 1995:18. See also in the same book, 'Mater et Magistra' pars. 35 and 43, as well as 'Pacem in Terris' pars. 9 and 11.

119. Rantete, J. M., *The African National Congress and the negotiated settlement in South Africa,* Pretoria: J. L. van Schaik, 1998:xv–xix.

120. Brierly, J. L., *The law of nations,* Oxford: Clarendon Press, 1963:144.
Marek, Krystyna, *Identity and continuity of states in public international law,* 1968:5–6.

121. O'Connel, D. P., *State succession in municipal and international law,* vol. 1, Cambridge: Cambridge University Press, 1967:4.
Von Glahn, G., *Law among nations,* New York: Macmillan 1986:111–113.

122. Makonnen, Y., *International law and the new states of Africa,* UNESCO, *Regional participation programme for Africa,* Addis Abeba 1983:133.

123. Sebidi, L. J., 'The dynamics of the black struggle and its implications for black theology,' in I. J. Mosala and B. Tihagale, eds., *The unquestionable right to be free,* Johannesburg: Skotaville Publishers, 1986:26.

124. *Harris v Minister of the Interior* 1952 (2) SA 428 (A). *Minister of the Interior v Harris* 1952 (4) SA 769 (A).

125. Davenport, T. R. H., 'Civil rights in South Africa, 1910–1960,' *Acta Juridica,* 1960:13.

126. Ramose, M. B., *African philosophy through ubuntu,* Harare: Mond Books Publishers, 1999.

127. The Promotion of National Unity and Reconciliation Act No. 34 of 1995. Case CCT 17/96.

128. *S v Makwanyane and Another* 1995 (3) SA 391 (CC). 1995 (6) BCLR 665 (CC) at pars 224–227; 241–251; 263 and 307–313.

129. Wiechers, M., 'Namibia: The 1982 constitutional principles and their legal significance.' *South African Yearbook of International Law,* vol. 15 1989/90:321.

130. *Kesavananda v State of Kerala* A.I.R. 1973 S.C. 1461. For an extensive discussion of this case see Morgan, D. G., 'The Indian "essential features" case,' *The International and Comparative Law Quarterly,* vol. 30, 1981:307–337.

131. Van Horn, Alison, 'Redefining "property": The constitutional battle over land redistribution in Zimbabwe,' *Journal of African Law,* 38(2) 1994:160.

132. MacGarry, B., *Land: For which people,* Gwelo: Mambo Press, 1994.
Riddell, R., *From Rhodesia to Zimbabwe: The land question,* Gwelo: Mambo Press, 1978.
Moyo, S., *The land question in Zimbabwe,* Harare: SAPES Books, SAPPHO, 1995.

133. Devine, D. J. 'The status of Rhodesia in international law,' *Acta Juridica,* 1979:403.

134. Alexandrowicz, C. H., 'New and original states: The issue of reversion to sovereignty,' *International Affairs,* 45(3) July 1969:471–473.

135. Davidow, J., *A peace in Southern Africa,* 1990:98.

136. Brueggemann, W., *the land,* Philadelphia: Fortress Press, 1977:5.

137. May, R. H., *The poor of the land,* New York: Orbis Books, Maryknoll, 1991:122.

138. Soyinka, W., *The burden of memory, the muse of forgiveness,* New York: Oxford University Press, 1999: 39 and 25.

Afrikaans Language Conflict

Boatamo Mosupyoe

The events of June 16, 1976, marked an explosion that was preceded by protracted failed negotiations between the South African government officials, teachers, and members of the school boards over Afrikaans, the language of white South Africans of Dutch origin. The saliency of the imposition of Afrikaans on black students did not obscure the fact that the insurrection was quintessentially a confluence of reactions against the system of apartheid as a whole. While the event can rightfully be defined as a single event in the long history of the struggle against apartheid that drafted masses of youth and students into the liberation movements, its broader social epistemological foundation that reflects the multiple structures from which it emerged as one of the challengers of Bantu education, one of the pillars of apartheid, cannot be ignored. The resilience of the students who took up the struggle against the imposition after their parents failed culminated with the apartheid officials, who were initially rigid, giving in for the first time in the history of the struggle against apartheid.

April 27, 1994, marked the first true democratic election in South Africa. The day brought about a new era that marked both the collapse of the 48 years of the Nationalist apartheid government and an end to three centuries of the struggle against injustices directed at black South Africans. The protracted opposition against apartheid assumed different forms, most notably the African National Congress (ANC) and the Pan African Congress (PAC), and waged unrelenting and complex resistance. Initially the resistance comprised of negotiations, peaceful demonstrations, defiance campaigns, and economic boycotts. The strategies changed after the

Sharpeville massacre, where the apartheid government shot and killed 69 people who were part of a peaceful demonstration.[1] Both organizations decided to go underground and wage guerilla warfare against the apartheid system. This culminated in the arrest, the treason trial, and finally the conviction of the leaders of the organizations, including Nelson Mandela and Walter Sisulu. After these leaders were sentenced to life imprisonment on Robben Island, the political struggle against apartheid experienced a respite that was to be broken by the June 16 uprising.

Although the failed negotiations around the imposition of Afrikaans[2] on black students are salient in the June 1976 uprising, the insurrection was quintessentially a confluence of reactions against the oppression of apartheid. The event may rightfully be defined as a single event in the long history of the struggle against apartheid that conscripted masses of the youth and students into the liberation movements. Its broader social epistemological foundation, however, reflecting the multiple structures from which it emerged as one of the challengers of Bantu education as one of the pillars of the apartheid system, cannot be ignored. That notwithstanding, the critical role of the students, though enhanced, is viewed in the context of that critical evaluation in this paper.

Lederach asserts that ethnic identity and not ideological differences account for conflicts.[3] The validity of the assertion cannot be disputed. The conflict that led to the June 16, 1976, uprising, however, departs from this assertion. This paper discusses how the social process of creation, that is, the shared experience of black South Africans from different ethnic groups, functioned to transcend ethnicity and enhance their position in negotiating against the imposition of the Afrikaans language on black students. The paper will also discuss the role of the students in the negotiations that, although ending in the brutal killing of students by police, succeeded for the first time in the history of the struggle against apartheid in forcing the apartheid government to abandon one of its pivotal policies of "pure apartheid."[4] The paper ends by situating the language conflict in the current theories of conflict as advanced by Galtung.[5]

The paper commences with the discussion of the events that led to the formation of the student organization that came to be known as the South African Students Movement (SASM). The discussion is necessary to provide both a context and a full understanding of the confluence of the structures that informed the students' actions as they attempted to negotiate with the government.

The development of political involvement of students in the early 1970s was marked by activities that expanded into high schools and secondary schools throughout the country. These happened in a very rapid manner that resulted in the formation of many different organizations. One of those organizations was SASM, which owes its origin to the African Student Movement (ASM), formed by students in SOWETO to address the failure rate of students in high schools.[6]

Multiple factors contributed towards this failure rate. First, it reflected the design of the apartheid system and systematic structural violence against blacks. Galtung's definition of structural violence as the progression of denial of needs that leads to conflict applies here.[7] Indeed, the lack and inferior quality of resources in black schools, the shortage of properly qualified teachers that sometimes resulted in the cancellation of classes for months, the pay rate for black teachers that was 75% less than their white counterparts, and the curriculum that was specifically designed to train blacks to be servile and of service to the whites, concretely functioned to set black students up for failure.[8] Furthermore, the fact that the structural violence mirrored in every aspect of apartheid fell drastically short of meeting the standard of viability, ethnicality, and just peace[9] increased the chances of conflict.

The beginnings of ASM came from a group of students in their last two years of high school

that joined together to address these obstacles. They identified students who had strengths in different subjects to teach others during the winter and summer vacations. These students not only sacrificed their school holidays but they also encouraged some teachers to join them. The idea spread to different high schools and gradually the numbers increased and culminated in the birth of ASM, which was launched in Rockville, SOWETO, at the Chiawelo Centre in 1970.[10]

ASM teamed up with a community organization called the Association of Education and Cultural Advancement (ASSECA), which was formed by adult community leaders who resolved to raise funds to sponsor projects that aimed at improving the pass rates in SOWETO schools. It was a mixed blessing that concurrently the highly politicized students in black universities were questioning and protesting against the apartheid system. Many of these students were expelled as a result. The public sector belonged to the apartheid system and therefore would not hire them. The private sector also feared the apartheid regime and would not dare hire them.[11]

The expelled students then became available as teachers and strengthened the efforts of high school students to confront the injustices of the apartheid educational system. They further imparted the philosophy of black consciousness to the secondary and high school students. The scope of focus for ASM then expanded to include a heightened political consciousness when addressing the imbalances engendered by the apartheid system in schools. These new teachers realized that the conviction of the ANC and PAC leaders, the banning of the organizations, and the migration to exile of the members of these organizations created a political vacuum that deprived the young generation knowledge of the history of the struggle against apartheid.[12]

With this renewed energy and the infusion of an overt political agenda, a handful of students in ASM then began an agenda of politicizing other students. They first approached students who were good in debate because their eloquence would serve a useful purpose in articulating the aims of ASM. They then focused on social clubs and organizations such as the Student Christian Movement (SCM). The SCM posed a challenge for various reasons. For a long time, the SCM had a monopoly of organizing student activities, and their religious agenda at the time totally rejected the inclusion of any language that would suggest opposition to apartheid. Their philosophy was predicated on the idea that they were students and not politicians even though their rhetoric was considered by some students a perpetuation and reinforcement of the apartheid biblical interpretations. They were also favored by school officials and the apartheid regime. Thus, the task of recruiting members into ASM was even more daunting. In this case, SASM strategy paralleled the horizontal capacity strategy that recognizes the importance of working with counterparts across the lines of division in order to succeed.

ASM also approached principals and teachers for support as a student movement. Most principals rejected the idea because of fear of reprisal from the Security Branch Police, the section of the South African government that was charged with repressing any opposition to the system of apartheid. There were a few exceptions like Tom Manthata, a teacher, and Lekgau Mathabathe, the principal of Morris Isaacson High School, which is located in SOWETO. Mathabathe not only allowed ASM to exist visibly in his school, but he also hired an expelled student from the University of the North (Turfloop), Abraham Onkgopotse Tiro. This was a tremendous show of courage and a great risk by Mathabathe, given who Tiro represented.

On April 29, 1972, Tiro, in his address at the graduation ceremony at the University of the North, rightfully criticized the Bantu education system and, among other things, said, "The day shall come when we shall be free, when every man and woman will breathe the air of freedom, and when that day shall come, no man no matter how many tanks he has shall reverse the course of freedom."

His speech shocked the racist university officials and J. L. Boshoff, the Rector of the University, and his council expelled him. This expulsion sparked the students' revolt against the repressive system of apartheid, which he denounced in his speech. The action, reaction, and counteraction by the apartheid regime, the students, and the black community spread throughout the country and subsequently led to the closure of

universities. Tiro's last words to Boshoff were, "For we can do nothing against the truth, but for the truth." He further said, "The expulsion has made me realize that one can be punished for saying two plus two make four."[13]

It was no surprise that the Department of Education refused to register Tiro as a teacher, but ASSECA agreed to pay his salary. Mathabathe was under tremendous pressure from both the department and the Security Branch Police to terminate his service, but he maintained his ground. Mathabathe would not even be deterred by their threats to exclude him from any future consideration for promotion.[14] Tiro served as a motivation to ASM as it expanded. Some of the student clubs and organizations such as SCM feared to lose their independence if they were to join ASM. Akin to Lederach's horizontal capacity strategy—that is, efforts to work with counterparts across the lines of division[15]—ASM then agreed to a dual identity arrangement such that the organizations became affiliates of ASM but maintained their autonomy.

This strategy proved invaluable since the organizations' non-political activities became a fertile ground for recruitment of members into ASM. ASM in the long run never missed an opportunity to make presentations at these activities and attract members. In January 1972 in Wilgespruit Roodepoort, after several months of hard work, ASM held a conference that was attended by all its affiliates, students from different high schools, as well as leading members of the South African Students Organisation and Black People's Convention.[16] Thus, a viable and visible representative organization with proper functional structures and presence in all the SOWETO high schools was launched.

In this context, the name of ASM was found to be restrictive and was thus changed to South African Student Movement (SASM), a nomenclature that included the so-called Coloreds and Indian students who were also adversely affected by the injustices of apartheid even though they were placed marginally higher up on the ladder. This move affirmed the growth of SASM and its ability to understand the need for interdependence in building alliances. The conference decided that the strategy should focus on organization and unity, and what better way of uniting the oppressed than collectively referring to them by one name—black. This strategy also countered the government classification of Indians, coloreds, and blacks as separate.

The other resolutions of SASM exemplify the social practice of creativity in conflict, including the students' comprehension of the Bantu education system. They were able to articulate this system as gutter tutelage to the masses specifically produced and fashioned to make it extremely difficult or impossible for blacks to get out of the gutter of illiteracy and low paid employment. SASM came up with solutions to circumvent the obstacles of Bantu education. The objectives included:

1. To confer with the principals in their principals' council on matters affecting students
2. To raise funds for educational purposes
3. To appeal to the community to help in education
4. To encourage and promote love for education
5. To relieve the shortage of schools and teachers
6. To organise additional tuition for students during school days and vacations
7. To give assistance and recommendation where schools are under construction or to be renovated
8. To encourage youth to be an asset to the community
9. To organise work campaigns
10. To work jointly with other student bodies/movements or black organizations/associations who are in sympathy with the aim and objectives of SASM
11. To promote a sense of unity and awareness among black students.[17]

The birth of SASM immediately provided a platform for secondary and high school students to work and voice long-standing suppressed feelings of anger and frustration. It also helped them to articulate, frame, and contextualize the impact of apartheid on their daily lives and education. SASM also owed part of its strength to the association with the South African Student Organisation (SASO)[18] and Black Peoples'

Convention (BPC). Students began coming out to question some of the aspects of the education they were receiving. More importantly, however, they began to justifiably see that the education they were receiving and the apartheid system were mutually inclusive and needed to be addressed accordingly. This political maturity and political acumen manifested in various concrete ways.

In 1971, SASM successfully organized a boycott of the celebration of the 10th anniversary of the Republic of South Africa. They equated the celebration to the symbolic affirmation of the continued oppression of the Black people of South Africa. In the same year SASM also made it clear that they were not going to participate in activities honoring Dr. Kamuzu Banda of Malawi, who came to South Africa at the invitation of the apartheid government and was considered a supporter of the system. Occasionally student leaders would substitute, much to the dismay of some principals and teachers, poems at morning assemblies with speeches that contested the Bantu Education system. Of course, these students would be expelled. The most remarkable achievement of SASM in the early 1970s found expression in their successful and effective obstruction of the various efforts of the South African Bureau of Racial Affairs (SABRA) to help the government to implement its racial discrimination against Blacks. SABRA was formed as an alternative to the South African Institute of Race Relations, which the Afrikaaners[19] considered to be too liberal. This organization was highly influenced by the Broederbond, the think tank of the apartheid system.

The Broederbond was formed in June 1918 and its objective included ensuring the preservation of apartheid, Afrikaaner nationalism, and, it could be argued, white supremacy. Under Prime Minister Hendrik Verwoerd,[20] the Broederbond policies became increasingly aggressive. Even at the end of the apartheid era just prior to the 1994 elections, most members of the departing white parliament were members of the Broederbond (including almost all of the National Party cabinet). The Broederbond engineered and supported SABRA's programme and its pursuit of "pure apartheid," which among other points meant the speedy and complete removal of blacks from "white areas." For whites, SABRA organized conferences where speakers would advocate tougher discrimination against Blacks.[21]

SABRA, with the support of the Broederbond, then designed a programme for Black students where they would be systematically encouraged to accept the homeland system[22] and the concept of "pure apartheid." SABRA strategy involved paying for trips and food for students of different ethnic groups one at a time to visit universities, which were themselves divided according to different ethnic groups. It was important that the groups take trips at different times since the strategy was to divide and conquer. SASM was quick to realize the objective of SABRA and mobilized students against the trips. The task was not easy and it resulted in a rift between SASM and SCM. SASM fully understood that it had to mediate the conflict with extreme tact. This meant recognizing the previous monopoly of SCM in organizing activities and also making sure that SCM did not feel marginalized. Antagonism of any nature within the students' ranks would defeat SASM's objective of unity.

When SASM realized its failure to convince some of the SCM members against the trip, they decided to attend meetings where an agent of SABRA, a black teacher by the name of Grootboom, was recruiting students. They asked him questions about the intentions of SABRA that Grootboom could not answer without exposing the real agenda of SABRA's trips. In view of Grootboom's poor performance, the SCM students needed no further convincing and the programme collapsed. This was not the only victory that SASM scored against SABRA. Another project was started by SABRA in 1973 aimed at the ethnicisation of high schools. The plan was to divide the existing schools into different ethnic groups, divide students along ethnic lines, dissolve the multi-ethnic school boards, and keep South African Blacks divided.

SABRA succeeded in declaring the Sekano Ntoane iTshiVenda and iXitsonga high school, which meant that the high school was only to admit students from iTshiVenda and iXitsonga speaking groups. Gradually SABRA hoped the rest of the SOWETO high schools would also be designated to a particular ethnic group in a system parallel to the homelands.[23] Although the principal and teachers were opposed to the idea,

their fear of the security police surpassed their desire to go against the apartheid machinery. Consequently, SABRA steamrolled the project over them without many students or the community noticing. However, when SASM became aware of the plan, they successfully disrupted a meeting held at Phiri Hall by teachers, principals, and multi-ethnic school board members with the intention of dissolving the boards.[24]

Though only a few months in existence, SASM's presence was beginning to be felt. Political activities within school campuses expanded SASM's scope of organizing and experience, enabling the student body to improve by learning more as time went by. Even more impressive was SASM's ability to completely win over SCM members, most markedly at its conference in Wilgespruit in 1973. It was here that two papers that reflected the complete embrace by SCM of the mutual exclusivity of education and the struggle against apartheid were read. One paper applauded the bold vocal stand of BPC and SASO against the apartheid system. The other paper condemned the complicity of the Christians toward apartheid.[25]

The Language Conflict: Mediation by Teachers, Community, and Sschool Boards

It was at this time when SASM was enjoying success that the apartheid government examined its language policy in Black schools. The aim of the Nationalist party since its inception in 1948 was to also elevate their language, Afrikaans, as an official language equally acceptable as English. The Nationalist government believed that raising the Afrikaans language would then effectively elevate their culture, national ideals, and eventually the Afrikaaner people.[26] Consequently the 1954 Bantu Education Act stipulated the immediate recognition of Afrikaans and English as the two official languages to be included immediately in school curricula.[27]

After a few years, the Nationalist government commissioned a study to assess the success of the use of Afrikaans as a medium of instruction in African schools. The results showed that 26% of secondary schools followed the 50/50 medium of instruction of English and Afrikaans. Forty-three percent were not teaching any subject in Afrikaans except Afrikaans itself. Further, since 1962 there had been a gradual decline from 33% to 26% of secondary schools that carried out the 50/50 language policy. The government was dismayed and resentful.[28] It realized that Black people still preferred English to Afrikaans and that their 50/50 policy failed to address the English/Afrikaans imbalance inas far as Blacks were concerned.

The government decided to come up with a language policy for secondary schools. The dictates of the language policy required that the medium of instruction from standard five (grade seven) to form five (senior year in high school) should be in English or Afrikaans. For schools under the Department of Bantu Education, the final decision on the medium of instruction at the secondary school level would rest with the Secretary of Bantu Education. As a result, the Secretary of Bantu Education issued Circular No. 2 of 1973 and stated that, for all secondary schools and standard five classes, the medium of instruction could be exclusively English, exclusively Afrikaans, and English and Afrikaans on 50/50 basis. The three alternatives as choices were undermined by the fact that the Secretary for Bantu Education was to approve the schools' selections.[29]

The government required that the dominant language spoken in white areas close to the Black schools should determine the adoption of either Afrikaans or English as a medium of instruction. This dictate clearly exposed how disingenuous the apartheid government was, for SOWETO in particular. SOWETO is located in Johannesburg, the financial capital of South Africa. The dominant white language was English. There would be no need then to even address this issue in a prolonged way if the apartheid government was honest in its intentions of the language policy. The determination of the government to implement Afrikaans as a medium of instruction was affirmed by two circulars in 1974 with conflicting directives.

One was Circular 6 of April 17, 1974, signed by the acting secretary, G. J. Rousseau. It was directed only to regional directors and circuit inspectors, reiterated the 50/50 policy, and offered an option of deviation from the policy with the approval of the Department of Education. On the other hand, the August 29 circular signed by W. C. Ackerman, the Southern Transvaal Regional Director, dictated "Uniform Approach in Schools," with clear, inflexible instructions. It stated that standard five and forms one and two should teach general science and practical subjects like home craft, needlework, and metalwork, through the medium of English; mathematics, arithmetic, and social studies through the medium of Afrikaans; and religious instruction, music and singing, and physical education through a vernacular medium.[30]

The circular further stipulated a rigid time frame of implementation. Instruction in Afrikaans would commence in 1975 in the standard five classes and in 1976 for secondary and high schools. That circular presented predicaments that would cause conflicts and tensions. The instructions of the circular explicitly required the closure of lines of communication and shut down the possibility of exemptions and deviations. Another tension was created by Ackerman's decision to send the circular directly to the school principals, a deliberate act to undermine the school boards. The school principals were instructed to ignore the school boards on matters related to the language policy.[31] The teachers, school boards, and parents engaged in numerous attempts to persuade the government to abandon its Afrikaans language policy or at the least to be flexible in its application.

Many reasons were given why the implementation of Afrikaans was impractical. In their negotiation with the Bantu Education officials, the parents asserted their right to choose a medium of instruction for their children. The teachers and school principals explained how they were better equipped to teach in English and far less qualified to teach in Afrikaans. This imposition, they accurately argued, contributed towards poor J.C. and Matric[32] results. Members of the school boards pointed out the differential treatment of Blacks; white, Indian, and colored schools could teach in either English or Afrikaans, while the 50/50 policy was imposed only on Africans.

When all of these negotiations failed, the parties adopted different strategies in the hope of winning over the apartheid officials. The negotiation by the Orlando Diepkloof and Machangana school boards was confrontational and up to the point. Other school boards, on the other hand, were apologetic, hoping to gain sympathy, while parents flooded the department of education with letters expressing their opposition to the language policy. Moreover, the African Teachers Association of South Africa (ATASA) sent a memorandum to the department protesting against the 50/50 policy, and again objecting to the principle that the choice of medium in an area should be decided mainly on the basis of which of the two official languages is dominant in the white community of the area concerned. In December 1974, a representative body of school boards from the Transvaal area of South Africa formed the Transvaal Council of School Boards, consisting of 91 delegates. The aim was to present a united voice to the apartheid Bantu education officials.[33]

In January 1975, this delegation met the Secretary for Bantu Education, F. J. Rousseau, the Regional Director for Northern Transvaal, and the Secretary for Education. They reiterated that African teachers were not equipped to teach in Afrikaans and that the parents' first choice was English as a medium of instruction for their children. The officials encouraged the delegation to apply for exemption. Many applications were submitted and they were all rejected with a statement upholding the implementation as part of the ministerial decision for a 12-year plan. The Federation did not give up. In April 1975, they submitted yet another petition to the Bantu Education Advisory Board addressing the unreasonableness of expecting standard five students to take a public exam immediately after the implementation of the 50/50 language policy in Afrikaans, arguing that students were not fully prepared. Again the Federation's efforts were in vain; nothing came out of those endeavors, and that left the teachers and principals dejected, saddened, helpless, and frustrated. The government felt victorious.

To punctuate its success the government turned its attention to breaking the teachers', members' of school boards, and principals' resistance to the implementation of the language policy. It unleashed its unlimited ability to disempower all of them. Schools that failed to imple-

ment the language policy would lose government subsidy and the services of teachers and members of school boards who displayed continued resistance to the policy would be terminated. Indeed, in February 1976 two members of the Meadowlands Tswana School Board, Mr. Letlape and Joseph Peele, were dismissed by the Department of Bantu Education. The deputy minister stated that the two members were dismissed in accordance with Regulation 4 (1) of Government Notice R429 of 1966 that allowed him to terminate the services of any board member considered of disservice to the Black community.[34]

In another case the government tried to be subtle in getting rid of a vocal opponent of the language policy, Jeremiah Mahlangu. An official of the apartheid Bantu education department, De Beer, forced the board to call for an early election. The board elected Mahlangu with 100% of the votes. In this context the real intention of the government was exposed when De Beer served Mahlangu with a letter terminating his services.[35] Eight additional members of different school boards were dismissed while other school members resigned in protest. These members declined conditional offers of reinstatement if they would withdraw their instructions to schools to use English and not Afrikaans as a medium of instruction.

As hopeless as the situation was, the parents and teachers decided to reopen the negotiations before the students were affected. To this end on April 26, 1976, ATASA met with the Secretary of Bantu Education, Dr. Van Zyl, who promised to open discussions with the minister of education. Van Zyl never came back with a response. Furthermore, the Federated School Board arranged to meet with Van Zyl on June 20, 1976, but that meeting would not take place because of the events of June 16, 1976.[36]

The Language Conflict: Mediation by Students

While the parents and teachers were engaged in futile negotiations with the government, the students experienced hardships imposed by the use of Afrikaans. The teachers were as unfamiliar with the language as the students were. The fact that teaching arithmetic and social sciences required the knowledge of technical terms that teachers did not possess compounded the issue. The government also failed to provide additional training to teachers; consequently, students would submit homework given to them in Afrikaans in English. Students were also expected to write the final national examinations in Afrikaans. One incident in Orlando West Junior Secondary/Phefeni Secondary sparked a huge controversy. One teacher administered corporal punishment to students who refused to do their homework in Afrikaans. The students were incensed and approached their school prefect, Seth Mazibuko, to intervene on their behalf. It was at this point that the students became aware of the futile negotiations by adults with the government to stop the implementation of Afrikaans as a medium of instruction. The students refused to accept the government's position and wrote the following letter to the principal:

> We as students of Phefeni Junior Secondary feel that these subjects that are taught in Afrikaans are difficult for us because even the teachers who are responsible for these subjects, they are also difficult for them they cannot teach them to perfection, so we will be glad if the Principal can call Mr. de Beer, so that we can explain to him.[37]

As expected, De Beer ignored the students and responded by delivering new Afrikaans textbooks to the school. In protest, the students burned all those books and expressed their disgust at De Beer's arrogance. On May 17, 1976, students at Orlando West Junior Secondary/ Phefeni Secondary refused to go to classes after the usual morning assembly, and instead they displayed placards simply expressing that they did not want to do social studies and mathematics in Afrikaans. They also demanded to meet with De Beer. Seth Mazibuko tried to intervene by reading them the minutes where the government clearly stated that the policy cannot be reversed. The students ignored him and insisted on opening the negotiation with De Beer. Of course, De Beer refused to come, and the principal could not honor De Beer's demand that he go to meet with him because the students had disabled his car.

Students continued to come to school but refused to attend classes taught by their teachers. They instead conducted their own classes in English. They also continued their attempt to open negotiations with the government. After consultations with the principal and the staff, the students wrote a letter to the regional director of Bantu education in which they outlined their grievances. They were again ignored. Consequently, the opposition to Afrikaans spread from one school to others and even to higher primary schools. The deteriorating situation compelled the Director of the Institute of Race Relations (SAIRR) to write a letter to de Villiers, a member of Parliament and also a member of the Executive Committee for the Institute, expressing concern.[38] De Villiers demanded an explanation from the Minister of Education, who responded by issuing a statement that clearly failed to refer to the imposition of Afrikaans as the problem and also gave a misleading impression that negotiations on the issue were ongoing. This is how the minister's statement read:

> The problem with regard to the strike of students in SOWETO is being dealt with on a low level at the moment, and negotiations have not yet reached a point of deadlock. Nor has the matter been referred to the secretary of the department although this might happen later. We will determine what the contributory causes are, but at the moment it is said that the students are striking because the teachers (according to the children) are not capable of conducting subjects in Afrikaans. Possibly the matter is not as simple as that.[39]

In the meantime, when school authorities reported their concerns about the class boycotts the government responded by calling in the police and insisting that students should be expelled. The Security Branch Police entered into both violent and non-violent confrontations with students.

The language controversy became a key focal point at the second National Conference of SASM on May 28, 1976. Students from all over SOWETO looked to SASM to provide leadership that would hopefully lead to the opening of the negotiations. Informed by the rigid stance of the government and their repeated refusal to honor a call to negotiations, student delegates made it clear that they also would not accept the language policy. SASM leadership then became the only hope remaining between the Department of Education and the students to bridge the extreme polarization. After much deliberation SASM decided to convene a meeting for June 13, 1976, at Donaldson Orlando Community Centre (DOCC) in Orlando East, to be attended by all the high schools in SOWETO. At this meeting SASM conceded that the government officials of the Department of Bantu Education replaced the open channels of communication with threats, persecution, and obstinacy. SASM also recognized that the students were unwilling to accept Afrikaans as a medium of instruction. Consequently, the students unanimously decided to organize a peaceful demonstration for Wednesday, June 16, 1976, with the hope of opening negotiations.[40]

Through the competent management of an elected Coordination Committee, students were able to spread the word about the plan of action to all the high schools, secondary schools, and higher primary schools. Some principals allowed students to address the students, albeit after school; others refused to give permission. The latter notwithstanding, SASM was able to find a way to inform all the schools concerned. Some leaders of SASM met with Winnie Mandela, who asked them if they were prepared for police reaction to the demonstration. Naively, the students concluded that since this was going to be a peaceful march the police would at worst react with tear gas and not bullets. Further, students were convinced that their planned demonstration was not known to the police. However, word did get out through two Black policemen, Saude and Masopa, to Lieutenant Kolonel Johannes Augstinus Kleingeld, the Station Commander at Orlando Police Station. Masopa learned about the demonstration from his son who was a student at Orlando High School. Fortunately for the students, Kleingeld decided that the matter had to wait until the following morning.[41]

There were two reasons why the plan had to be executed within 72 hours and be kept from the police. The half-yearly exams were scheduled for June 16 and writing the exams would imply

a capitulation to the language policy. Further, delaying the demonstration opened students to the risk of detention and interrogation by the Security Police should the information leak out, and the possible foil of the demonstration.

As planned, students from various schools in SOWETO converged in large numbers from different directions towards Orlando West Junior School/Phefeni Secondary, which was to be the assembly point for all high schools marching from the various parts of SOWETO. Meanwhile Colonel Kleingeld, acting on the information he received the previous night, sent three surveillance teams to three different schools—Madibane High School, Orlando West High School, and Orlando High School—to confirm the demonstrations. Eventually Kleingeld learned from the third team that there was indeed a huge demonstration by students. He assembled a group of Black and white policemen and armed them with .38- and .45-caliber revolvers. A Lieutenant Brandt made sure that the Alsatian police dogs were also taken along.[42] The loudspeaker was the only item that was visibly absent. As a result of the police violence that ensued, it became clear that the police had no interest in negotiations or a peaceful resolution to the conflict. They would not need a loudspeaker to warn the students.

When the police came in contact with the students, Lieutenant Colonel Kleingeld pulled one of three Sten submachine guns; it jammed and failed to fire. He then took the second one that Sergeant Ronald Anthony Lombard[43] was holding and without any warning shot into the crowd. This was followed by students dropping to the ground. This infuriated the students. Instead of scattering all over the place, the students went on the attack. They threw whatever they could get in their hands at the police. It was only then that the police realized that they had it all wrong. The assumption of easily intimidating the students failed. The violence that ensued resulted in the death of hundreds of students and spread throughout schools in South Africa. Although eventually, for the first time in South Africa's history, the government abandoned the 50/50 language policy, it acted too late to prevent the massacre of so many young students whose lives could have been spared if negotiations had been honored and pursued.

Conclusion

An analysis of the language controversy greatly benefits from some aspects of Galtung's framework and typology.[44] The Bantu education apartheid system allowed violence to occur vertically. The system not only disproportionately deprived Black students access to education, amongst other resources, but the inherent inequality, repression, and exploitation were managed from top to bottom.

Also applicable is Galtung's marginalization and fragmentation concepts. Through various methods, including the efforts of SABRA and Broederbond, the government unsuccessfully tried to prevent mobilization by dividing students into different ethnic groups for the purpose of advancing the total apartheid plan that would eventually turn SOWETO into a mirror image of the homelands. Further, the imposition of Afrikaans would ensure the condition of subservience. Since Afrikaans is only spoken in two countries in the world, forcing its use would limit the English proficiency of Blacks, which would adversely impact their ability to articulate the violence of apartheid to the world. Additionally, as Dr. Daniel Malan, a priest of the Dutch Reformed Church in 1908, said, "Raise the Afrikaans language, let it become the vehicle for our culture, our history, our national ideals, and you will also raise the people who speak it."[45]

The penetration and segmentation aspects of Galtung are less applicable in this analysis. Galtung defines these as "preventing conscience forming."[46] ASM achieved its objective of injecting political awareness into the student body. Even more remarkable was its ability to tactfully win over the SCM, the movement that was favored by the Security Police.

Finally, the loosely applied shifting position of the apartheid Bantu Education officials and the evolving requests and demands of the students and adults pertaining to the language controversy typify Galtung's notion of conflict as a transformation and not a conflict resolution process and Thomas Kuhn's paradigm shift.[47] Kuhn described this shift as a process of breaking conventionally recognized modes of problem identification and resolution, with the possible effect of creating new modes. The simple issue evolved into a complicated matter, with goal posts continuously shifting. The four circulars issued by Bantu Education officials contained either new or contradictory information. The confusing process confirmed the hardening attitude of the officials. On the other hand, the students refused to give in.

The systematic control of Black Africa under the racist system of apartheid permeated all levels of society. As illustrated, at the core of education and communication, the apartheid regime sought to control the black population. When the contradictions and exploitation of the language requirements were exposed, the government resorted to violence. It took decades to fully engage the international community with an awareness of the wholesale assault on human rights that the apartheid system relied upon. The negotiated end of apartheid, however, offers lessons for the potential role of global civil society to insist that negotiations be prioritized by governments and others who would resort to violence to protect perceived interests.

Notes

1. Mosupyoe, Boatamo. 1999. *Mediation of Patriarchy and Sexism by Women in South Africa.* New York: McGraw-Hill.
2. Afrikaans is a language created and mainly spoken by white South Africans of Dutch origin.
3. Lederach, John Paul. *Preparing for Peace: Confliction Transformation Across Cultures.* Syracuse, NY: Syracuse University Press.
4. The process by the South African apartheid government embarked to attain total separation from the Black majority.
5. Johan Galtung. 1996. *Peace by Peaceful Means: Peace and Conflict Development and Civilization.* London: Sage.
6. Mosegomi, Mosala. 2007. Birth of SASM. In *SOWETO Explodes,* ed. B. Y. Mosupyoe. Dubuque, IA: Kendall/Hunt, 2007, pp. 1–28.
7. Galtung, *Peace by Peaceful Means,* pp. 197–200.
8. Mosupyoe, Boatamo. 1999. *Mediation of Patriarchy and Sexism by Women in South Africa.* New York: McGraw-Hill, pp. 97–108.
9. Lederach, John Paul. Justpeace: The Challenge of the 21st century. In *European Centre for Conflict Prevention, People Building Peace: 35 Inspiring Stories from Around the World.* Utrecht: European Centre for Conflict Prevention, pp. 27–36.
10. Mosegomi, "Birth of SASM," pp. 1–28.
11. Ibid.

12. Mosegomi, Mosala. 2007. The NAYO Trial. In *SOWETO Explodes*, ed. B. Y. Mosupyoe. Dubuque, IA: Kendall/Hunt, p. 12.
13. Mafuna, Bokwe. 2003. On the Commemoration of the Life of Onkgopotse Abraham Tiro, http://www.azapo.org.za/speeches/speech21.htm.
14. Mosegomi, "Birth of SASM," pp. 20–28.
15. Lederach, "Justpeace," p. 30.
16. The Black People's Convention (BPC) was founded at the end of 1972 as part of the Black Consciousness Movement (BCM) in South Africa. Black in the context of BCM is an inclusive concept of historically oppressed peoples (Africans, coloureds, and Asian Indians) in then apartheid South Africa. The BCM was a product of historicultural and ideological imperatives that exposed the hypocrisy of white liberal college/university students of apartheid South Africa.
17. Security Police SASM Profile.
18. The South African Students' Organisation (SASO) was a body of South African students who resisted apartheid through political action. Students in this organisation broke away from the National Union of South African Students, which was based on white campuses, and its leadership positions were almost entirely taken by white students who not only ignored issues raised by Black students but also lacked understanding of and sensitivity to the Black experience under apartheid system. The organisation that played a major role in the Movement was formed in 1968, with Steve Biko as the first president of the organisation.
19. Euro-South Africans of Dutch descent. Most of them openly and unashamedly supported apartheid.
20. He is regarded as the architect of the racist apartheid system. He was the prime minister from 1958 to 1966. He was assassinated with a knife in 1966.
21. Mosegomi, Mosala. 2007. The Wrong Diagnosis. In *SOWETO Explodes*, ed. B. Y. Mosupyoe. Dubuque, IA: Kendall/Hunt, pp. 111–129.
22. These were arid areas that the apartheid system implemented so as to strip Black South Africans of their citizenship. They implemented the system with the hope that Blacks would become "citizens" of the "homeland." Under this system 13% of the land belonged to 80 million Blacks and 87% was given to the whites.
23. South African Institute of Race Relations Survey (1977), p. 119.
24. Mosegomi, Mosala. 2007. Concocting the Powder Keg. In SOWETO Explodes, ed. B. Y. Mosupyoe. Dubuque, IA: Kendall/Hunt, pp. 131-140.
25. Ibid.
26. Meredith, Martin. 1988. *In the Name of apartheid*. New York: Harper and Row.
27. Mosegomi, "The Wrong Diagnosis," p. 111.
28. Ibid.
29. Department of Education File 6/8/1 (1973).
30. Ibid.
31. Ibid.
32. Junior High School and High School.
33. Mosegomi, Mosala. 2007. Submit or Fight. In *SOWETO Explodes*, ed. B. Y. Mosupyoe. Dubuque, IA: Kendall/Hunt, pp. 143–145.
34. South African Institute of Race Relations Survey (1977), 53.
35. South African Institute of Race Relations, Volume 30, 139.
36. Mosegomi, "The Wrong Diagnosis," pp. 111–120.
37. Ibid., p. 123.
38. Ibid.
39. Ibid., p. 126.
40. Ibid., 138.
41. Ibid.
42. Ibid.
43. Mosegomi, Mosala. 2007. Embers of Soweto. In *SOWETO Explodes*, ed. B. Y. Mosupyoe. Dubuque, IA: Kendall/Hunt, p. 184.
44. Galtung, *Peace by Peaceful Means*.
45. Meredith, *Name of Apartheid*, p. 12.
46. Galtung, *Peace by Peaceful Means*, p. 93.
47. Kuhn, Thomas Samuel. 1970. *The Structure of Scientific Revolution*. Chicago: University of Chicago Press, p. 22.

Racialized Societies

David Covin

Howard Winant's work has served to illuminate this pathway.

Racialized societies are societies that function as they do in large part because of the meanings they ascribe to race. Racialized societies are characterized by the highly significant meanings they give to race and the effects these meanings give to the structures of the societies.

Constructs of race may be present in nonracialized societies, but they do not act with such agency as to determine the very character of the societies. Even among racialized societies, some are more racialized than others.

Here, no attempt is made to identify all racialized societies. Instead, the focus is on racialized societies in the Western Hemispheric African diaspora. Most of all, the study uses the U.S. as a template.

It may be that African diasporic societies contain among them the most highly racialized societies in the world. Indeed, St. Claire Drake, among others, identified African descendants in the U.S. as the most racially conscious people in the world. To the degree that this characterization is accurate, it may be a product of the society they inhabit, particularly as it affects them. While white people and others in the U.S. may be racially conscious, their racial consciousness pales beside that of black people in the country.

The Meaning of Race in Racialized Societies

Here the meanings assigned to race by societies are considered—not any objective definition of race, as it has been effectively established that there is currently no definition of race which has generic utility.

Race is what societies say it is. People belong to the races to which societies assign them. The concept is one of the most flexible in human usage. Not long ago it was possible to speak in all seriousness about the English race or the Roman race, the German race or the French race. Anglo-Saxons constituted a race, as did Slavs. People spoke knowingly about the Jewish race and the Aryan race.

Essentially the term is used as a way of grouping people. Those who are deemed to have certain characteristics in common are identified as members of the same race. There are no uniformities with respect to what those characteristics are. They may be a language they speak in common, they may be supposed moral attributes, they may be observed physical characteristics, they may be where they live, their religion, their social customs, a supposed common ancestry, or any combination of such factors. It may be stated, categorically, that race is a catch-all category, a nonsense category. But it is dear to human beings. Its definitions vary not only from place to place, but over time in the same place. Census categories are instructive in this regard.

In racialized societies definitions of race are among the most important social definitions. They assign characteristics associated with specific populations. They are definers of people. People are assigned social places, social spaces, and social roles on the basis of their racial characterizations. Racialized societies are hierarchical with place in the hierarchy determined to a great extent by race. Social place can be considered as designating a group's standing in the social hierarchy. It is a relative place. It is assigned with reference to other racial groups.

From *The Unified Black Movement in Brazil, 1978–2002.* © 2006 David Covin by permission of McFarland & Company, Inc., Box 611, Jefferson NC 28640 www.mcfarlandpub.com

The various races are also assigned specific spaces in society: spaces where they can live, worship, work, play; spaces where they can eat, travel, study, receive treatment, invest, perform, have voice or presence, and spaces where they cannot.

The U.S. System as a Template for Race in the Western Hemispheric Diaspora

Primarily because of the significance the study attributes to contexts, this work devotes a good deal of attention to racial conditions in the United States in a study which purports to treat a Brazilian political organization. By looking at the U.S. context one can develop a better understanding of how a particular form of racialization developed there. By comparing that setting with Brazil, insights can be gained on the specific elements of racialization developed in Brazil. By appreciating some of the features which produced the Southern Christian Leadership Conference in the U.S., one may be more alert to *different* features which produced the MNU in Brazil. Looking at the United States is, nevertheless, a shorthand. The study does not look at the other countries in the Western Hemisphere with significant African populations. It would have been possible to choose a country other than the U.S. or even multiple countries for this learning by comparison. One reason for limiting this type of juxtaposition to one country is to simplify the comparison.

Another reason to consider the U.S. experience is because Brazil and the MNU inhabit a world, an international space, dominated by the U.S. Brazilians can't help being influenced by what has happened and is happening in the U.S. It is important to look at the MNU in this internationally hegemonic context. At the same time, despite U.S. domination of the world, Brazil is not the U.S. African-descended people in Brazil differ from those in the U.S. That reality can be made explicit by setting the two situations side by side. Despite the repression of African-descended people in both countries, and despite the U.S. setting itself up as a world model, there are powerful reasons why scholars should not expect black people in Brazil to build structures

or to interact with each other as their U.S. counterparts do. A comparative examination of context enables the researcher to see that more clearly. To enable such comparison the work gives extensive consideration to racialization in the U.S.

Jim Crow

The Jim Crow system in the U.S. serves as an *ideal type* of spatial assignment by race because the spaces were statutory, they were written into law. Within the Jim Crow area each state and locality defined the spaces accessible to particular races. While the particular assignments were not uniform, what was uniform was that races were assigned spaces by law. The laws generally applied to the "white" and "black" races, though occasionally they accounted for other races as well. When no special provision was made for a nonwhite or nonblack group, decisions had to be made about which of the two more prominent races' spaces the *third party* group had access to.

The spaces were fungible to the benefit of the higher status group. For example, if the law required blacks and whites to be assigned separate sections in public buses, if the white section filled up, the black section of the bus could be reduced in size. This kind of section designation could work both ways—the black section could be expanded too if few white passengers were on the bus—but never to the point where white passengers could lose their seats. Black passengers were *always* at the risk of losing theirs. By the same token, if the law required that black and white people use separate public parks and there was only one public park, it was for whites.

White people were privileged by race though the legal fiction was that the law merely separated, it did not rank.

There were some spaces that were public in the sense that people of both races could use them: the public thoroughfares, public structures. But even within some public spaces the spaces *within* those spaces were limited to one race. Blacks and whites could not sit together in public theaters. One section of the theater was for whites, another for blacks. Blacks were not allowed to sit at lunch counters in public stores they were allowed to enter. Separation within public buses has already been noted. Sometimes spaces that were legally open to blacks were closed by custom. In some localities black people were not allowed to walk on the sidewalks, though such spaces were supposedly open to both races. In some localities black people had curfews—which meant they could use *no* public space after the designated hour.

Roles were assigned on the basis of race. The role of subservient, inferior, was reserved for black people. The position of overlord, superior, was designated for white people. Black people were expected to be humble and meek before white people, to take off their hats, to lower their eyes, to keep their heads bowed. They were expected to address white people formally—Mr., Master, Mrs., Miss. They were expected to get out of a white person's way, to hold the door for white people. They were expected to do what a white person told them—*any* white person.

White people, on the other hand, could call black people whatever they pleased. Almost always they used terms of familiarity—first names; nick names; a title, such as "uncle" or "auntie." This contributed to the tendency of black people to give their children grandiloquent names: King, Queen, Princess, Famous, General, Napoleon, Duke, Precious. If their children were going to be referred to by their first names, they at least were going to be known by a term of respect.

White people were expected to act imperiously to black people, to command them, to tolerate no disrespect. Black people were understood to have no rights a white person was bound to respect.

Politics were explicitly prohibited to black people by law and by custom. The political was exclusively "white folks' business."

All these patterns meant that there were certain roles forbidden black people. A black person couldn't be a judge, a mayor, a legislator. A black person couldn't be a police officer. No black person could be a physician who treated white patients or a lawyer who had white clients. A black person couldn't conduct a white orchestra or display a work of art in a white gallery. A black person couldn't teach white children or adults, or supervise white people in any way.

Black people's collective role, space, and place was to be the bottom of society—by law, by custom, and in fact.

In Jim Crow society definitions of race were critical. There could be no ambiguity. Life chances were allocated by race. If you were black, you had no chance of becoming white, *i.e.*, escaping the place, space, and role assigned to you by race.

The one-drop rule provided certainty. If one had any known African ancestry, the person was black. This was a legal definition. It was also customary where it was not legal. Its rootedness in ancestry, not appearance, led to the phenomenon of "passing."

Jim Crow, however, did not characterize all of the U.S. even when it was the legal order throughout the South. Its absence, however, did not change the racial hierarchy in places where Jim Crow did not exist. Nor did it alter the places, spaces, and roles assigned to black people—even when there was no legal order dedicated to enforcing it. The United States has been a racialized society from its inception. The meaning and the place of "blackness" was built into what it meant to live in the U.S. and to participate—or not—in its society. Jim Crow merely codified the *status quo*. The broader parameters of the order persisted in the absence of codification. Everybody lived within those parameters. Hence, whether in the North or South, segregation existed, either *de facto* or *de jure*. It was the same condition, merely at different levels of formality.

The Historical Trajectory of Race in the U.S.

During the Colonial Period

In each colony, over a period lasting up to half a century, through legislation, court decisions, and practice, the status of Africans and slaves was worked out. They constituted the bottom of the social order. That was the place for them and their descendants *in perpetuity*. It was understood to be a *permanent* condition.

It was also through law and practice that the definition of the African, the black, was worked out.

There was no instant, universal agreement in law. Indeed, a universal agreement in law was *never* established. But, nationally, in most places—in practice—the one-drop rule was accepted. Anyone with any known African ancestry was "African," "colored," "Negro," or "black." This constituted the floor of society to which no one else—whatever the other circumstances of their lives—could ever fall.

The trouble with mulattoes and zambos, quadroons and octoroons, paternal identity and maternal identity, was that these notions made African identity amorphous and changeable, *as it came to be in Brazil.* In a slave society it is critical to know who the people are who can be enslaved. Because for white people the society *was* "free." That meant they could not be subject to enslavement. Who was not white—who *was* black—was a crucial element of identity. Without having a clear and standard practice on this matter, the slaveocracy could not function. *In Brazil another pattern developed. Who was white—not who was black—became the critical divider of persons.*

In a slaveocracy, the society had to be wholly racialized and the definition of race fixed. The tricky matter in the United States was that the fixed definition of race could not come through the definition of who was white—the variation among white people was too great. Racial definition had to be based on who *was not* white, *i.e.*, who *was* black. This was, explicitly, *racial* slavery. Not just any somebody could be enslaved. This was a fate reserved for Africans and their descendants.

Unlike the Brazilian case, in North America the definition of black was both extreme and fixed because there was no dearth of white people. There was no need to incorporate non-white people into the social and political population. There were no significant leadership or skilled roles which would go unfilled without such incorporation. The definition of the African could be as broad as possible—as it ultimately came to be. Authentic white people had to be separated from mere pretenders. Genuine whiteness came from the absolute absence of African ancestry.

In a slave society in which the condition of slavery is based on race, a racialized slaveocracy, race becomes a critical component of every feature of life, if nothing else, because the society's most valuable commodity is a *racial* commodity.

One feature of a racialized commodity is that true personhood cannot be associated with it. A human being is not a commodity. Africans were the equivalent of money in the bank, acreage under cultivation, or heads of stock. Except that as commodities they were more valuable than other commodities because they could *create* other commodities. They could clear fields, plant and harvest them, raise stock, and create income which could be put in the bank.

Their lives had value only as commodities and every other aspect of them could be eliminated. Because society was racially defined, every feature of society was both racially defined and had racial meaning. The English colonies in North America were racialized slaveocracies.

An African who was not a slave had no place in the society. Some were present, but they were anomalies. They had no place. That is why their status was ambiguous. No one knew what to do with them *because they shouldn't have been there.*

Race in the United States as an Independent Country

When the 13 colonies broke with England and established themselves as a single country, they did not change the status of Africans either socially or politically. The new country remained racialized. It remained a racialized slaveocracy.

In fact, eventually, that condition became incorporated into the country's basic political document, the Constitution. It was done in a curious way—one might say in a hypocritical way—without ever mentioning slavery, Africans, or black people. But it was done most thoroughly, shaping the very nature of the state and the polity which constituted it. It is not overstating the case to say that arrangements for slavery dominate the U.S. Constitution.

In provisions which establish that slave states shall be more heavily represented in the House of Representatives than free states, that slave states shall play a greater role in the selection of the president through the Electoral College than free states, through forbidding an end to the international slave trade before 1808, in establishing that a slave *cannot* escape slavery anywhere in the constitutional jurisdiction of the United States, and in specifying that the only provision of the Constitution which cannot be changed is that which enables the slave trade to continue until 1808, the Constitution's arrangements for slavery dominate the document. It places the control of the national government in the hands of the slave-owning classes and establishes their property values as preeminent in the national state.

The Constitution is a testament to the codification of a national slaveocracy. Moreover, it works on two levels, state and national. Each slaveholding state's government is a slaveocracy. The national government over the country as a whole is a slaveocracy. This places the state as a perperrator and defendet of slavery as deeply into the political order as possible. According to the Constitution slaves are not citizens. They are not even counted among those who will be represented. Those who own them control the state.

A Democratic Social and Political Order?

This racialized slaveocracy purported to be a democracy, or in the parlance of the time, a republic. What these forms of government are popularly understood to mean is that the citizens are allowed some form of participation in the selection of the state and that they are guaranteed certain basic rights.

By that formulation the citizenry was much more restricted than it is today, but the general populace was nevertheless understood to receive the protection of basic rights. Not so for the enslaved who were understood to be neither citizens nor persons in the legal sense. Even when participatory citizenship rights were eventually extended to the general white, male population, they were not extended to the enslaved—who still did not possess legal personhood. As to the circumstance of free black people, it was tied much more closely to that of the slave population than to that of the free, white population.

The racial aspect of citizenship compounds the difficulty as is made clear by the end of the Civil War and the passage of the Civil War amendments, attempting, by political means, to

change the *place* and the *role* of African descendants in the society. Racialized slavery was political, but its political dimension was only one aspect of an entirely racialized society and polity. Class structure too was racial, as was status. Culture was racial. Families were racial. Wealth and social mobility were racial. Education, personal associations, and neighborhoods were racial, as were religions, language, cuisine, wardrobes, and customs. Identity was racial.

Getting rid of slavery was removing only the tip of the iceberg. As in Brazil, where abolition of slavery was much more gradual, abolition did not change the racialized character of the society. Because the whole society was racialized, "democracy" in the United States was racialized. One cannot have a democratic politics devoid of racialization when the class structure and culture are racial, when status and family relationships are racial, when wealth and social mobility are racial, when education and language are racial, when associations and wardrobes are racial, when neighborhoods, customs, and identities are racial. It is not possible. All these elements enter into politics and have political effects.

Through African Eyes

To this point this work has considered racialization from the stand-point of the dominant beliefs in society and the overall social and political structures. It has not considered it from the point of view of the African.

A premise of this study is that the African is an invention born in the Americas. The people who boarded the "black ships" on the Atlantic's eastern shore were not Africans. They knew themselves as Mandinka, Wolof, Dan, Fanti, Ashante, Hausa, Yoruba, Ibo, Ewe, Congo, Angola, Fulani, and on *ad infinitum*. African was a conception unknown to them.

Except for residence on the continent of Africa they had little apparently in common. They came from separate nations. They spoke often mutually unintelligible languages. They practiced different religions, shared few customs, acknowledged no common identity.

For those who survived the crossings, they shared at least the awful initiation into a new world whose parameters they could not remotely discern. But, other than that, they remained as distant from each other as their origins dictated.

Upon their recuperation from the horror of the middle passage, they were transported to many and varied places and commanded to undertake a wide variety of roles. There was nothing uniform about their situations—except that almost all of them were "owned" by other human beings.

Their "owners" imposed distinctions upon them which were both alien and incomprehensible: African savage (newly arrived), seasoned (adjusted to the slave system), home grown (born in the Americas), trusted, trustworthy, dangerous, manservant or womanservant, field hand, artisan, mixed race. The features of their daily lives were remarkably dissimilar.

Yet despite the measureless differences between them, and still further distinctions imposed upon them, these divisions were all trumped by their continent of origin, which they ultimately came to understand as race.

A terrible uniformity of place, space, and role was imagined for their persons—which as they knew—did no justice to the diversity and complexity among them. Over time many of them— particularly those who emerged as leaders of collective life—began to recognize the utility of a unitary identity for coping with their common oppression and exploitation. They then deliberately featured themselves as Africans, Aftos, coloreds, Negroes, blacks, Africans again. They too came to recognize in themselves, their ancestors, and their fellows around the globe the presence of a people who had never heretofore existed, the Africans. They conceived of themselves as members of a specific race. Not only had their presence in the new world been racialized, so had their imaginations.

The Racialized Societies of the African Diaspora in the Western Hemisphere

What happened in the U.S. happened, with significant variation, throughout the Americas. Societies were racialized. The preeminent racial distinctions were between Africans and Europeans. The role of indigenous peoples in racialization experienced the most variation from place to place. Often this was tied to survival rates of indigenous populations.

Revisiting what happened in the U.S. enables us to open a window onto what happened elsewhere. The U.S. experience provides examples both of variations and of underlying similarities among black people. Throughout the Western Hemisphere such differential experiences can be found within and between countries.

In the U.S. the northern and southern regions of the country established separate patterns of racialization. Both regions were tacialized, but the *patterns* were different. In the North slavery was gradually outlawed by state legislatures. In the South state legislatures not only continued slavery, but also strengthened the legislation and systems of enforcement under which it was maintained. While the number of black people in the North was comparatively small, most of them were free. The large black population in the South was almost entirely in bondage. An accompanying anomaly was that there was a tiny fraction of the free black population in the South composed of slaveholders.

Nevertheless, in both the North and South, irrespective of the standing of free or enslaved, the black population constituted the floor, the bottom of society. They had the least social standing of any racial group, and owned the least wealth. They had the least education, were the most criminalized, had the shortest life spans, the highest infant mortality rates, lived in the most wretched environments, had the least social mobility, and the least political efficacy.

While in the South, after Reconstruction, Jim Crow laws required the separation of the population by race and the political emasculation of the black population, the same conditions were realized in the North in the absence of law, by custom.

A civil rights movement could be mounted in the southern states because there were laws requiring racial separation which could be challenged as alien to the national legal system. No such challenge could be mounted in the North where no such legal impediments to black people existed, but where they were imposed by custom. In the North a system of racial superiority and inferiority had been sustained without the imposition of a legal system which required it. *The absence of a legal apparatus for maintaining a racialized social and political system is no indicator of whether such a system exists.*

Racialized societies rooted in slavery were established throughout the Western Hemispheric African diaspora. The implications for understanding these societies is that the condition, *and its remedies*, can neither be understood nor dismantled by restricting considerations to one place. What is critical to understanding race in the Western Hemisphere is understanding the collective position of African peoples there. Remedies, likewise, are most appropriate which take into account the situations throughout the hemisphere.

Take, for example, the respective African-descended populations of the U.S. and Brazil. Until the early 1940s the best evidence is that from the beginning of the 20th century the material conditions of black people in the U.S. and Brazil were roughly equivalent. Beginning with World War II and continuing with the postwar ruin of most of the world's industrialized economics, the U.S. emerged as the dominant economic power in the world, the driving engine of industrial modernization. From its position as the world's leading investor, and hence the major recipient of returns on investment the national economy was transformed. An important aspect of that transformation was the creation of a *substantial* middle class—*a class which had never before reached such dimensions*.

Concomitant with this national increase in wealth, a significant black middle class, consisting largely of industrial workers, was created. As the ranks of this class increased, the material condition of black people in the U.S. began to separate from those of Afro-Brazilians. By the year 2000, the U.S. black population, collectively, was unquestionably the wealthiest African-descended population in the world. On the other hand, the material circumstances of Afro-Brazilians had not dramatically improved over what they had been in the 1940s.

Yet in *both* countries the diasporic effect is inescapable. In both the U.S. and Brazil the black population was at the bottom of its respective material and social orders, the least educated, the most criminalized, the weakest link in the countries' economic well-being.

In the presence of racialized democracies and in the absence of strategies to develop and incorporate diasporic strategies in addressing these conditions, how likely is it that these situations will be remedied? To further explore that question this work examines the specific context which produced the MNU.

Brown v. Topeka Board of Education: Fifty Years Later

Otis L. Scott

Introduction

May of 2004 marked the fiftieth anniversary of the landmark Supreme Court decision, *Brown vs. Topeka Board of Education*. Across the nation countless events have been carried out in commemoration of the 1954 decision. It is safe to assert that most of these events hailed the significant role *Brown* played in dismantling the walls of Jim Crow segregation surrounding public schools in southern and border states of the United States.

This article is a general examination of the pre and post *Brown* eras with critical attention given to the extent to which the decision fulfilled the dreams of the proponents of public school desegregation. I contend that the effects of *Brown* must be examined within a heuristic model that demands we critically examine the responses of American society—especially its formal governing institutions—and secondly, its citizenry, to policies and practices of desegregation. In raising these concerns I also raise up the need for a critical examination of the concept of integration which has, and to a diminishing extent today, serves as the norm driving the discourse around public school desegregation.

Historical Context

The United States prior to the *Brown v. Board* decision of 1954 was for all intents and purposes an apartheid society. Policies and practices separating African Americans from white Americans

was a defining feature of this nation beginning in the seventeenth century. Segregation practices became engrained by habits of custom and heart. These practices were subsequently canonized into the ethos and processes of the nation's social systems at both the national and state levels simultaneously with the framing of a new governing experiment. An experiment resting on the bedrock proposition touting political equality. In fact, the United States was created with what the historian W.E.B. DuBois called the color line. This line has historically divided Black and whites into two distinct societies; separate and unequal. The metaphorical line is as much an issue today as it was at the dawn of the 20th century following the 1896 Supreme Court decision in *Plessy v Ferguson*. This decision established in legal concrete, that the races—meaning particularly African descended people and white people—must be kept separate in public spaces. This decision also had negative implications for other people racialized as a *minority* in the United States. Following habits of heart and mind in matters of race long in force in this nation, *Plessy* articulated this nation's policy on race. Namely, the separation of African people from whites was right, just and proper in order to maintain domestic tranquility and most importantly, white supremacy.

There were few spaces in public life in the United States where the operation of what became known as the "Jim Crow" doctrine of racial separation was more pronounced and more destructive than in public education. And no where were the practices of the pronouncement more destructive than when used to deny African American children living in border and southern states a quality education and the life enhancing opportunities derived from being educated.

Jim Crow's Children

This nation's dereliction in providing any form of a meaningful education for African Americans long predates the 1896 *Plessy* decision. The Virginia legislature as early as 1680 passed a law prohibiting Africans from gathering together for any reason. Doing so was punishable by "Twenty Lashes on the Bare Back well laid on" (Irons 2002). The intent of such severe legislation was seemingly to discourage slaves from forming their own schools and from meeting to conjure up plans to overthrow their masters. If Africans in colonial America received any form of education it was one heavily doused with biblical teachings counseling the virtues of obedience, supplication, faith in the deliverance of God and the benevolence of white people. Within the antebellum south any efforts at educating African men, women and children were typically clandestine. Throughout the south such efforts were almost always illegal. Slave owners feared that any form of literacy would lead to insurrection. One defender of this position asked in 1895, "Is there any great moral reason why we should incur the tremendous risk of having our wives and children slaughtered in consequence of our slaves being taught to read incendiary publications?" (Irons 2002).

The first institutionalized efforts to educate African Americans were made after the Civil War by the Reconstruction Congress. There is clear evidence that African Americans took advantage of the opportunity to learn to read and write (Bullock 1967). If one reviews the policy positions taken by African Americans elected and appointed to office during the brief period of Reconstruction, it will be revealed the extent to which newly freed African Americans expressed an unflagging desire for an education for both adults and especially for children. Reconstruction efforts were brought to a screeching halt after 1876 by virtue of the grand betrayal brokered between the political forces supporting the Republican, Rutherford B. Hayes and those supporting Democrat, Samuel B. Tilden. After receiving sufficient electoral votes to be declared president of the United States in 1877, Hayes began dismantling the fledgling political–legal infrastructure being crafted by African Americans

and their white allies for their inclusion into the civic culture of this nation. In effect, he sabotaged efforts by African Americans to become citizens by re-creating the ante bellum conditions for racists in both the north and the south to again get the upper hand in determining the racial etiquette of the south and the nation as a whole. For African Americans this meant a return to the abject status of racial pariah.

Typical of the educational environment for African Americans living in the post *Plessy* south is described by James T. Patterson (2001),

> *Schools for black people were especially bad-indeed primitive. . . . Sunflower County, Mississippi, a cotton plantation region, had no high schools for Blacks. In the elementary grades of the county's Black schools, many of the teachers worked primarily as cooks or domestics on the plantations. Most had no more than a fourth grade education (10).*

Continuing, he notes that,

> *In the 1948–49 school year, the average investment per pupil in Atlanta public school facilities was $228.05 for Blacks and $570.00 for whites. In 1949–50 there was an average of 36.2 Black children per classroom, compared to an average of 22.6 among whites (11).*

By the early 1950s just as in the preceding decades after the civil war, racial segregation was the hallmark of American apartheid. Public schools in the south and border states were the parade ground where Jim Crow marched and drummed out his message of separation, inequality and inferiority. Schools for African American children were the by products of systematic and institutionalized racism.

Chinks in the armor of Jim Crow began to appear in the decades of the 1940s primarily due to the activism of the National Association for the Advancement of Colored People (NAACP). The NAACP had won some important cases before the U.S. Supreme Court in controversies involving all white primary elections (*Smith v. Allwright* 1944) and segregated law schools (*Sweatt v. Painter*, 1950). The belated initiatives by presidents Franklin D. Roosevelt to open the nation's war industries to African American workers and Harry Truman's Executive Order desegregating the armed forces as the decade of the 1940s closed, at least gave notice that the Executive Branch was willing to address America's race dilemma.

The Brown Case

When the 1950s began Linda Brown had just turned six years old. In many respects she typified the thousands of African American children attending segregated public schools. She lived within walking distance, or a short car ride, of a white school in or near their neighborhood. In Linda's case there was a bit of an irony. She lived in an integrated neighborhood and regularly played with white school children. On occasion her white playmates even stayed overnight in her parent's home. Yet, she could not attend the white elementary school just a few blocks from her house. Instead she had to rise early each school morning, walk through a dangerous train switch yard, which was usually a hang out place for some of the town's derelicts and transients, catch a bus which took her to an all Black elementary school some two miles from her house.

Fed up with the color line and the indignities of public school segregation, Oliver Brown, Linda's father, challenged Topeka, Kansas' Jim Crow school system. The challenge came after his being unable to register his daughter in the white school near his house. Typically a mild mannered man—not having a record of activism—Oliver Brown sought out the assistance of the local branch of the NAACP headed by McKinley Burnett (Kluger 1976). Burnett is often times acknowledged as the understated and real hero of the Brown saga. It was he who developed the strategy, organized parents, pulled together the resources necessary to challenge the Topeka School Board's segregation policies (Irons 2002). It was McKinley Burnett who convinced the national NAACP to take on the Topeka case as part of a growing number of school segregation cases the national office was seriously considering.

The Brown case was initially heard before the District Court for the District of Kansas on February 28th, 1951. Robert L. Carter, an able and respected attorney with the NAACP Legal and Defense Fund argued for an injunction forbidding Topeka's public schools from segregating African American elementary school children from white children. By all accounts Carter's presentation was masterfully structured and convincingly presented to the District judges. Indeed, the judges of the District Court were moved to register their empathy for African American children deprived of the higher quality education typically provided to white children. On this point the Court noted, "Segregation of white and colored children in public schools has a detrimental effect on colored children" (Kluger 2002). But the judges refused to issue an injunction, resting their decision instead on the fact that the provisions of the 1896 *Plessy* decision which decreed that public schools were to be "separate but equal" was still the law of the land.

On October first of the same year, the Brown case was joined with other law suits from South Carolina, Delaware, Virginia, and the District of Columbia challenging public school segregation. While the end results of the case are well known and certainly represent a sea change in the application of the 14th amendment's equal protection clause to African American children, it was not the first challenge to segregated public schools. In 1849 a similar challenge in the Sarah Roberts case *(Roberts v. City of Boston)* was filed in Boston, Massachusetts. In 1947, seven years before the Brown decision, The California State Supreme Court declared that the segregated public school system in Orange County, in southern California, was discriminatory towards Mexican American elementary school children *(Mendez v. Westminster School District)*. In Kansas between 1881 and 1949 some eleven cases were filed challenging segregated schools. At the time Brown was argued before the U.S. Supreme Court, the racially segregated public school system was the norm in a good part of the nation. It was legally sanctioned or permitted in twenty four states.

The legal strategy leading to the cases comprising *Brown* deserves more attention than is the subject of this article. It is important to point out that the assault against public school segregation was well planned for in advance by some of the best legal minds both African American and white associated with the NAACP. The plans were underway earnestly in the 1930s with legal challenges being considered against segregation in graduate and professional schools, voting rights and housing (Greenberg 1994).

The chief architect of the desegregation strategy was Charles H. Houston, who was the dean of the Howard University Law School at the time he was also taking the lead in orchestrating a response to public school segregation. The core of the strategy was its focus on graduate and professional education institutions rather than elementary education. Houston's thinking was that by drawing on the equal provisions of *Plessy* and forcing states to build professional and graduate schools *equal* in all aspects to the white graduate and professional schools, he would overwhelm their ability to support two separate systems of graduate and professional education. Thus, making it impossible for states to maintain expensive dual systems of post secondary education and graduate systems. Using this strategy he won a landmark decision in 1936 when the Maryland Supreme Court ordered the University of Maryland's law school to admit Donald Murray, a Black student, rather than send him to an out of state law school. *(Murray v. Maryland)*. He won a similar case before the U.S. Supreme Court in 1938 *(Missouri ex rel Gaines v. Canada)*. The Supreme Court in this case found that the University of Missouri, though it did create a separate law school for Black students, the facility—in a building shared with a hotel and a movie theatre—provided a "privilege . . . for white students" which it did not provide for Black students.

In 1939 Houston's prize student, Thurgood Marshall, took over as the chief counsel for the NAACP and established the NAACP Legal Defense and Education Fund. By the late 1940s Marshall was of a mind that the "validity" of the segregation statutes which the NAACP had left unchallenged with its "equalization" strategy was insufficient as a strategy for dismantling segregation laws. At the time the elementary school cases were accepted by the NAACP, the organization's strategy was focused on proving that public school segregation imposed restrictions on African American school children which denied them equal protection of the laws as prescribed by the 14th amendment to the U.S. Constitution. Interestingly, Marshall and his brilliant team of colleagues drew from the research studies by social and behavioral scientists in making their case. In particular the doll studies by Professors Kenneth Clarke and his wife, Mamie were instrumental. Using black and white dolls the Clarkes' demonstrated that the actions of African American children in choosing white dolls in a testing situation and attributing to the dolls positive characteristics displayed the extent to which segregation had diminished their sense of identity and self esteem. Their studies, while controversial were sufficient to convincing the Justices of the destructive effects racial segregation can have on children.

Significance of *Brown*

To assert that the unanimous decision rendered by the Court on May 17, 1954 was of landmark proportions is now well supported. Given its message and the times the decision was tantamount to the earth tilting a few degrees off its normal axis. The Court's pronouncement that "separate educational facilities are inherently unequal," and thus constituting a denial of the equal protection clause of the 14th amendment was for its day a profound rebuke of the long standing provisions of the 1896 *Plessy* decision. In effect the Court said that African American children deserved to receive an opportunity for an education which constitutionally should be on par with that provided to most white children living in the South.

Because of many questions and uncertainties as how to implement the provisions of the decision, the Supreme Court delivered a *Brown II* decision a year later. This decision did not provide necessary direction to southern school boards or establish the standards they were to follow in desegregating their public schools. Instead, the Court established the vague principle that desegregation should proceed "with all deliberate speed." This limp edict allowed southern states, their school boards and their public officials, elected and appointed, a huge escape route from implementing fourteenth amendment provisions of the first *Brown* decision.

Critique of *Brown II*

Brown II was a failure. It failed to give sufficient guidance and direction to the federal courts in desegregation cases. As such, it did not hold states or courts accountable for implementing 14th amendment protections for African American public school children in the south. Thus, only the most courageous judges would venture on their own and rule in the favor of fourteenth amendment protections for African American school children. *Brown II* was also a failure in that it, in effect, succumbed to the deeply entrenched belief of white supremacy subscribed to by the great majority of white southerners and no few northerners. The Warren Court, notwithstanding its unanimous decision in *Brown I*, was not about the business of transforming southern racial values and practices. It had spoken loudly in extending the 14th amendment anew to African American children, but it was not about to take on—head to head—the ideology of white supremacy. The court had gone as far as it cared on the issue of state sponsored school desegregation.

And because of this the "with all deliberate speed" clause allowed southern politicians, policy makers of various stripes and the ordinary white citizens to dodge school desegregation. As noted above, the Supreme Court should have stepped in and ordered compliance with its order. It took no such action. As a result racial segregation in southern school districts changed very little between 1955 and 1964 (Patterson 2001). Regarding the glacial movement of desegregation in the south, James T. Patterson notes, "By early 1964, only 1.2 percent of black children in the eleven southern states attended school with whites" (Patterson, 2001). Similarly, northern schools were virtually untouched by desegregation until the mid 1970s. The major point here is that the adherents of *Brown* were unable to muster the political or moral might necessary to transform the decision into a national social/political strategy the object of which would have been to desegregate this nation's public schools.

The fact that this was not done is more of a comment on the unwillingness of this nation's leadership communities to advance desegregation than it is a negative comment on the failings of the U.S. Supreme Court. It is more a critical comment on the lack of a national will; a will undergirded by the moral premise that it is fundamentally wrong, intolerable and unacceptable for any of this nation's children to have to attend schools—especially those segregated by race—where they will predictably receive an inferior education. An education which will predictably—cause doors of opportunity to be closed in their faces.

While there were many millions of Americans of all ethnicities and social economic classes in agreement that African American children and children of color should have an opportunity for a quality education, there was never a national consensus of commitment to bringing about the radical changes in how this nation conducted the business of public school education. To wit, there was never a national will to make *Brown* other than the symbolization of an education norm. That this is the case is disturbingly illustrated by the strident and racist oppositional voices generated by both *Brown* decisions.

Resistance to the *Brown* Decisions

To state that the Supreme Court's desegregation decision caused severe undulations in the social, political and legal fabric of the south is to speak to the obvious. This was not a decision that most southerners were expecting although there were for decades growing signs of African American impatience with Jim Crow.

In the main, resistance to the *Brown* decisions was the order of the day in the south. While there was some reluctant compliance in states, e.g., Arkansas and Tennessee, in the main, resistance was fierce and unrelenting. Typically such resistance took three forms: litigation, privatization and terror. Most southern states challenged desegregation orders through the courts; thus, dragging out implementation. Privatization of public schools was a second form of resistance. White parents, with the aid of school officials and politicians, formed private academies and other institutions, often times using public funds as a way of evading desegregation. The third form of resistance was well known. Use of terror. White segregationists formed hate groups like the

White Citizen's Councils which became vehicles for the transport of hate speech and acts of violence against African Americans and any one or anything presumed to be a threat to segregation.

The most effective assault against the idealistic, albeit vague, mandates of the Supreme Court was launched by Presidents Richard Nixon, Ronald Reagan and George Bush, the elder. All three presidents were hostile to desegregation and especially when the federal courts ordered bussing as the device to accomplish the fact. The three, beginning with Nixon, sought to change what they felt was an overly active federal judiciary (with particular criticism aimed at the decisions by the Warren Court) by appointing conservative judges to the federal judiciary and to the Supreme Court. Appointees to the federal judiciary in the decades of the 70s and 80s were made by presidents committed to shaping a more conservative federal judiciary with judges having no zeal for enforcing civil rights laws. It is perversely ironical to note that during this era of redemption, President Ronald Reagan, with mean spirited intentions, nominated Clarence Thomas, the second African American to serve on the U.S. Supreme Court and no friend of civil rights causes, to replace Thurgood Marshall.

In a series of Supreme Court decisions beginning in 1974 and extending into the mid-nineties, the conservative voices on the Court and elsewhere in the federal judiciary essentially rendered a moribund *Brown*, dead. Examples of key decisions during this period were *Milliken v. Bradley* (1974); *Board of Education of Oklahoma City v. Dowell* (1991); *Freeman v. Pitts* (1992); *Missouri v. Jenkins* (1995).

In *Milliken*, a Detroit, Michigan case, the Court made *Brown* all but irrelevant for most northern cities by not approving desegregation plans combining city and suburban schools. In the *Board of Education of Oklahoma City v. Dowell* the Court ruled that school districts could be released from desegregation orders if they created "unitary"—meaning racially mixed-schools. In the *Freeman* case the Court provided that a school district could dismantle its desegregation plans without having to desegregate its faculty and provide students equal access to its programs. And finally, in *Missouri v. Jenkins,* the Court prohibited efforts to attract white suburban and private

school students voluntarily into city schools by using strong academic programs.

Today for all intents and purposes the idealistic, albeit toothless, provisions of *Brown* are memories of a failed future. This is because of the factors previously mentioned: a combination of a weak commitment by policy makers at all levels to enforce desegregation; a Supreme Court's unwillingness to pursue enforcement of its mandates; an intense backlash by both southerners and northerners against court ordered desegregation; no national will to undo segregated schools; the general inability of the African American civil rights community to mount an effective response to the "with all deliberate speed" clause which was used as subterfuge to desegregation.

Post *Brown* and Public School Resegregation

In a 2002 report, "Race in American Public Schools: Rapidly Resegregating School Districts," authored by Erika Frankenberg and Chungmei Lee, we are given a fresh and disturbing look at the nation's rush back to resegregation. A telling conclusion of their study is that,

"Virtually all public school districts . . . are showing lower levels of inter-racial exposure since 1986, suggesting a trend towards resegregation, and in some districts, these declines are sharp" (4).

These two scholars, as have several before them, note that since the mid 1980s African American and Latino students have become increasingly more segregated in public schools (Orwell and Eaton 1996). Again, the significant problematic here is—not that increasing racial isolation is underway, but the fact that the schools attended by African American and Latino students are more closely associated with "low parental involvement, lack of resources, less experienced and credentialed teachers, and higher teacher turnover all of which in combination exacerbate educational inequality for mostly minority student" (Frankenberg and Lee).

There is much good to say about having children of diverse backgrounds learning in the same classroom setting; attending the same schools. Indeed, if this nations is to become truly a democratic society, one which accepts multiculturalism as a fundamental characteristic of its being, we—children and their parents and other adults—must learn about each other with each other; children (and we) must learn to collaborate across gender, sexual orientation, social class, religious, ethnic and other lines, borders, and margins which function as social lines of demarcation. They must learn to see themselves in others. Which is to say that the struggle is to identify those aspects of who we are as distinct cultural beings which can be tapped for collaborative purposes, rather than placing emphasis on changing or muting our defining cultural attributes. But this is the ideal.

The reality of social formation in this nation is that its history of discrimination, the *minoritizing* and marginalizing of cultural groups is deeply institutionalized in habits of both heart and mind. We cannot escape who we are. No matter the feel good fluffy escapist attempts by popular culture outlets to portray contemporary American society as only challenged by the need for more sun blocker and the proliferation of trendy unproven weight loss schemes. The color line remains as a defining feature of who we are. Yet, as a nation we remain hopelessly deluded, believing that the sins of the past are in the past.

This is clearly evident when one looks at the state of public school education for African American children. These are children attending urban schools enter where they are not being prepared to take advantage of opportunities for social, economic, and education mobility. The education issue for the African American community is not one framed by who the child sits next to in a classroom, but whether or not the child is receiving a quality education at the school she/he is attending. The compelling social/education/political challenge for the African American community is not desegregation, but access to *quality education*. There is compelling and disturbing evidence that African Americans in too many of this nation's urban public schools are being drastically shortchanged.

It is clear to this writer that this nation has turned its back on issues relating to the civil rights of citizens. Such issues have always focused this nation on how some groups of citizens have fared at the hands of other citizens and the government. Especially condemning have been those recurrences of longstanding discrimination and acts of brutality carried out against people of color and especially African Americans. Too many people now believe that the civil rights legislation, namely, the 1965 Civil Rights and the 1964 Voting Rights Act and subsequent equal opportunity legislation have significantly addressed race and other forms of discrimination. As a result, so this line of thinking goes, the once existing barriers to opportunity have fallen. And as a result, no such impediments stand in the way of anyone's entry into or progress within America's institutional formations. Or so it is widely believed.

This is to say different strategies for addressing longstanding institutional practices which remain as barriers must be considered and adopted. This is especially the case given the fact that this nation has also turned its back on the normative provisions of the first *Brown* decision. In effect saying "we don't care if African American school children receive low quality education experiences."

What Is to Be Done?

The central question at this point concerns the responses to the fact that the promises of *Brown* have not been realized. In the main, I believe the responses should be framed, or at least influenced, by what have been the responses to efforts to effect public school desegregation. Indeed, there are salient lessons to be learned from this history. For example, one of the important lessons learned from *Brown* is that, at least for the foreseeable future, there is neither the national will nor leadership structures to reshape public schools. That is, to reshape them around value laden resource allocation practices designed to insure that all children have an opportunity to receive a high quality education experience. Another clearly delivered lesson is that the parents of children attending quality public schools in suburbs and exurbs are adamantly against any desegregation schemes which will take their children from neighborhood schools. And are only luke warm to any in-bussing efforts bringing urban children into suburban schools and neighborhoods. Another lesson learned and which must be heeded is that the African American civil rights and the broader civil rights communities and the progressive elements of the education communities were unable to develop the political education strategies needed to translate the promise of *Brown I* into policy directives and statutes compelling desegregation. Seemingly the thinking was that the Supreme Court decision in and of itself would prompt a transformation of racist attitudes and practices.

Given these and other lessons gained from the era of *Brown* and the predictable lack of appetite for more substantive approaches to institutional change in this nation, this writer is not surprised that the typical small "l" liberal approaches to addressing the shortcomings of the nation's response to public school desegregation. Contemporarily the strategies offered and righteously defended include the following in various iterations:

◆ Mounting a national campaign to educate Americans regarding the inequalities of education provided to urban dwelling African Americans and other people of color and the dire implications of this.

◆ Energizing civil rights organizations to take more aggressive lobbying tactics on behalf of access to quality education for all public school students.

◆ Filing law suits on behalf of aggrieved students of color.

◆ Energizing and holding public policy makers accountable for passing legislation designed to close education gaps and holding school officials accountable for implementing the expectations.

These strategies are in and of themselves are reasonable. They intend to lay claim on this nation's advocacy organizations, policy making and education structures for doing the right thing on behalf of public school children. Indeed, noble intentions. But, unfortunately, these strategies fail to take into account the history of responses this nation has made to the social justice claims by people of color. If the past is prologue, this writer simply does not put much faith in the likelihood that these approaches—even if adopted—would have the desired effect. The strategies place too much stock in normalistic and

gradualistic approaches to social change which historically have not met the needs or social objectives of people of color. These approaches rest on the presumptive belief that decision making processes are fair, equally accessible to prince and pauper alike, and are fundamentally committed to the concept and practices of a quality education for all children. The evidence supporting these beliefs is thin.

Given the gravity of the challenges facing African American children and given the responses by this nation to desegregation efforts along with the lessons learned from *Brown,* it is time for African Americans to give serious attention to other strategies. The social and cultural costs for not doing so are too horrifying to disregard. Simply stated, consider the life chances for a young person graduating from high school without the critical thinking skills, numeracy skills, reading skills and experiences with information technology today. Consider the life chances of someone who has dropped out of school before graduating.

I am recommending that African American parents, community members and leaders develop education strategies based on a fundamental proposition emanating from the social history of African people in this nation. The proposition is this. African Americans and any allies gained along the way must first and foremost take the responsibility for educating African American children. This proposition arises out of lessons from the social history of Africans in this land. The proposition is neither defeatist (likely to be a charge) nor cynical. Its truth is based in the truth of the social experiences of African Americans. This truth demonstrates that there have been only two instances in nearly four centuries of the African presence in this part of the diaspora where the federal government has willfully committed resources to educate African people.

The first was during the Reconstruction Era after the Civil War with the formation of the Freedmen's Bureau. According to historian, John Hope Franklin, the Bureau's most significant impact was providing education opportunities for newly freed slaves. The Bureau established and helped to administer an array of educational institutions from day schools to colleges (1966). The second instance of a federal commitment to addressing and repairing social damage done to

African Americans due to institutionalized and individual discrimination was during the administration of President Lyndon B. Johnson. The Johnson administration's advocacy of civil rights and equal opportunity legislation set the tone for improvements in education programs benefiting African American and poor children and for opening access to colleges and universities. Unfortunately, both of these instances were short lived and existed within the maelstrom of challenge and resistance, especially from white southerners.

Against this backdrop and given what we know about the nation's responses to the concept and practice of desegregation and given the grave consequences now facing African American students in too many inner city schools, I strongly recommend that another course of action be considered. African Americans must reorganize institutional resources, e.g., families, churches, civic and social organizations, etc., around a fundamental proposition. Namely, educating children is the primary responsibility of African Americans. Any one wishing to assist in this effort should be considered, but the primary responsibility rests with African Americans. Institutionalizing this proposition can take several delivery forms, among these are:

♦ Private schools—secular or sectarian
♦ Charter schools
♦ Gendered schools—all male or all female
♦ Charter magnet schools

These institutions would be open to all students, but the emphasis would be on providing African American students a high quality education experience that is culturally relevant. The considerable wealth (approximately 800 billion dollars in annual spending power) and talent from such sectors in the African American community such as: education, business, entertainment, churches, professional athletics and ordinary citizens must be marshaled and focused on providing education alternatives to African Americans. The capacity to do this is present. The will to do so must be bolstered and redirected. In short, African Americans must themselves take on this imperative project.

This is a much needed and long overdue approach to addressing the fact that this nation has

not taken the education interests of African American and most children of color seriously. Again, this step towards education independence and self reliance is dictated by the African American's social history. As pointed out above, this history is replete with incidences of betrayal and subterfuge by the institutions charged with protecting the rights of African Americans (Bell 2002). It seems foolhardy, and in fact, is culturally suicidal, to continue to depend on institution of education to prepare African American children to compete on equal footing with others in this nation. Lessons from African American history speak to the need for a drastically different education paradigm. The stakes for not doing so are much too high. A people simply cannot advance socially, economically, politically or culturally, if their children and subsequently, their adults, are miseducated at worst, and poorly educated at best.

In its final analysis, the need for an independent course of action rests on another critically important proposition. History is not kind to a people who deliver up their children to a society's institutions of education when these institutions like the others comprising the social order have been implicated in the historical oppression of the people.

References

Bullock, H. (1967). *A History of Negro Education in the South.* Cambridge, Massachusetts: Harvard University Press.

Bell, D. (2004). *Silent Covenants.* New York, New York: Oxford University Press.

Frankenberg, E. and Lee, C. (2002). *Race in American Public Schools: Rapidly Resegregating School Districts.* Cambridge, Massachusetts: The Civil Rights Project Harvard University.

Franklin, J. H. (1966). *From Slavery to Freedom.* New York, Vintage Books.

Greenberg, J. (1994). *Crusaders in the Courts: How a Dedicated Band of Lawyers Fought for the Civil Rights Revolution.* New York, New York: Basic Books.

Hochschild, J. (1984). *The New American Dilemma: Liberal Democracy and School Desegregation.* New Haven, Connecticut: Yale University.

Irons, P. (2002). *Jim Crow's Children.* New York, New York: Penguin Books.

Kluger, R. (1976). *Simple Justice: The History of Brown v. Board of Education and Black Americans' Struggle for Equality.* New York, New York: Alfred P. Knopf.

Orfield, G. and Eaton, S. (1996). *Dismantling Desegregation: The Quiet Reversal of Brown v. Board of Education.* New York, New York: The New Press.

Patterson, J. (2001). *Brown v. Board of Education: A Civil Rights Milestone and its Troubled Legacy.* New York, New York: Oxford University Press.

Court Cases Cited in Article

Roberts v. City of Boston, 59 Massachusetts. 198 (1849)

Plessy v. Ferguson, 163 U.S. 537 (1896)

University v. Murray, 169 Maryland 478 (1936)

Missouri ex. rel. Gaines v. Canada, 305 U.S. 337 (1938)

Mendez v. Westminster, S.D. California (1946)

Sweatt v. Painter, 339 U.S. 629 (1950)

Brown v. Board of Education of Topeka, 349 U.S. 294 (1954)

Brown v. Board of Education of Topeka, 349 U.S. 294 (1955)

Milliken v. Bradley, 418 U.S. 717 (1974)

Board of Education of Oklahoma City v. Dowell, 489 U.S. 265 (1991)

Freeman v. Pitts, 503 U.S. 467 (1992)

Missouri v. Jenkins, 515 U.S. 1139 (1995)

Bias: Impact on Decision Makers in Child Welfare

Rita Cameron Wedding, Ph.D.

The public child welfare agency is the system entrusted with protecting our nation's most vulnerable population—our children. Most people believe that kids are put in foster care because they have been abused or neglected by their parents or caretakers. But studies show that more subjective factors such as race may contribute to the overwhelming number of children of color who are placed into foster care each year. Black children are overrepresented in the child welfare system in every state. They are only 15 percent of the U.S. population, yet they represent over 36 percent of the children in foster care (Hill, *Synthesis of Research on Disproportionality in Child Welfare* 3). In 46 states they are 1 ? to 3 ? times more likely to be in the child welfare system than their representation in the general population (12). This fact may seem irrelevant to many people because, after all, *What's race got to do with it? The parents must have done something wrong or their kids would not have been taken away.* Despite the fact that research is clear that blacks are no more likely to abuse or neglect their kids than whites, studies show that race has a compelling influence on which children are removed and placed into foster care and their experiences once they are in care.

How is it that race can have such a profound influence on child welfare outcomes? Many children are put in foster care due to general neglect, which is often inconclusive and requires the decision maker to make a case for removal. Each decision point is influenced by perception,

interpretation, intuition and hunches that are documented in the case notes and available to influence decisions at each subsequent decision point. Discretionary decision making by mandated reporters, screeners, social workers and even judges such as determining "minimum acceptable level of care" can be highly susceptible to bias. According to the Race Matters Toolkit, "research across youth-serving systems shows that the more discretion that exists in decision-making, the more likelihood that youth of color, especially African American, Latino and Native American, will be treated more negatively than their white counterparts" (12). Although most of us would like to think of ourselves as color-blind and may even assert that we don't notice race, the fact is that we are inundated with racial stereotypes that reiterate themes about groups of people that can become the backdrop against which many decisions about child well-being are made.

Introduction

The purpose of this chapter is to discuss how the impact of stereotyping, implicit bias and institutional racism can influence decision making and result in patterns of discrimination in our major social institutions.

Much of this is unintentional because individuals have internalized codes and cues that allow the racialization process to continue even though formal laws of discrimination have been outlawed. This process is based on beliefs of white superiority and black inferiority. This racial legacy that socializes us to interpret, understand, and react to race in ways that, though sometimes unconscious, can preserve a racial hierarchy.

To the extent that institutional and agency practices mirror those of broader society, they look like routine business-as-usual acts that are unrelated to race, even though they have racial consequences.

Using Public Child Welfare as the example, this chapter explores how pervasive societal biases can distort decision making of well-meaning individuals within child welfare and other youth-serving institutions, e.g., education or juvenile justice, leading to disparate outcomes *without anyone seeming to notice.*

Statement of the Problem

"Black children are overrepresented in the child welfare system in every state. Native American/ American Indian and Alaska Native children are overrepresented in the jurisdictions in which they reside. Hispanic children are overrepresented in more than 10 states, and their representation in the child welfare system is on the rise" (Hill, An Analysis of Racial/Ethnic Disproportionality 1). Blacks and American Indians are the two most overrepresented groups, represented in foster care at twice their proportions in the census populations. The fact that such a disproportionate number of our nation's children who live in foster care are children of color goes largely unnoticed by most Americans because, in a colorblind society, we are conditioned not to notice race because "race doesn't matter." But in child welfare, race is associated with decisions of child protective services at most stages of decision making except one, and that is reentry (Hill, *Synthesis of Research on Disproportionality in Child Welfare* 1). In child welfare (as in all of our major social institutions) race matters!

In this chapter, the focus on African Americans (this term is used interchangeably with "blacks") is not intended to minimize the disparities faced by other groups like Native Americans who experience similar outcomes in child welfare. The purpose of this chapter is to explore the particular impact of ideologies, stereotypes, implicit bias and institutional racism on African Americans' increased risk for child welfare involvement.

Review of the Data

Disproportionality and Disparity are the two terms used most when describing child welfare outcomes. According to Barbara Needell, a researcher at UC Berkeley, "disproportionality is when a group makes up a proportion of those experiencing some event that is higher or lower than the group's proportion in the population. When we examine disparity we are comparing one group (e.g., regarding disproportionality, services, outcomes) to another group." (Needell, Webster and Armijo). Looking at California data, African American children represent 7.18 percent of the child population; however, they represent 27.72 percent of the children in foster care in 2006, nearly four times the percent in the population. Native American children are also disproportionately in care, representing .84 percent of the child population and 1.41 percent of the children in foster care in 2006 (Needell, Webster and Armijo).

Similarly, if county-level data is explored within California, disproportionality is further demonstrated. In San Francisco County, for example, African American children represent 8.12 percent of the child population and 66.98 of the children in foster care in 2006 (8.25 times higher than their percentage in the population). Therefore, black children are over 31 times more likely to be in care than white children (8.25/.26)!

Another way of looking at data around disproportionality relates to the rates per 1,000 children. In a group of 1,000 children representative of the diversity of the population of the state of California 7.73 of them would be in

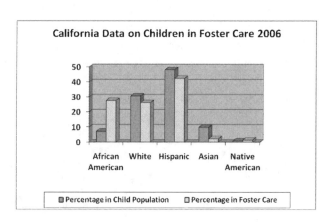

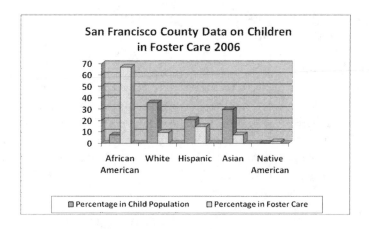

Rates in Foster Care Per 1000 Children

	California	San Francisco County
All Children	7.73	14.47
African American	29.83	119.36
White	6.58	3.80
Hispanic	6.81	10.15
Asian	1.77	3.62
Native American	12.94	94.41

foster care, while in a group of 1,000 African American children in the state of California 29.83 of them would be in foster care. Even further, in a group of 1,000 San Francisco County African American children 119.36 of them would be in foster care. The rate for white children in San Francisco County is 3.80 per 1,000. Note that 119.36/3.80 gives us the same 31-fold difference between black and white children as we saw when we looked at the disproportionality ratios, so these two methods for computing disparity ratios are equivalent (Needell, Webster and Armijo). The numbers are very high for Native American children in California and elsewhere throughout the country.

Many people assume that racial disproportionality is due to a greater incidence of abuse and neglect among black families. The data is clear that there is no prevalence of abuse or neglect by race. Yet, despite this, black children are more likely to be placed in foster care and to have different and poorer outcomes once they are in the system. Research shows that children of color in foster care and their families are treated differently from and not as well as whites. When we compare in-care outcomes of one race/ethnicity to another, the data shows alarming disparities in service delivery to children in care. Disparities for black children include: fewer and lower quality services, fewer foster parent support services, fewer contacts by caseworkers, less access to mental health services, less access to drug treatment services, and higher placement in detention or correctional facilities (Hill, *Synthesis of Research on Disproportionality in Child Welfare* 28). Other studies show that the child welfare system was less responsive to the needs of black families than white families, delaying intervention until black families' problems were perceived as chronic and failing to address the most pressing problems, such as poverty, ill health, inadequate housing and unsafe neighborhoods (Hill, *Synthesis of Research on Disproportionality in Child Welfare* 28). Clearly, the failure to mitigate problems with the greatest potential to put children at risk will contribute to disproportionality and disparity of blacks in child welfare. Black children pay an enormous price for this social inequity. According to Robert Hill, these children, while under state-mandated care, suffer far worse outcomes in terms of physical and mental health, educational performance, and access to basic services and resources (Hill, *Synthesis of Research on Disproportionality in Child Welfare* 1).

Because the data is not always clear about where, why and how bias occurs, many people reject the notion of racism, preferring instead to blame factors such as poverty and maltreatment for disproportionality and disparity outcomes in child welfare.

Explaining Disproportionality and Disparities: Poverty and Abuse

Public Child Welfare is largely a poor person's system, and poverty, as it conflates with race, increases the probability of child welfare involvement. As stated earlier, the disproportionate numbers of children in foster care are children of color, many of whom are poor, but poverty alone does not explain disproportionality. If disproportionality was just about poverty there would be a higher proportion of poor people from all racial/ethnic groups, including whites, in the system. Even though nationally Latinos have poverty rates comparable to blacks in most jurisdictions, their underrepresentation in child welfare is comparable to whites. If poverty caused disproportionality, you would expect to see more consistent patterns of overrepresentation of Latinos.

When we examine outcomes of middle-class white people, the indicators are much different. As stated earlier, white families are consistently underrepresented in the child welfare system; it is almost an anomaly to see white middle-class and wealthy families in crisis come into the child welfare system. Wealth does not inoculate families from crisis, but these families typically have private means that allow them to bypass the public

child welfare system even on the rare chance that they are referred to the system. Watching families in crisis has become part of the new entertainment genre. Families (predominately white) that appear on shows like *Dr. Phil, Wife Swap* and *Supernanny* display the most egregious examples of child abuse on primetime TV. Ironically, even though these families literally air their dirty laundry before all of America, they manage to fly under the radar of Child Protective Services.

When it comes to the involvement of blacks in Child Welfare, the inextricable link between poverty and "being black" is very clear. "One study using California data found that after controlling for poverty and maltreatment, African American children were more likely to be removed from their homes and placed in foster care compared to whites when income was accounted for" (Government Accountabilty Office 24). Among African Americans, 23 percent live below the poverty line compared to 6 percent of whites (Government Accountabilty Office 18). Poverty does not cause abuse, but the effects of poverty appear to interact with other risk factors, such as depression, isolation, teenage pregnancy, unemployment, substance abuse, and domestic violence, to increase the likelihood of maltreatment (Hill, 2006, Drake & Zuravin, 1998; English, 1998; Giovannoni, 1995, McRoy, 2004; Rose & Meezan, 1995,1996). Synthesis of Research on Disproportionality 17. Circumstances linked to poverty make black families more vulnerable to child welfare involvement. "Rather than visiting private doctos, poor families are likely to attend public clinics and emergency rooms for routine medical care; rather than hiring contractors to fix their homes, poor families encounter public building inspectors; rather than using their cars to run errands, poor mothers use public transportation. Middle class parents, on the other hand, are insulated from this degree of scrutiny. (Roberts 32) According to Roberts, the intensified supervision of poor families cannot account for their higher incidence of child maltreatment. But it does explain why so many poor and so few wealthier families are involved with child protective services (33). Obviously, regardless of how abuse and neglect comes to the attention of authorities, the important thing is that children are protected. But perceptions of risk as well as decisions about how to mitigate risk are dealt with differently depending on the race and social class of the families involved. Some people would argue that the state has more of an interest in punishing rather than helping poor people. Many decisions to place children in care are poverty related. Even when having subsidized housing is not the primary cause of removal, it is frequently at the center of caseworkers' decisions to place children in foster care. "The U.S. department of Health and Human services reports that children from families with housing problems are also more likely to stay in the system longer. The court appointed administrator of the District of Columbia foster care system determined that as many as half of the children in foster care could be immediately reunited with their parents if housing problems were resolved" (Roberts 35). Among families with housing problems, white families are offered housing services at almost twice the rate as black families (Roberts 21).

Poverty also affects the quality and level of services that families receive because many poverty related conditions are interpreted as neglect. Parental conduct or home conditions that appear innocent when the parents are affluent are often considered to be neglectful when the parents are poor (Roberts 38).

Under California law, general neglect is defined as the negligent failure of a parent or care-taker to provide food, clothing, shelter, or supervision where no physical injuries to the child have occurred (Roberts 33). Severe neglect occurs when the child's health is endangered, including severe malnutrition. Since many of the indicators child welfare agencies use to assess whether a child is at risk for maltreatment are conditions of poverty, even children who have never been mistreated and who are in no immediate danger may be removed from their homes (Roberts 38). For example, there are times that decisions to remove children are based on predictions. One social worker said he refused to return kids to their homes if they lived in a dangerous neighborhood. Most people wouldn't live in dangerous neighborhoods if they could afford to live elsewhere. This is just one example of how a condition of poverty, e.g., a dangerous

neighborhood, is the reason why children are not reunified. Social workers in another jurisdiction identified the following subjective factors that influenced their decisions to remove or reunify: lifestyle choices, poor character, family structure and social worker values.

- *Lifestyle*

  Examples are a dirty house, not unsafe, just nasty, and too many guys hanging around. These suggest potential, not actual harm.

- *Poor Character*

  The mother is perceived to have a bad attitude. The mother is labeled hostile or aggressive. According to Roberts, the attitude of the mother toward the social worker is often perceived as evidence of "risk" to the child. (66) Different parenting practices exhibited by a black mother which might be characterized as stern and not nurturing or the fact that the mother shows no contrition that her children are removed (Roberts) might also be used as evidence of risk.

- *Family Structure*

  Single mothers, children by different fathers, or absent fathers (always assumed to be uninvolved and "deadbeat") constitute "broken families" when compared to an "intact" white, middle-class, nuclear family that is always presumed to be responsible.

- *Personal Values of Caseworkers*

  The "apple doesn't fall too far from the tree" theory that presumes that child welfare or welfare involvement is generational treats removal as inevitable (Cameron Wedding and Molinar).

  Alone, these subjective factors may not be the grounds for removal, but they are routinely used in reports to bolster recommendations regarding removal or reunification. Furthermore, after the actual cause of removal (such as substance abuse or general neglect) is addressed these conditions will likely persist. Because these examples reflect conditions of poverty, the moral character of the client and personal values of the worker they may be impossible to reconcile in the eyes of the caseworker.

All families have rough spots; even in stable families parents can have a lapse in judgment or experience a medical related, financial or substance abuse crisis (prescribed or illegal). But poor families are less able to rebound when things get rough.

"Poor parents often cannot afford to pay others to care for their children when they are unable to, because they have to go to work, they are distraught, or they are high on drugs or alcohol. Nor can they afford to pay professionals to cover up their mistakes. They cannot buy services to mitigate the effects of their own neglectful behavior. Affluent substance-abusing parents, for example, can check themselves into a private residential drug treatment program and hire a nanny to care for their children during their absence. The state never has to get involved" (Roberts 36).

The conflation of social class and race intersect in ways that result in caseworkers making decisions about these families with minimum information. While white families are assumed to be resilient and capable of recovery, the negative assumptions that accrue to black families based on race, class, and gendered assumptions may result in what Roberts refers to as *vague definitions of neglect*. The majority of black children are removed for neglect, which is often subject to interpretation, hunches, and intuition. Intuition and hunches are by definition subjective, yet decision makers openly attribute their discretionary decision making (that determines the fate of many) to intuition as though it is based in science. "Vague definitions of neglect, unbridled discretion and lack of training form a dangerous combination in the hands of caseworkers charged with deciding fates of families. Unlike child abuse that can at least be substantiated with physical evidence the vague definition of neglect is highly susceptible to biased evaluations of harm based on the parent's race or class or on cultural differences in child rearing" (Roberts 55).

Stereotypes Promote Assumptions of Black Maternal Unfitness

Racial ideologies or stereotypes which are proliferated throughout society contain the coding and cues used to define and interpret groups. Racial paradigms which originated during slavery continue to stigmatize black people as problematic, predisposed to criminality, laziness, and immorality. Connotations that create a context for presumptions of black maternal unfitness can have a huge impact on how services are provided to black families.

According to Roberts, there is popular mythology that portrays black women as unfit to have children. The same set of stereotypes also supports the removal of black women's children. "It has been accepted that there is a fundamental problem with the black family," Megan McLaughlin, Executive Director of the Federation of Protestant Welfare Agencies, told Child Welfare Watch. "There are many people who believe that to save these children they have to take them from their families. It is a sense that black families are already broken, and you're saving these kids from broken black families" (Roberts 61).

The relationship between poverty and race is reflected in ideological images of black women as the Welfare Queens. "The 'welfare mother' is labeled a bad mother, who is content to sit around and collect welfare, shunning work and passing on her bad values to her offspring" (Roberts 61). "Case workers and judges can be unconsciously influenced by potent stereotypes of black mothers' unfitness when they make judgments about how to handle allegations of child maltreatment" (Roberts 66).

Is It Racism? Is It Bias?

"Race was not found in nature but made by people in power. Racial classifications provide a way to justify privilege and oppression by making inequity appear to be the result of natural differences."

—Ron Chisom, Executive Director, The Peoples Institute for Survival and Beyond (Casey, *Undoing Racism* 2).

Race, though used as a biological or genetic category, is in fact a social category that has no purpose other than to institutionalize the inequitable distribution of societal resources. "Race should not be thought of as merely the acts of a few misguided individuals such as skinheads or white supremacists, nor should it be defined only as acts deemed as hate crimes. Racism is neither random nor coincidental; it is intrinsic to the stratification of U.S. society (Cameron Wedding 2). "In the post-civil rights era racial discrimination in employment and housing, racially segregated schools, racism in the health-care and criminal justice systems, environmental racism, transportation racism, racial discrimination in voting procedures, racial bias in the mass media, race-based hate crimes, and plain old "everyday racism" in daily social interactions remain ubiquitous features of U.S. Society" (Neubeck, 2002; Bonilla-Silva, 2001; Fegin and Vera, 1995). Racism affects all of our social institutions because it is embedded in policies and, most specifically, the practices of often well-meaning people.

In the chapter "Defending Whiteness" (in this volume), I state that there are significant differences in the way racism is manifested in contemporary society compared to historic racism (racism that existed prior to the civil rights movement). There are three features that mark contemporary racism: 1) racism doesn't (necessarily) show malice; 2) racist attitudes and actions are often unintended; 3) racist attitudes can be unconscious.

- *Racism doesn't show malice*

  Historic racism showed a direct link between racial animus and actions which were incontrovertibly racist such as lynching or the use of racial epithets. But in contemporary society racism can and does exist even in the absence of anti-black sentiment. Actions that promote racist outcomes can be subtle and covert and reveal no evidence of discrimination. The question is: if the attitudes which lead to discriminatory actions do not show malice or motive, are they still racist? This is the dilemma of contemporary racism. One form of racism in

modern society is that which is manifested in behaviors or attitudes which are ordinary everyday acts void of any racial markers. But when actions occur unevenly or when decisions are differentially applied because of some (even unconscious) racial cue or influence, the resulting racial patterns or outcomes are racist ones. The assumption that individuals such as teachers, social workers or judges, who appear to be non-prejudiced and who do not possess anti-out-group or anti-black sentiments, are non-racist must be challenged because even individuals who "claim no prejudice" against blacks (and others) nonetheless discriminate in subtle but consequential ways" (Gaertner 168).

- *Racist attitudes can be unintended*

  According to colorblind ideology the litmus test for racism is intentionality. Asserting that statements or actions can't be racist unless they were "intended" as such will protect even the most obvious racist actions (Cameron Wedding 13).

- *Racist attitudes can be unconscious*

  Perhaps the most perplexing aspect of contemporary racism is unconscious or implicit bias.

According to Mahzarin Banaji, one of the Harvard researchers who studies implicit bias, most people judge according to unconscious stereotypes and attitudes or implicit prejudice. The process of judging is not necessarily rooted in anti-black sentiment, but rather a fundamental *mechanics of thought*. "Early on we learn to associate things that commonly go together and expect them to inevitably coexist (58). Exposed to images that juxtapose black men and violence, portray women as sex objects, imply that the physically disabled are mentally weak and the poor are lazy even the most consciously unbiased person is bound to make these accusations" (Banaji 58).

According to Banaji, because we automatically make such associations to help us organize our world, we grow to trust them, and they can blind us to those instances in which the associations are not accurate. Our implicit prejudice that arises from the ordinary and unconscious tendency to make associations (mechanics of thought) is distinct from conscious forms of prejudice such as overt racism or sexism. This distinction explains why people who are free from conscious prejudice may still harbor biases and act accordingly. "Although people may wish to act in egalitarian ways, implicit biases are a powerful predictor of how they actually behave" (Banaji). We've watched this scenario get played out numerous times recently in the press, a good example being shock jock Don Imus' insidiously racist reference to the Rutgers women's basketball team as "nappy-headed ho's." There are also intellectuals like William Bennett, the Secretary of Education for Ronald Regan, who said, "If you really want to reduce crime you can abort every black baby in New York City and the crime rate will go down." Dr. Bennett was quoting from a book entitled *Freakanomics* but, interestingly, though the authors did show a link between the legalization of abortion and a decrease in the crime rate in New York City, they did not in their research indicate race as a causal effect—as did Bennett.

Implicit bias is not what we say we believe, but what comes out of our mouths before we have a chance to censor ourselves. But just because ubiquitous ideologies or stereotypes that depict blacks as violent, criminal, etc., permeate our thoughts and leave these racial assumptions on the tips of our tongues, does it mean that we really believe them and does it necessarily mean that our thinking will be influenced by them? "An implicit attitude doesn't control our behavior in a be-all and end-all kind of way, but it flavors our behavior in a pretty consistent way," says Banaji.

Another recent example of implicit bias was the biased news reporting we witnessed during Hurricane Katrina. Blacks who were "finding" food were labeled "looters" while whites who were "finding" food were described as "finding food." The reporters most likely unconsciously selected terminology that corresponded to race: whites were finders and blacks were looters. The practice of attaching negative connotations to blacks has over time normalized the association of blacks and criminality.

Implicit bias has particular effects within child welfare and other youth-serving institutions. Preconceived ideas or stereotypes that are common themes promoted in the media and throughout popular culture construct a backdrop for how all black people can be judged. Racial stereotypes and myths are embedded into the "common sense" of well-meaning people, therefore decisions assumed to be based solely on the evidence can instead be framed by implicit prejudices such as those which depict blacks as bad parents.

Child Welfare

The presence of racism in child welfare outcomes is often difficult to detect. Acccording to the Synthesis on Research on Disproportionality studies have identified a pattern in which the overrepresentation of black children in foster care might be affected by the racial composition of the geographic areas in which they reside. Most small rural localities that have a small population of blacks tend not to be as concerned about disproportionality because there are so few blacks in their communities. Studies show, however, the "rates of out-of-home placement of minority children are higher in localities in which the proportion of minorities is relatively small (where they are more visible) han in local areas where the proportion of minorities is relatively large". (27) The overrepresentation of black children in foster care can be affected by racial composition of the geographic areas "Researchers found that the visibility pattern existed only for black children and not for any of the other three minority groups (American Indians, Asians, and Hispanics). More specifically, their findings revealed that black children were twice as likely to be placed in foster care in counties where they comprised 5 to 10 percent of the population than in counties where black children comprised 30 to 50 percent of the population" (Hill, *Synthesis of Research on Disproportionality in Child Welfare* 27).

As stated earlier, social class is a major indicator for child welfare involvement. Implicit social class biases can effect discretionary decisions by mandated reporters (teachers, medical professionals or law enforcement officers, all of whom are mandated by law to report reasonable suspicions of child abuse and neglect), investigators (people who investigate allegations of maltreatment), social workers and even judges when they are predisposed to assumptions of risk based on race and social class differences in child-rearing. Many child welfare personnel may unconsciously believe that ideal families are middle-class. In fact, low risk families are essentially middle-class families in which there are two parents, with at least one parent employed, with earnings from income rather than welfare, who live in a low-crime neighborhood. (Hill, *Synthesis of Research on Disproportionality in Child Welfare* 22) In Stephanie Coontz' book, *The Way We Never Were*, she talks about the mythical model white family that never existed. According to Coontz, "White families benefit from the presumptions of parental fitness.... Holding up white families as the superior standard against which all other families fail is entrenched in American culture" (Roberts 67). In contrast, poor one-parent families who are on welfare and live in high-crime neighborhoods are labeled high risk based on their circumstances, not their actions. "Black children are less likely than white children to have advantaged characteristics, e.g., two parents, employment from earnings and a low-crime neighborhood, but even when they do have the advantaged traits they are more likely to be placed in foster care than comparable white children." (Hill, *Synthesis of Research on Disproportionality in Child Welfare* 22). These families are always under scrutiny. Where spanking might be perceived as acceptable and the right of the parents in a middle-class family, the same exact discipline might be assumed to be abuse in a poor family.

According to Hill, research revealed both public and private hospitals over reported abuse and neglect among blacks and under reported maltreatment among whites. "Among the 805 cases of child abuse and neglect that came to the attention of hospital staff, 75 percent of black families were reported for maltreatment, compared to 60 percent of white families." (18.) Studies revealed cases of abusive head trauma that inflicted injuries were more often overlooked in white children than minority children.

Mental Health

Several studies revealed that mental health professionals who had internalized stereotypes of blacks as being more violent or aggressive more often diagnosed black patients as schizophrenic than white patients. Minority youth are more likely than white youth to be prescribed psychiatric medications such as Ritalin to control their aggressive behavior. Minority students are more likely than white youth to be labeled as "mentally or educationally retarded" and assigned to special education programs (or detention) in schools (Race Matters Toolkit).

Juvenile Justice

Implicit biases and stereotypes may influence perceptions and how officers interpret behaviors and evidence that is otherwise ambiguous. Juvenile justice research on police activity suggests several factors contributed to disparities between self-reported data on offense behavior and arrest data, including differences in the attitudes or perceived attitudes of African American and white youth upon arrest (Schiraldi). Thus, the *perception* of the attitudes of youths can influence decisions related to youth detention.

Bias in contemporary society is very hard to detect. The following discussion identifies three factors that operate in tandem to mask bias in decision-making.

Three Factors That Mask Bias in Major Social Institutions: Colorblindness, Stereotyping and Institutional Racism

Colorblindness

According to Omi and Winant in *Racial Formations in the United States*, "The notion of a colorblind society where no special significance, rights, or privileges attach to one's 'race' makes for an appealing ideology. Taken at face value, the concept reaffirms values of 'fair play' and 'equal opportunity'—ideals, some would argue, which constitute the very essence of our democratic way of life." (Omi and Winant 1). Colorblindness ideologies condition us not to be aware of and therefore make us unable to critique our implicit racial biases. Each semester when I ask my students to reflect on their implicit biases they find it very difficult, deferring instead to the refrain, "I don't notice race." But our country has been and continues to be anything but colorblind. From the inception of this nation to the present, "race has been a profound determinant of one's political rights, one's location in the labor market, and, indeed, one's identity" (Omi and Winant 1). In the post-civil rights era, one way we can obscure how race is still a determinant of social outcome is to discourage people from noticing race. Colorblind ideologies assert that "we are all on a level playing field" and "race doesn't matter." By not showing how racial markers in a colorblind society can promote racialized outcomes, people accept that outcomes such as disproportionality are the result of some inherent failings of the group or individual, and not an unjust social structure.

Colorblind ideologies provide the rules which regulate and control the public discourse on race. Fox News appears to be a proponent of colorblindness because it has established language and protocol for censoring people who violate the rules of racial discourse. On the *O'Reilly Factor* during coverage on Hurricane Katrina, host Bill O'Reilly called Jessie Jackson a "race-baiter" and a "Bush-hater." Fox News often criticizes people who expressly discuss race as "playing the race card" or "white bashing." Such public criticism provides the social conditioning needed to suppress public or private conversations about race. Many people fear that to stand up against racism would put them at risk professionally in terms of performance evaluations and job promotions, or cause them to be ostracized because, as the person who notices race, they are perceived as someone who "refuses to let race go and thus jeopardizes the possibility of a society in which race doesn't matter" (Guinier 37). The threat of being accused of "playing the race card" makes people very cautious about speaking out against racism, but by ignoring racism and not intervening we give our support to the existing power arrangements (Stewart and Hurtado 299).

But there is another reason why we must acknowledge race as well as culture. From a strictly professional standpoint, whether we are teachers, social workers, or health care professionals, we must understand race and its relationship to culture in order to deliver culturally competent services. *Research on Black families overwhelmingly shows that the behaviors and lifestyles of Black people are different from those of whites but still research priorities have emphasized educating blacks to conform to the values and behaviors of mainstream white Americans* (Peters, *Parenting of Young Children in Black Families*). Because of lack of awareness about race and culture caseworkers often misinterpret black parents' cultural traditions, demeanor, and informal means of handling family distress as neglect (Roberts 59). For example, cultural relativity allows us to respect black cultural traditions in which the children live with relatives other than parents as an African American family tradition that is strength-based rather than evidence of neglect. If we are "colorblind" we will inevitably default to a standard of service that is geared toward those who are white and middle-class (their traditions, values and parenting practices), thus we are bound to misdiagnose and misapply services and approaches which are likely to fail when families are unable to follow our colorblind approach to service delivery.

Stereotypes

A stereotype is a generalization of a group that is treated like an inherent characteristic that every person in this group is presumed to have. Stereotypes create a racial profile of the group which forms a backdrop or a frame of reference that informs our conscious or unconscious thinking. The fact that stereotypes are well-known by most people suggests their ubiquitousness and their ability to inform intuition, assumptions, perceptions, and the way we interpret what we see. "When I turn on the news each night what do I see again and again, Black men alleged to be killing, raping, mugging, stabbing, gangbanging, looting, rioting, selling drugs, pimping, ho-ing, having too many babies, dropping babies from tenement windows, fatherless, motherless, Godless, penniless. I believe we've becomes so used to this image of the black male predator that we are forever ruined by this brainwashing" (Moore 29).

From religious doctrine to popular culture with encoded racist and sexist messages that explain and legitimize why groups within society have greater or lesser access to its resources and institutions, ideologies are penetrated throughout all aspects of society (Jewell). In contemporary society, stereotypes that might affect practice are rarely made explicit. For example, few social workers acknowledge that their belief that black people have poor parenting skills influences their decision-making, yet in child welfare the assumption that *blacks have poor parenting skills* is so commonly accepted that people don't even flinch when it is presented to them as an example of implicit bias. They seem more surprised that it's considered a stereotype and not a fact. In one jurisdiction, when asked on a survey why more black children were removed, the answer *blacks have poor parenting skills* was ranked as the primary reason. Many social workers say they don't notice race, race doesn't matter, "I just follow the rules," but bias as it is informed by stereotypes (such as blacks have poor parenting skills) can result in differences, however slight, in the application of policies and procedures which can make a difference in decisions to remove children (Roberts). Individuals can participate in routine practices which are inadvertently biased under the guise of "just following the rules." For example, stereotypes which automatically associate one-parent families, particularly those headed by women, as "broken" families and therefore unfit might influence the decision to remove or reunify. From the perspective of the decision-maker, the decision was not based on stereotypes that characterize single parents as negligent, but rather on data that identifies single parent households as "high risk." Thus, the decision-maker is absolved of personal accountability because he or she "just followed the rules" (or complied with agency practice). In this example the decision-maker is left to conclude that his or her decision was based strictly on the facts and not how stereotypes might have impeded a fair, unbiased assessment of family strengths that might have led to a different outcome.

Institutional Racism

The third factor that masks bias in contemporary society and influences decision making is institutional racism, which "consists of established laws, customs, and practices which systematically reflect and produce intentionally and unintentionally racial inequalities in American society (Carter 200).

Institutional racism is hard to detect because it utilizes policies and practices which on the surface appear neutral to race; but when bias, conscious or unconscious, results in a difference in the implementation of policies it produces a racial effect or disparities. For example, although studies have found no prevalence of substance abuse along either racial or economic lines, black women were ten times more likely than white women to have their newborns placed in out-of-home care. Even though drug testing policies can be applied to all mothers, such policies will have a disparate effect on poor black mothers because of their reliance on county hospitals, which are more likely to mandate drug testing than are private physicians and health plans. Such differential testing practices reflect a higher incidence of reporting due to disparate testing practices and should not be interpreted as a higher incidence of drug exposure for black children (Roberts 51).

Policies related to drug testing seem like policies that affect everyone the same. As a result of colorblindness, few people question the fact that these tests are often located in county hospitals where predominantly poor black women were tested. The disparate impact is obvious. Whether the policy was designed to target black women or whether it just intended to protect children (and the fact that predominantly black mothers are tested is an unintended effect) the outcomes are the same. Thus, the differential application of policies in institutions can become a pathway into the child welfare system for poor women, while wealthy women with private health insurance and private physicians can bypass detection. In this way they avoid the stigma as well as the social and legal sanctions of having their children removed.

Institutional racism relies on racial practices such as colorblindness and stereotypes. Zero tolerance in schools, though touted as being a colorblind policy, is particularly detrimental to kids of color. On the surface it can be argued that the punishments under zero tolerance are unilateral; the principal has to act on all referrals the same, therefore all referrals of misconduct will result in some mandatory consequence such as a 3-day suspension (Verdugo). Principals might argue (as do judges regarding mandatory minimum sentencing), that the law has taken the discretionary decision-making out of their hands. Discretion may not be a factor once the incident of misconduct is referred to the principal, but a great deal of discretion can occur in the classroom as teachers decide which of the numerous daily offenses that occur will be handled informally, overlooked altogether, or result in referral. As these decisions occur on an unconscious level, the teacher may not realize that race influenced his/her decision to make a referral.

Bias Constructing a Perception of Risk

Most social work decisions are presumed to be based on facts which can document that maltreatment has occurred. But decisions of social workers, teachers, police officers and even judges occur within a cultural context infused with race, gender and class biases that are at least in part interpreted through the lens of agency and practitioner values. According to Hill, placing a child outside the home in a foster care placement is the result of many previous decisions, and decisions continue to be made once the child enters care. Decisions include the decision to make the report of potential child abuse or neglect, whether to accept or substantiate the report, placement into foster care, reunification with family, and return to foster care" (5).

Every decision-making point is susceptible to bias. Understanding how such biases manifest is the challenge that must be faced. Developing strategies and interventions that enhance services in youth-serving agencies like child welfare, juvenile justice and education is where we begin to address racial disproportionality.

Since racial biases are typically routine acts that are applied differentially by race and social class it is hard to detect on a case-by-case basis and often will not be noticed until larger patterns of bias are observable. Many people reject the validity of racism on the grounds that it cannot be proven, but while we stay head-locked in the debate of is it racism or isn't it the racialization process continues.

In order to interrogate racism in contemporary society we have to examine the use of language, connotations, terminology, expressions, attitudes, presuppositions, conjecture, assumptions, personal values, and intuition because all of these things are prone to prejudice.

What follows is a list of attitudes, language, and practices that can promote bias and influence outcomes across and within systems. As a transfer of learning tool it identifies how these factors can promote bias. This tool also suggests intervention strategies that can be utilized by anyone to intervene against everyday racism.

Intervention Strategies for Reducing Bias in Child Welfare and other Youth Serving Systems

Language, attitudes and actions can mask bias and result in the difference, however slight, in the application of policies and procedures across and within systems, e.g., child welfare, juvenile justice, education, etc.

Cultural misinterpretations are inevitable when there are such disparate cultural and social class differences between practitioners and the people they serve (Roberts). In a colorblind culture in which individuals are conditioned to not assess for bias, well-documented cases infused with biased interpretations can easily go undetected. Everyday wrongs that we cannot document are inherent in the ordinary everyday behavior of good, well-intentioned people (Banaji 64). By understanding how individual biases intersect with those of the agency and society, individuals can identify strategies that strengthen the information upon which their decisions are made.

GUIDELINES	DESCRIPTION	APPLICATION	NOTES
1. Terminology	Terms like "at risk," "minorities" and "disadvantaged" can influence how individuals/groups are perceived and subsequent case-planning.	Such terminology can promote bias before the facts are reviewed, even in the absence of any explicit mention of race/ethnicity.	Terminology also normalizes the status of whites by reinforcing the "otherness" of people of color.
2. Labeling	The use of words or expressions, e.g., resistant, hostile, aggressive, and druggie, or even using the word juvenile instead of child, can have negative overtones.	Labels can over time become associated with a particular ethnic (or gender) group. For example, labeling an entire group as having "poor parenting skills" can cause everyone who is a member of this group to be judged in this way. Labels, as they get passed from one employee/ agency to the next, can influence outcomes.	Choose language that's more specific to the facts and descriptive. Ambiguous language and terminology invite assumptions and allow stereotypes to "fill in the blanks."
3. Passive [voice]	Reports and documentation that use passive references can be misleading and can distort important aspects of the case.	For example, a court report entry that states "the mother understood" does not confirm her understanding. Active language would read "the mother stated that she was in agreement."	Such clarification will result in outcomes more consistent with facts than with biased interpretations of the facts.
4. Coding and Cues	Disparities in word choices. Using negative terminology and descriptions in reference to one group and positive or neutral terminology to describe another.	Hurricane Katrina was the best example; in which whites were described neutrally as "looking" for food" and blacks described negatively as "looting."	Coding associates black with evil, wicked or sinful and white as morally pure, spotless.

5. Stereotypes	Blatant stereotypes are easy to recognize. But any tendency to generalize group behavior or characteristics to individuals can disadvantage or advantage the individual.	Even stereotypes that are self-deprecating to one's own group such as "trailer park trash" should be challenged as such a term is deprecating to poor white people.	Even so-called positive stereotypes, e.g., Asian Model Minority, which implies that all Asians are smart, should be avoided in documentation.
6. Objectification	Referring to people according to their condition, problem or circumstance can cause them to be seen as the problem/condition rather than as people who might be experiencing this problem or condition.	Calling children placements, damaged, or illegitimate, or parents crackheads. Referring to removals as "bookings." Objectification focuses on deficits rather than strengths. It's hard to feel empathy toward people who are objectified.	In reporting and documentation put people first then their condition, e.g., rather than referring to a "mentally ill person" use "person with a mental illness."
7. Mimicking	Definition: To imitate closely as in speech, expression or gesture. Appropriating speech patterns or accents of a group through mimicry.	Such practices, even in jest, can be considered offensive, as mocking and derogatory, and will interfere with the assessment of family strengths.	
8. Policy Interpretation	"Zero Tolerance" has had a disproportionate impact on youth of color. Biases in perceptions result in disparities in zero-tolerance application.	Racial bias distorts how zero-tolerance policies are interpreted and applied.	Zero-tolerance policies can criminalize behaviors that would have otherwise been handled exclusively within schools.

9. Connotation	Words, terminology or expressions that imply a negative context such as "broken families" reinforce negative connotations about a group or things associated with a group, e.g., using the word "ghetto" has negative implications such as "That's ghetto."	Such words or terminology allow us to unconsciously draw negative conclusions and to problematize families, individuals or circumstances without prior knowledge or evidence.	Words like "intact" used in reference to family structure promote "two-parent" households as inherently good and imply that families without two parents are "broken" and inherently deficient.
10. Vague Definition of Neglect	Ambiguous charges of neglect are highly susceptible to biased evaluations of harm on the parent's race or class. (D. Roberts, p.55)	Individuals should choose words that are specific and not open to misinterpretation.	

References

Banaji, Mahzarin R. "How Ethical Are You." *Harvard Business Review* 56–64.

Cameron Wedding, Rita. "Defending Whiteness." Cameron Wedding, Rita and Michelle Renee Matisons. *Institutions, Ideologies, & Individuals: Feminist Perspectives on Gender, Race, & Class*. Dubuque: Kendall/Hunt Publishing Company, 2004. 1–27.

Carter, Robert T. "Expressions of Racial Indentity." *Off White: Readings on Race, Power and Society*. Ed. M. Fine, et al. Great Britain: Routledge Press, 1997.

Derezotes, Dennette M., John Poertner and Mark F. Testa, *The Overrepresentation of African American Children in the System*. Washington, DC: CWLA Press, 2005.

Gaertner, S. L. "Does white racism necessarily mean anti-blackness: Aversive racism and pro-whiteness." *Off White: Readings on Race, Power, and Society*. Ed. M. Fine, et al. Great Britain: Routledge Press, 1997.

Gladwell, Malcolm. *Blink*. New York: Little Brown and Company, 2005.

Government Accountabilty Office. "African American Children in Foster Care." 2007.

Guinier, L. *The Miner's Canary: Enlisting Race, Resisting Power, Transforming Democracy*. Cambridge: Harvard University Press, 2002.

Hill Collins, Patricia. *Black Feminist Thought: Knowledge, Consciousness, and the Politics of Empowerment*. New York: Routledge, 2000.

Hill, Robert B. "An Analysis of Racial/Ethnic Disproportionality and Disparity at the National, State, and County Levels." 2007.

"Synthesis of Research on Disproportionality in Child Welfare: An Update." October 2006.

Jewell, K. Sue. *From Mammy to Miss America and Beyond: Cultural Images and the Shaping of U.S. Social Policy*. New York: Routledge, 1993.

Jones, Teresa C. "Social Work Practice with African Americans." *Cultural Competence, Practice Stages, and Client Systems: A Case Study Approach*. Ed. Doman Lum. Belmont: Brooks/Cole, 2005. 59–87.

Kohl, Patricia L. "Unsuccessful In-Home Child Welfare Service Plans Following a Maltreatment Investigation: Racial and Ethnic Differences." 2007.

Moore, Michael. "Kill Whitey." *Ethnic America: Readings in Race, Class, and Gender*. Ed. Rita Cameron Wedding, Eric Vega and Gregory Y. Mark. Dubuque: Kendall/Hunt Publishing, 2003.

Needell, B, et al. *Child Welfare Services Reports for California*. 2007. 30 January 2008 <http://cssr.berkeley.edu/ucb_childwelfare>.

Needell, Barbara. "Child Welfare: Ethnic/Racial Disproportionality and Disparity." 21 September 2007.

Omi, Michael and Howard Winant, *Racial Formations in the United States From the 1960s to the 1990s*. New York: Routledge Press, 1994.

Peters, Marie Ferguson. "Parenting of Young Children in Black Families." McAdoo, Harriette Pipes. *Black Families*. Thousand Oaks: Sage Publications, 2007. 203–218.

Platt, Tony. "The Frightening Agenda of the American Eugenics Movement." 24 June 2003. 30 January 2008 <http://hnn.us/articles/1551.html>.

"Race Matters Toolkit." n.d. Annie C. Casey Foundation.

Roberts, Dorothy. *Shattered Bonds: The Color of Child Welfare*. New York: Basic Civitas Books, 2002.

Schiraldi, Vincent N. "Disproportionate Minority Contact in the Juvenile Justice System." *Disproportionate Representation of Minorities in Family Court*. Washington D.C., 2007.

Aida Hurtado, Aida and Stewart, Abigail. "Through the Looking Glass: Implications of Studying Whiteness for Feminist Methods." Fine Michelle, Weis Lois. *Off White: Readings on Race, Power, and Society*. New York: Routledge, 1997. 297–311.

The Annie E. Casey Foundation. "Race Matters: Family 2 Family." 2007.

Verdugo, Richard R. "Race-Ethnicity, Social Class, and Zero-Tolerance Policies: The Cultural and Structural Wars." *Education and Urban Society* (2002): 50–75.

Chapter Four Questions

Choose one answer.

1. Who indentified African Americans as the most racialized-conscious people?
    a. David Covin
    b. St. Claire Drake
    c. Otis Scott
    d. Rita Cameron-Wedding
    e. Mogobe Ramose

2. The Jim Crow system was
    a. statutory
    b. imaginary
    c. imaginary but unjust
    d. imaginary and just
    e. real and just

3. The one-drop blood rule is also known as the
    a. hypodescent rule
    b. racial discrimination
    c. gender discrimination
    d. Jim Crow law
    e. racial and gender discrimination rule

4. SASM stands for
    a. South African Student Movement
    b. South African Scholastic Moment
    c. South African Scholarly Moment
    d. South American School Movement
    e. None of the above

5. Who was expelled from the University of the North for speaking against racism?
    a. Lekgau Mathabathe
    b. Onkgopotse Tiro
    c. Tsiesti Mashinini
    d. Seth Mazibuko
    e. None of the above

6. In 1976 South African Soweto unrest was a rejection of what language as a medium of instruction?
    a. Spanish
    b. IsiZulu
    c. Afrikaans
    d. English
    e. Setswana

7. According to Lederach's opinion, what causes conflict?
   a. Ideological difference
   b. Ethnic identity
   c. Religion
   d. Languages
   e. Land
   f. Love of money

8. Who said, this "Raise the Afrikaans language let it become the vehicle for our culture, our history, our national ideals and you will raise the people who speak it"?
   a. F.W. De Klerk
   b. Daniel Malan
   c. Pik Botha
   d. P. W. Botha
   e. Van Zyl Slabbert

9. The first institutionalized efforts to educate African Americans were made
   a. in 1964
   b. after the Civil War
   c. during the Civil War
   d. during the civil rights movement
   e. when Rosa Parks refused to give up her seat on the bus

10. The first institutionalized efforts to educate African Americans were made by
    a. the Reconstruction Congress
    b. *Brown v. Board of Education* decision
    c. Charles Huston
    d. Thurgood Marshal
    e. President Barack Obama

11. According to Otis Scott, the chief architecture of desegregation strategy was
    a. Thurgood Marshall
    b. Jessie Jackson
    c. Charles Huston
    d. Barack Obama
    e. None of the above

12. The *Murray v. Maryland* decision was won in
    a. 1967
    b. 1936
    c. 1878
    d. 1545
    e. 1890

13. The decision on *Brown v. Board of Education* was announced on
    a. May 25, 1954
    b. May 3, 1954
    c. May 17, 1954
    d. May 1, 1954
    e. None of the above

14. What bests represents Ramose's cultural context of colonialization?
    a. Racist notions of false superiority by Europeans
    b. Dichotomies that adversely construct Africans as inferior
    c. Infidels who need to be Christianized
    d. Uncivilized indigenous people
    e. Barbarians

15. The Chimurenga War was fought in
    a. South Africa
    b. Zimbabwe
    c. Angola
    d. Lesotho
    e. Botswana

16. The Chimurenga War was specifically a war of
    a. liberation
    b. liberation of Zimbabweans against white domination
    c. liberation against Ian Smith
    d. Zimbabweans and South Africans against Eurodomination
    e. None of the above

17. Robert Mugabe is the president of
    a. Angola
    b. Lebowa
    c. Zimbabwe
    d. South Africa
    e. Lesotho

18. Black children
    a. are 2% of the population and represent over 36% of children in foster care
    b. are 15% of the population and represent over 56 % of children in foster care
    c. are 25% of the population and represent over 86% of children in foster care
    d. are 15% of the population and represent over 36% of children in foster care
    e. are 75% of the population and represent over 100% of children in foster care

19. According to Mahzarin Banaji, a Harvard researcher, most people judge others according to
    a. unconscious stereotypes
    b. attitudes
    c. implicit prejudice
    d. unconscious stereotypes, attitudes, and implicit prejudice
    e. racial lens

20. What factors pose increased risk for African Americans in child welfare system?
    a. Implicit bias, stereotypes, and ideologies that translate into institutionalized racism
    b. Implicit bias and stereotypes
    c. Stereotypes and ideologies
    d) Institutionalization
    e) None of the above, the system is efficient

Discuss the impact of bias and racism in the child welfare system.

What accounts for the denial of insitutionalized racism and bias in the child welfare system?

What is the significance of *Brown v. Board of Education*?

Discuss the strategy of Charles Huston and name the cases he won that eventually led to the *Brown v. Board of Education* landmark victory.

Discuss Covin's views on racialized societies.

Discuss the essence of Ramose's "I Conquer and Therefore I am the Sovereign."

Briefly discuss the events leading to the 1976 Soweto Uprising.

Discuss how Racialization plays out in Brazil.

CHAPTER 5

Pan-African Epistemology

Introduction to Chapter Five

Boatamo Mosupyoe

The articles in this chapter provide insights into how linguistics, concepts of monotony and multiplicity, applications of constructs like war proper, rebellion and terrorism, and pronunciation of suspicion have historically and currently constituted justification to declare war. After a persuasive examination of these factors Ramose, in his article "Wisdom in War and Peace," argues for a serious consideration of the reasons and causes of conflict and a resolution embracing peace through dialogue. Oyugi's reflection in "Human Rights in Africa" offers insights into the complexity and the dynamism of the concept of human rights. Oyugi questions in part the perception of human rights as universal since it is unmistakably affected by several factors. Oyugi notes the contradictions between the human rights ideology and the practices such as positive authority to control citizens' movements through passports, individual rights, and national security concerns, the exploitation by Heads of States of their positions that interprets opposition as treachery.

Canon, in his article "Elusive Quest," continues the dialogue with his examination of achievements and challenges Rwanda faces after the 1994 genocide. He argues that the "enigmatic Janus face" of Kagame and his government deserve praise, but ran short of distributing and decentralizing responsibilities to broader community constituencies. In order to curb protracted reconciliation and rescue the process from perceptions and realities of elusive quest a broader inclusive approach that supplants elitisms and incorporates programs that are rural, regional, peasant, and worker oriented, and have a district and regional focus. Oladipo Olusegun argues for a conception of Africa beyond the traditionalist lenses and towards dynamism that reflects a conjuncture of both. The latter will provide a viable approach that will mediate the tension engendered by the current African problem with efficacy.

With the article "Morality in Yoruba Thought: A Philosophical Analysis" Oladipo shares insights into the relationship of Morality and Religion in Yoruba culture. Olusegun considers a view that links morality only to religion as limited and undermining the "wider range of human activities" that informs human behavior and choices. Kwasi Wiredu completes the discourse in this chapter by reminding us through the discussion "The Need for Conceptual Decolonialization in African Philosophy that a thought process that involves analyzing concepts in African languages benefits the decolonialization of African philosophy constitutes the development of thought in Pan Africanism.

Wisdom in War and Peace

Mogobe B. Ramose

Introduction

It is a long time from the 'Black September' in Munich to the bright September 11 2001 in New York and Washington. The two events are bound together by the concept of terrorism. Another common factor shared by the two events is that the 'jihad' was in some way the inspiration for the attacks in Munich and the United States of America. As is well known, Israel and the United States of America are allies (Said 2002:2–3). It is part of the intention of the present essay to consider, albeit secondarily, whether these allies ascribe the same meaning to the concept 'terrorist.' Indeed, experience shows that in the context of international relations it is relatively easy to reach a common understanding on the meaning of 'terrorism' (Teichman 1989:505–517). But the same cannot be said with regard to the meaning of 'terrorist' (Primoratz 1990:130–133). For example, prior to September 11 2001, it was acceptable that the 'terrorist' of yesterday could discard this appellation permanently on the attainment of an honourable civilian status such as head of state (Gearty 1996:xiv–xv). Today, however, the acceptability of the transition from 'terrorist' to civilian is being called into question. The bright September 11 2001 in New York and Washington has brought about a rethinking on the meaning of terrorism with particular reference to the concept of 'terrorist.' It has at the same time made it necessary to examine the novel concepts of the 'strike against terror' and the 'war against terror'

in the context of the just war doctrine. The difficulty around these concepts within the context of the just war doctrine proceeds from the assumption that philosophically both the jihad and the just war doctrine share one common feature, namely, their teachings on why it is permissible to resort to war and, how war should be conducted. However, aside from this, there are vast differences between the two doctrines on war and, not least, partly because they each originate in different and conflicting religious foundations. Hence, even if the jihad is not translatable into 'holy war' without qualification, the idea of a 'just war' in the Christian tradition is by no means completely free of the claim to the divine sanction of war. However, this and other similar points of difference are not the primary focus of the present essay. Our primary preoccupation here is with the philosophical question of the permissibility of resort to war and how it should be conducted in view of the necessity to rethink the meaning of terrorism with particular reference to the concept of 'terrorist' in the light of the bright September 11 2001 in New York and Washington.

The Place of Philosophy in War and Peace

There is a widespread tendency among us humans to insist that on going through life our own way regardless of any timely and pertinent advice from those with past experience. This somewhat blind readiness to ignore advice seems to rest upon two pillars. One is the intuitive conviction that our own personal experience may, against all expectations, and despite what anybody else may say, turn out for the best. Another pillar is the impulsive dogma that we will succeed where everyone

"Wisdom in War and Peace" by M.B. Ramose from *After September 11: Globalization, War and Peace* ed. by C.W. Du Toit & G.L.A. Lubbe, Research Institute for Theology and Religion, University of South Africa, Pretoria. Reprinted by permission.

else has failed. We imagine our success will undermine any advice issuing from the experience of the past. More fundamental, however, is that both the paths of intuitive conviction and impulsive dogmatism ultimately question conventional wisdom. In short, they pose the question: what is wisdom?

This questioning may be justified on two grounds. The first is the appeal to our uniqueness; the claim that each and everyone of us is specifically and exclusively his or her own person. We can neither be anyone else nor can we be replaced. This view then is based on the assertion of our right to be different, and our insistence on recognition, respect and protection of this right to be different. But the right to be different does not in itself eliminate the minimum biological content, namely that although we are unique individuals we nonetheless belong to the same species. Nor does the right to be different erase the most basic ethical claim that we are all human beings. The second ground of justification is our ethical claim to the right to freedom. To be human is not only to be rational but to be free as well. Like the right to be different, the right to freedom demands recognition, respect and protection. Giving advice then may be construed as an interference in and infringement upon these rights. Thus, the voice of wisdom may be rejected on the basis that it is an unwarranted violation of both our rights to be different and free. This rejection of the voice of wisdom may be sustained only if it is assumed that these rights are infinite and without limit. But it is well known that in the context of human relations the view that there is no limit to the exercise of any right is both unreasonable and untenable. Therefore, the voice of wisdom may—in certain circumstances—justifiably impose limits upon our exercise of the rights to be free and different. This is particularly so with regard to humankind's experiences of peace and war over the ages.

Indeed, on the strength of the etymological definition of philosophy as the love of wisdom, it is apparent, in the light of the above, that philosophy may justifiably claim a special privilege to offer advice on all the facets of human experience. This special privilege is particularly pertinent to the matter of war and peace. Philosophy as practical wisdom is averse to dogmatism and absolutism. On the contrary, it is the disposition

to remain open and honest to reality without deciding beforehand the character and meaning of truth. Consequently, wisdom does not preclude justifying war in the name of unconditional pacifism. Nor does it sanction peace built upon inhumanity and injustice.

Human Rights and the Right to Self-Defence

The inscription of human rights into the just war doctrine reaffirms the insight that talk about the permissibility of war is meaningful only if it takes the right to self-defence seriously. The recognition of the right to self-defence as the ultimate reason for resort to war calls into question the use of any means in the conduct of war. In the course of this line of questioning, the phenomenon of war in history has been described variously as rebellion, war proper, in the Clausewitzean sense and, terrorism. Whatever the nuances and differences between all three descriptions, each one of them rests on an appeal to self-defence. Therefore, to the extent that the human rights discourse is the reaffirmation of the right to self-defence in that much it stands as the justification for rebellion, war proper and terrorism. In other words, rebellion, war and terrorism are specific descriptions of the logic of self-defence in particular circumstances. All three share a common point of departure, namely the recognition of the right to self-defence. The core problem arises when this recognition is used to justify self-defence by placing it as the basis to describe rebellion, war and terrorism. What often happens in this connection is that description is allowed to supersede and precede justification. It is therefore necessary to keep in mind that the justification for war is one thing whereas the justification for the conduct of war is quite another. It follows therefore that what is permissible in the context of *jus ad bellum* is not automatically and necessarily the licence to adopt and use any means in the conduct of war. Although, in specific cases, *jus ad bellum* and *jus in bello* are interconnected and, must therefore be considered holistically, it is also true that the two are experientially and conceptually separable. It is precisely this separation that must be preserved in our thinking about the right and the logic of self-defence. Once we ignore this separation, it becomes easy to find terrorism to be morally opprobrious whereas war may be found to be morally proper. Let us pursue this by focusing on Honore's defence of 'the right to rebel.'

Honore (1988:43) has advanced the following argument in defence of the 'right to rebel.'

> But suppose the campaigns of those who are denied human rights are ineffective. Surely the implication must be that the citizens to whom human rights are conceded and whom UDHR says may be compelled as a last resort to rebel are not merely to be excused when their patience snaps but are justified in rebelling. And if the moral justification for doing so consists in the fact that rebellion is the only means by which they can in the last resort assert their humanity, defend their ways of life or vindicate their independence, does it follow that they have a right to rebel? It is not merely that they regard themselves as justified because they see no alternative, or that the consequences of rebellion appear preferable to those of passive resistance, but that they have a right which others are bound to respect and which entitles them to the help, or at least the neutrality, of those who are not party to the dispute. Would it make sense to deny someone the right to do what he is compelled to do in the sense not of being coerced but of having no other means of vindicating his fundamental interests? Does not everyone, if the dilemma is presented, recognize such a right? To deny it would be to assert that people may be bound indefinitely to submit to conditions of life which we and they recognize as intolerable; that their interests may properly be disregarded and they themselves treated as unworthy of respect. It seems to me, therefore, that in a proper case there must be a right to rebel. It will not generally be a formal right, but neither is it a purely informal right grounded in the conventional morality of the international community. It possesses an intermediate, semi-formal status. It is based, that is, both on a certain conception of human dignity and on an interpretation of the political norms of the international community, including the principles, embodied in documents, which members of that community have endorsed.

According to Honore, then, by acknowledging the right to rebel, the international community would thereby be recognising, respecting and protecting human rights. This may be so provided one understands, like Honore (1988:36), that the right to rebel means:

> the right of an individual or group to resort to violence, if necessary on a large scale, in order either (a) to secure on behalf of individuals or groups conceived as exploited or oppressed a change in the government, structure or policies of the society to which they belong (radical rebellion), or (b) to resist on behalf of individuals or groups who are attached to their way of life a change in the government, structure or policies of their society which the rulers of the society intend to bring about (conservative rebellion), or (c) to secure on behalf of a group conceived as distinct the right to independence from the society to which it at present belongs (rebellion in aid of self-determination).

From the human-rights perspective underpinned by Von Clausewitz' (1976) definition of war as the continuation of politics by violent means, Honore's argument on the right to rebel is a reaffirmation of the right to self-defence. The rhetorical question arising from this is: from a purely logical point of view, does the right of self-defence, extend also to the 'terrorist'?

September 11 2001 and then War

Having failed to persuade the Taliban government to deliver to America Osama Bin Laden, the primary suspect behind the September 11, 2001 attacks in New York and Washington, the United States of America decided to wage war on the Al-Qaeda organisation supported by the Taliban government in Afghanistan. The immediate aims of the war were

- ◆ the total defeat of the Al-Qaeda organisation
- ◆ the arrest or killing of Osama Bin Laden
- ◆ the replacement of the Taliban government with another government acceptable to the United States

These then were the aims underling the 'strike against terror.' Added to them were the aims of identifying 'terrorists' anywhere in the world and then destroying and defeating them. In this way the 'strike against terror' limited to Afghanistan made its transition to the worldwide 'war against terror.' Was the decision to wage war consonant and consistent with the just war doctrine? Was the decision wise in any way? In an attempt to answer these questions, we will consider three instances in which the United States of America was involved in a war.

A Lesson from My Father

Not so long ago, former United States President, George Bush, the father of the incumbent President Bush, mobilised a segment of the international community to participate in the Gulf War. It was claimed that the reason for the war was Iraq's violation of the sovereignty of Kuwait. Yet, those who believed themselves to know better suggested that the Iraqi action against Kuwait posed a threat to the continued supply of oil to the West. Therefore, they argued, the defence of the oil supply to the West was the primary reason for the Gulf War.

> On November 29, 1990, in an unprecedented step, the United Nations Security Council authorized the use after January 15, 1991, of 'all necessary means' to achieve the withdrawal of Iraqi forces from the territory of Kuwait. On January 12 the Congress of the United States authorized President Bush to use American armed forces to implement that resolution. This too was unprecedented . . . Aggression had to be resisted and reversed. Moreover, no power could be permitted to dominate an area that contained resources so vital to the well-being of the international community (The road to war 1991:1).

Former United States Ambassador in the Middle East, Ambassador Akins (1991:48), reaffirmed this thus:

> American's hand on the oil valves of Arabia may be light but the United States will surely take control. Washington has no real choice, having shown no intention of exerting enough self-discipline to free itself from dependence on oil. America will not cut its consumption; it will not even consider a modest increase in gasoline prices. So the United States is constrained to look to the Persian Gulf for its oil and perhaps solutions to its energy problems.

Three years after the war, these views were confirmed by Mandelbaum (1995:35) in these terms:

> The crippling of Iraq's nuclear program was a byproduct of the war. (Desert Storm/Gulf War.) The official purpose was to evict Iraq from Kuwait. Restoring Kuwait's sovereignty was, in fact, a less important American interest than keeping Saddam Hussein from controlling a large part of the Persian Gulf's oil reserves. A sovereign Kuwait was also less important than a nonnuclear Iraq. But because it constituted an unambiguous violation of international law, the invasion and occupation of Kuwait provided the basis for the political support of the war attracted.

There is little doubt then that the defence of oil supplies to the West, and not the sovereignty of Kuwait, was the primary reason for the war against Iraq.

The protection and restoration of Kuwaiti sovereignty was at best a secondary reason for the war (Coffey 1989:23, Alexander 1990:2). From the point of view of the just war doctrine, the question that arises, is whether one sovereign state may wage war on behalf of another. Where one of the would-be belligerents makes a direct and express request to a third party, does such a request constitute sufficient ground for waging war on behalf of another sovereign state? It would appear that the traditional just war doctrine does not address this question directly and expressly. If this is a theoretical vacuum then it may be filled by the argument that, provided it is consistent with the relevant requirements pertaining to the *jus ad bellum*, the defence of human rights (McKeever 2000:110–111) may be invoked as justification for the declaration of war either by the sovereign state directly affected or by other sovereign states (Ramose 2000:205–206). Bearing in mind the distinction between the right to wage war—*jus ad bellum*—and the ethico-legal imperatives in the conduct of war—*jus in bello*—then it should not be difficult to realise that the recognition, respect and protection of human rights are the core of the just war doctrine. According to this argument, crimes against humanity must be added to the list of legitimate grounds for resort to a just war.

Iraq

In the war on Iraq, former President Bush declared that the removal of President Saddam Hussein from office was one of the aims of the Gulf War. This aim was not achieved despite attempts by the United States and Great Britain to encourage and support Iraqis in over-throwing President Saddam Hussein. To date, President Saddam Hussein is still the ruler of Iraq. He has become reconciled with Kuwait and is now the darling of the Arab world. In the meantime, former President Bush has either finished or is about to finish writing his, leaving the aging and almost forgotten legacy of safe havens in the north of Iraq. It is significant to note that Britain is America's sole partner in this legacy.

The lesson the Gulf War holds for the incumbent President Bush could be said to be the following:

◆ The right to wage war must be matched by a just cause consistent with the requirements of the just war doctrine. It is impermissible to wage war if the 'just cause' is either dubious or subordinated to a less credible reason for war.
◆ The fact that the presidency of Saddam Hussein has survived beyond the Gulf War implies that in any war the claim to victory is often limited and always elusive.

This is affirmed by the fact that the incumbent President Bush has followed the same route as his father in his 'war against terror' initiated against the Al-Qaeda in Afghanistan and thence world wide. One of the principal aims of this war was to remove the Taliban government from power. This aim has been achieved. However, the achievement of this aim has not resulted in the total elimination of the threat to the United States of America posed by the Al-Qaeda organisation.

Kosovo

Again not so long ago, former President Clinton mobilised a segment of the international community in a war against the Federal Republic of Yugoslavia. The reason for the war was said to be the gross human rights violations perpetrated by the Serbs on the ethnic Albanians in Kosovo. From the Serbs' point of view, the reason for 'ethnic cleansing' was to ensure that the ethnic Albanians would never again claim that they had a title to sovereignty over the territory of Kosovo. This struggle for sovereign title over Kosovo, now more than six hundred years old, is yet to be resolved. At the end of the war against the Federal Republic of Yugoslavia, NATO under the leadership of the United States, insisted that the solution to the territorial dispute was autonomy for the ethnic Albanians in Kosovo. However, the solution was not acceptable to the ethnic Albanians. Despite the massive destruction and arguably disproportionate amount of harm that NATO has inflicted upon the ethnic Albanians and the Serbs alike, the question of sovereignty over Kosovo remains, as before, a matter of life and death. The deep-seated convictions on either side of the ethnic divide have survived the NATO bombardments. The survival of these convictions questions the effectiveness of bombs in conflict resolution. In the massive destruction which they wrought in Yugoslavia, the bombs brought an end to gross human rights violations by the Serbs. However, the bombs failed to eradicate the ethnic Albanians and the Serbs' convictions about their sovereign title to Kosovo (Ramose 2000:214). The bombs may be silent, former President Slobodan Milosevic arraigned and facing charges on human rights violations in the International Court of Justice in The Hague, but the surviving convictions of the contending parties remain a real threat to the precarious peace in the Federal Republic of Yugoslavia.

It is suggested that President Bush could have drawn at least one lesson from this experience, namely bringing in bombs does not necessarily make peace. On the contrary, bombing tends to make the achievement of peace harder and much more elusive. Even the most powerful bomb cannot destroy the deeply-held convictions of a people. No doubt the bombs may kill particular individuals along with their convictions, but one of the qualities of convictions is that they are shared by others. Thus, one option is to kill all those who share similar convictions. Genocide? Without this, the survival of their convictions is guaranteed for as long as the conditions that give rise to them remain. This leads to the second option, namely to focus on the conditions that give rise to specific convictions posing a threat to political stability and peace.

The Second World War

More than half a century ago, elated by the news that the final assembly of the first atomic bomb had been completed on 5 August, President Truman authorised that the bomb be dropped over Hiroshima the next day.

> On the same day, the second atomic bomb was detonated over Nagasaki. Its effect was no less devastating than that of the first. The use of the second bomb can be explained not in terms of necessity, but only the momentum of events. On August 10, Japan made clear its intentions to surrender, and did so on August 14, and so the Second World War was over. The atomic age had begun (Yergin 1977:122).

It is indeed a moot point whether or not President Truman's use of the atomic bomb was motivated by military necessity. However, it is beyond question that the bomb was used. Its physical effects upon the Japanese born long after it was dropped are still felt in the affected cities today. There is also no doubt that the use of the atomic bomb ushered in the age of nuclear weapons diplomacy. In this context it is pertinent to reflect upon the prevailing MAD (mutual assured destruction) condition in the sphere of strategic nuclear military planning. Our thesis in this connection is that to hold city populations hostage under threat of a nuclear military strike is, if the threat is carried out, a violation of the principle of non-combatant immunity. Terrorism by nuclear weapons? Does the holding of city populations hostage under threat of a nuclear military strike amount to a specific kind of state terrorism?

One of the lessons to be drawn from the dropping of atomic bombs over Japan is that only military necessity should justify either the continuation of war or the use of specific weapons in war. Without this, both the principles of non-combatant immunity and proportionality are likely to be violated. Another lesson to be drawn is that the era of nuclear weapons diplomacy is in reality the MAD (Gompert 1977:301–313) situation in which the civilians of the respective potential adversaries, in particular, the United States and Russia, are held hostage by the terror of the nuclear military strike. This situation has appositely been referred to as the 'balance of terror.' Has the time now come to rename it 'balance by terrorism?' Even if we may find both appellations infelicitous and prefer mutual deterrence through the threat of a nuclear strike, it is impossible to argue convincingly against the ultimate violation of the principle of non-combatant immunity. The concept of theatre or limited nuclear war is at best an imaginary construction inconsistent with Von Clausewitz' definition of real war. It is therefore realistic to expect that once nuclear war breaks out it will become an all-out nuclear war. In such an eventuality the instant large scale and rapid destruction of life on our planet are assured (Goodwin 1981). A veritable nuclear omnicide will prevail and thus the principle of proportionality will have been violated. Politics will come to an end. Von Clausewitz' definition of war as the continuation of politics by violent means will also become meaningless since there will be no politicians to continue politics. Neither will there be a conqueror not a conquered. There will be no one to pronounce on the wisdom or folly of the 'balance of terror' or the 'balance by terrorism.' Is humanity condemned to nuclear terrorism without terrorists? The novel concept of 'war on terror' cannot be credible if it chooses to ignore this question.

Assessing the Lesson of My Father

We have drawn a few lessons from the three wars and reflected upon some of them. No doubt there are many more lessons to be learnt, but these are sufficient for our purposes. One of the lessons drawn from the Gulf War is that the pursuit of the right to self-defence must be based upon, and be consistent with, all the requirements of the just war doctrine. According to this doctrine, it is impermissible to wage war if the 'just cause' is either dubious or subordinated to a less credible reason for war. This particular lesson serves as the basis for posing the following question: since conclusive proof that Bin Laden and his Al-Qaeda organisation were responsible for the September 11 attacks is either the privilege of a few or is becoming increasingly elusive, does the probability that they were, constitute a sufficient reason for war?

> Americans do not need much convincing that Osama bin Laden is to blame for the attacks on Washington and New York City. Which is fortunate, because we may never have the forensic comfort of a videotape or signed contract. Clear links are almost impossible to find in shady terrorist networks designed to have none. To make matters murkier, the United States government is reluctant to share any evidence it may have. On Friday, White House press secretary Ari Fleischer said publicising evidence would compromise the investigation. While that argument makes sense from an intelligence standpoint, it may not fly diplomatically. And for now, the known case against bin Laden is circumstantial [http://www.cnn.com/2001/US/09/26/inv.intelligence.board].

Thus it is the logic of probability or, even more strongly, suspicion which emerges as the only basis for the decision to wage war on Al-Qaeda and 'terrorism' all over the world. Does suspicion constitute a ground for resort to war?

The person and alleged involvement of Bin Laden complicate the above question. For some he is a Jesus-like figure not only in terms of his physique but also with regard to his ability to appear and disappear at will. Others consider him to be the liberator in the apparent struggle between Islam and the West, led by the United States.

> No Arab forgets the humiliation of the loss of most of Palestine in 1948 and the rest in 1967. Arab honor was at stake and Arabs know they will have no peace as long as Palestinians are clamouring for justice. President Bush also understands this and in 1990 gave solemn

assurances to President Assad of Syria, President Mubarak of Egypt and King Fahd of Saudi Arabia that as soon as the Iraqi aggression in Kuwait was reversed he would devote his full attention to solving the Arab-Israeli conflict. The Arabs are holding him to his promise and he seems to be trying to fulfill it. Whether the administration's attention spell will be long enough to accomplish anything is not yet clear (Akins 1991:42).

The image of Bin Laden as the liberator appears to have been extended so far as to include the expectation that like Jesus, he will reappear at the Parousia, the Last Day of Judgement. In this image of Bin Laden he is portrayed as an enigma: a human figure who is the personification of surprise. If it is true that Bin Laden is responsible for the bright September 11 attacks then this is consistent with his image as an enigma. The timing, the manner and the targets of the attacks came as a complete surprise, as well as a shock to many people. That the bright September 11 attacks were completely unexpected is underlined by Democrat Senator, Robert Torricelli, in his call for a probe into the 'stunning' failure of the American Intelligence Service to uncover and derail the planned attacks. In his call for the probe, Senator Torricelli declared that

> In the months ahead there must be a thorough inquiry into the actions of our intelligence agencies in the days and weeks leading up to September 11th. The goal of this inquiry would not be to assess blame and ruin careers. It would have a much more important goal: determining what went wrong so we can prevent it from happening again [http://www.cnn.com/2001/US/09/26/inv.intelligence.board].

The prevention of future attacks is the core of the Senator's call for an investigation. If preventative measures had been effective, then the bright September 11 attacks would not have occurred. There would have been no surprise attack on the United States of America. It is critical to remember that the bright September 11 attacks were not the first time an attack had taken the United States of America by surprise.

The Japanese bombing of Pearl Harbour was also a surprise attack linked to the 'failure' of the United States Intelligence service. 'American officials did not think Japan would attack their country. To start war with so superior a power would be to commit national hara-kiri. To Western mode of thought, it made no sense. This rationalism was parallelled by a racism that led Americans to underrate Japanese abilities and will. Such views were held not only by common bigots but by opinion-makers as well. These preconceptions blocked out of American minds the possibility that Japan would attack an American possession.

As he was saying this, six of the carriers thought by traffic analysis to be lying in home waters were in fact plowing the seas north of Hawaii. They had launched airplanes for a Sunday morning attack on the Pacific Fleet at Pearl Harbor. Japan's strategic plan would prove unsuccessful. The attack so enraged and unified the American people that they would never tire of the struggle but would battle on to total victory. Yet Japan's tactical plan worked to perfection: the raid achieved *complete surprise*.

American intelligence had failed. Evidence warning of an attack could have overcome American preconceptions, but intelligence—which relied almost solely on the *diplomatic* transmissions via PURPLE—had found no such evidence. Japan sealed all possible leaks . . . And though war with Japan was indeed expected, that expectation did not—could not—imply knowledge of an attack on Pearl Harbor, for it is impossible in logic to leap from a general belief to a specific prediction.

Pearl Harbor was the greatest shock ever sustained by the United States (emphasis). It destroyed the national myth of isolation and invulnerability. This was one of the reasons the United States 'unencapsulated' itself after World War II and reached out to other nations in a network of alliances. And Pearl Harbor reverberated throughout the Cold War as a fear of *surprise attack*. The nation spent billions on early-warning radar lines and intelligence satellites and, for decades, kept its missiles ready to fire within minutes.

. . . probably with the surprise Japanese attack in the back of his mind, Truman ordered that plans be drawn for 'a comprehensive and coordinated foreign intelligence program for all federal agencies concerned with that type of activity.' A few months later Congress's Pearl Harbor committee recommended 'that there be a complete integration of army and navy intelligence agencies.' This gave powerful impetus to Truman's establishment a year later of the Central Intelligence Agency. As former President Herbert Hoover wrote in 1955 in a report of his Commission on Organization of the Executive Branch of the Government: The CIA may well attribute its existence to the attack on Pearl Harbor.

Does today's astonishing sophistication preclude surprise attacks? It does to a greater extent than it 1941, *but not entirely*. Though eyes-in-the-sky make it hard to mass troops, dispatch warships or launch airplanes or missiles undetected, not all messages will be radioed so that they can be intercepted, and—most important—not every leader can always be persuaded that his or her nation is going to be hit. But by searing into the American psyche the perils of insufficient intelligence, Pearl Harbor has taught the United States to gather more information and evaluate it better. That unforgotten lesson of a half-century ago still matters; it is why Americans, even today, remember Pearl Harbor (Kahn 1991/92:145–152 [my emphasis]).

As the surprise attack on Pearl Harbour gave birth to the Central Intelligence Agency. The surprise attacks on New York City and Washington are to give birth to yet another intelligence agency.

Just as the Japanese attack on Pearl Harbour impelled the United States to wage war on Japan so did the surprise attacks on New York City and Washington push the United States into waging war on the Al-Qaeda organisation in Afghanistan. By doing so, the United States has provided an indirect answer to our question whether or not suspicion constitutes a ground for resort to war. The answer is as follows: there is a link between the 'stunning' intelligence failure and the surprise attack. This link leaves only suspicion as the guide either to further an investigation before a final decision is made or to launch a timed action based mainly on suspicion. It would seem that the United States has chosen the latter option. This preference must be seen against the background that at this 'unipolar moment' the United States tends to act unilaterally and with condescension towards those who support her policies and actions.

> There is much pious talk about a new multilateral world and the promise of the United Nations as guarantor of a new post-Cold War order. But this is to mistake cause and effect, the United States and the United Nations. The United Nations is guarantor of nothing. Except in a formal sense, it can hardly be said to exist . . . What we have today is a pseudo-multilateralism: a dominant great power acts essentially alone, but, embarrassed at the idea and still worshipping at the shrine of collective security, recruits a ship here, a brigade there, and blessings all around to give its unilateral actions a multilateral sheen (Krauthammer 1991:25).

The spectacle and effect of the surprise attack appears to have strengthened the United States' hand in deciding on timed action based mainly on suspicion. Again, the horror of this unexpected attack seems to have injected into the decision a momentum impelling the United States ineluctably to launch its 'strike against terror.' The views of three former United States Secretaries of State are an indication of this impelling inevitability. According to Henry Kissinger (2001:9),

> President Bush wisely has warned that the attacks on New York and Washington amounted to a declaration of war. And in a war it is not enough to endure; it is essential to prevail. . . . moderation is a virtue only in those known to have an alternative. It is not in the interest of even the moderate Islamic nations that US—or Western—policy is perceived as cowering before the threat or actuality of terror. For the first victims of such a course would be the moderates in the Islamic world and, in the long run, all the populations of democracies. Having overcome the vast military and ideological threats of the last half century, we must now master this more indirect but perhaps even more insidious peril and turn it into a decisive victory.

The readiness and determination to wage war even if a 'threat' is the reason for war is unmistakable in Kissinger's view. His veiled reference to victory over the Cold War clearly begs the

question we raised above, namely whether or not humanity should be condemned to silence and passivity when faced with the threat of nuclear omnicide implicit in the 'balance by terror.' Yet another former American Secretary of State, James Baker (2001:8), expressed the view that:

> Once we determine who they are, we would go after the infrastructure and the assets of any country that harbours them, on whose soil they conduct their training. We know Afghanistan has been harbouring Osama bin Laden. A lot of people think he is the logical suspect. . . . We should tell the Taliban leadership that they have only a certain amount of time to deliver Osama bin Laden, and if they don't we will determine that they continue to harbour him and must suffer the consequences.

For Baker, the 'strike against terror' shall not be limited to Afghanistan if the Taliban government refused to co-operate. It shall be extended to 'any country' that hosts those responsible for the bright September 11 attacks. Here we detect the seminal idea of the 'war against terror.' Echoing James Baker on the desirability of imposing a deadline upon the Taliban government for the delivery of Osama bin Laden and, also endorsing the idea of the 'war against terror,' Madeleine Albright (2001:8) declared that:

> The United States was hit hard. We must respond in a way that is proportionate to what has happened. But it is not necessarily something that has to happen tomorrow. It is more important that it be done effectively than it be done quickly.

In one of the preceding paragraphs, Albright had already acknowledged that suspicion was the only basis for the belief that Osama bin Laden was responsible for the attacks. It goes without saying that even James Baker had admitted as much in the above citation. Read in context then, Albright's declaration is in effect an endorsement of timed action based on suspicion. Furthermore, it is curious that Madeleine Albright correctly invokes the principle of proportionality while at the same time endorsing the idea of a global 'war against terror.' The point we are making here is that Afghanistan is by no means the entire globe.

Therefore the principle of proportionality would require action restricted to Afghanistan but not extended world wide as demanded by the 'war against terror.'

It is precisely the views of the three former Secretaries of State that President George Bush subsequently reaffirmed.

> In some of his most forceful language yet, President Bush on Wednesday called suspected terrorist mastermind Osama bin Laden 'an evil man' who is bent on killing innocent civilians—a man who doesn't mind destroying women and children. He also said the terrorists who carried out the September 11 attacks 'underestimated the will and determination of the commander in chief' [http://www.cnn.com/2001/US/09/27/gen.america.under.attack].

The above leave us in no doubt of the President's will and determination to wage war on the basis of suspicion. While the President correctly decried bin Laden's intent to kill 'innocent civilians,' he was curiously oblivious of his similar intent to kill 'innocent civilians' through the use of nuclear weapons.

By the time the first 'strike on terror' was launched it was for those who did not 'need much convincing' and, for the greater part of the world populations only suspicion that was the basis for resort to war. Thus the 'strike against terror' introduced a new theoretical question with regard to the just war doctrine. The question now is whether or not suspicion may be included as one of the elements constituting a *justa causa*, that is, a necessary and sufficient reason for resort to war.

Language and War

By describing Osama bin Laden as 'an evil man,' President Bush subtly counterposed himself as the 'good man' in the struggle. By using this type of imagery the 'strike against terror' was transformed into the fundamental battle between 'good and evil.' The desideratum for this struggle is that the 'good' should prevail over the 'evil.' In terms of this reasoning, the 'strike against terror' is an ethical duty. Accordingly, all those on the side of 'good' are duty-bound to join the 'strike against

terror.' This has translated into the now familiar rhetoric that people must choose either to be for or against the United States of America. Since the desideratum is that the 'good' will prevail over the 'evil,' the expectation is that only the wicked minority will make a choice against the United States of America. And the wicked will perish in the course of the 'strike against terror.' However, as Said so appositely points out, the people of the United States do not in fact all stand as one on this. America is by no means an indissoluble entity of identical ideas and intentions represented by the Bush administration, 'America is not a monolith for the use of George Bush and Dick Cheney, but in fact contains many voices and currents of opinion which this government is trying to silence or make irrelevant' (Said 2002:2).

The 'strike against terror' has military connotations. It denotes a clinically precise and forceful military operation. It conjures up the image of devastating and disarming destruction. Survival is unimaginable once the 'strike against terror' is launched. But the problem with this clinically precise and forceful military operation is that it must be specific, focused and, therefore, limited. The limitation is a drawback insofar as it prevents the strike from reaching terrorism wherever it might be. For this reason an extension is necessary. It is precisely in response to the need for an extension of the strike against terrorism that the term 'war on terror' is used. This must be construed as azimuthal defence against terrorism.

It may well be reasoned that from the point of view of the struggle between 'good and evil,' both the 'strike against terror' and the 'war against terror' emerge as ethical imperatives imposing a duty on us to support them. Both are necessary and desirable to combat and overcome the 'evil' of terrorism. They are rational and ethically justified. They constitute the just cause, a reason to die for the fatherland—*pro patria mori*, as it were. Therefore, they are consistent with the just war doctrine. Accordingly, it is noble to die for the cause of the 'war against terror.' Ironically, this is precisely the same reasoning that underlies Bin Laden's peculiar (Sajoo 2001:8) interpretation of the jihad. The question then is not only who is on the side of the 'evil' of terrorism but, more, fundamentally, what is terrorism? Is it the logic of the right to self-defence that is the problem or, does the problem lie in the description and definition of terrorism? Surely, neither the description nor the definition of terrorism eliminates the right to self-defence? On the contrary, both the description and the definition of terrorism are inconceivable and blind without the recognition and reaffirmation of the right to self-defence.

The representation by the 'jihad' or 'holy war' adherents that 'terrorism' is an 'evil' has made the use of symbolism and innuendo even more necessary in the language of war and peace. Consider the following terms and note your own reactions as you read each one of them: 'homicide,' 'matricide,' 'fratricide,' 'genocide,' 'omnicide,' sororicide' 'pesticide,' 'suicide.' Each of these terms evokes specific expectations, for example, from the ethical and legal points of view. For instance, homicide is ethically repugnant and legally questionable. However, it may be legally excusable and ethically pardonable where sound and justifiable reasons can be provided. The assumption behind this kind of reasoning is that homicide can be rational in specific circumstances. It is precisely this assumption of rationality which underlies both the ethical and the legal justification of homicide. The same assumption underlies most of the terms except suicide and nuclear omnicide.

Suicide is associated with irrationality and irresponsibility. From the point of view of the observer, a person committing suicide must have gone beyond the threshold of reason. According to this reasoning, action taken beyond the threshold of reason is both irrational and irresponsible. It is against the background of this reasoning that we should understand the meaning of the term 'suicide bomber' in the language of war. In this language, the suicide bomber is someone whose action is prompted by both irrationality and irresponsibility. Accordingly, it is unnecessary to take the claims and actions of the suicide bomber seriously. Thus, the fact that the suicide bomber knowingly and purposely takes his or her own life deserves no special consideration. The 'irresponsibility' of taking the lives of others as well, is that which deserves attention and must be decried. It is important to question whether this characterisation of a suicide bomber is sound and fair. (Rees et al 2002:22–32) Pursuant to this inquiry we will consider the hallowed nobility of

pro patria mori and the existing threat of nuclear omnicide seriatim.

Pro patria mori is both an ethical and political maxim. Its ethical dimension justifies the claim that at times it may be necessary to choose death rather than suffer the loss of specific rights and values. This challenge to choose death is usually situated in the political terrain. Here we must remember that the political terrain includes the religious domain as well. Usually it is the interaction between religious and the political convictions which ultimately poses the challenge to choose death. Politics elevates those who choose to die in defence of their rights to the status of nobility. They have died a noble death. Although they have lost their lives, the loss itself is seen as both rational and responsible. The rationality and responsibility of death *pro patria mori* is deemed to be acceptable even though the loss of one's life might involve the loss of other people's lives as well as indeed is the case in war. The important point for us to remember is that the essence of *pro patria mori* is to choose death knowingly and purposely. Logically, the choice is the same one made by the suicide bomber. The irrationality and irresponsibility imputed to the suicide bomber is a political decision. This does not mean to say that it is by necessity always ethically justifiable. If the political decision to refuse to accord the status of nobility to the suicide bomber were reversed then it would become apparent that like the *pro patria mori*, suicide bombing is an act of the selfless self-sacrifice in order to give others life. In other words, acting *pro patria mori* and suicide bombing may logically be construed as martyrdom. From the point of view of Christian theology, we understand martyrdom in the following terms.

> God's demands on us become concrete in the practice of justice. Justice demands everything of the subject, everything without exception. In its concrete historical form the practice of justice demands not only that we give of our abilities and talents but also that we give of our life and even give that life itself; it demands a readiness to die in the interests of giving life (Sobrino 1984:58).

It is suspected that many other religions and theologies concur with this perspective. Justice is a concept that belongs to ethics. Once it is connected to politics then greater disagreement and conflict ensue. Since the ethical domain is controlled by those who wield political power, their control often denies the logical parity between *pro patria mori* and suicide bombing. By relegating suicide bombing to the realm of irrationality and irresponsibility those in political power portray suicide bombing as unethical. Clearly, this is a case in which language has been manipulated to achieve political objectives. Once the fallacy of the reasoning of political power is uncovered, then suicide bombing is not by necessity either irrational or unethical.

The supposed irrationality and irresponsibility of suicide bombing is also comparable to the existing threat of nuclear self annihilation: omnicide. The spectre of mutual assured destruction triggered by the major nuclear military powers has already been mentioned. The existence of this situation is legitimated by appeal to the rationality of the irrationality argument (Maxwell 1968:3–4). Briefly, the core of this argument is that each of the major nuclear military powers relies on the rationality of its counterpart. This reliance boils down to this; that the counterpart will never cross the threshold of rationality by making the irrational option to actually use nuclear weapons. This last mentioned option is deemed not only to be irrational but irresponsible as well. The reason why it is irrational and irresponsible is that it is suicidal. Thus nuclear omnicide is rejected on the grounds of rationality. But the rational is not by necessity the ethical. Accordingly, the rejection of nuclear omnicide on exclusively rational grounds leaves open the question whether or not nuclear omnicide is ethically justifiable. Leaving this question open underlines the fallacy that the rational is the ethical. It is curious that on purely legal grounds, the International Court of Justice determined that in 'an extreme circumstance of self-defence' it may be permissible to resort to the use of nuclear weapons. In other words, the Court endorsed the option of being irrational and irresponsible by committing suicide through nuclear omnicide (Burroughs 1997:21–22). If the option of nuclear omnicide is the epitome of martyrdom then it is logically and ethically on par with suicide bombing.

Victory in War

In the above citation, former Secretary of State, Henry Kissinger, declared that it is 'essential to prevail' in war. According to Von Clausewitz (1976:233–234), victory in war consists of 'three elements: (1) The enemy's greater loss of material strength. (2) His loss of morale. (3) His open admission of the above by giving up his intentions.' The continuation of the 'strike against terror' in Afghanistan shows that only partial victory has been achieved. At the time of writing, the 'war against terror' is mainly putative. There is no conclusive evidence that the enemy's has lost its morale irretrievably. Nor has the enemy made an open admission never ever to resist and fight again. Thus the 'war on terror' shall be protracted but without the certainty of victory in the Clausewitian sense. As this war unfolds it is important to ponder on how one of its principal supporters, British Prime Minister, Tony Blair, conducts it. He is keen and enthusiastic about the crushing of 'terrorists' anywhere in the world. However, a notable exception to this policy are the 'terrorists' on his doorstep, namely those pursuing the cause of a free, united and sovereign Ireland. It is indeed remarkable that Tony Blair consistently persists to fight these 'terrorists' with the legislative weapon known as the 'Prevention of Terrorism Act' but prefers to use violence in the fight against other 'terrorists.'

Conclusion

It has been shown that it is theoretically problematic to hold suspicion as a legitimate *justa causa* in the context of the just-war doctrine. It has also been suggested that despite the skilful use of warlike language, it is debatable whether the decision to launch the 'strike against terror' and the 'war against terror' was wise. Victory in both instances continues to be limited. Resort to bombing does not of necessity make peace or remove the cause of terrorism. Accordingly, the wise course appears to be an inquiry into the causes and reasons that give rise to terrorism. The reason for acts of 'terrorism' is not to be found in the acts themselves. Rather it lies in the existential conditions which provide cause for the contemplation and the implementation of such acts. Though it may be plausible, provided all peaceful alternative means have been exhausted, to track down the 'terrorists' and even 'strike against terror' on the plea of self-defence, it does not necessarily follow that this is the inevitable and strategic course to pursue. Once the reasons and cause have been identified, then genuine dialogue on how to eliminate them should follow. It seems wise then to seek peace through dialogue aimed at either changing or reconciling deep-seated convictions held by the contending parties.

References

Akins, J E 1991. The new Arabia. *Foreign Affairs,* 70(3), 36–49.

Albright, M 2001. Time to choose sides on the new battlefield. *Sunday Times* September 16, 8.

Alexander, M 1990. De rol van de NAVO in een veranderende wereld. *NAVO Kroniek,* 38(2), 1–6.

Baker, J 2001. Set deadline for Bin Laden's extradition. *Sunday Times,* September 16, 8.

Burroughs, J 1997. *The legality of threat or use of nuclear weapons.* LIT: Munster.

Coffey, J I 1989. Veiligheid in het Midden-Oosten: Kunnen de Bondgenoten het beter aanpakken? *NAVO Kroniek,* 37(5), 20–25.

Gearty, C (ed) 1996. *Terrorism.* Dartmouth: Aldershot.

Gompert, D C et al (ed) 1977. *Nuclear weapons and world politics.* New York: McGraw-Hill.

Goodwin, P 1981. *Nuclear war: The facts.* London: Ash & Grant.

Honore, T 1988. The right to rebel. *Oxford Journal of Legal Studies,* 8, 34–54.

Kahn, D 1991/92. The Intelligence failure of Pearl Harbor. *Foreign Affairs,* 70(5), 138–152.

Kissinger, H 2001. Moderation is no virtue against terrorism. *Sunday Times,* September 16, 9.

Krauthammer, C 1991. The unipolar moment. *Foreign Affairs,* 70(1), 23–33.

Mandelbaum, M 1995. Lessons of the next nuclear war. *Foreign Affairs,* 74(2), 22–37.

Maxwell, S 1968. Rationality and deterrence. *Adelphi Papers,* 50. London: International Institute for Strategic Studies.

McKeever, M 2000. The use of human rights discourse as a category of ethical argumentation in contemporary culture. *Studia Moralia,* 38, 103–125.

Primoratz, I 1990. What is terrorism?, *Journal of Applied Philosophy,* 7(2), 130–133.

Ramose, M B 2000. Only the sovereign may declare war, and NATO as well. *Studia Moralia,* 38, 197–216.

Rees, M et al 2002. Why suicide bombing . . . *Time Magazine,* April 15, 22–32.

Said, E 2002, Thoughts about America. *Al-Ahram Weekly.* [http://www.ahram.org.eg/weekly/2002], 1–7.

Sajoo, A B 2001. The ethics of the public square [http://www.polylog.org/them/2/asp4-en.htm.]

Sobrino, J 1984. *The true church and the poor.* O'Connell, M J (trans). Maryknoll, New York: Orbis.

Teichman, J 1989. How to define terrorism. *Philosophy,* 64, 3–15.

Von Clausewitz, C 1976. *On war.* Howard, M & Paret, P (ed and trans). Princeton, New Jersey: Princeton University Press.

Yergin, D 1977. *Shattered peace.* Harmondsworth, Middlesex: Penguin.

Human Rights in Africa

E. Oyugi

Human Rights is the twentieth-century name for the rise of individualism in the theory and practice of modern western societies, as informed by the calvinist and protestant spirit. Like all such catch-phrases, it is very political-theory-laden and refers to a historically situated problematic. It implies a general view of man in relation to society, of individuality (in the sense of the claim of a particular part against the whole), politics and government in relation to particular social formations.

Its study, therefore, presupposes an insightful acquaintance with the characters of the principle categories around which gravitate the various stands of civil society. Three main categories obtrude upon us. They are: social classes as they view for the hegemonic control of the political-economical life of a given class society; the state and its tendentious deployment as an instrument of oppression of one class (or an alliance of cognate classes) by an other; and the character of the prevailing class-dictatorship as it helps sustain the rule of one class over the others.

In this article, I intend to trace the development of the idea of human rights back to its historical taproots. This is necessary due to its protean character as revealed in the fact that it undergoes continuous changes, both in content and social function. Its internal complexities will be discussed with a view to gaining insight into the 'theoretical climate' which has provided a moral framework for tendentious 'ideological gaming' with it. I shall prioritize its post-colonial African manifestations for a much more closer analysis. The goal: a dialectical-materialist examination and evaluation of the prominent features of human

rights theory and practice in Africa today. The result: hypostatization of the human rights concept within the relative context of a political world divided into ideological units and sub-units and, thereby, unpacking the erroneous assumption underlying the contention that human rights have a universal character, and therefore, suspended above the reach of the convulsive effects of historical changes that occur in response to class struggles in post-colonial Africa.

The discussion of the nature and history of human rights permits intermittent reflection of a large and overarching question: is the notion of human rights an intellectual product of the enlightenment or not? For sure, history teaches us that it is much more ancient than we are prone to believe. We know that certain Greek cities accorded their citizens such rights as IOGORIA (equal freedom of speech) and ISONOMIA (equality before the law); both of which constitute prominent features of rights claimed in the modern world. In the Hellenistic period which sequelled the breakdown of the Greek city-states, the stoic philosophers formulated the doctrine of natural rights. These, they argued, belonged to all men at all times. Such natural rights, were conceived as though they didn't constitute particular privileges of citizens of particular cities. Every human being was entitled to these rights, by virtue of the simple fact of sharing humanity and rationality with everyone else.

Much later, the name of John Locke became closely associated with the classical formulation of the seminal ideas on the subject. The intellectual seeds of the Bill of Rights which was enacted in the English parliament after the 'Glorious Revolution' in 1689, can be traced to Locke's publication on the theory of government. These ideas find a faithful echo in the Declaration of

"Human Rights in Africa" by E. Oyugi in Quest, Vol. III, No. 1, June 1989, pp. 45–69. Reprinted by permission of African Studies Centre.

Independence issued by the American states in July 1776. It reads as follows:

"We hold these truths to be self-evident, that all men are created equal; that they are endowed by their creator with certain inalienable rights; that among these are life, liberty and the pursuit of happiness. . . ."[1]

The French Declaration of the Rights of man and citizen, issued by the constituent Assembly followed closely the English and American models. Not long after, the French Declaration Sweden and Holland (1809 and 1815) followed the English model and accordingly incorporated the concept of natural rights into the constitutional framework of their respective monarchies; leaving other nations to copy the American republic model.

It did not take long before the theory of natural rights spiraled out of national appeal into the ethereal layers of international concern. This took place as the United Nations was being created after the Second World War; when, as Winston Churchill put it: the most important task assigned to the newly created family of nations was "the enthronement of human dignity."[2]

But although designed to confer universal validity upon an immensely complex phenomenon, the Universal Declaration of Human Rights hardly fostered unmitigated consensus. In essence, it betrayed a surreptitious shift from natural law to natural rights. This happened to be at variance with the time-honored liberal traditions which had acted as a firm intellectual anchor to the vagrant European political philosophies. Among the mandarins of this intellectual discipline were: Hume, Bentham, Austin and most of the Hegelian idealists of the twentieth century. While some admitted a general concept of rights, the majority argued that rights belonged not to individuals but to societies or communities. The subsequent condemnation of the shift from natural law to natural rights, later found an eloquent expression in Leo Strauss' sentiments. He thought of it as an egoistic doctrine, which deserved to be sharply contrasted with the classical doctrine of natural law, the focus of which was on the law of a society, justice, duty and public interests.[3]

Germany, then the scion (and later the bastion) of idealist philosophy proclaimed a Declaration of Rights (by the nationalist German liberals in 1848) which veered tangentially from the antecedent individualistic cast of the Universal Declaration of Human Rights.* Whereas the American and French one asserted the right of Man, the German manifesto placed the emphasis on the realm of individualistic *Vertrag* and placing it on the collective interest and will of the corporate *Gesamtakt*.[4]

Space and thematic priority do not allow that this aspect of the problematic be dealt with in large. However, a few tentative remarks and observations are quite in order. An overarching question poses itself: can there be a discussion on rights which will shy away from touching on the social character of human life in the context of which the question of human rights is problematized? The answer is an out-right no. All rights on which an individual member of a given society can lay any legitimate or illegitimate claim

"are social at the very least in the sense that they imply the existence of society and that their function relates to society."[5]

These radical ideas find a profound articulation and elaboration in the writings of Marx who regarded the notion of the rights of man a bourgeois will-of-the-wisp, the attainment of which would require a dialectical detour through its own dialectical negation. This unmitigated hostility to the individualistic undertows of the wave of natural rights ideas hitting the shores of 18th century liberalism, derived its cogency from the axiom and belief (in humanity) that man is a species being and that humanity could be realized only when men ceased to think of themselves in bourgeois individualistic terms as individuals invariably bestowed with inalienable rights.

Human rights, we should be able to say by now, are "claims on the part of the individual against one, some or all members of a society."[6] It is a moral concept, the meaning and social function of which have a place only in a particular system of social organization. It derives from society, from its historical and structural needs. Collaterally, they also derive from man's needs, his powers, his powerlessness and the requirements of his self-fulfillment. In the final analysis, the notty is-sues we have been trying to unskein and outline above, boil down to a few outstanding questions, behind which lurk the controversy over the nature of man vis-a-vis society. I shall, therefore, attempt in the next section to look a little more 'closely at' the nature of class societies in their contextual relation to human rights.

Social Classes and the Contest for Their Relative Civil Rights

The most comprehensive and profound conceptualization of classes is found in the celebrated works on Lenin. In his book *The Great Beginning*, Lenin wrote: "Classes are large groups of people differing from each other by the place they occupy in a historically determined system of social production, by their relation (in most cases fixed and formulated in law) to the means of production, by their role in the social organization of labour and consequently by the dimensions of the share of social wealth of which they dispose and the mode of acquiring it. Classes are groups of people one of which can appropriate the labour owing to the different places they occupy in a definite system of social economy."[7]

Lenin's definition of classes is of great theoretical significance to a correct understanding of modern capitalist society in that, apart from articulating its fundamental features, it furnishes the guide and key to the class structure of modern social-economic formations. It also provides a reliable clue to the way social-power is distributed and consequently used in the maintenance of class rule.

The process by which classes profiled themselves out of rudimentary social formations of too long a story to be told in a paper with such a limited thematic scope. It should, however, suffice to mention that with the gradual increase in economic inequalities communities joined into relatively larger groupings, occasioning the forward match of the division of labour. As the productive forces increased, extra labour was required. For some time, neither the individual community nor the larger society could provide it. War became the only possible source of the desiderative extra labour. The prisoners of war were spared

death so they could be made to produce surplus products. With time, however, community-leaders who, by virtue of their one-up-manship in the management of the communities' social affairs, had found it advantageous to lay unilateral claim upon the control of surplus products, began to enslave their fellow-tribesmen by both 'legal and extra-legal' means which they devised.

Since the disintegration of the primitive-communal systems the history of class societies has been characterized by the ding-dong struggle between the antagonistic classes: freeman and slave, patrician and plebeian, nobleman and serf, capitalist and workman. Common to all these struggles is the antagonism between the oppressor and the oppressed; waging an incessant struggle—today secretly and tomorrow openly.

In the course of such struggles, each class reserves no effort to defend and extend the range of civil liberties and human rights—going to all lengths to multiply them (where they are inadequate), wrest them from the ruling classes (where they have been alienated) and consolidate them (where their legitimacy is in question). As Klenner correctly observes, such rights

"are neither eternal truths nor supreme values. . . . They are not valid everywhere nor for an unlimited time. They are rooted neither in the conscience of the individual, nor in God's plan of creation. They are of earthly origin . . . a comparatively late product of the history of human society and their implementation does not lie in everybody's interest. In their essentials, man's interests are not the same everywhere and they cannot even be the same in any particular country."[8]

Human rights, even in their eighteenth century Jeffersonian formulation—as rights of liberty and equality—are a battle cry for social change, vociferated by those members of a society who are socially disadvantaged in as far as the distribution of social powers concerned. They were invoked by the French revolutionaries to bring down the ancient regime, just as they helped usher in the Soviet Union of the Bolsheviks. A scientific conception of human freedom in general and human rights in particular can only be achieved once both are actualized and concretized in the relative context of social formations and class interests.

Thus, the demand for rights in the seventeenth and eighteenth centuries was a demand (by the then socially disadvantaged groups) against the existing state and authorities, against despotism and political disfranchisement of those who held different opinions. Bourgeois conception of human rights, for instance illegitimately abstracts the individual from society, casts him adrift from the necessary moorings of history and social practice and place the tendentious authority upon the impartial pretensions of a state suspended above the group or class interests, in the defence of which it is established.

It follows from the above contention that all human rights are political. Their legitimacy is a function of the hegemonical authority of the social group in whose interest they are promulgated by a given state. It is the state with all its instruments of power, throwing itself in the fray on the side of the ruling classes that can observe or protect them, or become delinquent, depending on the immediate and pressing protective or offensive needs of the ruling classes.

The State as the Tendentious Regulator of Human Rights

The classical relationship between power and democracy hinges on the nature of state. At the root of it stands the idea of power and subjugation of those who should not have any share in its deployment in particularizing or privatizing social gains.

History teaches us that the state has a long history of variegated forms. We encounter different forms of state in almost every epoch. At the time of monarchy, republic, aristocracy and "democracy" there appeared corresponding states. Take, for instance, the history of the slave-owning societies, we see that for all their different forms of governments, common to them all was power and subjugation. The slaves were therefore not considered citizens enjoying civil rights and duties. Anyone whose private life was devoid of political status was a slave. In such societies, a special machinery was required to safeguard the privileges of the slave-owning class. It gave special powers and rights to the slave-owners so that they could exploit the slaves with impunity. Human rights was therefore, the preserve of the slave-owning classes.

Under feudalism, the feudal state acted as the nobilities' organ for oppressing serfs and villains. Accordingly, the alignment of political power was in strict conformity with the amount of land owned. The peasants, despite their numerical superiority, were bound to the soil. Only lords and gentlemen enjoyed certain civil rights. The peasant had none at all. In fact their position was little different from that of the slaves—their counterparts in the preceding era. Under, the modern republican democracies, the state, despite its neutral pretenses, remained the instrument of exploitation of wage labour by capital.

A preliminary question, poses itself and enjoins upon us the need to answer the following: What are the characteristics of the state and its attendant institutions which have become an essential appurtenance of Western civilization. The experience of the West includes a great many forms of constitutional regimes. No doubt, not all of them were inspired by the same principles or gave reflection to the same set of social values and goals which the historically determined institution of the state was meant to achieve. Ordinarily, the above question should have called for an in depth tracing of the evolution of those principles and doctrines which informed the development of the state to its present forms, but space and thematic priority are conjointly not in favour of an elaborate pursuance of such an important, albeit (for now) irrelevant undertaking. A few remarks are, however, necessary.

Aristotle, elaborating and extending the range of Plato's theoretical accounts of the relationship between power and liberty, formulated classical distinctions between various forms and types of state and government and between different forms of constitutions. Such distinctions, however, fell short of addressing the modern constitutional problem of the division of powers intended to provide restraints in the exercise of power. Subtending both the Platonic and Aristotelian philosophy of the state was the idea of natural law which was deemed to be independent of the state. Aristotle's philosophical point of departure was the inequality of human nature. This was in direct opposition to the axiomatic contention by Seneca and Cicero who, remaining faithful to the fundamental ideas of the stoics argued for the natural equality of human nature. The difference between these two outlooks was a direct reflection of the differing social situations obtaining for both Aristotle and the Stoics.

Later on, Hegel, inspired by the German liberal tradition, tried to construct the state as an entity abstracted from the social and historical forces which, as we now know, create and condition it in empirical reality of social life. He did this by depicting civil society as the class of the social forces, to be transcended by the putative universality of the state.

The separation between civil society and the state proved fallacious when Karl Marx, basing his refutation on dialectical and historical materialism, argued that the objective arrangements of the state are just so many particular interests parading under the false banner of the general and the universal. Accordingly, every political institution, despite their specious claim to universal generality, only mask the particularistic, tendentious and egoistic interest of civil society.

Marx and Engels maintained that the state is primarily an instrument of oppression. Its most prominent institution is *"public forces,"* comprised of armed men, prisons, intelligence service, the police and the various constitutional appendages of oppression. Its function, therefore, is to ensure *peace and public order,* so as to permit the class or an alliance of classes in whose powerful interest it was fashioned, to exercise unquestionable hegemonical control over the others.

Having examined the concrete facts bearing on the state's development through the ages, we have been able to draw some tentative conclusions. In the first place, we have seen that the state arises with the appearance of stratification of society into antagonistic classes. Secondly, the state has, with historical invariability, always expressed the hegemonical will and aspirations of the ruling classes. The nature, scope and stage of class struggle defines, to the minutest details, who enjoys what kind of civil or human rights and even how their (human rights) class-struggle-inspired violations can be legitimized or justified. Every epoch, every generation and every historical situation gives rise to a class and a corresponding state machinery which aspires to assume the role of the subject society's general consciousness. For a time such a class will represent the *RES PUBLICA,* but after a while, with changes in the

distribution of social forces, this claim for universality no longer accords with the interests of society as a whole.

Around the core advantage of the class in whose service the state has been fashioned, cluster claims, liberties, powers and immunities, the unified existence which preclude the same for the oppressed sections of society. By this very token, human rights are rendered relativistic and can only be claimed or denied in strict accordance with the varying degree of human social agency as determined by the dynamics of class-societies.

Class Dictatorship and Human Rights

We have seen from the above that the state bureaucracy represents the practical illusion of the universality of modern political life and that by the same token it degenerates into an "institutional licence for sectorial interests."[9] Rights in general and socio-economic rights in particular usually involve the conception of human society as a productive system. They constitute and reflect the demands and denials about the allocation of what is socially produced. The essence of the above argument is best captured in the illuminating remarks by Alexis de Toqueville in his MEMOIR ON PAUPERISM:

> "There is nothing which, generally speaking, elevates and sustains the human spirit more than the idea of rights. There is something great and virile in the idea of right which removes from any request its suppliant character and places the one who claims it at the same level as the one who grants it. But the right of the poor to obtain society's help is unique in that, instead of elevating the heart of the man who exercises it, it lowers him."[10]

Outside the framework of positive law, with its legal and paralegal instruments which by nature, should come to the general citizenry not in muted parcels but in bold chiaroscuros, what individual rights should there be other than those that are devoid of positive recognition? The twilight character of human right ideology is far from being a fortuity. Beclouded by innumerable meta-juridical politics and factors which convert its jurisprudential character into juridical politics and consequently cut it free from its moorings in legal positivism, human rights is "a ship adrift on the sea of political rhetoric at the mercy of this or that ideological."[11]

The legal terrain from which it comes, is itself a tendentious instrument under the monopoly of the ruling social interests.

In the name of the "Preservation of Public Security" the state, on behalf of the ruling classes abridge, at will and to every extent, all the political as well as civil rights of those whose social interests are at variance with the official state of affairs. The right to peaceful demonstration is, for instance, almost all over Africa, granted (if at all) not on the basis of positive legal provisions, but rather on condition that it does not, in any way appear to offend the political-economic interests of the ruling elements. Even though, the post-colonial constitutional provisions bestow upon every individual the right to travel, the majority of African states still reserve the right of asserting positive authority to control the citizens' movement. This is done by considering the provisions of travelling documents a privilege and not a right of citizens. Like a victorian duenna, the state, dictating on behalf of the ruling forces in society, does not only suppress things, it forestalls them: it knows, in advance, what is bad for the children and will not admit in the nursery of national life anything that might offend the political sensibilities of the ruling classes.

The clash between personal liberties and the putative requirements of national security constitutes a challenge of and reaction to the class dictatorship of the ruling interests; occasioning the severe trenching upon the civil liberties and rights of those who bear the stigma of revolutionary politics. These rights are always not surrendered willingly on the alter of national security. In the majority of the cases, those to whom our people have entrusted the power to govern, infringe upon the rights with the overt mission of maintaining the prevailing authority and the corresponding social one-up-manship.

The social scheme that produces civil society cannot perpetuate itself if it does not try to "harmonize" the antagonistic interests of which it is made up. This minimum of harmony and cohesion, however, cannot be achieved except by trenching upon the right of those whose social interests are seen to antagonize prevailing interests of the ruling classes. The coercive characteristics of the over-developed state in post-colonial Africa are far from acquiring the subtle features, just as the classes it represents are still trying to profile themselves as self-confident classes-in-themselves. Most of the institutional instruments of the state's coercive authority are personalized beyond the parameters of the social schemes. The heads of states are personalized laws in themselves. And since their personal involvement in the social schemes transcended the positively given laws of the land, the urge to preserve the prevailing systems impels them to hypostatize the state and its crude instruments of coercion as a supra-human domain, situated above and even opposed to the rights of individuals. In most cases, the ambiguity of the heads of state's position as both Head of State and Head of Government is exploited by the ruling interests in such a way as to represent all opposition to the government as disloyalty to the state. Colin Leys illustrated this in the example of a district officer at Maseno, near Kisumu in 1972, who had the following to say with regard to the freedom of worship:

"Freedom of worship is guaranteed within the constitution, but this could be curtailed at any time when the government deemed it necessary."[12]

Behind such a statement lurks the functionalist theory of bureaucratic rule, the principle objective orientation of which is the execution of pragmatic measures in order to sustain the favourable features of the status quo. Of extremely less importance, for such a functional dictatorship, is the shaping of political decisions necessary for the formulation and deployment of institutional instruments duly informed by popular governance policies; hence the recent proliferation of 'Massnahmestaten,'[13] i.e. states or governments in which ordinances and administrative measures readily supplant the regulative legislative procedures. The interim result: even the legal-positivistically protected rights lose their immunity to the extra-legal 'Massnahmen.' The end result: blatant violation of human rights.

However, the personalities of the political leadership is in addition undoubtedly a decisive factor in the maintenance of the functional character of the dictatorship. If such human-rights-violating leaders, in whom all power is vested, concede more validity to autocratic, military considerations or if they chose to show no appreciation of broad democratic constitutional procedures, it is to be expected that when their civil leaderships are challenged, they will usually abolish those rules which derive their legitimacy from the constitution; particularly when these appear bothersome to them. This has been, with metronomic regularity, repeatedly demonstrated in African countries where the joint interests of the military and the bureaucracy is devoid of constitutional morality.

Notes

1. Kameka, E. & A. Erh Soon Tay, *Human Rights* (London, 1978) p.2.
2. Maurice Cranston, *What are Human Rights* (London, 1973) p.3.
3. Leo Strauss, *National Rights and History* (Chicago, 1953) p.181, 182.
4. Friedmann, W. *Legal Theory* (London, 1967) p.131, 182.
5. Pennock, J.P. & J.W. Chapman (eds.) *Human Rights* (New York, 1981) p.6.
6. Lenin, V.I. *Collected Works* (. . . ., 19 . . .) Vol.29. p.421.
7. Lenin, *Collected Works* vol 29. p.421.
8. Hermann Klenner, *Human Rights: Battle-cry for Social Change or a Challenge to Philosophy of Law*; paper circulated to participants in the World Congress on Philosophy of Law and Social Philosophy, Sidney/Canberra, Aug. 1977. p.8–9.
9. Avineri Shlomo, *The Social and Political Thoughts of Karl Marx*, (Cambridge, 1969) p.23.
10. A. de Tocqueville and G. de Beaumontion, *Social Reform*, edited and translated by S. Drescher (New York & London, 1968) p.17.
11. Kameka E. & Erh-Soon Tay (eds.), *Human Rights*, (London, 1978) p.38.
12. Colin Leys, *Underdevelopment in Kenya: the Political Economy of Underdevelopment* (London, 1975) p.246.
13. Daily Nation, 15 Jan. 1972.

Elusive Quest? The Political Economy of Reconciliation in Post Genocide Rwanda

Patrick Cannon, Ph.D.

To the extent that the events of 1994 were conditioned by poverty and resource scarcity, . . . possible solutions in the economic sphere will have to occur in tandem with reconciliation.[1]

A possible political economy interpretation of the above quote suggests that if a deep socioeconomic cleavage between the elite and the poor created a precondition for the political manipulation of and mass mobilization around ethnicity, then the economic policies adopted by the Rwandan Patriotic Front (RPF) after 1994 can help foster reconciliation if those policies address both the socioeconomic cleavage contributing to and the ethnic division resulting from the genocide.

This paper argues that while the RPF, after its first decade in power, has adopted standard neoliberal policies potentially sufficient to increase economic growth, due to structural constraints and choice, it has yet to tailor those policies to local conditions so that they address the marginalization of the masses and ensure a more equitable distribution of resources to reduce poverty. As a result, solutions in the economic sphere have not occurred in tandem with reconciliation, making the latter a protracted and tenuous process at best and an elusive quest at worst.

This paper substantiates its central argument in four parts. Part one explains why an examination of the political economy of reconciliation fills a lacuna in the literature on the genocide and especially its aftermath. Part two briefly reviews the economic and reconciliation challenges faced by the RPF on taking control of the country in July, 1994. Part three discusses the economic policies adopted by the RPF since 1994. Part four summarizes the gains accomplished through the RPF's

economic policies and then demonstrates how those economic policies, particularly its agrarian and land reform, privatization and military commercialism, maintain the longstanding socioeconomic cleavage; fail to include institutions that acknowledge and reduce the marginalization of the majority of rural dwellers; and ethnicize the economy.

Political Economy, the Genocide, and Reconciliation

Unpacked, the implied relationship between politics ("events of 1994") and economics ("poverty and resource scarcity") embodied in the above quote is consistent with other analyses of the political economy of the genocide:[2] to retain control over a shrinking economy a small, 'Hutu Power' faction, originating in the northern prefecture of Gisenyi and ensconced within the Habyarimana regime, effectively bundled long standing socioeconomic and regional cleavages—exacerbated by environmental scarcity, population growth and livelihood conflict—into a problem framed as an "outsider" ethnic minority (Tutsi) intent on imposing its dominance on an "indigenous" majority (Hutu), and a solution defined as (mostly) ethnic cleansing.

The analyses that address the political economy of the genocide contribute significantly to understanding the events of 1994. Placing an emphasis on regional and especially socioeconomic cleavages highlights the sometimes obscured reality that many Hutu perpetrators participated in the genocide for a variety of reasons other than fear (and hatred) of the 'other,' including the opening to settle old scores in land disputes, the opportunity to acquire land and houses, and the availability of employment opportunities for unemployed youth who joined the *Interahamwe* and *impuzimugambi* militias that carried out much of the killing. However, notwithstanding a few exceptions,[3] the political economy of genocide analyses do not consider the political economy of reconciliation. The inattention to reconciliation from a political economy perspective is understandable. Given the magnitude of the genocide, most scholars have focused their attention on identifying and understanding the causes of the genocide. Equally important, beyond convicting the planners of and participants in the genocide, reconciliation is an ambiguous and inherently contestable concept whose definition depends on one's explanation of 'who has to be reconciled with whom' which in turn depends on one's identification of the primary causes of the genocide.[4]

Given the complexity of the politics and conflicts of the Great Lakes Region, ranging from the ethnic pogroms in Burundi (1972 and 1993), the genocide in Rwanda, and the revenge killings of Hutu by the RPF in the aftermath of the genocide to the Rwandan Army's occupation of the eastern Democratic Republic of Congo from 1998 to 2002 (if not the present) to the complex social landscape within contemporary Rwanda, where some oppositions might be more pertinent than the Hutu versus the Tutsi, it is not explicitly evident 'who has to be reconciled with whom,' and what would be the focus of reconciliation—regional and/or class cleavages within Rwanda and/or the ethnic tension that emerged during and after the genocide.

In this paper, reconciliation refers to the ability of the RPF to ease the relentless pressure of economic hardship among the masses by addressing the marginalization, poverty and resource scarcity that created a precondition for the political manipulation of and mass mobilization around ethnicity; and its ability to mitigate the obvious ethnic tension that emerged during and after the genocide. Due to limited space, this analysis omits a detailed consideration of Great Lakes regional factors, such as the interdependence of the politics between Burundi, Rwanda and DRC.[5] Nonetheless, the decision to define and analyze reconcili-

ation in this way is consistent with the political economy of the genocide, the intersection between region, class and ethnicity in Rwanda in 1994 and after, and it avoids perpetuating an essentialist conception of ethnicity that inevitably leads to a fundamental misreading of Rwanda's conflict history.

A Twofold Challenge for the RPF

At the conclusion of the Rwandan civil war and genocide, the RPF faced the twofold challenge of economic reconstruction and reconciliation.[6] Economically, the RPF had to rebuild a devastated economy, identifiable only by the surviving shards of its eviscerated financial and institutional infrastructures. To promote reconciliation, the RPF also had to weld a society fractured by longstanding socioeconomic and regional cleavages and an ethnic division cultivated during and after the genocide.

Economic Reconstruction

When the RPF seized Kigali in July of 1994, it inherited a devastated economy. Declining commodity revenues, Habyarimana's[7] use of scarce government resources to fund the 1990–1994 civil war, and the systematic dismantling of the financial and institutional infrastructures by the fleeing interim government resulted in a thorough and complete declension of the Rwandan economy. World coffee prices started to decline in 1984 before collapsing in 1986 and significantly undercut Rwanda's major source of income; its coffee export receipts dropped from US $144 million in 1985 to US $30 million in 1993.[8] Volatile world tea prices and the collapse of the tin industry further eroded the country's export earnings.[9] Consequently, the precipitous drop in export earnings for coffee, tea, and tin combined to shred Rwanda's balance of payments: its external debts doubled between 1985 and 1989 and increased another 34 per cent between 1989 and 1992, reaching US $804.3 million.[10]

Exacerbating the country's economic difficulties, Habyarimana diverted scarce government resources and official development assistance toward funding the civil war. Whereas military expenditures accounted for 1.6% of Gross National Product (GNP) in 1989, it increased to 8.4% of GNP by 1994.[11] Additionally, while Habyarimana spent $10 million in 1989 on arms imports, he purchased nearly $80 million in arms by 1994.[12] Overall, between 1990 and 1994, Habyarimana diverted close to 40 per cent of Rwanda's budget to military purposes,[13] while the size of the army expanded six-fold, from about 5,000 to more than 30,000.[14]

Realizing it had lost the civil war, the fleeing interim government concluded its brief rule by systematically dismantling the country's financial and institutional infrastructures. Absconding with 17–24 billion Rwandan francs—more than twice that in circulation at the time—and with the foreign currency holdings of the central bank, the fleeing interim government dismantled the country's financial system.[15] Moreover, it also looted government ministries, schools, and businesses of most assets and emptied the country of its trained civil service and professional staff, thereby destroying the country's institutional infrastructure.[16] As a result, by 1994 Rwanda's real annual Gross Domestic Product (GDP) growth registered at *negative* 49 per cent;[17] inflation climbed to 64 per cent;[18] Gross National Income (GNI) per capita plummeted to US $140 from US $370 in 1990;[19] and farmers failed to produce a tea or coffee harvest for that year.[20] Indeed, by the time the RPF came to power, Rwanda had become the poorest country on earth, according to the World Bank, and most international development experts concurred that they had never seen a country so laid to waste.[21]

Reconciliation

Welding a society fractured by socioeconomic and regional cleavages and the ethnic tension during and after the genocide completed the twofold challenge confronting the RPF. Socioeconomic stratification pervaded pre- and post-independent Rwanda: while the elite monopolized access to land, state resources, the private sector, and higher education, the vast majority—around 90 per cent of the population—farmed the steep hills, mostly as subsistence farmers, and lived in poverty.[22]

The gap between the elite and the poor reached its apex in the decade preceding the civil war and the genocide. In contrast to the successful image of Rwanda marketed by the World Bank and other members of the international development community as a developing country committed to rural development and livelihoods and despite a several year period of increased food and coffee production and improvements in transport infrastructure,[23] the reality more closely resembled an African Potemkin Village whose optimistic façade masked extreme socioeconomic stratification caused by elite monopolization of land and access to non-farm employment and income, more expensive and evaporating social services, and increased taxes.

By 1984, 15 per cent of the farmers owned 50 per cent of land, while 26 per cent had become landless.[24] Forty-three percent of all farming households lacked enough land to subsist on.[25] By 1990, according to some estimates, the percentage of landless remained steady at about a quarter of the rural population, and in some districts that figure approached 50 per cent.[26] Duress sales due to people selling their land on the informal land market to buy food and other necessities prompted the sustained, if not dramatic, incidence of landlessness. Having access to more non-farm employment and income, most of the land owning elite, who were connected to the Habyarimana regime, became richer after 1984 while the poor became poorer. According to Uvin, the income share of the richest decile in Rwanda increased from 22 per cent in 1982 to 52 per cent in 1994.[27] Uvin calculated further that by the end of the 1980s, "approximately half of Rwanda's society must . . . be considered ultra-poor, up to 40 percent more poor, 9 per cent non-poor, and 1 per cent positively rich."[28]

More expensive and evaporating social services and increased taxes in the late 1980s and into the early 1990s exacerbated the economic hardship and marginalization of the dispossessed rural dwellers. In compliance with the 1990 IMF and World Bank structural adjustment loans, the Habyarimana government devalued the Rwandan franc, which increased prices, even for non-imported items; imposed a "cost-sharing" austerity program that required citizens pay higher fees for fewer public services, including access to water; and increased local taxes, all the while the elite flaunted its considerable wealth and excessive consumption.[29]

By the early 1990s, then, the elite campaign to appropriate the remaining shares of land and income, declining and more expensive social services and increased taxes in a severely stratified pre genocide Rwanda deepened a long-standing cleavage in social cohesion along socioeconomic lines. Such a cleavage—exacerbated by mounting environmental scarcity, population growth, and livelihood loss[30]—contributed to the political milieu of the early 1990s that produced the willing executioners of the genocide among those who benefited and those who sought to benefit from such an arrangement. State employees wanted to protect their privileged positions, army personnel—ranging from soldiers to senior officers—feared demobilization and the unemployed joined the militias to acquire the spoils secured through intimidation, murder, and theft.[31]

While the socioeconomic cleavage lined the tinderbox of the genocide with the kindling, the competition between regional, Hutu elite for access to and control over state power (and resources) ignited the fuse that set in motion the killing machine that devoured moderate Hutu and Tutsi from April to July in 1994. While the Kayibanda government (1962–1973) awarded key political positions to Hutu from his home region of Gitarama in central Rwanda,[32] Habyarimana, his successor, disenfranchised Hutu from the center and south in favor of patrons and clients from the north,[33] especially his wife's prefecture, Gisenyi.

During Habyarimana's Second Republic (1973–1994) Hutu from Gisenyi occupied one-third of the top jobs in government and almost all leadership positions in the security forces and controlled the vast majority of development projects.[34] Most likely, since 1973 Hutu from the south were as discriminated as Tutsi.[35] By the late 1980s the interregional competition between elites narrowed to deadly infighting among Habyarimana's inner circle (the *akazu*) that rejected the president's anticipated successor because it would strip the akazu of power and control over a rapidly shrinking economy. The outcome of the akazu infighting led to a *genocidaire* controlled government and, along with the intensifying socioeconomic stratification, it also instilled a profound distrust of and alienation from the state among the masses, which increasingly refused to attend commune meetings, perform obligatory communal labor

(ubukonde), and cut down coffee trees to grow food crops.[36]

Given that the interim government chose to frame Rwanda's problem and solution in ethnic terms, the RPF also had to address a complex ethnic division that emerged in two varieties after July, 1994: between Hutu perpetrators and Tutsi survivors; and between a Tutsi dominated government and the Hutu majority who considered the post genocide government as foreign because most of its members had grown up in Uganda.[37] It is important to stress that to suggest an ethnic division exists in contemporary Rwanda is not the same as saying essentialist and corporate conceptions of ethnicity were the primary cause of the genocide, as the above discussion has attempted to elucidate: "it is politics that makes ethnicity important . . . not ethnicity which invariably defines politics."[38] Nonetheless, for many Hutu the "social structure and the cultural strangeness embodied in [the RPF] makes it an alien form of power."[39] Indeed, post genocide Rwanda, according to Lemarchand, "is more profoundly divided" between Hutu and Tutsi than ever.[40] So, even though no ancient tribal animosity between Hutu and Tutsi exists—a misunderstanding often associated with the history of conflict in Rwanda—the interim government constructed a virulent ethnic divide that still influences the politics and quotidian reality in Rwanda. In sum, the choice of economic policies adopted by the RPF and how it decides to distribute the gains from those policies will influence the extent to which Rwandan society will be able to weld the socioeconomic and regional cleavages contributing to and the ethnic division resulting from the genocide.

The RPF Quest for Competitiveness: Economic Policies in Post Genocide Rwanda

To establish normalcy, qualify for official development assistance, and integrate Rwanda more substantially into the global economy, the RPF embraced an export oriented development strategy, supported by exchange rate and trade liberalization, agrarian and land reform, and privatization policies, as well as military commercialism. Though the RPF entertains a long-term ambition to transform Rwanda from a commodity exporter to a technology based services economy, or the "Grenada of Africa,"[41] the most the RPF can accomplish in the immediate future is to ascend from a subaltern to a competitive niche in the global economy. Lacking a diversified economy and skilled citizenry, Rwanda's most direct connection to and, realistically, its only option to become more competitive within the global economy is through the export of primary commodities and handicrafts. While coffee, tea, and tin had been established but inconsistent and insufficient foreign currency earners, the RPF has sought to enhance its revenue capacity through legal and extralegal means. To increase commodity production, the Rwandan Parliament recently passed agrarian and land reform legislation. To meet its immediate financing needs in the aftermath of the genocide, the RPF, through military commercialism, aggressively carved out a niche in the global coltan commodity chain. Though the coltan boom was ephemeral and now contributes rather sparingly to government revenue, from 1998 to 2002 it was, arguably, the most significant economic policy of the last decade, and as a result of the growing struggle between Rwanda, Uganda, and the new South Africa over control of the expanding markets in parts of East Central Africa, military commercialism might very well presage future production, distribution, and management models in several countries of the Great Lakes region.

Exchange Rate and Trade Liberalization Since 1994

To a large extent, the economic policies embraced by the RPF since 1994 resume the reforms introduced by the Habyarimana regime in 1990. At that time, in need of foreign currency both to pay for imports and to sate the acquisitive appetites of the elite, Rwanda submitted to a structural adjustment program with the IMF and World Bank and commenced its exchange rate and trade liberalization and privatization reforms.[42] However, the civil war interrupted Rwanda's reform process and did not resume until after the conclusion of the genocide.

After the genocide the RPF faced similar pressures. In dire need of official development assistance, and—similar to the majority of developing countries—without an alternative to the neoliberal development strategy, the RPF commenced its economic reconstruction process with standard exchange rate and trade liberalization reforms. Apropos to the exchange regime, the RPF introduced a fully liberalized and market determined exchange rate system; established a licensed foreign exchange bureau; and abolished all current account restrictions.[43] In regard to trade liberalization, the RPF reduced the maximum tariff rate from 100 per cent before 1995 to currently between 25–30 per cent.[44] It also reduced the number of non-zero tariff bands from 40 to 3.[45] Additionally, the RPF eliminated the coffee export tax in 1999 and joined the Common Market for Eastern and Southern Africa (COMESA) in 2004. For goods imported and that originate from COMESA, the RPF slashed tariffs by 90 per cent.[46] Based on its trade liberalization reforms, the government of Rwanda's development strategy relies on its traditional, "official" exports of coffee, tea, cassiterite tin, and handicrafts and from 1998 to 2002 the often, "unofficial" export of coltan.

Since 1994 the RPF has taken limited steps towards increasing coffee production, mostly through investing in washing and processing facilities and supporting fair trade coffee cooperatives. While Rwanda has made a very slight inroad into the premium blend fair trade coffee market, coffee output, Rwanda's main cash crop, fell by nearly 80 per cent between 1990 and 2001.[47] By 2003, coffee production continued its downward trend, while tea output registered a modest increase over the last several years.[48] Recent attempts to export cassava paste to the ethnic food market in France show some potential but have yet to contribute in any meaningful way to government revenue.[49] In addition, exports of cassiterite tin, hides, and handicrafts increased in output and value during the first decade of reconstruction,[50] though not enough to register a noticeable increase in export earnings.

Agrarian and Land Reform

In November 2004 Rwanda's Parliament passed agrarian and land reform legislation, perhaps the most important reform since the genocide, given the relationship between access to land, income and poverty in pre and post genocide Rwanda. Driven by demographic and economic pressures, the primary purpose of the new legislation is to maximize and commercialize agricultural production through regional specialization, or the practice of monocropping, where the government will determine the type of crop grown, depending on location. The expected outcomes of the reform take three forms: to generate increased export revenue; to create more employment opportunities in the formal economy through agro-processing jobs; and to minimize food insecurity.

To a significant extent, the RPF's version of agrarian and land reform recycles the efforts of Habyarimana to do so commencing in the late 1970s. Similar to Habyarimana's Second Republic, the impetus for reform for the current government of Rwanda stems from demographic and economic pressures. Increasing at a rapid clip of nearly 2% per year, the population now totals nearly 8 million (in a country the size of Maryland) and population density reads at an overcrowded 350 people per square kilometer, leading to a considerable fragmentation of land holdings. Whereas the average landholding at the household level registered at 2 hectares in 1960, it dropped to 0.7 hectare in 1990 and has continued its downward trend; currently at least 60 per cent of households' land holdings measure at less than 0.5 hectare.[51] While the majority of rural dwellers endure a subsistence living on tiny landholdings—usually inherited or rented—a significant share of land, often parceled in plots of 50 hectares or more, is controlled by a rich elite mainly from urban areas.[52] Many of these larger holdings often fail to maximize production capacity because of a disinterest in commercial farming by those who control them.[53] Consequently, the current, simultaneous fragmentation and overproduction on small holdings will not be able to sustain subsistence farming indefinitely while the under production on large plots inhibits the maximization and commercialization of agricultural production. Left unreformed, the current arrangement of subsistence farming coexisting with larger holdings adverse to commercial farming can not generate increased revenue—definitely a dire need—for the RPF.

To wrest land, the scarcest factor of production, from the Charybdis of fragmentation and overproduction and the Scylla of under production on large plots, the agrarian and land reform legislation intends to consolidate smaller holdings into a minimum of one hectare, provide credit and investment incentives to large landholders to spur commercial farming, and impose cultivation of particular crops, depending on location of region. In doing so, the RPF aims to change the current agricultural production system from a consumer to a market driven system, where, ostensibly, many rural dwellers will become wage laborers on the large holdings converted to agro industries, thus earning enough money to purchase rather than grow food and thereby minimize food insecurity. Whether the newly legislated reforms will produce the expected outcomes is unclear. Since independence authorities have repeatedly attempted (1959, 1960, 1961, and 1976) to legislate the land market and formalize the remaining vestiges of the traditional *igikingi*, *isambu*, and *ubukonde* systems largely diluted by a nearly century long process of the individualization and monetization of the informal land market introduced during Belgium colonization.[54]

Privatization

Initiated in 1996, Rwanda's privatization strategy included enhancing the government's institutional capacity for the sale of state-owned enterprises (SOEs) and then auctioning those parastatals. To enhance institutional capacity, the government established a regulatory agency to set tariffs, grant licenses, and prevent companies from acting as private monopolies.[55] Further, it created an Independent Private Sector Federation to replace the former government controlled Chamber of Commerce, and, to facilitate the privatization and deregulation of it utilities, introduced an Independent Regulatory Agency. Such institutional reforms have enabled the sale of 37 out of 53 state-owned enterprises. While most of the sold SOEs were small enterprises, the government has sold its airline, Rwanda Air Express, and it has finalized the sale of shares of Pfunda tea factory. In June 2003, the government sold 55% of Pfunda to LAB International, one of the three major buyers of tea at the Mombasa Auction. Though Electogaz, the water and electricity provider, will remain under state ownership, in May 2003, the government signed a five-year management contract for private firms to manage that parastatal. Finally, the government sold majority shares in Prime Holdings, which developed three hotel projects during 2003, to private investors.[56]

Military Commercialism and the Global Coltan Commodity Chain

Faced with disappointing and uncertain prospects in enhancing the country's economic competitiveness through traditional exports, the RPF capitalized on the confluence of a security threat, new product development in global communications and electronics industries, and the entrepreneurial skills of its military leaders to secure a niche in the global coltan commodity chain. After an incursion into Zaire in 1996, from 1998 to 2002, the RPA occupied eastern DRC in response to continued threats from exiled Rwandan Armed Forces (ex-FAR) and *Interahamwe*. During that period, products in the communications and electronics industries, ranging from cell phones to playstations, generated a significant global demand for coltan. To capitalize on its presence in the DRC and the global demand for coltan, the leaders of the RPA captured the coltan mines and trade in eastern DRC and established a distribution network, earning Rwanda much needed revenue.

In response to incursions by ex-FAR and milita members, the RPA first ventured into Zaire to address the threat in 1996, before its eventual occupation of the area from August 1998 to September 2002. While the RPF maintained that its presence in eastern DRC was strictly for security purposes, several independent reports suggested that Rwanda's presence was to exploit DRC's natural resources, specifically its profitable coltan mines.[57] Between 1998 and 2002, the RPA and its Congolese surrogate, the Rassemblement Congolais pour la Democratic (RCD), seized the coltan mines in Maniema, South and North Kivu, and Katanga.[58] As a result, the RPA monopolized 60–70 per cent of the coltan exported from the DRC, flying it directly from airstrips near mining sites to Kigali or Cyangangu.[59]

Once the RPA acquired a secure supply of coltan, it also developed an efficient distribution system, which continues to operate.[60] Essentially, the RPA, through its supply and distribution networks, is a textbook example of what Dietrich calls military commercialism, where military officers create corporate-military businesses in order to generate income for themselves and their politico-military (state) apparatus.[61] Once the RPA established control of most of eastern DRC's coltan trade, it expanded its military commercialism throughout the region by establishing a broad network of subsidiaries and enterprises, ranging from the selling of mining licenses to the collection of taxes and customs duties to the management of water, power and transportation facilities. During a seventeen-month period, from 2000 to 2001, it is estimated that the RPA earned $18 million a month[62] from its control of the DRC's coltan mines and trade. While coltan revenue had dropped significantly since 2002, the network of subsidiaries and enterprises still provide some revenue for the RPF. Consequently, Rwanda's military commercialism emerged as the most important source of revenue for the government of Rwanda from the late 1990s to 2002.

Institutional Stasis and the Tenuous Connection between Economic Policy and Reconciliation

While the RPF, after its first decade in power, has adopted standard neoliberal policies potentially sufficient to increase economic growth, due to structural constraints and choice, it has yet to tailor those policies to local conditions so that they address the marginalization of the masses and ensure a more equitable distribution of resources to reduce poverty. This section summarizes the gains accomplished through the RPF's economic policies and then demonstrates how those economic policies, particularly its agrarian and land reform, privatization and military commercialism, maintain the longstanding socioeconomic cleavage; fail to include institutions that acknowledge and reduce the marginalization of the majority of rural dwellers; and ethnicize the economy.

Results of Economic Policies

Since 1995, the Rwandan economy has been one of the fastest growing in Africa and indeed the world. Between 1995 and 2001, GDP growth registered an average of 12.5 per cent per year,[63] and dropped to about 8 per cent per annum between 2002 and 2003, still more than double the average for sub-Saharan Africa. Though still heavily aid dependent, burdened by unsustainable, external debt,[64] and lacking a diversified economy, average incomes are now roughly back to their pre-genocide level, and the RPF has made real progress in rebuilding the shattered school and health-care systems.[65] In short, most analysts agree that the RPF has demonstrated much skill in its handling of the country's economic reconstruction, though substantial work remains.

Persistent Cleavages and Institutional Stasis

For the most part, possibly through intent but probably as a result of circumstance, the RPF's agrarian and land reform and privatization and military commercialism policies buttress rather than challenge Rwanda's longstanding socioeconomic cleavage. In its own way each policy diverts resources to the elite rather than achieving a semblance of balance between the vanguard and the rearguard of the economy, resulting in an identifiable trend of enhancing elite rather than mass interests.

Specific provisions of the agrarian and land reform, such as the plans for land consolidation, registration, and access to credit all favor richer farmers with larger holdings and, most likely, a source of non-farm income.[66] For example, due to the expense of surveying and registration of land, many rural dwellers most likely will not participate and, even if they do, they most likely will not be competitive for loans or programs to enhance productivity. Most analysts expect agrarian and land reform to benefit large landholders willing to produce for the commercial market. In addition, some researchers suggest that, "land consolidation policies are unlikely to increase land productivity significantly,"[67] and agricultural specialization, or monocropping on consolidated fields, could lead to increased rates of soil erosion.[68] Either outcome would disproportionately threaten the tenuous livelihoods of the majority of rural dwellers.

Similarly, the RPF's privatization and military commercialism policies also maintain the status quo of the socioeconomic cleavage. A significant overlap exists between the managers of the privatization and military commercialism programs: senior members of the Rwandan Army and civilians well connected to them. Currently, senior members of the army control the Office National Des Transports en Commun, the Office Rwandais d'Information, the state television station, and Electrogaz.[69] Additionally, senior members of the military and Kigali businessmen connected to them control the profits and offshoot businesses associated with the coltan trade and the Rwandan expropriation of the economies in Kisangani and other areas in eastern DRC.[70] The main point, here, is that an elite controls the gains of the most profitable economic policies, and it is unclear whether those profits are being used for private business or public investment. Thus, whereas the Habyarimana regime cultivated an elite through the allocation of government jobs, military positions and development projects, the Kagame regime might be recreating such a group among those who manage the privatization and military commercialism programs.

At this point, one might argue that a deep socioeconomic cleavage between the elite and the poor is pervasive throughout Africa and does not preclude or even influence reconciliation in post genocide Rwanda. Further, one might also argue that given the structural constraints faced by Rwanda as a primary commodity producer in a global economy often hostile to such countries, its dependence on IMF and World Bank debt relief and loans and international aid in general, and the inefficiency and corruption rife in the First and Second Republics, it is inevitable that the RPF embraced the standard neoliberal policy prescriptions, whether they fit local conditions and address local problems or not. In response to the first possible criticism, while it is true that a wide divide exists between the rich and poor in countries in the region and on the continent, with the exception of Burundi and, currently, Sudan, those countries have not experienced a genocide making the Rwandan situation a special case, practically *sui generis*. Moreover, this paper argues that the inability to link economic policies to minimizing the socioeconomic cleavage conditioning the genocide does not preclude reconciliation but will at the least make it a tenuous and protracted process. More significantly, as a rebuttal to the second possible criticism, again, it is reasonable to argue that Rwanda is basically hemmed in and constrained in its policy choices due to its subordinate status in the global economy. However, the type of institutions needed to address local conditions do not run counter to an export oriented, market driven development strategy, which leads to the second main point of this section: whether through intent or circumstance, the RPF's economic policies have yet to include institutions that acknowledge and attempt to reduce the marginalization of rural peasants. The inability of the RPF to do so manifests most clearly (and recently) in the 2004 agrarian and land reform, but also in the privatization program.

The agrarian and land reform legislation creates at least two new institutions to implement the new policy: a Land Center to provide technical and administrative support to the National Land Commission; and national, provincial, and district land commissions to manage the consolidation, surveying, and registering of land.[71] To date, it appears that MINITERE[72] will determine the mission, program, and membership for the provincial and district land commission. Significantly, MINITERE omits peasant representation in the provincial and district land commission, making reform a top down process. While legitimate management and human capital issues might partly explain the exclusion of peasant representation in commission membership, the decision might also reflect the governing style of the RPF. The cooperatives originating in the 1970s ended up creating a venue where the rank and file often challenged the leadership.[73] Perhaps in an effort to avoid delay and criticism and opposition form rural dwellers, the new reform will most likely continue to avoid engaging them in discussions and decision making about the future of agricultural production.

A similar trend of peasant exclusion also appears in the privatization program. As noted earlier, thirty-seven out of fifty-three SOEs have been privatized. Of those thirty-seven privatized SOEs, the vast majority has been sold to wealthy Rwandans, foreign individuals, and foreign firms (nearly one-third of all enterprises sold).[74] Approximately three SOEs have been auctioned to peasant/worker cooperatives.[75] While the lack

of investment capital and educated workers would make the sale of hotel and tourism, industry, mining, energy and services parastatals to worker cooperatives a chimera, the sale of agriculture, agro-industry, and other low-tech, low to semi-skilled enterprises is possible,[76] but has not been given serious consideration by the government. Such cooperatives could establish an institutional structure that would promote a common goal for and cooperation among rural Rwandans,[77] as well as integrate them into the formal economy.

Given the change in leadership and demographic shifts after the genocide, perhaps it is inevitable that the economic policies adopted by the RPF after 1994 would lead to an ethnicized economy, where returning Tutsi control the vast majority of investment capital in current day Rwanda and remaining members of the moderate Hutu elite have been essentially crowded out of key strategic and lucrative positions. Returning members of the Tutsi diaspora—numbering more than 700,000 and virtually replacing those who perished in the genocide—have monopolized the formal economy, occupying businesses and shops abandoned by fleeing Hutus and financed by the resources they arrived with. Thus, even before the commencement of privatization, the demographic shifts in the aftermath of the genocide created a dichotomized economy: Hutus occupy the land, working as subsistence farmers, while Tutsis have captured the town-based, monetized, formal sectors.[78] In an early assessment of the potential for privatization in post genocide Rwanda, Prunier concluded, "privatization of state enterprises [does] not sound very realistic in the present context unless one means [they're] being taken over by the Ugandans,"[79] referring to both military and civilian returnees.

The potential consequences of the RPF's decision not to complement its economic policies with institutions that acknowledge and address the marginalization of the majority of rural dwellers and the current Tutsi monopolization of the economy are twofold. First, the PRF might have missed an important opportunity to recreate social capital relationships of trust; restore the rural community torn asunder by the genocide; and to cultivate a civil society to counterbalance the power of the state.[80] Second, the RPF ignores the useful advice, "that with appropriate policies the government in Kigali could win over [many Rwandans], those who are partisans of neither side."[81] According to the Newburys, "literally millions of Rwandans do not see themselves as partisans of one or the other camp (i.e., neither the RPF nor the army of the former Habyarimana regime)."[82] In combination with the RPF's choice not to address seriously the country's still severe socioeconomic stratification, the decisions to exclude peasant representation in agrarian and land reform and most aspects of privatization and to ignore the post genocide ethnic division between Hutu and Tutsi probably will do little to attract support from the people most affected by the RPF's economic policies.

After its first decade in power in post genocide Rwanda, the RPF has evolved into an enigmatic, Janus-faced regime. While it has used its skill and resourcefulness to commence a relatively promising economic reconstruction of the country, it has yet to tailor those policies to local conditions so that they reduce the longstanding socioeconomic cleavage; include institutions that acknowledge and reduce the marginalization of the majority of rural dwellers; and acknowledge and address the ethnicized economy in post genocide Rwanda. In short, solutions in the economic sphere have not occurred in tandem with reconciliation, making the latter a protracted and tenous process at best and an elusive quest at worst. To make reconciliation less protracted, if not elusive, the RPF might consider the adoption of more rural/regional development programs, embrace peasant representation in district and provincial land commissions, promote peasant/worker cooperatives, and perhaps even adopt an affirmative action program. To put such a burden on the RPF is grossly unfair. After all, it faces serious economic constraints from its subaltern status in a global economy hostile and unforgiving toward primary commodity producers. And, it receives insufficient support from an often indifferent, if not callous, international political community. However, if the RPF fails to address the country's socioeconomic cleavage, the marginalization of peasants, and its ethnic division at this critical juncture in its country's history, it will have missed perhaps a rare opportunity to help liberate Rwanda from its violent past and possible future.

Notes

1. UN Economic Commission on Africa, *Economic Report on Africa 2003* (http://www.uneca.org/era2003/), p. 125.
2. Most of the following authors cited are not technically political economists and, in fact, represent an array of disciplines, ranging from history to development studies. Nonetheless, their writings address issues fundamental to a political economy approach to the genocide. See Peter Uvin, *Aiding Violence, The Development Enterprise in Rwanda* (West Hartford, CT: Kumarian Press, 1998), *Development, Aid and Conflict Reflections from the Case of Rwanda* (Helsinki: UNU/WIDER, 1996), and "Rwanda: Social Roots of Genocide," in Nafziger et al, (eds) *War, Hunger and Displacement: The Origins of Humanitarian Emergencies*, volume 2 (Oxford: Oxford University Press, 2000); Gerard Prunier, *The Rwanda Crisis. History of a Genocide* (New York: Columbia University Press, 1997) and "Rwanda: the Social, Political and Economic Situation," *Writenet (UK) June 1997, pp. 1–11*; Catherine Newbury and David Newbury, "Identity, Genocide, and Reconstruction in Rwanda, Paper prepared for the Conference on Les Racines de la Violence dans la Region des Grands Lacs, Parlement Europeen, Bruxelels, 12–13 janvier 1995; David Newbury and Catherine Newbury, "Bringing the Peasants Back In: Agrarian Themes in the Construction and Corrosion of Statist Historiography in Rwanda," *The American Historical Review*, Volume 105, Issue 3 (also at http://www.historycooperative.org); David Newbury, "Understanding Genocide," *African Studies Review*, Volume 41, No. 1 (April 1998), 73–97; Catherine Newbury, "Rwanda: Recent Debates Over Governance and Rural Development," in *Governance and Politics in* Africa, Goran Hyden and Micael Bratton, eds., (Boulder: Lynn Rienner Publisher, 1992), pp. 193–218; Justin MacDermott, "The Livelihood Conflicts Approach on Trial in Rwanda: Towards a Political Critique," *Development Studies Instiute Working Paper No. 01-21* (London School of Economics and Political Science, 2001); Andy Storey, "Structural Adjustment, State Power and Genocide: the World Bank and Rwanda," Paper presented at the conference on 'The global constitution of "failed states": consequences of a new imperialism?', Suxxes, 18–20 April 2001; and Saskia Van Hoyweghen, "The Urgency of Land and Agrarian Reform in Rwanda," *African Affairs*, Volume 98, No. 392 (July 1999), pp. 353–372.
3. See Prunier, *The Rwanda Crisis*, and especially Saskia Van Hoyweghen, "Urgency of Land and Agrarian Reform in Rwanda."
4. See Rene Lemarchand, "Genocide in the Great Lakes: Which Genocide? Whose Genocide?" *African Studies Review*, Volume 41, Number 1 (April 1998), pp. 3–16.
5. While each country has an autonomous history, the politics in one clearly influences those in another.
6. Due to space limitations, security, the third challenge of the RPF, is omitted here. For a detailed discussion of

Rwanda's security after 1994, see Institute for Security Studies, "Rwanda: Security," 2003. http://www.isa.org/za/AF/profiles/Rwanda/SecInfo.html; and Patrick Cannon, "Economic Reconstruction, Security and Reconciliation in Post Genocide Rwanda," Paper delivered at Second Genocide Conference, California State University, Sacramento, October 14–16 2004.

7. Between independence and the conclusion of the 1994 civil war and genocide, Rwanda had two presidents, Kayibanda from 1962 to 1973, and Habyarimana from 1973 to April 1994. An interim president and government replaced Habyarimana after his death in April 1994 and ruled until it fled to Zaire in July, 1994.

8. Peter Uvin, "Rwanda: Social Roots of Genocide," in Nafzigr et al, (eds) *War, Hunger, and Displacement,* p. 175. Cited in J. MacDermott, "The Livelihood Conflicts Approach," p. 12.

9. World Bank, *Rwanda: Country Assistance Evaluation* (Washington, D.C.: World Bank, 2004) p. 1.

10. R. Anderson, "How Multilateral Development Assistance Triggered the Conflict in Rwanda," *Third World Quarterly*, Vol. 21, No. 3, (2000), p. 448.

11. K. Emizet, "The massacre of refugees in Congo: a case of UN peacekeeping failure and international law," *The Journal of Modern African Studies*, Vol. 38, No. 2 (2000), p. 165.

12. Emizet, 2000, p. 165.

13. Anderson, 2000, p. 448.

14. Catherine Newbury and David Newbury, "Identity, Genocide, and Reconstruction," p. 11.

15. Danida, *The International Response to Conflict and Genocide: Lessons from the Rwanda Experience* (http://www.um.dk/Publikationer/Danida/English/Evaluations/1997_rwanda/b4/c3.asp), 1997; Prunier, *The Rwanda Crisis*, p. 321.

16. Peter Gourevitch, *We Wish to Inform You that Tomorrow We Will be Killed with our Families. Stories from Rwanda* (New York: Farrar, Straus and Giroux, 1998), pp. 162, 169.

17. Institute for Security Studies, "Rwanda, Economy," http://www.iss.org.za/AF/profiles/Rwanda/Economy.html 2003.

18. Orla Ryan, "Rwanda's Struggle to Rebuild Economy," BBC News. 2004

19. World Bank, 2004, p. 31.

20. Gourevitch, 1998, p. 229.

21. *Ibid.*, pp. 270, 229.

22. In terms of ethnicity, whereas Tutsi comprised the elite during the pre-independence era, Hutu constituted most—but not all—of the elite after 1962. After 1962, Tutsi, though clearly the victims of systematic discrimination, still managed a larger portion of representation with respect to their demographic share in the management of state-owned enterprises, banking, and the private sector. Nonetheless, the Hutu governments after 1962 limited Tutsi influence to the economic realm and retained their stranglehold on the country's political and economic institutions. See A. Bell-Fialkoff, *Ethnic Cleansing* (New York: St. Martin's Press, 1999), p. 185.

23. Catherine Newbury, "Rwanda: Recent Debates," p. 193.

24. Uvin, "Rwanda: Social Roots of Genocide," p. 169, cited in MacDermott, p. 11.

25. Peter Uvin, *Aiding Violence*, p. 57. Cited in Storey, 2001, p. 6.

26. Herman Musahara and C. Huggins, "Land Reform, Land Scarcity and Post Conflict Reconstruction. A Case Study of Rwanda," *Eco-Conflicts*, Volume 3, Number 3, October 2004, pp. 1–4.

27. Uvin, "Rwanda: Social Roots of Genocide," p. 169. Cited in MacDermott, 2001, p. 27.

28. Uvin, *Development, Aid and Conflict Reflections from the Case of Rwanda*, p. 25.

29. Catherine Newbury and David Newbury, "Identity, Genocide and Reconstruction," p. 9.

30. MacDermott, 2001.

31. Storey, 2001, p. 8

32. David Newbury, "Understanding Genocide," p. 7.

33. *Ibid.*, p. 18.

34. Storey, p. 4.

35. Uvin, "Rwanda: Social Roots of Genocide," p. 165. Cited in MacDermott, p. 23.

36. David Newbury and Catherine Newbury, "Bringing the Peasants Back In," p. 26.

37. Prunier, "Rwanda: the Social, Political and Economic Situation," 1997.

38. Catherine Newbury and David Newbury, "Identity, Genocide and Reconstruction," p. 16.

39. Prunier, *The Rwanda Crisis*, p. 371.

40. Wilson's Quarterly (2000) 'Rwanda's Tangled Web', Review of "Hate Crimes" by Rene Lemarchand, in Transition (2000: Nos. 81–82), *Wilson's Quarterly* 24 (3): 117–119.

41. C. Onyango-Obbo, "Special Report on Rwanda: Rwanda Can only Win the Grenada Way, or with 'Cambodian Magic,'" from *The Monitor*, August 21, 2001, p. 3.

42. M. Chossudovsky, *The Globalisation of Poverty: Impacts of IMF and World Bank Reforms* (London and New Jersey: Zed Books: Penang: Third World Network, 1997).

43. Rwanda Ministry of Finance and Economic Planning (2003) *Annual Economic Report 2003* (Kigali: Government of Rwanda), p.38.

44. Rwanda Ministry of Finance and Economic Planning (2004) 'Privatisation Status—April 2004' (Kigali: Government of Rwanda), p. 38.

45. *Ibid.*, p. 38.

46. Rwandan Ministry of Finance and Planning, 2003, p. 24.

47. UN ECA, *Economic Report on Africa 2003*, p. 121.

48. Rwandan Ministry of Finance and Planning, 2003, p. 14.

49. Interview with Jean Claude Kayisinga, Coffee Program Coordinator, PEARL PROJECT. Butare, Rwanda, July, 2005.

50. Rwandan Ministry of Finance and Planning, 2003, p. 14.

51. Mushara and Huggins, "Land Reform," p. 1.

52. *Ibid.*, p. 3.

53. Van Hoyweghen, p. 367.

54. See Van Hoyweghen, Prunier, Mushara and Huggins, and Catherine Newbury, *The Cohesion of Oppression*, (New York: Columbia University Press, 1988).

55. Rwanda Ministry of Finance and Economic Planning, 2003, p. 15

56. ECA, 2003, pp. 113–116; Rwandan Ministry of Finance and Economic Planning, 2003, p. 41; Rwandan Ministry of Finance and Economic Planning, 2004.

57. See International Peace Information Service (IPIS), *Supporting the War Economy in the DRC: European Companies and the Coltan Trade* (Brussels: IPIS), 2002; Steven Jackson, "Nos Richesses Sont Pillees: Economies de Guerre et Rumeurs de Crime dans les Kivus, Republique Democratique du Congo," *Politique Africaine*, no. 84, 2001 and *Fortunes of War: the coltan trade in the Kivus*, (New York: Social Science Research Council), 2003; Tim Raeymaekers, *Network War: An Introduction to Congo's Privatised Conflict Economy* (Brussels: IPIS), 2002; UN Panel of Inquiry, "Panel of Experts on the Illegal Exploitation of Natural Resources and Other Forms of Wealth of the Democratic Republic of Congo," S/2002/357, its Addendum, S/2001/1072, the Interim Report, S/2002/565, and the Final Report, S/2002/146; All Party Parliamentary Group on the Great Lakes Region and Genocide Prevention (APPG), *Cursed by Riches: Who Benefits from Resource Exploitation in the Democratic Republic of Congo* (London: British Parliament), 2002. Found in cassiterite tin, columbo-tantalite, or coltan, contains two rare metals with similar atomic structures: columbium (niobioum, Nb) and tantalum (Ta) (Raeymaekers, 2002). While cassiterite tin had been mined in the Kivus since colonial times, the demand to separate the coltan from the tin and the technology needed to do so did not emerge until the 1990s (Jackson, 2003: 7). An essential metal in the making of capacitors, a key component in mobile phones, laptop computers, video cameras, playstations, and automotive electronics (Raeymaekers, 2002), capacitor and chip manufactures, such as AMD, Hitachi, Intel, and NEC, and members of the high-tech industry, such as Compaq, Dell, Ericsson, HP, IBM, Lucent, Nokia, and Siemens, (IPIS, 2002: 10–15) created the surge in global demand, which more than doubled between 1993 and 2000 (IPIS, 2002: 10–15; Jackson, 2003: 7). The West Australian company Sons of Gwalia, the world's biggest tantalum producer, could not meet the demand, which was soon filled by mines in eastern DRC, where coltan mining began in 1996 (Jackson, 2003: 7). By November 2000, the price of coltan shot up from $30–40 USD/lb to over $300 USD/lb before dropping to its previous level after March 2001 (Jackson, 2003: 7; Final Report; APPG, 2002)

58. APPG, 2002; International Peace Information Service (IPIS), 2002, p. 9.

59. Final Report, p. 18.

60. Three RPA controlled *comptoirs*, or trading posts, Rwanda Metals, Grands Lacs Metals, and SOMIGL (Societe des Mines des Grands Lacs) receive deliveries of coltan directly from diggers working in riverbeds and mines in North and South Kivu, Maniema, and Katanga. In turn, the RPA comptoirs sell the metal to several international trading companies: Eagle Wings Resources International, Finmining, Raremont, and Cogecom, among others. Using international transport companies, such as ABAC, Steinweg, Ulba Aviakompania, and Sabena/Swiss Cargo, the international trading companies sell and deliver the coltan to Ulba Metallurgical Plant in Kazakhstan, the American firms Trinitech and Cabot, Ningxia in China, and H.C. Stark in Germany, where the coltan is processed into tantalum powder and then sold to the electronics industry where the powder is used to manufacture capacitors (Final Report, 2002a: 18–20; IPIS, 2002: 10–15).

61. C. Dietrich, "The Commercialization of Military Deployment in Africa," *African Security Review*, Volume 9, 2000; Raeymaekers, 2002; IPIS, 2002, p. 20.

62. Jackson: 2001; Jackson: 2003, p. 11.

63. World Bank: 2004, p. 4.

64. African Forum and Network on Debt and Development: 2004; World Bank: 2004, p. 6.

65. *Economist*: 2004, p. 3.

66. See Musahara and Huggins.

67. *Ibid.*, p. 2.

68. *Ibid.*, p. 3.

69. Prunier, *The Rwanda Crisis*, p. 387. Though the Prunier reference is from 1997, it is still valid.

70. It has been estimated that 60 to 70 per cent of coltan revenue has been reinvested in the military, leaving between 30 to 40 per cent unaccounted for.

71. See Musahara and Huggins.

72. Misistere Des Terres, De L'environment, Des Forets, De L'eau et Des Resources Naturelles.

73. Van Hoyweghen, p. 359.

74. See Rwanda Ministry of Finance and Economic Planning, "Privatisation Status—April 2004."

75. *Ibid.*

76. To a limited extent, the RPF has already initiated such a strategy. For example, the Nkora coffee factory has been sold to Cooperative UPROCA and Maraba Coffee is a worker owned cooperative, as is the Nyagatare dairy, purchased by cooperative KOABOMU (Rwandan Ministry of Finance and Economic Planning, 2004).

77. Whether organized as a producer cooperative or an employee stock ownership enterprise, both would be consistent with privatization. Though cooperatives will not quickly or substantially reduce income inequality and completely eliminate ethnic tensions, their increased presence could begin to change the perception of the Hutu majority that it is being ruled by a foreign, alien government unconcerned about its plight.

78. Prunier, "Rwanda: the Social, Political and Economic Situation," pp. 3, 7.

79. *Ibid.*, p. 8.

80. Van Hoyweghen, p. 359.

81. Catherine Newbury and David Newbury, "Identity, Genocide and Reconstruction," p. 21.

82. *Ibid.*, p. 19.

Toward a Philosophical Study of African Culture: A Critique of Traditionalism

Oladipo Olusegun

What should be the attitude of the African philosopher to the cultural heritage of his people?

This question, which is a significant offshoot of the debate on the question of African philosophy—i.e. the question of what we may mean when we talk of 'African Philsopshy'[1]—is likely to occupy a significant position in the history of African philosophy. Indeed, there is a sense in which answers given to it can be used as a basis for grouping African philosophers into different schools of thought. The reason why this is the case should not be difficult to fathom. For if the function (or, at any rate, one of the important functions) of philosophy is the critical examination of 'the intellectual foundations of our life, using the best modes of knowledge for human well-being,'[2] then the issue of how an African philosopher should relate (intellectually) to the cultural heritage of his people cannot but attract the philosopher's reflective and critical attention, moreso at a time when his people are confronted with a crisis of self-identity of no mean proportion.

Broadly speaking, there are two schools of thought on this issue. First, there are those Bodunrin aptly christens 'traditionalists,' that is those philosophers who are concerned with 'the discovery of authentic African ideas and thought systems uninfluenced by alien accretions.'[3] For this school of thought, the African philosopher should be engaged in a combination of two tasks. First, he should attempt to defend African cultures against all false ideas about them that have been perpetrated by Western scholarship. Second, he

"Towards a Philosophical Study of African Culture: A Critique of Traditionalism" by Oladip Olusegun, *Quest*, Vol. III, No. 2, December 1989. Reprinted by permission of Africa Studies Centre.

should describe these cultures and their various elements as they really are. The task of the African philosopher, then, for this school of thought, should be to promote an understanding of African belief systems through the exposition of their logical structure and the assumptions on which they are based.[4]

The second school of thought, on the other hand, argues, very persuasively I think, that given the fact that Africans are engaged in socio-economic and cultural reconstruction, the African philosopher, rather than content himself with a mere exposition of the logical structure of African belief systems, should engage in the important task of critically examining the intellectual foundations of African forms of life. And the point of doing this is to trace the source, and course of development, of our present troubles and see the best ways in which they can be tackled.[5]

In this paper, I reject the approach of the traditionalists in the study of African culture for three important reasons. First, by assuming that Africans have a world-view that is uniquely their own and which can be contrasted with the scientific world-view believed to be characteristically Western, they imply that African societies and Western societies 'operate on two basically opposed mental capacities.'[6] To so conclude is to rule out the possibility that forms of life may overlap in terms of practical and theoretical ends which they serve and that this overlap may provide a basis for comparative assessment of the rationality or irrationality of beliefs or categories of belief. Second, the traditionalists' position leads to the absurd conclusion that every belief or social practice is rational. This is because it assumes that all that is required of a belief in order for it to be rational, is that it is comprehensible by fitting into a given cultural matrix. Yet, it should be clear that we can understand a belief, see its point or function in a belief system and still insist that it is not rational. This may be the case, for example, in a situation in which we see the belief or world-outlook has not been effective in enabling the people to achieve the goals for which it provides a basis. Finally, the traditionalists do not seem to recognise the close connection between collective world-outlooks and their socio-economic basis, nor do they take account of the changing nature of these world-outlooks themselves, in connection with the changes occurring in the society as a whole. They assume, quite erroneously, that African world-views are static and, therefore, that a romantic glorification of the past should be the primary task of African philosophers. They thus misunderstand the nature of the connection between critical philosophy and socio-cultural development.

Before we start discussing these matters in detail, let us give a summary of the views of the traditionalists, so as to bring into sharper focus the main strands of their position.

In main, the position of the traditionalists is an attempt to justify African culture 'against external contempt and underestimation.'[7] It is a concerted effort at repudiating the image of African societies painted by some Western anthropologists (James Frazer, Edward Tylor, Max Muller etc.) who—having taken for granted the universal validity of the logico-scientific criteria of rationality developed within the context of Western cultural activities—saw in African belief systems and ritual practices a bundle of false hypotheses about man and nature which did not correspond to any objective reality.

On the basis of the assumption that 'each race is endowed with a distinctive nature and embodies, in its civilisation, a particular spirit,'[8] the traditionalists reject any attempt at placing African beliefs on the rationality scale in terms of criteria of rationality developed within the context of human and social activities which are products of a world-view which, for the traditionalists, differs in significant respects, if not totally, from the African world-view. Their view on what should be the attitude of the African philosopher to the world-view of his people, either expressed or implied in their works, is this. That since cultures differ in the way they interpret experiences because they operate with different assumptions about

the nature of reality, a people's culture can be understood only by unearthing those assumptions, theories and concepts in terms of which they interpret experiences. And since different interpretations of experience yield different philosophies, no philosophy can claim to have the final word on the meaning of existence as experienced.[9] This being the case, the argument continues, philosophy in Africa cannot benefit from what is called a 'universalist view' of its concerns. To be relevant to the African situation, it has to be 'a reflection on the cultural experience, or the exposition of the basic assumptions, concepts and theories which underlie African cultural experience and activities.'[10] In other words, it should primarily be concerned with a rational justification of African belief systems and the assumptions on which they are based. The whole point of doing this, of course, is to correct the distortions of African world-views that is a direct result of attempts by some Western anthropologists to superimpose alien criteria of rationality on them. The tr. can therefore be seen to be arguing, not only that there are no context-free norms of rationality, but also that African belief systems constitute a distinct form of life, the justification of which should be the primary preoccupation of African philosophers.

It should be clear from the summary of the position of the tr. given above, that they have some point in their favour. It is a fact, for instance, that a people's interpretation of life may differ from culture to culture. Even within the same culture, interpretations may differ from person to person and from one period to an other.[11] But if people's reactions to experiences are so conditioned—environmentally and historically—there should be no doubt that there can be no absolute way which represents the 'true' way of interpreting such experiences. It is therefore the case that no philosophy can escape the influence of the assumptions and concepts which provide the framework within which reality is interpreted in the cultural milieu in which it operates. Thus any philosophical activity in Africa, if it is to be authentically African, must relate consciously to those assumptions and concepts which underlie the African cultural experience.

The error of the traditionalists, then, lies neither in their contention that reality is open to different interpretations (this, of course, is an empirical fact), nor in their characterization of philosophy as a cultural activity. Rather, the error lies in the move they make from the acknowledgement of these facts to the conclusion that there is a picture of the world that is peculiarly African and that there is a distinctively African form of rationality—the justification of which, in their view, should be the preoccupation of the African philosopher. For, as I intend to show in the course of the discussion, one can admit these facts and still argue that the different interpretations of reality under consideration are complementary rather than contradictory and, therefore, that there is a sense in which we can talk of diffusion of criteria of rationality between, and within, cultures.

But first, let it be noted that the idea of a distinctive African mode of thought or form of rationality can be traced to the very beginnings of modern African thought,[12] which developed as 'part of a comprehensive process of reflection by African intelligentsia upon our historical being,'[13] a process which itself was set in motion by the colonial experience. The significance of this idea is best captured in the meaning of the twin concepts of 'African personality' and 'Negritude.' These concepts provided rallying points for a concerted and articulate reaction by the African intelligentsia to the denigration of the African experience by the imperialists. They also provided the intellectual foundation for some socio-political doctrines—'African Socialism' for example—that later became the framework for political action in some African countries. Thus, by postulating a distinctive African mode of thought whose coherence and rationality can only be seen within the framework of African conceptions of reality and the social activities they engender, our tr. (in contemporary African philosophy) are heirs to a significant intellectual tradition. The significance of this intellectual tradition consists in replacing the conception of Africans 'as untamed in their intellectual activities and so incapable of making distinctions between intellectual categories'[14] with the image of a people with 'a coherent system of institutions and customs, animated by spiritual and moral principles of the highest order.'[15]

But to what extent can we say that the insight provided by this tradition of thought, which may be adequate for the interpretation of the African reality as defined by the colonial experience, is also adequate for the task of post-colonial socio-economic reconstruction?

In considering this question, let us examine the claim of the traditionalists that Africans have a unique mode of thought, with distinctive criteria of rationality.[16] This with a view to seeing whether or not there is any kind of justification for the 'great divide' between African and Western cultures as suggested by Levy-Bruhl.

The traditionalists, as we can see, postulate a kind of theoretical consensus among Africans. They see 'beneath the various manifestations of African civilization and beneath the flood of history which has swept the civilization along willy-nilly, a solid bedrock which might provide a background for certitudes; in other words, a system of beliefs.'[17] The bedrock of this system of beliefs they see, curiously enough, in the work of a European missionary, Father Tempels,[18] whose 'avowed purpose in undertaking the study of Bantu philosophy was to arrive at the understanding of the profound workings of the Bantu mind in order to facilitate the integration of Christian principles within its schemes of values.'[19] Thus, for them, the nature of 'African Metaphysics' is captured in the saying: 'The African identifies being with life, or rather with life-force'[20] and if anybody was in doubt what the 'African mode of knowing' is, he simply needed to be reminded that this mode of knowing is a holistic one in which dualisms such as that between man and nature, subject and object, mind and matter, are totally absent[21]—a sentiment poetically expressed by Senghor when he writes:

> The African is, as it were, shut up in his black skin. He lives in the primordial night. He does not begin by distinguishing himself from the object, the tree or stone, the man or animal or social event. He does not keep it at a distance. He does not analyse it.
>
> Once he has come under its influence, he takes it like a blind man, still living, into his hands. He does not fix or kill it. He turns it over and over in his supple hands, he fingers it, he feels it. The African is one of the warms created on the third day . . . a purely sensory field. Subjectively at the end of his antennae, like an insect, he discovers the other. He is *moved* to his bowels, going out in a centrifugal movement

from the subject to the object on the waves sent out by the other.[22]

This kind of metaphysics and epistemology which constitutes the 'African Mindset' is contrasted with a uniform 'Western Mindset' which, again uniquely, is analytic and consequently, institutes all kinds of dichotomies: between man and nature, subject and object, body and mind etc. Again we have to return to Senghor, the apostle of Negritude, for a proper characterization of this contrast. He writes:

> The life-surge of the African, his self-abandonment, to the *other* is thus actuated with reason. But here reason is not the eye-reason of the European, it is the *reason-by-embrace* which shares more the nature of *logos* than *ratio*. Ratio is compass, setsquare and sextant, measure and weight where *logos*, before its Aristotelian tempering, before it became diamond, was living speech, which to the most typically human expression of neuro-sensory-impression, does not cast the object untouched, into rigid logical categories. African speech in raising itself to the Word, rubs and polishes things to give them back their original colour, with their grain and their veins, shooting through the rays of light to restore their transparency, penetrating his sureality, or rather their unyielding reality, in its freshness. Classical European reason is analytical and makes use of the object. African reason is intuitive and participates in the object.[23]

These contrasts prepare the ground for the relativist claim that, in trying to understand a people through their cultural expressions, we must judge each culture both in terms of its basic assumptions about reality and in terms of its goals.[24]

But I ask: can the traditionalists be right? Is there, in fact, any basis (empirical or theoretical) for the kind of water-tight distinction they draw between African and European 'Mindsets' such that the two are mutually exclusive?

Now, it can be argued, *contra* the traditionalists, that the only thing we can legitimately talk about, given the diversities among the people of Africa, is not any metaphysical or mythic unity, but a variety of the metaphysical world-views of myriad races and cultures.[25] In this view, the

thesis of a collective African philosophy is nothing but 'a smokescreen' behind which each author is able to manipulate his own philosophical views. It has nothing beyond this ideological function, it is an indeterminate discourse with no object.[26]

However, to argue in this manner is to imply that the thesis of a unique African mindset is an empirical claim, which it is not. It is, in the words of Prof. Irele, "not so much a descriptive analysis of African culture but a synthetic vision."[27] In bringing out the inadequacies of the traditionalists project, therefore, we have to move beyond this rather cheap critique of their position to a more penetrating analysis of its underlying assumptions. And in doing this, the issue that urgently presses for attention is the issue of the extent to which traditionalists are right in postulating a kind of rigid and unbridgeable gap between the 'African Mindset' and the 'European Mindset,' between the African mode of knowing which is both emotional and rhythmic and the European mode of knowing which is characteristically descriptive and analytical. The question, again, is this: Can the traditionalists be right?

The answer to this question cannot but be negative. For there is no society without some science and technology, and in every society, there is mutual interplay between 'forms of life'; between, for example, the religious and scientific forms of life. It is a known fact, for instance, that in traditional African societies there methods of healing and diagnosis which relied purely on naturalistic principles like those that now obtain in modern (Western) medicine. It was not every disease that had to be attributed to the agency of the gods, malevolent spirits etc.[28] So, it is incorrect to assert that traditional Africans were totally unscientific in their activities—both practical and intellectual. In any case, we do know, as aforementioned, that there has always been a mutual interplay between forms of life. This can be seen from the observation that religion and science have always interacted.[29] For example:

> The alchemists experimental techniques and low-level empirical knowledge made a large contribution to chemistry, but interestingly, their experimentation and study of nature seems to have been imbued with an attitude that is religious in nature.[30]

However, a more telling blow on the position of the traditionalists is the realisation that even in Western societies, there are scientists who are deeply religious and also people who still believe in and practice witchcraft.[31] This situation vividly suggests that forms of life need not be mutually exclusive; indeed they can be, and are in many cases, complementary.

Given the observations made above, it should be clear that there is no basis for the kind of rigid distinction between 'Mindsets' made by the traditionalists. We can see that there is a kind of overlap between those conceptions of reality and modes of knowing that are thought to be unique each to Africans and Europeans. This situation, in my view, provides some justification for some attempts at assessing *some* African traditional beliefs in terms of (Western?) sciento-technical criteria of rationality.

This issue of rationality brings me to the examination of a fundamental assumption which underlies the position of the traditionalists. This is the assumption that a system of beliefs is rational once we can understand it within the context of the socio-cultural activities which define it. That this assumption is fundamental to the position of the traditionalists can be seen in the dogmatic manner in which they venerate what they regard as the distinctive African mode of thought. As Prof. Bodunrin puts it:

> They hardly see why others may refuse totally to share their esteem for the system they describe. They do not raise philosophical issues about the system (because for them no philosophical problems arise once we "understand" the system); therefore they do not attempt to give a philosophical justification of the belief system or the issues that arise it.[32]

We can, for instance, find elements of this kind of attitude in Sodipo's analysis of the Yoruba conception of cause and chance and the scientific conception.[33] Sodipo has done this with a view to showing, not only the differences between them, but also that the Yoruba conception 'fits very well into the Yoruba traditional systems of belief, especially our religious belief system.'[34] Nowhere in the analysis is any attempt made to answer the very important question as to which of the two

conceptions is more efficacious in dealing with experience. The same attitude can be noticed in the exposition of Chewa cultural ideals and systems of thought attempted by D.N. Kaphagawani and H.F. Chidani'modizi in their illuminating article, "Chewa Cultural Ideals and Systems of Thought as Determined from Proverbs: A preliminary Anaylsis."[35] We see in this article that, although Chewa culture stresses the connection between knowledge and action, it is, at the same time, protective of authority. Like most traditional cultures, it stresses the preservation of tradition as against a critical engagement with it. The question that arises then is this: should a philosophical study of a people's culture, or better still aspects of it, be a mere exposition of the logical structure of the people's beliefs or should it go beyond that to consider the implications of such beliefs for human productive activities? Like Sodipo, the authors of the article just mentioned appear to have settled for the first option; for nowhere in their article is any attempt made to resolve the tension in Chewa culture between a concept knowledge that stresses action and that which favours the preservation of tradition. But, how justified is this kind of attitude?

Let me, in examining this issue, quickly make a logico-epistemological point, which is that a belief, activity or practice is not justified simply because it is understandable and, therefore, has a point or rationale. The fallacy involved in the inference from the fact that a belief has point to the conclusion that it is rational, becomes clear when we consider the following. It is, for example, a fact that the major super powers (the United States of America and the Union of Soviet Socialist Republics) spend astronomical amounts of money on arms build-up. Surely they can be said to have a point in doing this, which is to say that the arms race, although frightening, had a kind of deterrent effect; that it could ensure what was fondly called balance of power (terror) between the contending powers. But, as it is now becoming obvious to the super powers, we cannot say that this action is rational given the following: First, the fact that the arms-race tended to exacerbate world tension, both in terms of its scope and intensity; second the fact that money wasted on instruments of destruction could be used, not only to improve these developed (developing?) societies, but also to aid genuinely poor nations which find it difficult to sustain for their peoples the barest conditions for survival; finally there is the fact that the monumental arms build-ups constitute serious health hazards to the world and its inhabitants. Or, to take a less volatile example, in political terms, a man who has an acquisitive urge for cars and satisfies this urge by piling them up, when there are people around him who are in dire need of means of sustenance, can provide a rationale for this action. But can we say that this action is rational?

The above illustrations are given in an attempt to show that it does not follow from the mere fact that a belief or action has a point that it is rational. From these examples, although the super powers or the rich man many provide some rationale for their actions, such actions could still be judged to be irrational. Thus we may agree with the traditionalists that believe in magic, witchcraft, oracles, spirits etc. have a point in the context of the societies in which they exist and yet find them wanting on the rationality scale.

But here the argument may still be inconclusive. The traditionalists could argue, and I think with some justification, that they are not claiming that all beliefs are rational, but that the criteria of rationality in terms of which beliefs are assessed should not be external to the forms of life in which they obtain. But why should this be so, given the fact that forms of life are not mutually exclusive and they do overlap to a considerable degree?

It seems to me that the position of the traditionalists on this matter rests on their failure to make a clear distinction between the issues involved in this debate. The two issues that are being conflated by our traditionalists are these: (i) the question of how best to study the thought systems of our peoples; and (ii) the question of whether there is any justification for employing so-called alien criteria of rationality in assessing the beliefs of our peoples.

While the position of the traditionalists can be seen as an adequate answer to the first question (for how do we study a thought system without understanding the point or rationale of the belief that are its major elements?), it surely cannot be an adequate answer to the second question. This is because, as I have tried to show, we may see

the point of a belief or activity within the context of a given culture, we may see the function(s) it performs in that culture and still insist that it is not a rational belief. But on what grounds do we base this insistence? Can it be because it does not correspond to a given reality or that it does not appear to be the best alternative in a given situation? In short, on what grounds are we justified in questioning a belief when it has been established that it fulfils certain functions within the culture in which it exists?

I do not think that a legitimate case can be made for the claim that a belief is not rational because it does not correspond to some given reality. To argue in this manner is to suggest that we can have a starting point for knowledge which is without presuppositions and that there is 'a meaning-in-itself which understanding seeks to uncover.'[36] Yet, we do know that 'understanding is grounded in a network of beliefs and practices out of which the very fabric of our lives are woven,'[37] and, consequently, that there is nothing like an absolute set of standards of judgement and value against which all beliefs and cultural practices can be meansured.[38] On this point I agree with the traditionalists. But are we then to say, on the basis of this admission, that all beliefs and practices are equally valid as means of realising societal goals and objectives?

My answer to this question is definitely negative. For if it were the case that every belief or societal practice is equally effective for the realisation of societal goals and objectives, we should always be satisfied with our beliefs and societal practices: there would be no need for comparing alternative systems of belief in terms of the extent to which they enhance or hinder attempts to deal with experience by those who hold them; Africans would not have had the colonial experience in the first place, let alone the socio-cultural disorientations engendered by that experience. Indeed, if it were true that every belief or social practice is equally effective for the realisation of goals, there would be no need for philosophy as a critique of reason (pure or practical), for literature as a form of social consciousness or science as a search for better ways of enhancing the conditions of mankind. That we have all these activities is enough indication that, among alternatives, there is a sense in which we can say that one belief or set of beliefs and social practices is better than others as a means of dealing with experience.

Thus we should be prepared to see our conceptions of reality, modes of knowing etc. as presuppositions whose limitations can be revealed when compared with the presuppositions of other forms of life in terms of the extent to which they are adequate as means of realising our objectives. These goals are not static; they are usually defined or redefined in terms of the nature of our encounter and interaction with nature and one another. There is therefore a constant need for a critical engagement with our culture, our world-views, assumptions and values. This should be done with a view to determining these beliefs and activities that can best enhance our ability to accomplish our goals, both theoretical and practical.

Inability (refusal?) to see the close connection between a people's world outlook, their values, assumptions and prejudices, on the one hand, and the means through which man comes to terms with his environment, on the other hand, makes the traditionalists see a form of life as a closed system; they view it as something static, a commodity as it were, which could be preserved, revived, bought and sold and exhibited by a people. Hence their recommendation of an approach to a philosophical study of African thought systems that emphasizes the mere exposition of the logical structure of a world outlook which is just a product of a given socio-economic formation, and their belief that any attempt to subject some aspects of this world outlook to critical analysis, in the face of present realities, is a betrayal of the African experience. But we do know that a culture is not a finished product. It is something that is constantly in the making in consonance with the dynamics of the continuous evolution of human societies.[39] It is, therefore, not something we want to preserve in all cases. Rather it is something, aspects of which we may want to reevaluate, depending on the nature of our socio-economic reality and the ends (both theoretical and practical) which we have set for ourselves. Thus what determines which aspects of our culture (beliefs, social practices and values) to promote and which to consider anachronistic are the demands of action as defined by our socio-economic reality at any point in time.

Now, if we acknowledge the fact that the socio-economic reality of Africa today is characterized by a "search for culture" which, no doubt, has its roots in the socio-economic disorientations engendered in African societies by the colonial experience, and if this search manifests itself in the form of a dilemma poignantly characterized by Bodunrin when he writes:

> We want to forget our colonial past. We want to forget the unfavourable image of us painted by, chiefly, the Western man. At the same time, however, we are anxious to improve the lot of our people. We want technological development,[40]

then it should not be difficult to see the need for African philosophers to be very critical in their study of African thought systems. And the question we need to constantly ask is not so much the question of what we were (a question which our traditionalists are never tired of asking) but the related questions of what we are and where we are going. These are questions which suggest, 'not a mere analysis of the past to the point of its arrival today, but a rational examination of present ends.'[41] Answers to these questions should not only illuminate the present, but also suggest a project for the future.

It therefore becomes clear that neither the insight offered by the traditionalists nor the programme of action they recommend for African philosophers can be regarded as providing a proper model for the understanding of the African condition or an appropriate recommendation for the resolution of the African crisis of identity. The important task for the African philosopher, then— if he is genuinely interested in seeing Africa emerge from the morass of ignorance, hunger and want in which she is presently submerged—is not the demonstration of the uniqueness of the African world outlook nor even a defence of the 'thoughts of the crowd.' The important thing, it seems to me, is to show the contribution which that world outlook has made to the determination of the African condition. Where this is seen to be negative, the search should be directed to an alternative outlook or combination of outlooks. An authentic African philosophy has to be a philosophy of action. It certainly cannot be a combative phenomenological sketch of the African world outlook.

Nothing in this point implies that we jettison all our traditional beliefs, social practices and values. Rather, the suggestion is that we critically analyse them with a view to determining which of their elements we can retain and which we can jettison in the light of contemporary socio-economic realities in Africa. It should therefore be obvious that nothing in the critical approach to the study of African thought implies a wholesale inculcation of the "scientific spirit." Rather the point is that we should not hesitate to imbibe aspects of that "spirit," or any other "spirit" for that matter, that we think, in combination with some useful aspects of our traditional world outlooks, can serve us better in the struggle for survival in a largely competitive world.[42]

Notes

1. Significant contributions to the debate on this issue include the following: Kwasi Wiredu "On an African Orientation in Philosophy," *Second Order: An African Journal of Philosophy*, July 1972, reprinted in Kwasi Wiredu, *Philosophy and an African Culture* (Cambridge University Press, 1980), pp. 26–36, Paulin Hountondji, *African Philosophy: Myth and Reality*, translated by Henry Evans with the collaboration of Jonathan Ree, (London: Hutchinson University Press for Africa, 1983), pp. 33–107; P.O. Bodunrin, "The Question of African Philosophy," *Philosophy: The Journal of Royal Institute of Philosophy*, April, 1981, vol. 56, No. 216, pp. 161–179; Odera Oruka, "The Fundamental Principles in the Question of 'African Philosophy'"—*Second Order*, Vol. IV, Number 1, January 1975, pp. 44–55; Olabiyi Yai, "Theory and Practice in African Philosophy: The Poverty of Speculative Philosophy," *Second Order*, Vol. VI, Number 2, July 1977, pp. 3–30; and K.C. Anyanwu, *The African Experience in the American Market Place*, (New York: Exposition Press, 1983), 119pp.

2. Kwasi Wiredu, *Philosophy and an African Culture*, (Cambridge University Press, 1980), p. 62.

3. P.O. Bodunrin in P.O. Bodunrin (ed.), *Philosophy in Africa: Trends and Perspectives*, (University of Ife Press Ltd., 1985), p. XI.

4. See, for instance, Okot p'Bitek, *African Religions in Western Scholarships* (Kampala, Nairobi and Dar es Salaam: East African Literature Bureau, 1970); and K.C. Anyanwu, *The African Experience in the American Market Place*, (New York: Exposition Press, 1983), 119pp.

5. Representative figures of this school of thought include Profs. Kwasi Wiredu, P.O. Bodunrin and Paulin Hountondji. See, for instance, Kwasi Wiredu, 1980, *op.cit.*, P.O. Bodunrin, 1981, *op.cit.* and Paulin Hountondji, 1983, *op.cit.*

6. Isidore Okpewho, "Myth and Rationality," *Ibadan Journal of Humanistic Studies*, No. 1, April 1981, pp. 31–32.

7. Paulin Hountondji, "Reason and Tradition" in H. Odera Oruka and D.A. Masolo (eds.), *Philosophy and Cultures*, Proceedings of the 2nd Afro-Asian Philosophy Conference, October/November, 1981 (Nairobi: Bookwise Ltd., 1983), p. 143.

8. Abiola Irele, *The African Experience in Literature and Ideology*, (London: Heinemann Educational Books Ltd., 1981), p. 70.

9. See K.C. Anyanwu, "Philosophy and African Culture," *The Philosopher: An Annual Magazine of the National Association of Philosophy Students*, University of Ife Branch, Vol. 2, No. 1, December 1984, p. 16.

10. K.C. Anyanwu, 1983, *op.cit.*, p. 42.

11. It should be noted, however, that our traditionalists do not seem to appreciate the temporal dimensions of the variations in the interpretation of experiences within, and between, cultures, hence, they erroneously present African world-views as static and unchanging.

12. For a lucid and comprehensive history of the development of this thought, see Abiola Irele, 1981, *op.cit.*, pp. 67–116 and Abiola Irele, Introduction to Paulin Hountondji, 1983, *op.cit.*, pp. 7–30. A useful account of the development of this thought, particularly its political aspect, can be found in Olsanwuche Esedebe, "The Emergence of Pan-African Ideas" in Onigu Otite (ed.) *Themes in African Social and Political Thought*, (Enugu: Fourth Dimension Publ., 1978), pp. 75–103.

13. Abiola Irele, 1983, *op.cit.*, p. 11.

14. Isidore Okpewhe, *op.cit.*, p. 31.

15. Abiola Irele, 1981, *op.cit.*, p. 97.

16. Now that the ideological battle for the recognition of the humanity of Africans has been won, we can settle down to a critical examination of some of those claims that were crucial pillars of this battle. We have to do this in order to map out realistic programmes for African development in all its interlocking facets.

17. Paulin Hountondji, 1983, *op.cit.*, p. 59.

18. Placide Tempels, *Bantu Philosophy*, (Paris: Presence Africaine, 1959).

19. Abiola Irele, 1983, *op.cit.*, p. 16.

20. L.S. Senghor, *Prose and Poetry*, edited and translated by John Reed and Clive Wake, (London, Nairobi, Ibadan and Lusaka: Heinemann African Writers Series, 1976), p. 36.

21. See K.C. Anyanwu, 1983, *op.cit.*, pp. 61–75.

22. L.S. Senghor, 1976, *op.cit.*, pp. 29–30. The emphasis in the quotation is Senghor's.

23. *Ibid.*, pp. 33–34. All emphases are that of Senghor.

24. See K.C. Anyanwu, 1983, *op.cit.*, p. 26.

25. This argument is put up by Anthony Appieh in his article, "Soyinka and the Philosophy of Culture" in P.O. Bodunrin (ed.), 1985, *op.cit.*, p. 257.

26. See Paulin Hountondji, 1983, *op.cit.*, p. 62.

27. Abiola Irele, 1981, *op.cit.*, p. 73.

28. Cf. Tola Olu Pearce, "Medical Systems and the Nigerian Society" in Olayiwola A. Erinosho (ed.), *Nigerian Perspectives in Medical Sociology* (published by the Department of Anthropology, College of William and

Mary Williamsburg, Virginia U.S.A., 1982), pp. 119–120; and Godwin Sogolo, "On a Socio-Cultural Conception of Health and Disease" in A.T. Tymieniecka (ed.) *Analecta Husserliana*, Vol. XX, 1986, pp. 159–173.

29. For a very interesting historical account of this kind of interaction between science and religion, See R. Hooykaas, *Religion and the Rise of Modern Science* (Edinburgh and London: Scottish Academic Press, 1972).

30. J.B. Maund, "Rationality of Belief—Intercultural Comparisons" in S.I. Benn and G.W. Mortimore, *Rationality and the Social Sciences* (London, Henley and Boston: Routledge and Kegan Paul, 1976), pp. 46–47.

31. Cf. Kwasi Wiredu, 1980, *op.cit.*, pp. 37–50.

32. P.O. Bodunrin, 1981, *op.cit.*, pp. 172–173.

33. J.O. Sopido, "Notes on the Concept of Cause and Chance in Yoruba Traditional Thought," *Second Order: An African Journal of Philosophy*, Vol. II, Number 2, July 1973, pp. 12–20.

34. P.O. Borundin, 1981, *op.cit.*, p. 174.

35. *Journal of Social Science*, University of Malawi, Vol. 10, 1983, pp. 100–110.

36. Lawrence M. Hinman, "Can a Form of Life be Wrong?", *Philosophy*, July 1983, Vol. 58, No. 225, p. 350.

37. *Ibid.*, p. 349.

Globalization and Economic Fundamentalism

E. J. Kelsey

Globalisation of markets, we are told, will provide the solution to poverty and lift the standard of living for everyone in the world. Liberation of market forces allows the world's limited human, natural and financial resources to be used most efficiently, thereby maximising global wellbeing (as measured in monetary terms). To achieve that goal, the owners of capital must be free to seek out the highest return with the least impediment. That requires the free movement of money, products, services and (some) information across borders—which, in turn, means dismantling and proscribing any laws, policies and regulations that act as barriers and subordinating social, cultural, environmental and political priorities to the primacy of the market.

This entails a major paradigm shift from the Keynesian, interventionist welfare state which most OECD countries pursued post-World War II and is the antithesis of the New International Economic Order which newly independent former colonies advocated in the early 1970s. Paradigm shifts of this magnitude involve a significant redistribution of wealth and power between and within countries. They do not just happen. They have to be rationalised and legitimated through a process that converts the ideology of the new regime into a new orthodoxy. That new orthodoxy must secure adherence from a sufficiently powerful section of the elite, and preferably the consent, or at least the acquiescence, of a significant number of the regime's subjects. As South Africans know better than most, when rule rests

primarily on repression it is unstable as well as unjust, and is likely to be unsustainable when its victims rebel. In an address of mine I examined the politics of economic globalisation. I want to investigate this ideological dimension of globalisation today.

Many critics of globalisation depict it as a new era of imperialism dominated by the major super powers and the associated capital. Significantly, supporters of globalisation are also now proclaiming a new era of United States-led imperialism. The *New York Times* on 31 March 2002 quoted the observation of conservative columnist Charles Krauthammer 'that no country has been so dominant culturally, economically, technologically and militarily in the history of the world since the Roman Empire.' The features editor of the *Wall Street Journal*, Max Boot, proclaimed more bluntly that 'Afghanistan and other troubled lands today cry out for the sort of enlightened foreign administration once provided by self-confident Englishmen in jodhpurs and pith helmets' (*New York Times*, 31 March 2002).

In ideological terms, there are clear parallels. In the previous era of imperialism, the hegemonic ideology was sourced in a combination of Enlightenment philosophy, Christian doctrine and scientism. The evangelists belonged to a loosely connected network of colonial officials, Christian missionaries, aboriginal protectionists, entrepreneurs, explorers and adventurers, publishers and novelists, among others. Their institutional bases were provided, courtesy of imperial governments and private elites, through their colonial administrations, their courts, their churches, their newspapers, their charities, their banks and their companies. The primary beneficiaries were the capitalists and to a lesser extent, a carefully

"Globalization and Economic Fundamentalism" by E.J. Kelsey from *After September 11: Globalization, War and Peace* ed. by C.W. Du Toit & G.L.A. Lubbe, Research Institute for Theology and Religion, University of South Africa, Pretoria. Reprinted by permission.

nurtured but subordinated native elite. Their ideology was absolutist: there was no alternative. Any who struggled to defend their traditional ways or seek out new paths were, by definition, 'enemies of the Empire.' Brutal repression was rationalised, not simply as a means to ensure the loyal servants of the Empire could fulfil their God-given duty, but as part of a civilising mission that would benefit their victims. As John Stuart Mill (1962:136) argued in his celebrated essay *On Liberty:* 'Despotism is a legitimate mode of government in dealing with barbarians provided the end be their improvement.'

Today, there are new missionaries at the frontier. Their ideology is sourced in the scientism of neoclassical economics, the primacy of property rights and the supremacism of Western values and institutions. The evangelists are a loosely connected network of economists, politicians, government technocrats, financiers, CEOs and managers, lobbyists, consultants, spin doctors, journalists and more. Their institutional bases are provided, courtesy of the major powers and private elites, by the IMF, World Bank, World Trade Organisation, OECD, transnational corporations, investment institutions, credit-rating agencies, World Economic Forum, International Chamber of Commerce, *The Economist, Wall Street Journal* and CNN, the Heritage Foundation and business roundtables, elite university business schools, the ministries of finance and central banks. As with their predecessors, their mission is not simply to extend the reach of their Empire. They insist that only the gospel of globalisation can bring a permanent end to world poverty, bad government and war. These true believers preach their own version of There Is No Alternative (TINA)—that globalisation is an evolutionary process which is both inevitable and irreversible. In the words of current WTO director-general, and one-time New Zealand Prime Minister, Mike Moore (1997): 'We evolved from families, to tribes, to the city state, to the nation state and now to global and regional economic and political arrangements.' The disciples of economic fundamentalism consider it their civilising duty variously to convince, cajole, bully, threaten, destabilise, overthrow or even to eliminate any who seek to maintain a different regime or promote a new one.

Critics such as economic historian Eric Hobsbawm (2000) have challenged claims that globalisation is irresistible and inevitable as misleading and self-serving. The development of new technologies, such as air transport, telecommunications and information technology, is indeed permanent and irreversible. Such technologies condense distances of time and space, with significant impacts on production techniques and their geographical location. That, in turn, has created a new international division of labour and undermined the power of workers. But not everything can be globalised. There will always be a need and demand for locally produced goods and services. Nor can countries afford to build their futures primarily on the new 'knowledge economy.' The short-lived dot.com bubble and scandals like the Enron/Arthur Andersen affair have exposed the mercurial nature of technology and services sectors whose value often rests more on perception than on substantive products. Equally, technology has enhanced the capacity of speculative finance capital to seek instant returns. But it also increases the risk of 'economic earthquakes.' While those tremors have so far been contained, a systemic crisis is ever-threatening.

Hobsbawm draws a distinction between changes in technology, production and finance, and the regulatory dimension of globalisation, such as the abolition of trade barriers and market liberalisation, which he sees as a secondary phenomenon. Despite claims that states are no longer relevant in the global era, the international economic institutions whose task it is to oversee the transition in economic paradigms still rest on the power of states. Those states, in turn, require social stability and political legitimation at the nation level to survive, which implies some regulation of economic activity. Even with a rapidly expanding system of international economic laws and institutions, capital must conform to the laws and institutions of those states. While small and poorer countries have less autonomy than major powers to choose their own economic policies without reference to the global economy, they can—and may well—move in the opposite direction when confronted with market failure or social upheaval.

Connected to, but analytically distinct from these dimensions is the ideology that promotes free-market fundamentalism. Once the ideology of

TINA is deflated and people and governments dare to suggest that the new Emperor has no clothes, the international regulatory regime looks much less invincible. People can begin to explore alternative models of production and investment that utilise the genuinely irreversible new technologies in more economically, socially and ecologically progressive ways.

It is hardly surprising, then, that a massive investment has been made to secure the rapid and comprehensive implementation of structural adjustment programmes and embed them in ways that are costly to reverse. The standard agenda, known colloquially as the Washington Consensus, demands:

- fiscal discipline through lower government spending and repayment of public debt;
- privatisation of state enterprises and assets;
- reduction of progressive income tax and broadening of the tax base through consumption taxes;
- the levying of tariffs on border protections and ultimate removal of direct and 'disguised' trade barriers;
- increased foreign investment by liberalising entry rules, guarantees of non-discrimination and investment protection, and lifting of capital controls;
- deregulation of domestic markets, including removal of all subsidies and industry support, and the promotion of competition;
- monetary policy that focuses exclusively on price stability and is administered through a politically independent central bank;
- liberalisation of financial markets, with market-determined interest rates;
- devaluation, followed by exchange rate management that aims to maintain international competitiveness; and
- guaranteed protection of private property rights.

Sympathetic studies consider structural adjustment to be successful if these policies have been implemented; the outcomes are simply assumed to be beneficial. These studies usually describe a two-stage process.[1] Initiation of radical change is achieved through rapid-fire strategies that are antidemocratic, but highly effective. Because 'there is no alternative,' there is no need to conduct research, explore options or engage in debate. One prominent study conducted by the Washington-based Institute for International Economics in 1993 explored the success of techniques used by governments in a range of richer and poorer countries. Their aim was to produce a manual for so-called 'technopols' implementing structural adjustment programs (Williamson 1994). They hypothesised a range of techniques, all of which were present in the case study of my own country, New Zealand:

- capture of economic policy-making by a team of committed technocrats, primarily in the ministry of finance and the central bank;
- capture of economic policy-making in the governing party by politicians who are committed more to the structural adjustment programme than to their own or their party's political survival;
- support from a well-resourced, influential and activist private sector, both locally and overseas, who are installed as the authorised voices of the 'national interest';
- an ideologically coherent programme where each new policy forms part of an integrated whole, so that individual policies cannot easily be isolated and reversed;
- implementation through change teams which are insulated from those bureaucrats, politicians, unions or interest groups who are likely to resist;
- beginning in a period of actual or manufactured crisis, taking full advantage of the honeymoon by blaming the costs of change on the legacy of the previous administration;
- adopting a *blitzkrieg* approach which moves so far and so fast that critics cannot keep pace;
- fostering sympathetic and uncritical media; and
- marginalising and discrediting potential critics by dismissing them as vested interests who place personal gain ahead of national well-being, or as dinosaurs unable to grasp the need for change.

Ideally, a period of consolidation follows, during which the new 'orthodoxy' is normalised and more deeply embedded. Successive governments continue to operate within the redesigned institutional structures, policies and laws. If this can be led by a nominally social democratic party, so much the better. The core economic changes can be maintained, while new governments address the most serious market failures and socially disruptive impacts. Older intellectuals and activists in political parties, the bureaucracy, media and universities now offer variations within the new paradigm. New generations are unaware that other paradigms even exist. The major beneficiaries sound the fire alarms, issuing dire warnings of capital flight and economic disaster at the first signs of deviation. Popular expectations—it is hoped—adjust to this new reality. Provided a grumbling acquiescence is maintained, and no major economic or social crises precipitate capitulation by the government, the evolutionary process of globalisation can proceed unopposed.

Such one-dimensional theories have a fundamental flaw: what happens if the policies fail to deliver the anticipated benefits and the resulting social distress, political disempowerment or economic earthquakes provoke fundamental challenges to the now prevailing orthodoxy?

Harvard economist Dani Rodrik (2000:177, 180), has labeled this the 'political trilemma of the world economy.' International economic integration can coexist with a nation state, but only if that state acts in ways that do not impede economic transactions. In other words, there is no space for popular groups to access and influence national economic policy-making, and developmental goals are subordinated to maintaining international market confidence. 'The over-arching goal of nation-states in this world would be to appear attractive to international markets' (Rodrik 2000:182). Under this option, the notion of 'good governance' requires a largely depoliticised state. It is incompatible with democratic ideals of mass politics based on an unrestricted franchise, a high degree of political mobilisation and political institutions that are responsive to mobilised groups. Put another way, if we want to retain the nation state, we have to choose between mass politics and international economic integration. We cannot have both.

Rodrik goes on to suggest another option: to combine international economic integration and mass politics through a form of global federalism that brings together diverse international political forums and regulatory institutions. Like the 1995 report of the UN Commission for Global Governance entitled *Our Global Neighbourhood* (1995), this assumes that the representatives of mineworkers, women refugees, the urban poor and dispossessed indigenous landowners can sit alongside the owners of capital, such as RTZ, Shell, Coca-Cola and SmithKleinBeecham and exert equal influence in a global forum.

Rodrik concedes that the more likely scenario is either the combination of global economic integration and limited government (the model currently promoted as the neoliberal orthodoxy), or a revival of protectionism as nation states face a popular backlash against the impacts of globalisation.

This poses interesting challenges for countries that have already been taken a long way down the globalisation path and offers important lessons for countries still in the 'initiation' phase. My own country, New Zealand, has become famous, or infamous, since 1984 for implementing the most radical free-market policies is the OECD—some claim, in the world. That bastion of neoliberalism, *The Economist*, variously described it as 'the sort of socialism of which millionaires approve,' 'trail-blazing economic reforms,' 'out-Thatchering Mrs Thatcher,' and 'a paradise for free-marketeers—if not for those New Zealanders who have lost their jobs . . .' The initial political architect, finance minister Roger Douglas (1993: ch 10), has subsequently made a career out of advising other governments of how to achieve such radical change, offering such advice as:

Once the programme begins to be implemented, don't stop until you have completed it. The fire of opponents is much less accurate if they have to shoot at a rapidly moving target.

and

Consensus among interest groups on quality decisions rarely, if ever, arises before they are made and implemented. It develops after they are taken, as the decisions deliver satisfactory results to the public.

There are four features that I would particularly like to highlight about the 'New Zealand Experiment':[2] the long-term impact of globalisation on the economy and the country's infrastructure; the social costs of massive redistribution of wealth within the country; the compound effect of neo-colonialism on indigenous Maori; and the political implications for democratic government and sovereignty.

Supporters of the experiment point to key economic gains: consistently low inflation, operating surpluses over seven consecutive years, significantly reduced government expenditure, lower top personal and corporate income tax rates, and large-scale repayment of government debt. Competition has improved efficiency and choice. Many services are more flexible and responsive. And the monocultural, centralised welfare state has been forced to diversify.

These indicators disguise the systematic decline of New Zealand into a pathologically dependent, vulnerable and underperforming economy. Although successive social democratic and conservative governments did everything the Washington Consensus required of them, New Zealand's OECD ranking continued to decline: from ninth in 1970 to twenty-first of twenty-six countries in 2001. During the main 'initiation' phase from 1985 to 1992 the average growth across OECD countries was 20%; New Zealand's economy shrunk by 1%. Over the longer range of 1986 to 1998, the relative growth rates of Australia and New Zealand, which were previously comparable, diverged significantly.

While public debt was repaid, total foreign debt now exceeds 105% of GDP. Private savings are among the lowest in the OECD. A chronic deficit in the current account of the balance of payments neared 7% of GDP in September 2000, and is predicted to hover between 3.5% and 4.5% over the next two years. This has to be bridged by asset sales, more overseas borrowing, or government reserves. The figure partly reflects persistent trade deficits, due to import dependency, unstable commodity export markets and the damage caused by rigid anti-inflation policies on interest and exchange rates. A 1998 survey of 45 countries showed that New Zealand was one of five to have lost market share over the past six years, a trend that was predicted to continue for several

more years. New Zealand was ranked 20th out of 25 OECD countries on export growth performance indicators.

Significantly, the major contributor to the balance of payments deficit is the deficit on investment income. Foreign companies with no long-term commitment to New Zealand control the financial, media, transport, telecommunications, energy, forestry and resource infrastructure of the country. An ideologically driven privatisation programme, with no regulation of access, price and quality—the product of an equally ideological commitment to light-handed regulation—allowed the new foreign owners to maximise their short-term profits with no obligation to maintain the long-term capacity of the infrastructure. From 1996 to 1998, they took 92% of the accumulated profit on foreign direct investment as dividend. The share of the country's income from domestic production that remains available to fuel the New Zealand economy, after net profits, income and dividends remitted abroad are accounted for, is at a fifty-year low.

During the past year the government has been forced to renationalise Air New Zealand and parts of the rail track. It has launched a new government-owned bank to serve the needs of poor and regional citizens. It has instructed the state-owned television company to broaden its pursuit of commercial returns to promote national culture and current affairs. It has also, reluctantly and minimally, recognised market failure and begun to reregulate electricity and telecommunications, the share market, company takeovers, and workplace health and safety.

But people still have no guaranteed access to core services. Nor is there any strategic programme for the development of a sustainable infrastructure of the 21st century. Indeed, the Third Way social democratic government elected in late 1999 remains evangelically committed to globalisation, further foreign direct investment and new free-trade agreements. There are real concerns that the government might even soften its landmark anti-nuclear policy in return for US agreement to begin negotiations on a free-trade and investment agreement, whose merits it refuses to debate.

The social costs have been equally dramatic. By 1996 around one in five New Zealanders, and one-third of the country's children, were living in poverty—more than double the numbers in 1988. Alongside a deepening feminisation of poverty, indigenous Maori and immigrant Pacific Islands and refugee families have been most seriously affected. Inequality also grew. Between 1984 and 1996, the richest 5% of New Zealanders increased their share of the national income by 25%, and the top 10% of the population increased theirs by 15%. The share of the national income received by the bottom four-fifths of New Zealanders fell, with the poorest proportionately losing most. Dependence on charity, such as food banks, continues to increase. Charities also serve as bankers for the poor, who cannot afford accounts at the privatised banks which the government insists they must have to receive any welfare payments. There has been a resurgence of poverty-related illnesses such as glue ear, diabetes, pneumonia, mental health disorders, tuberculosis, whooping cough and meningitis. New Zealand reportedly has the highest youth suicide rate in the OECD.

For many indigenous Maori, who now comprise 15% of the population, this represents the latest phase of a colonisation process that began in 1840 when sovereignty over their country was seized by the English, despite a treaty that guaranteed them continued control of their resources and political self-determination. Recent settlements of treaty grievances have been designed so as to perpetuate the commodification and commercialisation of fisheries, land, forests, water within the market-led economy, and primarily benefit Maori elites and their white advisors. Meanwhile, deepening poverty, inequality, unemployment and exclusion from essential social services is a daily reality in most urban and rural Maori communities.

By the late 1990s most New Zealanders recognised that the neo-liberal Emperor had no clothes. But the *blitzkrieg* approach to structural adjustment, especially between 1984 and 1988, and 1991 and 1993, left most ordinary people apathetic and decimated the unions and the political left. Anger at the unaccountability of government did force the introduction of a proportional representation electoral system in 1996. But with the complicity of both major parties complicit in the 'revolution,' and no effective opposition, the consolidation process was by then largely complete. Rather than explore real alternatives, the new social democratic government has promoted

the contradictory projects of 'nation-building' and 'globalisation with a social face.' The result is a market-led approach to nation-building where maintaining investor confidence takes precedence over the long-term needs of the country and interests of New Zealand's people. In essence, New Zealand is now firmly locked into Rodrick's option 1: globalisation overseen by a limited state. How long this can be sustained is a critical question for New Zealanders, as it is for countries with Third Way governments everywhere.

Let me now compare and contrast this with the experience of economic fundamentalism in Argentina and the deep crisis now facing that once affluent country. I was privileged to visit Argentina in August 2001 (just as the government announced major cuts to government salaries and pensions) and to visit the northern Tucuman region as well as Buenos Aires. Given those circumstances, it was chilling that the first responses to both my presentations on the New Zealand Experiment drew direct parallels with structural adjustment in Argentina.

Argentina's neoliberal revolution began when the military dictatorship seized power in 1976. The democratically elected government of Alphonsin tried a new direction in the mid-1980s, and failed. His successor Carlos Menem (later jailed for his part in running guns during conflicts in Croatia and Ecuador/Peru) campaigned on a populist theme in 1989, but promptly embraced neoliberalism after the election. Supported by the IMF, he and finance minister Domingo Cavallo engaged on a programme of trade liberalisation, removed restrictions on capital flows, recklessly privatised most state assets and activities, and adopted a currency board arrangement that guaranteed convertibility of the peso to the US dollar. Rampant inflation quickly fell from 78% to 4%. The budget deficit was eliminated and public debt was repaid. Argentina's economy recovered rapidly, recording strong export growth and high levels of foreign direct investment. But a large portion of domestic industry and production was destroyed, leaving Argentina dependent on imports. The privatisations were at bargain prices, profit-stripping by foreign owners became rampant, they failed to reinvest in the infrastructure and price hikes were prohibitive. Massive inflows of capital kept the growth rate buoyant. Even with the Mexican peso crisis in 1995, real per capita GDP growth averaged 4.3% between 1991 and 1998. But the situation was unsustainable.

By 1998 South America was confronted by the contagion effects of the 1997 currency crisis, the slowing of the world economy and a strong US dollar. Argentina began a rapid economic decline. Much of the blame is attributed to the inflexibility of the exchange rate and the inappropriateness of US monetary settings that applied automatically to Argentina. In January 1999 neighbouring Brazil responded to a chronic currency crisis by abandoning the hard peg with the US dollar and floating the real. The resulting massive devaluation gave it a competitive advantage over Argentina in international markets and within the free-trade area of Mercosur. The combination of Brazil's exchange rate and lower costs, especially for labour, made it difficult for Argentine exporters and domestic producers to compete in a slowing international economy. Capital mobility enabled investors to relocate to Brazil, compounding the Argentine recession. Unemployment mounted, especially in the regions. The burden fell directly on businesses and workers with flow-on effects for families, communities and entire regions. Official unemployment had reached 18% by mid-2001. 'Fortunate' workers were reemployed under the table at below the minimum wage and without legal entitlements.

As central government revenue fell and public external debt grew, foreign lenders increased the risk premium. The debt burden mushroomed. The currency board prevented the government from funding its fiscal needs by expanding the money supply or devaluing to reduce debt denominated in the domestic currency. Although the central government could not create new money, provincial governments responded to falling revenues by issuing their own local currency in the form of limited-term bonds. In Tucuman province, for example, these were known as *bonos*. While these had parity with the peso and US dollar, they could only be used within the province. As pesos became scarcer and revenue continued to fall, *bonos* were supplemented by tickets redeemable in specified stores. By mid-2001 provincial workers such as teachers were being paid in a mixture of *bonos*, tickets and salary deferred for six months. Buenos Aires

province then issued its own version of limited-term bonds, the *Patacom*. Privatised electricity and telephone companies announced that they would accept Patacoms as part payment. Even McDonalds announced a new meal—the *Patacombo*—that could only be bought with the new currency. The central government vainly attempted to control the rapidly expanding money supply by legalising a national system of regional bonds that could be used to pay taxes and would be deducted from the region's revenue entitlement from central government.

In July 2001 the government announced plans to alter the currency peg to a combination of the US dollar and the Euro. Speculation that the government might default on its sovereign debt and/or abandon the currency board raised the risk premium again. As government revenue continued to decline, the share dedicated to debt repayments grew. In August 2001 default was imminent. The IMF made refinancing conditional on a zero-deficit budget that limited government expenditure to actual revenue. As demands for social spending and income support grew, the government cut all central government wages and pensions by 13%.

This further reduced domestic demand and intensified popular unrest. Militant unemployed people, known as *piqueteres*, blockaded the main arterial routes across the country. Pensioners, public servants, unions, left-wing parties, the 'mothers of the disappeared' and many others staged massive protests in central Buenos Aires. Students occupied the universities. Middle-class families with no waged incomes struggled to survive. A growing number of the poor were starving. The crisis deepened in December 2001 as the government seized the state pension fund, limited cash withdrawals by nationals to US$250 a week and imposed capital controls. On 20 December, amidst predictions of imminent debt default, the government imposed a 30-day state of emergency.

As the social and economic costs of maintaining convertibility mounted, the IMF continued to provide ad hoc bailouts to ensure the payment of interest on foreign loans, imposing in turn conditions of ever-stricter fiscal austerity. While pro-market critics of the IMF strategy urged writedowns of the debt coupled with full dollarisation, a group of prominent academic economists

(Portnoy et al 2001) called for an alternative economic strategy rooted in Argentina:

> Historical experience and the modern world are definite: countries which assume the responsibility of driving their own destiny prosper. Only a fundamentalist or inverted vision of globalisation yields before the power of the great transnational and local actors, in policies and negotiations which gather links in the chain of dependence. We believe that the reason why the country is in this struggling situation is the result of a bad articulation of the way of the modern world and we must radically modify our responses to the challenges and opportunities of globalisation. To recognise the restrictions of an autonomous economic policy does not mean giving up a policy with a realistic vision and a sense of national development.

By late December 2001 the people of Argentina had rebelled. Within a month the country saw five presidents. Ultimately, the government defaulted on its debt, abandoned the currency board and devalued the peso. In a time of deep crisis, the supposedly unthinkable once again became possible. A battle continues to rage between nationalists, who demand primacy for domestic economic interests, social well-being and popular democratic participation, and the advocates of even deeper integration into the global economy and an even more limited central state.

I have chosen to focus on Argentina and New Zealand as distinct but parallel examples of full-blown economic fundamentalism. In both cases the contradictions between the expansion of global capitalism and the maintenance of social well-being and political legitimacy are starkly exposed. In New Zealand's case, the result is a state of suspended animation, induced by successful political management under the rubric of the Third Way. It remains to be seen how long the transfer of power from the citizens of a nation state to the representatives of international capital can be sustained. In Argentina's case, the country and its people face a traumatic social, economic and political crisis to which there is no simple solution. A majority is now convinced that the way forward requires a new economic paradigm. The neoliberal hegemony has been thoroughly shattered and attempts to reinstate those policies will be vigorously contested. But the social and political cost of achieving that understanding has been devastating.

When ideological dogmatism takes hostage the processes and substance of economic policy-making at national and international levels, there is no room to debate these issues before the contradictions reach a crisis point. It leaves no space for constructive dialogue that validates alternative models of development and genuinely empowers people to make their own choices about the kind of world they want to live in, respecting the right of all others to do the same.

New Zealand and Argentina may seem light years away from the ideological fundamentalism that is perceived to underpin the attacks in the US on September 11 and the US response. But, as I indicated before, the deepening division between wealth and poverty created by economic globalisation is often expressed through nationalist and religious fundamentalism. When those reactions are met by naked imperialism, expressed through a combination of military force and economic fundamentalism, the existing tensions are set to intensify. Far from being an inevitable evolutionary process, the evangelical pursuit of economic globalisation carries with it the seeds for its own destruction. The costs of that destruction tend to fall hardest on those who are already the most vulnerable. The pursuit of peace and justice on a global scale requires of us to expose these contradictions and, as academics, to create the intellectual space in which genuine alternatives can be debated and legitimised.

Notes

1. For example see Haggard, S & Kaufman, R (eds) 1992; Bates, R & Krueger, A 1993.
2. See generally Kelsey, E J 1995.

References

Bates, R & Krueger, A 1993. *Political and economic interactions in economic policy reform.* Oxford: Blackwell.
Douglas, R 1993. *Unfinished business.* Auckland: Random.
Haggard, S & Kaufman, R (eds) 1992. *The politics of economic adjustment.* New Jersey: Princeton University Press.

Hobsbawm, E 2000. *The new century: In conversation with Antonio Polito*. London: Abacus.

Kelsey, E J 1995. *Economic fundamentalism. The New Zealand experiment: A world model for structural adjustment?* London: Pluto.

Mill, J S [1962] 1985. *Ultalitarianism. On liberty: Essays on Bentham*, 136. London: Fontana.

Moore, M 1997. Speech to University of Canterbury Seminar on International Liberalisation, 25 August.

Portnoy, L et al 2001. *Towards the Phoenix plan: Proposals for a strategy of reconstruction of the Argentine economy for growth with equality.* Buenos Aires: University of Buenos Aires.

Rodik, D 2000. How far will international economic integration go? *Journal of Economic Perspectives* 14(1), 177, 182.

UN Commission for Global Governance 1995. *Our global neighbourhood*. New York: United Nations.

Williamson, J 1994. In search of a manual for technopols, in Williamson, J (ed), *The political economy of policy reform*, 9-11. Washington DC: Institute for International Economics.

Proverbs as a Source of African Philosophy: A Methodological Consideration

Heinz Kimmerle

Introduction

Traditional African philosophy has been handed down through the centuries only partially by means of written documents. Primarily written sources of philosophy we find above all in ancient Egypt and in Ethiopia. Cheikh Anta Diop, a historian, philosopher, and politician in Senegal, and others have tried to gain acceptance for the theory that the wisdom of ancient Egypt is the cradle not only of African philosophy, but also to a remarkable extent of Western philosophy. This remains rather hypothetical, but there is no doubt that the documents of the ancient Egyptian mysteries are important sources of African philosophy.

Ethiopian philosophical texts are of enormous value, too, although I feel that African philosophers themselves have not come close to giving them the attention they deserve. The particular value of these sources for African philosophy, however, lies not so much in the fact that they were written down, but much more importantly in that as early as the fifth century AD they amalgamated Western and African thought from the standpoint of an African culture. Thus they can fulfil a historic-propaedeutic function for current African thought, in which similar processes are taking place on a large scale.

Political philosophy, produced during the period of the struggle for independence and the first phase of the creation of independent African states, and academic philosophy, as practised since the 1950s in the philosophy departments of African universities, were put into writing in the same way as texts in a culture with primarily written forms of communication and the transmission of traditions. The writings of Senghor and Nkrumah, Cabral and Touré, Kenyatta and Nyerere were discussed in Africa during the fifties and sixties on a broad scale. And since the emergence of African universities a vivid debate on African philosophy has taken place. To be sure, the spreading and availability of these texts is a major problem in Africa, because they are more often to be found, and in a more complete form, in libraries outside Africa than in the collections of African institutes and universities.

However, if it is true, as I have stated elsewhere,[1] that the work of the 'sages' in traditional African culture is characteristic of the specifically African in the philosophy of this continent, which is also contained in these texts, we can assume that important philosophical elements can be found in the primarily oral tradition. The pronouncements of the 'sages,' of which only remnants are currently written down, have to be seen as speech acts which did not occur in isolation within African languages, but were embedded in a tradition of narration and counselling.

Within a framework of thought determined by Western philosophy, I feel that the first task should be to deconstruct the generally accepted opposition of written and oral communication. Thinking in terms of oppositions, for instance in regard to cultures having or lacking a form of writing ('lettered' and 'unlettered' cultures), belongs to the tradition of Western metaphysical thought since Plato and Aristotle. The philosophical systems of Plato and Aristotle, the Neoplatonists and the thinkers of the Middle Ages—Descartes, Spinoza and Leibniz, Bacon, Hume and Locke, Kant, Fichte, Schelling and Hegel, to mention only a

"Proverbs as a Source of African Philosophy: A Methodological Consideration" by H. Kimmerle in *Embracing the Baobab Tree: The African Proverb in the 21st Century*, edited by W. Saayman. Reprinted by permission of Unisa Press, University of South Africa.

few of the best-known—are constructed by means of oppositions: the heavenly and the sublunary spheres, theory and practice, the single and the many, good and evil, right and wrong, true and false, etc. To obtain a clear view of traditional African philosophy, it is very important that the difference between primarily oral and primarily written forms of communication and tradition is not interpreted in this traditional way as indicating that they are mutually exclusive or in opposition to each other.

African philosophers are certainly aware that the transition from primarily oral to primarily written forms of communication and tradition, which typified the situation in philosophy during the fifties, has resulted in both profit and loss. Odera Oruka from the University of Nairobi has stated that with the introduction of writing as the primary medium of communication and transmission, memory slackens.[2] The coherent structure of life which exists when communications are on a primarily oral level is slowly dying out in the current situation, so that many invaluable philosophically wise teachings, among other things, are being lost for good.

It is recognised that various African peoples (for instance in what are now Liberia, Sierra Leone, Nigeria and Cameroon) have known writing, in the sense of writing down what was said, in a particular period of their history. However, because writing of this sort had no clear function in the coherent communication and the handing down of traditions, it sank into oblivion.[3] Currently, opinions vary among African philosophers with regard to the significance of written texts as compared to primarily oral transmissions. In his *Critique of ethnophilosophy*, Hountondji, from Cotonou in Benin, maintains that philosophy without written texts cannot be recognised as such, while Olabiyi Yai—a countryman of Hountondji who was educated in Ibadan in Nigeria and is currently teaching in Gainesville, Florida—places an especially high value on the role and significance of orally transmitted philosophical thought. The latter refers to Finnegan's research in which the specific significance of orally transmitted cultural matter is clearly elaborated.[4]

Credit must go to Jacques Derrida for having developed a new concept of writing in his book *De la grammatologie* (Paris 1967). Previously lettered and unlettered cultures were regarded as opposites to each other, with writing seen as a sign for the spoken word, which itself figures as a sign for a thing. Derrida overcomes this with a concept of writing which is not based on a theory of signs, and in which the writing is of secondary importance. Bearing the theory of signs in mind, and then going beyond it, Derrida emphasizes—continuing from Lacan—that there is no final indicated thing, that everything which is indicated (signifié) is also a indicator (significant) and that this continues in an everlasting chain. In this way writing can be lifted out of its secondary position. What is written has the advantage over what is heard in that it can be constantly reread and reinterpreted. An ultimate valid interpretation is not only impossible, but is no longer sought. This leads to difficult questions about the concept of truth. As far as the concept of writing is concerned, the result is that writing is no longer conceived of as a (by definition secondary) sign, but a 'trace,' which is read in an of itself endless context of references.

If writing is understood in this manner as a 'visible and readable trace,' one can postulate that it is as old as spoken language. Footprints in the sand, a broken branch or scattered stones are just as much forms of writing as scratches on rocks or gourds, scars indicating membership of a family or sex, warpaint on the body, little pictures representing words (hieroglyphics), or the letters of an alphabet. There is not more of a hierarchy among the various types of writing than there is between written and spoken language. Derrida makes clear that spoken language has been given precedence in the history of Western metaphysics from Plato's thesis in his *Seventh letter* that truth cannot be written down, via Rousseau's characterising of writing as simply an aid to remembering what has been said verbally, to Hegel's belief that, because of its relatively immaterial character, spoken language is closer to the idea than any type of writing. According to Derrida this means that Western metaphysics is not only characterised by a logocentrism in which 'logos,' that is, rational thinking, stands at the center, but also by a phonocentrism, which prefers the *phone*, the voice or the spoken language, to what is written.

In Derrida's thinking, which must lead to a revaluation of the relationship between primarily oral and primarily written communication and transmission, a paradoxical change of direction occurs at this point. He draws a line from logocentrism via phonocentrism to ethnocentrism, and in the following manner. On the one hand, the thinking of the Western metaphysicist regards writing as a sign which is secondary to spoken language, and on the other hand, this same thinking expresses a clear preference for lettered cultures as opposed to unlettered cultures in which oral communication is of primary importance. This is completely inconsistent because Western metaphysical thought, in concurrence with the higher evaluation of spoken language, should give preference to those cultures in which oral communication and transmission of traditions are of primary importance. This paradox, however, is not a fault in the development of Derrida's thinking, but is inherent in Western metaphysical thinking. It is in this that the ethnocentrism becomes evident. According to Derrida, this ethnocentrism also appears in the work of Lévi-Strauss when he expresses his great admiration for 'wild thinking' and gives fairly nostalgic descriptions of the innocence and beauty of natural peoples, because in this connection he maintains the opposition of lettered and unlettered cultures.

In Derrida's thinking the opposition between spoken language and writing, as well as every hierarchical relationship between them, is dropped. They stand side by side, constantly fulfilling different functions of language. They are equally original and both have their history of origin in the process of hominisation as such. Because they are both functions of language, these functions overlap: oral forms of communication and transmission always contain elements of writing as well, and in writing, elements of the spoken language are always present. In the first case, reference can be made to fixed formulas in language and to the significant arrangements connected to certain situations of speech; consider religious or judicial rituals, or the situation of narration and listening which appears to play an important role in African communities. In the second case, the presence of elements of oral language in writing is expressed in certain styles and genres, even if these do not directly demand an oral presentation.

Language as the Source of Philosophy

Language is the medium in which philosophy works. Philosophy draws its questions and the possible answers from language. That is not just the case since the 'linguistic turn' in the history of Western philosophy, through which idealistic philosophy's paradigm of consciousness was replaced by the paradigm of the concrete languages. It can be seen particularly in a number of great philosophies in the Western tradition where something is stated in language and by means of language, which previously could not be said, but which is very expressive, even though occasionally it can take some time before such new expressions become accepted. Kant's term 'transcendental' and the meaning he gave to the word 'critique' are just as striking examples of this as Hegel's 'an sich,' 'für sich' and 'an und für sich,' or Heidegger's 'In-der-Welt-sein,' or the formulations that 'the language talks,' 'the thing things' which are still very difficult even today. Aristotle clearly related his method to language when he started from 'legethai' (what 'one says') and then tried to create clarity and precision within it.

Seen in this light, the work of Placide Tempels and the other ethno-philosophers, who endeavour to draw a philosophy from the language of an African people, is original philosophical work. Language is understood very broadly: it includes grammatical structure as well as the meanings of words and word combinations; and also myths, poetry and stories, sayings and proverbs play an important role. Apparently it has no effect on the result if a *Belgian* missionary tries to describe the thinking of a Bantu people, the *Luba*, as long as he speaks the language of this people well. The Ruandan theologian and philosopher Alexis Kagame has confirmed through extensive language research the propositions of the Belgian Tempels, which in general—despite initial strong criticism—have penetrated on a large scale into the research and the teaching of African philosophy.

In this manner the ethno-philosophers stand precisely at the point of transition from primarily oral to primarily written forms of expression in African philosophy. It is a misconception to think that they wish to present the collective thinking of a people, expressed in its language, as philosophy, as Hountondji in particular has remarked critically.[5] They are individuals, philosophical authors, who clarify and define the philosophical thoughts present in a language. One can also say—and here I agree with the words of Oluwole from Lagos—that ethno-philosophers examine the way in which sayings and proverbs, certain ideas and ideals, and also myths, poetry and narratives form the 'philosophical substratum of the thinking of a people.'[6] That this process can necessitate an enormous interpretative effort is made clear by Oluwole with a Yoruba proverb: 'Let the eyes see, but keep the mouth shut,' in which the following ethical clue is hidden: 'It is not ALL things your eyes see that your mouth should report.' It is then relevant to ask at which point seeing and keeping silent should merge.

Philosophical work in language and about language can also be carried out without the creation of written texts. The sages (wise teachers, both male and female) formulate their advice about difficult practical questions of life and about the riddles of the universe and human life in a conversation which frequently results in a saying or a proverb. They use proverbs in a specific way and are often themselves the 'inventors' of proverbs with a philosophical content. Their advice or story doesn't result directly in an instruction as to what should be done in a particular situation. The proverb is formulated in such a general way that an interpretation is required, and only then does the concrete advice appear. Moreover, the advice can more easily be remembered if it takes the form of a terse saying or proverb. Other people who give advice or who are telling a story or speak in another way can also be the originators of proverbs, philosophical proverbs included.

In this way, sayings and proverbs are elements of the written in an oral transmission. Gyekye from Ghana explicitly mentions the sages as possible inventors of proverbs.[7] Even if the individual origin of a proverb cannot be demonstrated, at some point it had to be used for the first time. It implies an *auctor* ('originator'), an author. Konaté from the Ivory Coast emphasises that it is important to make clear the connection between proverbs and their authors in the situation of primarily oral transmission. According to him a proverb may be connected with an ethnic group or people, but its origin is not a 'collective production.' The first use is always individual and personal. Because a certain formulation finds a broad echo in a community, it becomes part of the general usage and ultimately sinks into the collective memory.[8] Of course, not all proverbs have a philosophical content. However, there is a special relationship between proverbs and philosophy to the extent that philosophy has its primary place in the medium of spoken language.

This does not mean, of course, that proverbs do not play a role in the written sources of traditional African philosophy. Very important documents of Ethiopian philosophy from the sixteenth and seventeenth century such as the *Maxims* of Skendes and the *Hatata* of Zera Yacob, were written down only because there was an occasional quest to do it. They are just the written version of a primarily oral teaching and advice for practical life problems.

Let me summarise in a scheme the various sources of African philosophy and the place of proverbs within them:

Primarily oral sources	Primarily written sources
Language	Ancient Egyptian
Sages and others	Ethiopian philosophy
Ethno-philosophy	5th–17th century
Symbols eg Adincra	Political and academic
symbols in Ghana	philosophy in 20th century
---> Proverbs <---	----> Proverbs <-----

Proverbs and Philosophy

Some of the African philosophers who use a partially ethno-philosophical method place special emphasis on the proverbs in their language. This is true of Abraham from Ghana, who has been living for a long time already in California, Mbiti from Kenya, who taught at the Makerere University in Uganda and currently works in Switzerland, Wiredu from Ghana, currently at the University of Southern Florida in Tampa, and Gyekye, also from Ghana and at the moment living in Washington DC.[9] The latter gives a survey of the sources of traditional African philosophy and discusses the particular significance of proverbs. The following are mentioned as sources: 'proverbs, myths and folktales, folk songs, rituals, beliefs, customs, and traditions of the people . . . its art symbols and its sociopolitical institutions and practices.' After referring to the philosophical impact of the 'symbolic character' of African art, Gyekye deals with a number of arguments for the specifically philosophical significance of proverbs, which can be found in the book by Mbiti. According to Mbiti they are 'repositories of traditional beliefs, ideas, wisdom and feelings.' But we have to take into account that their philosophical content 'is mainly situational.'[10]

The Akan use a proverb to express the close relationship of proverbs to situations: 'If the occasion has not arisen, the proverb does not come' or in a positive version: 'When the occasion arises, it calls for a proverb.' Thus it may be necessary to know the local facts belonging to a particular proverb. If the Akan say: 'No one sells his chicken without a reason,' a situation is imagined in which everyone knows that a chicken is a valuable possession. For the Akan, proverbs are also often conclusions drawn from a story or a fable. After a story is told in which someone's egotistical behaviour has painful results, Ananse, a spider who as a rule provides clever solutions in different situations, concludes: 'If you do not let your neighbour have nine, you will not have ten.'

With this last proverb in mind, I suggested in my first book on African philosophy that not only the situation in which a proverb is used should be involved in the interpretation, but also the one in which it arises. Frequently this situation will have to be extrapolated from the proverb itself. In the example under discussion, a situation is supposed in which peaceful neighbours are living together in a village. One can contrast this with people who are nomadic or live alone, that is to say, have a lifestyle in which this situation does not, or does not yet, exist. Sedentary life only provides advantages if the peace among neighbours is maintained, if competition and envy are not dominant. Accordingly this proverb can be interpreted not simply as a 'rejection of ethical egoism,' as happens in Gyekye's book, but the interpretation is given an extra dimension in which the imagined social situation, as it is embedded in a cultural-historic context, has to be regarded as significant.[11]

According to Gyekye, the special relationship between proverbs and philosophy for the Akan rests on the affinity between a proverb and a palm tree, which can be etymologically demonstrated: in Twi, the language of the Akan, a proverb is 'ebe,' a palm tree is 'abe.' The products of the palm tree—palm oil, palm wine, palm soap, etc—are produced by means of distillation. It seems surprising at times that these products can be got from a palm tree. Production involves a great deal of work. Similarly, proverbs are distilled from everyday language. They form terse, compressed formulations and often enough they have an enigmatic, elliptical or even a cryptic character. This applies especially to proverbs with a clear philosophical content. One example is a proverb about destiny, which no one can avoid: 'Unless you die of God, let living man kill you, and you will not perish,' and one about African logic, which is often expressed in metaphors: 'There are no crossroads in the ear.' This last example is interpreted by Gyekye as an Akan formulation of the principle of contradiction.

This characteristic of Akan proverbs can be directly compared to Hegel's explanation of the process of philosophising. Hegel emphasises above all the density of philosophical concepts. According to him, the process which must lead to this density is a difficult one; he talks about the 'effort of the concept' or also about the task of bringing something 'to the concept.' In the foreword to his *Grundlinien der Philosophie des Rechts* (Berlin 1821) there is the famous statement: 'Philosophie ist ihre Zeit in Gedanken erfaßt.' Russell describes in more detail this character of philosophy which apparently runs parallel to proverbs and the process of their creation. In the foreword to his *History of Western philosophy* (London 1946) he says, without referring to the close relationship between philosophy and language which is assumed here: 'I have tried . . . to exhibit each philosopher as . . . a man in whom were crystallized and concentrated thoughts and feelings which, in a vague and diffused form, were common to a community of which he was a part.'

How Systematic Should Philosophy Be?

In order to make a comparison with African proverbs, Gyekye takes examples which are formulated as aphorisms from Western and Eastern philosophies. By so doing he wishes to show that the Akan proverbs which he mentions and interprets are the equal of these examples. Thus the Akan proverb 'No destiny is the same as another' is placed next to Socrates' statements 'Virtue is knowledge' or 'No one willingly does wrong' and Confucius' aphorism 'He who learns but does not think is lost, he who thinks but does not learn is in danger.' Reference is also made to the fragments of the pre-Socratics, in which important philosophical ideas are summarised in a few short sentences. However, Gyekye is not satisfied with the philosophy in proverbs. On the one hand, he regards certain proverbs as true philosophy; on the other hand he wants more. He wants to explain the philosophical system of the Akan. In this connection proverbs are 'sources' for this system.

Gerald J Wanjohi from Nairobi is also working on the explanation of an African philosophy on the basis of proverbs, in his case the philosophy of the Gikuyu. Without any doubt the first question is: Which proverbs have a philosophical content and can be considered philosophy or a source for philosophy? Gyekye and Wanjohi have at their disposal an extensive collection of the proverbs in Twi and the language of the Gikuyu.[12] They can select philosophically relevant proverbs from this material and other sources. As a second step, it is important to classify the proverbs according to certain themes. Thematic classification also takes place in other areas of the research into proverbs outside philosophy. The principles for classification are always taken from outside to a certain extent: proverbs on family life, women, history, good behaviour, destiny, life after death, etc.

Selecting and classifying proverbs with a philosophical content has to remain provisional. It depends on the understanding of the philosopher which proverbs he or she will regard as philosophical. In principle all proverbs can turn out to be used as a source of philosophy or as a subject of philosophical interpretation.

Proverbs are mostly not the only source which is used in order to find out or to reconstruct what the philosophy of an African people is. Gyekye is trying to build up a system in which the whole of the Akan philosophy can be expressed. For that purpose the proverbs are one of the principal sources. But there are other important sources: the language itself, the customs of the people, art, religion, political life, etc. All these have been the subject of different scientific disciplines. Therefore,

an interdisciplinary approach is necessary: linguistics, cultural anthropology, art criticism, religious studies and political sciences can help to investigate these areas. And it is vital to speak with the sages in the villages about their philosophical ideas. As a result 'The Akan conceptual scheme' can be reconstructed.

In organising the material of the proverbs, in his work Wanjohi follows the systematic classification of philosophy as it has been worked out in Western traditions. In 1990 he published a contribution to the theory of knowledge of the Gikuyu, in which, at the same time, the epistemological status of the proverbs in question was demonstrated as 'philosophical.'[13] In addition he is working on contributions to metaphysics and the philosophy of religion, ethics and political philosophy, and other systematic disciplines in the Gikuyu philosophy. One can question whether the classification system of Western philosophy is not too much the guide to the different divisions and subdivisions of the philosophy of an African people.

I feel that the working methods of both African colleagues also give rise to the following question: How systematic should philosophy be? They are not alone in working in this way: Charles S Bird and Ivan Karp are the general editors of a series of books published in Bloomington/Indianapolis under the title *African systems of thought*. Hasn't the attempt to find a more or less complete system been inspired by the example of the great systems of Western philosophy? I mention only Aristotle, Thomas, Descartes, Spinoza, Hegel, Whitehead and the contemporary German philosopher Hermann Schmitz. I realise that this attempt of African philosophers is also motivated by resistance to assertions from the colonial period that 'the Africans' would not be capable of logical and systematic thought. It could have seemed that African philosophies would be considered the equal to those in the West only if they were systematically constructed.

Within Western philosophies, however, the precedence of systematic philosophising is no longer valid. During the Romantic period a preference for epigrams arose, and the entire philosophical programme of this period was only fragmentally developed. In the work of Nietzsche, the breakthrough of aphoristic philosophy as 'great' philosophy took place. In *Sein und Zeit* (Tübingen

1927) Heidegger arrived at a project of the destruction of the metaphysical systems in Western history, and nowadays Derrida occupies himself with the deconstruction of these systems. Wittgenstein, in his early work, argued according to a series of propositions which did reveal a certain systematic construction; however, his later work is clearly aphoristic. The idea of 'language games,' which is central to that work, is also characteristic of his writing style. In the *Negative Dialektik* (Franfurt am Main 1966) Adorno criticised systematic philosophising broadly and penetratingly, and argued in favour of developing models which relate to particular concrete situations, and for making visible constellations which can change, depending on the appearance of the historical context. At the same time that these authors were criticising systematic philosophy and attempting to break it down, art took on an important function both in and for their philosophy.

In the later work of Heidegger the relationship between philosophy (thinking) and language was placed in a totally new dimension. After everything that has happened in the history of Western philosophy, after a gigantic accumulation of traditions and a steadily rising flood of written documents, it turned out to be an extremely difficult task to return to *speaking simply*, without there being a diminution in quality. In this connection, Heidegger tried to reconstruct what was thought in certain words by tracing their etymology. He was busy collecting basic words for thinking from his own language, as the ancient Greek philosophers had done. In this way he worked at the task of finding 'another beginning' for philosophy (or as he himself said: thinking). In doing this he experienced the existence of a close relationship between thinking and poetry, that they 'are neighbours.' When he was quite old, he began to study Chinese in order to be able to read Lao Tse in the original.

Whatever the case may be, it is not my concern to replace the precedence of systematic philosophy with the precedence of aphoristic or any other non-systematic philosophies. Up to a certain point philosophy will be and remain systematic;[14] this is already a given by the meaning of argumentation in and for every philosophy. Systematic philosophising, also in the form of 'open systems,' is, however, only one type of philosophy, besides which aphoristic, epigrammatic, fragmentary and other forms of philosophy have their own right and value. That makes room for a multiple use of proverbs as philosophy and as sources of philosophy. On the one hand, a collection of proverbs is not a philosophical book. Philosophically relevant proverbs have to be recognised as such, selected and organised thematically, before they can play a role as philosophy. On the other hand, JC Thomas's warning is appropriate here. He writes in his introduction to Ackah's book about *Akan ethics* (Accra 1988, p. 20) that 'the temptation must . . . be avoided to impose system and order on what is not systematically presented.'

It is not up to me to decide whether, and to what extent, African philosophies should be systematic. Given the significance of proverbs for philosophy and the special significance which they have in primarily oral communication and transmission, I would like to conclude with my question: How systematic should African philosophy be? As far as Africa is concerned, only African philosophers can give an answer to this question. It will depend on this answer how they will deal with proverbs and other non-primarily written sources in their philosophical work, how they will use proverbs as philosophy and as a source of philosophy.

Notes

1. H. Kimmerle: *Afrikanische Philosophie als Weisheitslehre?* In R. A. Mall/D. Lohmar (eds), *Philosophische Grundlagen der Interkulturalität.* Amsterdam/Atlanta, Ga. 1993 (Studien zur interkulturellen Philosophie 1), p. 159–180.
2. H. Odera Oruka: *Sagacity in African Philosophy. International Philosophical Quarterly* 23 (1983), see pages 391–392.
3. K. Wiredu: *Philosophy and an African culture.* Cambridge 1980, p. 40, note 3.
4. P. J. Hountondji: *African philosophy. Myth and reality.* London 1983, p. 55; O. Yai: *Theory and practice in African philosophy. The poverty of speculative philosophy. Second Order* 6 (2) (1977); R. Finnegan: *Oral literature in Africa.* Oxford 1970.
5. P. J. Hountondji, oc., Part 1, chapters 1 and 2.
6. S. B. Oluwole: *Witchcraft, reincarnation and the God-Head.* Lagos 1992, pp. 56–60; see also for the following.
7. K. Gyekye: *An essay on African philosophical thought. The Akan conceptual scheme.* Cambridge 1987, p. 19.

8. Y. Konaté: *Le syndrome Hampaté Bâ ou Comment naissent les proverbes*. Quest. *An International African Journal of Philosophy* 8, 2 (1994), p. 23–44.

9. W. E. Abraham: *The mind of Africa.* Chicago 1962; J. S. Mbiti: *African Religions and Philosophy.* London 1969; K. Wiredu, oc. (in note 3); K. Gyekye, oc. (in note 7).

10. Gyekye, oc., pp. 13–15; see for the following 16–23.

11. H. Kimmerle: *Philosophie in Afrika—afrikanische Philosophie.* Frankfurt am Main 1991, pp. 46 and 123.

12. J. G. Christaller: *A collection of 3 600 Twi Proverbs.* Basel 1879; R. S. Rattray: *Ashanti proverbs.* Oxford, 1916; G. Barra: *1 000 Gikuyu proverbs.* London 1960; N. Njururi: *Gikuyu proverbs.* London 1969.

13. G. J. Wanjohi: *The philosophy of Gikuyu proverbs. An epistemological contribution.* In: H. Oosterling/F. de Jong (eds), *Denken unterwegs. Philosophie im Kräftefeld sozialen und politische Engagements. Festschrift für Heinz Kimmerle zu seinem 60. Geburtstag.* Amsterdam 1990, pp. 383–394.

14. It is important to note that what is at stake here is the *presentation* of philosophical thought, not the thought itself (or 'thinking-as-philosophy' à la Heidegger on page 95 above). I am referring primarily to the outward aspect of philosophy therefore.

Morality in Yoruba Thought: A Philosophical Analysis

Oladipo Olusegun

What is morality? How is it related to other means of regulating human conduct, for example law, in society? What is its origin and on what does its hold on persons in society rest? What is the logical structure of moral language? Are moral statements propositions, commands or mere expressions of feelings? These, and many other questions, have been central to moral discourse in the history of (Western) philosophy. In this essay, however, I do not intend to address (at least directly) any of these intricate issues. My concern is, rather, a modest one. It is to examine the nature of morality in Yoruba thought with a view to determining, through philosophical analysis, the extent to which it is tenable to assert that:

> With the Yoruba, morality is certainly a fruit of religion. They do not make any attempt to separate the two, and it is impossible for them to do so without disastrous consequences. What have been named *tabu* took their origin from the fact that people discerned that there were things which were morally approved or disapproved by the Deity.[1]

In this essay I argue that this is an unnecessarily one-sided interpretation of the Yoruba ethical system. It fixates overmuch evidences tending to one end of the axis to the neglect of their complements, and thus arriving at partial or utterly erroneous conclusions,[2] I also contend that it rests on a misconception of the nature of morality and its relationship to religion. But, first, what are the basic elements of Yoruba ethics? On

"Morality in Yoruba Thought" by Oladipo Olusegun, *Quest*, Vol. I, No. 2, December 1987. Reprinted by permission of African Studies Centre.

what basis is the assertion made that, in Yoruba thought, morality and religion are inseparable?

The Yoruba stress the importance of character *(iwa)* in human life. This, we are told, is the case, not only because 'man's well-being here depends on his character,'[3] but also, and perhaps more importantly, because 'his place in Afterlife is determined by *Olodumare* (the Deity) according to his deserts.'[4] Morality in Yoruba thought is therefore given expression in the concept of *Iwa*.

> *Iwa*, according to the Yoruba, is the very stuff which makes life a joy because it is pleasing to God. It is therefore stressed that good character must be the dominant feature of a person's life. In fact, it is one thing which distinguishes a person from the brute. . . . A person of good character is called *Omoluwabi*. . . . "One who behaves as a well-born"; and a person of bad character is *enia—k'enia*—"A mere caricature of a person."[5]

The components of a good character include the following: chastity before marriage, particularly on the part of the woman, hospitality, particularly to strangers, opposition to selfishness, kindness involving generosity, abhorrence of wickedness, high regard for truth and rectitude, condemnation of stealing, covenant breaking and falsehood, and hypocrisy, protection of women by men, high regard for honour and due respect to old age.[6]

The question then is this: What is the basis of these components of good character that constitute the defining elements of Yoruba ethics? Are they, essentially, social in origin?

For some scholars on Yoruba beliefs, these elements of good character are inextricably linked to the people's religion, particularly their conception of the Deity, Prof. Bolaji Idowu, for instance, writes:

The real source and norm of the unrestricted, universally recognised and binding moral values in the religion of the Yoruba is *Olodumare*. They derive immediately from His own divine nature as revealed to the Yoruba. . . . In Him alone can be resolved the ever-baffling problem of right conduct which are inevitably encountered in the divinities or ancestral sanctions.[7]

And the argument in support of this position, simply put, is this: That since the sense of right and wrong is necessary for morality and since, for the Yoruba, this sense of right and wrong is an endowment of Olodumare (he is the one, we are told, that put in a person *Ifa aya*—'the oracle of the heart' which 'guides man and determines his ethical life,')[8] then it follows that Yoruba moral values cannot be separated from their conception of the Deity. The implication here, of course, is that without their conception of the Deity the people's moral orientation may have been other than we know it to be.

In examining this position I consider two interrelated issues: First, the issue of whether the existence of a sense of right and wrong sufficiently explains the set of moral rules given expression, in Yoruba thought, in the concept of *Iwa* and the patterns of conduct these engender. Second, the issue of whether, in fact, the people's moral values cannot be separated from their conception of the Deity.

Let us, in considering the first issue, grant a point. This is that a sense of right and wrong, whatever its nature, is necessary for morality. Without this sense, the question of what constitutes proper conduct within society would not have arisen in the first place, and, of course, without this there would not have been any need for classifying human conduct or behaviour, according to whether it is good or bad, right or wrong. Consequently, neither would the need for praising or blaming people for their actions or training them to behave in certain desirable ways in the society have arisen. It is because we are able to recognise certain actions as good or bad, right or wrong that we are able to define the limits of proper or permissible conduct within society, praise or blame people for their actions, and also shape their moral outlook in ways that we think will enable them to function as good members of the society. Having granted this point, however, we need to ask: what is the nature of this sense of right and wrong?

Let us, for our purposes in this essay, agree with Prof. Bolaji Idowu that this sense of right and wrong is a faculty (what is called in Yoruba *Ifa aya*) and, since the Yoruba believe that *Olodumare* is the maker of human beings and every other thing in the universe, also agree that it is an endowment of the Deity. But does it follow from this that the Deity also determines the nature of the set of rules which a person should obey and the modes of conduct he should adopt in society, in giving fulfilment to the sense of right and wrong with which he is endowed?

If we follow Prof. Idowu in giving an affirmative answer to this question and assert, as he does, that Olodumare is the real source of the unrestricted universally recognised and binding moral values of the *Yoruba*, then we shall have to explain the following issues. First, we have to explain how it comes to be that 'contradictions and confusions' result from 'taking the divinities as the norm of moral obligation,'[9] particularly when we are wont to maintain that these divinities are ministers of *Olodumare*? Second, we have to explain the fact which is revealed in their institutionalized practices that the Yoruba are 'a pragmatic people who place great stock on expediency. . . .'[10] I take these issues in turn with a view to bringing into sharper focus the errors (theoretical and factual) the position under examination harbours.

In considering the first issue, it should be noted that, apart from the belief in a Deity *(Olodumare)*, another important element of the Yoruba cosmological world-view, which makes many writers on African beliefs to regard them as an 'incurably religious' people, is the belief in 'minor gods.' But, as Prof. Bolaji Idowu observes, there are certain incompatibilities in the norms of behaviour and moral obligations 'inspired by the cults' associated with them. We have an example of this kind of 'contradictions and confusions' 'about what should be done and what should not be done' in this Yoruba poem quoted by Prof. Idowu. (Here I only give the English translation).

Olufon it is who gave me birth, I must not drink palm-wine, *Orisa - Ogiyan* it is who gave me birth, I must not drink palm-wine, *Osun* of

Iponda however, forbids me maize-wine palm-wine it is which he orders me to drink.'[11]

But why is this so? Prof. Idowu, rather than tackle this important question, simply disregards these divinities as norms of moral obligation and proceeds, unperturbed, to declare that: 'The real source and norm of the unrestricted, universally recognised and binding moral values in the religion of the Yoruba is Olodumare.'[12]

This certainly cannot be a satisfactory posture on this matter. For if these divinities are, as Prof. Idowu and many other writers on African beliefs are wont to argue, ministers who 'serve the will of Olodumare in the creation and theocratic government of the world,'[13] then the question of how it comes to be that there are 'contradictions and confusions' in taking them as norms of morality has to be seriously tackled. In tackling this question one thing is clear: we cannot disregard these divinities as norms of morality, for it is a fact of life in Yoruba societies that certain moral obligations flow from the people's conception of them. The only option that is left for us then is to have another look at the people's belief about the nature of these divinities, with a view to reassessing their nature.[14] The hypothesis I put forward here in this regard is that these divinities do not have, strictly speaking, the kind of direct connection with the Deity many of our writers say the Yoruba believe they have. For, besides the fact that they are 'generally acknowledged to be in every case traceable to a human being'[15] and that the value attached to each of them is dependent on the 'strength and universality of the course to which it ministers,'[16] we can also see that the attitude of the people to them—because it is essentially pragmatic and utilitarian—cannot be regarded as a religious attitude, the kind one would expect the people to have towards them if they are believed to have any direct links with the Deity.

It thus seems to be the case that, for the Yoruba, there are other sources of moral obligation than the Deity, and unless we are able to show that these other sources are of a typically religious nature—a proposition we may not be able to defend given the evidence available[17]—then we shall have to admit that other considerations that may not have anything to do with

religion also serve to underpin the moral rules and patterns of behaviour we associate with the Yoruba.

This brings us to a consideration of the second issue which anybody who asserts that morality in Yoruba thought is inseparable from their conception of the Deity will have to contend with. This is closely connected with the fact that a look at some of the proverbs and institutionalized practices of the people, rather than reveal a consistency and coherence of outlook we would expect a world-outlook totally anchored on a conception of the Deity to display, betrays what one would call an essentially this-worldly and pragmatic orientation.

It is not uncommon, for example, to find in the repertoire of Yoruba proverbs those which, when taken together, are inconsistent and also some which sanction moral values that are clearly at variance with the values we would expect of a religion-based moral system. Here are some examples.'[18]

1. *fija f'Olorun ja f'owo leran* (Let God fight for you don't try and avenge yourself.)
2. *O fun mi l'ewugudugbe, mo fun o l'ebo-toro, afinju iwo lajo fun ra wa* (You fed me with poison that turns me into a bloated, swollen-up sack, I gave you a poison that peeled off your skin. We have fed each other with vantage poisons).
3. *Eni ti ko gbon ni aawe ngbo* (only a fool suffers from hunger while he is fasting.)
4. *Kaka ki omode pa agba l'ayo, agba a fi ogbo agba gbe e* (rather than loose a game of *ayo* to a child, the older person should save the day by resorting to the wisdom of the elders).

Now, it can be seen that the first two proverbs recommend certain moral values that appear inconsistent; whereas the first one abhors retaliation, the second one recommends it. The third and fourth proverbs, on the other hand, seem to suggest that there is nothing bad in resorting to some unconventional methods to achieve one's objectives. The implication of the third one, as Prof. Oyekan Owomoyela rightly points out, is that: 'if one proclaims to be fasting and remembers to appear hungry, there is no reason why one may not gorge oneself in the secrecy of one's home.'[19] And the fourth one says that an elder may simply cheat in a game of *ayo* to forestall a situation in which a child defeats him.

What these proverbs seem to make clear is that the Yoruba do not have a set of timeless, internally consistent moral values which directly derive from their conception of the Deity and therefore can consistently be used for adjudging human actions as right or wrong, good or bad; the rightness or goodness of an action is determined by certain factors, not the least of which is the interest of the human agent himself. So much for proverbs.

Let us now consider some institutionalized practices of the people. Do they, in any fundamental sense, reflect a religion-sanctioned system of moral values? Our answer here, again, cannot but be negative. We are not unfamiliar, for instance, with the notoriously famous, and perhaps peculiar, method of collecting debts—the *Osomalo* strategy—from 'an incorrigible debtor' which is described by Samuel Johnson in his book, *The History of the Yorubas*, in these terms.

> When a creditor who has obtained judgement for debt finds it impossible to recover any thing out of the debtor, he applies to the town authorities for a licensed destrainor. This individual is called *Ogo*, he is to *d'ogo ti* i.e. to sit on the debtor (as it were). For that purpose he enters the premises, seeks the debtor, or ensconces in his apartment until he makes his appearance, and then he makes himself an intolerable nuisance to him and to the members of the family generally until the money is paid.[20]

This, perhaps, is done without any consideration for the debtor's financial health. Yet this is a society in which, we are told, hospitality, opposition to selfishness, abhorrence of wickedness, kindness involving generosity are components of a good character that derive from the people's conception of the Deity! But, lest the objection is raised that the payment of debts is a purely contractual and, therefore, legal matter which should be removed from the realm of the moral, thereby underplaying this glaring inconsistency we note in the interpretation of the people's moral beliefs in terms of their conception of the Deity and this

institutionalized method of collecting debts, I should quickly give another example; this time from a realm of business transactions. Here I quote Oyekan Owemoyela. He writes:

> Their conduct of market transactions in general provides corroborative proof of the Yoruba belief that the cunning shall inherit the earth. It is well known that Africans hardly ever assign fixed prices to their merchandise; rather the buying and selling of commodities match the wits and patience of the seller and the purchaser, awarding the ultimate benefit to whichever party is endowed with those qualities. Among the Yoruba the process has been developed into a fine art with well-understood rules. Even though each of the participants knows that the other is in effect maneuvering to "cheat," she is not incensed because she too is scheming to profit at her expense.[21]

A business ethics based on people's conception of the Deity indeed!

Now, when we add to the institutionalized practices we have mentioned the fact that even the 'verbal art form, *oriki* (eulogistic address)' is used to celebrate 'subjects—people, animals, diseases, natural formations and human actions'[22]— that are 'not necessarily benevolent or edifying,' then we cannot but wonder whether the interpretation of the nature of Yoruba moral values under consideration in this essay is not a deliberate distortion designed to serve some nationalistic or religious ends.

But perhaps we are unfair in our interpretation, after all, it may be argued, we do not, because of the existence of divergencies between Islamic or Christian ethics enunciated in the scriptures and the practice of the believers, deny that these norms of behaviour are really there to guide conduct. This would have been an appropriate riposte but for the fact that, in the case of the Yoruba, the institutionalized practices we have mentioned are not at all seen as being inconsistent with the belief in a Deity who is their maker, the way a deviation from the norms of Islamic or Christian ethics would be regarded as an egregious deviation a sin. In any case, how de we establish the claim that Yoruba moral values are products of the religion of the people directly linked to their conception of the Deity, particularly when it is realized that in Yoruba traditional religion, as in the religions of many African traditional societies, revelation simply has no place?

We may even ask: what explains the separation which many of our Christian converts, for example, often try to effect between 'Christian ethics' and what they now call, as a result of conversion, 'pagan ethics,' if indeed the Deity is the source of all moral values and observances and if, as Prof. Idowu says, there is only one God of which people have different conceptions?[23]

The major implication that follows from our analysis thus far can be put in the following terms: whereas it is the case that certain norms of behaviour can be associated with the people's conception of the Deity, these norms certainly do not exhaust the variety of such norms we have in Yoruba societies; there are certainly other moral values that arise out of the attempt by the people to grapple with the various dimensions of human existence. The reason why this is so should be clear. Morality, because it is inextricably linked to human action, covers a wider range of human activities and experiences than religion. This explains its variety and the range of its diversity, not only from one society to the other, but also, within the same society, from time to time. And so the diversity in Yoruba moral values and the apparent contradictions between some of them we earlier on noticed in our analysis, do not constitute a negative commentary on the character of the people. It is, besides being a clear reflection of the dynamic character of traditional Yoruba societies—which are noted, not only for the sophistication of their political systems and the intensity of their economic activities, but also for their robust, if at times inconsistent, world-outlook—also, as Dr (Mrs) Oluwole points out, an indication of the fact that the Yoruba 'give due cognizance to human interests in moral matters.'[24]

It should be clear then, from this analysis, that the existence of a sense of right and wrong, even, the admission that this is given by the Deity, does not sufficiently explain the nature of moral rules, and the authority they have on people's conduct, in Yoruba societies. The interpretation of Yoruba moral values wholly in terms of religion can thus be an expression of the tendency on the part of our experts on African beliefs, particularly those in Religious Studies, to give a one-sided view of the beliefs they interpret thereby distorting them. Religion 'is *part* of life, not an orientation towards the whole of it.'[25] It cannot therefore serve as an adequate means of explaining the nature of morality which—whether understood as 'a set of rules for the regulation of conduct'[26] or as 'patterns of conduct viewed in relation to such rules'[27]—necessarily 'accompanies all deliberate human actions'[28] and thus has a wider scope. To realize this fact is, not only to begin to pave the way for a clear understanding of the reason why 'many African societies in times past have generated diverse ethics,' but also, and more importantly, to begin to lay a solid foundation for an adequate comprehension of the set of factors that shape our ethical orientations and moral preferences in contemporary society.[29]

Notes

*The Yoruba can be found in South-Western Nigeria and some parts of the Republic of Benin and Togo.

1. E. Bolaji Idowu, *Olodumare: God in Yoruba Belief*, (London: Longman Group Limited, 1962), p. 146.
2. Oyekan Owomoyela, "The Pragmatic Humanism of Yoruba Culture," *Journal of African Studies*, vol. 8, Number 3 fall 1981, p. 126.
3. E. Bolaji Idowu, *op. cit.*, p. 154.
4. E. Bolaji Idowu, *ibid*.
5. *Ibid*. pp. 154–155.
6. For a comprehensive discussion of these components of Yoruba ethics, see E. Bolaji Idowu, *Ibid.*, pp. 154–166.
7. E. Bolaji Idowu, *Ibid.*, p.154.
8. *Ibid*.
9. *Ibid.*, p. 152.
10. Oyekan Owomoyela, *op. cit.*, p. 127.
11. E. Bolaji Idowu, *op. cit.*, p. 153.
12. *Ibid.*, p. 154.
13. *Ibid.*, p. 57.
14. It should be noted that this is a very large issue which cannot be treated in detail in this paper.
15. N.A. Fadipe, *The Sociology of the Yoruba*, edited by Francis Olu Okediji and Oladejo O. Okediji, (Ibadan: Ibaban University Press, 1970), p. 262.
16. *Ibid*.
17. Among these divinities for instance, we have deified ancestors and, even deities 'introduced in response to certain diseases and life hazards.'
18. The first two of these four proverbs and their translations are taken from Dr. Niyi Oladeji's paper, "Language signposts in Yoruba pragmatic Ethics: An Analysis of Selected Yoruba Proverbs," an unpublished paper read at the conference on Ethics in African Societies organized by the Department of Philosophy, Obafemi

Awolowo University, Ile-Ife, Nigeria, 1st–4th July 1987, p. 3. The last two are taken from Oyekan Owomoyela, *op. cit.*, p. 128.

19. Oyekan Owomoyela, *Ibid.*
20. Samuel Johnson, *The History of the Yorubas*, (Lagos: C.M.S. (Nigeria) Bookshops, 1948), pp. 130–131.
21. Oyekan Owomoyela, *op. cit.*, p. 127.
22. *Ibid.*
23. CF. E. Bolaji Idowu, *African Traditional Religion: A Definition*, (London: SCM Press Ltd., 1973), p. 146.
24. S.B. Oluwole, "The Rational Basis of Yoruba Ethical Thinking," *The Nigerian Journal of Philosophy: Journal of the Department of Philosophy, University of Lagos*, vol. 4, Nos 1 & 2, 1984, p. 23.
25. Venon Pratt, *Religion and Secularisation* (London and Basingstoke: Macmillan and Co. Ltd., 1970), p. 45.
26. Kwasi Wiredu "Morality and Religion in Akan Thought," paper presented at the 2nd Afro–Asian philosophy conference, October/November 1981, p. 2. The paper is published in H. Odera Oruka and D.A. Masolo (eds.), *Philosophy and Cultures*, (Nairobi: 1983) The reference here is to the original manuscript.
27. *Ibid.*
28. Emerita S. Quito "Value as a Factor in Social Action," *International Social Science Journal*, vol. XXXVI, No. 4, 1984, p. 604.
29. This is a slightly modified version of a paper read at the conference on Ethics in African Societies, organized by the Department of Philosophy, Obafemi Awolowo University, Ile-Ife, Nigeria, 1st–4th July 1987. I am grateful to Dr. A.G.A. Bello of the Department of Philosophy, University of Ibadan, Nigeria, for his useful comments on an earlier draft of the paper.

The Need for Conceptual Decolonization in African Philosophy

Kwasi Wiredu

In June 1980 at the UNESCO conference on "Teaching and Research in Philosophy in Africa" I advocated a program of conceptual decolonization in African philosophy.[1] In the present discussion I wish to pursue this idea further. I write now with an even greater sense of urgency, seeing that the intervening decade does not seem to have brought any indications of a widespread realization of the need for conceptual decolonization in African philosophy.

By conceptual decolonization I mean two complementary things. On the negative side, I mean avoiding or reversing through a critical conceptual self-awareness the unexamined assimilation in our thought (that is, in the thought of contemporary African philosophers) of the conceptual frameworks embedded in the foreign philosophical traditions that have had an impact on African life and thought. And, on the positive side, I mean exploiting as much as is judicious the resources of our own indigenous conceptual schemes in our philosophical meditations on even the most technical problems of contemporary philosophy. The negative is, of course, only the reverse side of the positive. But I cite it first because the necessity for decolonization was brought upon us in the first place by the historical superimposition of foreign categories of thought on African thought systems through colonialism.

This superimposition has come through three principal avenues. The first is the avenue of language. It is encountered in the fact that our philosophical education has generally been in the medium of foreign languages, usually of our erstwhile colonizers. This is the most fundamental,

subtle, pervasive and intractable circumstance of mental colonization. But the two other avenues, though grosser by comparison, have been insidious enough. I refer here to the avenues of religion and politics. Through these have been passed to us legacies of long-standing religious evangelization, in the one case, and political tutelage, in the other. I can only touch the tips of these three tremendous historical icebergs in one discussion.

Take first, then, the linguistic situation. By definition, the fundamental concepts of philosophy are the most fundamental categories of human thought. But the particular modes of thought that yield these concepts may reflect the specifics of the culture, environment and even the accidental idiosyncracies of the people concerned. Conceptual idiosyncracy, although an imponderable complication in human affairs, probably accounts for a vast proportion of the conceptual disparities among different philosophical traditions, especially the ones in which individual technical philosophers are deeply implicated. Think, then, of the possible enormity of the avoidable philosophical deadwood we might be carrying through our historically enforced acquisition of philosophical training in the medium of foreign languages. Of course, a similar pessimistic soul-searching is altogether in place even among the natives of any given philosophical tradition vis-a-vis their historical inheritance. This is, in fact, much in evidence in contemporary Western philosophy, for example. But the position is graver in our situation of cultural otherness, for even ordinary common sense would deprecate needlessly carrying other peoples garbage.

What exactly are the concepts am I thinking of here? There is a large bunch of them, but let me mention only the following: Reality, Being, Existence, Thing, Object, Entity, Substance, Property,

Quality, Truth, Fact, Opinion, Belief, Knowledge, Faith, Doubt, Certainty, Statement, Proposition, Sentence, Idea, Mind, Soul, Spirit, Thought, Sensation, Matter, Ego, Self, Person, Individuality, Community, Subjectivity, Objectivity, Cause, Chance, Reason, Explanation, Meaning, Freedom, Responsibility, Punishment, Democracy, Justice, God, World, Universe, Nature, Supernature, Space, Time, Nothingness, Creation, Life, Death, Afterlife, Morality, Religion.

In regard to all these concepts the simple recipe for decolonization for the African is: Try to think them through in your own African language and, on the basis of the results, review the intelligibility of the associated problems or the plausibility of the apparent solutions that have tempted you when you have pondered them in some metropolitan language. The propositions in question may be about topics that have no special involvement with Africa, but they may well be about the internalities of an African thought system.

By the sheer fact of our institutional education, we are likely to have thought about some at least of these concepts and problems framed in terms of them using English or French or some such language. The problem is that thinking about them in English almost inevitably becomes thinking in English about them. It is just an obvious fact, in Philosophy at least, that one thinks most naturally in the language of one's education and occupation. But in our case this means thinking along the lines of conceptual frameworks which may be significantly different from those embedded in our indigenous languages. In virtue of this phenomenon, we constantly stand the danger of involuntary mental de-Africanization unless we consciously and deliberately resort to our own languages (and culture). It turns out that this form of self-knowledge is not easy to attain, and it is not uncommon to find highly educated Africans proudly holding forth on, for instance, the glories of African traditional religion in an internalized conceptual idiom of a metropolitan origin which distorts indigenous thought structures out of all recognition.

There is no pretence, of course, that recourse to the African vernacular must result in instantaneous philosophic revelation. The chances, on the contrary, are that philosophical errors are evenly distributed among the heterogeneous races of humankind. Suppose, for example, that the concept,

much employed in, say, English philosophical discourse seems to lose all meaning when processed in a given African language. This consequence may conceivably be due to an insufficiency in the African language rather than to an intrinsic defect in the mode of conceptualization of the foreign language or culture concerned. How does one determine whether this is so or not? The only way, I suggest, is to try to reason out the matter on independent grounds. By this I mean that one should argue in a manner fathomable in both the African and the foreign language concerned. With that accomplished, it would be clear that the considerations adduced are not dependent on the peculiarities of the African language in question. In general, failure to heed this requirement is one of the root causes of the kinds of conceptual idiosyncracies that, in part, differentiate cultural traditions of thought.

Notice that if such independent grounds can be adduced, relativism is false. In many of the things I have written elsewhere, I have argued against relativism.[2] Here I will take it for granted that the theory is false and proceed to give some illustrations of the procedure of conceptual decolonization that I have been talking about, so far, in a rather general way. Let us attend, to start with, to the cluster of epistemological concepts in the list of basic concepts given above. We mentioned Truth, Fact, Certainty, Doubt, Knowledge, Belief, Opinion and some more. Now, one very powerful motive for the persistent wrestling with these concepts in Western epistemology has been the desire to overcome skepticism, and one very influential form of skepticism has been the clear and simple form of it encountered in Descartes' methodological skepticism. Interestingly, classical Greek skepticism was more complex in its argumentation than the Cartesian version. But, possibly, partly because of its devastating simplicity and lucidity, it is the latter that has become the driving force of epistemological inquiry. At peak, the skeptical problem à la Descartes is simply that so long as my cognition is subject to the possibility of error, it is uncertain; and so long as it is uncertain, it falls short of knowledge. In the Meditations the program of doubt starts with the observation that the senses have proved deceptive in the past and consequently cannot be trusted to give us knowledge. This consideration is reinforced with the reflection that, in any case, all our perceptual beliefs might very well be dream illusions. These two degrees of doubt still leave simple a priori propositions, such as those of elementary school arithmetic, unscathed. But not for long, for soon Descartes invokes the hypothesis of an all powerful God, or for fear of the impiety of the idea, 'some malicious demon of the utmost power' who might make me 'go wrong every time I add two and three or count the sides of a square.'[3] Aside from the dramatic imagery of the hypothesis, what it means is simply that none of our cognition's or at least none of those considered up to that point are exempt from the possibility of error. And this is the sole reason why all claims to certainty must be suspended. As is well known, the only thing that proves capable of breaking the suspension is the Cogito, the contention that 'I think therefore I am,' which, in the eyes of Descartes, is guaranteed against, not just error, but indeed the very possibility of it. From all which it is apparent that for Descartes certainty means the impossibility of error.

It is important to note that this conception of certainty is not peculiar to Descartes in Western philosophy. It has held sway in that tradition, before and since Descartes, over the minds of innumerable philosophers of differing persuasions. For example, the logical positivist position that empirical knowledge is incapable of certainty was predicated upon the single consideration that such cognitions are perpetually open to the possibility of error. This notion was also entertained (very notably) by C. I. Lewis, the 'conceptual pragmatist' and other non-positivists in contemporary philosophy.[4] Yet, on a little reflection, this understanding of certainty is, or should be, seen to be rather surprising, for exemption from the possibility of error is nothing short of infallibility. Accordingly, the quest for certainty[5] becomes the quest for infallibility—as chimerical a quest as ever there was. Certainly, neither Descartes nor the logical positivists and others are known to have laid explicit claims to infallibility in any part of their knowledge. How, then, has this quest for infallibility gone on in actual practice for so long and exercised so controlling a force in Western epistemology? The answer is that this is probably due to the fact that it has almost always—not quite always, because it is

explicit in Plato[6]—gone on concealed under the designation of certainty.[7]

But, now, that concealment seems to be at all possible only in a language like English. I find it hard to think that anyone could so much as make a beginning of such concealment in my own language, namely, Akan. In this language to say 'I am certain' I should have to say something which would translate back into English in some such wise as 'I know very clearly' (Minim pefee or Minim koronyee) or 'I very much know' (Minim papaapa). For the more impersonal locution 'It is certain' we would say something like 'It is indeed so' (Ampa) or 'It is true' (Eye nokware) or 'It is rightly or very much so' (Ete saa potee)[8] or 'It is something lying out there' (Eye ade a eda ho). None of these turns of phrase has the slightest tendency to invoke any intimations of infallibility. To suggest that in order to say of something that ete saa potee I must claim exemption from the possibility of error would strike any average or above average Akan as, to say the least, odd in the extreme. (The Akans are given to methodological understatement.) Any Akan will tell you, even at a pre-analytical level of discourse, that just because it is possible for me to go wrong, it does not follow that I can never go right. A popular adage says 'If you look carefully, you find out' (Wo hwehwe asem mu a wuhu mu.)

This is not, by any means, to imply that skepticism is unknown in Akan society. But in that environment a skeptic is not one who is moved to doubt the possibility of knowledge through viewing certainty under the pretensions of infallibility. S/he is simply an akyinyegyefo, literally, one who debates, in other words, one who is apt to question or challenge received beliefs. And the challenges are ones that are inspired by more stringent criteria of justification (whether in perceptual or conceptual discourse) than is customary. This form of skepticism is akin to the variety which is manifested in the disputing of, say, the belief in God on the grounds that good reasons are lacking. That is a well established usage of the concept of skepticism in English discourse. In comparison with it, the skepticism of Descartes, even as a methodological foil, seems highly misconceived. And the essential reason is not because it is not supportable by Akan linguistic categories or epistemologic intuitions, but rather that it involves a fallacy, namely, that of confusing certainty with infallibility of which all judicious thinking should steer clear, whether in the medium of Akan, English or Eskimo. The relevance of Akan language here is only this: that (in my opinion) any Akan who reflects on the matter from the standpoint of his or her own language is very unlikely to be drawn into that fallacy.

I will illustrate this relevance further by means of another example still involving Descartes. His Cogito has already acquired quite a place in African philosophy, dialectically speaking. Mbiti has commented, by implication, that 'I think therefore, I am' betrays an individualist outlook, to which he has counterposed what he takes to be the African communalist axiom: 'I am because we are, and since we are, therefore I am.'[9] Before Mbiti, Senghor had expressed a characteristic 'participatory' reaction to the Cogito on behalf of the African: Spurning "the logician's conjunction 'therefore'" as unnecessary, "the Negro African," according to Senghor, "could say, 'I feel, I dance the Other; I am."[10] But, by far the most conceptually interesting African comment on Descartes' claim was that by Alexis Kagame who pointed out that throughout the Bantu zone a remark like 'I think, therefore I am' would be unintelligible for "the verb 'to be' is always followed by an attribute or an adjunct of place. I am good, big etc., I am in such and such a place, etc. Thus the utterance '. . . therefore, I am' would prompt the question 'You are . . . what . . . where?"[11] Kagame's point holds very exactly in the Akan language also, and I would like to amplify it a little and explore some of its consequences for the Cogito and other philosophical suppositions.

For our present purposes the most relevant fact regarding the concept of existence in Akan is that it is intrinsically spatial, in fact, locative; to exist is to be there, at some place.[12] 'Wo ho' is the Akan rendition of 'exist.' Without the 'ho,' which means 'there,' in other words, 'some place,' all meaning is lost. 'Wo,' standing alone, does not in any way correspond to the existential sense of the verb 'to be,' which has no place in Akan syntax or semantics. Recur now to 'I think, therefore I am,' and consider the existential component of that attempted message as it comes across in Akan. In that medium the information communicated can only be that I am there, at some place; which

means that spatial location is essential to the idea of my existence. It is scarcely necessary to point out that this is diametrically opposed to Descartes' construal of the particular cogitation under scrutiny. As far as he is concerned, the alleged fact that one can doubt all spatial existences and yet at the some time be absolutely certain of one's existence under the dispensation of the Cogito implied that the 'I,' the ego, exists as a spiritual, non-spatial, immaterial entity. The incongruity of this sequence of thought, quite apart from any non sequiturs, must leap to the Akan eye. There is, of course, nothing sacrosanct about the linguistic categories of Akan thought. But, given the prima facie incoherence of the Cartesian suggestion within the Akan conceptual framework, an Akan thinker who scrutinizes the matter in his or her own language must feel the need for infinitely more proof of intelligibility than if s/he contemplated it in English or some cognate language. On the other hand, if on due reflection, the Akan thinker becomes persuaded of the soundness of Descartes' argumentation, that would not necessarily be a loss to conceptual decolonization, for that program does not envisage the automatic refusal of all foreign food for thought. I might mention, though, for what it is worth, that in my own case the exercise proves severely negative.

Negative or not, the implications of the Akan conception of existence for many notable doctrines of Western metaphysics and theology require the most rigorous examination. It is well known that inquiries into the explanation of the existence of the universe enjoy a high regard among many Western metaphysicians and is one of the favorite pursuits of philosophical theology. However, a simple argument, inspired by the locative conception of existence embedded in the Akan language, would seem, quite radically, to subvert any such project: To have a location is to be in the universe. Therefore, if to exist means to be at some location, then to think of the existence of the universe is to dabble in sheer babble. This reasoning does not, by the way, mean that it is so much as false to say that the universe exists. More drastically, it means that it does not make sense to say of the universe either that it exists or that it does not exist. But this same impropriety must obviously afflict any idea of a being who supposedly brought the universe into existence. If one cannot speak of the universe either as existing or not existing then neither can one speak of its having been brought into existence. Since the Akans, in fact, generally believe in a supreme being, it must occur to the student of Akan thought that the Akan conception of that being cannot be of a type with, say, the ex-nihilo creator of Christianity but rather must be of the character of a quasi demiurgic cosmic architect.[13]

Here now comes the challenge of conceptual decolonization. Have Akan Christians, of whom there are many, confronted the conceptual disparity thus revealed and opted for the Christian notion in consequence of critical reflection or have they perhaps unconsciously glossed over them or, worse still, assimilated the Akan conceptions to those of Christianity or vice versa? One answer that any of them would be exceedingly ill-advised to attempt would be to say that religious matters are not a subject of argument or analysis but, instead, of faith. For where two incompatible faiths are available through indigenous culture and foreign efforts of proselytism, to go along with the latter for no conscious reason would be the quintessence of supine irrationality. It would, besides, betray a colonized mentality. Again, the suggestion is not that profession of the Christian persuasion on the part of an African is automatically a mark of the colonial mentality. In general, only the unreasoning profession of a religion with an association with colonialism merits that description.

Actually, if it comes to that, the unreasoning profession of any religion, indigenous or foreign, is not a model of intellectual virtue. The Akans believe traditionally that the existence of the supreme being, as conceived by them, is so obvious that no one need teach it to a child. (Hardly any Akan adult brought up in Akanland can be ignorant of the Akan saying Obi nkyere akwadaa Nyame, which means 'No one teaches the child the supreme being.') The implication is not that no reflection goes into the acquisition of the belief, but rather that it takes only a little of it. If so, the least an Akan thinker who embraces a foreign conception of the Supreme being can do, if s/he is mindful of the Akan tradition, is to make sure that there are good reasons for that metaphysical belief mutation. Otherwise s/he cannot escape attributions of the colonial mentality. I myself do not believe either in the Akan

or the Christian or any kind of supreme being, though (a) I find the Akan concept more intelligible than the Christian one (which, in truth, I find of zero intelligibility) and (b) I am of the opinion that the locative concept of existence found in the Akan language is more conducive to sound metaphysics than its rivals.[14] Although, my convictions in these matters are quite stout, I enjoy no sense of infallibility, and I do not rule out the possibility of being argued out of them in one direction or another. I might stress in the present connection, though, that on any appropriate occasion I would be prepared to try quite industriously to offer rational justifications for these intellectual commitments or avoidances. Hopefully, I might thereby be able to make some little progress towards freeing my own mind of any vestiges of the colonial mentality. It is, at all events, impossible to overemphasize the necessity for the rational evaluation of religious belief in contemporary African philosophy, for the unexamined espousal of foreign religions, often in unleavened admixture with indigenous ones, is the cause of some of the severest distortions of the African consciousness.

It is equally obvious that Africa has suffered unspeakably from the political legacies of colonialism. Unhappily she continues in this sphere to suffer, directly or indirectly, from the political tutelage of the West. This is due to a variety of causes, frequently not of Africa's own making. But it is impossible not to include in the inventory of causes the apparently willing suspension of belief in African political traditions on the part of many contemporary African leaders of opinion. After years of subjection to the untold severities of one-party dictatorships in Africa, there is now visible enthusiasm among many African intellectuals and politicians for multi-party democracy. Indeed, to many, democracy seems to be synonymous with the multi-party system. This enthusiasm is plainly not unconnected with foreign pressures; but there is little indication, in African intellectual circles, of a critical evaluation of the particular doctrine of democracy involved in the multi-party approach to government. Yet that political doctrine seems clearly antithetical to the philosophy of government underlying traditional statecraft. The advocates of the one-party system at least made an effort to link that system with African traditional forms of government. That linkage was uniformly spurious, and in some cases, perhaps disingenuous.[15] But there was at least an intent to harmonize the contemporary practice of politics in Africa with what was considered viable in the traditional counterpart. The lack of evidence of any such intent in more recent times must raise legitimate fears of a new lease of life for the colonial mentality in contemporary African political thought.

What, then can we learn from the traditional philosophy of government that might be of relevance to the contemporary quest for democracy? Traditional African governments displayed an interesting variety of forms. But amidst that variety, if the anthropological evidence is anything to go by, there was a certain unity of approach, at any rate among a large number of them.[16] And that unity consisted in the insistence on consensus as the basis of political decision-making. Now, this conception of decision-making is very distinct from that which makes the will of the majority, by and large, decisive. Since majorities are easier to come by than consensus, it must be assumed that the decided preference for consensus was a deliberate transcending of majoritarianism. Assuredly, it was not an unreflecting preference; it can be shown to have been based on reflection on first principles. And the most fundamental principle here is not far to seek. It may be stated as follows: In any council of representatives—traditional councils usually consisted of representatives elected by kinship units—the representative status of a member is rendered vacuous in any decision in which s/he does not have an impact or an involvement. And any such voiding of the will constitutes a deprivation of the right of the representative, and through him, of his constituency to be represented in the making of the decision that affects their interests (broadly construed). By any reckoning, that should be considered a violation of a human right.

It is or should be well-known that majoritarian democracy, that is, the form of democracy involving more than a single party in which, in principle, the party that wins the most parliamentary seats forms the government, is apt to render the will of a substantial minority of no effect, or almost of no effect, in the making of many important decisions affecting their interests. It is,

then, from a consensus-oriented standpoint, a system that is frequently deleterious of genuine representation, that is, representation beyond parliamentary window-dressing. It is obvious, by the same token, that a democracy based on consensus must of necessity be of a non-party character, not in the sense that political associations must be proscribed, which, of course would be authoritarian, but simply in the sense that majority at the polls need not be an exclusive basis of government formation. Perhaps, some proponents and practitioners of the one-party system confused the one-party with the non-party concept. May the former never return to Africa!

The detailed and systematic working out of a system of the sort barely hinted at above in the contemporary world, as distinct from the comparatively simpler circumstances of traditional times, must encounter many difficulties. But its serious exploration would at least show some sensitivity to the need for intellectual decolonization in African political life. Besides it might conceivably lead to a system that might bring peace and the possibility of prosperity.

Most of the considerations relating to the need for decolonization urged in this discussion were derived from facts about language. I was, accordingly, constrained to focus on the only African language about which I am somewhat confident. Africans from other linguistic areas are invited to compare and, if appropriate, contrast, using their own languages. The principle of decolonization will, however, remain the same. My own hope is that if this program is well enough and soon enough implemented, it will no longer be necessary to talk of the Akan of Yoruba or Luo concept of this or that, but simply of the concept of whatever is in question with a view to advancing philosophical suggestions that can be immediately evaluated on independent grounds.

Nor, is the process of decolonization without interest to non-African thinkers, for any enlargement of conceptual options is an instrumentality for the enlargement of the human mind everywhere.

Notes

1. K. Wiredu: *Philosophical Research and Teaching in Africa: Some Suggestions [Toward Conceptual Decolonization].* In: Teaching and Research in Philosophy: Africa. Paris 1984.

2. See, for example, (a) *Philosophy and an African Culture*. London 1980, p. 216–232, (b) *Are there Cultural Universals?* In: Quest. Philosophical Discussions 4, No. 2 (1990).

3. *The Philosophical Writings of Descartes*. Vol. II. Transl. J. Cottingham, R. Stoothoff and D. Murdoch. New York 1984, p. 14.

4. See Norman Malcolm's critique of Lewis and others on this issue in his *The Verification Argument*. In: M. Black (ed), Philosophical Analysis (1950).

5. Of the great Western philosophers none, perhaps, was more scathing of this quest for certainty than John Dewey, witness his *The Quest for Certainty*. New York 1930 (1960²). Yet, in the apparent resurgence of pragmatism in recent times it is not clear how well and truly the allurements of that ideal have been resisted, all the fulminations against 'foundationalism' notwithstanding.

6. See Plato: *The Republic*, for example, V, 478. In the translation by F. MacDonald Cornford. New York 1945, p. 185.

7. Infallibility has marched on with other disguises too, such as Indubitability, Incorrigibility, Absolute validity, etc. For example, some of the logical positivists, such as Schlick (but unlike Neurath) insisted that an 'observation sentence' (as also an analytic one) is indubitable or absolutely certain in the sense that it makes 'little sense to ask whether I might be deceived in regard to its truth.' See M. Schlick: *The Foundation of Knowledge*. In: A.J. Ayer (ed), Logical Positivism. Glencoe 1959, p. 225. Compare O. Neurath: *Protocol Sentences* in the same volume.

8. An entry in a dictionary written long ago by German scholars is quite useful: (a) J. G. Christaller, C. W. Locher and J. Zimmermann: *A Dictionary, English-Tshi (Asanti)*. Basel 1874, p. 46: **Certain, it is** —, ewom ampa; **Certainly**, adv. ampa, nokware, potee.

9. J.S. Mbiti: *African Religions and Philosophy*. London 1991, p. 108.

10. L.S. Senghor: *The African Road to Socialism (1960)*. In: On African Socialism. Transl. M. Cook. New York 1964.

11. A. Kagame: *Empirical Apperception of Time and the Conception of History in Bantu Thought*. In: P. Ricoeur (ed), Cultures and Time. Paris 1976, p. 95.

12. In his *An Essay on African Philosophical Thought* Kwame Gyekye very correctly insists on the locative character of the Akan concept of existence. (See Cambridge 1987, p. 179 and 181).

13. See further, K. Wiredu: (a) *Universalism and Particularism in Religion from an African Perspective*. In: Journal of Humanism and Ethical Religion, Vol. 3, No. 1, 1990. Reprinted in D. Kolak and R. Martin (eds), Self, Cosmos, God. New York 1992 under the title Religion from an African Point of View and (b) *African Philosophical Tradition: A Case Study of the Akan*. In: The Philosophical Forum XXIV, No. 1–3, (1992–93), p. 41 ff.

14. I am aware of the objection that a locative conception of existence will have to be dumb in respect of the existence of abstract objects, like, say, numbers. My reply is that abstract objects are objects only in a figurative sense, and figurative locations are not hard to come by.

15. The extremely useful anthology of *Readings in African Political Thought*. London 1975, that was edited by G.-C.M. Mutiso and S.W. Rohio included in its VIIth part some of the best arguments for and against the one-party system.

16. See, for example, M. Fortes and E.E. Evans-Pritchard (eds): *African Political Systems*. Oxford 1940.

Chapter Five Questions

Choose one answer.

1. By "Elusive Quest" Cannon means
   a. protracted efforts at reconciliation
   b. military commercialism policies
   c. deep socioeconomic image
   d. democracy
   e. All of the above

2. Who is the President of Rwanda?
   a. Hutu Tutsi
   b. Tutsi Hutu
   c. Paul Kagame
   d. James Kimonyo
   e. RFP

3. RPF stands for
   a. Rapulane Patriotic Place
   b. Rwanda Patriotic Front
   c. Reconciliation Political Place
   d. Rwanda Patriotic Forms
   e. None of the above

4. In his argument for just war, Ramose posits
   a. suspicion as a legitimate reason to declare war
   b. suspicion as a legitimate reason to declare war is needed
   c. suspicion as a legitimate reason to declare war is a good doctrine
   d. suspicion as a legitimate reason to declare war is theoretically problematic
   e. suspicion as a legitimate reason to declare war and kill terrorists

5. What does IOGORIA mean?
   a. Freedom of speech
   b. Freedom of the press
   c. Equal freedom of the press
   d. Equality before the law
   e. Equal freedom of speech

6. What does ISONOMIA mean?
   a. Equality before the law
   b. Equality representation in the Constitution
   c. Equal representation in the legal system
   d. The Bill of Rights
   e. Freedom of speech

7. Bodurin traditionalists see themselves as concerned with
   a. African ideas
   b. Discovery of authentic African ideas
   c. African philosophy
   d. Authentic African ideas
   e. Western scholarship

8. Which of these concepts does Wiredu think will lead to conceptual decolonization in African philosophy if thought out in African languages?
   a. Thing, object, substance
   b. Statement, opinion, belief
   c. Fact, truth, proposition
   d. Mind, soul, spirit
   e. All of the above

9. Wiredu's views on relativism are
   a. true
   b. false
   c. worth exploring
   d. western thought
   e. an African concept

Discuss how language can be framed to vilify the opponent and justify war.

Discuss how class dictatorship affects human rights in Africa.

Discuss why Canon describes the RPF in its first decade of rule in Rwanda as an "enigmatic Janus-faced regime."